THE ADOPTION OPTION COMPLETE HANDBOOK

2000–2001

Christine Adamec

PRIMA PUBLISHING

PRIMA PUBLISHING and colophon are registered trademarks of Prima Communications, Inc.

Library of Congress Cataloging-in-Publication Data

Adamec, Christine A.

   The adoption option complete handbook, 2000–2001 / Christine Adamec

     p.   cm.

   Includes bibliographical references and index.

   ISBN 0-7615-2007-4

   1. Adoption—United States handbooks, manuals, etc. 2. Adoption—Canada Handbooks, manuals, etc. I. Title.

HV875.55.A277	1999
362.73'4'0973--dc21	99-41662
	CIP

99 00 01 02 BB 10 9 8 7 6 5 4 3 2 1

Printed in the United States of America

How to Order

Single copies may be ordered from Prima Publishing, P.O. Box 1260BK, Rocklin, CA 95677; telephone (916) 632-4400. Quantity discounts are also available. On your letterhead, include information concerning the intended use of the books and the number of books you wish to purchase.

Visit us online at www.primalifestyles.com

Contents

Acknowledgments

I would like to thank my ever-supportive husband, John Adamec, for all his help while I researched and edited this book. In addition, I would like to thank Steve Kirsh, an experienced adoption attorney in Indianapolis, Indiana, and former president of the American Academy of Adoption Attorneys, for his help with creating the attorney questionnaire. Thanks also to Jerri Ann Jenista, M.D., for her help with many different elements of the book. Many other people assisted me with this book, including my very knowledgeable contributors. Finally, thanks to the hundreds of adoption professionals who responded to my questionnaires.

Introduction

Call it creativity or serendipity—or maybe you could call it a message from God. Or perhaps it is "all of the above." But sometimes, something clicks—an idea darts into your brain from nowhere, and you just know that it's a good one and wonder why you never realized it before. That's what happened to me one day, when the idea for this book suddenly hit and it all made sense.

I am a freelance writer and an adoptive mom. I've written books about adoption and other topics over the past fifteen years. One day, my two lives, as freelance writer generalist and as adoption author and advocate, converged. I was reading through entries in the *Writer's Guide to Book Editors, Publishers, and Literary Agents*, as I have many times before and thinking once again how much I liked the practical and helpful information and the quotations from real people who were editors and literary agents.

Suddenly I realized that this format would work well with adoption. People who wanted to adopt needed comparative information on what kind of families agencies and attorneys were seeking, what kinds of children they were placing, how much they charged, and much more. They didn't have any place or source for such information. I also knew that often people call an agency that isn't a good fit for them, and they give up, not knowing that many other agencies in and outside their state could help them. I knew this was also true of adoption attorneys. If prospective parents called one attorney and were discouraged, they might think there were no other options. But there are many options available today for the person who wants to adopt—more so now than in many years past.

As the idea evolved in my mind, I also knew there was only one publisher who could produce the book I wanted: Prima Publishing. The result is in your hands.

In a way, I compare the research for this book to the quest for adopting a child. Many people will tell you that it's impossible or, at best, too hard. Do something else. Don't take a chance.

I don't agree with those people. I think it's good to pursue your dreams and once in awhile do something difficult but worthwhile. I hope you will listen to the hopeful voice inside yourself, too. The information in these pages can get you started if you want to adopt a child. For most of you, adoption is a goal within your grasp. But you must act. Pick up the phone, write a letter, or send an e-mail. Get started! The end result—your child—is so worth it that words fail even a writer to express the feeling adequately.

I have one suggestion for you. If you like this book, as I hope you will, perhaps you would consider buying a copy for your local library and giving it to your reference librarian. Your donation could result in the creation of more happy families through adoption.

THE LAY OF THE BOOK

This book is divided into chapters covering specific topics. Chapter 1 covers adoption basics, including some information that may surprise you. Chapter 2 is dedicated to adoption agencies, including the responses of over two hundred agencies to my questionnaire. Read what they have to say about their criteria for adoptive parents, the services they offer, fees they charge, and more.

Chapter 3 covers adoption attorneys, including an essay by Sam Totaro, Jr., a prominent adoption attorney, who describes how to create a good relationship with your lawyer. The chapter also includes data from over one hundred noted adoption attorneys, drawn from questionnaires they returned to me.

Chapter 4 on adoption in Canada, includes a comprehensive practical article by Jennifer Smart, followed by a listing of adoption agencies and support groups in Canada.

Adoptive parent support groups are the subject of Chapter 5, beginning with an essay from Alan Wasserman, president of a key support group, followed by a list of adoptive parent groups nationwide.

Chapter 6 covers adopting a baby in the United States and includes my ten-point Adoption Option Plan. This chapter also includes important information on open adoption from agency director Maxine Chalker.

Chapter 7 covers some basics and provides extremely valuable advice from agency co-director Jean Nelson-Erichsen on information you need at the time you adopt your child and for months thereafter. Don't miss this chapter if you have even the slightest interest in international adoption.

You may be interested in adopting an older child. If so, you need to read Chapter 8. Or perhaps you want to adopt a baby but are interested in an infant of another race or a baby with medical problems. An essay by Peggy Soule, an experienced adoption advocate, covers the myths and realities of adopting children with special needs.

Chapter 9 provides valuable information for after you adopt, such as the medical evaluation on your newly adopted child, by Jerri Ann Jenista, an experienced pediatrician and adoptive mother of five children. A unique article on food and adopted children by R. Dubucs is offered in this chapter, followed by my discussion on how to explain adoption to your child and to others.

The Appendix lists adoption organizations, state adoption offices, and adoption publications, and includes a quick-reference glossary.

Good luck!

CHAPTER ONE

STARTING OUT: ADOPTION BASICS AND MUST-KNOWS

For most of us, when we think about making a major, life-changing commitment, we feel thrilled and eager at the thought of the adventure that lies ahead. And yet, at the same time, the idea of such a change can induce fear as doubts crowd in. Should you get married? Take that job? Adopt a child? It's exhilarating to imagine your life with your child and all the wonderful times you'll have together. It's also scary to consider the process of adoption and problems that might crop up.

Knowledge is power. Learning as much as you can about adoption and adoption organizations can really help. This chapter covers very important adoption basics. Chapters Two and Three contain detailed information provided by agencies and attorneys.

WHO ADOPTS AND WHO NEEDS FAMILIES?

To begin, who are the people who adopt? Who are children who need families?

Who Adopts?

Most adopters are married middle-class people with good educations. For example, a 1999 report from the National Center for Health Statistics (NCHS) revealed that 60% of the adoptive mothers in their survey had some college education or were college graduates and post graduates. But many other people also adopt: singles of both sexes, those with low incomes, people who are disabled, large families and divorced individuals. Don't eliminate yourself as a candidate.

Who Are Adopted Children and Why Do They Need Families?

Adopted children are of all races and ethnicities, although it may be easier and faster to adopt a nonwhite child. Public (government) agencies typically do not place newborns who have no health or social issues.

There are about 500,000 children in foster care in the United States. President Clinton has supported the adoption of foster children who cannot be returned to their parents. Although no one knows exactly how many children fall into that category, it has been estimated that if even 5 percent could be adopted, that would equal 25,000 children placed. Most foster children have been abused or neglected, but many can do well in adoptive families. With new federal and state laws, it is hoped that increasing numbers of foster children will escape the extended warehousing system that foster care has become and move into loving families.

Thousands of babies and older children live in foreign orphanages worldwide. International adoptions could double or triple, and there would still be plenty of children in orphanages who need parents. Some people think that, since so many children need families, adopting them should be free. It doesn't work that way, because of agency, travel, and other expenses.

In general, the older the child, the more difficult the transition to a new culture and language. (It is also true that the older an American child is, the more difficult the transition to a family.) Agencies can provide much more information.

Children with Special Needs

"Special needs" is a phrase used when an agency thinks it could be hard to find a family for a child. This may mean a child is nonwhite, has a disability, or is older. It could also mean the child is in a group of siblings. Medical special needs are very different from social, emotional, and behavioral special needs. Many families find medical problems far less daunting than emotional problems. (Read Peggy Soule's essay on children with special needs in Chapter Eight.)

WHAT KIND OF FAMILIES ARE AGENCIES AND ATTORNEYS LOOKING FOR?

Many state and private adoption agencies and adoption attorneys are interested in married applicants. Some seek members of a particular religion. In the past, many agencies set an age limit of forty, but most have raised the bar to forty-five or thrown out age limits altogether.

Single people may adopt through numerous agencies, although in some cases, they may only be eligible to adopt children with special needs. Singles are not banned from adopting in any state and may also adopt children from some (but not all) other countries.

Whether gays and lesbians may adopt depends partly on state laws. If a state bans discrimination, an agency complies. If not, agencies decide for themselves. One way to ascertain an agency's policy is to ask whether they accept applications from singles. If the agency discourages singles, gays and lesbians should move on. If the agency accepts singles, ask about its policy on gays and lesbians.

How healthy must you be? Adopting parents should be in good health but that does not preclude some illnesses or disabilities. The main point is, could you care for a child through his or her growing years? As a result, a person with HIV would generally be turned down.

Categories of people unlikely to be accepted are those with a child abuse record or felony convictions.

HOW LONG DOES IT TAKE TO ADOPT?

Forget the five-year waiting period you're used to hearing about. My questionnaire respondents reported waits of a year or less. Many agencies said they would start the homestudy within weeks of receiving an application. Don't expect immediate action of course, and do try to exercise some patience.

IT CAN BE CONFUSING AT FIRST

The adoption process can feel like a minefield of confusing words and phrases. You'll need to navigate a landscape of "birthmothers," (women who place their children for adoption) and "homestudies" (evaluations of the family), "adoption agencies" and "social workers" and "adoption attorneys." Let's start with adoption agencies.

WHAT DO ADOPTION AGENCIES DO?

Throw out your image of the crabby social worker clutching a clipboard. Social workers come in all ages, races and temperaments. Nearly all are very nice! Their main goal: to find good parents for children who need families.

Adoption Agencies Have Different Goals

Most adoption agencies are nonprofit organizations licensed by the state in which they operate. Agencies differ in goals, the types of children they place, and the families they seek. Some agencies cover the gamut, from placing healthy newborns to finding families for abused foster children. Others manage only intercountry adoptions, and some specialize in placing children from only one or two countries. Some agencies concentrate on "domestic" adoption only: placing children from the United States (or, in Canada, children from Canada). A few agencies specialize in placing children with special needs.

Why is this important to know? Because it can save you time and money. If you're interested in adopting a child from the United States, it would be silly to apply to agencies specializing in intercountry adoption. If you want to adopt a healthy baby, it would be foolish to try to adopt from an agency that primarily places children with special needs. And yet, this is what some people do. I have known of families who spent years working with an agency that would never place the child they wanted, although other agencies could and would have helped, if asked.

Agencies also differ in the types of services they offer. Some provide classes, seminars, and other services. Nearly all perform a "homestudy." A few agencies concentrate on the homestudy and do not place children with families. The homestudy is the assessment and evaluation of the prospective family, including self-assessment.

Now let's get into some details about the main types of agencies.

Public Agencies

State social services adoption organizations place foster children for adoption. As a result of the Adoption and Safe Families Act of 1997, public agencies must return children to their families or terminate parental rights and place children for adoption within about fifteen months of a child's entry into foster care.

Some foster children are born healthy but have suffered from years of neglect and abuse. Some children are amazingly resilient and survive relatively intact. They are not the norm. This is why social workers are concerned when adopting parents think, "Okay, Jimmy was severely abused and lived in twelve foster homes and never celebrated a birthday in his eight years of life. But heck, with a little love, he'll be just fine." Jimmy may do well in his new adoptive home, but he'll probably test the patience of new parents for some time until they all reach an accommodation.

Some foster children were not born healthy and some were born to drug-addicted or alcohol-abusing mothers. Some children have fetal alcohol syndrome (FAS), were born premature, or had very low birth weight.

At least half of all foster children are black or biracial. In past years, whites were actively discouraged from adopting black or biracial children. With passage of the Multiethnic Placement Act (MEPA), public agencies may no longer use race as the primary factor in selecting families for children.

The Kind of Families State Agencies Seek. State adoption agencies seek families that are flexible. At the same time, they want families who can set limits. People with parenting experience seem to do better than childless people. There's some indication that parents who are not college graduates do better at rearing foster children. Experts speculate this is because high school graduates have realistic expectations for children. This doesn't mean a college graduate would make a bad parent; it means a parent must be able to accept a child's abilities. If your child must grow up to be rich and famous, don't adopt a foster child. Or any child.

To Learn More. To learn more about adopting a foster child, contact your state social services office. You can view photos of "waiting children" on the "Faces of Children" Web site (www.adopt.org) jointly managed by the National Adoption Center and Children Awaiting Parents (CAP).

Private Adoption Agencies

There are several thousand private adoption agencies in the United States. I sent questionnaires to 2,000 agencies and received replies from over 200. This was a good return for several reasons. First, it's hard to convince 10 percent of any group to respond to a questionnaire. Second, some agencies that are licensed for adoption, don't do any adoptions. Most of my respondents are very active in the adoption field.

I asked agency staff the questions that many people hoping to adopt would *like* to know but are often afraid to ask, questions about waiting times, types of children they place, fees, adoptions that fall through after placement, whether they've been sued and lost, and so forth.

Agencies that responded were all sizes. Holt International Children's Services, for example, placed nearly a thousand children in 1998. Most agencies place far fewer; if an agency places over a hundred children per year, it is doing very well.

Many agency directors are adoptive parents and some are adopted adults or birthparents (people who chose adoption for their children in the past). An agency doesn't have to be run by someone personally involved with adoption to do wonderful work, but sometimes it helps to know that the people you are dealing with have a personal connection to the work.

Don't Sign Up Until You Learn More About the Agency.   Some adoption agencies are very effective, others are average, and some are incompetent or bad. Be an educated consumer. One point my agency and attorney respondents made repeatedly was that prospective parents don't do enough research.

Learn as much as possible about an agency before making a commitment. Verify that the agency is licensed. Call the Better Business Bureau to find if there have been any complaints against it. Talk to people who adopted children from that agency. Sometimes people are blunt about agencies in Internet chatgroups, but keep in mind some people may be unreasonably dissatisfied.

Ask the agency whether it has been sued or has had complaints. An agency may have been sued unfairly, but if it has been sued repeatedly, this could indicate a problem. Ask whether it has a grievance procedure.

Find out what pre- and post-adoption services the agency provides. Ask for handouts or brochures. If the agency offers articles to read and a great deal of helpful information, this is a good sign.

Start with agencies in your home state. Learn about their policies, types of children they place, fees, and so forth. If your state is not listed in this book, check listings for nearby states and other states—many agencies place children in other states. Some agencies place children in most states in the United States and Canada.

WHAT DO ADOPTION ATTORNEYS DO?

If you want to adopt a baby, think about asking an attorney to help. As many as two-thirds of all infant adoptions are nonagency adoptions. Many attorneys are adoptive parents who like the idea of helping a family form by adoption. Be sure to read Attorney Sam Totaro, Jr.'s essay on establishing rapport with your attorney in Chapter 3.

As with adoption agencies, carefully screen an attorney before you sign up. Ask for names of others who have adopted using an attorney's services. Find out what the local adoptive parent groups think of the attorney. You want someone with a good track record who is effective and honest. Many adoption attorneys are members of the American Academy of Adoption Attorneys, an organization based in Washington. D.C. A few are members of the National Council For Adoption, an adoption organization also based in Washington, D.C. Membership in one or both of these groups is good but no guarantee.

The role of the adoption attorney varies greatly from state to state because of state laws. In some states, attorneys provide almost a "turnkey" service, from finding a pregnant woman interested in placing her baby to doing legal paperwork and ultimately hand-ing you the baby. In other states, attorney's services are restricted; for example, they may be able to tell you how to locate a pregnant woman but can't find someone for you. Once you've located a pregnant woman interested in adoption, an attorney can assist you.

The main down side to nonagency adoption is you risk having the birthmother change her mind before placement. This is emotionally and financially painful.

Some people purchase adoption cancellation insurance to cover expenses if a U.S. birthmother has a change of heart. MBO Insurance Brokers in Menlo Park, California provides insurance for payments made by adoptive parents. The insurance program, originally created by an adoptive father, is underwritten by Kemper. For more information, contact MBO Insurance at 800-833-7337.

BASICS OF INTERNATIONAL AND DOMESTIC ADOPTION

One decision you need to make is whether to adopt domestically or internationally. Even if you are certain which you want, you should consider both options. Why? Because it's better to be running *toward* your preferred option, than primarily running *away* from an option you fear and know nothing about. If you fear domestic adoption, you may decide to adopt a child from another country. Yet a domestic adoption might be a good choice for you. Or you may be interested in international adoption but have never been out of the country and don't know if you could handle it, so you forego this choice. With information, you may make the same choice you were leaning toward before, but it will be a reasoned choice.

International Adoptions

Nearly 16,000 children from other countries were adopted by Americans in 1998, up from fewer than 8,000 in 1989. Most of these adoptions were managed by private agencies, although some parents received assistance from attorneys or private facilitators. Canadians adopted 2,000 children from other countries in 1998.

In 1998 and 1999, most internationally adopted children came from China and the former Soviet Union. Their health may be good or poor: Some doctors view all children adopted from other countries to have potential, if not currently diagnosable, special needs. Most children adopted from other countries are infants over 6 months or toddlers. About 10 percent are older children and another 10 percent are siblings or twins.

Some agencies are experienced and provide a great deal of information and "handholding." Others know less and are not very helpful. You can't tell who is good or bad by looking at fees alone—some bad agencies charge a lot. Never assume you will adopt a "better baby" because of a high price. Conversely, don't assume an agency with low fees is automatically the best choice.

Consider health aspects. Children in Thailand and Vietnam are exposed to diseases not common in the United States or Eastern Europe. Some Russian children are born to alcoholic mothers. Some agencies provide videotapes of children, especially from Eastern Europe. It's important to obtain as much medical information as possible, but you can never get as much as you'd probably like. Read Dr. Jenista's essay on medical evaluations of adopted children in Chapter Nine.

Be Prepared Before You Travel. Get your passport in order: Don't wait until the last week. Ask your agency for a list of everything you should do and check off items as you do them. Contact adoptive parents who recently traveled about availability of health and baby care needs in the country. Learn a few words of the language before you go. Check the Centers for Disease Control Web site for a travel advisory on needed immunizations and other information (www.cdc.gov/travel/travel.html). Canadians may wish to check this travel site: www.hc-sc.gc.ca/hpb/lcdc/osh/tmp_e.html.

Adopting a child from another country is an adventure! Thousands of parents each year can attest to this fact. If you are prepared and have a good idea of what to expect, (you can never know everything), the experience will be far more positive for you.

U.S. (Domestic) Adoptions

The majority of agencies and attorneys placing children in the United States concentrate on babies. Newborns may be healthy but have "special needs" because they are black or biracial or have a medical problem. To some agencies, every child is considered special needs except healthy white infants.

An increasing number of domestic adoption agencies support the concept of "open adoption." There are many definitions but in general, open adoption means the agency offers birthmothers choices. Sometimes birthmothers review special, nonidentifying resumes of prospective adoptive parents, and sometimes they meet once, on a first-name basis. Open adoption could also mean an exchange of identities and that an ongoing relationship is expected. If you are considering this option, ask your agency or attorney exactly what to expect. (Read agency director Maxine Chalker's essay on open adoption in Chapter 6.) Numerous agencies offer the gamut of options, from complete confidentiality to full disclosure of identities.

WHAT IF YOU'RE CANADIAN?

"Are you going to say ANYTHING at all about Canadians adopting children?" asked one adoptive parent, who added, "Most books just ignore us." My heart sank when I heard that statement, because I've been guilty in the past of ignoring people from Canada who wish to adopt children. So I have included a chapter dedicated to Canadians adopting children, including an essay written by a Canadian mom, followed by listings of Canadian adoption agencies, adoptive parent groups, and government organizations.

HOW MUCH DOES IT COST TO ADOPT A CHILD?

One area that often causes considerable consternation to prospective parents is cost. Will adopting a child put you in—or close to—bankruptcy? Despite media stories about adoptions costing $50,000 and up, adoption expenses are often considerably less than *half* that amount. In one form of adoption, the state pays you. If you adopt a foster child, you may be eligible (and should apply) for an adoption subsidy for the child. This is a monthly payment continuing until the child reaches adulthood and is meant to defray expenses. Often the child continues to be eligible for Medicaid (state medical insurance) benefits too.

Types of Fees Agencies Charge

Most people don't think about it, but social workers and other employees at adoption agencies are paid salaries. Adoption agencies are not magically exempted from paying telephone bills, rent, electric bills, and so forth as well. As a result, agencies charge adoption fees to people who want to adopt. It drives social workers crazy when applicants constantly complain about fees or cite the $25,000 they spent on fertility options, thinking they should now get a break on adoption fees.

Most agencies charge an application fee. Application fees can range from $50 to $500 or more. Based on the responses of agencies to my questionnaire, the average application fee is $225.

Most agencies also charge a homestudy fee. Homestudy fees usually start at $1,000, depending on the agency. Based on responses to my questionnaire, the average home study fee is $1,200.

The placement fee, usually the largest fee charged by agencies runs from $3,000 and up, with an average of about $7,000. Placement fees do not include travel expenses.

Some agencies charge adopting parents a sliding scale fee instead of a flat placement fee. This is a percentage of the parent's gross or net income. Many religious agencies favor sliding scales, although some nonsectarian agencies use the sliding scale method as well.

International Adoption Fees

International adoption agencies may have other fees in addition to application, homestudy, and placement fees. For example, they may charge for translation of documents. There are almost always travel expenses and often are foreign legal or court fees and a required orphanage donation.

In my questionnaire, I asked international adoption agencies for a breakdown of fees and the total expense to adopt. The average total expense for adopting from China (including travel) was $14,950. Total expenses to adopt from Russia (the former Soviet Union) were higher. The average reported by agencies was $20,685. Guatemala, another popular country, had average total expenses of $22,000.

Fees That Attorneys Charge

Of course, lawyers charge for their services too. Some attorneys specialize in adoption while others only do this work as a sideline. (I asked each attorney what percent of his or her practice was devoted to adoption.) Others assist adoption agencies. Some do both. Some charge a phone consultation fee. The average cost of a first-time office visit is $240.

Many attorneys want a retainer, an amount against which they charge their hourly rate. When the retainer is paid varies. Some attorneys request the retainer when you begin using their services. Others want a retainer when a match is made between you and a birthmother. (There are other policies as well.)

A retainer shows you are serious about adopting. Here's how it works, very basically. If an attorney wants a retainer of $1,500 and charges $150 per hour, then that would cover ten hours of work. If the attorney does more than ten hours of work, he or she bills for more. Among fifty attorneys who charged retainers, the average is about $1,900.

Other Expenses

Many states allow the payment of a birthmother's "living expenses" through an attorney or adoption agency. Some states put a dollar limit on the amount. Most states also require adopting families to have a homestudy, so that is another expense incurred in a private adoption.

Often the largest expense, eclipsing legal fees, is payment for the obstetrician and hospital. Costs can range from $5,000 to $10,000, or more if there are medical complications. Many pregnant women are eligible for or are on Medicaid or have health insurance. If not, the adopting parents may have to pay this bill.

If you adopt a child from another state, you will usually need to hire an attorney or adoption agency in that state. They help you ensure the adoption complies with the provisions of the Interstate Compact on the Placement of Children (ICPC). ICPC governs how interstate adoptions are handled. Do not take a child from one state to another unless the agency or attorney assures you it is okay to do so. Never rely on the statement of birthparents alone, because it's unlikely they know about or understand ICPC.

HOW CAN YOU AFFORD TO ADOPT?

How do people afford adopting a child? Some use savings. Others dip into retirement plans. Some use credit cards and others take out bank loans. One popular source of income is family. Sometimes a church or community group will help you raise funds for the adoption of a particular child.

Many corporations offer adoption grants. The average grant is $3,000. Do not assume you'd know if your corporation offered them. Ask your human resources department if this benefit is part of your company's work/family package.

Helpful IRS Changes

The IRS now allows a tax credit for expenses of up to $5,000 per adoption. (You must have paid fees of $5,000 or more for the full credit.) The IRS has published a booklet on this and can provide special forms. Another major break for adopters is that an adoption grant from your employer, up to $5,000, is now considered "excludable" income, which means you don't pay taxes on it.

FEARS AND REALITIES OF ADOPTION

Many different aspects of adoption can be scary. The following table illustrates the common fears and realities of adoption.

FEAR	REALITY
Most birthmothers change their minds about adoption.	Most don't.
You'll have to wait five years to adopt.	Normal waits are one to two years or less.
Adopted kids will grow up to have problems.	Most children adopted as infants or toddlers stack up well against nonadopted children.
The agency might give me a sick child.	A good agency or attorney will give you all available medical information. They cannot and should not issue guarantees.
I'll never find the right child.	Most people who persist do succeed at adopting.
I won't love an adopted child as my own.	Most adoptions, even high-risk ones, turn out successful, well-bonded families.

DO MANY U.S. ADOPTIONS FALL THROUGH?

A common fear is that you'll find your child and adopt and then the whole thing will fall apart. You've probably heard of someone who adopted a child and took the child home, only for the birthmother to change her mind. Maybe you decide adopting is too dangerous. Are you right?

No. There are no guarantees, but most birthparents who choose adoption follow through after the baby is with the adoptive parents. In many states, once the consent form is signed, it is irrevocable. That means the birthmother can't take the child back later on.

What if a biological father ("birthfather") shows up to stake his claim to a child? This occasionally happens. How state laws address unmarried birthfathers vary. (In the case of married birthfathers, however, his permission is mandatory.) Some states say that if the birthfather did not register on a state "putative father" registry, he must not be interested. Other states allow a brief time for a birthfather to take action after the birth. About half the states allow "prebirth consent," in which a biological father signs a consent before a child is born.

When possible, it's best to obtain consent from both biological parents. Also when possible, it's a good idea to obtain verbal agreement from a birthparents' parents. Not everyone agrees, because of privacy issues. However, if birthparents don't tell their parents they are planning an adoption, when the baby is born, the birthgrandparents may talk the birthmother out of placing her child.

Looking at Some Numbers. In my questionnaire, I asked agencies in how many cases an adoption had fallen through after placement because of a birthparent challenge. Of 143 agencies that responded unequivocally, 81 percent had had no problem. Twelve agencies (8 percent) said they had had one such incident. Six (4 percent) said they had had two incidents. Seven percent had three or more such incidents.

I didn't specifically state I wanted the number of placements challenged in 1998, assuming most would give me 1998 data. But many told me of the number of adoptions that had *ever* fallen through because of a birthparent challenge. For example, one agency had five cases out of 500 in their entire experience, a rate of 1 percent.

Here are comments I received:

- None since 1983.
- In ten years, in four of 940 placements have children been returned to birthparents.
- Of approximately 700 placements, there have been approximately ten such cases.
- Under 1 percent, and none after the ten-day revocation period.

Now let's look at attorneys. In response to, "In how many of your cases has an adoptive parent been placed with a child but lost the child due to a birthparent challenge?" of the sixty-four unequivocal responses, thirty-seven (57 percent) said zero. In eight cases, attorneys said they had one such instance (12.5 percent) and in nine cases, that they'd had two (3 percent). Six percent reported three or more cases. (See individual entries by attorneys in Chapter 3.)

Here are some comments:

- In over 1,000 adoptions, only five fall-throughs *after* the placement was made.
- One out of approximately forty-five cases.
- Less than 1 percent.
- One, and that case is still pending and expecting a positive outcome.

Beyond the Numbers. One way to avoid problems is to look at the birthmother's personal situation. The characteristics in the following chart may predict whether a birthmother will change her mind about adoption. Remember: This chart is not foolproof. A birthmother could fit every category that indicates not changing her mind and then change her mind anyway. The probability is lower in certain circumstances, but there are no guarantees.

BIRTHMOTHERS CONSIDERING ADOPTION

Less Likely to Change Mind	*More Likely to Change Mind*
Women over age 18	Women under 18; the younger, the worse the risk
Pregnant women planning to return to school or work	Pregnant women with no plans for after baby is born
Women who have broken off with birthfather	Women with a continuing relationship with birthfather
Women who live away from their parents	Women who live with their parents
Women who have a friend or relative who placed baby for adoption	Unmarried women who have a friend or relative who decided to parent baby
Women whose mothers think adoption is a good idea	Women whose mothers think placing the baby for adoption is a bad idea
Women whose fathers are college graduates	Women whose fathers are not college or high school graduates
Women who are high school (or higher) graduates	Women who are high school dropouts
Women who go to church	Women who are not religious

CONTINUES

BIRTHMOTHERS CONSIDERING ADOPTION, CONTINUED

Less Likely to Change Mind	*More Likely to Change Mind*
Women who grew up in a two-parent home	Women raised by a single parent
Women not on public assistance or food stamps	Women on public assistance or food stamps; the longer on assistance, the lower probability they will choose adoption

HOW TO USE THIS BOOK

Chapter Two includes replies to my questionnaire from over 200 adoption agencies nationwide. I asked each agency to send a copy of their agency license, and most did. I also contacted state licensing offices to verify that the agencies were licensed, but it's up to you to check on the agency you choose, because circumstances can change. A wonderful director may retire and be replaced by someone less wonderful. The field of adoption is very dynamic.

Where should you start? Go directly to your state? That would be a good starting place. Should you read *only* information on your state? No! Agencies in other states may fulfill your needs better than agencies in your state. Look at the list of agencies that place in other states and find detailed information on these agencies in the state where they are based.

Do the same for adoption attorneys—read about lawyers in your state, then neighboring states. Then review the list of attorneys who work with families throughout the country (and even outside the country).

When you identify agencies or attorneys that interest you, call or e-mail them. Ask if they might be able to work with you. They may wish to send you brochures and other information. Read what they send. Agencies say a common mistake of applicants is not reading the information the agency provides.

The last sections of the book covers postplacement. Jean Nelson-Erichsen of Lost Ninos International Adoption Center describes what you need to know and do right after adopting from another country. My own essay on explaining adoption can help when your child is old enough to start asking questions.

MY GOAL FOR YOU

I researched, wrote, and edited this book because I wanted to give you practical information that other books don't provide. I want you to know that it is possible to get details on agencies and attorneys, and to adopt.

Adoption is a wonderful option for children and families. Join the club of happy adoptive families! I hope my book will help you find your child, out there somewhere.

CHAPTER TWO

ALL ABOUT
ADOPTION AGENCIES

Adoption agencies are very important organizations. They educate prospective parents on relevant issues, assess family readiness to adopt, and help families with self-assessment. Agencies often recommend adoptive parent groups as well as books and newsletters. Many agencies provide a great deal of "hand holding" along the way. Most importantly, adoption agencies link children to their new parents.

This chapter offers information based on responses from over 200 adoption agencies, including what kind of children they place, what kind of families they seek, the fees they charge, and much more. I recommend you read the entries for your own state and neighboring states, as well as agencies from other states that may work well for you.

If you find an agency that sounds promising, call or e-mail the agency for further information. I strongly advise you to consider more than one agency—at least five or six—before settling on the one that seems right for your family.

Read the list of representative and helpful advice to adopters who are just starting out. Then read the list of what adoption agency workers wish adopting parents would memorize. And read the list of basic do's and don'ts, gleaned from the advice that agency respondents provided. Agency workers are offering you very helpful and practical advice, so I urge you to pay attention.

AGENCIES THAT PLACE IN ALL OR MOST STATES*

Agency	State	Places Children In
Villa Hope International Adoption	AL	All states
Adoption Care Center	AZ	All states
God's Children International Adoption Agency	CA	All states
Independent Adoption Center	CA	All states
North Bay Adoptions	CA	Many states
Adoption Alliance	CO	All states for international
Adoption Choice Center	CO	All states
Adoption Options	CO	All states

CONTINUES

AGENCIES THAT PLACE IN ALL OR MOST STATES*, CONTINUED

Agency	State	Places Children In
Colorado Christian Services	CO	Many states
Friends of Children of Various Nations	CO	All states
Small Miracles	CO	All states except NY, CT, and WI
Lutheran Social Services of New England	CT	All states
A Bond of Love Adoption	FL	All states except CT
Adoption Source	FL	All states
Advocates for Children and Families	FL	All states
All About Adoptions	FL	All states
An Angel's Answer	FL	All states except NY
Gift of Life Adoption Agency	FL	All states
One World Adoption Services	FL	All states
Adoption Planning, Inc.	GA	All states except CT and NY
Hope for Children	GA	Many states
Open Door Adoption	GA	All states
Hawaii International Child	HI	Many states
Children's Adoption Services	ID	All states
Family Resource Center	IL	All states
Uniting Families Foundation	IL	All states
Americans for African Adoption	IN	All states; Canada; Americans overseas
Families Thru International Adoption	IN	All states; Americans overseas
Heart of America Adoption Center	KS	All states
Nine Months Adoptions	KS	All states
Beacon House Adoption	LA	All states
St. Gerard's Adoption Network	LA	CA, FL, LA, NY, NJ, PA, TX
Maine Adoption Placement Service	ME	All states; Americans overseas
Adoption Resource Center	MD	All states
Adoptions Together, Inc.	MD	All states
Cradle of Hope Adoption Center	MD	All states
Creative Adoptions	MD	All states; Americans overseas
World Child	MD	All states; Americans overseas
Wide Horizons for Children	MA	CT, MA, NH, CT, NY, RI, and VT
Children's Home Society of Minnesota	MN	Many states
New Horizons Adoption Agency	MN	All states
Reaching Arms International	MN	Many states
Mississippi Children's Home Society	MS	All states; Americans overseas
Southern Adoptions	MS	All states; Americans overseas
Children's Hope International	MO	All states

AGENCIES THAT PLACE IN ALL OR MOST STATES*, CONTINUED

Agency	State	Places Children In
Highlands Child Placement Services and Maternity Home	MO	All states
LIGHT House	MO	All states
Love Basket	MO	All states
Small World Adoption Foundation	MO	Many states
New Hope Christian Services	NH	All states; Canada
Golden Cradle Adoption Services	NJ	All states
Reaching Out Thru International Adoption	NJ	All states
La Familia, Inc.	NM	All states
Rainbow House International	NM	All states
Triad Adoption and Counseling Services	NM	All states except NY
Happy Families Information Center	NY	Many states
New Life Adoption Agency	NY	All states
Frank Adoption Center	NC	All states
Adoption By Gentle Care	OH	All states
Building Blocks Adoption Services	OH	All states
Private Adoption Services	OH	All states
Deaconess Home Pregnancy and Adoption Services	OK	All states except AR
Adventist Adoption and Family Services	OR	All states
Adoption Service Information Agency, Inc. (A.S.I.A.)	OR	All states
Cascade International Children's Services	OR	All states
Holt International Children's Services	OR	All states
Journeys of the Heart Adoption Services	OR	All states
Orphans Overseas	OR	All states
PLAN Loving Adoptions Now	OR	All states; military overseas
Adoption Services, Inc.	PA	All states except NY
Adoptions From the Heart	PA	International and minority, all states
Adoptions International	PA	All states
Jewish Family and Children's Services	PA	International adoption, all states
Kaleidoscope of Family Services	PA	Many states
Gift of Life Adoption Service	RI	All states
Little Treasures Adoption Services	RI	All states
Andrel Adoptions	TX	All states; Canada
Gladney Center	TX	All states
Great Wall China Adoption	TX	All states; Americans overseas
Los Ninos International Adoption Agency	TX	All states

CONTINUES

AGENCIES THAT PLACE IN ALL OR MOST STATES*, CONTINUED

Agency	State	Places Children In
Texas Cradle Society	TX	All states for international. Most states for domestic except NY
Adopt an Angel	UT	All states
Wasatch International Adoptions	UT	All states; military overseas
Adoption Advocates International	WA	All states; Americans overseas
Americans Adopting Orphans	WA	All states; Americans overseas
New Hope Child and Family Agency	WA	International adoption, all states
Pauquette Children's Services	WI	International adoption, all states

* Many agencies will place children with special needs out of state. Don't limit yourself to this chart if you're interested in adopting a child with special needs. Also note that some agencies that place in many states will also place in Canada. Check with those agencies to find out.

HOW WOULD YOU ADVISE PROSPECTIVE ADOPTERS JUST STARTING OUT?

Here is some helpful advice from adoption agencies. Read and heed!

- Do your homework, stay flexible, keep realistic expectations, and above all, keep a sense of humor!—Bay Area Adoption Services, Mountain View, CA
- Don't give up—anything you have to go through is worth it when you receive your child.—Small Miracles Foundation of the Rockies, Englewood, CO
- Be good consumers, read between the lines. Choose an agency that gives you time, attention, straight answers, one you feel will advocate for you and seems like a good fit (not just paper shufflers).—Thursday's Child, Inc., Bloomfield, CT
- Be open-minded—there is no such thing as a "dumb" question. Balance patience with perseverance and be completely open and honest with yourself and each other (if a couple).—Bethany for Children and Families, Moline, IL
- Advocate for yourselves; no one will do it better. Ask hard questions; trust your heart.—Family Resource Center, Chicago, IL
- Read widely, ask many questions, and order a copy of the current year's *Report on Intercountry Adoption* from International Concerns for Children, 911 Cypress Dr., Boulder, CO 80303, for $25.—Beacon Adoption Center, Great Barrington, MA
- Attend free information meetings at several agencies and talk to those who have adopted through those agencies.—Wide Horizons for Children, Waltham, MA
- Deal with infertility; grieve and say goodbye to "the child that would have been;" resolve the desperation.—Catholic Social Services of Washtenaw County, Ann Arbor, MI
- Get information from a minimum of 10 different agencies who offer what the client is looking for. Ask specific questions, such as what is the agency refund policy, what

happens to fees paid if the country closes, etc. Once an agency is selected, take copious notes and keep a detailed diary. Copy every document you prepare for the adoption. Read everything you can about adoption. Join support groups.—Small World Adoption Foundation, Ballwin, MO

- Know the strengths of your family; don't compromise on what is *most* important to you.—Community Maternity Services, Albany, NY
- Educate yourself about all options—domestic vs. international. Explore country options, agency options. Talk to other adoptive families.—Family Adoption Consultants, Macedonia, OH
- Be flexible and persevere; there is a child who needs you.—Orphans Overseas, Portland, OR
- Get as much info as possible. Check licensing of providers. Check references.—Adoptions International, Inc., Philadelphia, PA

WHAT DO YOU WISH YOU COULD MAKE ADOPTIVE PARENTS MEMORIZE?

- To be more empathetic, supportive of birthparents.—Adoption Care Center, Scottsdale, AZ
- Adoptive parents and agencies have the same goal—good homes for children.—Dillon Southwest, Scottsdale, AZ
- Education and self-exploration first—adoption process second. Adoption is not a right; it's a service to families, a duty to children.—Adoption Horizons, Eureka, CA
- The sooner you turn in your paperwork the sooner your homestudy will be done.—Families for Children, Sacramento, CA
- There are no guarantees!—Adoption Alliance, Aurora, CO
- Never promise more openness than you feel comfortable with. Think about your child's possible needs for contact with birthparents. Put those needs before your own fears.—Small Miracles Foundation of the Rockies, Englewood, CO
- Adoption takes Patience (capital 'P') but it's worth the effort.—Thursday's Child, Inc., Bloomfield, CT
- All parenting is a leap of faith.—Advocates for Children and Families, North Miami Beach, FL
- The baby that is meant for us will eventually be placed with us in our home.—Adoption Planning, Inc., Atlanta, GA
- God's timing in their receiving a child is perfect.—Covenant Care Services, Macon, GA
- Be genuinely kind to birthparents. The child is their child until they sign consents requesting that you adopt their child.—Ad-In, Inc., Indianapolis, IN
- Being parents is about the *relationship* you have with your child—not giving birth or looking like that child.—Wide Horizons for Children, Waltham, MA
- There are risks in adoption! Either take some or forget adoption!—Adoption Associates, Jenison, MI

- 1. Birthmothers change their minds. 2. Adoption is as emotional an experience as pregnancy (if not more so). 3. Adoption shouldn't be viewed as a "second choice!"—Adoption Advocates, Kansas City, MO
- Be patient: Forever families take a while.—Universal Adoption Services, Jefferson City, MO
- 1. If at first you don't succeed keep trying—never give up. 2. Think of all the paperwork and process as your swollen ankles, labor, and delivery. When you hold your child the pain is forgotten.—Family Connections, Inc., Cortland, NY
- Treat your agency staff as you want to be treated.—Heaven Sent Children, Murfreesboro, TN
- Stop imagining "What if..."—Andrel Adoptions, Austin, TX
- They need to read, read, read! As well as attend adoption workshops.—Texas Cradle Society, San Antonio, TX
- In international adoptions there are no promises. We are at the mercy of the foreign governments and institutions, and things can go wrong.—Wasatch International Adoptions, Ogden, UT
- Trust your instincts and go slowly.—Jewish Family Service of Tidewater, Virginia Beach, VA

TOP TEN AGENCY DO'S AND DON'TS FOR ADOPTERS

I searched for patterns among the responses to my agency questionnaire and found these helpful hints, stated by many agencies.

1. Don't be in a big hurry and rush into something without thinking about it first. Panic and desperation are not your friends.
2. Do your agency paperwork. If you procrastinate, you can delay a placement.
3. Don't call the agency every day. Monthly (or weekly, if you must) is better.
4. Be honest. Lying could cause your application to be turned down.
5. If you want the agency to guarantee you a perfect child, think again. Even healthy children can have problems later. Do, however, obtain as much information as you can.
6. Listen to your agency: Don't assume outsiders know more. The Internet is not always right!
7. Read the brochures and handouts the agency gives you. They answer most questions.
8. Be understanding of birthparents and don't look down your nose at them.
9. Don't set artificial deadlines, like "I want to adopt by Christmas" or your birthday or some other date on your calendar. The process won't follow your schedule.
10. If you adopt from another country, realize that countries have their own rules and the agency can't change them.

INFORMATION FROM INDIVIDUAL ADOPTION AGENCIES

Cautionary Note: The information that follows is drawn from an adoption agency questionnaire I submitted, primarily from February to June 1999. In some cases, so much information was provided to me that I could not include it all.

Listing in this book is in no way a guarantee of services nor should it be considered to be an endorsement. Readers should thoroughly check out personally any adoption agency before applying. Do not apply to an adoption agency until you have considered at least several agencies, for comparison purposes.

The information provided here may have changed since June 1999, and thus you should verify policies, fees, and other data. The purpose of providing this information is to give you not only data on each agency but also information that can be used for comparison purposes. I have checked and double-checked the responses, and my transcribed data but errors of omission and commission may have crept in; if so, I apologize for them.

ALABAMA

LIFELINE CHILDREN'S SERVICES, INC.

Respondent: Chuck Johnson, Director
In charge of social services: Lea Anne Parker, Supervisor
2908 Pump House Rd., Birmingham, AL 35243
(205) 967-0811 • Fax: (205) 969-2137
www.lifelineadoption.org
Year first licensed by state: 1981

Agency provides services for: U.S. adoption; children with special needs; infants; homestudy if parents working with another agency; postplacement services; maternity home; contract for international adoptions.

What states do your adoptive parent clients come from? Alabama. Special needs, all states.

States/countries your birthparents/adopted children come from: All states.

What was the goal of your agency when first organized? What is the goal of your agency now? Provide Christian homes to birthmoms and children. Now: Same.

Nonrelative children placed in 1998: 42

Percent of adoptive placements under 6 mos.: 50–75%

Special expertise of staff: Licensed social workers: adoption counselor.

In 1998, what was the average time from when a prospective adoptive parent applied to when he or she received a homestudy? Varied according to type of child. Caucasian: 2–4 years; African-American: 6 mos. or less; Biracial: 6 mos. or less.

What made you decide to work in the adoption field? Each of us is dedicated to Christian, pro-life work.

Agency criteria for adoptive parents you work with: Varies according to type of child.

How do you screen adoptive parents? Fingerprints, child abuse [checks], references, medicals, financial status, personal health and habits, mental health, homestudy, insurance coverage.

What kind of medical information do you seek from birthparents? All personal and family medical history, prenatal care history, birth history, HIV status.

What kind of medical information do you seek on older children? Same as above, with pediatric care added plus HIV status.

What percent of your U.S. adoptions are nonwhite children? 50%

Do you have a waiting list of prospective parents? Yes, for Caucasian. Very short for African-American or Biracial.

Is it all right if adopting parents you work with are on waiting lists of other agencies or attorneys? Yes.

Are your adoption fees based on a sliding scale? No.

Do you have an application fee? If yes, what is the amount of the application fee? Yes. Varies.

What is your placement fee? Based on expenses, by law.

My agency: Offers confidential adoptions; "semi-open" adoptions; meetings between birthparents and adoptive parents; birthparents pick adoptive parents from bios/resumes; offers full disclosure of names between birth and adoptive parents.

Does your agency provide videotapes of children needing adoption? Case by case basis. Usually on Web site.

Are you an adoptive parent, adopted person, or birthparent? Adoptive parent.

In how many cases with your agency has an adoptive parent been placed with a child but lost the child due to a birthparent challenge? Never after legal period but three times during risk period.

Has your agency lost any adoption litigation filed against you by an adoptive parent or birthparent? No.

VILLA HOPE INTERNATIONAL ADOPTION

Respondent: Jeanne Wear, Executive Director
6 Office Park Circle, Suite 218, Birmingham, AL 35223
(205) 870-7359 • Fax: (205) 871-6629
E-mail: villahope@worldnet.att.net • www.pbwebstuff.com/villahope
Year first licensed by state: 1988

Agency provides services for: International adoption; homestudy if parents working with another agency; postplacement services.

What states do your adoptive parent clients come from? Any state.

Services provided adopting parents: Required readings of books and/or articles on adoption; private meeting with in-state families to discuss all aspects of the adoption process.

States/countries your birthparents/adopted children come from: Bolivia, Ecuador, Peru, China, Vietnam, Russia (Alabama only).

What was the goal of your agency when first organized? What is the goal of your agency now? To provide assistance to poor and homeless children throughout the world and to facilitate international placements of legally adoptable orphaned and abandoned children. Now: Same.

Nonrelative children placed in 1998: 46

Special expertise of staff: Adoptive parents on staff; licensed social workers.

In 1998, what was the average time from when a prospective adoptive parent applied to when he or she received a homestudy? 6–8 weeks

Average time from homestudy to placement of child: 6–9 mos.

What made you decide to work in the adoption field? Involvement in AID program.

Agency criteria for adoptive parents you work with: Varies with program; determined by individual countries.

How do you screen adoptive parents? Through preliminary application form initially and the homestudy process, which includes criminal background checks.

What kind of medical information do you seek on older children? What is available from the specific country according to their laws and regulations.

Do you have a waiting list of prospective parents? No.

Is it all right if adopting parents you work with are on waiting lists of other agencies or attorneys? Yes.

Are your adoption fees based on a sliding scale? If yes, what are the sliding scale criteria? Yes. Family income.

Do you have an application fee? If yes, what is the amount of the application fee? Yes. $150

What is your homestudy fee (if a flat rate)? $850

What is your placement fee? Varies with country. We include postplacement fees. Villa Hope's actual placement fee is $2,700–2,900

If applicable, what is the average document language translation fee? $20/page

If international adoption, what are average travel expenses? Varies ($2,000–5,000, depending on country).

If you place children from other countries please list the estimated *entire* average cost to adoptive parents for each country. All programs average $16,000–18,000, Russia program averages $20,000.

Does your agency provide videotapes of children needing adoption? For some programs.

Has your agency lost any adoption litigation filed against you by an adoptive parent or birthparent? No, we have never had a lawsuit against our agency.

ALASKA

CATHOLIC SOCIAL SERVICES

Respondent: Elaine Cordova, Director, Adoption/Pregnancy Support
In charge of social services: Elaine Cordova
3710 E. 20th Ave., Anchorage, AK 99508
(907) 276-5590 • Fax: (907) 258-1091
E-mail: ecordova@css.ak.org
Year first licensed by state: 1970

Agency provides services for: International adoption (agent for Holt International); U.S. adoption; children with special needs; infants; homestudy if parents working with another agency; postplacement services.

What states do your adoptive parent clients come from? Alaska.

Services provided adopting parents: Classes with other prospective parents; required readings of books and/or articles on adoption; special needs training.

States/countries your birthparents/adopted children come from: Alaska and through international agencies.

What is the goal of your agency? Finding and securing permanent homes for children.

Nonrelative children placed in 1998: 12

Percent of adoptive placements under 6 mos.: 95%

Special expertise of staff: Psychologists.

In 1998, what was the average time from when a prospective adoptive parent applied to when he or she received a homestudy? 2 mos.

Average time from homestudy to placement of child: 9 mos.

What made you decide to work in the adoption field? Few resources in the state.

Agency criteria for adoptive parents you work with: Healthy, stable.

How do you screen adoptive parents? Thorough training, interviews, homestudy.

How do you screen birthparents? Through interviews and counseling.

What kind of medical information do you seek from birthparents? Free disclosure of health history as well as prenatal.

What kind of medical information do you seek on older children? Physical examination.

What percent of your U.S. adoptions are nonwhite children? 50%

About what percent are children with medical problems? 10%

Do you have a waiting list of prospective parents? No.

Is it all right if adopting parents you work with are on waiting lists of other agencies or attorneys? Yes.

Are your adoption fees based on a sliding scale? No.

Do you have an application fee? If yes, what is the amount of the application fee?
Yes. $75

What is your homestudy fee (if a flat rate)? $550–850

What is your placement fee? $5,500

Do adopting parents also pay fees for medical and hospital expenses for birth-mother and baby when they have no insurance? If yes, what is the average fee paid? Yes. Usually covered by Medicaid; when not, $2,000 is average.

My agency: Offers confidential adoptions; semi-open adoptions; meetings between birthparents and adoptive parents; birthparents pick adoptive parents from bios/resumes; full disclosure of names between birth and adoptive parents.

In how many cases with your agency has an adoptive parent been placed with a child but lost the child due to a birthparent challenge? 0

Has your agency lost any adoption litigation filed against you by an adoptive parent or birthparent? No.

FAIRBANKS COUNSELING AND ADOPTION

Respondent: Melody Jamieson, Adoption Coordinator
912 Barnette St., Fairbanks, AK 99709
(907) 456-4729 • Fax: (907) 456-4623
Year first licensed by state: 1972

Agency provides services for: International adoption (homestudy and postplacement only); U.S. adoption; children with special needs; infants; homestudy if parents working with another agency; postplacement services; counseling for adoption issues.

What states do your adoptive parent clients come from? Alaska.

Services provided adopting parents: Classes with other prospective parents (in collaboration with other agencies); required readings of books and/or articles on adoption; parenting discussions.

States/countries your birthparents/adopted children come from: Alaska (birthparents). Adopted children all over the United States and the rest of the world.

What was the goal of your agency when first organized? What is the goal of your agency now? To provide adoption services/birthparent services and counseling (individual and family) and teen pregnancy prevention. Now: Basically the same plus counseling for children in foster care and any child of any age with abuse and neglect issues.

Nonrelative children placed in 1998: 8

Percent of adoptive placements under 6 mos.: 95%

Special expertise of staff: Adoptive parents on staff; licensed social workers; psychologists; therapists; adoption counselor/coordinator has 30 years experience in all kinds of adoptions.

In 1998, what was the average time from when a prospective adoptive parent applied to when he or she received a homestudy? 2 weeks to begin; usually finished in 2–3 mos.

Average time from homestudy to placement of child: 8–9 mos.

What made you decide to work in the adoption field? Challenging, rewarding, love to work with families and children

Agency criteria for adoptive parents you work with: All families are considered on a case-by-case basis.

How do you screen adoptive parents? We ask for references, criminal clearances, financial and health information, and we talk with the family.

How do you screen birthparents? Talk with them and get releases to verify the information they give us, such as medical.

What kind of medical information do you seek on older children? As complete a history as we can locate.

What percent of your U.S. adoptions are nonwhite children? 50%

About what percent are children with medical problems? Severe: Approximately 10%. Mild or at risk for: Approximately 50%.

Do you have a waiting list of prospective parents? Yes, a short one—5–10 families at a time.

Is it all right if adopting parents you work with are on waiting lists of other agencies or attorneys? Yes.

Are your adoption fees based on a sliding scale? No.

Do you have an application fee? If yes, what is the amount of the application fee? Yes. $75

What is your homestudy fee (if a flat rate)? $900

What is your placement fee? $5,025

Do adopting parents also pay fees for medical and hospital expenses for birth-mother and baby when they have no insurance? If yes, what is the average fee paid? Yes; happens very rarely. $7,000–8,000

My agency: Offers confidential adoptions (only by birthparent request); semi-open adoptions; meetings between birthparents and adoptive parents; birthparents pick adoptive parents from bios/resumes; full disclosure of names between birth and adoptive parents. We strongly encourage open/identified adoptions. All our families are prepared for open adoption.

Does your agency provide videotapes of children needing adoption? Yes, occasionally.

In how many cases with your agency has an adoptive parent been placed with a child but lost the child due to a birthparent challenge? 0

Has your agency lost any adoption litigation filed against you by an adoptive parent or birthparent? No.

ARIZONA

ADOPTION CARE CENTER

Respondent: Rick DiMaggio, Agency Administrator
In charge of social services: Danielle Saquier
8233 Via Paseo Del North E 250, Scottsdale, AZ 85258
(602) 922-8838 • Fax: (602) 922-8823
Year first licensed by state: 1990

Agency provides services for: U.S. adoption; homestudy if parents working with another agency; postplacement services.

What states do your adoptive parent clients come from? All.

Services provided adopting parents: Parenting discussions; individual family counseling.

States/countries your birthparents/adopted children come from: All.

What was the goal of your agency when first organized? What is the goal of your agency now? Child placement. Now: Same.

Nonrelative children placed in 1998: 14

Percent of adoptive placements under 6 mos.: 93%

Special expertise of staff: Licensed social workers; adoption counselors.

In 1998, what was the average time from when a prospective adoptive parent applied to when he or she received a homestudy? 2 mos.

Average time from homestudy to placement of child: 10 mos.

Agency criteria for adoptive parents you work with: Open; reasonable expectation of placement within 1 year.

How do you screen adoptive parents? Review of homestudy.

How do you screen birthparents? Personal evaluation, blood screens, etc.

What kind of medical information do you seek from birthparents? Comprehensive social/medical history.

What kind of medical information do you seek on older children? Complete medical history.

What percent of your U.S. adoptions are nonwhite children? 12%

Do you have a waiting list of prospective parents? No.

Is it all right if adopting parents you work with are on waiting lists of other agencies or attorneys? Yes.

Are your adoption fees based on a sliding scale? No.

Do you have an application fee? No.

What is your homestudy fee (if a flat rate)? $850

What is your placement fee? $18,000

Do adopting parents also pay fees for medical and hospital expenses for birth-mother and baby when they have no insurance? If yes, what is the average fee paid? Yes. $4,500

My agency: Offers confidential adoptions; semi-open adoptions; meetings between birthparents and adoptive parents; birthparents pick adoptive parents from bios/resumes.

In how many cases with your agency has an adoptive parent been placed with a child but lost the child due to a birthparent challenge? 2

Has your agency lost any adoption litigation filed against you by an adoptive parent or birthparent? No.

DILLON SOUTHWEST

Respondent: Marsha Usdane, ACSW, CISW, Director
In charge of social services: Marsha Usdane
3014 N. Hayden Rd. #101, Scottsdale, AZ 85251
(602) 945-2221 • Fax: (602) 945-3956
E-mail: mlusdane@aol.com
Year first licensed by state: 1983

Agency provides services for: International adoption; children with special needs; infants; homestudy if parents working with another agency; postplacement services.

What states do your adoptive parent clients come from? Arizona.

Services provided adopting parents: Classes with other prospective parents; group discussions about adoption; parenting discussions; nurses teaching care for first-time parents.

States/countries your birthparents/adopted children come from: Korea. We also network with other agencies for families adopting from other countries.

What was the goal of your agency when first organized? What is the goal of your agency now? To find good homes for children in need of homes. Now: Same.

Nonrelative children placed in 1998: 35

Special expertise of staff: Adoptive parents on staff; licensed social workers; therapists.

In 1998, what was the average time from when a prospective adoptive parent applied to when he or she received a homestudy? Within 2 weeks.

Average time from homestudy to placement of child: 6 mos. or less.

What made you decide to work in the adoption field? Adoptive parent who saw the need for a good agency that could find homes for international children.

Agency criteria for adoptive parents you work with: Our requirements are those of the country we are doing the study for plus those we feel are important for a child (physically, emotionally, financially able to care for a child).

How do you screen adoptive parents? 1. Self-screening process of an all-day group education meeting; 2. Adoptive homestudy.

What kind of medical information do you seek on older children? We receive information from our counterpart agency in Korea.

Do you have a waiting list of prospective parents? No.

Is it all right if adopting parents you work with are on waiting lists of other agencies or attorneys? No.

Are your adoption fees based on a sliding scale? No.

Do you have an application fee? If yes, what is the amount of the application fee? Yes. $250

What is your homestudy fee (if a flat rate)? $950

Do adopting parents also pay fees for medical and hospital expenses for birthmother and baby when they have no insurance? No.

If international adoption, what are average travel expenses? $1,400 to Korea.

If you place children from other countries, please list the estimated _entire_ average cost to adoptive parents for each country. Korean program: $13,000, including homestudy, postplacement. For other countries, preapplication, $50; application, $250; homestudy, $950; postplacement, $950.

My agency: Offers confidential adoptions.

Does your agency provide videotapes of children needing adoption? Rarely.

Are you an adoptive parent, adopted person, or birthparent? Adoptive parent.

In how many cases with your agency has an adoptive parent been placed with a child but lost the child due to a birthparent challenge? 0

Has your agency lost any adoption litigation filed against you by an adoptive parent or birthparent? No.

CALIFORNIA

ADOPT A SPECIAL KID

Respondent: Vali Ebert, MSW, Assistant Director, Programs
In charge of social services: Vali Ebert
287 17th St., Suite 207, Oakland, CA 94612-4123
(510) 451-1748 • Fax: (510) 451-2023
www.adoptaspecialkid.org
Year first licensed by state: 1973

Agency provides services for: U.S. adoption; children with special needs.

What states do your adoptive parent clients come from? 21 counties in Northern California.

Services provided adopting parents: Classes with other prospective parents; required readings of books and/or articles on adoption; group discussions about adoption; parenting discussions; family events (picnics, parties, baseball games, shows); buddy families (prospective parents are matched with experienced families).

States/countries your birthparents/adopted children come from: Any state, mostly California. We don't work with birthparents.

What was the goal of your agency when first organized? What is the goal of your agency now? Promote the adoption of special needs children. Now: Same.

Nonrelative children placed in 1998: 22

Special expertise of staff: Adoptive parents on staff.

In 1998, what was the average time from when a prospective adoptive parent applied to when he or she received a homestudy? 1 mo.

Average time from homestudy to placement of child: 6 mos.

What made you decide to work in the adoption field? Helping under-served, mal-treated children.

Agency criteria for adoptive parents you work with: We try to be as inclusive as possible while following state regulations.

How do you screen adoptive parents? Interview process, fingerprints, child abuse clearance, personal and employment references, medical report.

What kind of medical information do you seek from birthparents? We receive birthparent information from the child's social worker. This varies between regions and custodial agencies, but is usually very thorough.

What kind of medical information do you seek on older children? Same as above.

What percent of your U.S. adoptions are nonwhite children? Over 50%

About what percent are children with medical problems? 20%

About what percent are children with emotional problems? 80%

Do you have a waiting list of prospective parents? No.

Is it all right if adopting parents you work with are on waiting lists of other agencies or attorneys? No.

Are your adoption fees based on a sliding scale? No fees.

Do you have an application fee? No.

What is your homestudy fee (if a flat rate)? 0

My agency: Offers confidential adoptions.

Does your agency provide videotapes of children needing adoption? No.

In how many cases with your agency has an adoptive parent been placed with a child but lost the child due to a birthparent challenge? 0

Has your agency lost any adoption litigation filed against you by an adoptive parent or birthparent? No.

ACCEPT - AN ADOPTION AND COUNSELING CENTER

Respondent: Bee Brown Ph.D., Executive Director
In charge of social services: Marge Hurwitz, LCSW
339 S. San Antonio Rd., Los Altos, CA 94022
(650) 917-8090 • Fax: (650) 917-8093
E-mail: accepadopt@aol.com
Year first licensed by state: 1991

Agency provides services for: International adoption; U.S. adoption; children with special needs; homestudy if parents working with another agency; postplacement services.

What states do your adoptive parent clients come from? Northern California only (we are a local service agency).

Services provided adopting parents: Required readings of books and/or articles on adoption. We do all counseling individually and we provide this as a free service.

States/countries your birthparents/adopted children come from: Peru, Guatemala, Chile, Bulgaria, Russia, Ukraine, China, Taiwan, India, Nepal, Hong Kong.

What was the goal of your agency when first organized? What is the goal of your agency now? To find loving, safe homes for orphaned children. Now: Same.

Nonrelative children placed in 1998: 137

Percent of adoptive placements under 6 mos.: 10%

Special expertise of staff: Adoptive parents on staff; licensed social workers; psychologists; therapists.

In 1998, what was the average time from when a prospective adoptive parent applied to when he or she received a homestudy? 2–3 mos. This is because the state is slow clearing state fingerprints and child abuse checks.

Average time from homestudy to placement of child: 10 mos.

Agency criteria for adoptive parents you work with: We have a very open policy.

How do you screen adoptive parents? Anyone with a history of drug, alcohol abuse, drunk driving, spousal abuse, etc., we will not work with.

What kind of medical information do you seek on older children? As much as we can get.

What percent of your U.S. adoptions are nonwhite children? 2 per year.

Do you have a waiting list of prospective parents? Yes.

Is it all right if adopting parents you work with are on waiting lists of other agencies or attorneys? Yes.

Are your adoption fees based on a sliding scale? No.

Do you have an application fee? If yes, what is the amount of the application fee? Yes. $150

What is your homestudy fee (if a flat rate)? $1,800 for domestic; $2,450 for international.

If international adoption, what are average travel expenses? $4,000

If you place children from other countries, please list the estimated *entire* average cost to adoptive parents for each country. Peru, $12,000; Russia/Ukraine, $23,000; China, $15,000; Guatemala, $21,000; Bulgaria, $19,000.

Does your agency provide videotapes of children needing adoption? Yes, whenever possible.

In how many cases with your agency has an adoptive parent been placed with a child but lost the child due to a birthparent challenge? 0

Has your agency lost any adoption litigation filed against you by an adoptive parent or birthparent? No.

ADOPTION CONNECTION

Respondents: Lynne Fingerman, MSW; Randie Bencanann, LCSW, Co-directors
In charge of social services: Rachel Breuer, Outreach Coordinator
3272 California St., San Francisco, CA 94118
(415) 202-7494 • Fax: (415) 351-2707
E-mail: families@adoptionconnection.org • www.adoptionconnection.org
Year first licensed by state: 1985

Agency provides services for: U.S. adoption.

What states do your adoptive parent clients come from? California.

Services provided adopting parents: Classes with other prospective parents; group discussions about adoption; parenting discussions.

States/countries your birthparents/adopted children come from: All states.

What was the goal of your agency when first organized? What is the goal of your agency now? To facilitate open domestic adoptions. Now: Same, but also provide postplacement services for adoptive families.

Nonrelative children placed in 1998: 120

Percent of adoptive placements under 6 mos.: 99%

Special expertise of staff: Adoptive parents on staff; licensed social workers; therapists; attorney; adoptee.

In 1998, what was the average time from when a prospective adoptive parent applied to when he or she received a homestudy? 2 mos.

Average time from homestudy to placement of child: 1 year

What made you decide to work in the adoption field? Many of us have personal experience with adoption, as well as interest in the well-being of children and families.

Agency criteria for adoptive parents you work with: Age, marital status. Number of children in the home is not necessarily limiting for potential adoptive parents.

How do you screen adoptive parents? They need to complete a homestudy, which includes interviews with a social worker, fingerprint and child abuse clearance, references, medical and financial reports, and home visits.

How do you screen birthparents? Telephone and in-person interviews, collection of medical records, and autobiographical information.

What kind of medical information do you seek from birthparents? Exclusive self-reported medical and social history, plus doctor's reports.

What kind of medical information do you seek on older children? Medical reports and other appropriate assessments as needed.

What percent of your U.S. adoptions are nonwhite children? 15%

Do you have a waiting list of prospective parents? Yes.

Is it all right if adopting parents you work with are on waiting lists of other agencies or attorneys? Yes.

Are your adoption fees based on a sliding scale? If yes, what are the sliding scale criteria? Yes. Combined household income.

Do you have an application fee? If yes, what is the amount of the application fee? Yes. $100

What is your homestudy fee (if a flat rate)? $850–2,300

What is your placement fee? $750–2,100

Do adopting parents also pay fees for medical and hospital expenses for birth-mother and baby when they have no insurance? If yes, what is the average fee paid? Yes. $3,000–5,000

My agency: Offers confidential adoptions; semi-open adoptions; meetings between birthparents and adoptive parents; birthparents pick adoptive parents from bios/resumes; offers full disclosure of names between birth and adoptive parents.

Does your agency provide videotapes of children needing adoption? No.

Are you an adoptive parent, adopted person, or birthparent? Adopted person.

In how many cases with your agency has an adoptive parent been placed with a child but lost the child due to a birthparent challenge? 2% of our placements have been reclaimed prior to birthparents signing relinquishment papers.

Has your agency lost any adoption litigation filed against you by an adoptive parent or birthparent? No.

ADOPTION HORIZONS

Respondent: Sherill Chand, Executive Director
In charge of social services: Sherill Chand
302 4th St., Eureka, CA 95501
(707) 444-9909 • Fax: (707) 442-6672
Year first licensed by state: 1982

Agency provides services for: International adoption; U.S. adoption; children with special needs; infants; homestudy if parents working with another agency. Our affiliate, the Birth Parent Center, facilitates open, independent adoptions.

What states do your adoptive parent clients come from? Mostly California, but for some programs any state.

Services provided adopting parents: Classes with other prospective parents; required readings of books and/or articles on adoption; group discussions about adoption; parenting discussions; individual counseling on infertility, loss, and marital issues.

States/countries your birthparents/adopted children come from: Birthparents mostly California. Children: 30% from China and Vietnam, 30% from California, foster adoptions.

What was the goal of your agency when first organized? What is the goal of your agency now? To fill a void of services in Northern California and to reduce the wait for a child, access to children worldwide. Now: Ensure professional, learning-based services. Support quality of adoptive placement. Do less, better.

Nonrelative children placed in 1998: 20

Percent of adoptive placements under 6 mos.: 50%

Special expertise of staff: Adoptive parents on staff; licensed social workers; therapists; parenting teachers; credentialed educators; peer mentors; pastoral counselors.

In 1998, what was the average time from when a prospective adoptive parent applied to when he or she received a homestudy? 2–3 mos.

Average time from homestudy to placement of child: 6 mos.

What made you decide to work in the adoption field? I was a family life educator and realized families needed education before adoption and that learning skills would serve children by creating a more prepared pool of adoptive families.

Agency criteria for adoptive parents you work with: We will work with anyone who can meet the criteria of our several programs. Our main criteria are an approved homestudy and adoption process customized for the requested program.

How do you screen adoptive parents? Initial phone interview, two-hour orientation, two-hour consultation, application, pre-social–worker interview in some cases, four session individual homestudy.

How do you screen birthparents? In affiliate program only, three pre-application counseling sessions with therapist, one- to two-hour intake interview, medical and social records, and references, ongoing weekly contact with social worker and therapist.

What kind of medical information do you seek from birthparents? Full information going back three generations, prenatal records, any psychosocial records, and self-history.

What kind of medical information do you seek on older children? Everything that is available. May request developmental or physical evaluations be done prior to match.

What percent of your U.S. adoptions are nonwhite children? 10%

About what percent are children with medical problems? 10%

About what percent are children with emotional problems? 10%

Do you have a waiting list of prospective parents? No.

Is it all right if adopting parents you work with are on waiting lists of other agencies or attorneys? Yes, in some programs.

Are your adoption fees based on a sliding scale? No. Offer scholarships and loans to eligible families.

Do you have an application fee? If yes, what is the amount of the application fee? Yes. $75

What is your homestudy fee (if a flat rate)? Varies on kind of homestudy from $500–3,500.

What is your placement fee? Varies with program from $750–7,500.

Do adopting parents also pay fees for medical and hospital expenses for birthmother and baby when they have no insurance? If yes, what is the average fee paid? Yes. $3,500–5,000

If applicable, what is the average document language translation fee? $600–1,000. Includes other services.

If international adoption, what are average travel expenses? $2,500 per person.

If you place children from other countries, please list the estimated *entire* average cost to adoptive parents for each country. China, $17,000 with two people traveling; Vietnam, $20,000 with two people traveling.

My agency: Offers confidential adoptions; semi-open adoptions; meetings between birthparents and adoptive parents; birthparents pick adoptive parents from bios/resumes; offers full disclosure of names between birth and adoptive parents.

Does your agency provide videotapes of children needing adoption? Yes.

In how many cases with your agency has an adoptive parent been placed with a child but lost the child due to a birthparent challenge? 0

Has your agency lost any adoption litigation filed against you by an adoptive parent or birthparent? No.

ADOPTION SERVICES INTERNATIONAL

Respondent: Marilyn F. Adams, M.A., Executive Director
In charge of social services: Lisa Browne, LCSW, Social Work Supervisor
2021 Sperry Ave., Suite 35, Ventura, CA 93003
(800) 704-4841 • Fax: (805) 644-9270
E-mail: asicas@aol.com
Year first licensed by state: 1984

Agency provides services for: International adoption; U.S. adoption; infants; homestudy if parents working with another agency; postplacement services; parent support groups; parent preparation workshops; homeland tours; international boutique; library of books, videos, and tapes; family gathering days; culture camp.

What states do your adoptive parent clients come from? California.

Services provided adopting parents: Classes with other prospective parents; required readings of books and/or articles on adoption; group discussions about adoption; parenting discussions.

States/countries your birthparents/adopted children come from: Russia, Romania, China, Nepal, India, Pacific Islands, Vietnam, Guatemala, Brazil, Korea, Philippines.

What was the goal of your agency when first organized? To find families for Korean orphans.

Nonrelative children placed in 1998: 96

Percent of adoptive placements under 6 mos.: 20%

Special expertise by staff: Adoptive parents on staff; licensed social workers; therapists.

In 1998, what was the average time from when a prospective adoptive parent applied to when he or she received a homestudy? 4 mos.

Average time from homestudy to placement of child: 1–2 mos.

What made you decide to work in the adoption field? I have experience with adopting children myself and foster-parenting many children. I have always worked in human service agencies and this sounded like a good match.

Agency criteria for adoptive parents you work with: Must be married 1 year; must meet criteria of foreign country. No other restrictions.

How do you screen adoptive parents? We meet all legal requirements, do a preliminary interview, and listen to our social workers' opinions of the parents.

What kind of medical information do you seek from birthparents? We only receive what foreign agency can or will provide, usually very little.

What kind of medical information do you seek on older children? Complete medical from doctor or clinic in foreign country plus special tests if indicated.

About what percent are children with medical problems? 5%

Do you have a waiting list of prospective parents? Yes.

Is it all right if adopting parents you work with are on waiting lists of other agencies or attorneys? Yes.

Are your adoption fees based on a sliding scale? No.

Do you have an application fee? No.

What is your homestudy fee (if a flat rate)? $1,800

What is your placement fee? $2,700

If applicable, what is the average document language translation fee? $10 per page.

If international adoption, what are average travel expenses? $1,200–2,300 per program.

My agency: Offers confidential adoptions.

Does your agency provide videotapes of children needing adoption? No.

Are you an adoptive parent, adopted person, or birthparent? Adoptive parent.

In how many cases with your agency has an adoptive parent been placed with a child but lost the child due to a birthparent challenge? 0

Has your agency lost any adoption litigation filed against you by an adoptive parent or birthparent? No.

ALTERNATIVE FAMILY SERVICES

Respondent: Jesse Aldrich Strassman, MSW, Adoption Services Coordinator
In charge of social services: Jim Gold, LCSW, Associate Director
25 Division St., Suite 201, San Francisco, CA 94103
(415) 626-2700 • Fax: (415) 626-2760
E-mail: altfamser@aol.com
Year first licensed by state: 1973

Agency provides services for: U.S. adoption; children with special needs; postplacement services.

What states do your adoptive parent clients come from? California.

Services provided adopting parents: Classes with other prospective parents; required readings of books and/or articles on adoption; group discussions about adoption; parenting discussions.

States/countries your birthparents/adopted children come from: California.

What was the goal of your agency when first organized? What is the goal of your agency now? Foster care (therapeutic). To provide children with an alternative to institutional care. Now: Reunification, foster care, adoption.

Nonrelative children placed in 1998: 0 (new program)

Percent of adoptive placements under 6 mos.: 0%

Special expertise of staff: Adoptive parents on staff; licensed social workers; psychologists.

In 1998, what was the average time from when a prospective adoptive parent applied to when he or she received a homestudy? 3–4 mos. We began our program in January 1999.

Average time from homestudy to placement of child: We haven't yet placed a child.

What made you decide to work in the adoption field? My graduate internship with a national advocacy agency that worked on adoption issues.

Agency criteria for adoptive parents you work with: Case-by-case basis. No specific criteria except family must be able to support itself prior to child being placed. If the family experiences a major change, loss, pregnancy, we try to give the family a year to stabilize prior to placement.

How do you screen adoptive parents? Telephone, orientation meeting, training, homestudy process.

What kind of medical information do you seek from birthparents? County obtains this information.

What kind of medical information do you seek on older children? As much as possible.

Do you have a waiting list of prospective parents? No.

Is it all right if adopting parents you work with are on waiting lists of other agencies or attorneys? No.

Are your adoption fees based on a sliding scale? No.

Do you have an application fee? No.

My agency: Offers meetings between birthparents and adoptive parents; offers full disclosure of names between birth and adoptive parents.

Does your agency provide videotapes of children needing adoption? Yes, sometimes.

Has your agency lost any adoption litigation filed against you by an adoptive parent or birthparent? No.

BAL JAGAT (CHILDREN'S WORLD)

Respondent: Hemlata Momaya, MSW, Executive Director
In charge of social services: Hemlata Momaya
9311 Farralone Ave., Chatsworth, CA 91311
(818) 709-4737 • Fax: (818) 772-6377
E-mail: BJCW@earthlink.net • www.adopt.baljagat.org
Year first licensed by state: 1983

Agency provides services for: International adoption; children with special needs; infants; homestudy if parents working with another agency; postplacement services.

What states do your adoptive parent clients come from? Almost all from California, but occasionally we help parents in other areas. Any state.

Services provided adopting parents: Required readings of books and/or articles on adoption; group discussions about adoption; parenting discussions; personal orientation and group preparation before travel. Our own publication, "Adoption Times."

States/countries your birthparents/adopted children come from: In 1998 our children arrived from India, China, Vietnam, Romania, Russia, Haiti, Marshall Island, and Pakistan. This year we expect children from Guatemala and Thailand.

What was the goal of your agency when first organized? What is the goal of your agency now? To help orphaned children be placed in adoptive homes and offer them a chance to grow in a family with love. Now: It is the same goal today. All children deserve a life to live, be loved, and grow in a family.

Nonrelative children placed in 1998: 83

Percent of adoptive placements under 6 mos.: More than 10%

Special expertise of staff: Adoptive parents on staff; licensed social workers; psychologists; therapists.

In 1998, what was the average time from when a prospective adoptive parent applied to when he or she received a homestudy? 2 mos.

Average time from homestudy to placement of child: 8–10 mos. Depends on country.

What made you decide to work in the adoption field? My degree in social work, specializing in family and child welfare, past experience working with orphaned children, love for children, and commitment to helping innocent lives and to making a small change in these innocent lives.

Agency criteria for adoptive parents you work with: Under age 45 for infant, not too large families, one divorce only, proper and stable married couple, proper income, adequate living conditions, married for more than 2 years, not newly married couples, and much more.

How do you screen adoptive parents? By interviewing them in person, no group meetings, and asking questions about everything.

What kind of medical information do you seek from birthparents? Foreign orphanages get some information from birthparents if possible.

What kind of medical information do you seek on older children? AIDS, hepatitis B test, full checkups, TB test in India, vaccination reports, etc.

Is it all right if adopting parents you work with are on waiting lists of other agencies or attorneys? No.

Are your adoption fees based on a sliding scale? No.

Do you have an application fee? If yes, what is the amount of the application fee? Yes. $300

What is your homestudy fee (if a flat rate)? $1,500

If international adoption, what are average travel expenses? About $2,000

If you place children from other countries, please list the estimated *entire* average cost to adoptive parents for each country. China, $10,000; India, $12,000 (although there are some inexpensive programs in India); Vietnam, $10,000; Romania, $12,000; Russia, $10,000; Thailand, $9,000; Guatemala, $16,000. This cost does not include travel, hotel, or homestudy.

My agency: Offers confidential adoptions; semi-open adoptions; full disclosure of names between birth and adoptive parents in some cases.

Does your agency provide videotapes of children needing adoption? Yes, for Russia.

In how many cases with your agency has an adoptive parent been placed with a child but lost the child due to a birthparent challenge? 0

Has your agency lost any adoption litigation filed against you by an adoptive parent or birthparent? No.

BAY AREA ADOPTION SERVICES

Respondent: Andrea Stawitcla, Executive Director
In charge of social services: Devon Rubin, LCSW, Supervisor of Social Work
465 Fairchild #215, Mountain View, CA 94043
(650) 964-3800 • Fax: (650) 964-6467
E-mail: baas@baas.org • www.baas.org
Year first licensed by state: 1984

Agency provides services for: International adoption; children with special needs; infants; postplacement services.

What states do your adoptive parent clients come from? Northern California only.

Services provided adopting parents: Classes with other prospective parents; required readings of books and/or articles on adoption; annual conference for adoptive parents and professionals; annual picnic; networking and workshops taught by social work staff.

States/countries your birthparents/adopted children come from: China, Guatemala, Russia, India, Philippines, Taiwan, Japan, Vietnam, Cambodia.

What was the goal of your agency when first organized? What is the goal of your agency now? To find homes for orphaned and abandoned children worldwide. Now: Still the same plus ongoing support for adoptive families.

Nonrelative children placed in 1998: 100+

Percent of adoptive placements under 6 mos.: 40–50%

Special expertise of staff: Adoptive parents on staff; licensed social workers; psychologists; therapists; bilingual (Spanish and Chinese).

In 1998, what was the average time from when a prospective adoptive parent applied to when he or she received a homestudy? 1–3 mos.

Average time from homestudy to placement of child: 6–12 mos., but can often be longer.

What made you decide to work in the adoption field? The belief that I could make a difference in the lives of children overseas.

Agency criteria for adoptive parents you work with: Must be 25; a citizen; if married, married for 1 year; and reside in one of the 12 counties in which we are licensed.

How do you screen adoptive parents? Our process is somewhat self-screening; prospective adoptive parents must complete a series of preadoption classes prior to the homestudy; some drop out at that point. Then the social worker completes the process during the course of the homestudy.

What kind of medical information do you seek from birthparents? Most of our adoptions are abandonments, so no information is known.

What kind of medical information do you seek on older children? Everything that is available.

About what percent are children with medical problems? Less than 10%

Do you have a waiting list of prospective parents? Yes.

Is it all right if adopting parents you work with are on waiting lists of other agencies or attorneys? Yes.

Are your adoption fees based on a sliding scale? No.

Do you have an application fee? If yes, what is the amount of the application fee? Yes. $175

What is your homestudy fee (if a flat rate)? $2,220

What is your placement fee? 0. Fees are paid directly to the program overseas. We provide postplacement services for up to $550.

If applicable, what is the average document language translation fee? $500–1,000

If international adoption, what are average travel expenses? $1,000–3,000

If you place children from other countries, please list the estimated *entire* average cost to adoptive parents for each country. China, $14,000–16,000; Philippines, $2,000; Colombia, $7,000; India, $5,000–8,000; Guatemala, $12,000–17,000; Vietnam, $15,000.

My agency: Offers confidential adoptions; offers semi-open adoptions.

Does your agency provide videotapes of children needing adoption? No.

In how many cases with your agency has an adoptive parent been placed with a child but lost the child due to a birthparent challenge? 0

Has your agency lost any adoption litigation filed against you by an adoptive parent or birthparent? No. Have never been sued.

FAMILIES FOR CHILDREN

Respondent: Amy Hokom, Adoption Supervisor
In charge of social services: Ursula DeVere, Executive Director
2650 Auburn Blvd., Suite C-206, Sacramento, CA 95821
(916) 974-8744 • Fax: (916) 487-1494
E-mail: ffc@families4children.com • www.families4children.com
Year first licensed by state: 1989

Agency provides services for: U.S. adoption; children with special needs; infants; homestudy if parents working with another agency.

What states do your adoptive parent clients come from? California.

Services provided adopting parents: Classes with other prospective parents; parenting discussions.

States/countries your birthparents/adopted children come from: California.

What is the goal of your agency now? To provide high-quality foster care and adoption services to special needs children.

Nonrelative children placed in 1998: 10

Percent of adoptive placements under 6 mos.: 5%

Special expertise of staff: Adoptive parents on staff; licensed social workers; therapists.

In 1998, what was the average time from when a prospective adoptive parent applied to when he or she received a homestudy? 3 mos.

Average time from homestudy to placement of child: 3–6 mos.

What made you decide to work in the adoption field? Helping children in need.

Agency criteria for adoptive parents you work with: Must comply with state regulations and live in California.

How do you screen adoptive parents? Fingerprints; child abuse index; 12 hours of training; CPR/first aid; individual and couple interview; questionnaires.

How do you screen birthparents? We rarely work with birthparents. Almost all of our children come from the foster care system.

What kind of medical information do you seek on older children? Everything that is available.

What percent of your U.S. adoptions are nonwhite children? 20%

About what percent are children with medical problems? 50%

About what percent are children with emotional problems? 80%

Do you have a waiting list of prospective parents? No.

Is it all right if adopting parents you work with are on waiting lists of other agencies or attorneys? No.

Are your adoption fees based on a sliding scale? No.

Do you have an application fee? If yes, what is the amount of the application fee? Yes. $50

What is your homestudy fee (if a flat rate)? $950

My agency: Offers confidential adoptions; semi-open adoptions; meetings between birthparents and adoptive parents; birthparents pick adoptive parents from bios/resumes; offers full disclosure of names between birth and adoptive parents.

Does your agency provide videotapes of children needing adoption? No.

In how many cases with your agency has an adoptive parent been placed with a child but lost the child due to a birthparent challenge? 0

Has your agency lost any adoption litigation filed against you by an adoptive parent or birthparent? No.

Is there anything that I have not asked you that is important? We focus on children who were removed from their parents and will not be going back because their parents did not meet reunification requirements.

FAMILY CONNECTIONS ADOPTIONS

Respondent: Audrey Foster, Executive Director
In charge of social services: Audrey Foster
P.O. Box 576035, Modesto, CA 95357
(209) 869-8844 • Fax: (209) 869-7334
E-mail: familycn@pacbell.net
Year first licensed by state: 1983

Agency provides services for: International adoption; U.S. adoption; children with special needs; homestudy if parents working with another agency; postplacement services; adoption education.

What states do your adoptive parent clients come from? California.

Services provided adopting parents: Classes with other prospective parents; required readings of books and/or articles on adoption; group discussions about adoption; parenting discussions; post-adoption support.

States/countries your birthparents/adopted children come from: Any U.S. state (most from California), Vietnam, China, Russia, India, Korea, Romania, Bulgaria, plus other countries families may have a referral from.

What was the goal of your agency when first organized? What is the goal of your agency now? Recruit families for waiting children. Now: Same.

Nonrelative children placed in 1998: 191

Special expertise of staff: Adoptive parents on staff; licensed social workers; therapists; attorney.

In 1998, what was the average time from when a prospective adoptive parent applied to when he or she received a homestudy? 4 mos.

Average time from homestudy to placement of child: 1 year

Agency criteria for adoptive parents you work with: If married, married 2 years.

How do you screen adoptive parents? Using state requirements: fingerprints, medicals, references.

What kind of medical information do you seek on older children? Everything that exists.

What percent of your U.S. adoptions are nonwhite children? 75%

About what percent are children with medical problems? 40%

About what percent are children with emotional problems? 60%

Do you have a waiting list of prospective parents? No.

Is it all right if adopting parents you work with are on waiting lists of other agencies or attorneys? For intercountry adoption only.

Are your adoption fees based on a sliding scale? No.

Do you have an application fee? If yes, what is the amount of the application fee? Yes. $100

What is your homestudy fee (if a flat rate)? $1,100 (including application fee) for U.S. adoptions; $1,500 (including all fees) for international.

What is your placement fee? There is postplacement fee ranging from $500–$1,000, depending on services requested by country.

If applicable, what is the average document language translation fee? No average available.

My agency: Offers confidential adoptions; semi-open adoptions; meetings between birthparents and adoptive parents.

Does your agency provide videotapes of children needing adoption? Yes.

Are you an adoptive parent, adopted person, or birthparent? Adoptive parent.

In how many cases with your agency has an adoptive parent been placed with a child but lost the child due to a birthparent challenge? 0

Has your agency lost any adoption litigation filed against you by an adoptive parent or birthparent? No.

GOD'S CHILDREN INTERNATIONAL ADOPTION AGENCY

Respondent: James Molter, Executive Director
In charge of social services: Joanne Olson, MSW
P.O. Box 320, Trabuco Canyon, CA 92678
(949) 858-7621
E-mail: adopt@godschildrenadoptions.org • www.godschildrenadoptions.org
Year first licensed by state: 1996

Agency provides services for: International adoption; postplacement services; education.

What states do your adoptive parent clients come from? All states.

Services provided adopting parents: Classes with other prospective parents; required readings of books and/or articles on adoption; group discussions about adoption; parenting discussions.

States/countries your birthparents/adopted children come from: Russia, Ukraine, China, Poland, Mexico, South Pacific, Vietnam, Belarus.

What was the goal of your agency when first organized? What is the goal of your agency now? To provide all necessary services to adoptive parents and their children before, during, and after the placement. Now: Same.

Nonrelative children placed in 1998: 24

Special expertise of staff: Adoptive parents on staff; licensed social workers; attorney.

In 1998, what was the average time from when a prospective adoptive parent applied to when he or she received a homestudy? 48 hours

Average time from homestudy to placement of child: 4–5 mos.

What made you decide to work in the adoption field? Dire need to provide all necessary information for parents.

Agency criteria for adoptive parents you work with: Must be at least 25 years old. The rest is on a case-by-case basis.

How do you screen adoptive parents? State and INS standards in addition to our own standards.

What kind of medical information do you seek from birthparents? All available.

What kind of medical information do you seek on older children? All, especially red-flag issues, as determined by American Academy of Pediatrics.

Do you have a waiting list of prospective parents? Yes.

Is it all right if adopting parents you work with are on waiting lists of other agencies or attorneys? No.

Are your adoption fees based on a sliding scale? No.

Do you have an application fee? If yes, what is the amount of the application fee? Yes. $100

What is your homestudy fee (if a flat rate)? $1,500

What is your placement fee? $4,500

If applicable, what is the average document language translation fee? $400 per dossier

If international adoption, what are average travel expenses? $3,000

If you place children from other countries, please list the estimated *entire* average cost to adoptive parents for each country. $14,000–20,000

My agency: Offers confidential adoptions; semi-open adoptions; meetings between birthparents and adoptive parents; birthparents pick adoptive parents from bios/resumes; full disclosure of names between birth and adoptive parents.

Does your agency provide videotapes of children needing adoption? Yes.

Are you an adoptive parent, adopted person, or birthparent? Adoptive parent.

Has your agency lost any adoption litigation filed against you by an adoptive parent or birthparent? N/A

HEARTSENT ADOPTIONS, INC.

Respondent: Val Free, Executive Director
In charge of social services: Val Free
15 Altarinda Rd., Suite 100, Orinda, CA 94563
(925) 254-8883 • Fax: (925) 254-8866
E-mail: heartsent@earthlink.net • www.heartsent.org
Year first licensed by state: 1995

Agency provides services for: International adoption; children with special needs; infants; homestudy if parents working with another agency; postplacement services; education and post-adoption counseling.

What states do your adoptive parent clients come from? We can work with families in Northern California for the homestudy and families in any state to complete adoption.

Services provided adopting parents: Classes with other prospective parents; required readings of books and/or articles on adoption; group discussions about adoption; parenting discussions; travel preparation; classes with adoption-related issues.

States/countries your birthparents/adopted children come from: China, Taiwan, Vietnam, Russia, Ukraine, Guatemala.

What was the goal of your agency when first organized? What is the goal of your agency now? Kind process, parents helping parents, affordable, education. Now: Same.

Nonrelative children placed in 1998: 47

Special expertise of staff: Adoptive parents on staff; licensed social workers; therapists; physician.

In 1998, what was the average time from when a prospective adoptive parent applied to when he or she received a homestudy? 1 mo.

Average time from homestudy to placement of child: Depends on the country and particular case; China, 8–10 mos.; Vietnam, 6 mos.; Russia/Ukraine, 7–9 mos.

Agency criteria for adoptive parents you work with: Follow guidelines set by California; at least 25 years old; if married, at least 1 year; must be a U.S. citizen; single men or women, couples may apply.

How do you screen adoptive parents? Interview with director; required criminal clearances through state of California and FBI. Meetings with social worker.

What kind of medical information do you seek on older children? As much as is available, depending on the country.

About what percent are children with medical problems? 5%

Do you have a waiting list of prospective parents? No.

Is it all right if adopting parents you work with are on waiting lists of other agencies or attorneys? Yes—depends on case.

Do you have a sliding scale? No.

Do you have an application fee? If yes, what is the amount of the application fee? Yes. $200

What is your homestudy fee (if a flat rate)? $2,400 (includes application fee).

What is your placement fee? Depends on country; China/Taiwan, $3,900; Vietnam, Russia, Ukraine, depends on liaison agency fees.

Do adopting parents also pay fees for medical and hospital expenses for birthmother and baby when they have no insurance? If yes, what is the average fee paid? Yes. (Taiwan and Guatemala only.) $6,000 approximately.

If applicable, what is the average document language translation fee? $500–700 (Taiwan and China).

If international adoption, what are average travel expenses? Depends on country and length of stay. Single: China, $1,500; Taiwan, $1,000–1,500.

If you place children from other countries, please list the estimated entire average cost to adoptive parents for each country. Including homestudy: China, $12,700; Taiwan, $15,400–18,400; Vietnam, $15,800; Eastern Europe $17,000–22,400.

My agency: Offers confidential adoptions.

Does your agency provide videotapes of children needing adoption? No.

Are you an adoptive parent, adopted person, or birthparent? Adoptive parent.

Has your agency lost any adoption litigation filed against you by an adoptive parent or birthparent? No.

HOLY FAMILY SERVICES ADOPTION & FOSTER CARE

Respondent: Debra E. Richardson, LCSW, Executive Director
In charge of social services: Debra E. Richardson
402-A South Marengo Ave., Pasadena, CA 91101-3113
(626) 578-1156 • Fax: (626) 578-7321
E-mail: HFSAdopt@aol.com • www.hfs.org
Year first licensed by state: 1949

Agency provides services for: International adoption; U.S. adoption; children with special needs; infants; homestudy if parents working with another agency; postplacement services.

What states do your adoptive parent clients come from? California: Los Angeles, Orange, Ventura, Riverside, and San Bernardino counties—our licensed areas.

Services provided adopting parents: Classes with other prospective parents; required readings of books and/or articles on adoption; group discussions about adoption; parenting discussions; support group for adoptive parents awaiting placement.

States/countries your birthparents/adopted children come from: California.

What was the goal of your agency when first organized? What is the goal of your agency now? To provide no-cost counseling and assistance to birthparents choosing adoption for their child. Now: To promote quality family opportunities for children without regard to race, religion, sex, or ethnic origin, through counseling, education, and continuing support activities. We're celebrating our fiftieth anniversary during the fiscal year July 1999–2000.

Nonrelative children placed in 1998: 93

Percent of adoptive placements under 6 mos.: 70%

Special expertise of staff: Adoptive parents; licensed social workers; registered nurse.

In 1998, what was the average time from when a prospective adoptive parent applied to when he or she received a homestudy? 4 mos.

Average time from homestudy to placement of child: 18 mos.

What made you decide to work in the adoption field? After 25 years of working with physically and emotionally disturbed children, I wanted to make a difference in the early life of a child and of many children. This is the perfect opportunity to do so.

Agency criteria for adoptive parents you work with: Prospective adoptive parents should be at least 21 years of age, in good (not necessarily perfect) health, and, if married, married for at least 1 year.

How do you screen adoptive parents? Personal interviews, personal references, job references, fingerprint clearances (state and FBI), child abuse index, TRWs, and DMV printouts.

How do you screen birthparents? Personal interviews, personal and family medical history.

What kind of medical information do you seek on older children? Physical, developmental, and psychological testing.

What percent of your U.S. adoptions are nonwhite children? 63%

About what percent are children with medical problems? 25%

About what percent are children with emotional problems? 18%

Do you have a waiting list of prospective parents? Yes.

Is it all right if adopting parents you work with are on waiting lists of other agencies or attorneys? Yes.

Are your adoption fees based on a sliding scale? If yes, what are the sliding scale criteria? Yes. 11% of gross annual income with cap at $9,000, plus a one-time $1,500 birthparent medical fee.

Do you have an application fee? If yes, what is the amount of the application fee? Yes. $100

What is your homestudy fee (if a flat rate)? $1,500 for domestic adoption in California and $2,000 for interstate and international adoption.

What is your placement fee? Included in adoption fees.

Do adopting parents also pay fees for medical and hospital expenses for birthmother and baby when they have no insurance? No.

My agency: Offers confidential adoptions; semi-open adoptions; meetings between birthparents and adoptive parents; birthparents pick adoptive parents from bios/resumes; offers full disclosure of names between birth and adoptive parents.

Does your agency provide videotapes of children needing adoption? No.

Has your agency lost any adoption litigation filed against you by an adoptive parent or birthparent? No.

INDEPENDENT ADOPTION CENTER

Respondent: Bruce Rappaport, Ph.D., Executive Director
In charge of social services: Kathleen Silber, MSW, ACSW, Associate Executive Director
391 Taylor Blvd., Suite 100, Pleasant Hill, CA 94523
(925) 827-2229 • Fax: (925) 603-0820
E-mail: iacorg@earthlink.net • www.adoptionhelp.org
Year first licensed by state: 1994

Agency provides services for: U.S. adoption; children with special needs; infants; home-study if parents working with another agency; postplacement services.

What states do your adoptive parent clients come from? All states. Licensed in California, North Carolina, Georgia, Indiana, New York, and Connecticut.

Services provided adopting parents: Classes with other prospective parents; required readings of books and/or articles on adoption; group discussions about adoption; parenting discussions; training on open adoption.

States/countries your birthparents/adopted children come from: All states.

What was the goal of your agency when first organized? What is the goal of your agency now? To make fully open adoption available to prospective adoptive parents and to serve women facing untimely pregnancy nationwide. Now: Same.

Nonrelative children placed in 1998: 174

Percent of adoptive placements under 6 mos.: 95%+

Special expertise of staff: Adoptive parents on staff; licensed social workers.

In 1998, what was the average time from when a prospective adoptive parent applied to when he or she received a homestudy? 2 mos.

Average time from homestudy to placement of child: 6–18 mos.

What made you decide to work in the adoption field? Before establishing the Center in 1982, I worked for several years as director of an infertility clinic. There I realized how few solutions were available to couples for whom infertility treatments were not successful.

Agency criteria for adoptive parents you work with: Our sole criterion is that adoptive parents be willing to participate in a fully open adoption. That is, that adoptive parents and birthparents share full identifying information and there is an opportunity for ongoing contact with the birthparents.

How do you screen adoptive parents? Adoptive parents are screened through the homestudy process, which includes visits with one of our social workers as well as the state-mandated background checks.

How do you screen birthparents? Our birthparent intake counselors conduct interviews that include questions about drug/alcohol use during pregnancy and other risk factors. A counselor also meets with the birthparents. Adopting parents meet the birthparents at a match meeting and participate in open adoption counseling together.

What kind of medical information do you seek from birthparents? Birthparents complete background history forms, which include medical history.

What kind of medical information do you seek on older children? A psychological evaluation is required, and the birthmother signs a release of pediatric records and medical records from the hospital where the child was born.

What percent of your U.S. adoptions are nonwhite children? About 40% are of mixed or non-Caucasian ethnicity.

About what percent are children with medical problems? About 20% have some drug exposure.

Do you have a waiting list of prospective parents? No.

Is it all right if adopting parents you work with are on waiting lists of other agencies or attorneys? Yes.

Are your adoption fees based on a sliding scale? If yes, what are the sliding scale criteria? Yes. Gross yearly household income.

Do you have an application fee? No.

What is your homestudy fee (if a flat rate)? Included.

Do adopting parents also pay fees for medical and hospital expenses for birthmother and baby when they have no insurance? If yes, what is the average fee paid? Yes. $2,000, paid only if they are willing to do so. Adoptive parents may indicate in the preparation process whether they are willing to work with birthparents who have high expense needs.

If international adoption, what are average travel expenses? $2,500

If you place children from other countries, please list the estimated entire average cost to adoptive parents for each country. $3,500–10,000

My agency: Offers meetings between birthparents and adoptive parents; birthparents pick adoptive parents from bios/resumes; full disclosure of names between birth and adoptive parents.

Does your agency provide videotapes of children needing adoption? No.

In how many cases with your agency has an adoptive parent been placed with a child but lost the child due to a birthparent challenge? 0

Has your agency lost any adoption litigation filed against you by an adoptive parent or birthparent? No.

INFANT OF PRAGUE ADOPTION SERVICE

Respondent: Karen Spencer, Community Relations
In charge of social services: Judith Casson, MSW, Executive Director
6059 N. Palm Ave., Fresno, CA 93704
(559) 447-3333 • Fax: (559) 447-3322
Year first licensed by state: 1953

Agency provides services for: U.S. adoption; children with special needs; infants; homestudy if parents working with another agency; postplacement services.

What states do your adoptive parent clients come from? California.

Services provided adopting parents: Classes with other prospective parents; required readings of books and/or articles on adoption; group discussions about adoption; parenting discussions; annual picnic; newsletter; post-adoption services.

States/countries your birthparents/adopted children come from: California.

What was the goal of your agency when first organized? What is the goal of your agency now? To provide caring counseling for unwed mothers and place their children in loving, adoptive homes. Now: To provide quality counseling for all involved as we find quality homes for children in need of adoption.

Nonrelative children placed in 1998: 34

Percent of adoptive placements under 6 mos.: 90%

Special expertise of staff: Adoptive parents on staff; licensed social workers (MSWs); two social workers with over twenty years experience in adoption.

In 1998, what was the average time from when a prospective adoptive parent applied to when he or she received a homestudy? 3 mos.

Average time from homestudy to placement of child: 10 mos.

What made you decide to work in the adoption field? Opportunity to make a difference. Commitment to pro-life alternatives to crisis pregnancies. Belief in maintaining professional agency adoption services.

Agency criteria for adoptive parents you work with: Three-year marriage; live in one of eleven San Joaquin counties.

How do you screen adoptive parents? Criminal and health clearance, education, counseling, and home clearance.

How do you screen birthparents? Health history and prenatal care history to find appropriate home for each child needing adoption.

What kind of medical information do you seek from birthparents? Form provided by California Department of Social Services (AD67, AD67A).

What kind of medical information do you seek on older children? Birth records and medical records as complete as possible.

What percent of your U.S. adoptions are nonwhite children? 15%, when including Hispanic as white. 40% when not including Hispanic as white.

About what percent are children with medical problems? 40% with potential problems.

Do you have a waiting list of prospective parents? Yes.

Is it all right if adopting parents you work with are on waiting lists of other agencies or attorneys? Yes.

Are your adoption fees based on a sliding scale? If yes, what are the sliding scale criteria? Yes. Base fee, plus a percentage of family's income.

Do you have an application fee? If yes, what is the amount of the application fee? Yes. $500 enrollment fee. Other fees: $2,500 payable at the first education group meeting. $1,000 to $5,000 payable at the home visit. $2,500 payable at the time child enters home.

Do adopting parents also pay fees for medical and hospital expenses for birth-mother and baby when they have no insurance? If yes, what is the average fee paid? Yes. Up to a maximum of $2,000, only after child is placed.

My agency: Offers semi-open adoptions; meetings between birthparents and adoptive parents; birthparents pick adoptive parents from bios/resumes; full disclosure of names between birth and adoptive parents.

Does your agency provide videotapes of children needing adoption? No.

In how many cases with your agency has an adoptive parent been placed with a child but lost the child due to a birthparent challenge? None.

Has your agency lost any adoption litigation filed against you by an adoptive parent or birthparent? No.

LILLIPUT CHILDREN'S SERVICES

Respondent: William H. Fuser, Executive Director
In charge of social services: Cheryle Roberts, LCSW, Social Work Supervisor
130 East Magnolia, Stockton, CA 95202
(209) 943-0530 • Fax: (209) 943-6829
E-mail: LCSadopt@aol.com • www.lcsadopt.org
Year first licensed by state: 1991

Agency provides services for: U.S. adoption; children with special needs.

What states do your adoptive parent clients come from? California.

Services provided adopting parents: Classes with other prospective parents; required readings of books and/or articles on adoption; group discussions about adoption; parenting discussions.

States/countries your birthparents/adopted children come from: California.

What was the goal of your agency when first organized? What is the goal of your agency now? To provide emergency shelter. Now: To provide permanent families for children.

Nonrelative children placed in 1998: 30

Percent of adoptive placements under 6 mos.: 5%

Special expertise of staff: Licensed social workers.

In 1998, what was the average time from when a prospective adoptive parent applied to when he or she received a homestudy? 4–6 mos.

Average time from homestudy to placement of child: 1–3 mos.

Agencies criteria for adoptive parents you work with: Minimum age: 24.

How do you screen adoptive parents? Mostly it's self-screening. A thorough home-study determines appropriateness of applicants.

What kind of medical information do you seek on older children? All that is available and relevant.

What percent of your U.S. adoptions are nonwhite children? 35%

About what percent are children with medical problems? 10%

About what percent are children with emotional problems? 20%

Do you have a waiting list of prospective parents? Yes.

Is it all right if adopting parents you work with are on waiting lists of other agencies or attorneys? No.

Are your adoption fees based on a sliding scale? No. No fees.

Do you have an application fee? No.

Do adopting parents also pay fees for medical and hospital expenses for birthmother and baby when they have no insurance? No.

My agency: Offers semi-open adoptions; meetings between birthparents and adoptive parents.

Does your agency provide videotapes of children needing adoption? No.

In how many cases with your agency has an adoptive parent been placed with a child but lost the child due to a birthparent challenge? 0

Has your agency lost any adoption litigation filed against you by an adoptive parent or birthparent? No.

NORTH BAY ADOPTIONS

Respondent: Cindy Gallaher, President, Board of Directors
In charge of social services: Lizbeth Hamlin-Haims
862 3rd St., Santa Rosa, CA 95404
(707) 570-2940 • Fax: (707) 570-2943
E-mail: nbadopt@wco.com • www.wco.com/~nbadopt
Year first licensed by state: 1991

Agency provides services for: International adoption; children with special needs; infants; homestudy if parents working with another agency; postplacement services.

What states do your adoptive parent clients come from? California, Nevada, Georgia, Maine, Michigan, New York, New Jersey, Oregon, Washington, Wisconsin, Connecticut, Massachusetts—all over the United States.

Services provided adopting parents: Classes with other prospective parents; required readings of books and/or articles on adoption; group discussions about adoption; parenting discussions.

States/countries your birthparents/adopted children come from: Mexico, Guatemala, El Salvador, Colombia, Ecuador, Nicaragua, Trinidad, China, Vietnam, India.

What was the goal of your agency when first organized? What is the goal of your agency now? To find permanent, loving homes for children who need them. Now: Same.

Nonrelative children placed in 1998: 30

Percent of adoptive placements under 6 mos.: 10%

Special expertise of staff: Adoptive parents; licensed social workers; therapists.

In 1998, what was the average time from when a prospective adoptive parent applied to when he or she received a homestudy? 3–4 mos.

Average time from homestudy to placement of child: 8 mos.

What made you decide to work in the adoption field? I have three internationally adopted children of my own. I believe adoption is a wonderful way to build a family and to provide a family for those who are educated about what it involves.

Agency criteria for adoptive parents you work with: Minimum of 25 years of age, no felony record; one parent must be a U.S. citizen

How do you screen adoptive parents? Through the homestudy process, fingerprint, and criminal–child abuse and background checks. The education sessions also serve as a self-screening tool for parents.

What kind of medical information do you seek on older children? We take whatever is available.

Do you have a waiting list of prospective parents? No.

Is it all right if adopting parents you work with are on waiting lists of other agencies or attorneys? No.

Do you have an application fee? No.

What is your homestudy fee (if a flat rate)? $2,400. Program fee: $500. Total fee of $3,500 includes $150 apllication fee and $450 fee for classes.

If applicable, what is the average document language translation fee? Usually included in foreign fee.

If international adoption, what are average travel expenses? $2,500 for one person.

If you place children from other countries, please list the estimated *entire* average cost to adoptive parents for each country. Vietnam, $17,000; China, $14,000; Guatemala, $23,000; Colombia, $10,000.

Does your agency provide videotapes of children needing adoption? No

Are you an adoptive parent, adopted person, or birthparent? Adoptive parent.

In how many cases with your agency has an adoptive parent been placed with a child but lost the child due to a birthparent challenge? 0

Has your agency lost any adoption litigation filed against you by an adoptive parent or birthparent? No.

COLORADO

ADOPTION ALLIANCE

Respondent: Virginia Appel, Executive Director
In charge of social services: Virginia Appel
3090 S. Jamaica Crt., Suite 106, Aurora, CO 80014
(303) 337-1731 • Fax: (303) 337-5481
E-mail: info@adoptall.com • www.adoptall.com
Year first licensed by state: 1989

Agency provides services for: International adoption; U.S. adoption; children with special needs; infants; homestudy if parents working with another agency; postplacement services.

What states do your adoptive parent clients come from? Colorado for domestic adoptions; entire United States for international adoptions.

Services provided adopting parents: Classes with other prospective parents; required readings of books and/or articles on adoption; group discussions about adoption; parenting discussions.

States/countries your birthparents/adopted children come from: Birthparents come from entire United States for designated or identified adoption. Children from United States and around the globe.

What was the goal of your agency when first organized? What is the goal of your agency now? To provide safe, loving, permanent homes for children. Now: Same.

Nonrelative children placed in 1998: 64

Percent of adoptive placements under 6 mos.: 15%

Special expertise of staff: Adoptive parents; licensed social workers; therapists.

In 1998, what was the average time from when a prospective adoptive parent applied to when he or she received a homestudy? 4–6 weeks

Average time from homestudy to placement of child: 6–9 mos.

What made you decide to work in the adoption field? First internship in graduate school (22 years ago) was in adoption agency. I was hooked!

Agency criteria for adoptive parents you work with: Flexible; depends on program.

How do you screen adoptive parents? Fingerprinted through Colorado Bureau of Investigation (or FBI for international), screened through Central Registry for Child Protection, medicals, reference letters, therapists' reports, detailed family assessment.

How do you screen birthparents? They complete social/medical background information form.

What kind of medical information do you seek on older children? Current physician's report and other available medical reports.

What percent of your U.S. adoptions are nonwhite children? 15%

About what percent are children with medical problems? 5%

About what percent are children with emotional problems? 25%

Do you have a waiting list of prospective parents? No.

Is it all right if adopting parents you work with are on waiting lists of other agencies or attorneys? Yes.

Are your adoption fees based on a sliding scale? No.

Do you have an application fee? If yes, what is the amount of the application fee? Yes. $150

What is your homestudy fee (if a flat rate)? $1,000–1,200

What is your placement fee? Varies depending on program.

Do adopting parents also pay fees for medical and hospital expenses for birthmother and baby when they have no insurance? If yes, what is the average fee paid? Yes. $5,000

If international adoption, what are average travel expenses? $1,500 for singles; $3,000 for couple.

If you place children from other countries, please list the estimated *entire* average cost to adoptive parents for each country. Vietnam, Russia, Guatemala, Romania, $18,000–20,000; Colombia, $8,000–10,000; China, $12,000–14,000.

My agency: Offers confidential adoptions; semi-open adoptions; meetings between birthparents and adoptive parents; birthparents pick adoptive parents from bios/resumes; full disclosure of names between birth and adoptive parents.

Does your agency provide videotapes of children needing adoption? Yes, for some international programs.

In how many cases with your agency has an adoptive parent been placed with a child but lost the child due to a birthparent challenge? 0

Has your agency lost any adoption litigation filed against you by an adoptive parent or birthparent? No.

ADOPTION CHOICE CENTER, INC.

Respondent: Ellen Levy, Director and Placement Supervisor
In charge of social services: Ellen Levy
729 South Cascade, Suite 2, Colorado Springs, CO 80903
(719) 473-4444 • Fax: (719) 444-0186
Year first licensed by state: 1989

Agency provides services for: U.S. adoption; infants; homestudy if parents working with another agency; postplacement services.

What states do your adoptive parent clients come from? All states.

States/countries your birthparents/adopted children come from: All states.

What was the goal of your agency when first organized? What is the goal of your agency now? Infant adoptions within United States. Now: Same.

Nonrelative children placed in 1998: 16

Percent of adoptive placements under 6 mos.: 95%

Special expertise of staff: Licensed social workers; therapists; attorney.

In 1998, what was the average time from when a prospective adoptive parent applied to when he or she received a homestudy? 4 weeks

Average time from homestudy to placement of child: We specialize in designated adoptions. Most situations come with potential placements in tow.

Agency criteria for adoptive parents you work with: As long as individuals are fit, healthy, good moral character, stable, etc.

How do you screen adoptive parents? Personal meeting.

How do you screen birthparents? Personal meeting.

What kind of medical information do you seek from birthparents? Personal information questionnaire.

What kind of medical information do you seek on older children? Medical records.

What percent of your U.S. adoptions are nonwhite children? Less than 25%

Do you have a waiting list of prospective parents? No.

Is it all right if adopting parents you work with are on waiting lists of other agencies or attorneys? Yes.

Are your adoption fees based on a sliding scale? No.

Do you have an application fee? If yes, what is the amount of the application fee? Yes, but we often waive. $500

What is your homestudy fee (if a flat rate)? $2,000

What is your placement fee? $850 for postplacement supervision.

Do adopting parents also pay fees for medical and hospital expenses for birthmother and baby when they have no insurance? If yes, what is the average fee paid? Yes. Wide range.

My agency: Offers confidential adoptions; semi-open adoptions; meetings between birthparents and adoptive parents; birthparents pick adoptive parents from bios/resumes; full disclosure of names between birth and adoptive parents.

Does your agency provide videotapes of children needing adoption? No.

In how many cases with your agency has an adoptive parent been placed with a child but lost the child due to a birthparent challenge? 0

Has your agency lost any adoption litigation filed against you by an adoptive parent or birthparent? No.

ADOPTION OPTIONS

Respondent: Carol Holliday Lawson, Executive Director
In charge of social services: Carol Holliday Lawson
2600 S. Parker Rd., #2-320, Aurora, CO 80014
(303) 695-1601 • Fax: (303) 695-1626
E-mail: adoptopt@henge.com • www.adoption-options.com
Year first licensed by state: 1981

Agency provides services for: International adoption; U.S. adoption; children with special needs; infants; homestudy if parents working with another agency; postplacement services; provide nonidentifying information for adult adoptees.

What states do your adoptive parent clients come from? All states.

Services provided adopting parents: Classes with other prospective parents; required readings of books and/or articles on adoption; group discussions about adoption; parenting discussions.

States/countries your birthparents/adopted children come from: Colorado.

What was the goal of your agency when first organized? What is the goal of your agency now? To provide services for all members in the adoption area respective of age, race, religion, etc. Now: Same.

Nonrelative children placed in 1998: 39

Percent of adoptive placements under 6 mos.: 95%

Special expertise of staff: Adoptive parents; licensed social workers; MSWs and BSWs.

In 1998, what was the average time from when a prospective adoptive parent applied to when he or she received a homestudy? 2–4 weeks to start, 4–6 weeks to complete.

Average time from homestudy to placement of child: 16 mos.

What made you decide to work in the adoption field? After working in child protection, I could see the value of adoption in breaking the cycle of deprivation, child abuse, etc.

Agency criteria for adoptive parents you work with: Will place up to five children. No age limit, although birthparents usually choose, so over 50 not an easy age to place.

How do you screen adoptive parents? Assessment during homestudy, family assessment tool, ecomaps, genograms. Second opinion by placement supervisor.

How do you screen birthparents? Ongoing assessment by birthparent counselor, completion of social/medical health reports.

What kind of medical information do you seek from birthparents? AIDS test plus normal medical background information.

What kind of medical information do you seek on older children? Pediatric report, psychological.

What percent of your U.S. adoptions are nonwhite children? 35%

About what percent are children with medical problems? 10%

About what percent are children with emotional problems? 5%

Do you have a waiting list of prospective parents? Yes.

Is it all right if adopting parents you work with are on waiting lists of other agencies or attorneys? Yes for minority or special needs, no for Anglo program.

Are your adoption fees based on a sliding scale? If yes, what are the sliding scale criteria? Yes. Based on income.

Do you have an application fee? If yes, what is the amount of the application fee? Yes. $100

What is your homestudy fee (if a flat rate)? $1,200

Do adopting parents also pay fees for medical and hospital expenses for birthmother and baby when they have no insurance? No.

If applicable, what is the average document language translation fee? $700

If international adoption, what are average travel expenses? $5,000

If you place children from other countries, please list the estimated *entire* average cost to adoptive parents for each country. Belarus and Russia, $15,580; with travel, approximately $20,000–22,000.

My agency: Offers confidential adoptions; semi-open adoptions; meetings between birthparents and adoptive parents; birthparents pick adoptive parents from bios/resumes.

Does your agency provide videotapes of children needing adoption? No.

Are you an adoptive parent, adopted person, or birthparent? Birthparent.

In how many cases with your agency has an adoptive parent been placed with a child but lost the child due to a birthparent challenge? 4

Has your agency lost any adoption litigation filed against you by an adoptive parent or birthparent? No.

ADOPTIONS ADVOCACY AND ALTERNATIVES

Respondent: Joanne Gallagher, LCSW, Director
2500 S. College, Ft. Collins, CO 80525
(970) 493-5868 • Fax: (970) 472-0352
Year first licensed by state: 1992

Agency provides services for: International adoption; infants; homestudy if parents working with another agency; postplacement services.

What states do your adoptive parent clients come from? Mostly Colorado.

Services provided adopting parents: Classes with other prospective parents; required readings of books and/or articles on adoption; group discussions about adoption; parenting discussions; training.

States/countries your birthparents/adopted children come from: Colorado, Arizona, Illinois.

What was the goal of your agency when first organized? What is the goal of your agency now? To offer therapeutic intervention and support for birthparents and adoptive parents. Now: Same.

Nonrelative children placed in 1998: 25

Percent of adoptive placements under 6 mos.: 24%

Special expertise of staff: Adoptive parents; licensed social workers; psychologists; therapists.

In 1998, what was the average time from when a prospective adoptive parent applied to when he or she received a homestudy? 3 mos.

Average time from homestudy to placement of child: 8 mos.

What made you decide to work in the adoption field? Infertility and adoption experience.

Agency criteria for adoptive parents you work with: Under age 50, no more than two kids, commitment to process for closure to infertility work.

How do you screen adoptive parents? CBI, FBI, central registry, adoptive homestudy process.

How do you screen birthparents? Self-report, home visits, medical records. Testing, work with other professionals.

What percent of your U.S. adoptions are nonwhite children? 33%

Do you have a waiting list of prospective parents? Yes.

Is it all right if adopting parents you work with are on waiting lists of other agencies or attorneys? No.

Are your adoption fees based on a sliding scale? No.

Do you have an application fee? If yes, what is the amount of the application fee? Yes. $960

What is your homestudy fee (if a flat rate)? $2,850

What is your placement fee? $2,850

Do adopting parents also pay fees for medical and hospital expenses for birthmother and baby when they have no insurance? If yes, what is the average fee paid? Yes. Up to $1,500

My agency: Offers confidential adoptions; semi-open adoptions; meetings between birthparents and adoptive parents; birthparents pick adoptive parents from bios/resumes; full disclosure of names between birth and adoptive parents.

Does your agency provide videotapes of children needing adoption? No.

Are you an adoptive parent, adopted person, or birthparent? Adoptive parent.

In how many cases with your agency has an adoptive parent been placed with a child but lost the child due to a birthparent challenge? 1

Has your agency lost any adoption litigation filed against you by an adoptive parent or birthparent? No.

COLORADO CHRISTIAN SERVICES

Respondent: Elizabeth Rich Bolz, LCSW, Placement Supervisor
In charge of social services: Elizabeth Rich Bolz
4796 S. Broadway, Suite 110, Englewood, CO 80110
(303) 761-7236 • Fax: (303) 783-5708
E-mail: ccserv@uswest.net • www.christianservices.org
Year first licensed by state: 1963

Agency provides services for: U.S. adoption; children with special needs; infants; homestudy if parents working with another agency; postplacement services.

What states do your adoptive parent clients come from? All states.

Services provided adopting parents: Classes with other prospective parents; group discussions about adoption.

States/countries your birthparents/adopted children come from: Colorado and Oklahoma.

What was the goal of your agency when first organized? What is the goal of your agency now? Originally Colorado Christian Services was a group home for teenagers who didn't have anywhere to live. Gradually the focus shifted to providing adoptive services. Now: To continue to serve children and families.

Nonrelative children placed in 1998: 18

Percent of adoptive placements under 6 mos.: 98%

Special expertise of staff: Licensed social workers; therapists.

In 1998, what was the average time from when a prospective adoptive parent applied to when he or she received a homestudy? 6 mos.

Average time from homestudy to placement of child: 18 mos.

What made you decide to work in the adoption field? I love children and strongly adhere to the mission and vision of Colorado Christian Services.

Agencies criteria for adoptive parents you work with: Between the ages of 21–45, married a minimum of 2 years, adequate financial resources and health insurance, history of infertility, active members of a Christian faith.

How do you screen adoptive parents? Telephone (initially) and then by social worker through family assessments.

How do you screen birthparents? Through contact with birthparents we determine whether they are a good fit for the agency.

What kind of medical information do you seek from birthparents? We gather as much social and medical history on the parents as is available.

What kind of medical information do you seek on older children? As much as possible.

What percent of your U.S. adoptions are nonwhite children? 5%

About what percent are children with medical problems? 1%

Do you have a waiting list of prospective parents? Yes.

Is it all right if adopting parents you work with are on waiting lists of other agencies or attorneys? Yes.

Are your adoption fees based on a sliding scale? No.

Do you have an application fee? If yes, what is the amount of the application fee? Yes. $300–500, depending on program,

What is your homestudy fee (if a flat rate)? $1,200

What is your placement fee? $500

Do adopting parents also pay fees for medical and hospital expenses for birthmother and baby when they have no insurance? Yes. It is rarely not covered by insurance.

My agency: Offers confidential adoptions; semi-open adoptions; meetings between birthparents and adoptive parents; birthparents pick adoptive parents from bios/resumes; full disclosure of names between birth and adoptive parents.

Does your agency provide videotapes of children needing adoption? No.

In how many cases with your agency has an adoptive parent been placed with a child but lost the child due to a birthparent challenge? 0

Has your agency lost any adoption litigation filed against you by an adoptive parent or birthparent? No.

FRIENDS OF CHILDREN OF VARIOUS NATIONS

Respondent: Connie Higgins, Assistant Director
1562 Pearl St., Denver, CO 80203
(303) 837-9438 • Fax: (303) 837-9848
E-mail: fcvn@webaccess.net
Year first licensed by state: 1973

Agency provides services for: International adoption; U.S. adoption; children with special needs; infants; homestudy if parents working with another agency; postplacement services; postplacement/adoption counseling; search; support groups; cultural events.

What states do your adoptive parent clients come from? All states.

Services provided adopting parents: Classes with other prospective parents; required readings of books and/or articles on adoption; group discussions about adoption; parenting discussions.

States/countries your birthparents/adopted children come from: United States, China, India, Vietnam, Russia.

Nonrelative children placed in 1998: 30

Special expertise of staff: Adoptive parents on staff; licensed social workers; therapists.

In 1998, what was the average time from when a prospective adoptive parent applied to when he or she received a homestudy? Study is started on receipt of formal application.

Average time from homestudy to placement of child: 6 mos.–1 year

What made you decide to work in the adoption field? I'm an adoptee and have adopted children.

Agency criteria for adoptive parents you work with: Determined by the countries we work with.

How do you screen birthparents? Per state regulations.

What kind of medical information do you seek from birthparents? As much as possible.

What kind of medical information do you seek on older children? As much as possible.

Do you have a waiting list of prospective parents? No.

Is it all right if adopting parents you work with are on waiting lists of other agencies or attorneys? No.

Are your adoption fees based on a sliding scale? No.

Do you have an application fee? If yes, what is the amount of the application fee? Yes. Preliminary, $50; formal, $50.

What is your homestudy fee (if a flat rate)? $1,200

What is your placement fee? $900

Do adopting parents also pay fees for medical and hospital expenses for birthmother and baby when they have no insurance? Yes, United States only.

If international adoption, what are average travel expenses? Determined by the country.

If you place children from other countries, please list the estimated *entire* average cost to adoptive parents for each country. India, $11,400; Vietnam $10,200 plus travel; Russia, $23,000; China, $19,000. (Vietnam and China include homestudy and postplacement supervision.)

My agency: Offers confidential adoptions; semi-open adoptions; meetings between birthparents and adoptive parents; birthparents pick adoptive parents from bios/resumes; full disclosure of names between birth and adoptive parents.

Does your agency provide videotapes of children needing adoption? Yes, waiting children only.

Are you an adoptive parent, adopted person, or birthparent? Adoptive parent, adopted person.

In how many cases with your agency has an adoptive parent been placed with a child but lost the child due to a birthparent challenge? 0

Has your agency lost any adoption litigation filed against you by an adoptive parent or birthparent? No.

LITTLEST ANGELS INTERNATIONAL

Respondent: Sandra S. Whitton, Executive Director
In charge of social services: Sandra S. Whitton
1512 Grand Ave. #216, Glenwood Springs, CO 81601
(970) 945-2949 • Fax: (970) 928-2020
E-mail: ltlst@aol.com • www.co-biz/angels-international
Year first licensed by state: 1995

Agency provides services for: International adoption; U.S. adoption; children with special needs; infants; homestudy if parents working with another agency; postplacement services; foster care.

What states do your adoptive parent clients come from? Colorado and other states if birthmother is in Colorado.

Services provided adopting parents: Required readings of books and/or articles on adoption; group discussions about adoption; parenting discussions.

States/countries your birthparents/adopted children come from: All states and Cambodia.

Nonrelative children placed in 1998: 9

Percent of adoptive placements under 6 mos.: 98%

Special expertise of staff: Licensed social workers; psychologists; physician; attorney.

In 1998, what was the average time from when a prospective adoptive parent applied to when he or she received a homestudy? 6 mos.

Average time from homestudy to placement of child: 6 mos.

What made you decide to work in the adoption field? I felt I was called. In our rural locale, there was no reasonably priced agency.

How do you screen adoptive parents? Initial meeting, questionnaire, required medicals, fingerprints, Colorado child registry, references.

How do you screen birthparents? Medical information, relinquishment counseling.

What kind of medical information do you seek from birthparents? Diabetes, full general health, HIV, TB, hepatitis B and C.

What kind of medical information do you seek on older children? Full child study, including social and medical.

What percent of your U.S. adoptions are nonwhite children? 2%

Do you have a waiting list of prospective parents? Yes.

Is it all right if adopting parents you work with are on waiting lists of other agencies or attorneys? Yes.

Are your adoption fees based on a sliding scale? No.

Do you have an application fee? If yes, what is the amount of the application fee? Yes. $250

What is your homestudy fee (if a flat rate)? $750

What is your placement fee? $750

Do adopting parents also pay fees for medical and hospital expenses for birthmother and baby when they have no insurance? If yes, what is the average fee paid? Yes. $3,500

If applicable, what is the average document language translation fee? $800

If you place children from other countries, please list the estimated *entire* average cost to adoptive parents for each country. Only Cambodia $13,000.

My agency: Offers confidential adoptions; semi-open adoptions; meetings between birthparents and adoptive parents; birthparents pick adoptive parents from bios/resumes; offers full disclosure of names between birth and adoptive parents.

Does your agency provide videotapes of children needing adoption? No.

In how many cases with your agency has an adoptive parent been placed with a child but lost the child due to a birthparent challenge? 3

Has your agency lost any adoption litigation filed against you by an adoptive parent or birthparent? No. Never had any.

SMALL MIRACLES FOUNDATION OF THE ROCKIES

Respondent: Brenda Retram, Director, Adoption Services
5555 DTC Pky., Suite B-2100, Englewood, CO 80111
(303) 220-7611 • Fax: (303) 694-2622
E-mail: smallmiracles@msn.com • www.smallmiracles.com
Year first licensed by state: 1992

Agency provides services for: U.S. adoption; infants; homestudy if parents working with another agency; postplacement services.

What states do your adoptive parent clients come from? We work with all states except New York, Connecticut, and Wisconsin.

Services provided adopting parents: Classes with other prospective parents; required readings of books and/or articles on adoption; group discussions about adoption; parenting discussions.

States/countries your birthparents/adopted children come from: Colorado.

What was the goal of your agency when first organized? What is the goal of your agency now? To make the adoption process time-limited as is the biological process—placement in 9 mos. or less. Now: Same.

Nonrelative children placed in 1998: 46

Percent of adoptive placements under 6 mos.: 100%

Special expertise of staff: Adoptive parents on staff; licensed social workers; psychologists; therapists.

In 1998, what was the average time from when a prospective adoptive parent applied to when he or she received a homestudy? 2 mos.

Average time from homestudy to placement of child: 4 mos.

What made you decide to work in the adoption field? Adoptive parent.

Agency criteria for adoptive parents you work with: Age not over 50, 2 years of marriage, no more than one child in home, infertile.

How do you screen adoptive parents? Fingerprints, child abuse registry, current physicals, references, 1040 (IRS), employment verifications, infertility history, interviews and written autobiographies, adoption education classes.

How do you screen birthparents? Interviews, counseling, HIV testing, assessment of drug/alcohol use.

What kind of medical information do you seek from birthparents? Social/medical history form, prenatal records including HIV test results.

What kind of medical information do you seek on older children? Study of child report, complete medical records.

What percent of your U.S. adoptions are nonwhite children? 25%

Do you have a waiting list of prospective parents? Yes.

Is it all right if adopting parents you work with are on waiting lists of other agencies or attorneys? Yes.

Are your adoption fees based on a sliding scale? If yes, what are the sliding scale criteria? Yes, for minority placements. No, for Caucasian placements.

Do you have an application fee? If yes, what is the amount of the application fee? Yes. $495 in-state, $550 out-of-state.

Do adopting parents also pay fees for medical and hospital expenses for birthmother and baby when they have no insurance? If yes, what is the average fee paid? Yes. $1,000

My agency: Offers confidential adoptions; semi-open adoptions; meetings between birthparents and adoptive parents; birthparents pick adoptive parents from bios/resumes.

Does your agency provide videotapes of children needing adoption? No.

Are you an adoptive parent, adopted person, or birthparent? Adoptive parent.

In how many cases with your agency has an adoptive parent been placed with a child but lost the child due to a birthparent challenge? 7 over 7 years.

Has your agency lost any adoption litigation filed against you by an adoptive parent or birthparent? No.

CONNECTICUT

DOWNEY SIDE

Respondent: Carolyn Goodridge, Area Director
In charge of social services: Carolyn Goodridge
23264 Silas Deane Hwy., Rocky Hill, CT 06067
(860) 257-1694 • Fax: (860) 257-1698
Year first licensed by state: 1991

Agency provides services for: U.S. adoption; children with special needs; postplacement services.

What states do your adoptive parent clients come from? Connecticut.

Services provided adopting parents: Classes with other prospective parents; group discussions about adoption; parenting discussions; support groups.

States/countries your birthparents/adopted children come from: All states.

What was the goal of your agency when first organized? What is the goal of your agency now? To find homes for the children in the foster care system in the United States. Now: Same.

Nonrelative children placed in 1998: 15

Percent of adoptive placements under 6 mos.: 0%

Special expertise by staff: Adoptive parents on staff; licensed social workers; attorney.

In 1998, what was the average time from when a prospective adoptive parent applied to when he or she received a homestudy? 4 mos.

Average time from homestudy to placement of child: 1 year or less

What made you decide to work in the adoption field? Parents were foster parents. Worked in public foster care agency before private agency placing older children.

Agency criteria for adoptive parents you work with: At least 18 years old with no actual upper range, depending on the age of child requested. Children in home considered as part of placement decision. Can't have criminal record in past 5 years. Protective services check is also done.

How do you screen adoptive parents? Paperwork, classes, criminal checks, child abuse checks, references, medical, home visits.

What kind of medical information do you seek from birthparents? Request medical backgrounds from family's agency.

What kind of medical information do you seek on older children? Birth records and all medical history.

What percent of your U.S. adoptions are nonwhite children? 30%

About what percent are children with emotional problems? 100%

Do you have a waiting list of prospective parents? Yes.

Is it all right if adopting parents you work with are on waiting lists of other agencies or attorneys? No.

Are your adoption fees based on a sliding scale? No.

Do you have an application fee? If yes, what is the amount of the application fee? Yes. Commitment fee is $50 for single, $75 for couple.

What is your homestudy fee (if a flat rate)? None.

What is your placement fee? None.

My agency: Offers confidential adoptions.

Does your agency provide videotapes of children needing adoption? Yes.

In how many cases with your agency has an adoptive parent been placed with a child but lost the child due to a birthparent challenge? 0

Has your agency lost any adoption litigation filed against you by an adoptive parent or birthparent? No.

LUTHERAN SOCIAL SERVICES OF NEW ENGLAND, INC.

Respondent: Lynn Gabbard, Adoption Program Manager, Connecticut
In charge of social services: Kristina Backhaus, Director of Adoptions
2139 Silas Deane Hwy., Suite 201, Rocky Hill, CT 06067-2336
(860) 257-9899 • Fax: (860) 257-0340

Agency provides services for: International adoption; U.S. adoption; children with special needs; infants, homestudy if parents working with another agency; postplacement services; relative adoptions; stepparent adoptions.

What states do your adoptive parent clients come from? All states.

Services provided adopting parents: Classes with other prospective parents; required readings of books and/or articles on adoption; group discussions about adoption; parenting discussions; monthly support groups; parent auxiliary group.

States/countries your birthparents/adopted children come from: Birthparents, primarily Connecticut; adopted children, all states and Russia, Romania, Bulgaria, China, Vietnam, Marshall Islands.

What is the goal of your agency now? To find appropriate families for children in need of permanence.

Nonrelative children placed in 1998: 20

Percent of adoptive placements under 6 mos.: 50%

Special expertise of staff: Adoptive parents on staff; licensed social workers.

In 1998, what was the average time from when a prospective adoptive parent applied to when he or she received a homestudy? 2–3 mos.

Average time from homestudy to placement of child: 11 mos.

What made you decide to work in the adoption field? I'm an adoptive parent of seven children.

Agency criteria for adoptive parents you work with: Varies.

How do you screen adoptive parents? Interviews, primarily; police check; protective service check; references, etc.

How do you screen birthparents? Interviews.

What kind of medical information do you seek from birthparents? As much as possible.

What kind of medical information do you seek on older children? As much as possible.

What percent of your U.S. adoptions are nonwhite children? 10–20%

About what percent are children with medical problems? 10–20%

About what percent are children with emotional problems? 5%

Do you have a waiting list of prospective parents? No.

Is it all right if adopting parents you work with are on waiting lists of other agencies or attorneys? No.

Are your adoption fees based on a sliding scale? No.

Do you have an application fee? If yes, what is the amount of the application fee? Yes. $250

What is your homestudy fee (if a flat rate)? $1,500

What is your placement fee? Varies.

Do adopting parents also pay fees for medical and hospital expenses for birthmother and baby when they have no insurance? Yes, at times.

If international adoption, what are average travel expenses? $1,500

If you place children from other countries, please list the estimated *entire* average cost to adoptive parents for each country. Russia, $15,500; Bulgaria, $15,000; Vietnam, $15,000; China, $12,000; Romania, $12,000–15,000.

My agency: Offers confidential adoptions; semi-open adoptions; meetings between birthparents and adoptive parents; birthparents pick adoptive parents from bios/resumes; full disclosure of names between birth and adoptive parents.

Does your agency provide videotapes of children needing adoption? Yes.

Are you an adoptive parent, adopted person, or birthparent? Adoptive parent.

In how many cases with your agency has an adoptive parent been placed with a child but lost the child due to a birthparent challenge? 5

Has your agency lost any adoption litigation filed against you by an adoptive parent or birthparent? No.

THURSDAY'S CHILD, INC.

Respondent: Iris Arenson-Fuller, Executive Director
In charge of social services: Roxanne Feeney, MSW, Supervisor and Barbara Presson-Nilsson, LICSW
227 Tunxis Ave., Bloomfield, CT 06002
(860) 242-5941 • Fax: (860) 243-9898
E-mail: tcexecdir@aol.com • www.adoptthursdayschild.org
Year first licensed by state: 1981

Agency provides services for: International adoption; U.S. adoption; children with special needs; infants; homestudy if parents working with another agency; postplacement services; parent support; adoption-related counseling; post-adoption support; some foreign assistance.

What states do your adoptive parent clients come from? Connecticut and out-of-state for foreign final decree programs, China, Guatemala, Russia, and Bulgaria. Others as available. Also do out-of-state Hindu adoption sponsorships for India.

Services provided adopting parents: Classes with other prospective parents; required readings of books and/or articles on adoption; group discussions about adoption; parenting discussions; social events; parent support.

States/countries your birthparents/adopted children come from: Connecticut and other states/agencies approved to work here according to Connecticut laws and restrictions. Presently, Bulgaria, China, Guatemala, India, Russia, Vietnam. Programs change; others may become available.

What was the goal of your agency when first organized? What is the goal of your agency now? To provide flexible, caring, personalized family-centered (as well as child-centered) adoption services and to focus on international, minority, older and special needs domestically, although we sometimes place healthy local babies. Now: Same.

Nonrelative children placed in 1998: 20

Percent of adoptive placements under 6 mos.: 10%

Special expertise of staff: Adoptive parents on staff; licensed social workers; therapists; postgraduate-level supervisors (Ph.D./expert in transnational transracial adoptions).

In 1998, what was the average time from when a prospective adoptive parent applied to when he or she received a homestudy? 2 weeks

Average time from homestudy to placement of child: 6–12 mos.

What made you decide to work in the adoption field? I was an adoptive parent, volunteer birthparent consultant, child advocate, for many years prior to founding agency.

Agency criteria for adoptive parents you work with: Flexible but varies with specific country requirements.

How do you screen adoptive parents? Carefully and ethically according to state, federal, and foreign country requirements but always with caring support and flexibility, attending to individual needs and differences. We are not thrilled with groups, preferring individualized preparation and hooking up to experienced adoptive and birth families.

How do you screen birthparents? With same caring, personalized approach. We are honest with them and tell them early on if we cannot meet their needs.

What kind of medical information do you seek from birthparents? As much as possible. Social, personal, genetic and medical. Form revision in process, but we don't do many local adoptions.

What kind of medical information do you seek on older children? Same. Little information available internationally. We get as much as we can.

Do you have a waiting list of prospective parents? No.

Is it all right if adopting parents you work with are on waiting lists of other agencies or attorneys? No.

Are your adoption fees based on a sliding scale? No.

Do you have an application fee? If yes, what is the amount of the application fee? Yes. $200 locally; smaller out-of-state registration fee.

What is your homestudy fee (if a flat rate)? $1,500–2,000

What is your placement fee? Varies with program; usually $3,000–3,500

Do adopting parents also pay fees for medical and hospital expenses for birthmother and baby when they have no insurance? Yes.

If applicable, what is the average document language translation fee? Included in most fees. Is $350–500 for program not included.

If international adoption, what are average travel expenses? Varies. We hook up with good resources but do not get into this, as it fluctuates too much.

If you place children from other countries, please list the estimated *entire* average cost to adoptive parents for each country. $15,000–22,000 or so.

My agency: Offers confidential adoptions; semi-open adoptions; meetings between birthparents and adoptive parents; birthparents pick adoptive parents from bios/resumes.

Does your agency provide videotapes of children needing adoption? Yes, when available.

Are you an adoptive parent, adopted person, or birthparent? Adoptive parent.

In how many cases with your agency has an adoptive parent been placed with a child but lost the child due to a birthparent challenge? 0

Has your agency lost any adoption litigation filed against you by an adoptive parent or birthparent? No.

D.C. (DISTRICT OF COLUMBIA)

ADOPTION SERVICE INFORMATION AGENCY (ASIA)

Respondent: Mary S. Durr, Director of Professional Services, Executive Director, VA Branch
In charge of social services: Mary S. Durr
7720 Alaska Ave. NW, Washington, DC 20012
(202) 726-7193 • Fax: (202) 722-4928
E-mail: ASIADC@AOL.com • www.asia-adopt.org
Year first licensed by state: 1981

Agency provides services for: International adoption; U.S. adoption; children with special needs; infants; homestudy if parents working with another agency; postplacement services.

What states do your adoptive parent clients come from? We work in all states, depending upon the program. The Korean program is limited to District of Columbia, Maryland, Virginia, North Carolina and West Virginia. The domestic program is limited to District of Columbia, Maryland, and Virginia.

Services provided adopting parents: Classes with other prospective parents; required readings of books and/or articles on adoption; group discussions about adoption; parenting discussions.

States/countries your birthparents/adopted children come from: We place children from Korea, China, India, Vietnam, Sri Lanka, Russia, and Thailand.

What was the goal of your agency when first organized? What is the goal of your agency now? To place children in permanent loving homes. Now: To recruit and prepare parents for intercountry adoption, to maintain working relationships with overseas entities placing children in the United States, to facilitate placement, and to provide supervision and support. To provide counseling to birthparents and adoptive parents, homestudies, etc. in domestic adoption.

Nonrelative children placed in 1998: 103

Percent of adoptive placements under 6 mos.: 50%

Special expertise of staff: Adoptive parents on staff; licensed social workers; psychologists.

In 1998, what was the average time from when a prospective adoptive parent applied to when he or she received a homestudy? 3–5 mos.

Average time from homestudy to placement of child: 4–10 mos.

What made you decide to work in the adoption field? Interest in service to children.

Agency criteria for adoptive parents you work with: Depends on the program client is working with.

How do you screen adoptive parents? Interviewing applicants, plus the verifying documents necessary in homestudy process are the main tools.

How do you screen birthparents? Counseling process is the basic tool.

What kind of medical information do you seek on older children? Intercountry program dictates what information is available.

What percent of your U.S. adoptions are nonwhite children? 40%

Do you have a waiting list of prospective parents? Yes.

Is it all right if adopting parents you work with are on waiting lists of other agencies or attorneys? No.

Are your adoption fees based on a sliding scale? If sliding scale, what are the criteria? Yes. Depending on income, but fee is between $5,000 and $12,000 for domestic.

Do you have an application fee? If yes, what is the amount of the application fee? Yes. $150

What is your placement fee? Overall fee is $5,000–12,000 for domestic.

If applicable, what is the average document language translation fee? Depends on country. 0 to $750.

If international adoption, what are average travel expenses? $1,850–3,000

My agency: Offers confidential adoptions; semi-open adoptions; meetings between birthparents and adoptive parents; birthparents pick adoptive parents from bios/resumes; offers full disclosure of names between birth and adoptive parents.

Does your agency provide videotapes of children needing adoption? Yes, when available.

In how many cases with your agency has an adoptive parent been placed with a child but lost the child due to a birthparent challenge? 0

Has your agency lost any adoption litigation filed against you by an adoptive parent or birthparent? No.

DELAWARE

ADOPTION HOUSE, INC.

Respondent: Leah Tenenbaum, Executive Director
In charge of social services: Leah Tenenbaum
Suite 101 Webster, 3411 Silverside Rd., Wilmington, DE 19810
(302) 477-0944 • Fax: (303) 477-0955
E-mail address: adopt@adoptionhouse.com • www.adoptionhouse.com
Year first licensed by state: 1998

Agency provides services for: International adoption; U.S. adoption; infants; homestudy if parents working with another agency; postplacement services.

What states do your adoptive parent clients come from? All states.

Services provided to adopting parents: Classes with other prospective parents; required readings of books and articles on adoption; group discussions about adoption; parenting discussions; special 20-hour training for adoption issues.

States/countries your birthparents/adopted children come from: All over United States, Russia, Ukraine, Moldova, Romania, Guatemala, China.

What was the goal of your agency when first organized? What is the goal of your agency now? To assist birthmothers with unplanned pregnancies and to help adoptive couples to adopt. Now: Same.

Nonrelative children placed in 1998: 1 (new agency).

Percent of adoptive placements under 6 mos.: All domestic placements.

Special expertise of staff: Adoptive parents on staff; licensed social workers; therapists; attorney.

What made you decide to work in the adoption field? I was adopted myself and wanted to assist others.

Agency criteria for adoptive parents you work with: We do not discriminate on the basis of age, race, religion, or number of children. All couples who qualify after a valid homestudy may adopt.

How do you screen adoptive parents? References, fingerprints, employer references, and the homestudy.

How do you screen birthparents? Through questionnaires and physician reports.

What kind of medical information do you seek from birthparents? As much as possible.

Do you have a waiting list of prospective parents? No.

Is it all right if adopting parents you work with are on waiting lists of other agencies or attorneys? Yes.

Are your adoption fees based on a sliding scale? No.

Do you have an application fee? No.

What is your homestudy fee (if flat rate)? $1,000

What is your placement fee? Varies; charge on an hourly basis at $125 per hour.

Do adopting parents also pay fees for medical and hospital expenses for birthmother and baby when they have no insurance? Yes.

If applicable, what is average document language translation fee? $150

If international adoption, what are average travel expenses? $1,500

If you place children from other countries, please list the estimated _entire_ average cost to adoptive parents for each country. China, $16,000; Guatemala, $22,000; Russia, $20,000; Romania, $19,000.

My agency: Offers confidential adoptions; semi-open adoptions; meetings between birthparents and adoptive parents; birthparents pick adoptive parents from biographies.

Does your agency provide videotapes of children needing adoption? Yes.

Are you an adoptive parent, adopted person, or birthparent? Adopted person.

In how many cases with your agency has an adoptive parent been placed with a child but lost the child due to a birthparent challenge? 0

Has your agency lost any adoption litigation filed against you by an adoptive parent or birthparent? No.

FLORIDA

A BOND OF LOVE ADOPTION AGENCY

Respondent: Suzanne Martin, Executive Director
1800 Siesta Dr., Sarasota, FL 34329
(941) 957-0064 • Fax: (941) 954-5134
E-mail: abondoflove@juno.com
Year first licensed by state: 1992

Agency provides services for: International adoption; U.S. adoption; children with special needs; infants; homestudy if parents working with another agency; postplacement services; counseling.

What states do your adoptive parent clients come from? All but Connecticut.

Services provided adopting parents: Classes with other prospective parents; required readings of books and/or articles on adoption; group discussions about adoption; parenting discussions.

States/countries your birthparents/adopted children come from: All states.

What was the goal of your agency when first organized? What is the goal of your agency now? To provide services to the triad. Now: Same.

Nonrelative children placed in 1998: 29

Percent of adoptive placements under 6 mos.: 99%

Special expertise of staff: Licensed social workers; attorney; adoptee on staff.

In 1998, what was the average time from when a prospective adoptive parent applied to when he or she received a homestudy? 1 week

Average time from homestudy to placement of child: 1 year

What made you decide to work in the adoption field? Best friend and nephew adopted.

Agency criteria for adoptive parents you work with: Minimum age for adoptive parents is 25; married for 2 years.

How do you screen adoptive parents? Homestudies, in-person meeting.

How do you screen birthparents? In-person meetings.

What kind of medical information do you seek from birthparents? Prenatal medical information; self-report on personal and family medical.

What kind of medical information do you seek on older children? Medical reports.

What percent of your U.S. adoptions are nonwhite children? 25%

Do you have a waiting list of prospective parents? Yes.

Is it all right if adopting parents you work with are on waiting lists of other agencies or attorneys? Yes.

Are your adoption fees based on a sliding scale? If yes, what are the sliding scale criteria? Yes. Only for special needs situations.

Do you have an application fee? If yes, what is the amount of the application fee? Yes. $350

What is your homestudy fee (if a flat rate)? $1,500

What is your placement fee? $15,000

Do adopting parents also pay fees for medical and hospital expenses for birth-mother and baby when they have no insurance? If yes, what is the average fee paid? Yes. $4,000

My agency: Offers confidential adoptions; semi-open adoptions; meetings between birthparents and adoptive parents; birthparents pick adoptive parents from bios/resumes; full disclosure of names between birth and adoptive parents.

Does your agency provide videotapes of children needing adoption? No.

In how many cases with your agency has an adoptive parent been placed with a child but lost the child due to a birthparent challenge? 0

Has your agency lost any adoption litigation filed against you by an adoptive parent or birthparent? No.

ADOPTION SOURCE, INC.

Respondents: Jill Scott and Sheila Nestler, Owners
2245 Corporate Blvd. NW, Suite 230, Boca Raton, FL 33431
(561) 912-9229 or (800) 877-78 CHILD • Fax: (561) 912-9912
Year first licensed by state: 1997

Agency provides services for: International adoption; children with special needs; infants; homestudy if parents working with another agency; postplacement services; counseling services; parenting classes.

What states do your adoptive parent clients come from? We place children in all states as well as [with] U.S. citizens living abroad.

Services provided adopting parents: Classes with other prospective parents; required readings of books and/or articles on adoption; group discussions about adoption; parenting discussions; private counseling services with social workers and psychologist.

States/countries your birthparents/adopted children come from: Russia, China, Romania, Mexico.

What was the goal of your agency when first organized? What is the goal of your agency now? To have a relatively small, personal agency, owned and run by adoptive parents who themselves experienced all the emotions of the process. To maintain consistent one-to-one service throughout the process. Now: Continue to believe strongly in personalized, caring, ethical service. We walk our clients through each step of the program, assisting in each step with constant communication.

Nonrelative children placed in 1998: 20

Special expertise of staff: Adoptive parents on staff; licensed social workers; psychologists; therapists; physician; attorney.

In 1998, what was the average time from when a prospective adoptive parent applied to when he or she received a homestudy? $1\frac{1}{2}$ mos.

Average time from homestudy to placement of child: 4 mos.

What made you decide to work in the adoption field? Our education was nursing and we are both adoptive parents who worked with the local courts testifying and advocating for children in abuse and neglect cases. After the adoption of our own children, we wanted to help other children find permanent placement.

Agency criteria for adoptive parents you work with: Married more than 2 years; singles; income meeting U.S. criteria; approved homestudy.

How do you screen adoptive parents? Homestudy; abuse registry clearance; psychological evaluation; law enforcement clearance.

What kind of medical information do you seek on older children? Birth weight, height, head circumference, immunization history, medical evaluation, developmental milestones, video.

About what percent are children with medical problems? 10%

Do you have a waiting list of prospective parents? No.

Is it all right if adopting parents you work with are on waiting lists of other agencies or attorneys? No.

Are your adoption fees based on a sliding scale? No.

Do you have an application fee? If yes, what is the amount of the application fee? Yes. $250

What is your homestudy fee (if a flat rate)? $1,200

What is your placement fee? $6,000–14,000 depending on program. We waive fees for special needs children.

If applicable, what is the average document language translation fee? Most programs include translation; the programs that do not are $250.

If international adoption, what are average travel expenses? $2,500

If you place children from other countries, please list the estimated *entire* **average cost to adoptive parents for each country.** China, $15,000 (including agency fee); Eastern Europe, $15,000–25,000 (depending on region).

My agency: Offers confidential adoptions.

Does your agency provide videotapes of children needing adoption? Yes

Are you an adoptive parent, adopted person, or birthparent? Adoptive parent.

Has your agency lost any adoption litigation filed against you by an adoptive parent or birthparent? No. We have never been involved or named in a lawsuit.

ADVOCATES FOR CHILDREN AND FAMILIES

Respondent: Laurie Slavin, Executive Director
In charge of social services: Laurie Slavin
16831 NE Sixth Ave., NM Beach, FL 33162-2408
(305) 653-2474 • Fax: (305) 653-2746
E-mail: adoptact@worldnet.att.net • adoptionflorida.org
Year first licensed by state: 1992

Agency provides services for: International adoption (homestudies and referrals); U.S. adoption; children with special needs; infants; homestudy if parents working with another agency; postplacement services.

What states do your adoptive parent clients come from? All states.

Services provided adopting parents: Classes with other prospective parents; group discussions about adoption; parenting discussions.

States/countries your birthparents/adopted children come from: All states and many countries. Most foreign birthparents from Central America and the Caribbean.

What was the goal of your agency when first organized? What is the goal of your agency now? 1. To streamline social services and legal services in one entity, and 2. To terminate parental rights on voluntary surrenders or abandonment in an expedited manner. Now: To make good matches that will withstand time. To tailor each adoption to the needs of the parties.

Nonrelative children placed in 1998: 30–50 every year.

Special expertise of staff: Adoptive parents on staff; licensed social workers; therapists; attorney.

In 1998, what was the average time from when a prospective adoptive parent applied to when he or she received a homestudy? 45 days

Average time from homestudy to placement of child: 9–15 mos.

What made you decide to work in the adoption field? Adoptive parent support group activity.

Agency criteria for adoptive parents you work with: Case-by-case. We rely on homestudy recommendation for the most part.

How do you screen adoptive parents? Abuse and criminal record checks, medical, homestudy, reference letters, personal interviews.

How do you screen birthparents? Personal interviews, criminal record checks, medical records.

What kind of medical information do you seek from birthparents? Drug and alcohol screen results, proof of pregnancy, prenatal medical records, checklist completed by birthfamily.

What kind of medical information do you seek on older children? Birth and delivery records, pediatric records, immunization records, checklist completed by birth family.

What percent of your U.S. adoptions are nonwhite children? 40%

About what percent are children with medical problems? 10%

Do you have a waiting list of prospective parents? Yes.

Is it all right if adopting parents you work with are on waiting lists of other agencies or attorneys? Yes.

Are your adoption fees based on a sliding scale? No, but we reduce fees for financial need of family.

Do you have an application fee? If yes, what is the amount of the application fee? Yes. $1,000

What is your homestudy fee (if a flat rate)? $1,500

What is your placement fee? Varies with actual cost. Approximately $8,000 plus costs.

Do adopting parents also pay fees for medical and hospital expenses for birthmother and baby when they have no insurance? If yes, what is the average fee paid? Yes. Average medical if no insurance, $5,000–7,000.

My agency: Offers confidential adoptions; semi-open adoptions; meetings between birthparents and adoptive parents; birthparents pick adoptive parents from bios/resumes; full disclosure of names between birth and adoptive parents.

Does your agency provide videotapes of children needing adoption? No.

Are you an adoptive parent, adopted person, or birthparent? Adoptive parent.

In how many cases with your agency has an adoptive parent been placed with a child but lost the child due to a birthparent challenge? 5 of over 500 placements.

Has your agency lost any adoption litigation filed against you by an adoptive parent or birthparent? No.

ALL ABOUT ADOPTIONS, INC.

In charge of social services: Judy Houser
503 East New Haven Ave., Melbourne, FL 32901
(407) 723-0088 • Fax: (407) 952-9813
E-mail: grassadopt@aol.com • members.aol.com/grassadopt
Year first licensed by state: 1993

Agency provides services for: International adoption; U.S. adoption; children with special needs; infants; homestudy if parents working with another agency; postplacement services.

What states do your adoptive parent clients come from? All states.

States/countries your birthparents/adopted children come from: Primarily from Florida. We are working on a foreign program.

What was the goal of your agency when first organized? What is the goal of your agency now? Primarily to conduct homestudies for prospective adoptive parents. Now: To place children.

Nonrelative children placed in 1998: 40

Percent of adoptive placements under 6 mos.: 98%

Special expertise of staff: Attorney.

In 1998, what was the average time from when a prospective adoptive parent applied to when he or she received a homestudy? We only accept prospective adoptive parents with a current homestudy.

Average time from homestudy to placement of child: Usually not more than 6 mos.

What made you decide to work in the adoption field? It was a transition from intermediary to agency.

How do you screen adoptive parents? Consultation plus homestudy.

How do you screen birthparents? Personal interviews. Birthparent packets are not sent via mail.

What kind of medical information do you seek on older children? Medical records.

Do you have a waiting list of prospective parents? Yes.

Is it all right if adopting parents you work with are on waiting lists of other agencies or attorneys? Yes.

Are your adoption fees based on a sliding scale? If yes, what are the sliding scale criteria? Yes. Depends on the case. Age, race, sibling group, etc.

Do you have an application fee? No. Consultation fee: $250.

What is your homestudy fee (if a flat rate)? $1,500, including the postplacement visits and final report.

Do adopting parents also pay fees for medical and hospital expenses for birthmother and baby when they have no insurance? If yes, what is the average fee paid? Yes. $8,500

My agency: Offers confidential adoptions; semi-open adoptions; meetings between birthparents and adoptive parents.

Does your agency provide videotapes of children needing adoption? No.

In how many cases with your agency has an adoptive parent been placed with a child but lost the child due to a birthparent challenge? 0

Has your agency lost any adoption litigation filed against you by an adoptive parent or birthparent? No.

AN ANGEL'S ANSWER ADOPTION AGENCY

Respondent: Lyn Dinkmeyer, Director of Case Management
In charge of social services: Lyn Dinkmeyer
98 SE 6th Ave., Suite 3, Delray Beach, FL 33483
(561) 276-0660
Year first licensed by state: 1992

Agency provides services for: U.S. adoption; children with special needs; homestudy if parents working with another agency; postplacement services.

What states do your adoptive parent clients come from? All states except New York.

Services provided adopting parents: Classes with other prospective parents; required readings of books and/or articles on adoption; group discussions about adoption; parenting discussions.

States/countries your birthparents/adopted children come from: Florida.

What was the goal of your agency when first organized? What is the goal of your agency now? To assist with placements of special needs children; to assist in placements involving the ICPC [Interstate Compact for the Placement of Children] support service to out-of-state attorneys, agencies. Now: ICPC, special needs, assist in designated adoptions. Support service to out-of-state attorneys, agencies.

Nonrelative children placed in 1998: 8

Percent of adoptive placements under 6 mos.: 95%

Special expertise of staff: Adoptive parents on staff; licensed social workers; psychologists.

In 1998, what was the average time from when a prospective adoptive parent applied to when he or she received a homestudy? 30 days

Average time from homestudy to placement of child: 6 mos.

What made you decide to work in the adoption field? I like helping people.

Agency criteria for adoptive parents you work with: No law enforcement problems.

How do you screen adoptive parents? Homestudy, FDLE, and abuse checks.

How do you screen birthparents? Personal interview, HIV, drug screen, RPR, sonogram (at adoptive parents' expense).

What kind of medical information do you seek from birthparents? Health history, copy of medical records from treating physician.

What kind of medical information do you seek on older children? Medical records where possible.

What percent of your U.S. adoptions are nonwhite children? 15%

About what percent are children with medical problems? 15%

Do you have a waiting list of prospective parents? Yes.

Is it all right if adopting parents you work with are on waiting lists of other agencies or attorneys? Yes.

Are your adoption fees based on a sliding scale? No.

Do you have an application fee? If yes, what is the amount of the application fee? Yes. $500

What is your homestudy fee (if a flat rate)? $1,500

What is your placement fee? $3,500–5,000

Do adopting parents also pay fees for medical and hospital expenses for birthmother and baby when they have no insurance? If yes, what is the average fee paid? Yes. $3,000–6,000

My agency: Offers confidential adoptions; semi-open adoptions; meetings between birthparents and adoptive parents; birthparents pick adoptive parents from bios/resumes.

Does your agency provide videotapes of children needing adoption? No.

Are you an adoptive parent, adopted person, or birthparent? Adoptive parent.

In how many cases with your agency has an adoptive parent been placed with a child but lost the child due to a birthparent challenge? 0

Has your agency lost any adoption litigation filed against you by an adoptive parent or birthparent? No.

CHILDREN'S HOME SOCIETY, WESTERN DIVISION

Respondent: Carol Tullius, MSW, Adoption Program Coordinator
In charge of social services: Carol Tullius
P.O. Box 19136, Pensacola, FL 32523-9136
(850) 494-5990 • Fax: (850) 494-5981
E-mail: chs013ctull@pcola.gulf.net

Agency provides services for: International adoption; U.S. adoption; children with special needs; infants; homestudy if parents working with another agency; postplacement services.

What states do your adoptive parent clients come from? Primarily Florida; we are only licensed in Florida.

Services provided adopting parents: Group discussions about adoption.

States/countries your birthparents/adopted children come from: Florida Panhandle.

What was the goal of your agency when first organized? What is the goal of your agency now? To provide permanency for children in need. Now: Same.

Nonrelative children placed in 1998: 53

Percent of adoptive placements under 6 mos.: 75%

Special expertise of staff: Adoptive parents on staff; MSWs.

In 1998, what was the average time from when a prospective adoptive parent applied to when he or she received a homestudy? 2 years

Average time from homestudy to placement of child: 2 years

What made you decide to work in the adoption field? Wanted to make a difference in the lives of children.

Agency criteria for adoptive parents you work with: It varies from program to program.

How do you screen adoptive parents? Interview and eligibility requirements.

How do you screen birthparents? Interviews.

What kind of medical information do you seek on older children? Physician records, hospital records.

What percent of your U.S. adoptions are nonwhite children? 50%

Do you have a waiting list of prospective parents? Yes.

Is it all right if adopting parents you work with are on waiting lists of other agencies or attorneys? Yes.

Are your adoption fees based on a sliding scale? If yes, what are the sliding scale criteria? Yes, some. They are based on household income.

Do you have an application fee? If yes, what is the amount of the application fee? Yes. $300

What is your homestudy fee (if a flat rate)? Varies.

Do adopting parents also pay fees for medical and hospital expenses for birthmother and baby when they have no insurance? If yes, what is the average fee paid? Yes. Varies; up to $2,000.

If applicable, what is the average document language translation fee? Varies.

If international adoption, what are average travel expenses? Average $2,000.

If you place children from other countries, please list estimated *entire* cost to adoptive parents for each country. $12,000

My agency: Offers confidential adoptions; semi-open adoptions; meetings between birthparents and adoptive parents; birthparents pick adoptive parents from bios/resumes.

Does your agency provide videotapes of children needing adoption? No.

In how many cases with your agency has an adoptive parent been placed with a child but lost the child due to a birthparent challenge? 0. I am not going to place if I feel there is going to be a problem.

Has your agency lost any adoption litigation filed against you by an adoptive parent or birthparent? No.

EVERYDAY BLESSINGS

Respondent: (Sister) Claire M. LeBoeuf, CSC, Director
In charge of social services: Dianne Reeger, BSW
P.O. Box 1264, Thonotosassa, FL 33592
(813) 982-9226 • Fax: (813) 986-0298
E-mail: everybless@aol.com
Year first licensed by state: 1998

Agency provides services for: International adoption; U.S. adoption; children with special needs; infants; homestudy if parents working with another agency; postplacement services.

What states do your adoptive parent clients come from? Majority from Florida; accept out-of-state families as well.

Services provided adopting parents: Classes with other prospective parents; required readings of books and/or articles on adoption; group discussions about adoption; parenting discussions; MAPP training.

States/countries your birthparents/adopted children come from: Majority from Florida; accept out-of-state and out-of-country as well.

What is the goal of your agency now? To provide safe, stable, and permanent homes for children; to involve birthparents in the selection process; to make adoptions affordable to all families who qualify.

Special expertise of staff: Licensed social workers.

In 1998, what was the average time from when a prospective adoptive parent applied to when he or she received a homestudy? 1 mo. or less

What made you decide to work in the adoption field? Personal experience supported the fact that birthparents were less reluctant to release children for adoption when they had the opportunity to meet adoptive parents at least one time.

Agency criteria for adoptive parents you work with: Comply with all state requirements. No age restrictions, nor any other.

How do you screen adoptive parents? As directed by the laws of the State of Florida.

How do you screen birthparents? Level of willingness to release child for adoption and to receive support throughout the process.

What kind of medical information do you seek on older children? General health of the child; request birth records.

Do you have a waiting list of prospective parents? Yes.

Is it all right if adopting parents you work with are on waiting lists of other agencies or attorneys? Yes.

Are your adoption fees based on a sliding scale? If yes, what are the sliding scale criteria? Yes. Determined for each family.

Do you have an application fee? If yes, what is the amount of the application fee? Yes. $100

What is your homestudy fee (if a flat rate)? $1,000 (for families not registered with Everyday Blessings).

What is your placement fee? Determined for each family.

Do adopting parents also pay fees for medical and hospital expenses for birthmother and baby when they have no insurance? No.

My agency: Offers meetings between birthparents and adoptive parents; birthparents pick adoptive parents from bios/resumes and videotapes.

Does your agency provide videotapes of children needing adoption? No.

In how many cases with your agency has an adoptive parent been placed with a child but lost the child due to a birthparent challenge? No.

Is there anything I have not asked you that is important? Many children need homes; adoption can be an affordable and pleasant experience.

GIFT OF LIFE ADOPTION AGENCY, INC.

Respondent: Lisa Davis, Executive Director
In charge of social services: JoAnn Welch, LCSW
4437 Park Blvd., Pinellas Park, FL 33781
(727) 549-1416 • Fax: (727) 548-8174
E-mail: giftoflifeadoptions@E-mail.msn.com • www.giftoflifeadoptions.org
Year first licensed by state: 1993

Agency provides services for: International adoption; U.S. adoption; children with special needs; infants; homestudy if parents working with another agency; postplacement services.

What states do your adoptive parent clients come from? All states.

Services provided adopting parents: Classes with other prospective parents; group discussions about adoption; parenting discussions.

States/countries your birthparents/adopted children come from: Florida.

What was the goal of your agency when first organized? What is the goal of your agency now? To provide services to children and families that will cultivate honesty, support, understanding, and love. Agency is dedicated to children and the quality of their lives. Now: Same.

Nonrelative children placed in 1998: 144

Percent of adoptive placements under 6 mos.: 98%

Special expertise of staff: Licensed social workers; attorney.

In 1998, what was the average time from when a prospective adoptive parent applied to when he or she received a homestudy? 2 mos.

Average time from homestudy to placement of child: 8–12 mos.

What made you decide to work in the adoption field? Founders' experience; that is, one is an adopted child and one family is foster and adoptive parent.

Agency criteria for adoptive parents you work with: Ability to provide healthy, happy, structured environment for child.

How do you screen adoptive parents? Through formal application, background screenings, personal and professional references, and homestudy.

How do you screen birthparents? Through personal interview and medical histories.

What kind of medical information do you seek on older children? Hospital records, pediatrician records.

What percent of your U.S. adoptions are nonwhite children? 2%

Do you have a waiting list of prospective parents? Yes.

Is it all right if adopting parents you work with are on waiting lists of other agencies or attorneys? No.

Are your adoption fees based on a sliding scale? No.

Do you have an application fee? If yes, what is the amount of the application fee? Yes. $200 preapplication; $4,800 application.

What is your homestudy fee (if a flat rate)? $900

What is your placement fee? $15,000; total, $20,000 (homestudy included in this fee).

Do adopting parents also pay fees for medical and hospital expenses for birth-mother and baby when they have no insurance? No.

If international adoption, what are average travel expenses? $4,000

If you place children from other countries, please list the estimated *entire* average cost to adoptive parents for each country. In-state: Russia/Ukraine, $21,800; China, $16,000. Out-of-state: Russia/Ukraine, $20,000; China, $14,200.

My agency: Offers confidential adoptions; semi-open adoptions; meetings between birthparents and adoptive parents; birthparents pick adoptive parents from bios/resumes; offers full disclosure of names between birth and adoptive parents.

Does your agency provide videotapes of children needing adoption? Yes, for international.

In how many cases with your agency has an adoptive parent been placed with a child but lost the child due to a birthparent challenge? 1

Has your agency lost any adoption litigation filed against you by an adoptive parent or birthparent? Yes.

ONE WORLD ADOPTION SERVICES, INC.

Respondent: Margaret T. Snider, MSW, Executive Director
In charge of social services: Margaret T. Snider
1030 S. Federal Hwy., Suite 100, Hollywood, FL 33020
(954) 922-8400 • Fax: (954) 922-4575
E-mail: adoptbaby@aol.com
Year first licensed by state: 1995

Agency provides services for: International adoption; U.S. adoption; children with special needs; infants; homestudy if parents working with another agency; postplacement services.

What states do your adoptive parent clients come from? All states.

Services provided adopting parents: Classes with other prospective parents; required readings of books and/or articles on adoption; parenting discussions.

States/countries your birthparents/adopted children come from: Russia (children) and Florida (most birthparents).

What was the goal of your agency when first organized? What is the goal of your agency now? To provide full, comprehensive, professional services to adoptive and birthparents, 24/7. Now: Same.

Nonrelative children placed in 1998: 70

Percent of adoptive placements under 6 mos.: 85%

Special expertise: Executive director has thiry-three years' experience in both domestic and foreign adoption.

In 1998, what was the average time from when a prospective adoptive parent applied to when he or she received a homestudy? 2–3 mos.

Average time from homestudy to placement of child: 6–9 mos.

What made you decide to work in the adoption field? I had been a birthmother.

Agency criteria for adoptive parents you work with: We evaluate each situation on its individual merits.

How do you screen adoptive parents? 1. Preliminary phone screen; 2. office visit; 3. homestudy evaluation.

How do you screen birthparents? 1. Phone screen; 2. receipt of medical records; 3. home visits; 4. criminal background checks.

What kind of medical information do you seek from birthparents? 1. Previous medical history; 2. current physical exam; 3. drug screen, hepatitis, and VDRL; 4. sonogram/amniocentesis if necessary.

What kind of medical information do you seek on older children? 1. Hospital records (at birth); 2. immunization and pediatric visits; 3. any ER or hospital visits; 4. health department records.

What percent of your U.S. adoptions are nonwhite children? 25%

About what percent are children with medical problems? 30%

About what percent are children with emotional problems? 10%

Do you have a waiting list of prospective parents? Yes.

Is it all right if adopting parents you work with are on waiting lists of other agencies or attorneys? Yes.

Are your adoption fees based on a sliding scale? If yes, what are the sliding scale criteria? Yes. The circumstances of the placement.

Do you have an application fee? If yes, what is the amount of the application fee? Yes. $300

What is your homestudy fee (if a flat rate)? Domestic, $1,200; international, $1,500.

What is your placement fee? Varies.

Do adopting parents also pay fees for medical and hospital expenses for birthmother and baby when they have no insurance? If yes, what is the average fee paid? Yes. $3,000–6,000

If applicable, what is the average document language translation fee? Varies by country and agency.

If international adoption, what are average travel expenses? $3,500

If you place children from other countries, please list the estimated *entire* average cost to adoptive parents for each country. Russia, $20,000–25,000.

My agency: Offers confidential adoptions; semi-open adoptions; meetings between birthparents and adoptive parents.

Does your agency provide videotapes of children needing adoption? Yes.

Are you an adoptive parent, adopted person, or birthparent? Birthparent.

In how many cases with your agency has an adoptive parent been placed with a child but lost the child due to a birthparent challenge? 1

Has your agency lost any adoption litigation filed against you by an adoptive parent or birthparent? No.

TEDI BEAR ADOPTIONS, INC.

Respondent: Tedi Martin Hedstrom, Executive Director
In charge of social services: Rebecca Kimball, Staff Social Worker
415 N. Pablo Ave., Suite 100, Jacksonville Beach, FL 32250
(904) 242-4995 • Fax: 904-242-8951
E-mail: tedibearh@aol.com • www.tedibearadoptions.org
Year first licensed by state: 1997

Agency provides services for: International adoption; U.S. children with special needs; infants (sometimes); homestudy if parents working with another agency; postplacement services.

What states do your adoptive parent clients come from? All states.

Services provided adopting parents: Classes with other prospective parents; required readings of books and/or articles on adoption; group discussions about adoption; parenting discussions: support groups.

States/countries your birthparents/adopted children come from: Mexico, Guatemala, Kazakhstan, China, Vietnam, Russia, Romania, Moldova, Bulgaria, Bolivia, Marshall Islands, Hong Kong, Philippines, U.S. special needs.

What is the goal of your agency? To find stable, loving homes for children who need parents and to provide major support for adoptive families before, during, and after their adoptions.

Nonrelative children placed in 1998: 76

Percent of adoptive placements under 6 mos.: 30%

Special expertise of staff: Adoptive parents on staff; licensed social workers; psychologists; therapists; physician; attorney.

In 1998, what was the average time from when a prospective adoptive parent applied to when he or she received a homestudy? 6 weeks

Average time from homestudy to placement of child: 6 mos.

What made you decide to work in the adoption field? We adopted a daughter in China after having three sons by birth. Saw orphans in China and had to do something to help.

Agency criteria for adoptive parents you work with: Very flexible. We go by individual country requirements.

How do you screen adoptive parents? Medical evaluations; financial, employer, and personal references; background checks; major interview process.

What kind of medical information do you seek on older children? All available, head circumference, updated measurements, videos, and pictures.

What percent of your U.S. adoptions are nonwhite children? 40%

About what percent are children with medical problems? 30%

About what percent are children with emotional problems? 10%

Do you have a waiting list of prospective parents? Yes.

Is it all right if adopting parents you work with are on waiting lists of other agencies or attorneys? Yes.

Are your adoption fees based on a sliding scale? No.

Do you have an application fee? If yes, what is the amount of the application fee? Yes. $500

What is your homestudy fee (if a flat rate)? $1,000 domestic; $1,500 international. Also charges an agency fee of $3,500.

My agency: Offers confidential adoptions.

Does your agency provide videotapes of children needing adoption? Yes.

Are you an adoptive parent, adopted person, or birthparent? Adoptive parent.

In how many cases with your agency has an adoptive parent been placed with a child but lost the child due to a birthparent challenge? 0

Has your agency lost any adoption litigation filed against you by an adoptive parent or birthparent? No.

GEORGIA

ADOPTION PLANNING, INC.

Respondent: Rhonda L. Fishbein, MA, JD, Executive Director
In charge of social services: Wendy Willman, MSW; Sheila Cohen, MS, MSW; Rhonda Fishbein
17 Executive Park Ave., Suite 480, Atlanta, GA 30329
(404) 248-9105 • Fax: (404) 248-0419
E-mail: rlfishbein@earthlink.net
Year first licensed by state: 1990

Agency provides services for: International adoption; U.S. adoption; infants; homestudy if parents working with another agency; postplacement services.

What states do your adoptive parent clients come from? All states except New York and Connecticut.

Services provided adopting parents: Required readings of books and/or articles on adoption; group discussions about adoption; parenting discussions.

States/countries your birthparents/adopted children come from: Mostly Georgia.

What was the goal of your agency when first organized? What is the goal of your agency now? After working several years as an attorney practicing in the area of private adoption, Ronnie Fishbein identified several needs of birthparents and prospective adoptive parents that could only be met by a licensed child-placing agency. The goal was to support these prospective parents and birthparents in their goal toward adoption. Now: To support prospective adoptive parents and birthparents in their adoption plans and to give control over the process to these birthparents and prospective adoptive parents.

Nonrelative children placed in 1998: 21

Percent of adoptive placements under 6 mos.: 100%

Special expertise of staff: Adoptive parents on staff; attorney.

In 1998, what was the average time from when a prospective adoptive parent applied to when he or she received a homestudy? 6 weeks after required documents are received.

Average time from homestudy to placement of child: Approximately under 1 year for a black or biracial infant; 1 to $1\frac{1}{2}$ years for a Caucasian child.

What made you decide to work in the adoption field? We do this to help birthparents find loving homes for their children and to help adoptive couples make their dreams of parenting come true.

Agency criteria for adoptive parents you work with: All individual couples with a favorable homestudy.

How do you screen adoptive parents? Homestudy process, which includes interviews and backup documentation.

How do you screen birthparents? One-on-one interviews; written questionnaires; medical screening; counseling; criminal background checks.

What kind of medical information do you seek from birthparents? All available medical and social background information.

What kind of medical information do you seek on older children? All available medical and social background information from hospitals and pediatrician.

What percent of your U.S. adoptions are nonwhite children? 50%

Do you have a waiting list of prospective parents? No.

Is it all right if adopting parents you work with are on waiting lists of other agencies or attorneys? Yes, with notification to us.

Are your adoption fees based on a sliding scale? If yes, what are the sliding scale criteria? Yes, for black/biracial. 10% of gross income (minimum of $5,200, maximum of $8,000).

Do you have an application fee? If yes, what is the amount of the application fee? Yes. Caucasian, $50 preliminary application fee and $300 application fee. Black or biracial, $50 application fee.

What is your homestudy fee (if a flat rate)? $1,200 plus mileage for a homestudy and $300 for a homestudy review if homestudy done by another agency.

What is your placement fee? $22,000 (Caucasian child); $5,200–8,000 (black or biracial child).

Do adopting parents also pay fees for medical and hospital expenses for birth-mother and baby when they have no insurance? No.

My agency: Offers semi-open adoptions; meetings between birthparents and adoptive parents; birthparents pick adoptive parents from bios/resumes; full disclosure of names between birth and adoptive parents.

Does your agency provide videotapes of children needing adoption? No.

Are you an adoptive parent, adopted person, or birthparent? Adoptive parent.

In how many cases with your agency has an adoptive parent been placed with a child but lost the child due to a birthparent challenge? Under 1% and 0% after the 10-day revocation period.

Has your agency lost any adoption litigation filed against you by an adoptive parent or birthparent? No.

ADOPTION SERVICES, INC.

Respondent: Janice M. Driggers, Executive Director
In charge of social services: Janice M. Driggers
P.O. Box 278, Pavo, GA 31778
(912) 859-2654 • Fax: (912) 859-2412
E-mail: adopt@surfsouth.com
Year first licensed by state: 1988

Agency provides services for: U.S. adoption; homestudy if parents working with another agency; postplacement services; homestudy for families to work with our agency. We search for children for them.

What states do your adoptive parent clients come from? Georgia.

Services provided adopting parents: Group discussions about adoption; parenting discussions.

States/countries your birthparents/adopted children come from: All states.

What was the goal of your agency when first organized? What is the goal of your agency now? To recruit adoptive homes for children with special needs. Now: Same.

Nonrelative children placed in 1998: 43

Special expertise of staff: Adoptive parents on staff; licensed social workers.

In 1998, what was the average time from when a prospective adoptive parent applied to when he or she received a homestudy? 4 mos.

Average time from homestudy to placement of child: 8 mos.

Agency criteria for adoptive parents you work with: Age is not a factor.

How do you screen adoptive parents? Financial stability, parenting skills, criminal history, motivation, physical stamina, expectation.

What kind of medical information do you seek on older children? All available.

What percent of your U.S. adoptions are nonwhite children? 60–70%

About what percent are children with medical problems? 10–15%

About what percent are children with emotional problems? 75%

Do you have a waiting list of prospective parents? No.

Is it all right if adopting parents you work with are on waiting lists of other agencies or attorneys? No.

Are your adoption fees based on a sliding scale? No.

Do you have an application fee? If yes, what is the amount of the application fee? Yes. $25

What is your homestudy fee (if a flat rate)? $1,000 (for non-special needs).

What is your placement fee? $5,000 for each sibling, billed as purchase of service $11,000; for first child.

Do adopting parents also pay fees for medical and hospital expenses for birthmother and baby when they have no insurance? No.

Does your agency provide videotapes of children needing adoption? No.

In how many cases with your agency has an adoptive parent been placed with a child but lost the child due to a birthparent challenge? 0

Has your agency lost any adoption litigation filed against you by an adoptive parent or birthparent? No.

COVENANT CARE SERVICES

Respondent: Iris M. Archer, Executive Director
In charge of social services: Iris M. Archer
3950 Ridge Ave., Macon, GA 31210
(912) 741-9829 or (800) 226-5683 • Fax: (912) 741-9842
Year first licensed by state: 1989

Agency provides services for: International adoption; U.S. adoption; children with special needs; infants; homestudy if parents working with another agency; postplacement services; foster care; crisis counseling.

What states do your adoptive parent clients come from? Primarily Georgia but for minority or special needs children anywhere in the United States.

Services provided adopting parents: Classes with other prospective parents; group discussions about adoption; referral services.

States/countries your birthparents/adopted children come from: Primarily Georgia.

What was the goal of your agency when first organized? What is the goal of your agency now? Covenant Care is a nondenominational Christian ministry. To provide high-quality social services to young pregnant women and to offer adoption services into two-parent Christian families. Now: Primarily the same except we are in the process of adding a counseling and mentoring program for young women.

Nonrelative children placed in 1998: 22

Percent of adoptive placements under 6 mos.: 98%

Special expertise of staff: Adoptive parents on staff; all caseworkers have a minimum of a BS or BA degree plus two staff have a master's degree.

In 1998, what was the average time from when a prospective adoptive parent applied to when he or she received a homestudy? 1–2 years

Average time from homestudy to placement of child: Usually a couple receives a child within 18 mos.

What made you decide to work in the adoption field? Most of the staff are involved with CCS because this is a Christian ministry.

Agency criteria for adoptive parents you work with: 25–45 years old; married 3 years for a first marriage, 5 years for a second or subsequent; members of the same Christian church (no specific denomination required); only one other child (Caucasian adoption only).

How do you screen adoptive parents? Initial screening: Each couple completes a preapplication form, signs the CCS statement of faith, and submits a pastor evaluation form.

How do you screen birthparents? All birthparents are acceptable; however we do require an HIV test.

What kind of medical information do you seek on older children? Physical exams, any other neurological or developmental screening as required.

What percent of your U.S. adoptions are nonwhite children? 40–45%

Do you have a waiting list of prospective parents? Yes.

Is it all right if adopting parents you work with are on waiting lists of other agencies or attorneys? No.

Are your adoption fees based on a sliding scale? Yes. (Our fees collected represent approximately one third of our overall budget.)

Do you have an application fee? If yes, what is the amount of the application fee? Yes. $125

What is your homestudy fee (if a flat rate)? $1,000

Do adopting parents also pay fees for medical and hospital expenses for birthmother and baby when they have no insurance? If yes, what is the average fee paid? Yes. Usually less than $100, however it has been around $4,000.

My agency: Offers confidential adoptions; semi-open adoptions; meetings between birthparents and adoptive parents; birthparents pick adoptive parents from bios/resumes.

Does your agency provide videotapes of children needing adoption? No.

In how many cases with your agency has an adoptive parent been placed with a child but lost the child due to a birthparent challenge? Only once and the child was placed under legal risk and was in the home for one week.

Has your agency lost any adoption litigation filed against you by an adoptive parent or birthparent? Yes. Two birthfathers moved for legitimation but the children were not placed with an adoptive family.

THE GIVING TREE

Respondent: Lesli Greenberg, Executive Director
In charge of social services: Lesli Greenberg
1842 Clairmont Rd., Decatur, GA 30033
(404) 633-3383 • Fax: (404) 633-3348
E-mail: giving2323@aol.com • www.thegivingtree.org
Year first licensed by state: 1997

Agency provides services for: U.S. adoption; children with special needs; homestudy if parents working with another agency; postplacement services; adoptive family support services.

What states do your adoptive parent clients come from? Georgia.

Services provided adopting parents: Classes with other prospective parents; required readings of books and/or articles on adoption; group discussions about adoption; parenting discussions.

What was the goal of your agency when first organized? What is the goal of your agency now? Recruit permanent families for children in foster care and provide support to families of adoption. Now: Same.

Nonrelative children placed in 1998: 5

Special expertise of staff: Therapists; adopted adults.

In 1998, what was the average time from when a prospective adoptive parent applied to when he or she received a homestudy? 3 mos.

Average time from homestudy to placement of child: 4 mos.

What made you decide to work in the adoption field? Started in CPS [child protective services] and foster care 12 years ago.

Agency criteria for adoptive parents you work with: Follow state law only.

How do you screen adoptive parents? Personal interview with executive director, application, adoptive parent training.

What percent of your U.S. adoptions are nonwhite children? 70%

About what percent are children with medical problems? 20%

About what percent are children with emotional problems? 90%

Do you have a waiting list of prospective parents? No.

Is it all right if adopting parents you work with are on waiting lists of other agencies or attorneys? Yes.

Are your adoption fees based on a sliding scale? No.

Do you have an application fee? If yes, what is the amount of the application fee? Yes. $25

What is your homestudy fee (if a flat rate)? $800

What is your placement fee? Purchase of service from state child is in custody with varies from state to state.

Do adopting parents also pay fees for medical and hospital expenses for birth-mother and baby when they have no insurance? No.

My agency: Offers confidential adoptions.

Does your agency provide videotapes of children needing adoption? Yes, if provided by state agencies.

Has your agency lost any adoption litigation filed against you by an adoptive parent or birthparent? No.

HOPE FOR CHILDREN, INC.

Respondent: Mark Johnson, Executive Director
In charge of social services: Kent Brand, Director of Social Services
1515 Johnson Ferry Rd., Suite 200, Marietta, GA 30062
(770) 977-0813 • Fax: (770) 973-6033
www.hopeforchildren.org
Year first licensed by state: 1991

Agency provides services for: International adoption; U.S. adoption; children with special needs; infants, homestudy if parents working with another agency, postplacement services.

What states do your adoptive parent clients come from? 27 states

Services provided adopting parents: Classes with other prospective parents; required readings of books and/or articles on adoption; group discussions about adoption; parenting discussions.

States/countries your birthparents/adopted children come from: China, India, Romania, Cambodia, Jamaica, Russia.

What was the goal of your agency when first organized? Maintain number of adoptions; stabilize personnel; solidify all international programs.

Nonrelative children placed in 1998: 70

Percent of adoptive placements under 6 mos.: 35%

Special expertise by staff: Adoptive parents on staff; licensed social workers; psychologists; attorney.

In 1998, what was the average time from when a prospective adoptive parent applied to when he or she received a homestudy? 1 mo.

Average time from homestudy to placement of child: 12 mos.

What made you decide to work in the adoption field? Desire to save children's lives.

How do you screen adoptive parents? We have one full-time individual who receives and responds to every adoptive parent call.

How do you screen birthparents? One-on-one meeting by licensed social worker.

What percent of your U.S. adoptions are nonwhite children? 65%

About what percent are children with medical problems? 10%

Do you have a waiting list of prospective parents? Yes.

Is it all right if adopting parents you work with are on waiting lists of other agencies or attorneys? No.

Are your adoption fees based on a sliding scale? No.

Do you have an application fee? If yes, what is the amount of the application fee? Yes. $250

What is your homestudy fee (if a flat rate)? $1,600

What is your placement fee? International, $6,250; domestic, $11,250.

If international adoption, what are average travel expenses? $3,000

If you place children from other countries, please list the estimated *entire* average cost to adoptive parents for each country. Romania, $20,000; Cambodia, $18,000; China, $16,000; Jamaica, $10,000; India, $16,000.

My agency: Offers confidential adoptions; semi-open adoptions; meetings between birthparents and adoptive parents; birthparents pick adoptive parents from bios/resumes.

In how many cases with your agency has an adoptive parent been placed with a child but lost the child due to a birthparent challenge? 0

Has your agency lost any adoption litigation filed against you by an adoptive parent or birthparent? No.

THE OPEN DOOR ADOPTION AGENCY, INC

Respondent: Walter E. Gilbert, CEO
In charge of social services: Jane Gilbert
P.O. Box 4, Thomasville, GA 31799
(912) 228-6339 • Fax: (912) 228-4726
Year first licensed by state: 1987

Agency provides services for: International adoption; U.S. adoption; children with special needs; infants; homestudy if parents working with another agency; postplacement services.

What states do your adoptive parent clients come from? All states.

Services provided adopting parents: Classes with other prospective parents; required readings of books and/or articles on adoption; group discussions about adoption; parenting discussions.

States/countries your birthparents/adopted children come from: Georgia, Florida, Russia, China, Ukraine, Poland, Latvia, Ecuador.

What was the goal of your agency when first organized? What is the goal of your agency now? To offer adoption as an alternative to abortion. Now: We originally planned to bring orphaned children from abroad to Christian adoptive families in the United States.

Nonrelative children placed in 1998: 70

Percent of adoptive placements under 6 mos.: 80%

Special expertise of staff: Psychologists; adoptee; MBA; CPA; paralegal.

In 1998, what was the average time from when a prospective adoptive parent applied to when he or she received a homestudy? 3 mos.

Average time from homestudy to placement of child: 9 mos.

What made you decide to work in the adoption field? After arranging a trip to Russian orphanages for the agency as a consultant, I fell in love with the orphan children. Helping the children and finding families for them became my driving passion.

Agency criteria for adoptive parents you work with: Aged 25–45 years for domestic adoptions (no maximum for international). Married $2\frac{1}{2}$ years or single woman. Christian adoptive parents. No infertility requirements or limit on number of children.

How do you screen adoptive parents? By the above criteria, homestudies, references, and criminal checks.

How do you screen birthparents? We screen for those who are serious about placing for adoption.

What kind of medical information do you seek from birthparents? Complete social and medical histories.

What kind of medical information do you seek on older children? Any major medical, emotional, psychological, or behavior problems.

What percent of your U.S. adoptions are nonwhite children? 50%

About what percent are children with medical problems? 5%

About what percent are children with emotional problems? 10%

Do you have a waiting list of prospective parents? Yes.

Is it all right if adopting parents you work with are on waiting lists of other agencies or attorneys? Yes.

Are your adoption fees based on a sliding scale? No.

Do you have an application fee? If yes, what is the amount of the application fee? Yes. $100

What is your homestudy fee (if a flat rate)? $1,200

What is your placement fee? $22,000 for domestic Caucasian child; $8,000 African-American child; $2,000 for child from China; $5,000 for child from Latin America; $8,500 for child from Russia.

If applicable, what is the average document language translation fee? $500

If international adoption, what are average travel expenses? $3,000–5,000

If you place children from other countries, please list the estimated *entire* average cost to adoptive parents for each country. China, $14,700; Latvia, $18,000; Russia, $20,000; Ecuador, $23,000.

My agency: Offers confidential adoptions; semi-open adoptions; meetings between birthparents and adoptive parents; birthparents pick adoptive parents from bios/resumes.

Does your agency provide videotapes of children needing adoption? Yes.

In how many cases with your agency has an adoptive parent been placed with a child but lost the child due to a birthparent challenge? 0

Has your agency lost any adoption litigation filed against you by an adoptive parent or birthparent? No.

HAWAII

HAWAII INTERNATIONAL CHILD, INC.
Respondent: Kristine Altwies, Executive Director
P.O. Box 240486, Honolulu, HI 96824-0486
(808) 377-0881 • Fax: (808) 373-5095
E-mail: adopt@h-i-c.org
Year first licensed by state: 1975

Agency provides services for: International adoption; U.S. adoption; children with special needs; infants; homestudy if parents working with another agency; postplacement services.

What states do your adoptive parent clients come from? Hawaii, New York, New Jersey, California, and many others.

Services provided adopting parents: Classes with other prospective parents; required readings of books and/or articles on adoption; group discussions about adoption; parenting discussions.

States/countries your birthparents/adopted children come from: Russia, China, Cambodia, Ukraine.

What was the goal of your agency when first organized? What is the goal of your agency now? As a Holt partner agency we brought 2,500 infants from Korea initially. Now: To find as many good homes for orphaned children as we can, and to help end the pain of infertility.

Nonrelative children placed in 1998: 75

Percent of adoptive placements under 6 mos.: 5%

Special expertise of staff: Adoptive parents on staff; licensed social workers; therapists; attorney.

In 1998, what was the average time from when a prospective adoptive parent applied to when he or she received a homestudy? 3 weeks

Average time from homestudy to placement of child: 4 mos.

What made you decide to work in the adoption field? Love of children and desire to do important work.

Agency criteria for adoptive parents you work with: None as such. Must pass typical state requirements.

How do you screen adoptive parents? Read application, review standard requirement papers. Talk to them if we have special concerns. Complete or read homestudy.

What kind of medical information do you seek on older children? All available.

What percent of your U.S. adoptions are nonwhite children? Less than 10% of U.S.-born children; 80% of foreign-born children.

About what percent are children with medical problems? Less than 5%

Do you have a waiting list of prospective parents? No.

Is it all right if adopting parents you work with are on waiting lists of other agencies or attorneys? Yes.

Are your adoption fees based on a sliding scale? No.

Do you have an application fee? If yes, what is the amount of the application fee? Yes. $100

What is your homestudy fee (if a flat rate)? $950

What is your placement fee? $5,000

Do adopting parents also pay fees for medical and hospital expenses for birth-mother and baby when they have no insurance? If yes, what is the average fee paid? Yes. Varies.

If applicable, what is the average document language translation fee? $25/page (varies).

If international adoption, what are average travel expenses? Standard airfare, hotel, etc.

If you place children from other countries, please list the estimated *entire* average cost to adoptive parents for each country. Russia and China, $15,000–20,000; Cambodia, $12,000.

My agency: Offers confidential adoptions; semi-open adoptions; meetings between birthparents and adoptive parents; birthparents pick adoptive parents from bios/resumes; full disclosure of names between birth and adoptive parents.

Does your agency provide videotapes of children needing adoption? Yes.

In how many cases with your agency has an adoptive parent been placed with a child but lost the child due to a birthparent challenge? 2

Has your agency lost any adoption litigation filed against you by an adoptive parent or birthparent? No.

IDAHO

CHILDREN'S ADOPTION SERVICES, INC.

Respondent: Helen Fairbourn, Executive Director
In charge of social services: Betty Griffin, Social Work Director
2308 N. Cole Rd., Suite #E, Boise, ID 83704
(208) 376-0558 • Fax: (208) 376-1931
E-mail: info@adoptcasi.org • www.adoptcasi.org
Year first licensed by state: 1992

Agency provides services for: International adoption; U.S. adoption; children with special needs; infants; homestudy if parents working with another agency; postplacement services.

What states do your adoptive parent clients come from? Any state in the United States.

States/countries your birthparents/adopted children come from: Domestic: All states. China, Ukraine, Haiti.

What was the goal of your agency when first organized? To unite families through adoption.

Nonrelative children placed in 1998: 90

Percent of adoptive placements under 6 mos.: 80%

Special expertise of staff: Adoptive parents on staff; licensed social workers.

In 1998, what was the average time from when a prospective adoptive parent applied to when he or she received a homestudy? Average time to complete a homestudy is about a month.

Average time from homestudy to placement of child: About 1 year.

What made you decide to work in the adoption field? Too many children without families; wanted to help.

Agency criteria for adoptive parents you work with: Adopted parents must be 15 years older than children they adopt. We do not put an age limit in general. Determination made on individual basis. For international adoptions, this regulation is set by the country. We do not have a cut-off for number of children already in home. Based on individual family and their ability to handle another child(ren).

How do you screen adoptive parents? Through the application process.

How do you screen birthparents? Through counseling with them on an individual basis.

What kind of medical information do you seek from birthparents? We have them provide information by filling out a standard comprehensive genetic background packet.

What kind of medical information do you seek on older children? Current medical reports from doctors, dentists, etc., along with their birthing information.

About what percent are children with medical problems? 5%

About what percent are children with emotional problems? 10%

Do you have a waiting list of prospective parents? Yes.

Is it all right if adopting parents you work with are on waiting lists of other agencies or attorneys? Yes.

Are your adoption fees based on a sliding scale? No.

Do you have an application fee? If yes, what is the amount of the application fee? Yes. $100

What is your homestudy fee (if a flat rate)? $500–800

What is your placement fee? $5,000 plus medical.

Do adopting parents also pay fees for medical and hospital expenses for birthmother and baby when they have no insurance? If yes, what is the average fee paid? Yes. $3,500

If applicable, what is the average document language translation fee? $500

If international adoption, what are average travel expenses? $3,000–5,000

My agency: Offers confidential adoptions; semi-open adoptions; meetings between birthparents and adoptive parents; birthparents pick adoptive parents from bios/resumes; full disclosure of names between birth and adoptive parents. [We] do try to avoid disclosing any identifying information. The birthmother and adoptive parents agree on degrees of openness accepted prior to adoption.

Does your agency provide videotapes of children needing adoption? If it comes with the program.

In how many cases with your agency has an adoptive parent been placed with a child but lost the child due to a birthparent challenge? 2 or 3

Has your agency lost any adoption litigation filed against you by an adoptive parent or birthparent? No. So far we haven't had any litigation filed.

NW SERVICES, INC.

Respondent: Kimberly Huitt, Executive Director
303 Palo Alto Dr., Caldwell, ID 83605
(208) 459-6772 • Fax: (208) 459-0968
E-mail: khuitt@aol.com
Year first licensed by state: 1997

Agency provides services for: U.S. adoption; infants; homestudy if parents working with another agency; postplacement services; birthparent counseling; interstate processing.

What states do your adoptive parent clients come from? Mainly Idaho but accept out-of-state families (all states).

Services provided adopting parents: Classes with other prospective parents; required readings of books and/or articles on adoption.

States/countries your birthparents/adopted children come from: Idaho.

What was the goal of your agency when first organized? What is the goal of your agency now? Facilitate newborn adoptions, provide free services to birthparents and adoptive families. Now: Same.

Nonrelative children placed in 1998: 3

Percent of adoptive placements under 6 mos.: 90%

Special expertise of staff: Licensed social workers; cross-cultural.

In 1998, what was the average time from when a prospective adoptive parent applied to when he or she received a homestudy? As soon as they finish paperwork. It depends on them; immediate services from us thereafter.

Average time from homestudy to placement of child: 2 mos.–2 years (varies). Birthparents choose adoptive family.

What made you decide to work in the adoption field? Love for adoption, personal experience with infertility, wanted to make it easier for people to adopt so started agency.

Agency criteria for adoptive parents you work with: None; few restrictions as possible.

How do you screen adoptive parents? Homestudy.

How do you screen birthparents? Interviews, collateral contacts.

What kind of medical information do you seek from birthparents? All possible information available.

What kind of medical information do you seek on older children? All possible information available.

What percent of your U.S. adoptions are nonwhite children? 80%

About what percent are children with medical problems? 5%

Do you have a waiting list of prospective parents? Yes.

Is it all right if adopting parents you work with are on waiting lists of other agencies or attorneys? Yes.

Are your adoption fees based on a sliding scale? No.

Do you have an application fee? If yes, what is the amount of the application fee? Yes. $100

What is your homestudy fee (if a flat rate)? $450

What is your placement fee? $6,500

Do adopting parents also pay fees for medical and hospital expenses for birth-mother and baby when they have no insurance? If yes, what is the average fee paid? Yes. $2,000–3,000

My agency: Offers confidential adoptions; semi-open adoptions; meetings between birthparents and adoptive parents; birthparents pick adoptive parents from bios/resumes; full disclosure of names between birth and adoptive parents.

Does your agency provide videotapes of children needing adoption? No.

Are you an adoptive parent, adopted person, or birthparent? Adopted person.

In how many cases with your agency has an adoptive parent been placed with a child but lost the child due to a birthparent challenge? 0

Has your agency lost any adoption litigation filed against you by an adoptive parent or birthparent? No.

ILLINOIS

BETHANY FOR CHILDREN AND FAMILIES

In charge of social services: Bill Steinhauser, Vice President
P.O. Box 697, Moline, IL 61265
(309) 797-7700 or (319) 724-9169 • Fax: (309) 324-2437 or (319) 324-2437
E-mail: ilbethany@aol.com

Agency provides services for: U.S. adoption; children with special needs; infants; home-study if parents working with another agency; postplacement services; counseling.

What states do your adoptive parent clients come from? Illinois and Iowa.

Services provided adopting parents: Classes with other prospective parents; required readings of books and/or articles on adoption; group discussions about adoption; parenting discussions.

States/countries your birthparents/adopted children come from: Illinois, Iowa, and some from the other 48 states.

What was the goal of your agency when first organized? Founded in 1899 as a union mission with a goal of the improvement, moral, industrial, and religious education of such persons in the city of Rock Island, Illinois as it can reach and bring under its influence of its work.

Nonrelative children placed in 1998: 3

Special expertise of staff: Licensed social workers; therapists.

In 1998, what was the average time from when a prospective adoptive parent applied to when he or she received a homestudy? 2 mos.

What made you decide to work in the adoption field? Community need for adoptive services.

Agency criteria for adoptive parents you work with: Each home is looked at individually for strengths, resources, and needs. As many cases now involve birthparents in the selection of an adoptive home. We are attempting to have a varied selection of homes with different circumstances for birthparents to choose from.

How do you screen adoptive parents? Homestudy process; multiple interviews with adoptive worker; personal references; attendance by adoptive parents at adoption class; checks of child abuse registry; and criminal records backgrounds.

How do you screen birthparents? Multiple interviews with birthparents; medical information reviews; counseling with agency therapists provided.

What kind of medical information do you seek on older children? Birth information, medical records since birth, biological parent and sibling medical histories.

What percent of your U.S. adoptions are nonwhite children? 33%

About what percent are children with medical problems? 33%

Do you have a waiting list of prospective parents? Yes.

Is it all right if adopting parents you work with are on waiting lists of other agencies or attorneys? Yes.

Are your adoption fees based on a sliding scale? If yes, what are the sliding scale criteria? Yes. Fees can be negotiated on an individual basis depending on income, resources, and circumstances.

Do you have an application fee? No.

What is your homestudy fee (if a flat rate)? $18

What is your placement fee? $57

Do adopting parents also pay fees for medical and hospital expenses for birthmother and baby when they have no insurance? No. This is negotiable. We have not encountered such a situation in years.

My agency: Offers confidential adoptions; semi-open adoptions; meetings between birthparents and adoptive parents; birthparents pick adoptive parents from bios/resumes; full disclosure of names between birth and adoptive parents.

Does your agency provide videotapes of children needing adoption? No.

In how many cases with your agency has an adoptive parent been placed with a child but lost the child due to a birthparent challenge? 1

Has your agency lost any adoption litigation filed against you by an adoptive parent or birthparent? No.

CATHOLIC CHARITIES OF THE ARCHDIOCESE OF CHICAGO

Respondent: Kathryn Herrera, Adoption Program Assistant
In charge of social services: Norene Chesebro, LCSW, Director of Maternity/Adoption Department
651 West Lake St., Chicago, IL 60661
(312) 655-7086 • Fax: (312) 236-5384
E-mail: ccadoptions@earthlink.net • www.ccaoc.org

Year first licensed by state: Catholic Charities of the Archdiocese of Chicago has been in existence since long before the State of Illinois began licensing child welfare agencies. We were instrumental in the development of the Illinois Department of Children and Family Services, around 1968.

Agency provides services for: International adoption; U.S. adoption; children with special needs; infants; postplacement services; adoptive parent support groups; adoption/subsidized guardianship preservation program; post-adoption search and reunion services.

What states do your adoptive parent clients come from? Predominantly Cook County, Illinois, although we will soon be able to work with families from other states for our Polish-American program.

Services provided adopting parents: Classes with other prospective parents; required readings of books and/or articles on adoption; group discussions about adoption; parenting discussions; individual preparation concerning intercountry adoption issues.

States/countries your birthparents/adopted children come from: Historically, predominantly Illinois. China, Russia, Romania, and Mexico. We have recently begun a new program with Poland.

What was the goal or mission of your agency when it was first organized? What is the goal or mission of your agency now? To fulfill the Church's role in the mission of charity by providing compassionate, competent, and professional services to improve the quality of personal and family life while respecting the unique resources of each individual. Now: Catholic Charities aims to improve personal and family life for those of every age, race, and creed, but has a special place in its heart for those most vulnerable in society—the children. The mission of the Maternity/Adoption Department is to find safe, nurturing, permanent families for children.

Nonrelative children placed in 1998: 29

Percent of adoptive placements under 6 mos.: 40%

Special expertise of staff: Licensed social workers; psychologists: therapists.

In 1998, what was the average time from when a prospective adoptive parent applied to when he or she received a homestudy? 4 mos.

In 1998, what was the average time from the homestudy to the placement of a child? This varies from program to program, and can range from less than one month to 18 months or longer.

Agency criteria for adoptive parents you work with: These are program-specific.

How do you screen adoptive parents? Prospective adoptive parents actively participate in educational and individual work to help them evaluate their own readiness for adoption and the type of child that they are best able to parent.

How do you screen birthparents? We provide counseling around making the best plan for themselves and their child(ren).

What kind of medical information do you seek from birthparents? Comprehensive medical background information for both birthparents, including medical history for members of their families of origin.

What kind of medical information do you seek on older children? All available birth records; any other medical history information; current medical information; developmental milestone history; current social, emotional, psychomotor, and cognitive developmental assessment; applicable educational information; length of time they have been in care; how/why they entered substitute care; any and all family history information available.

What percent of your U.S. adoptions are nonwhite children? For fiscal year 1998, 62%

About what percent are children with medical problems? For fiscal year 1998, 10–15%

About what percentage of your adoptions are children with emotional problems? 10%

Do you have a waiting list of prospective parents? Yes.

Is it all right if adopting parents you work with are on waiting lists of other agencies or attorneys? No.

Are your adoption fees based on a sliding scale? If yes, what are the sliding scale criteria? Yes. Fees are determined by program.

Do you have an application fee? If yes, what is the amount of the application fee? Yes. $250

What is your homestudy fee (if a flat rate)? $3,500. Waived for domestic waiting children.

What is your placement fee? The lesser of $9,500 or 12% of family income. Waived for domestic waiting children.

Do adopting parents also pay fees for medical and hospital expenses for birthmother and baby when they have no insurance? No.

If international adoption, what are average travel expenses? Varies greatly, from $800–$3,800 or higher.

If you place children from other countries, please list the estimated *entire* average cost to adoptive parents for each country. Mexico, $18,000; Poland, $20,000–23,000.

My agency: Offers confidential adoptions; semi-open adoptions; meetings between birthparents and adoptive parents; birthparents pick adoptive parents from bios/resumes.

Does your agency provide videotapes of children needing adoption? Yes.

In how many cases with your agency has an adoptive parent been placed with a child but lost the child due to a birthparent challenge? 0

Has your agency lost any adoption litigation filed against you by an adoptive parent or birthparent? No.

HOPE FOR THE CHILDREN

Respondents: Gail Tittle, Associate Director and Brenda Kranse Eheart, Director
In charge of social services: Gail Tittle
1530 Fairway Dr., Rantoul, IL 61866
(217) 893-4673 • Fax: (217) 893-3126
Year first licensed by state: 1994

Agency provides services for: U.S. adoption; children with special needs; postplacement services; post-adoption services.

What states do your adoptive parent clients come from? Primarily Illinois.

Services provided adopting parents: Classes with other prospective parents; group discussions about adoption; parenting discussions. We have weekly parent training for six weeks.

States/countries your birthparents/adopted children come from: Illinois.

What was the goal of your agency when first organized? What is the goal of your agency now? To place special needs children in permanent homes. Now: Same.

Nonrelative children placed in 1998: 14

Percent of adoptive placements under 6 mos.: 20%

Special expertise of staff: Adoptive parents on staff; therapists.

In 1998, what was the average time from when a prospective adoptive parent applied to when he or she received a homestudy? About 2 mos.

Average time from homestudy to placement of child: 3 mos.

What made you decide to work in the adoption field? Wanted to work in permanency for children

Agency criteria for adoptive parents you work with: No specific age requirements; licensing limits number of children in home to six, and we place two to four children with each family, as we need to be able to place this number of children with the family.

How do you screen adoptive parents? Application, then phone interviews and reference checks, followed by in-person interviews.

What kind of medical information do you seek from birthparents? Mental health, medical history, family history.

What kind of medical information do you seek on older children? Full medical information.

What percent of your U.S. adoptions are nonwhite children? 87%

About what percent are children with medical problems? 33%

About what percent are children with emotional problems? 54%

Do you have a waiting list of prospective parents? Yes.

Is it all right if adopting parents you work with are on waiting lists of other agencies or attorneys? No.

Are your adoption fees based on a sliding scale? No.

Do you have an application fee? No.

What is your homestudy fee (if a flat rate)? 0

What is your placement fee? 0

My agency: Offers confidential adoptions; meetings between birthparents and adoptive parents.

Does your agency provide videotapes of children needing adoption? No.

Are you an adoptive parent, adopted person, or birthparent? Adoptive parent.

In how many cases with your agency has an adoptive parent been placed with a child but lost the child due to a birthparent challenge? 0

Has your agency lost any adoption litigation filed against you by an adoptive parent or birthparent? No.

FAMILY RESOURCE CENTER

Respondent: Richard Pearlman, Executive Director
5828 N. Clark St., Chicago, IL 60660
(773) 334-2300 • Fax: (773) 334-8228
E-mail: adoption@f-r-c.org
Year first licensed by state: 1988

Agency provides services for: International adoptions, U.S. adoptions, children with special needs; infants, homestudy if parents working with another agency; postplacement services.

What states do your adoptive parent clients come from? All states, including New York and Connecticut.

Services provided adopting parents: Classes with other prospective parents.

States/countries your birthparents/adopted children come from: Illinois.

What was the goal of your agency when first organized? What is the goal of your agency now? To improve and facilitate the adoption process. Now: To focus on improving existing programs.

Nonrelative children placed in 1998: 98

Percent of adoptive placements under 6 mos.: 80%

Special expertise of staff: Adoptive parents on staff; licensed social workers.

In 1998, what was the average time from when a prospective adoptive parent applied to when he or she received a homestudy? 1 mo.

Average time from homestudy to placement of child: Varies widely depending on whether it is domestic or international.

What made you decide to work in the adoption field? I found it interesting. I wanted to be of service.

Agency criteria for adoptive parents you work with: Interested in fiber of character and willingness and ability to act responsibly.

How do you screen adoptive parents? Through homestudy, references, tax returns, FBI background checks.

How do you screen birthparents? Willing to help a range of clients.

What kind of medical information do you seek from birthparents? Complete our form plus a copy of the hospital records for the child's birth.

What kind of medical information do you seek on older children? See above, plus a developmental assessment.

What percent of your U.S. adoptions are nonwhite children? 20%

About what percent are children with medical problems? 3%

Do you have a waiting list of prospective parents? Yes.

Is it all right if adopting parents you work with are on waiting lists of other agencies or attorneys? Yes.

Are your adoption fees based on a sliding scale? No.

Do you have an application fee? If yes, what is the amount of the application fee? Yes. $450

What is your homestudy fee (if a flat rate)? $1,350

What is your placement fee? $4,000–18,900

Do adopting parents also pay fees for medical and hospital expenses for birthmother and baby when they have no insurance? Yes, in some situations.

If international adoption, what are average travel expenses? $5,000

If applicable, what is the average document language translation fee? $500

My agency: Offers confidential adoptions; semi-open adoptions; meetings between birthparents and adoptive parents; birthparents pick adoptive parents from bios/resumes; full disclosure of names between birth and adoptive parents.

Does your agency provide videotapes of children needing adoption? No.

In how many cases with your agency has an adoptive parent been placed with a child but lost the child due to a birthparent challenge? 2

Has your agency lost any adoption litigation filed against you by an adoptive parent or birthparent? No.

ST. MARY'S SERVICES

Respondent: Barbara O'Hara, Assistant Director
In charge of social services: Juanita Burdick, Executive Director
717 W. Kirchoff Rd., Arlington Heights, IL 60005
(847) 870-8181 • Fax: (847) 870-8325
E-mail: stmary@interaccess.com • http://homepage.interaccess.com/~stmary/home.htm
Year first licensed by state: 1946

Agency provides services for: International adoption; U.S. adoption; infants; homestudy if parents working with another agency (case-by-case); postplacement services; maternity counseling and expenses (medical and living).

What states do your adoptive parent clients come from? Illinois.

Services provided adopting parents: Classes with other prospective parents; required readings of books and/or articles on adoption; group discussions about adoption; parenting discussions.

States/countries your birthparents/adopted children come from: Illinois.

What was the goal of your agency when first organized? What is the goal of your agency now? "Every Child Deserves a Good Home." Now: Same.

Nonrelative children placed in 1998: 25

Percent of adoptive placements under 6 mos.: 98%

Special expertise of staff: Adoptive parents on staff; licensed social workers; adoptees.

In 1998, what was the average time from when a prospective adoptive parent applied to when he or she received a homestudy? 3 mos.

Average time from homestudy to placement of child: 1 year

Agency criteria for adoptive parents you work with: Priority to childless under 40, Judeo/Christian ethic, flexibility with race, openness.

How do you screen adoptive parents? Phone intake, letters, group assessment, homestudy.

How do you screen birthparents? Phone intake or referral, assessment, team evaluation.

What kind of medical information do you seek on older children? All available.

What percent of your U.S. adoptions are nonwhite children? 40%

About what percent are children with medical problems? 10% drug exposure in utero.

Do you have a waiting list of prospective parents? Yes.

Is it all right if adopting parents you work with are on waiting lists of other agencies or attorneys? No.

Are your adoption fees based on a sliding scale? If yes, what are the sliding scale criteria? Yes. 15% of adjusted gross.

Do you have an application fee? If yes, what is the amount of the application fee? Yes. $500

What is your homestudy fee (if a flat rate)? $1,500

What is your placement fee? 15% of adjusted gross income.

Do adopting parents also pay fees for medical and hospital expenses for birthmother and baby when they have no insurance? No.

My agency: Offers confidential adoptions; semi-open adoptions; meetings between birthparents and adoptive parents; birthparents pick adoptive parents from bios/resumes.

Does your agency provide videotapes of children needing adoption? No.

In how many cases with your agency has an adoptive parent been placed with a child but lost the child due to a birthparent challenge? 1

Has your agency lost any adoption litigation filed against you by an adoptive parent or birthparent? No.

UNITING FAMILIES FOUNDATION

Respondent: Lynn L. Wetterberg, Executive Director
In charge of social services: Jude Tanter, Social Work Supervisor
95 W. Grand Ave., Suite 206, P.O. Box 755, Lake Villa, IL 60046
(847) 356-1452 • Fax: (847) 356-1584
E-mail: unitingfam@aol.com • http://members.aol.com/unitingfam/index.html
Year first licensed by state: 1997

Agency provides services for: International adoption; children with special needs; infants; homestudy if parents working with another agency; postplacement services; educational training for pre-adoptive families; conferences.

What states do your adoptive parent clients come from? All states.

Services provided adopting parents: Classes with other prospective parents; required readings of books and/or articles on adoption; group discussions about adoption; parenting discussions.

States/countries your birthparents/adopted children come from: Russia, Romania.

Nonrelative children placed in 1998: 11

Special expertise of staff: Adoptive parents on staff; licensed social workers.

In 1998, what was the average time from when a prospective adoptive parent applied to when he or she received a homestudy? 80% were completed in 3 mos. or less.

Average time from homestudy to placement of child: 73% had placements within 7 mos. of application.

What made you decide to work in the adoption field? I have two adopted children.

Agency criteria for adoptive parents you work with: Married at least 1 year.

How do you screen adoptive parents? We look for families who make the commitment to completing our educational program and wish to pursue international adoption with the full understanding of all the risks involved.

What kind of medical information do you seek on older children? Any available.

About what percent are children with medical problems? 10%

Do you have a waiting list of prospective parents? Yes.

Is it all right if adopting parents you work with are on waiting lists of other agencies or attorneys? Yes.

Do you have an application fee? No.

What is your homestudy fee (if a flat rate)? $2,500 (includes educational training).

What is your placement fee? Russia/agency fee, $4,000; Russia/foreign fee, $6,000; Romania/agency fee, $4,000; Romania/foreign fee, varies.

Do adopting parents also pay fees for medical and hospital expenses for birth-mother and baby when they have no insurance? No.

Does your agency provide videotapes of children needing adoption? Yes, when available.

In how many cases with your agency has an adoptive parent been placed with a child but lost the child due to a birthparent challenge? 0

Has your agency lost any adoption litigation filed against you by an adoptive parent or birthparent? No.

INDIANA

AD-IN, INC. ADOPTION AND INFERTILITY SPECIALISTS
Respondent: Meg Sterchi, ACSW, LCSW, Executive Director
In charge of social services: Meg Sterchi
8801 N. Meridian St., Suite 105, Indianapolis, IN 46260
(317) 573-0891 • Fax: (317) 254-1870
E-mail: msterchi@iquest.net
Year first licensed by state: 1995

Agency provides services for: A homestudy and postplacement agency, not a placing agency. Homestudy if parents working with another agency; postplacement services; birthparent counseling; short-term foster care; reunification services; community education.

What states do your adoptive parent clients come from? Indiana.

Services provided adopting parents: Classes with other prospective parents; group discussions about adoption; parenting discussions.

States/countries your birthparents/adopted children come from: Indiana; some interstate adoptions with other states; also provide international adoptive homestudies for many agencies that are not located in central Indiana (variety of countries).

What was the goal of your agency when first organized? What is the goal of your agency now? The mission of AD-IN, Inc. is to provide professional and responsive services to birthparents and adoptive couples/families. AD-IN, Inc. specializes in adoptive homestudies and supervision, counseling, short-term foster care, reunification services, and community education. Now: Same.

Percent of adoptive placements under 6 mos.: 90%

Special expertise of staff: Adoptive parents on staff; licensed social workers; therapists.

In 1998, what was the average time from when a prospective adoptive parent applied to when he or she received a homestudy? Usually begin within one week; complete in 3–6 weeks (can be expedited if necessary).

Average time from homestudy to placement of child: Depends on the facilitating attorney/international agency. Usually 9–12 mos.

What made you decide to work in the adoption field? The adoption of my son, Grant. A desire to make the adoption process more friendly, supportive, and educational.

Agency criteria for adoptive parents you work with: There are no age criteria or maximum number of children in the home.

How do you screen adoptive parents? AD-IN, Inc. complete social histories, marital relationship/family values interviews, and limited criminal background checks on all household members. They require complete physical examinations; financial statements; references; verification of birth, marriage, and divorce decrees; autobiographies of prospective adoptive parents; home assessment; and an adoptive parent group meeting.

How do you screen birthparents? AD-IN, Inc. provides birthparent counseling to help birthparents assess their personal situation and the viability of making an adoption plan. AD-IN, Inc. provides emotional support for birthparents wanting to make an adoption plan.

What kind of medical information do you seek on older children? AD-IN, Inc. requests that birthparents provide medical history information and provides a medical release to the child's physician. International: AD-IN, Inc. relies on the facilitating agency to obtain medical information.

What percent of your U.S. adoptions are nonwhite children? 25%

About what percent are children with medical problems? 5%

About what percent are children with emotional problems? 10%

Do you have a waiting list of prospective parents? Yes.

Do you have an application fee? No.

What is your homestudy fee (if a flat rate)? U.S./domestic, $900; international, $1,000.

What is your placement fee? AD-IN, Inc. has an adoptive supervision fee. U.S./domestic, $400; international, $500.

Do adopting parents also pay fees for medical and hospital expenses for birthmother and baby when they have no insurance? If yes, what is the average fee paid? Yes. $5,000–7,000 for medical fees plus legal expenses.

My agency: Offers confidential adoptions; semi-open adoptions; meetings between birthparents and adoptive parents; birthparents pick adoptive parents from bios/resumes; full disclosure of names between birth and adoptive parents.

Are you an adoptive parent, adopted person, or birthparent? Adoptive parent.

In how many cases with your agency has an adoptive parent been placed with a child but lost the child due to a birthparent challenge? 0

Has your agency lost any adoption litigation filed against you by an adoptive parent or birthparent? No.

ADOPTION RESOURCE SERVICES, INC.

Respondent: Ruth A. Mark, MA, ACSW, Executive Director
In charge of social services: Ruth A. Mark
810 W. Bristol, Suite R., Elkhart, IN 46514
(219) 262-2499 • Fax: (219) 262-3485
Year first licensed by state: 1986

Agency provides services for: U.S. adoption; infants.

What states do your adoptive parent clients come from? Indiana.

Services provided adopting parents: Required readings of books and/or articles on adoption; grief therapy; homestudies.

States/countries your birthparents/adopted children come from: Indiana.

What was the goal of your agency when first organized? What is the goal of your agency now? To provide excellent counseling for both birth and adoptive parents. The focus of all our work is the healthy emotional development of every child we place, by assisting birth and adoptive couples to work through their grief and thereby return to emotional health. Also by providing much nonidentifying information to both birthparents and adopting couples about each other so all can trust each other. Now: To do all of the above and continue to exist in these very, very difficult times for adoption culture, where too few really care about the desperate need all of our children have for a stable, two-parent family.

Nonrelative children placed in 1998: 11

Percent of adoptive placements under 6 mos.: 100%

Special expertise of staff: Adoptive parents on staff; licensed social workers; therapists; attorney. One attorney does all our legal work for the adoptions.

In 1998, what was the average time from when a prospective adoptive parent applied to when he or she received a home study? 2 weeks–1 mo.

Average time from homestudy to placement of child: $8\frac{1}{2}$ mos.

What made you decide to work in the adoption field? I substitute-taught in the alternative school for kids who were kicked out of school and saw what happens to kids when they are badly parented or came from a single-parent home. I wanted to give kids a chance in life by providing them with excellent, stable, two-parent homes with parents who are ready and able to be parents.

Agency criteria for adoptive parents you work with: Between ages 25 and 46; married 3 years or more if a first marriage, 5 years or more if either has been married before; stable, solid marriage; residents of Indiana; no more than three children; unable to have a child; physically and emotionally healthy; no third marriages.

How do you screen adoptive parents? If they meet above requirements I interview them to assess emotional health and marriage relationship, and evaluate whether or not they are working through infertility appropriately and together. If I'm satisfied, I give them a homestudy packet, which includes a 20-page individual assessment, reference letters, etc. I evaluate what they return to me, then do a homestudy, which includes six to seven hours of interviewing alone and together in their home. Then I assess all of above to see whether our staff believes they will be excellent adoptive parents. [Also] check sex abuse registry (state).

How do you screen birthparents? Counselor meets with them regularly, does a psycho-social-physical history, communicates with birthmother's doctor, has an HIV screen done, has a drug screen done, talks with family members when possible, has birthparents do background information and medical history.

What kind of medical information do you seek on older children? Medical records from prenatal medical care, hospital records, medical records from birth to the present.

What percent of your U.S. adoptions are nonwhite children? 10%

Do you have a waiting list of prospective parents? No.

Is it all right if adopting parents you work with are on waiting lists of other agencies or attorneys? Yes, if agency. It is not ideal and they must be honest with us at all times if another placement may be materializing. I'm strongly opposed to attorney placement, so would under no circumstance work with a couple who was working with an attorney.

Do you have an application fee? If yes, what is the amount of the application fee? Yes. $125 application and first interview fee.

What is your homestudy fee (if a flat rate)? $1,100

What is your placement fee? We only discuss this with adoptive couples who are seriously interested in working with us.

Do adopting parents also pay fees for medical and hospital expenses for birthmother and baby when they have no insurance? Yes.

My agency: Offers confidential adoptions; semi-open adoptions; meetings between birthparents and adoptive parents; birthparents pick adoptive parents from bios/resumes. First names always.

Does your agency provide videotapes of children needing adoption? No.

In how many cases with your agency has an adoptive parent been placed with a child but lost the child due to a birthparent challenge? 0. We are very diligent in our work with birthfathers and would not place a child if the birthfather was challenging the adoption.

Has your agency lost any adoption litigation filed against you by an adoptive parent or birthparent? No. We would not place a child if the birthparents had any grounds to challenge the adoption and are very diligent and honest in our work with adoptive parents.

AMERICANS FOR AFRICAN ADOPTIONS, INC.

Respondent: Cheryl Carter-Shotts
8910 Timberwood Dr., Indianapolis, IN 46234-1952
(317) 271-4567 • Fax: (317) 271-8739
www.africanadoptions.org
Year first licensed by state: 1986

Agency provides services for: International adoption; children with special needs; infants.

What states do your adoptive parent clients come from? Across the U.S. and Canada. Can also work with military families stationed anywhere and European families.

Services provided adopting parents: Because our families are scattered, we network them together via phone and e-mail.

States/countries your birthparents/adopted children come from: East and West Africa.

What was the goal of your agency when first organized? What is the goal of your agency now? To place African orphans with qualified adoptive couples and single women. Now: Same.

Special expertise of staff: Adoptive parents on staff.

In 1998, what was the average time from when a prospective adoptive parent applied to when he or she received a homestudy? 1 mo.

Average time from homestudy to placement of child: 8–12 mos.

What kind of medical information do you seek from birthparents? All children are tested for HIV 1 and 2, hepatitis, TB, and syphilis, and are examined as needed by U.S. or Canadian embassy and in-country (Africa) doctors.

Do you have a waiting list of prospective parents? No.

Is it all right if adopting parents you work with are on waiting lists of other agencies or attorneys? No.

Are your adoption fees based on a sliding scale? No.

Do you have an application fee? If yes, what is the amount of the application fee? Yes. $250

What is your homestudy fee (if a flat rate)? $750

What is your placement fee? Included in $750.

If applicable, what is the average document language translation fee? We escort. $1,500 for one or two children.

If you place children from other countries, please list the estimated *entire* average cost to adoptive parents for each country. $8,000

My agency: Offers confidential adoptions.

Does your agency provide videotapes of children needing adoption? No.

Are you an adoptive parent, adopted person, or birthparent? Adoptive parent.

In how many cases with your agency has an adoptive parent been placed with a child but lost the child due to a birthparent challenge? 0

Has your agency lost any adoption litigation filed against you by an adoptive parent or birthparent? No.

CATHOLIC CHARITIES

Respondent: Debbie Schmidt, Adoption Director
In charge of social services: Debbie Schmidt
315 E. Washington Blvd., Ft. Wayne, IN 46802
(219) 439-0242 • Fax: (219) 439-0250
E-mail: djschmidt@fw.diocesefwsb.org
Year first licensed by state: 1922

Agency provides services for: International adoption; children with special needs; infants; homestudy if parents working with another agency; postplacement services.

What states do your adoptive parent clients come from? Indiana, but will accept families with completed homestudies from other states for special needs children.

Services provided adopting parents: Classes with other prospective parents; required readings of books and/or articles on adoption; group discussions about adoption; parenting discussions.

States/countries your birthparents/adopted children come from: Primarily Indiana.

What was the goal of your agency when first organized? What is the goal of your agency now? To help the poor. Now: Multi-services: Refugee, school counseling, counseling aging, parenting, case management, child care.

Nonrelative children placed in 1998: 170

Percent of adoptive placements under 6 mos.: 20%

Special expertise of staff: Adoptive parents on staff; licensed social workers; therapists; attorney.

In 1998, what was the average time from when a prospective adoptive parent applied to when he or she received a home study? 60 days after completion of training and paperwork.

Agency criteria for adoptive parents you work with: Varies depending on request for adoption (i.e., infant, special needs).

How do you screen adoptive parents? Homestudy.

How do you screen birthparents? Will accept all.

What kind of medical information do you seek on older children? Medical passport.

What percent of your U.S. adoptions are nonwhite children? 50%

About what percent are children with medical problems? 50%

About what percent are children with emotional problems? 60%

Do you have a waiting list of prospective parents? Yes.

Is it all right if adopting parents you work with are on waiting lists of other agencies or attorneys? Yes.

Are your adoption fees based on a sliding scale? No.

Do you have an application fee? If yes, what is the amount of the application fee? Yes. Infant, $80; special needs, none.

What is your homestudy fee (if a flat rate)? $900

What is your placement fee? 12% of adjusted gross income ($7,500–12,500).

Do adopting parents also pay fees for medical and hospital expenses for birth-mother and baby when they have no insurance? If yes, what is the average fee paid? Yes. Included in placement fee.

My agency: Offers meetings between birthparents and adoptive parents; birthparents pick adoptive parents from bios/resumes; full disclosure of names between birth and adoptive parents.

Does your agency provide videotapes of children needing adoption? No.

In how many cases with your agency has an adoptive parent been placed with a child but lost the child due to a birthparent challenge? 0

Has your agency lost any adoption litigation filed against you by an adoptive parent or birthparent? No.

FAMILIES THRU INTERNATIONAL ADOPTION

Respondent: Keith M. Wallace, Executive Director
In charge of social services: Gary May
991 South Kenmore, Evansville, IN 47714
(812) 479-9900 or (888) 797-9900 • Fax: (812) 479-9901
E-mail: adopt@ftia.org • www.ftia.org
Year first licensed by state: 1995

Agency provides services for: International adoption; children with special needs; homestudy if parents working with another agency; postplacement services.

What states do your adoptive parent clients come from? All 50 states and expatriates overseas.

Services provided adopting parents: For families who utilize our social worker, there are required readings, counseling, etc. For families using other homestudy agencies, we rely on their social workers.

States/countries your birthparents/adopted children come from: China, Russia, Guatemala, Vietnam, Ukraine.

Nonrelative children placed in 1998: 100

Percent of adoptive placements under 6 mos.: 10% (infants, 7–12 mos.: 75% of placements.)

Special expertise of staff: Adoptive parents on staff; licensed social workers; psychologists; attorney; educator with learning disability certification.

In 1998, what was the average time from when a prospective adoptive parent applied to when he or she received a homestudy? 30–45 days

Average time from homestudy to placement of child: China, 9 mos.; Russia, 6 mos.; Guatemala, 8 mos.; Vietnam, 5 mos.

What made you decide to work in the adoption field? We believe there is no higher calling or purpose than to serve the children of the world.

Agency criteria for adoptive parents you work with: No specific criteria. We work with all adoptive parents and discuss what is best for each family.

How do you screen adoptive parents? We rely on our social worker for local families and we rely on the homestudy agencies for their recommendation. FTIA then reviews the homestudy and the entire dossier before submitting it to the foreign adoption officials.

What kind of medical information do you seek on older children? We seek complete medical and social background on all older children. We obtain additional information when required by our families or when we determine the medical information we've received is not sufficient.

About what percent are children with medical problems? 10%

Do you have a waiting list of prospective parents? No.

Is it all right if adopting parents you work with are on waiting lists of other agencies or attorneys? Yes.

Are your adoption fees based on a sliding scale? If yes, what are the sliding scale criteria? Yes. It depends on the country.

Do you have an application fee? If yes, what is the amount of the application fee? Yes. $200

What is your homestudy fee (if a flat rate)? $1,025

What is your placement fee? China, Russia, and Guatemala, $4,600; Vietnam, $4,200.

Do adopting parents also pay fees for medical and hospital expenses for birthmother and baby when they have no insurance? No.

If applicable, what is the average document language translation fee? $500

If international adoption, what are average travel expenses? We negotiate with airlines and work with consolidators for the best prices available for our families. Prices may vary. The travel, including airfare, hotels, and all ground transportation averages as follows: China, $1,900; Russia, $3,300–4,000; Guatemala, $925–1,100; Vietnam, $3,750–4,000.

If you place children from other countries, please list the estimated *entire* average cost to adoptive parents for each country. China, $12,000, exclusive of homestudy; Russia, $18,000, exclusive of homestudy; Guatemala, $21,000, exclusive of homestudy; Vietnam, $17,000, exclusive of homestudy.

My agency: Offers confidential adoptions.

Does your agency provide videotapes of children needing adoption? Yes, for Russia.

Are you an adoptive parent, adopted person, or birthparent? Adoptive parent.

In how many cases with your agency has an adoptive parent been placed with a child but lost the child due to a birthparent challenge? 0

Has your agency lost any adoption litigation filed against you by an adoptive parent or birthparent? No.

LDS SOCIAL SERVICES

Respondent: Dennis D. Perkins, Agency Director
In charge of social services: Dennis D. Perkins
333 Founders Rd., Suite 200, Indianapolis, IN 46077
(317) 872-1749 • Fax: (317) 872-1756
Year first licensed by state: 1982

Agency provides services for: U.S. adoption; children with special needs; infants; post-placement services.

What states do your adoptive parent clients come from? Indiana and Kentucky.

Services provided adopting parents: Required readings of books and/or articles on adoption; group discussions about adoption.

States/countries your birthparents/adopted children come from: Indiana and Kentucky.

What is the goal of your agency now? To provide quality adoption services to birthparents and adoptive families.

Percent of adoptive placements under 6 mos.: 90%

Special expertise by staff: Licensed social workers; therapists.

In 1998, what was the average time from when a prospective adoptive parent applied to when he or she received a homestudy? 3 mos.

Average time from homestudy to placement of child: $1\frac{1}{2}$ years

What made you decide to work in the adoption field? A desire to see children raised in a stable, nurturing environment.

Agency criteria for adoptive parents you work with: 1. Members of the Church of Jesus Christ of Latter-Day Saints. 2. Up to 45 years of age.

How do you screen adoptive parents? 1. Interviews. 2. Criminal history check. 3. Reference letters.

How do you screen birthparents? Interviews.

What kind of medical information do you seek from birthparents? 1. Current medical report from physician. 2. Medical background information on birthparents and their extended family is gathered.

What kind of medical information do you seek on older children? Current medical report by physician.

What percent of your U.S. adoptions are nonwhite children? 15%

About what percent are children with medical problems? 10%

About what percent are children with emotional problems? 5%

Do you have a waiting list of prospective parents? Yes.

Is it all right if adopting parents you work with are on waiting lists of other agencies or attorneys? Yes.

Are your adoption fees based on a sliding scale? If yes, what are the sliding scale criteria? Yes. 10% of gross annual income up to maximum of $10,000. Minimum fee is $4,000.

Do you have an application fee? If yes, what is the amount of the application fee? Yes. $400

What is your homestudy fee (if a flat rate)? $600

What is your placement fee? 10% of gross annual income up to maximum of $10,000. Minimum fee of $4,000, minus the application and homestudy fee.

Do adopting parents also pay fees for medical and hospital expenses for birthmother and baby when they have no insurance? No.

My agency: Offers confidential adoptions; semi-open adoptions; meetings between birthparents and adoptive parents; birthparents pick adoptive parents from bios/resumes.

Does your agency provide videotapes of children needing adoption? No.

In how many cases with your agency has an adoptive parent been placed with a child but lost the child due to a birthparent challenge? 0

Has your agency lost any adoption litigation filed against you by an adoptive parent or birthparent? No.

LUTHERAN SOCIAL SERVICES OF IN

Respondent: Kathy Gallup, Adoption Specialist
In charge of social services: Stan Veit, Executive Director
P.O. Box 11329, Fort Wayne, IN 46857
(219) 426-3347 • Fax: (219) 424-2248
Year first licensed by state: 1901

Agency provides services for: International adoption; U.S. adoption; infants; homestudy if parents working with another agency; postplacement services; searches.

What states do your adoptive parent clients come from? Indiana.

Services provided adopting parents: Classes with other prospective parents; parenting discussions; support groups.

States/countries your birthparents/adopted children come from: Indiana. Sometimes an interstate, but this is usually in an identified situation.

What was the goal of your agency when first organized? What is the goal of your agency now? Find homes for abandoned infants. Now: Serve and care for others through the love of Christ.

Nonrelative children placed in 1998: 8

Percent of adoptive placements under 6 mos.: 100%

Special expertise of staff: Adoptive parents on staff; licensed social workers; therapists.

In 1998, what was the average time from when a prospective adoptive parent applied to when he or she received a homestudy? 12 weeks

Agency criteria for adoptive parents you work with: Married 2 years; not currently working on fertility issues; regular attendance of Christian congregation; practice Christian faith.

How do you screen adoptive parents? Interviews, asking the above questions at the initial contact.

What kind of medical information do you seek from birthparents? We obtain a release to send to doctor and hospital for all medical records. Request drug and HIV testing.

What percent of your U.S. adoptions are nonwhite children? 79%

Do you have a waiting list of prospective parents? Yes.

Is it all right if adopting parents you work with are on waiting lists of other agencies or attorneys? Yes.

Are your adoption fees based on a sliding scale? If yes, what are the sliding scale criteria? Yes. 12% of gross income; minimum $2,500, maximum $7,500.

Do you have an application fee? If yes, what is the amount of the application fee? Yes. $10

What is your homestudy fee (if a flat rate)? $1,250 for domestic; $1,500 for international.

Do adopting parents also pay fees for medical and hospital expenses for birthmother and baby when they have no insurance? If yes, what is the average fee paid? Yes. $4,500

If international adoption, what are average travel expenses? $3,000

My agency: Offers confidential adoptions; semi-open adoptions; meetings between birthparents and adoptive parents; birthparents pick adoptive parents from bios/resumes.

Does your agency provide videotapes of children needing adoption? No.

In how many cases with your agency has an adoptive parent been placed with a child but lost the child due to a birthparent challenge? 0

Has your agency lost any adoption litigation filed against you by an adoptive parent or birthparent? No.

IOWA

ADOPTION INTERNATIONAL, INC.

Respondent: Irene M. Yarigin, President/Adoption Program Director
In charge of social services: Irene M. Yarigin
900 55th St., West Des Moines, IA 50266
(515) 224-0500 • Fax: (515) 221-1904
E-mail: info@adoptchild.com • www.adoptchild.com
Year first licensed by state: 1997

Agency provides services for: International adoption from Russia.

What states do your adoptive parent clients come from? Iowa and the Midwest.

Services provided adopting parents: Required readings of books and/or articles on adoption; parenting discussions; personal assistance helping children adapt to new environment (i.e., Russian translation when necessary).

States/countries your birthparents/adopted children come from: Russia.

What was the goal of your agency when first organized? What is the goal of your agency now? Adoption International, Inc. is dedicated to finding American parents for Russian orphans. Our policy is based on our belief that every child has the right to a loving, nurturing family. Now: To accomplish the above and offer our adoptive parents the highest quality of personalized service. We uncomplicate the international adoption experience and make families as comfortable as possible throughout the process.

Nonrelative children placed in 1998: 15

Special expertise of staff: Licensed social workers; physician; attorney.

In 1998, what was the average time from when a prospective adoptive parent applied to when he or she received a homestudy? 4–5 weeks

Average time from homestudy to placement of child: 3–4 mos.

What made you decide to work in the adoption field? Our president, Irene Yarigin, is Russian and has always cared about all children. She is a teacher, and her entire professional career has been with children and students. All Adoption International, Inc. staff care for abandoned children and are grateful to the many American families willing to adopt these children from abroad.

Agency criteria for adoptive parents you work with: At least one parent must be an American citizen. There are no age requirements; however, most adoptive parents are 25–55 years old. Singles and divorcees are permitted to adopt. Singles must have above-average financial ability and have a plan for child care if they work. If married, a stable marriage must be evidenced, with the ability to financially care for the child. Adoptive parent(s) must receive their state's and INS approval for adoption.

How do you screen adoptive parents? Parents have to meet our general requirements, be able to provide a caring and nurturing environment, and be a morally and financially stable family. They must complete a homestudy with a positive recommendation to adopt by a certified adoption investigator. They also must have a record check from their division of criminal investigation and a child abuse record check.

How do you screen birthparents? We obtain all medical and legal documents available in Russia. Legal documents show how and why the child has been given the status of an orphan. We usually have detailed information on the child's parents. Medical history is also registered and given to the adoptive parents.

What kind of medical information do you seek from birthparents? All medical information is provided by the Russian authorities. All available information about the parents, pregnancy, and child's health condition is kept by the orphanage until the child is adopted. All information is shared with prospective parents.

What kind of medical information do you seek on older children? We receive the same information no matter what the child's age. We receive reports from the various specialists at the orphanage (such as surgeon, dermatologist, neurologist, psychiatrist, etc.) as well as vaccination charts.

Do you have a waiting list of prospective parents? No.

Is it all right if adopting parents you work with are on waiting lists of other agencies or attorneys? Yes.

Are your adoption fees based on a sliding scale? No.

Do you have an application fee? If yes, what is the amount of the application fee? Yes. $200

What is your homestudy fee (if a flat rate)? Varies. $450–650

What is your placement fee? $16,000 for one child; $24,000 for two.

If international adoption, what are average travel expenses? $6,000–7,000 for two people.

If you place children from other countries, please list the estimated *entire* average cost to adoptive parents for each country. Only working in Russia. Approximate total expenses for one child is $22,000 plus $8,000 for each additional child, if two people travel.

Does your agency provide videotapes of children needing adoption? Yes.

My agency: Offers confidential adoptions. Most of our adoptions are kept closed, however birthparents' names are usually on court documents. Also, in cases of older children when relatives are still alive, the child may keep contact with their birth family should they wish.

In how many cases with your agency has an adoptive parent been placed with a child but lost the child due to a birthparent challenge? 0

Has your agency lost any adoption litigation filed against you by an adoptive parent or birthparent? No.

LUTHERAN SOCIAL SERVICES OF IOWA
Respondent: Nancy Seymour, MSW, Infant Adoption Coordinator
In charge of social services: Nancy Seymour
310 West Kanesville, Suite #2, Council Bluffs, IA 51503
(712) 323-1558 • Fax: (712) 323-7588
Year first licensed by state: 1900s

Agency provides services for: U.S. adoption; children with special needs; infants; home-study if parents working with another agency; postplacement services.

What states do your adoptive parent clients come from? Iowa.

Services provided adopting parents: Classes with other prospective parents; required readings of books and/or articles on adoption; group discussions about adoption; parenting discussions.

States/countries your birthparents/adopted children come from: Iowa.

What was the goal of your agency when first organized? What is the goal of your agency now? Services for families and orphans. Now: Lutheran Social Services of Iowa, a ministry of the Evangelical Lutheran Church in America, is called by God to respond to our neighbors according to their needs.

Nonrelative children placed in 1998: 2. Infant adoption program just reopened in 1999 with four infant placements this year.

Percent of adoptive placements under 6 mos.: 2%

Special expertise of staff: Adoptive parents on staff; licensed social workers; therapists; birthmother on staff.

Do you have a waiting list of prospective parents? No.

Is it all right if adopting parents you work with are on waiting lists of other agencies or attorneys? Yes.

Are your adoption fees based on a sliding scale? Yes.

Do you have an application fee? No.

Do adopting parents also pay fees for medical and hospital expenses for birth-mother and baby when they have no insurance? Yes.

My agency: Offers meetings between birthparents and adoptive parents; birthparents pick adoptive parents from bios/resumes; full disclosure of names between birth and adoptive parents.

Does your agency provide videotapes of children needing adoption? No.

In how many cases with your agency has an adoptive parent been placed with a child but lost the child due to a birthparent challenge? 0

Has your agency lost any adoption litigation filed against you by an adoptive parent or birthparent? No.

KANSAS

ADOPTION BY GENTLE SHEPHERD

Respondent: Richard Van Deelen, Director
In charge of social services: Kelly Lachney, Social Work Supervisor
6405 Metcalfe Ave., Suite 318, Overland Park, KS 66202
(913) 432-1353 • Fax: (913) 432-1378
www.gentleshepherd.com
Year first licensed by state: 1983

Agency provides services for: U.S. adoption; infants; homestudy if parents working with another agency; postplacement services.

What states do your adoptive parent clients come from? We typically work with adoptive parents from Kansas and Missouri. We do accept homestudies from families in other states.

Services provided adopting parents: Required readings of books and/or articles on adoption.

States/countries your birthparents/adopted children come from: Typically the birthparents live in Kansas and Missouri.

What is the goal of your agency now? To serve birthparents and adoptive families.

Nonrelative children placed in 1998: 16

Percent of adoptive placements under 6 mos.: 100%

Special expertise of staff: Licensed social workers.

In 1998, what was the average time from when a prospective adoptive parent applied to when he or she received a homestudy? 4–6 weeks

Average time from homestudy to placement of child: Less than 1 year.

What made you decide to work in the adoption field? I enjoy helping couples build their family.

Agency criteria for adoptive parents you work with: Married 2 years and no more than three divorces.

How do you screen adoptive parents? Criminal background checks, child abuse/neglect screen, employer letters, health letters, reference checks, financial worksheet.

How do you screen birthparents? We spend as much time as necessary to learn about the birthparent.

What kind of medical information do you seek from birthparents? We try to get as much accurate information as possible: questionnaire and discussion.

What percent of your U.S. adoptions are nonwhite children? 20–25%

About what percent are children with medical problems? Less than 10%

Do you have a waiting list of prospective parents? Yes.

Is it all right if adopting parents you work with are on waiting lists of other agencies or attorneys? Yes.

Are your adoption fees based on a sliding scale? No.

Do you have an application fee? If yes, what is the amount of the application fee? Yes. $350, applied to the homestudy fee.

What is your homestudy fee (if a flat rate)? $1,000

What is your placement fee? $7,000

Do adopting parents also pay fees for medical and hospital expenses for birth-mother and baby when they have no insurance? If yes, what is the average fee paid? Yes. $5,000

My agency: Offers confidential adoptions; semi-open adoptions; meetings between birthparents and adoptive parents; birthparents pick adoptive parents from bios/resumes.

Does your agency provide videotapes of children needing adoption? No.

In how many cases with your agency has an adoptive parent been placed with a child but lost the child due to a birthparent challenge? 0

Has your agency lost any adoption litigation filed against you by an adoptive parent or birthparent? No.

ADOPTION CHOICES, INC.

Respondent: Virginia L. Frank, Executive Director
In charge of social services: Child Placement Supervisor
413 S. 10th St., Atchison, KS 66002
(800) 898-6028 • Fax: (405) 749-0412
E-mail: adoption@ionet.net • www.adoptionchoices.org
Year first licensed by state: 1998

Agency provides services for: International adoption; U.S. adoption; infants.

What states do your adoptive parent clients come from? Several from Georgia, Texas, and Pennsylvania; other states as well.

Services provided adopting parents: Required readings of books and/or articles on adoption.

States/countries your birthparents/adopted children come from: Oklahoma, Kansas, California, Washington, Hawaii, Marshal Islands, Arkansas. A few other states as well.

Nonrelative children placed in 1998: 75

Percent of adoptive placements under 6 mos.: 95%

Special expertise of staff: Licensed social workers; nurse and employees with degrees in similar field; women who have placed a child for adoption.

Average time from homestudy to placement of child: 6–8 mos.

What made you decide to work in the adoption field? I was raised by a single mom and most of my friends were pregnant before high school graduation. I wanted to help women make good decisions for themselves and their children.

How do you screen birthparents? First interview on the phone; then we have a face-to-face interview.

What kind of medical information do you seek on older children? All available medical records for doctors and hospitals.

What percent of your U.S. adoptions are nonwhite children? 20%

Do you have a waiting list of prospective parents? Yes.

Is it all right if adopting parents you work with are on waiting lists of other agencies or attorneys? Yes.

Are your adoption fees based on a sliding scale? No.

Do you have an application fee? If yes, what is the amount of the application fee? Yes. $150

What is your homestudy fee (if a flat rate)? $600

What is your placement fee? $14,500

Do adopting parents also pay fees for medical and hospital expenses for birthmother and baby when they have no insurance? If yes, what is the average fee paid? Yes. $2,000–3,000

If applicable, what is the average document language translation fee? $500

If you place children from other countries, please list the estimated *entire* average cost to adoptive parents for each country. Republic of the Marshall Islands, $18,000 (includes medical).

My agency: Offers confidential adoptions; semi-open adoptions; meetings between birthparents and adoptive parents; birthparents pick adoptive parents from bios/resumes.

Does your agency provide videotapes of children needing adoption? No.

In how many cases with your agency has an adoptive parent been placed with a child but lost the child due to a birthparent challenge? 0

Has your agency lost any adoption litigation filed against you by an adoptive parent or birthparent? No.

ADOPTION & COUNSELING SERVICES

Respondent: Nancy Bean, Director, Social Worker
10045 Hemlock, Overland Park, KS 66212
(913) 383-8448
Year first licensed by state: 1983

Agency provides services for: Does homestudies and counseling. Does not do placements. Infants; homestudy if parents working with another agency; postplacement services; private adoption (birth and adoptive families).

What states do your adoptive parent clients come from? Kansas, Missouri.

Services provided adopting parents: Required readings of books and/or articles on adoption; parenting discussions.

States/countries your birthparents/adopted children come from: Kansas and Missouri. I work with agencies that facilitate adoption internationally.

What was the goal of your agency when first organized? What is the goal of your agency now? To complete homestudies. Now: To help to educate adoptive and birthparents so that they will become healthy adoptive families.

Special expertise of staff: Licensed social workers.

In 1998, what was the average time from when a prospective adoptive parent applied to when he or she received a homestudy? 2 mos.

Average time from homestudy to placement of child: 3–18 mos.

What made you decide to work in the adoption field? I fell into it. It fit well with my interest in families and children.

Agency criteria for adoptive parents you work with: None, within reason.

How do you screen adoptive parents? Personal interviews, verification paperwork, references.

How do you screen birthparents? Personal interviews, paperwork.

What percent of your U.S. adoptions are nonwhite children? Few.

About what percent are children with medical problems? Few.

Do you have a waiting list of prospective parents? No.

Is it all right if adopting parents you work with are on waiting lists of other agencies or attorneys? Yes.

Are your adoption fees based on a sliding scale? No. Hourly fee for services.

Do you have an application fee? No.

What is your homestudy fee (if a flat rate)? Usually $700–1,000; $80/hour for service.

My agency: Offers semi-open adoptions; meetings between birthparents and adoptive parents; birthparents pick adoptive parents from bios/resumes; full disclosure of names between birth and adoptive parents.

Does your agency provide videotapes of children needing adoption? No.

In how many cases with your agency has an adoptive parent been placed with a child but lost the child due to a birthparent challenge? 0

Has your agency lost any adoption litigation filed against you by an adoptive parent or birthparent? No.

HEART OF AMERICA ADOPTION CENTER, INC.

Respondent: Jennifer Jackson-Rice, Program Director
In charge of social services: Jennifer Jackson-Rice
108 E. Poplar, Olathe, KS 66061
(913) 764-1888 • Fax: (913) 764-5012
www.haac-adopt.com
Year first licensed by state: 1991

Agency provides services for: International adoption; U.S. adoption; infants; homestudy if parents working with another agency; postplacement services.

What states do your adoptive parent clients come from? All states.

Services provided adopting parents: Required readings of books and/or articles on adoption; group discussions about adoption; parenting discussions; legal services.

States/countries your birthparents/adopted children come from: Kansas, Missouri, New York.

What was the goal of your agency when first organized? What is the goal of your agency now? Reassure pregnant women desiring a secure future for their expected newborns and to alleviate the confusion and anxiety of couples hoping to adopt. Now: Same.

Nonrelative children placed in 1998: 15

Percent of adoptive placements under 6 mos.: 100%

Special expertise of staff: Licensed social workers; attorney.

In 1998, what was the average time from when a prospective adoptive parent applied to when he or she received a homestudy? 1 mo.

Average time from homestudy to placement of child: $1\frac{1}{2}$ years

Agency criteria for adoptive parents you work with: Age 25–55, married for 2 years.

How do you screen adoptive parents? Orientation and homestudy process.

How do you screen birthparents? Intake and ongoing, contact.

What kind of medical information do you seek from birthparents? Any and all. We request medical records from doctor.

What kind of medical information do you seek on older children? Medical records from doctor.

What percent of your U.S. adoptions are nonwhite children? 35%

Do you have a waiting list of prospective parents? Yes.

Is it all right if adopting parents you work with are on waiting lists of other agencies or attorneys? Yes.

Are your adoption fees based on a sliding scale? No.

Do you have an application fee? If yes, what is the amount of the application fee? Yes. $950

What is your homestudy fee (if a flat rate)? $950

What is your placement fee? $6,000

Do adopting parents also pay fees for medical and hospital expenses for birth-mother and baby when they have no insurance? If yes, what is the average fee paid? Yes. $3,000

If international adoption, what are average travel expenses? $5,000

If you place children from other countries, please list the estimated *entire* average cost to adoptive parents for each country. Russia, $25,000; Guatemala, $25,000; China, $20,000; Vietnam, $20,000.

My agency: Offers semi-open adoptions; meetings between birthparents and adoptive parents; birthparents pick adoptive parents from bios/resumes; full disclosure of names between birth and adoptive parents.

Does your agency provide videotapes of children needing adoption? No.

In how many cases with your agency has an adoptive parent been placed with a child but lost the child due to a birthparent challenge? 0

Has your agency lost any adoption litigation filed against you by an adoptive parent or birthparent? No.

---

9 MONTHS ADOPTIONS

Respondent: T. Sean Lance, Executive Director
8676 West 96th St., Suite 200, Overland Park, KS 66212
(800) 768-7009 or 913-383-9774
E-mail: adoptions@ninemonths.org • www.ninemonths.org
Year first licensed by state: 1991

Agency provides services for: International adoption; U.S. adoption; children with special needs; infants; homestudy if parents working with another agency; postplacement services; all types of adoption situations.

What states do your adoptive parent clients come from? All states.

Services provided adopting parents: One-on-one customized adoption education.

States/countries your birthparents/adopted children come from: All states, Russia, China, Guatemala, Vietnam.

What was the goal of your agency when first organized? To provide loving stable homes for all children.

Nonrelative children placed in 1998: 100

Percent of adoptive placements under 6 mos.: 97%

Special expertise of staff: Adoptive parents on staff; licensed social workers; psychologists; therapists; attorney.

In 1998, what was the average time from when a prospective adoptive parent applied to when he or she received a homestudy? 2–3 weeks

Average time from homestudy to placement of child: 9–18 mos., traditional; 1–4 mos., minority; 9–12 mos., international.

What made you decide to work in the adoption field? Saw a great need to provide outstanding services to birthparents and adoptive families on a national level.

Agency criteria for adoptive parents you work with: Varies.

How do you screen adoptive parents? Homestudy primarily.

How do you screen birthparents? Extensive counseling, social history, and medical history.

What percent of your U.S. adoptions are nonwhite children? 40%

About what percent are children with medical problems? 5%

Do you have a waiting list of prospective parents? Yes.

Is it all right if adopting parents you work with are on waiting lists of other agencies or attorneys? Yes.

Are your adoption fees based on a sliding scale? No.

Do you have an application fee? If yes, what is the amount of the application fee? Yes. Varies by program.

What is your homestudy fee (if a flat rate)? $950

What is your placement fee? Varies by program. $6,500

Do adopting parents also pay fees for medical and hospital expenses for birthmother and baby when they have no insurance? If yes, what is the average fee paid? Yes. $6,000. They have the option to be selected for these situations.

If applicable, what is the average document language translation fee? $500

If international adoption, what are average travel expenses? $4,000–6,000

If you place children from other countries, please list the estimated *entire* average cost to adoptive parents for each country. China, $12,500; Vietnam, $14,500; Russia, $13,900–16,900; Guatemala, $22,500.

My agency: Offers confidential adoptions; semi-open adoptions; meetings between birthparents and adoptive parents; birthparents pick adoptive parents from bios/resumes; full disclosure of names between birth and adoptive parents.

Does your agency provide videotapes of children needing adoption? Yes, international.

In how many cases with your agency has an adoptive parent been placed with a child but lost the child due to a birthparent challenge? 0

Has your agency lost any adoption litigation filed against you by an adoptive parent or birthparent? No.

KENTUCKY

ADOPTIONS OF KENTUCKY, INC.

Respondent: Carolyn S. Arnett, Attorney and President
In charge of social services: Karen Klompus, MC, Executive Director
One Riverfront Plaza, Suite 1708, Louisville, KY 40202
(502) 585-3005 • Fax: (502) 585-5369
E-mail: ckarnett@aol.com
Year first licensed by state: 1994

Agency provides services for: U.S. adoption; infants; postplacement services; homestudies for independent adoptions.

What states do your adoptive parent clients come from? Primarily Kentucky.

Services provided adopting parents: Classes with other prospective parents; orientation and training; initial informative consultation (3 hours).

States/countries your birthparents/adopted children come from: Primarily Kentucky.

What is the goal of your agency now? To find good homes for newborn infants and young children and to provide homestudy services to adoptive parents wishing to work with this agency.

Nonrelative children placed in 1998: 35

Percent of adoptive placements under 6 mos.: 100%

Special expertise of staff: Adoptive parents on staff; licensed social workers; attorney; counselor.

In 1998, what was the average time from when a prospective adoptive parent applied to when he or she received a homestudy? 2–3 mos.

Average time from homestudy to placement of child: 6 mos.–1 year

What made you decide to work in the adoption field? A court assignment.

Agency criteria for adoptive parents you work with: We have no age limit, although they must be at least 21, and we have no limit to the number of children they can have.

How do you screen adoptive parents? They must provide state criminal checks, personal and credit reference, medical forms, and a completed application. An adoption worker meets with them at least two times to discuss the application, supporting documents, their home life, married life, childhood, etc.

How do you screen birthparents? We obtain a completed form including medical and social history and current information such as addresses, workplace, etc.

What kind of medical information do you seek on older children? All medical records will be obtained from any hospital, pediatrician, and/or doctor.

What percent of your U.S. adoptions are nonwhite children? 17%

Do you have a waiting list of prospective parents? Yes.

Is it all right if adopting parents you work with are on waiting lists of other agencies or attorneys? Yes.

Are your adoption fees based on a sliding scale? No.

Do you have an application fee? No.

What is your homestudy fee (if a flat rate)? $1,000 agency; $1,500 independent.

What is your placement fee? $2,000. The total agency fee is $8,500, which includes all of the above plus $2,500 for the supervision and court report and $3,000 for the birthparent(s)' attorney.

Do adopting parents also pay fees for medical and hospital expenses for birthmother and baby when they have no insurance? If yes, what is the average fee paid? Yes. $5,000

My agency: Offers semi-open adoptions; meetings between birthparents and adoptive parents; birthparents pick adoptive parents from bios/resumes; full disclosure of names between birth and adoptive parents.

Does your agency provide videotapes of children needing adoption? No.

In how many cases with your agency has an adoptive parent been placed with a child but lost the child due to a birthparent challenge? 0

Has your agency lost any adoption litigation filed against you by an adoptive parent or birthparent? No.

KENTUCKY ONE CHURCH ONE CHILD ADOPTION AGENCY

Respondent: Wanda Walker, Executive Director
In charge of social services: Nalo S. McWilliams, Social Services Director
1730 West Chestnut St., Louisville, KY 40203
(502) 561-6827 / (800) 248-8671 • Fax: (502) 561-1899
E-mail: kococ@bellsouth.net • www.Kyadoption.qpg.com
Year first licensed by state: 1995

Agency provides services for: Children with special needs; postplacement services; support groups for families; mentoring programs for children in foster care awaiting placement; mental health seminars for healthcare professionals, foster families, and social work students.

What states do your adoptive parent clients come from? Kentucky.

Services provided adopting parents: Classes with other prospective parents; required readings of books and/or articles on adoption; group discussions about adoption; parenting discussions.

States/countries your birthparents/adopted children come from: Kentucky. Inclusive of all counties in the state. The children are in the custody of the state Department of Social Services (DSS).

What was the goal of your agency when first organized? What is the goal of your agency now? To provide increased adoptive placements for children in foster care, particularly those who are African American or biracial. Now: To provide increased adoptive placements for children in foster care, particularly those who are African

American or biracial. This program offers tremendous untapped opportunities to recruit and support prospective adoptive parents from all sectors of the community and to provide hundreds of special needs children of all races with the permanent families they need.

Nonrelative children placed in 1998: 4

Percent of adoptive placements under 6 mos.: 0%

Special expertise of staff: Therapists.

In 1998, what was the average time from when a prospective adoptive parent applied to when he or she received a homestudy? 14–16 weeks, depending on turning in of required information and completed home consultations.

Average time from homestudy to placement of child: 3 mos.–1 year. Because we contract with DSS, we must rely on their timetable to set up preplacement meetings, visitation schedules, subsidy information, and anything pertaining to the child's welfare, as they are the guardians until placement.

Agency criteria for adoptive parents you work with: The prospective parent can be single, legally divorced, married (at least 2 years), between the ages of 21–65, rent or own their own home/apartment, and be able to provide for another person in their home with adequate bedroom and living space.

How do you screen adoptive parents? Any prospective family interested in adopting through this agency must complete a ten-week group preparation course, in which our agency requests state/city/county police record checks, a state child abuse registry check, references from various sources, and scheduled home consultations.

What kind of medical information do you seek on older children? We request all information held by DSS that pertains to the child's background. They usually have all information from birth to current.

What percent of your U.S. adoptions are nonwhite children? 80%

About what percent are children with medical problems? 75%

About what percent are children with emotional problems? 85%

Do you have a waiting list of prospective parents? Yes.

Is it all right if adopting parents you work with are on waiting lists of other agencies or attorneys? Yes.

Are your adoption fees based on a sliding scale? No.

Do you have an application fee? If yes, what is the amount of the application fee? Yes. $75

What is your homestudy fee (if a flat rate)? $1,500

Do adopting parents also pay fees for medical and hospital expenses for birthmother and baby when they have no insurance? No.

My agency: Offers confidential adoptions.

Does your agency provide videotapes of children needing adoption? No

In how many cases with your agency has an adoptive parent been placed with a child but lost the child due to a birthparent challenge? 0

Has your agency lost any adoption litigation filed against you by an adoptive parent or birthparent? No.

LOUISIANA

BEACON HOUSE ADOPTION SERVICES

Respondent: Anne R. Hughes, Administrator
In charge of social services: V. Ann Buie, Administrator of Social Services
750 Louisiana Ave., Suite C, Baton Rouge, LA 70817
(225) 387-6365 • Fax: (225) 387-1051
E-mail: beaconhouse@att.net • www.adopting.com/BeaconHouse
Year first licensed by state: 1990

Agency provides services for: International adoption; U.S. adoption; homestudy if parents working with another agency; postplacement services.

What states do your adoptive parent clients come from? All states.

Services provided adopting parents: Required readings of books and/or articles on adoption; parenting discussions.

States/countries your birthparents/adopted children come from: All states; Romania, Russia, Guatemala, Bulgaria.

What was the goal of your agency when first organized? What is the goal of your agency now? To make infants available for adoption to U.S. families. Now: To support the building of families by adoption and provide all necessary services.

Nonrelative children placed in 1998: 25

Percent of adoptive placements under 6 mos.: 100%

Special expertise of staff: Adoptive parents on staff; licensed social workers; psychologists; attorney.

In 1998, what was the average time from when a prospective adoptive parent applied to when he or she received a homestudy? 8 weeks

Average time from homestudy to placement of child: We only began providing homestudy services in 1998, so we can't answer this.

What made you decide to work in the adoption field? As an attorney I became involved through other agencies, then elected to open an agency.

Agency criteria for adoptive parents you work with: We are open to all ages, parents with children, and single parents.

How do you screen adoptive parents? Requirements are approved homestudy, criminal record check, child abuse clearance if their state can provide it, letters of reference, health statements from physicians, proof of income and expenses, application form and accessory forms, pictures, birth certificates, verification of marriage/divorce/death, life insurance in acceptable amounts, miscellaneous other information.

How do you screen birthparents? Social and medical histories; drug and HIV screenings; monitoring; prenatal care.

What percent of your U.S. adoptions are nonwhite children? 5%

Do you have a waiting list of prospective parents? Yes.

Is it all right if adopting parents you work with are on waiting lists of other agencies or attorneys? Yes.

Are your adoption fees based on a sliding scale? No.

Do you have an application fee? If yes, what is the amount of the application fee? Yes. $15 to receive packet; $250 full application fee to be submitted with packet.

What is your homestudy fee (if a flat rate)? $750

What is your placement fee? $6,000

Do adopting parents also pay fees for medical and hospital expenses for birth-mother and baby when they have no insurance? If yes, what is the average fee paid? Yes. $8,000

If international adoption, what are average travel expenses? $5,000

If you place children from other countries, please list the estimated *entire* average cost to adoptive parents for each country. Romania, $17,000; Guatemala, $22,000; Russia, $15,000–16,000 (depends on age of child); Bulgaria, $17,000.

My agency: Offers confidential adoptions; semi-open adoptions, only if requested by both parties.

Does your agency provide videotapes of children needing adoption? Yes, international only.

Are you an adoptive parent, adopted person, or birthparent? Adoptive parent.

In how many cases with your agency has an adoptive parent been placed with a child but lost the child due to a birthparent challenge? 0

Has your agency lost any adoption litigation filed against you by an adoptive parent or birthparent? No.

ST. ELIZABETH FOUNDATION

Respondent: Lillie Petit Gallagher, Director
In charge of social services: Lillie Petit Gallagher
8054 Summa Ave., Baton Rouge, LA 70809
(225) 769-8888 • Fax: (225) 769-6874
E-mail: sefound1@aol.com • www.sefoundation.com

Agency provides services for: U.S. adoptions.

What states do your adoptive parent clients come from? Mostly Louisiana, some Wisconsin and Pennsylvania.

Services provided adopting parents: Individualized homestudy adoption education component.

States/countries your birthparents/adopted children come from: Birthparents come from all over the United States, mostly from the South.

What was the goal of your agency when first organized? What is the goal of your agency now? To assist young women in the community who were dealing with an untimely pregnancy and to win against abortion by giving the girls a choice. Now: To provide services to young women who are pregnant and are considering adoption as a choice for the unborn child.

Nonrelative children placed in 1998: 18

Percent of adoptive placements under 6 mos.: 100%

Special expertise by staff: Adoptive parents on staff; licensed social workers; therapists; attorney.

In 1998, what was the average time from when a prospective adoptive parent applied to when he or she received a homestudy? 1 year

Average time from homestudy to placement of child: About 6 mos.–1 year

What made you decide to work in the adoption field? A local businessman and a personal friend wanted to give something back to the community. He wanted to provide services to young pregnant women like the Edna Gladney agency in Fort Worth does. I had a history as a community activist, so he asked me to help him to get it off the ground. Ten years later, I'm still here.

Agency criteria for adoptive parents you work with: Married 3 years; no more than one marriage for each person; at least 24 years old.

How do you screen adoptive parents? Through formal applications, criminal records check, fingerprints, letters of recommendation.

How do you screen birthparents? Family history, drug screens, prenatal care.

What kind of medical information do you seek from birthparents? All medical and genetic information from maternal and paternal side of birthmother and birthfather is required.

What percent of your U.S. adoptions are nonwhite children? 40%

Do you have a waiting list of prospective parents? Yes.

Is it all right if adopting parents you work with are on waiting lists of other agencies or attorneys? Yes.

Are your adoption fees based on a sliding scale? If yes, what are the sliding scale criteria? Yes. $9,500 for minority adoption; $16,000 for a second baby for couples who adopted before 1997; $22,000 placement fee payable only after placement.

Do you have an application fee? If yes, what is the amount of the application fee? Yes. $500

What is your homestudy fee (if a flat rate)? $1,500

What is your placement fee? $22,000

My agency: Offers confidential adoptions; semi-open adoptions; meetings between birthparents and adoptive parents; birthparents pick adoptive parents from bios/resumes; full disclosure of names between birth and adoptive parents.

Does your agency provide videotapes of children needing adoption? No.

In how many cases with your agency has an adoptive parent been placed with a child but lost the child due to a birthparent challenge? 1. (We have placed 175 babies.)

Has your agency lost any adoption litigation filed against you by an adoptive parent or birthparent? No.

ST. GERARD'S ADOPTION NETWORK, INC.

Respondent: Kent S. DeJean, President, Executive Director
In charge of social services: Dr. Berke Veillon
P.O. Box 769, Eunice, LA 70535
(318) 457-1111
Year first licensed by state: 1986

Agency provides services for: U.S. adoption; homestudy if parents working with another agency; postplacement services.

What states do your adoptive parent clients come from? Louisiana, New York, New Jersey, Pennsylvania, Texas, California, and Florida.

States/countries your birthparents/adopted children come from: Louisiana, Tennessee, and Midwest.

What was the goal of your agency when first organized? What is the goal of your agency now? To promote adoption as a viable alternative to abortion. Now: Same.

Percent of adoptive placements under 6 mos.: 100%

Special expertise of staff: Licensed social workers; psychologists; attorney.

In 1998, what was the average time from when a prospective adoptive parent applied to when he or she received a homestudy? 1 mo.

Average time from homestudy to placement of child: 2 years

What made you decide to work in the adoption field? My general partner introduced me to this field twelve years ago. I have developed an understanding of birthmothers and an appreciation of adoptive parents.

Agency criteria for adoptive parents you work with: Ages 18 and up; no criminal record; couple must be married; physically and mentally healthy; single parents allowed.

How do you screen adoptive parents? All adoptive parents must meet minimal requirements of licensing: five letters of recommendation, doctor's statement, criminal clearances, financial audit, homestudy, autobiographies, copy of marriage record and birth certificate.

How do you screen birthparents? All birthparents must complete social and medical questionnaires, must be under the care of a medical doctor who can be called to obtain medical records, and documentation must be received from birthmother to verify availability.

What kind of medical information do you seek from birthparents? Social and genetic history and all medical records of pregnancy are obtained.

What kind of medical information do you seek on older children? All past medical records are obtained and a thorough medical exam is done on child.

What percent of your U.S. adoptions are nonwhite children? 5%

About what percent are children with medical problems? 5%

About what percent are children with emotional problems? 5%

Do you have a waiting list of prospective parents? Yes.

Is it all right if adopting parents you work with are on waiting lists of other agencies or attorneys? Yes.

Are your adoption fees based on a sliding scale? If yes, what are the sliding scale criteria? Yes. $4,000–8,000

Do you have an application fee? If yes, what is the amount of the application fee? Yes. $100

What is your homestudy fee (if a flat rate)? $1,500 for in-state adoptive parents.

What is your placement fee? $4,000–8,000

Do adopting parents also pay fees for medical and hospital expenses for birthmother and baby when they have no insurance? If yes, what is the average fee paid? Yes. $7,000

My agency: Offers confidential adoptions; semi-open adoptions; meetings between birthparents and adoptive parents.

Does your agency provide videotapes of children needing adoption? No.

In how many cases with your agency has an adoptive parent been placed with a child but lost the child due to a birthparent challenge? 0

Has your agency lost any adoption litigation filed against you by an adoptive parent or birthparent? No.

MAINE

MAINE ADOPTION PLACEMENT SERVICE (MAPS)

Respondent: Dawn C. Degenhardt, Executive Director
P.O. Box 772, Houlton, ME 04730
(207) 532-9358 • Fax: (207) 532-4122
E-mail: maps@ainop.com • www.ainop.com/maps/
Year first licensed by state: 1977

Agency provides services for: International adoption; U.S. adoption; children with special needs; infants; homestudy if parents working with another agency; postplacement services; housing, counseling, training, education, etc. to birthmothers.

What states do your adoptive parent clients come from? All states and U.S. citizens living abroad.

Services provided adopting parents: Classes with other prospective parents; required readings of books and/or articles on adoption; group discussions about adoption; parenting discussions.

States/countries your birthparents/adopted children come from: All states; Russia, Ukraine, Kazakhstan, Romania, India, Nepal, China, Vietnam, Cambodia, Sierra Leone, Brazil, and Guatemala.

What was the goal of your agency when first organized? What is the goal of your agency now? To place special needs children from U.S. with their forever families. Now: To provide adoption services and humanitarian aid to orphaned and abandoned children as well as counseling and sheltering to homeless pregnant teens/women in America and abroad.

Nonrelative children placed in 1998: 368

Special expertise of staff: Adoptive parents on staff; licensed social workers; therapists; attorney; RN.

In 1998, what was the average time from when a prospective adoptive parent applied to when he or she received a homestudy? 1–4 mos.

Average time from homestudy to placement of child: 6 mos.–2 years depending on program or child request.

What made you decide to work in the adoption field? My husband and I adopted nine children ourselves. I am the founder and executive director.

Agency criteria for adoptive parents you work with: Over 25 years of age; married 2 years; number of children determined by program or foreign country.

How do you screen adoptive parents? Through the social worker and the homestudy process. Families usually screen themselves out if placement is not appropriate.

How do you screen birthparents? Counseling.

What kind of medical information do you seek from birthparents? Everything current and past, including family history.

What kind of medical information do you seek on older children? Everything that is available.

Do you have a waiting list of prospective parents? Yes. We also have a list of waiting children.

Is it all right if adopting parents you work with are on waiting lists of other agencies or attorneys? Yes. Not without our knowledge.

Are your adoption fees based on a sliding scale? No.

Do you have an application fee? If yes, what is the amount of the application fee? Yes. $350 for domestic, $1,000 for international.

What is your homestudy fee (if a flat rate)? $2,000–3,500; exceptions are made for special needs children from the United States.

What is your placement fee? Varies with program.

If applicable, what is the average document language translation fee? $1,000–1,500

If international adoption, what are average travel expenses? $3,000–4,000

My agency: Offers confidential adoptions; semi-open adoptions; meetings between birthparents and adoptive parents; birthparents pick adoptive parents from bios/resumes; full disclosure of names between birth and adoptive parents.

Does your agency provide videotapes of children needing adoption? Yes, when possible.

Are you an adoptive parent, adopted person, or birthparent? Adoptive parent.

In how many cases with your agency has an adoptive parent been placed with a child but lost the child due to a birthparent challenge? 0

Has your agency lost any adoption litigation filed against you by an adoptive parent or birthparent? No.

ST. ANDRE HOME, INC.

Respondent: Sister Theresa Therrien, LCSW, Adoption Casework Supervisor
In charge of social services: Sister Theresa Therrien and Donna Baker, LCSW, Director of Professional Services
283 Elm St., Biddeford, ME 04005
(207) 282-3351 • Fax: (207) 282-8733
E-mail: saint_andre@aol.com
Year first licensed by state: 1954

Agency provides services for: International adoption; U.S. adoption; children with special needs; infants; homestudy if parents working with another agency; postplacement services.

What states do your adoptive parent clients come from? Maine.

Services provided adopting parents: Required readings of books and/or articles on adoption; group discussions about adoption.

States/countries your birthparents/adopted children come from: Any state in the United States and any country they [adoptive parents] wish to adopt from.

What was the goal of your agency when first organized? What is the goal of your agency now? To come to the aid of pregnant teens. Now: Caring for women and children in need.

Percent of adoptive placements under 6 mos.: 50%

Special expertise of staff: Licensed social workers.

In 1998, what was the average time from when a prospective adoptive parent applied to when he or she received a homestudy? 1 mo.

Average time from homestudy to placement of child: 1 year

What made you decide to work in the adoption field? I enjoy working with people one-on-one. My religious community asked me if I wanted to work here.

Agency criteria for adoptive parents you work with: For our infant program, maximum age 42. For other programs, it depends on the agency they are adopting from.

How do you screen adoptive parents? We do a thorough homestudy.

How do you screen birthparents? Birthparents receive counseling from our licensed social workers.

What kind of medical information do you seek from birthparents? Everything we can obtain.

What kind of medical information do you seek on older children? Everything we can obtain from birthparents, medical personnel, and records.

What percent of your U.S. adoptions are nonwhite children? 25%

About what percent are children with medical problems? 25%

Do you have a waiting list of prospective parents? Yes.

Is it all right if adopting parents you work with are on waiting lists of other agencies or attorneys? No.

Are your adoption fees based on a sliding scale? No.

Do you have an application fee? If yes, what is the amount of the application fee? Yes. Only for our own infant program, $300.

What is your homestudy fee (if a flat rate)? $2,325. $1,000 for all other adoptions.

What is your placement fee? $3,500, only for our own infant program.

Do adopting parents also pay fees for medical and hospital expenses for birthmother and baby when they have no insurance? No.

If applicable, what is the average document language translation fee? Each person sees to this with networking agency.

If international adoption, what are average travel expenses? Each person takes care of this on their own.

My agency: Offers confidential adoptions; semi-open adoptions; meetings between birthparents and adoptive parents; birthparents pick adoptive parents from bios/resumes.

Does your agency provide videotapes of children needing adoption? No.

In how many cases with your agency has an adoptive parent been placed with a child but lost the child due to a birthparent challenge? 1

Has your agency lost any adoption litigation filed against you by an adoptive parent or birthparent? No.

MARYLAND

ADOPTION ALLIANCES

Respondent: Myra Hettleman, Senior Supervisor, Children's and Adoption Services
In charge of social services: Louise Scheraier, Coordinator
6 Park Center Ct., Suite 211, Owings Mills, MD 21117
(410) 581-1031 • Fax: (410) 356-1031
E-mail: adoption@jfs.org • www.jfs.org
Year first licensed by state: Early 1900s

Agency provides services for: International adoption; U.S. adoption; children with special needs; infants; homestudy if parents working with another agency; postplacement services.

What states do your adoptive parent clients come from? Maryland for domestic agency adoptions.

Services provided adopting parents: Classes with other prospective parents; group discussions about adoption; parenting discussions.

States/countries your birthparents/adopted children come from: Maryland.

What was the goal of your agency when first organized? What is the goal of your agency now? Services for Jewish families. Now: Placement of children in safe and loving families; helping birthparents evaluate parenting options and obtain support; life-long support and services.

Nonrelative children placed in 1998: 16

Percent of adoptive placements under 6 mos.: 50%

Special expertise of staff: Licensed social workers; attorney.

In 1998, what was the average time from when a prospective adoptive parent applied to when he or she received a homestudy? Begin within a week, complete in 10 days.

Average time from homestudy to placement of child: 1 year

What made you decide to work in the adoption field? Commitment to children and building families.

Agency criteria for adoptive parents you work with: Flexible.

How do you screen adoptive parents? Comply with state requirements.

How do you screen birthparents? Interviews, work with other medical, social work providers.

What kind of medical information do you seek from birthparents? Everything available.

What kind of medical information do you seek on older children? Everything possible.

What percent of your U.S. adoptions are nonwhite children? 20%

About what percent are children with medical problems? 5%

About what percent are children with emotional problems? 5%

Do you have a waiting list of prospective parents? Yes.

Is it all right if adopting parents you work with are on waiting lists of other agencies or attorneys? Yes. Would need to discuss.

Are your adoption fees based on a sliding scale? If yes, what are the sliding scale criteria? Yes. 15% of income to $15,000.

Do you have an application fee? If yes, what is the amount of the application fee? Yes. $200

What is your homestudy fee (if a flat rate)? $1,200

What is your placement fee? 15%

Do adopting parents also pay fees for medical and hospital expenses for birth-mother and baby when they have no insurance? Yes.

If you place children from other countries, please list the estimated *entire* average cost to adoptive parents for each country. Just beginning international adoption.

My agency: Offers confidential adoptions; semi-open adoptions; meetings between birthparents and adoptive parents; birthparents pick adoptive parents from bios/resumes; full disclosure of names between birth and adoptive parents.

Does your agency provide videotapes of children needing adoption? Yes.

In how many cases with your agency has an adoptive parent been placed with a child but lost the child due to a birthparent challenge? 1. (For 1 week.)

Has your agency lost any adoption litigation filed against you by an adoptive parent or birthparent? No.

ADOPTION RESOURCE CENTER, INC.

Respondent: Frances Aherns, Executive Director
In charge of social services: Frances Aherns
6630 Baltimore National Pike, 205A, Baltimore, MD 21228
(410) 744-6393 • Fax: (410) 744-1533
E-mail: adoptrc@aol.com • www.adoptionresource.com
Year first licensed by state: 1991

Agency provides services for: International adoption; homestudy if parents working with another agency; postplacement services.

What states do your adoptive parent clients come from? All states.

States/countries your birthparents/adopted children come from: Russia, China, Guatemala, Latvia.

What was the goal of your agency when first organized? What is the goal of your agency now? To make a placement plan which best meets the needs of the child. Now: Same.

Nonrelative children placed in 1998: 56

Special expertise of staff: Adoptive parents on staff; licensed social workers.

In 1998, what was the average time from when a prospective adoptive parent applied to when he or she received a homestudy? 1–2 mos.

Average time from homestudy to placement of child: 2–10 mos.

Agency criteria for adoptive parents you work with: Depends on foreign country's requirements.

How do you screen adoptive parents? Homestudy process.

What kind of medical information do you seek on older children? As much as possible—country basically determines available information.

Do you have a waiting list of prospective parents? No.

Is it all right if adopting parents you work with are on waiting lists of other agencies or attorneys? No.

Are your adoption fees based on a sliding scale? No.

Do you have an application fee? If yes, what is the amount of the application fee? Yes. $200

What is your homestudy fee (if a flat rate)? $1,200

What is your placement fee? $4,000

Do adopting parents also pay fees for medical and hospital expenses for birthmother and baby when they have no insurance? No.

If applicable, what is the average document language translation fee? $350

If international adoption, what are average travel expenses? $2,000 plus airfare.

If you place children from other countries, please list the estimated *entire* average cost to adoptive parents for each country. China, $20,000; Guatemala, $22,000; Latvia, $20,000; Russia, $30,000–32,000.

Does your agency provide videotapes of children needing adoption? Yes.

Are you an adoptive parent, adopted person, or birthparent? Adoptive parent.

Has your agency lost any adoption litigation filed against you by an adoptive parent or birthparent? No.

ADOPTIONS TOGETHER, INC.

Respondent: Janice Pearse, International Director
In charge of social services: Janice Gadwater, Executive Director
5740 Executive Dr., Suite 108, Baltimore, MD 21228
(410) 869-0620 • Fax: (410) 869-8419
E-mail: adoptintl@aol.com • www.adoptionstogether.com
Year first licensed by state: 1990

Agency provides services for: International adoption; U.S. adoption; children with special needs; infants; homestudy if parents working with another agency; postplacement services; placement of older children on Maryland Registry with in-state and out-of-state families.

What states do your adoptive parent clients come from? All states.

Services provided adopting parents: Classes with other prospective parents; required readings of books and/or articles on adoption; group discussions about adoption; parenting discussions.

States/countries your birthparents/adopted children come from: Maryland and District of Columbia. China, Vietnam, Russia, Latvia, Lithuania, Colombia, El Salvador, Guatemala, Chile, Mexico.

What was the goal of your agency when first organized? What is the goal of your agency now? Build healthy, secure, loving families by providing quality child placement services and life-long guidance to all individuals touched by adoption. Now: Same.

Nonrelative children placed in 1998: 180

Percent of adoptive placements under 6 mos.: About half.

Special expertise by staff: Adoptive parents on staff; licensed social workers; psychologists; therapists; attorney.

In 1998, what was the average time from when a prospective adoptive parent applied to when he or she received a homestudy? 1–2 weeks

Average time from homestudy to placement of child: Varies with program.

What made you decide to work in the adoption field? The adoption of my second child.

Agency criteria for adoptive parents you work with: Domestic: If married, at least 1 year. Younger parent less than 45 at application. International: Varies per country criteria.

How do you screen adoptive parents? Through the homestudy process.

How do you screen birthparents? Through counseling services.

What kind of medical information do you seek on older children? As much as possible.

What percent of your U.S. adoptions are nonwhite children? 50%

Do you have a waiting list of prospective parents? Yes.

Is it all right if adopting parents you work with are on waiting lists of other agencies or attorneys? No.

Are your adoption fees based on a sliding scale? If yes, what are the sliding scale criteria? Yes. Domestic only.

Do you have an application fee? If yes, what is the amount of the application fee? Yes. $500

What is your homestudy fee (if a flat rate)? $1,100

Do adopting parents also pay fees for medical and hospital expenses for birthmother and baby when they have no insurance? Yes.

If applicable, what is the average document language translation fee? $300–500 (included in many program fees).

If international adoption, what are average travel expenses? $3,500

If you place children from other countries, please list the estimated *entire* average cost to adoptive parents for each country. Most average about $20,000.

My agency: Offers confidential adoptions; semi-open adoptions; meetings between birthparents and adoptive parents; birthparents pick adoptive parents from bios/resumes; full disclosure of names between birth and adoptive parents.

Does your agency provide videotapes of children needing adoption? Yes.

Are you an adoptive parent, adopted person, or birthparent? Adoptive parent.

In how many cases with your agency has an adoptive parent been placed with a child but lost the child due to a birthparent challenge? 8 since 1990.

Has your agency lost any adoption litigation filed against you by an adoptive parent or birthparent? No.

THE BARKER FOUNDATION

Respondent: Julianne Bodnar, Director of Client Services
In charge of social services: Julianne Bodnar, U.S. Program and Michelle Hester, International Program
7945 MacArthur Blvd., Suite 206, Cabin John, MD 20818
(301) 229-8300 • Fax: (301) 229-0074
E-mail: bfinfo@atlantech.net • www.barkerfoundation.org
Year first licensed by state: 1947

Agency provides services for: International adoption; U.S. adoption; children with special needs; infants; homestudy if parents working with another agency; postplacement services; counseling; education; support groups.

What states do your adoptive parent clients come from? Maryland, Virginia, District of Columbia, other states for minority and special needs for U.S. program and international program.

Services provided adopting parents: Classes with other prospective parents; required readings of books and/or articles on adoption; group discussions about adoption; parenting discussions.

States/countries your birthparents/adopted children come from: Maryland, Virginia, District of Columbia for U.S. program. India, Vietnam, China, Colombia, Bulgaria, Chile, Guatemala for international program.

Nonrelative children placed in 1998: 84

Special expertise of staff: Adoptive parents on staff; licensed social workers; therapists.

In 1998, what was the average time from when a prospective adoptive parent applied to when he or she received a homestudy? 2 mos.

Average time from homestudy to placement of child: Varies according to program.

How do you screen birthparents? Work with all inquiries.

What kind of medical information do you seek on older children? Lots of measurements for height, weight, head circumference; lab tests (if facilities are reliable) for hepatitis B, HIV, etc.

What percent of your U.S. adoptions are nonwhite children? 50%

Do you have a waiting list of prospective parents? No.

Is it all right if adopting parents you work with are on waiting lists of other agencies or attorneys? Yes for domestic adoptions if we are aware. No for international program.

Are your adoption fees based on a sliding scale? If yes, what are the sliding scale criteria? Yes, international only. Applicant's income.

Do you have an application fee? If yes, what is the amount of the application fee? Yes. $400

What is your homestudy fee (if a flat rate)? $1,600

What is your placement fee? Varies according to total fee.

Do adopting parents also pay fees for medical and hospital expenses for birth-mother and baby when they have no insurance? If yes, what is the average fee paid? Yes. Agency has cap for total expenses and fees that can be paid; cap is $20,000.

If applicable, what is the average document language translation fee? Depends on country.

If international adoption, what are average travel expenses? Depends on country.

If you place children from other countries, please list the estimated *entire* average cost to adoptive parents for each country. China, $16,000–18,000; Colombia, $20,000–23,000; India, $15,000–16,000; Guatemala, $24,000–26,000; Bulgaria, $23,000–24,000.

My agency: Offers confidential adoptions; semi-open adoptions; meetings between birthparents and adoptive parents; birthparents pick adoptive parents from bios/resumes.

Does your agency provide videotapes of children needing adoption? No.

In how many cases with your agency has an adoptive parent been placed with a child but lost the child due to a birthparent challenge? 0

Has your agency lost any adoption litigation filed against you by an adoptive parent or birthparent? No.

CRADLE OF HOPE ADOPTION CENTER

Respondent: Linda Perilstein, Executive Director
In charge of social services: Leslie Nelson, Director of Social Services
8630 Fenton St., Suite 310, Silver Spring, MD 20910
(301) 587-4400 • Fax: (301) 588-3091
E-mail: cradle@cradlehope.org • www.cradlehope.org
Year first licensed by state: 1991

Agency provides services for: International adoption; homestudy if parents working with another agency; postplacement services.

What states do your adoptive parent clients come from? All states and other countries.

States/countries your birthparents/adopted children come from: Russia, China, Guatemala, and Ukraine.

What was the goal of your agency when first organized? What is the goal of your agency now? To assist abandoned children in need of loving homes and to provide humanitarian aid to the orphanages caring for them. Now: Same.

Nonrelative children placed in 1998: 200

Percent of adoptive placements under 6 mos.: 5%

Special expertise of staff: Adoptive parents on staff; licensed social workers; attorney.

In 1998, what was the average time from when a prospective adoptive parent applied to when he or she received a homestudy? 3 mos.

In 1998, what was average time from homestudy to placement of child? 6 mos.

Agency criteria for adoptive parents you work with: Our criteria is quite flexible. We work with singles and couples between 30 and 55 years of age.

How do you screen adoptive parents? Through the homestudy process.

What kind of medical information do you seek from birthparents? We seek as much information as is available from foreign orphanages.

What kind of medical information do you seek on older children? Same as above.

Do you have a waiting list of prospective parents? Yes.

Is it all right if adopting parents you work with are on waiting lists of other agencies or attorneys? Yes.

Are your adoption fees based on a sliding scale? If yes, what are the sliding scale criteria? Yes, homestudy and postplacement fees only. Income.

Do you have an application fee? If yes, what is the amount of the application fee? Yes. $500

What is your placement fee? Varies, depending on programs.

If applicable, what is average document language translation fee? $950

If international adoption, what are average travel expenses? $5,000–7,000

If you place children from other countries, please list the estimated *entire* average cost to adoptive parents for each country. $20,000–25,000

Does your agency provide videotapes of children needing adoption? Yes.

Are you an adoptive parent, adopted person, or birthparent? Adoptive parent.

In how many cases with your agency has an adoptive parent been placed with a child but lost the child due to a birthparent challenge? 0

Has your agency lost any adoption litigation filed against you by an adoptive parent or birthparent? Yes.

CREATIVE ADOPTIONS, INC.

Respondents: Philippa J. Street, Executive Director and Kendra Roberson,
Program Director
In charge of social services: Kendra Roberson
10750 Hickory Ridge Rd., Suite 108, Columbia, MD 21044
(301) 596-1521 • Fax: (301) 596-0346
E-mail: cai@creativeadoptions.org • www.creativeadoptions.org
Year first licensed by state: 1990 in Florida; 1994 in Maryland.

Agency provides services for: International adoption; children with special needs; infants; homestudy if parents working with another agency; postplacement services.

What states do your adoptive parent clients come from? All states and overseas
(Germany).

Services provided adopting parents: Required readings of books and/or articles on
adoption; group discussions about adoption; informational meetings at conferences
and workshops, exhibits.

States/countries your birthparents/adopted children come from: Russia, Ukraine,
Latvia, Hungary, China, Vietnam, Colombia, Jamaica.

**What was the goal of your agency when first organized? What is the goal of your
agency now?** International child placing agency, with all the necessary pre- and
postplacement supports. Now: Same.

Nonrelative children placed in 1998: 70

Percent of adoptive placements under 6 mos.: 15%

Special expertise of staff: Licensed social workers; psychologists.

**In 1998, what was the average time from when a prospective adoptive parent
applied to when he or she received a homestudy?** Approximately 2 mos. from
application to final homestudy report.

Average time from homestudy to placement of child: Range: 2–24 mos. Average time:
2–3 mos.

What made you decide to work in the adoption field? As a psychologist by background, I began to do homestudies for prospective adoptive families, and the tangible rewards for all members of the triad, once the process is handled ethically,
sensitively, and efficiently were overwhelming!

Agency criteria for adoptive parents you work with: All our eligibility criteria are
essentially mandated either by INS and/or the birth country of the child. Therefore, the only agency criteria per se is that the adoptive family be "good enough,"
committed and able to provide a nurturing, protective environment.

How do you screen adoptive parents? 1. Preliminary intake; 2. application interview;
3. homestudy or homestudy review and endorsement; 4. ongoing consultations
with homestudy provider, if not our agency; 5. ongoing assessment during the pre-referral and pre-travel process; 6. psychological evaluation if indicated.

How do you screen birthparents? As we work internationally only, our agency does not directly screen birthparents. In countries in which a private adoption is occurring, our facilitators understand that all measures must be taken to provide the birthparent(s) with all options and support prior to relinquishment.

What kind of medical information do you seek on older children? Any and all medical information available, plus a request for specific evaluations if indicated. Most typically, birth weight, height, head circumference, current weight, height, head circumference, lab testing results for hepatitis, AIDS, syphilis, developmental information, history of disease, illness, speech and language assessment, general psychological assessment, vaccination records, placement history, any birth family history, information about labor and delivery process.

Do you have a waiting list of prospective parents? Yes.

Is it all right if adopting parents you work with are on waiting lists of other agencies or attorneys? Yes, depending on status of case.

Are your adoption fees based on a sliding scale? If yes, what are the sliding scale criteria? Yes, for Maryland. Gross family income less than $50,000.

Do you have an application fee? If yes, what is the amount of the application fee? Yes. $275

What is your homestudy fee (if a flat rate)? $1,200

What is your placement fee? $4,000

Do adopting parents also pay fees for medical and hospital expenses for birthmother and baby when they have no insurance? No.

If international adoption, what are average travel expenses? This is very dependent on country of interest for example, Eastern Europe is about $5,000 for couple.

If you place children from other countries, please list the estimated *entire* average cost to adoptive parents for each country. These figures include estimate for travel, accommodations, and living expenses in-country: Russia, $19,000–20,000; Ukraine, $19,000–20,000; Hungary, $20,000–22,000; Latvia, $18,000; China, $18,000–19,000; Vietnam, $19,000–20,000; Columbia, $11,000–13,000; Jamaica, $6,000–10,000.

My agency: Offers confidential adoptions. (Many countries provide semi-open adoptions in that birth families' names are provided.)

Does your agency provide videotapes of children needing adoption? Yes.

In how many cases with your agency has an adoptive parent been placed with a child but lost the child due to a birthparent challenge? Of approximately 700 placements, there have been approximately 10 such cases.

Has your agency lost any adoption litigation filed against you by an adoptive parent or birthparent? No. In fact, we have never been sued to date!

WORLD CHILD, INC.

Respondent: Sherrell J. Goolsby, Executive Director
In charge of social services: Sherrell J. Goolsby
9300 Columbia Blvd., Silver Spring, MD 20910
(301) 588-3000 • Fax: (301) 588-7879
Year first licensed by state: 1983

Agency provides services for: International adoption; U.S. adoption; infants; homestudy if parents working with another agency; postplacement services.

What states do your adoptive parent clients come from? All states and Americans abroad, and some foreign nationals abroad.

Services provided adopting parents: Classes with other prospective parents; required readings of books and/or articles on adoption; group discussions about adoption; parenting discussions.

States/countries your birthparents/adopted children come from: Russia, Ukraine, Romania, Bulgaria, Kazakhstan, China, Vietnam, Guatemala, Bolivia, El Salvador, Peru, Mexico, at present.

What was the goal of your agency when first organized? What is the goal of your agency now? To place children from Latin America and then from anywhere in the world. Now: To place children who need homes primarily from other countries. Train families and provide support and referral afterwards.

Nonrelative children placed in 1998: 285

Percent of adoptive placements under 6 mos.: 10%

Special expertise of staff: Adoptive parents on staff; licensed social workers; attorney.

In 1998, what was the average time from when a prospective adoptive parent applied to when he or she received a homestudy? 2 mos.

Average time from homestudy to placement of child: 7 mos.

What made you decide to work in the adoption field? My first job out of social work school in 1972 was working with pregnant girls at a maternity home.

Agency criteria for adoptive parents you work with: We place as few restrictions on families as possible. Most are placed by foreign countries or our state regulations.

How do you screen adoptive parents? For local parents, an in-person interview plus those things required by state and good practice such as police checks, child abuse checks, fire and health inspections, references, etc. For others, we rely heavily on referral agencies, request copies of above requirements, interview by phone, and send some training material.

Do you have a waiting list of prospective parents? No.

Is it all right if adopting parents you work with are on waiting lists of other agencies or attorneys? Yes.

Are your adoption fees based on a sliding scale? No.

Do you have an application fee and if so, what is the amount? Yes. $125

What is your homestudy fee (if a flat rate)? $1,100

What is your placement fee? $3,500

Do adopting parents also pay fees for medical and hospital expenses for birth-mother and baby when they have no insurance? No.

If international adoption, what are average travel expenses? $3,000–3,500

If you place children from other countries, please list the estimated *entire* average cost to adoptive parents for each country. (Including travel) Russia, Ukraine, Kazakhstan, $21,000; Bulgaria and Romania, $13,000; China and Vietnam, $15,000; El Salvador, Guatemala, Mexico, $20,000; Bolivia and Peru, $14,000.

My agency: Offers semi-open adoptions; meetings between birthparents and adoptive parents; full disclosure of names between birth and adoptive parents.

Does your agency provide videotapes of children needing adoption? Yes, when possible.

Are you an adoptive parent, adopted person, or birthparent? Adoptive parent.

In how many cases with your agency has an adoptive parent been placed with a child but lost the child due to a birthparent challenge? 0

Has your agency lost any adoption litigation filed against you by an adoptive parent or birthparent? No.

MASSACHUSETTS

THE CHILDREN'S INTERNATIONAL ADOPTION PROJECT

Respondent: Nancy Conant, Director
In charge of social services: Nancy Conant
10 Langford Rd., Plymouth, MA 02360
(508) 747-3331 • Fax: (508) 746-6847
E-mail: childrensproject@worldnet.att.net
Year first licensed by state: 1996

Agency provides services for: International adoption; U.S. adoption; homestudy if parents working with another agency; postplacement services.

What states do your adoptive parent clients come from? Massachusetts.

States/countries your birthparents/adopted children come from: Romania, Bulgaria, Poland, Vietnam, China, United States.

What was the goal of your agency when first organized? What is the goal of your agency now? To place children of foreign heritage in permanent loving homes in the United States. Now: Same. Have included a domestic program.

Nonrelative children placed in 1998: 1 (new agency). Child was a newborn and first completed adoption. Three more are pending.

Special expertise of staff: Small agency. Licensed social workers on staff.

In 1998, what was the average time from when a prospective adoptive parent applied to when he or she received a homestudy? 6–8 weeks

Average time from homestudy to placement of child: $1\frac{1}{2}$ mos. for completed adoption.

What made you decide to work in the adoption field? Have large family of my own, enjoy working with family and children, want to make a difference in the lives of some children.

Agency criteria for adoptive parents you work with: Must be 21, married for 1 year, demonstrate stability in marriage, finances, background. Singles accepted.

How do you screen adoptive parents? Physical, emotional, financial [screening]. Autobiography required.

How do you screen birthparents? Intake form, birthparent workbook to be completed with the assistance of a social worker. Encourage at least four counseling sessions to develop plan, assess conditions, be informed.

What kind of medical information do you seek from birthparents? Present health, exam reports, statement from doctor stating applicant free from communicable diseases.

What kind of medical information do you seek on older children? All that is available; present health, HIV, hepatitis, TB, family and social background.

Do you have a waiting list of prospective parents? No.

Is it all right if adopting parents you work with are on waiting lists of other agencies or attorneys? No.

Are your adoption fees based on a sliding scale? No.

Do you have an application fee? If yes, what is the amount of the application fee? Yes. $200

What is your homestudy fee (if a flat rate)? $1,800

What is your placement fee? International, $4,000 agency fee; domestic, $3,000–9,000 depending on specific adoption plan and whether or not in-state or out-of-state.

Do adopting parents also pay fees for medical and hospital expenses for birthmother and baby when they have no insurance? If yes, what is the average fee paid? Yes. Varies.

If international adoption, what are average travel expenses? Varies.

If you place children from other countries, please list the estimated *entire* average cost to adoptive parents for each country. $20,000–25,000 per country. It varies.

My agency: Offers confidential adoptions; semi-open adoptions; meetings between birthparents and adoptive parents; full disclosure of names between birth and adoptive parents.

Does your agency provide videotapes of children needing adoption? Yes, if available.

In how many cases with your agency has an adoptive parent been placed with a child but lost the child due to a birthparent challenge? 0

Has your agency lost any adoption litigation filed against you by an adoptive parent or birthparent? No.

BEACON ADOPTION CENTER

Respondent: Deborah McCurdy, LICSW, Adoption Supervisor
In charge of social services: Deborah McCurdy
66 Lake Buel Rd., Great Barrington, MA 01230
(413) 528-2749
Year first licensed by state: 1990

Agency provides services for: International adoption; U.S. adoption (minority children only); children with special needs; infants; homestudy if parents working with another agency; postplacement services.

What states do your adoptive parent clients come from? We serve residents of the 413 phone area of western Massachusetts.

Services provided adopting parents: Classes with other prospective parents; required readings of books and/or articles on adoption; group discussions about adoption; parenting discussions; preparation/education through interviews (pre- and post-placement); homestudies; postplacement services.

States/countries your birthparents/adopted children come from: All countries and states that place children in Massachusetts. We do local service (homestudy, pre- and postplacement services) and families select their placing agency.

What was the goal of your agency when first organized? What is the goal of your agency now? To bring together children in need of homes and their permanent families, no matter where in the world the children are living. Now: Same.

Nonrelative children placed in 1998: 24

Percent of adoptive placements under 6 mos.: Maybe 20%

Special expertise of staff: Adoptive parents on staff; licensed social workers; therapists; many years of experience in intercountry adoption; considerable administrative expertise and experience.

In 1998, what was the average time from when a prospective adoptive parent applied to when he or she received a homestudy? 1–2 weeks to begin the home-study; average of $2\frac{1}{2}$–3 mos. to complete (including document preparation).

Average time from homestudy to placement of child: Average is hard to determine; usual range was 9–15 mos. for international adoptions, 1–2 mos. in the case of minority infants.

What made you decide to work in the adoption field? A strong desire to help children in need of parents and families seeking children.

Agency criteria for adoptive parents you work with: No fixed criteria beyond a strong desire on the part of both parents to adopt and a reasonable life expectancy, plus an absence of felonies. We place with singles and couples.

How do you screen adoptive parents? Adoptive parent interviews, child abuse clearances, police clearances, doctors' letters, a home visit, references, and any other state-required screening methods that apply.

What kind of medical information do you seek on older children? As much medical information as is available through the placing agency, orphanage, or international adoption clinic.

What percent of your U.S. adoptions are nonwhite children? 0%

About what percent are children with medical problems? 5–10%

Do you have a waiting list of prospective parents? No.

Is it all right if adopting parents you work with are on waiting lists of other agencies or attorneys? Yes. We assume that everyone will be selecting a licensed placing agency before the homestudy is completed, to locate and place the child.

Do you have an application fee? If yes, what is the amount of the application fee? Yes. $175

What is your homestudy fee (if a flat rate)? $1,650 (paid in installments).

What is your placement fee? No placing fee per se (except that charged by the chosen placing agency). We have a postplacement fee of $900, paid in installments, for postplacement visits and reports.

If international adoption, what are average travel expenses? Depends on the country.

If you place children from other countries, please list the estimated *entire* average cost to adoptive parents for each country. We encourage parents to choose agencies that are reasonable in cost, so that they can keep their total costs between $9,000 and $20,000.

My agency: Offers confidential adoptions; semi-open adoptions; meetings between birthparents and adoptive parents; birthparents pick adoptive parents from bios/resumes; full disclosure of names between birth and adoptive parents.

Are you an adoptive parent, adopted person, or birthparent? Adoptive parent.

In how many cases with your agency has an adoptive parent been placed with a child but lost the child due to a birthparent challenge? 0

Has your agency lost any adoption litigation filed against you by an adoptive parent or birthparent? No.

Is there anything I have not asked you that is important? There are many more children waiting for families, in all parts of the world, than will ever find homes.

FULL CIRCLE ADOPTIONS AND FAMILY BUILDING CENTER, INC.

Respondent: Marla Ruth Allisan, J.D., LICSW, Director
In charge of social services: Marla Ruth Allisan
39 Main St., Northampton, MA 01060
(413) 587-0007 • Fax 413-584-1624
E-mail: adoption@javanet.com • www.adoption-ma.com
Year first licensed by state: 1996

Agency provides services for: International adoption; U.S. adoption; children with special needs; infants; homestudy if parents working with another agency; postplacement services. We specialize in infant interstate (domestic) adoptions.

What states do your adoptive parent clients come from? Mostly New England but increasingly other states as well (including Wisconsin, Alabama) and Europe.

Services provided to adopting parents: Classes with other prospective parents; required readings of books and articles on adoption; group discussions about adoption; parenting discussions; "while you wait" group.

States/countries your birthparents/adopted children come from: Throughout the United States. We network with other agencies for international adoption.

What was the goal of your agency when first organized? What is the goal of your agency now? To serve children and families, and to promote conscientious care of the "full circle" of families involved in adoption. Now: Same.

Nonrelative children placed in 1998: 16. Note: We have placed over 30 so far (August 1999) in 1999.

Percent of adoptive placements under 6 mos.: 99%

Special expertise of staff: Adoptive parents on staff; licensed social workers; therapists; attorney; doctoral-level social worker; professionals who are adopted, birthparents, and adoptive parents.

In 1998, what was the average time from when a prospective adoptive parent applied to when he or she received a homestudy? No waiting time.

Average time from homestudy to placement of child: We measure profile to match: 6–18 mos.

Agency criteria for adoptive parents you work with: No restrictions as to age, religion, number of children in the home, years of marriage, marital/relation status, sexual orientation.

How do you screen adoptive parents? Homestudy.

How do you screen birthparents: Clinical assessment and interview.

What kind of medical information do you seek from birthparents? We have an exceptionally thorough form that we are happy to share.

What kind of medical information do you seek on older children? All available medical records.

What percent of your U.S. adoptions are nonwhite children? I don't define children as nonwhite. We have placed mostly Caucasian newborns. Four have had part Hispanic/Filipino and/or African-American heritage.

About what percent are children with medical problems? Healthy newborns except where special needs is requested.

Do you have a waiting list of prospective parents? No.

Is it all right if adopting parents you work with are on waiting lists of other agencies or attorneys? Yes.

Are your adoption fees based on a sliding scale? No, but we have other means of assisting families of moderate means.

Do you have an application fee? If yes, what is the amount of the application fee? Yes. $200

What is your homestudy fee? $2,000

What is your placement fee? Depends on services provided. Call us for fee schedule.

Do adopting parents also pay fees for medical and hospital expenses for birth-mother and baby when they have no insurance? If yes, what is the average fee paid? Yes, but we are excellent at getting birthmothers insured. We've only had one case where Medicaid or insurance was not available and birthmother delivered at a charity hospital. The most our families have paid is 20% when birthmother had an 80/20 plan.

If international adoption, what are average travel expenses? Varies.

My agency: Offers confidential adoptions (if requested); semi-open adoptions; meetings between birthparents and adoptive parents; birthparents pick adoptive parents from biographies; full disclosure of names between birth and adoptive parents.

Does your agency provide videotapes of children needing adoption? No.

In how many cases with your agency has an adoptive parent been placed with a child but lost the child due to a birthparent challenge? 0

Has your agency lost any adoption litigation filed against you by an adoptive parent or birthparent? No.

JEWISH FAMILY SERVICE OF METROWEST

Respondent: Dale A. Eldridge, LICSW, BCD, Coordinator, Adoptive Parent Services
475 Franklin St., Framingham, MA 01702
(508) 875-3100 • Fax: (508) 875-4373
E-mail: dae28@aol.com
Year first licensed by state: 1983

Agency provides services for: International adoption; U.S. adoption; infants; homestudy if parents working with another agency; postplacement services; pre-adoption planning and education; post-adoption consultation.

What states do your adoptive parent clients come from? Massachusetts.

Services provided adopting parents: Classes with other prospective parents; required readings of books and/or articles on adoption; group discussions about adoption; parenting discussions.

States/countries your birthparents/adopted children come from: Any state for domestic program; international program, primarily Russia and China with some placements in Hungary, Romania, Cambodia so far. (We work collaboratively with international placement agencies.)

What was the goal of your agency when first organized? What is the goal of your agency now? We are a nonprofit nonsectarian family service agency providing a wide range of services. Now: Same.

Nonrelative children placed in 1998: 26

Percent of adoptive placements under 6 mos.: 85%

Special expertise of staff: Adoptive parents on staff; licensed social workers; therapists; attorney.

In 1998, what was the average time from when a prospective adoptive parent applied to when he or she received a homestudy? 10 mos.

Average time from homestudy to placement of child: 8 mos.

What made you decide to work in the adoption field? Initially it was the need for an additional staff person in the program (ours is a family service agency). Increasingly it is my fascination with it and affinity with adoptive parents.

Agency criteria for adoptive parents you work with: We are flexible regarding these issues. For domestic adopter the birthparents are considering those issues in selecting the parents. Age is less of an issue for us than overall health.

How do you screen adoptive parents? The homestudy process involves five meetings (last one at home), medical and background checks, personal references, as well as clients participation in a ten-session group series. We get to know our families well in the process.

How do you screen birthparents? In person or by phone (if at a distance) to help them examine their options, either parenting or adoption planning. We provide ongoing counseling to ensure that they are comfortable with their decision, attempting to empower them throughout the process.

What kind of medical information do you seek on older children? Any available medical records.

What percent of your U.S. adoptions are nonwhite children? 30%

About what percent are children with medical problems? 25%

Do you have a waiting list of prospective parents? No.

Is it all right if adopting parents you work with are on waiting lists of other agencies or attorneys? No.

Are your adoption fees based on a sliding scale? If yes, what are the sliding scale criteria? Yes. Combined adjusted gross income.

Do you have an application fee? If yes, what is the amount of the application fee? Yes. $190

What is your homestudy fee (if a flat rate)? $1,200–3,000

What is your placement fee? $1,440–3,600

Do adopting parents also pay fees for medical and hospital expenses for birthmother and baby when they have no insurance? If yes, what is the average fee paid? Yes. $2,000–5,000

If you place children from other countries, please list the estimated *entire* **average cost to adoptive parents for each country.** We work collaboratively with international placement agencies. Total costs are in the vicinity of $20,000, depending on the country and program.

My agency: Offers confidential adoptions; semi-open adoptions; meetings between birthparents and adoptive parents; birthparents pick adoptive parents from bios/resumes; full disclosure of names between birth and adoptive parents.

Does your agency provide videotapes of children needing adoption? No.

In how many cases with your agency has an adoptive parent been placed with a child but lost the child due to a birthparent challenge? 0

Has your agency lost any adoption litigation filed against you by an adoptive parent or birthparent? No.

WIDE HORIZONS FOR CHILDREN

Respondent: Vicki Peterson, Executive Director
In charge of social services: Heather Arnes, Louise Plesha
38 Edge Hill Rd., Waltham, MA 02451
(781) 894-5330 • Fax: (781) 899-2769
E-mail: vicki@whfc.org • www.whfc.org
Year first licensed by state: 1975

Agency provides services for: International adoption; U.S. adoption; children with special needs; infants; homestudy if parents working with another agency; postplacement services; post-adoption, both cultural and educational.

What states do your adoptive parent clients come from? Primarily Massachusetts, New Hampshire, Connecticut, New York, Rhode Island, New Jersey, and Vermont. We also accept clients by referral in other states for some programs (China, Guatemala, India, Russia).

Services provided adopting parents: Classes with other prospective parents; group discussions about adoption; parenting discussions; cultural events; educational symposiums; social gatherings.

States/countries your birthparents/adopted children come from: Any state (primarily New England).

What was the goal of your agency when first organized? What is the goal of your agency now? To find good homes for Vietnamese children orphaned by the war. Now: To find a loving family for every child who doesn't have one.

Nonrelative children placed in 1998: 454

Percent of adoptive placements under 6 mos.: 33%

Special expertise of staff: Adoptive parents on staff; licensed social workers; therapists; physician; bilingual staff: Chinese, Spanish, Hindi, and Russian.

In 1998, what was the average time from when a prospective adoptive parent applied to when he or she received a homestudy? 3–4 mos.

Average time from homestudy to placement of child: 1 year

What made you decide to work in the adoption field? Family history of adoption while growing up. I am also an adoptive parent.

Agency criteria for adoptive parents you work with: Parents need to be accepting of differences and able to cope with adjustment issues. One parent needs to be at home for a minimum of two months after placement.

How do you screen adoptive parents? Application, interviews, and participation in a four-hour group.

How do you screen birthparents? Counselors meet with them minimum of four times before taking relinquishment, usually over many months.

What kind of medical information do you seek from birthparents? All medical history on birthparents, birthgrandparents, and siblings. Information on substance abuse before and during pregnancy.

What kind of medical information do you seek on older children? Pediatric medical report.

What percent of your U.S. adoptions are nonwhite children? 25%

About what percent are children with medical problems? 25%

Do you have a waiting list of prospective parents? No.

Is it all right if adopting parents you work with are on waiting lists of other agencies or attorneys? No.

Are your adoption fees based on a sliding scale? No.

Do you have an application fee? If yes, what is the amount of the application fee? Yes. $100

What is your homestudy fee (if a flat rate)? $3,400. Service fee includes homestudy fee, placement fee, and legalization.

Do adopting parents also pay fees for medical and hospital expenses for birthmother and baby when they have no insurance? If yes, what is the average fee paid? Yes. For domestic adoptions only, $2,000.

If applicable, what is the average document language translation fee? $100–300

If international adoption, what are average travel expenses? $3,000 per person

If you place children from other countries, please list the estimated *entire* average cost to adoptive parents for each country. China, $13,560; Colombia, $18,000; domestic, $19,500; Guatemala, $19,750; India, $15,000; South Korea, $16,700; Lithuania, $19,500; Moldova, $18,250; Russia, $15,000; Philippines, $12,500.

My agency: Offers confidential adoptions; semi-open adoptions; meetings between birthparents and adoptive parents; birthparents pick adoptive parents from bios/resumes.

Does your agency provide videotapes of children needing adoption? Yes, only from Russia.

Are you an adoptive parent, adopted person, or birthparent? Adoptive parent.

In how many cases with your agency has an adoptive parent been placed with a child but lost the child due to a birthparent challenge? 2. In both cases, the adopting parents willingly returned baby soon after placement. Neither case went to court.

Has your agency lost any adoption litigation filed against you by an adoptive parent or birthparent? No.

MICHIGAN

ADOPTION ASSOCIATES, INC.

Respondent: Richard Van Deelen, President
In charge of social services: Richard Van Deelen
1338 Baldwin, Jenison, MI 49428
(616) 667-0677 • Fax: (616) 667-0920
E-mail: adopt@adoptassoc.com • www.adoptassoc.com
Year first licensed by state: 1989

Agency provides services for: international adoption; U.S. adoption; children with special needs; infants; homestudy if parents working with another agency; postplacement services; networking instruction.

What states do your adoptive parent clients come from? Michigan mostly.

Services provided adopting parents: Classes with other prospective parents; required readings of books and/or articles on adoption; group discussions about adoption; parenting discussions; networking.

States/countries your birthparents/adopted children come from: Birthparents: United States. Adopted children: China, Russia, Moldova, Romania, Guatemala.

What was the goal of your agency when first organized? What is the goal of your agency now? To promote adoption. Now: Same.

Nonrelative children placed in 1998: 175

Percent of adoptive placements under 6 mos.: 70%

Special expertise of staff: Adoptive parents on staff; licensed social workers; birthmothers.

In 1998, what was the average time from when a prospective adoptive parent applied to when he or she received a homestudy? 2 weeks

Average time from homestudy to placement of child: 6–10 mos.

What made you decide to work in the adoption field? It's a positive option for all in triad!

Agency criteria for adoptive parents you work with: Almost none!

How do you screen adoptive parents? Very careful homestudies.

How do you screen birthparents? Careful initial appointments.

What kind of medical information do you seek from birthparents? Extensive: all we can get.

What kind of medical information do you seek on older children? Access to medical records, medical history.

What percent of your U.S. adoptions are nonwhite children? 32%

Is it all right if adopting parents you work with are on waiting lists of other agencies or attorneys? Yes.

Are your adoption fees based on a sliding scale? No.

Do you have an application fee? No.

What is your homestudy fee (if a flat rate)? $1,000

What is your placement fee? Time and expenses: $120/hr. $7,000 added if it's an agency match.

Do adopting parents also pay fees for medical and hospital expenses for birthmother and baby when they have no insurance? If yes, what is the average fee paid? Yes. $2,000–5,000

If applicable, what is the average document language translation fee? $500

If international adoption, what are average travel expenses? $3,000

If you place children from other countries, please list the estimated *entire* average cost to adoptive parents for each country. Guatemala, $20,000–22,000; China, $16,000; Moldova, $20,000–22,000; Romania, $20,000–22,000; Russia, $22,000.

My agency: Offers confidential adoptions; semi-open adoptions; meetings between birthparents and adoptive parents; birthparents pick adoptive parents from bios/resumes.

Does your agency provide videotapes of children needing adoption? Yes.

Are you an adoptive parent, adopted person, or birthparent? Adoptive parent.

In how many cases with your agency has an adoptive parent been placed with a child but lost the child due to a birthparent challenge? Before termination of parental rights: 20%. After termination of parental rights: 0%.

Has your agency lost any adoption litigation filed against you by an adoptive parent or birthparent? No.

ADOPTION CONSULTANTS INC.

Respondent: Elaine Canner, MSCSW, UP, Executive Director
In charge of social services: Elaine Canner
43422 West Oaks Dr. #274, Novi, MI 48377
(248) 788-0542 • Fax: (248) 788-0542
Year first licensed by state: 1996

Agency provides services for: International adoption; U.S. adoption; children with special needs; infants; homestudy if parents working with another agency. We also accept homestudies from other agencies for our international programs.

What states do your adoptive parent clients come from? Mainly Michigan, Ohio, Texas and Illinois (but any state okay). We have worked with Canadians.

Services provided adopting parents: Classes with other prospective parents; parenting discussions.

States/countries your birthparents/adopted children come from: Russia, Guatemala, Egypt (if Moslem family). New programs: Vietnam, Cambodia. No longer working in Ukraine; may resume in the future.

What was the goal of your agency when first organized? What is the goal of your agency now? To facilitate adoption for children in need around the world (and in the United States) where we can work to assist a wide variety of prospective parents. We do not approve everyone but have no age, income, or religious restrictions. We have assisted persons with a disability to adopt (on a case-by-case basis). Now: Same as above and to expand to other countries. We also provide humanitarian aid and insist that families working with us give something back to the country they adopt from.

Nonrelative children placed in 1998: 78

Percent of adoptive placements under 6 mos.: 23%

Special expertise of staff: Adoptive parents on staff; licensed social workers; psychologists; therapists. Board member is attorney; adoptive parents on board of directors.

In 1998, what was the average time from when a prospective adoptive parent applied to when he or she received a homestudy? Under 6 weeks unless they wanted to wait or go slowly.

Average time from homestudy to placement of child: 3–12 mos.

What made you decide to work in the adoption field? I am an adoptive parent with social and psychology background who worked contractually in adoption and also felt some difficulty I had adopting was due to narrow-minded goals or discrimination.

Agency criteria for adoptive parents you work with: No age, family size, income, or religious requirements.

How do you screen adoptive parents? State criminal and child abuse check, interview, reference check.

How do you screen birthparents? We work with any potential birthparents and their significant other/family (no screening).

What kind of medical information do you seek from birthparents? We try to obtain detailed medical history, including information about siblings, parents, and birthfather.

What kind of medical information do you seek on older children? As much as we can get. For international adoption we ask for all information. One of the reasons we stopped working in Ukraine was lack of detailed medical information and difficulty with cooperation.

What percent of your U.S. adoptions are nonwhite children? 0%

Do you have a waiting list of prospective parents? No.

Is it all right if adopting parents you work with are on waiting lists of other agencies or attorneys? Yes.

Are your adoption fees based on a sliding scale? If yes, what are the sliding scale criteria? Yes. We reduce fees or waive some; it depends on the case. We have done some adoptions for $0.

Do you have an application fee? If yes, what is the amount of the application fee? Yes. $200–500, depending on program.

What is your homestudy fee (if a flat rate)? $800

What is your placement fee? $2,000–3,000 depending on program.

Do adopting parents also pay fees for medical and hospital expenses for birthmother and baby when they have no insurance? If yes, what is the average fee paid? Yes. Domestic and part of country fee for Guatemala program (birthmother program).

My agency: Offers confidential adoptions; semi-open adoptions; meetings between birthparents and adoptive parents; birthparents pick adoptive parents from bios/resumes; full disclosure of names between birth and adoptive parents.

Does your agency provide videotapes of children needing adoption? Yes.

Are you an adoptive parent, adopted person, or birthparent? Adoptive parent.

In how many cases with your agency has an adoptive parent been placed with a child but lost the child due to a birthparent challenge? 0

Has your agency lost any adoption litigation filed against you by an adoptive parent or birthparent? No.

ADOPTIONS OF THE HEART, INC.

Respondent: Cathy Larsen, Executive Director
In charge of social services: Cathy Larsen
4295 Summerwind Ave. NE, Grand Rapids, MI 49525
(616) 365-3166 • Fax: (616) 365-2955
E-mail: adoptaid@iserv.net
Year first licensed by state: 1998

Agency provides services for: International adoption; U.S. adoption; children with special needs; infants, homestudy if parents working with another agency, postplacement services. Will consider all requests on case-by-case basis.

What states do your adoptive parent clients come from? Michigan.

Services provided adopting parents: Classes with other prospective parents; required readings of books and/or articles on adoption; group discussions about adoption; parenting discussions.

States/countries your birthparents/adopted children come from: Open to all.

What was the goal of your agency when first organized? What is the goal of your agency now? Find appropriate homes for children in need. Now: Same.

Percent of adoptive placements under 6 mos.: 25%

How many nonrelative children/adoptions did your agency place in 1998? 0 (new agency)

Special expertise by staff: Adoptive parents on staff; licensed social workers.

In 1998, what was the average time from when a prospective adoptive parent applied to when he or she received a homestudy? 2–3 mos.

What made you decide to work in the adoption field? Passion to maximize difficult situations for children in need of homes, birthparents unable to raise their children, and parents who wished to raise (more) children.

Agency criteria for adoptive parents you work with: All on a case-by-case basis; very open to any family meeting criteria of the State of Michigan that is appropriate, nurturing, and able to adopt.

How do you screen adoptive parents? References, state police and Children's Protective Services check, interviews, physicals for preliminary screening. Entire homestudy: above plus parenting inventory, worksheets, many interviews, home visit.

How do you screen birthparents? Via independent counseling services.

What kind of medical information do you seek from birthparents? All.

What kind of medical information do you seek on older children? All.

What percent of your U.S. adoptions are nonwhite children? 50%

About what percent are children with emotional problems? 50%

Do you have a waiting list of prospective parents? No.

Is it all right if adopting parents you work with are on waiting lists of other agencies or attorneys? Yes.

Are your adoption fees based on a sliding scale? No.

Do you have an application fee? If yes, what is the amount of the application fee? Yes. $50

What is your homestudy fee (if a flat rate)? $900 for singles, $1000 for couples.

What is your placement fee? None; legal fee: $500

Do adopting parents also pay fees for medical and hospital expenses for birthmother and baby when they have no insurance? If yes, what is the average fee paid? Yes. They may; it's their choice.

If you place children from other countries, please list the estimated *entire* average cost to adoptive parents for each country. $13,000–18,000 with outside agencies

My agency: Offers confidential adoptions; semi-open adoptions; meetings between birthparents and adoptive parents; birthparents pick adoptive parents from bios/resumes; full disclosure of names between birth and adoptive parents.

Does your agency provide videotapes of children needing adoption? No.

In how many cases with your agency has an adoptive parent been placed with a child but lost the child due to a birthparent challenge? 0

Has your agency lost any adoption litigation filed against you by an adoptive parent or birthparent? No.

AMLYN ADOPTION RESOURCES
Respondent: Karin Stollman, MSW, CSW, Director
In charge of social services: Karin Stollman
4190 Telegraph Rd., Suite 3100, Bloomfield Hills, MI 48302
(248) 644-5463, in-state: (800) 722-7197 • Fax: (248) 646-4345
Year first licensed by state: 1995

Agency provides services for: U.S. adoption; infants; homestudy if parents working with another agency; postplacement services.

What states do your adoptive parent clients come from? The agency is licensed in Michigan. I can work with families nationwide with the exception of New York and Connecticut.

Services provided adopting parents: Parenting discussions.

States/countries your birthparents/adopted children come from: Mostly Michigan. Some Texas (Hispanic children).

What was the goal of your agency when first organized? What is the goal of your agency now? I have recently taken over this agency (October 15, 1998). The couple that started this agency began in 1995 when the adoption laws changed and birthmothers were allowed to pick the adoptive couples. Now: We would like to expand to international adoption and eventually foster care. We are currently working on a Web site to allow adoptive couples to receive information and show their profiles.

Nonrelative children placed in 1998: 25

Percent of adoptive placements under 6 mos.: 100%

Special expertise of staff: Licensed social workers; psychologists; attorney.

In 1998, what was the average time from when a prospective adoptive parent applied to when he or she received a homestudy? It depended on how quickly they needed it. If they had a birthmother and were just waiting for a homestudy, I have done them within 48 hours.

Average time from homestudy to placement of child: 6 mos.–1 year

What made you decide to work in the adoption field? I worked contractually for this agency doing homestudies and postplacements for a year. I found it very rewarding. When the couple decided they wanted to retire I decided to take over the agency. This is a very challenging and difficult job. You are dealing with peoples' emotions from two different angles: the birthparents and the prospective adoptive couple.

How do you screen adoptive parents? Homestudy.

How do you screen birthparents? Individual interviews and counseling.

Do you have a waiting list of prospective parents? Yes.

Is it all right if adopting parents you work with are on waiting lists of other agencies or attorneys? Yes.

Are your adoption fees based on a sliding scale? No.

Do you have an application fee? If yes, what is the amount of the application fee? Yes. $300

What is your homestudy fee (if a flat rate)? $1,200

What is your placement fee? We have agency fees. These fees depend on how much counseling a birthmother needs, what month she is in, when she contacts our agency.

Do adopting parents also pay fees for medical and hospital expenses for birthmother and baby when they have no insurance? If yes, what is the average fee paid? Yes. Often, no medical fee; insurance co-pay $1,000–2,000.

My agency: Offers confidential adoptions; semi-open adoptions; meetings between birthparents and adoptive parents; birthparents pick adoptive parents from bios/resumes.

Does your agency provide videotapes of children needing adoption? No.

In how many cases with your agency has an adoptive parent been placed with a child but lost the child due to a birthparent challenge? 3

Has your agency lost any adoption litigation filed against you by an adoptive parent or birthparent? No.

CATHOLIC SOCIAL SERVICES OF WASHTENAW CO.

Respondent: Lois Plantefaber, MSW, Program Director
In charge of social services: Lois Plantefaber
4925 Packard Rd., Ann Arbor, MI 48108
(734) 971-9781 • Fax: (734) 971-2730
E-mail: loisplant@aol.com
Year first licensed by state: 1959

Agency provides services for: U.S. adoption; infants; homestudy if parents working with another agency; postplacement services.

What states do your adoptive parent clients come from? Michigan (primarily).

Services provided adopting parents: Classes with other prospective parents; required readings of books and/or articles on adoption; group discussions about adoption; parenting discussions.

States/countries your birthparents/adopted children come from: Michigan (primarily).

What was the goal of your agency when first organized? What is the goal of your agency now? To provide services to "unmarried mothers" and "childless married couples." Now: To provide child-centered, values-based, home-finding services for children.

Nonrelative children placed in 1998: 25

Percent of adoptive placements under 6 mos.: 100%

Special expertise of staff: Adoptive parents on staff; licensed social workers; therapists; adoptees on staff.

In 1998, what was the average time from when a prospective adoptive parent applied to when he or she received a homestudy? 2 weeks

Average time from homestudy to placement of child: 6 mos.

What made you decide to work in the adoption field? I began in 1973 by "happenstance," took a break between 1977 and 1988; again, by happenstance came back into adoption and it felt like coming home.

Agency criteria for adoptive parents you work with: The only eligibility requirement is that they live within 60 miles of Ann Arbor.

How do you screen adoptive parents? Mutual screening process through the family assessment (homestudy), which also includes references and criminal clearances.

How do you screen birthparents? Other than values-based options counseling, we don't.

What kind of medical information do you seek from birthparents? Three-generational history based on form provided by geneticists.

What percent of your U.S. adoptions are nonwhite children? 30%

Do you have a waiting list of prospective parents? Yes.

Is it all right if adopting parents you work with are on waiting lists of other agencies or attorneys? Yes.

Are your adoption fees based on a sliding scale? No.

Do you have an application fee? If yes, what is the amount of the application fee? Yes. $250

What is your homestudy fee (if a flat rate)? $1,300

What is your placement fee? $500–1,000

Do adopting parents also pay fees for medical and hospital expenses for birthmother and baby when they have no insurance? If yes, what is the average fee paid? Yes. $300

My agency: Birthparents pick adoptive parents from bios/resumes; offers full disclosure of names between birth and adoptive parents.

Does your agency provide videotapes of children needing adoption? No.

In how many cases with your agency has an adoptive parent been placed with a child but lost the child due to a birthparent challenge? Average two changes of plan per year.

Has your agency lost any adoption litigation filed against you by an adoptive parent or birthparent? No. We've had none filed.

CHILD AND FAMILY SERVICES OF WESTERN MICHIGAN, INC.

Respondent: Nancy Arbuckle, MA, LPC, Infant Adoption Coordinator
412 Century Ln., Holland, MI 49423
(616) 396-2301 • Fax: (616) 396-8070

Agency provides services for: U.S. adoption; children with special needs; infants; homestudy if parents working with another agency; postplacement services.

What states do your adoptive parent clients come from? Michigan.

Services provided adopting parents: Classes with other prospective parents; required readings of books and/or articles on adoption; group discussions about adoption; parenting discussions.

States/countries your birthparents/adopted children come from: Michigan.

What was the goal of your agency when first organized? What is the goal of your agency now? Child welfare: adoption, foster care, pregnancy counseling. Now: To provide a broad range of social services: adoption, foster care, youth mentoring, pregnancy counseling, family and individual counseling.

Nonrelative children placed in 1998: 15

Percent of adoptive placements under 6 mos.: 20%

Special expertise of staff: Adoptive parents on staff; licensed social workers; psychologists; therapists; infant mental health specialist.

In 1998, what was the average time from when a prospective adoptive parent applied to when he or she received a homestudy? 1 mo.

Average time from homestudy to placement of child: 9 mos.

What made you decide to work in the adoption field? General interest in children's issues.

Agency criteria for adoptive parents you work with: No specific criteria, except married couples as well as singles.

How do you screen adoptive parents? Police and protective services background check references, intensive homestudy.

How do you screen birthparents? Birthparents work intensively with a pregnancy counselor, provide detailed medical history.

What kind of medical information do you seek on older children? Any/all available.

What percent of your U.S. adoptions are nonwhite children? 10%

About what percent are children with emotional problems? 75%

Do you have a waiting list of prospective parents? No.

Is it all right if adopting parents you work with are on waiting lists of other agencies or attorneys? No.

Are your adoption fees based on a sliding scale? No.

Do you have an application fee? If yes, what is the amount of the application fee? Yes. $50

What is your homestudy fee (if a flat rate)? $1,800

What is your placement fee? $800 plus $750 for legal fees.

My agency: Offers full disclosure of names between birth and adoptive parents.

Does your agency provide videotapes of children needing adoption? No.

Are you an adoptive parent, adopted person, or birthparent? Adoptive parent.

In how many cases with your agency has an adoptive parent been placed with a child but lost the child due to a birthparent challenge? 0

Has your agency lost any adoption litigation filed against you by an adoptive parent or birthparent? No.

CHILD AND PARENT SERVICES

Respondent: Cathy Eisenberg, Executive Director
In charge of social services: Cathy Eisenberg
30600 Telegraph Rd., Suite 2215, Bingham Farms, MI 48025
(248) 646-7790 • Fax: (248) 646-4544
www.childandparentservices.com
Year first licensed by state: 1987

Agency provides services for: International adoption; U.S. adoption; infants; homestudy if parents working with another agency; postplacement services; interstate adoption; attorney-assisted adoptions; birthparent counseling.

What states do your adoptive parent clients come from? Primarily Michigan.

Services provided adopting parents: Classes with other prospective parents; required readings of books and/or articles on adoption; group discussions about adoption; parenting discussions; educational programs; seminars.

States/countries your birthparents/adopted children come from: Primarily Michigan; facilitate placements in all states and many countries.

What was the goal of your agency when first organized? What is the goal of your agency now? Helping to build families through adoption; always remaining committed to the best interests of the child. Now: Same.

Nonrelative children placed in 1998: 25. Facilitated an additional 50 placements.

Percent of adoptive placements under 6 mos.: 99%

Special expertise of staff: Adoptive parents on staff; licensed social workers; psychologists.

In 1998, what was the average time from when a prospective adoptive parent applied to when he or she received a homestudy? Within 2 mos.

Average time from homestudy to placement of child: 1 year

What made you decide to work in the adoption field? Adoptive parent of two children.

Agency criteria for adoptive parents you work with: We consider all situations on a case-by-case basis.

How do you screen adoptive parents? Homestudy, criminal background check, protective services check, medical exam, reference letters, verification of income, home visit to evaluate the suitability of home environment.

How do you screen birthparents? Intake interview, medical background questionnaire, and hospital and prenatal summary, including all medical records.

What percent of your U.S. adoptions are nonwhite children? 10%

Do you have a waiting list of prospective parents? Yes.

Is it all right if adopting parents you work with are on waiting lists of other agencies or attorneys? Yes.

Are your adoption fees based on a sliding scale? No.

Do you have an application fee? If yes, what is the amount of the application fee? Yes. $300

What is your homestudy fee (if a flat rate)? $1,100

What is your placement fee? Depends on birthparent expenses, generally in the $8,000–10,000 range.

Do adopting parents also pay fees for medical and hospital expenses for birthmother and baby when they have no insurance? If yes, what is the average fee paid? Yes. $9,000–18,000 depending on medical costs.

My agency: Offers confidential adoptions; semi-open adoptions; meetings between birthparents and adoptive parents; birthparents pick adoptive parents from bios/resumes; full disclosure of names between birth and adoptive parents.

Does your agency provide videotapes of children needing adoption? No.

Are you an adoptive parent, adopted person, or birthparent? Adoptive parent.

In how many cases with your agency has an adoptive parent been placed with a child but lost the child due to a birthparent challenge? 0

Has your agency lost any adoption litigation filed against you by an adoptive parent or birthparent? No.

FAMILY ADOPTION CONSULTANTS

Respondent: Lorene Cook, Director
In charge of social services: Kathleen Luz, Assistant Director
421 W. Crosstown Pkwy., P.O. Box 50489, Kalamazoo, MI 49005
(616) 343-3316 • Fax: (616) 343-3359
E-mail: info@facadopt.org • www.facadopt.org
Year first licensed by state: 1983

Agency provides services for: International adoption; U.S. adoption; children with special needs; infants; homestudy if parents working with another agency; postplacement services.

What states do your adoptive parent clients come from? Michigan and Ohio.

Services provided adopting parents: Required readings of books and/or articles on adoption; group discussions about adoption; parenting discussions.

States/countries your birthparents/adopted children come from: Michigan and other states, Korea, China, Philippines, Guatemala.

What was the goal of your agency when first organized? What is the goal of your agency now? To recruit and prepare adoptive families for homeless children. Now: Same.

Special expertise of staff: Adoptive parents on staff; licensed social workers; physician.

In 1998, what was the average time from when a prospective adoptive parent applied to when he or she received a homestudy? 2 weeks

Average time from homestudy to placement of child: Depends on program.

Agency criteria for adoptive parents you work with: Per foreign country requirements.

How do you screen adoptive parents? Very carefully.

How do you screen birthparents? Personal interview.

What kind of medical information do you seek from birthparents? Full disclosure.

What kind of medical information do you seek on older children? Full disclosure.

Do you have a waiting list of prospective parents? Yes.

Is it all right if adopting parents you work with are on waiting lists of other agencies or attorneys? Yes.

Are your adoption fees based on a sliding scale? If yes, what are the sliding scale criteria? Yes. Income.

Do you have an application fee? No.

Do adopting parents also pay fees for medical and hospital expenses for birthmother and baby when they have no insurance? If yes, what is the average fee paid? Yes. Individual.

If international adoption, what are average travel expenses? $2,500–5,000

If you place children from other countries, please list the estimated *entire* average cost to adoptive parents for each country. Korea, $15,500; Philippines, $7,600 plus travel; China, $11,200 plus travel; Guatemala, $18,000 plus travel.

My agency: Offers confidential adoptions; semi-open adoptions; meetings between birthparents and adoptive parents; birthparents pick adoptive parents from bios/resumes; full disclosure of names between birth and adoptive parents.

Does your agency provide videotapes of children needing adoption? Yes.

Are you an adoptive parent, adopted person, or birthparent? Adoptive parent.

In how many cases with your agency has an adoptive parent been placed with a child but lost the child due to a birthparent challenge? 2

Has your agency lost any adoption litigation filed against you by an adoptive parent or birthparent? No.

MORNING STAR ADOPTION RESOURCE SERVICES, INC.

Respondent: Rose Williams, Executive Director
In charge of social services: Rose Williams
26711 Woodward Ave., Suite 209, Huntington Woods, MI 48070
(248) 399-2740 • Fax: (248) 399-1764
Year first licensed by state: 1987

Agency provides services for: International adoption; U.S. adoption; infants; homestudy if parents working with another agency; postplacement services.

What states do your adoptive parent clients come from? Michigan.

Services provided adopting parents: Classes with other prospective parents.

States/countries your birthparents/adopted children come from: All over the United States and from over 20 countries.

What was the goal of your agency when first organized? What is the goal of your agency now? To assist families who desired to adopt through educational and adoption placement services, without the judgmental attitude that denies families for reasons unrelated to their ability to parent. Now: Same.

Nonrelative children placed in 1998: About 140

Percent of adoptive placements under 6 mos.: 80%

Special expertise of staff: Adoptive parents on staff; licensed social workers.

In 1998, what was the average time from when a prospective adoptive parent applied to when he or she received a homestudy? 45 days

Average time from homestudy to placement of child: 15 mos.

What made you decide to work in the adoption field? I didn't decide, I just fell into it by accident and I absolutely love it (the world of adoption).

Agency criteria for adoptive parents you work with: Extremely flexible, no criminal record. Family must be stable and have income and resources to support child.

How do you screen adoptive parents? Through homestudy process, which requires criminal and child abuse background check, three character references, and three in-person interviews.

How do you screen birthparents? Through meetings with social workers, copies of medical records, and medical questionnaires that ask about social and medical history.

What kind of medical information do you seek from birthparents? Health history and social history.

What kind of medical information do you seek on older children? Medical reports and social history.

What percent of your U.S. adoptions are nonwhite children? 15–20%

Do you have a waiting list of prospective parents? No.

Is it all right if adopting parents you work with are on waiting lists of other agencies or attorneys? Yes.

Are your adoption fees based on a sliding scale? No.

Do you have an application fee? If yes, what is the amount of the application fee? Yes. $50 plus $150

What is your homestudy fee (if a flat rate)? $950

What is your placement fee? $5,000 if family finds birthmother, $6,000 if we find birthmother.

Do adopting parents also pay fees for medical and hospital expenses for birthmother and baby when they have no insurance? If yes, what is the average fee paid? Yes. (Very rare.) $4,000

My agency: Offers confidential adoptions; semi-open adoptions; meetings between birthparents and adoptive parents; birthparents pick adoptive parents from bios/resumes; full disclosure of names between birth and adoptive parents.

Does your agency provide videotapes of children needing adoption? No.

In how many cases with your agency has an adoptive parent been placed with a child but lost the child due to a birthparent challenge? Before release, 2–3%. After release, 0%.

Has your agency lost any adoption litigation filed against you by an adoptive parent or birthparent? No.

OAKLAND FAMILY SERVICES

Respondent: Nancy Rebar, Associate Director, Family Preservation
In charge of social services: Nancy Rebar
114 Orchard Lake Rd., Pontiac, MI 48431
(248) 858-7766 • Fax: (248) 858-8227
E-mail: ofs@ofs-family.org
Year first licensed by state: 1921

Agency provides services for: U.S. adoption; children with special needs; infants; homestudy if parents working with another agency; postplacement services.

What states do your adoptive parent clients come from? Michigan.

Services provided adopting parents: Classes with other prospective parents; support groups.

States/countries your birthparents/adopted children come from: All states.

What was the goal of your agency when first organized? What is the goal of your agency now? Child welfare. Now: Our mission is to provide quality treatment, education, and prevention services to meet human service needs in the community.

Nonrelative children placed in 1998: 19

Percent of adoptive placements under 6 mos.: 3 of 19 children

Special expertise of staff: Licensed social workers; therapists.

In 1998, what was the average time from when a prospective adoptive parent applied to when he or she received a homestudy? 1 mo. There is no waiting for homestudy.

Average time from homestudy to placement of child: 3 mos.

What made you decide to work in the adoption field? Field placement in grad school.

Agency criteria for adoptive parents you work with: Need to be residents of Michigan, in contiguous counties, in good physical and emotional health/stability.

How do you screen adoptive parents? Preplacement assessment interviews, references, clearances, via protective services and criminal record clearances.

How do you screen birthparents? Interviews.

What kind of medical information do you seek from birthparents? All available. Form is 13 pages long.

What kind of medical information do you seek on older children? All available. Use same form.

What percent of your U.S. adoptions are nonwhite children? 50%

About what percent are children with medical problems? 25%

About what percent are children with emotional problems? 75%

Do you have a waiting list of prospective parents? Yes.

Is it all right if adopting parents you work with are on waiting lists of other agencies or attorneys? Yes.

Are your adoption fees based on a sliding scale? If yes, what are the sliding scale criteria? Yes. Ability to pay.

Do you have an application fee? If yes, what is the amount of the application fee? Yes. $175 preapplication and $200 application.

What is your homestudy fee (if a flat rate)? $1,000

Do adopting parents also pay fees for medical and hospital expenses for birthmother and baby when they have no insurance? If yes, what is the average fee paid? Yes. Less than $400.

My agency: Offers confidential adoptions; semi-open adoptions; meetings between birthparents and adoptive parents; birthparents pick adoptive parents from bios/resumes; full disclosure of names between birth and adoptive parents.

Does your agency provide videotapes of children needing adoption? Yes, sometimes.

In how many cases with your agency has an adoptive parent been placed with a child but lost the child due to a birthparent challenge? 0

Has your agency lost any adoption litigation filed against you by an adoptive parent or birthparent? No.

Is there anything I have not asked you that is important? In Michigan, adoptive parents must pay birthparent counseling costs. They may assist in medical, living expenses that are "reasonable" and that must be documented to court.

MINNESOTA

CHILDREN'S HOME SOCIETY OF MINNESOTA

Respondent: Margi Miller, Supervisor, International Adoptions
In charge of social services: Nancy Ward
2230 Como Ave., St. Paul, MN 55108
(651) 646-6393 • Fax: (651) 646-0436
E-mail: General@chsm.com • www.chsm.com
Year first licensed by state: 1989

Agency provides services for: International adoption; U.S. adoption; children with special needs; infants; homestudy if parents working with another agency; postplacement services.

What states do your adoptive parent clients come from? Minnesota, Wisconsin, and partner agencies from 35 other states.

Services provided adopting parents: Classes with other prospective parents; required readings of books and/or articles on adoption; group discussions about adoption; parenting discussions. International adoption preparation with the workbook, "With Eyes Wide Open."

States/countries your birthparents/adopted children come from: Minnesota, Korea, India, China, Vietnam, Russia, Bulgaria, Romania, Guatemala, Colombia, Ecuador, Peru, Bolivia, Honduras, Mexico, Greece.

What was the goal of your agency when first organized? What is the goal of your agency now? To find loving homes for children who were sent on the orphan trains. Now: Children's Home Society of Minnesota is committed to helping children thrive; to building and sustaining safe, loving families; and to providing opportunities for individual growth.

Nonrelative children placed in 1998: 450

Percent of adoptive placements under 6 mos.: 75%

Special expertise of staff: Adoptive parents on staff; licensed social workers; psychologists; therapists; attorney.

In 1998, what was the average time from when a prospective adoptive parent applied to when he or she received a homestudy? 4 mos.

Average time from homestudy to placement of child: 6–8 mos.

What made you decide to work in the adoption field? Experience as an adoptive parent.

Agency criteria for adoptive parents you work with: Age 22 and older; if married, two-year marriage; usually up to age 50 to adopt an infant.

How do you screen adoptive parents? State-required background checks, medical certificate, three references, counseling records reviewed if applicable, 2 years recovery if chemical dependency background, and active participation in recovery group.

How do you screen birthparents? Individual counseling appointments.

What kind of medical information do you seek on older children? If U.S.-born children, all available records, if internationally born, tests for HIV, hepatitis B, TB, vaccination records, any available birthparent background, and orphanage or nursery health records.

What percent of your U.S. adoptions are nonwhite children? 5%

About what percent are children with medical problems? With known problems, 30%.

Do you have a waiting list of prospective parents? No.

Is it all right if adopting parents you work with are on waiting lists of other agencies or attorneys? Yes, as long as they discuss this with us.

Are your adoption fees based on a sliding scale? What are your sliding scale criteria? Yes. For homestudy fees, $700–2,200 for incomes between $25,999 and $80,000.

Do you have an application fee? If yes, what is the amount of the application fee? Yes. $4,500 for local families; $250 for families from partner agencies.

My agency: Offers semi-open adoptions, with first names exchanged; meetings between birthparents and adoptive parents; birthparents pick adoptive parents from their bios/resumes; full disclosure of identities between birthparents and adoptive parents.

Does your agency provide videotapes of children needing adoption? Yes.

Are you an adoptive parent, adopted person, or birthparent? Adoptive parent.

In how many cases with your agency has an adoptive parent been placed with a child but lost the child due to a birthparent challenge? About 1%.

Has your agency lost any adoption litigation filed against you by an adoptive parent or birthparent? No.

LUTHERAN SOCIAL SERVICE OF MINNESOTA

Respondent: Betchen Oberdorfer, MSW, LICSW, LMFT, Director, Adoption and
Counseling Program
In charge of social services: Mark Peterson, CEO of Lutheran Social Services
2414 Park Ave. South, Minneapolis, MN 55404
(612) 879-5221 • Fax: (612) 871-0354
Year first licensed by state: Early 1900s.

Agency provides services for: International adoption; U.S. adoption; children with special
needs; infants; homestudy if parents working with another agency; postplacement services.

What states do your adoptive parent clients come from? Mostly Minnesota, but some
from Florida, East and West Coasts, and Midwest.

Services provided adopting parents: Classes with other prospective parents; group discussions about adoption; cross-cultural training, counseling, and parenting; pregnancy counseling.

States/countries your birthparents/adopted children come from: Birthparents predominantly from Minnesota, international mostly from Colombia and Bulgaria, but
also other countries.

What was the goal of your agency when first organized? Finding permanent homes
for orphaned children.

Nonrelative children placed in 1998: 75

Percent of adoptive placements under 6 mos.: 60%

Special expertise of staff: Adoptive parents on staff; licensed social workers; psychologists; therapists; physician.

**In 1998, what was the average time from when a prospective adoptive parent
applied to when he or she received a homestudy?** 2 weeks, except for those
wanting healthy Caucasian infants; then could be 1–2 years, as we don't want couples to pay for a study then wait years for a child, needing to continually update
the study.

Average time from homestudy to placement of child: Varies country by country.
Average is 14 mos.

What made you decide to work in the adoption field? Have two adopted children.

Agency criteria for adoptive parents you work with: Varies with the program (International, Minnesota Infant and Toddler, Special Needs) and country.

How do you screen adoptive parents? Professional staff interview; check references;
do criminal background checks; visit the home.

How do you screen birthparents? All are welcome. Do inclusive medical and social
histories.

What kind of medical information do you seek on older children? Complete medical
and developmental.

What percent of your U.S. adoptions are nonwhite children? 2% infants, 50% older
children.

About what percent are children with medical problems? 20%

About what percent are children with emotional problems? 80% of older children.

Do you have a waiting list of prospective parents? Yes, for healthy Caucasian infants.

Is it all right if adopting parents you work with are on waiting lists of other agencies or attorneys? Yes, for Minnesota infants and international. No for special needs.

Are your adoption fees based on a sliding scale? No, but special needs has no cost.

Do you have an application fee? If yes, what is the amount of the application fee? Yes. $90

What is your homestudy fee (if a flat rate)? $4,500 international; $5,950 for Minnesota Infant and Toddler program.

Do adopting parents also pay fees for medical and hospital expenses for birthmother and baby when they have no insurance? No.

If international adoption, what are average travel expenses? Varies between $2,500 and $7,000; depends on length of stay and program.

My agency: Offers confidential adoptions; semi-open adoptions; meetings between birthparents and adoptive parents; birthparents pick adoptive parents from bios/resumes; full disclosure of names between birth and adoptive parents.

Does your agency provide videotapes of children needing adoption? Yes.

Are you an adoptive parent, adopted person, or birthparent? Adoptive parent.

In how many cases with your agency has an adoptive parent been placed with a child but lost the child due to a birthparent challenge? None due to challenge. Three placed as legal risk from hospital and birthmother reclaimed before signing consents.

Has your agency lost any adoption litigation filed against you by an adoptive parent or birthparent? No.

NEW HORIZONS ADOPTION AGENCY, INC.

Respondent: Marlys Ubben, Executive Director
In charge of social services: Linda Roggow
P.O. Box 623, Frost, MN 56033
(507) 878-3200 • Fax: (507) 878-3132
E-mail: nhaa@means.net
Year first licensed by state: 1987

Agency provides services for: International adoption; U.S. adoption; children with special needs; infants; homestudy if parents working with another agency; postplacement services; birthparent counseling.

What states do your adoptive parent clients come from? All states.

Services provided adopting parents: Classes with other prospective parents; required readings of books and/or articles on adoption; group discussions about adoption; parenting discussions; support family.

States/countries your birthparents/adopted children come from: Guatemala, Vietnam, Russia, Ukraine, Haiti, India, United States: Iowa, Minnesota, South Dakota.

What was the goal of your agency when first organized? What is the goal of your agency now? Facilitate the placement of special needs children with adoptive families qualified to meet their needs. Assist birthparents in an unplanned pregnancy to locate and place with a loving adoptive family in a healthy and supportive environment. Now: Facilitate the placement of all children in need of a loving, stable home with families qualified to meet their needs. Assist birthparents in an unplanned pregnancy to locate and place their child with a loving adoptive family in a healthy and supportive environment.

Nonrelative children placed in 1998: 85

Percent of adoptive placements under 6 mos.: 75%

Special expertise of staff: Adoptive parents on staff; licensed social workers.

In 1998, what was the average time from when a prospective adoptive parent applied to when he or she received a homestudy? 1 mo.

Average time from homestudy to placement of child: 1 year

What made you decide to work in the adoption field? Love of children and respect for adoption.

Agency criteria for adoptive parents you work with: Single or married (if married, minimum 2 years); active Christian; 22–45 years of age (or special permission).

How do you screen adoptive parents? Preapplication, application, homestudy, references, criminal and child abuse checks, medicals, 1040, employment verification, bank letter.

How do you screen birthparents? Individual counseling.

What kind of medical information do you seek from birthparents? All background medical on them, their parents, brothers/sisters,aunts/uncles, grandparents; HIV results.

What kind of medical information do you seek on older children? Full medical; all background medical that we can obtain; HIV on international; hepatitis B.

What percent of your U.S. adoptions are nonwhite children? 60%

About what percent are children with medical problems? 10%

About what percent are children with emotional problems? 15%

Do you have a waiting list of prospective parents? Yes.

Is it all right if adopting parents you work with are on waiting lists of other agencies or attorneys? Yes.

Are your adoption fees based on a sliding scale? No.

Do you have an application fee? If yes, what is the amount of the application fee? Yes. $75

What is your homestudy fee (if a flat rate)? $1,950

What is your placement fee? $10,000; international varies.

Do adopting parents also pay fees for medical and hospital expenses for birthmother and baby when they have no insurance? No.

If applicable, what is the average document language translation fee? Depends on country.

If international adoption, what are average travel expenses? Depends on country.

If you place children from other countries, please list the estimated *entire* average cost to adoptive parents for each country. Guatemala, $13,000 plus travel; Ukraine, $17,000, including travel; Vietnam, $11,400, plus travel; Russia, $15,200, including travel.

My agency: Offers confidential adoptions; semi-open adoptions; meetings between birthparents and adoptive parents; birthparents pick adoptive parents from bios/resumes; full disclosure of names between birth and adoptive parents.

Does your agency provide videotapes of children needing adoption? Yes, sometimes.

Are you an adoptive parent, adopted person, or birthparent? Adoptive parent.

In how many cases with your agency has an adoptive parent been placed with a child but lost the child due to a birthparent challenge? 0

Has your agency lost any adoption litigation filed against you by an adoptive parent or birthparent? No.

REACHING ARMS INTERNATIONAL, INC.
Respondent: Nila M. Neumiller, Executive Director
In charge of social services: Jasmine Sims
904 Main St., Suite 330, Hopkins, MN 55343
(612) 932-9331 • Fax: (612) 932-4215
E-mail: raiadopt@raiadopt.com
Year first licensed by state: 1993

Agency provides services for: International adoption; U.S. adoption; children with special needs; infants; homestudy if parents working with another agency; postplacement services.

What states do your adoptive parent clients come from? All states.

Services provided adopting parents: Classes with other prospective parents; group discussions about adoption; parenting discussions; international representative visits the home to help with older child adoptions, adjustments with language barriers, and overall attachment and bonding.

States/countries your birthparents/adopted children come from: Texas, Illinois, Minnesota, Ukraine, Russia, Guatemala, Haiti.

What was the goal of your agency when first organized? What is the goal of your agency now? To find families for orphans from Eastern Europe and to provide for those who remain in orphanages. Now: The same plus found children's homes throughout the world.

Nonrelative children placed in 1998: 110

Percent of adoptive placements under 6 mos.: 30%

Special expertise of staff: Adoptive parents on staff; licensed social workers; therapists; educators; licensed teachers; internationals who train in cultural issues for parents.

In 1998, what was the average time from when a prospective adoptive parent applied to when he or she received a homestudy? 3 weeks–2 mos.

Average time from homestudy to placement of child: 3 mos.

What made you decide to work in the adoption field? I am an ordained pastor; this is a ministry for me.

Agency criteria for adoptive parents you work with: No limits for either as long as the nation has no limits. We adhere to each nation's laws.

How do you screen adoptive parents? They must be Jewish or Christian with no criminal history. They must be married 3 years, healthy, and financially stable.

How do you screen birthparents? It's the minority of our work. Screening is based on birthparent history, health, emotional stability, support system, etc.

What kind of medical information do you seek from birthparents? A packet created by Minnesota that details a medical family history.

What kind of medical information do you seek on older children? A profile of birth records and growth measurements as well as character and personality. We also gain as much data as possible on the social history of the child.

What percent of your U.S. adoptions are nonwhite children? 40%

About what percent are children with medical problems? Less than 10%

About what percent are children with emotional problems? 50%

Do you have a waiting list of prospective parents? No.

Is it all right if adopting parents you work with are on waiting lists of other agencies or attorneys? Yes.

Are your adoption fees based on a sliding scale? No.

Do you have an application fee? If yes, what is the amount of the application fee? Yes. $2,00

What is your homestudy fee (if a flat rate)? $1,500

What is your placement fee? $4,000 for one child

Do adopting parents also pay fees for medical and hospital expenses for birthmother and baby when they have no insurance? If yes, what is the average fee paid? Yes. $1,200

If applicable, what is the average document language translation fee? $3,500 for complete adoption processing.

If international adoption, what are average travel expenses? $3,500

If you place children from other countries, please list the estimated *entire* average cost to adoptive parents for each country. $9,700 for children over $2\frac{1}{2}$ years. $17,700 for infants.

My agency: Offers confidential adoptions; semi-open adoptions; meetings between birthparents and adoptive parents; birthparents pick adoptive parents from bios/resumes; full disclosure of names between birth and adoptive parents.

Does your agency provide videotapes of children needing adoption? Yes.

Are you an adoptive parent, adopted person, or birthparent? Adoptive parent.

In how many cases with your agency has an adoptive parent been placed with a child but lost the child due to a birthparent challenge? 1

Has your agency lost any adoption litigation filed against you by an adoptive parent or birthparent? No.

WELLSPRING ADOPTION AGENCY, INC.

Respondent: Robert D. Vincent, Executive Director
In charge of social services: Ann Jones
111 Third Ave. South, Minneapolis, MN 55401
(612) 379-0980 • Fax: (612) 332-1839
Year first licensed by state: 1990

Agency provides services for: International adoption; U.S. adoption; infants; homestudy if parents working with another agency; postplacement services.

What states do your adoptive parent clients come from? Primarily Minnesota, but all other states as well.

Services provided adopting parents: Classes with other prospective parents; required readings of books and/or articles on adoption; group discussions about adoption; parenting discussions; classes on how to talk to your child about adoption and other topics.

States/countries your birthparents/adopted children come from: Primarily Minnesota but all other states as well.

What was the goal of your agency when first organized? What is the goal of your agency now? To provide services to birth and adoptive families who want to pursue independent adoption. Now: To provide services to birth and adoptive families who want to pursue independent adoption, to educate the public about adoption, and to promote laws which make adoption easier and more positive for everyone.

Nonrelative children placed in 1998: 77

Percent of adoptive placements under 6 mos.: 95%

Special expertise of staff: Adoptive parents on staff; licensed social workers; psychologists; therapists; adopted adults.

In 1998, what was the average time from when a prospective adoptive parent applied to when he or she received a homestudy? 3 mos.

Average time from homestudy to placement of child: 13 mos.

What made you decide to work in the adoption field? I am an adoptive parent and want to promote adoption as a positive way to build families.

Agency criteria for adoptive parents you work with: None.

How do you screen adoptive parents? Through the adoption study process, beginning with an initial intake meeting where basic background information is obtained and details of our program are discussed to make sure we are a "good fit" for a specific family.

How do you screen birthparents? Through an initial meeting, during which basic background information is obtained, including self-reports of health history and drug use during pregnancy. A verification of pregnancy and release for medical records are then obtained.

What kind of medical information do you seek from birthparents? A 27-page social and medical background is required by law and prepared by the Department of Human Services.

What kind of medical information do you seek on older children? All medical records and information about the child's behavior and problems from the caregiver or guardian.

What percent of your U.S. adoptions are nonwhite children? 2%

About what percent are children with medical problems? 5%

Do you have a waiting list of prospective parents? No.

Is it all right if adopting parents you work with are on waiting lists of other agencies or attorneys? Yes

Are your adoption fees based on a sliding scale? If yes, what are the sliding scale criteria? Yes. Adoptive parent income determines cost of adoption study. Fees range from $950 to $3,250 for incomes up to $60,000.

Do you have an application fee? No.

What is your homestudy fee (if a flat rate)? Varies.

What is your placement fee? $500–3,000 depending on birthparent work.

Do adopting parents also pay fees for medical and hospital expenses for birthmother and baby when they have no insurance? If yes, what is the average fee paid? Yes. Approximately $4,000

My agency: Offers confidential adoptions; semi-open adoptions; meetings between birthparents and adoptive parents; birthparents pick adoptive parents from bios/resumes; full disclosure of names between birth and adoptive parents.

Does your agency provide videotapes of children needing adoption? No.

Are you an adoptive parent, adopted person, or birthparent? Adoptive parent.

In how many cases with your agency has an adoptive parent been placed with a child but lost the child due to a birthparent challenge? 0

Has your agency lost any adoption litigation filed against you by an adoptive parent or birthparent? No.

MISSISSIPPI

HARDEN HOUSE ADOPTION PROGRAM
Respondent: Patricia Digby, Program Director
In charge of social services: Patricia Digby
110 N. Gaither, Fulton, MS 38843
(601) 862-2386 • Fax: (601) 862-7382
E-mail: hardenad@network-one.com
Year first licensed by state: 1996

Agency provides services for: U.S. adoption; children with special needs; infants; home-study if parents working with another agency; postplacement services.

What states do your adoptive parent clients come from? Mississippi.

Services provided adopting parents: Classes with other prospective parents; required readings of books and/or articles on adoption; group discussions about adoption; parenting discussions; support group for parents and children.

States/countries your birthparents/adopted children come from: All states.

What was the goal of your agency when first organized? What is the goal of your agency now? Find families willing to take special needs children in Mississippi. Now: Find families for any children free for adoption.

Nonrelative children placed in 1998: 16

Special expertise of staff: Licensed social workers; therapists; attorney.

In 1998, what was the average time from when a prospective adoptive parent applied to when he or she received a homestudy? 4–6 mos.

Average time from homestudy to placement of child: 6 mos.–1 year

What made you decide to work in the adoption field? Worked in child protective ser-vices and saw the need for permanency for those children.

Agency criteria for adoptive parents you work with: Aged 23–65; stable income; clear background checks; fire hazard clearances.

How do you screen adoptive parents? Background checks, reference checks, etc.

What kind of medical information do you seek from birthparents? As much medical background as available from social worker.

What kind of medical information do you seek on older children? As much as is available.

What percent of your U.S. adoptions are nonwhite children? 5%

About what percent are children with emotional problems? 100%

Do you have a waiting list of prospective parents? Yes.

Is it all right if adopting parents you work with are on waiting lists of other agencies or attorneys? Yes.

Are your adoption fees based on a sliding scale? If yes, what are the sliding scale criteria? Yes. Not charged a fee yet; work off a grant.

Do you have an application fee? No.

What is your homestudy fee (if a flat rate)? $850 if not special needs.

What is your placement fee? Have not charged a fee yet; all special needs so far.

Do adopting parents also pay fees for medical and hospital expenses for birthmother and baby when they have no insurance? If yes, what is the average fee paid? Yes. Have not placed infant yet.

My agency: Offers confidential adoptions; semi-open adoptions; meetings between birthparents and adoptive parents; birthparents pick adoptive parents from bios/resumes.

Does your agency provide videotapes of children needing adoption? No.

In how many cases with your agency has an adoptive parent been placed with a child but lost the child due to a birthparent challenge? 0

Has your agency lost any adoption litigation filed against you by an adoptive parent or birthparent? No.

MISSISSIPPI CHILDREN'S HOME SOCIETY

Respondent: Nancy Knight Miller, Adoption Director
In charge of social services: John Ross, Community Services Director
1900 N. West St., Suite A, Jackson, MS 39202
(601) 352-7784 • Fax: (601) 968-0028
E-mail: msmiller@bellsouth.net • www.mchsfsa.org
Year first licensed by state: 1912

Agency provides services for: U.S. adoption; children with special needs; infants; homestudy if parents working with another agency; postplacement services.

What states do your adoptive parent clients come from? All states and outside of the United States (Germany).

Services provided adopting parents: Classes with other prospective parents; required readings of books and/or articles on adoption; group discussions about adoption; parenting discussions.

States/countries your birthparents/adopted children come from: All states, but primarily Mississippi.

What was the goal of your agency when first organized? What is the goal of your agency now? To place children into safe, nurturing and permanent homes. Now: "Building Foundations for Families."

Nonrelative children placed in 1998: 46

Percent of adoptive placements under 6 mos.: 75–80%

Special expertise of staff: Licensed social workers; attorney.

In 1998, what was the average time from when a prospective adoptive parent applied to when he or she received a homestudy? 4–6 weeks

Average time from homestudy to placement of child: 9 mos.

Agency criteria for adoptive parents you work with: Don't have any specific criteria. Birthparents are looking for different types of families.

How do you screen adoptive parents? Background checks, police record checks, child abuse registry checks, references, interviews, parenting classes.

How do you screen birthparents? Individual assessments; gather medical/social information for adoptive family.

What kind of medical information do you seek on older children? Same as above, plus all previous medical records, counseling records, etc.

What percent of your U.S. adoptions are nonwhite children? 65%

About what percent are children with medical problems? 5–10%

About what percent are children with emotional problems? 5–10%

Do you have a waiting list of prospective parents? No.

Is it all right if adopting parents you work with are on waiting lists of other agencies or attorneys? Yes.

Are your adoption fees based on a sliding scale? Yes.

Do you have an application fee? No.

What is your homestudy fee (if a flat rate)? $850 plus $50 an hour for travel.

Do adopting parents also pay fees for medical and hospital expenses for birthmother and baby when they have no insurance? If yes, what is the average fee paid? Yes, in about 5% of cases. Most clients have Medicaid (95%).

My agency: Offers confidential adoptions; semi-open adoptions; meetings between birthparents and adoptive parents; birthparents pick adoptive parents from bios/resumes; full disclosure of names between birth and adoptive parents.

Does your agency provide videotapes of children needing adoption? No.

In how many cases with your agency has an adoptive parent been placed with a child but lost the child due to a birthparent challenge? 0

Has your agency lost any adoption litigation filed against you by an adoptive parent or birthparent? No.

SOUTHERN ADOPTIONS

Respondent: Kathy Lahr, CEO
In charge of social services: Ray McNair
Route 8, Box 106B, Philadelphia, MS 39350
(800) 499-6862 • Fax: (601) 656-6561
E-mail: southadopt@aol.com • www.soadopt.qpg.com
Year first licensed by state: 1995

Agency provides services for: International adoption; infants; homestudy if parents working with another agency; postplacement services.

What states do your adoptive parent clients come from? All states and overseas.

Services provided adopting parents: Classes with other prospective parents; required readings of books and/or articles on adoption; group discussions about adoption; parenting discussions.

States/countries your birthparents/adopted children come from: Brazil, Romania, Russia, China, Honduras, Costa Rica, Mexico, Chile, Lithuania, Thailand, Philippines.

What was the goal of your agency when first organized? What is the goal of your agency now? To help babies/children in need of love. Now: Same.

Percent of adoptive placements under 6 mos.: 95%

Special expertise of staff: Adoptive parents on staff; licensed social workers; psychologists; therapists; physician; attorney.

In 1998, what was the average time from when a prospective adoptive parent applied to when he or she received a homestudy? 1 week

Average time from homestudy to placement of child: 4 mos.

What made you decide to work in the adoption field? I love babies/children.

Agency criteria for adoptive parents you work with: No certain age; they can have children, be divorced, be single. Older couples may apply.

How do you screen adoptive parents? Through our ministry in God; we do not ask for a couple to be of any certain religion, just to believe in God.

Do you have an application fee? No.

What is your homestudy fee (if a flat rate)? $700 in Mississippi and Alabama.

If applicable, what is the average document language translation fee? $500 for most; $2,000 for a few.

If international adoption, what are average travel expenses? Some countries we have babies escorted here. For others, $700–2,000.

If you place children from other countries, please list the estimated *entire* average cost to adoptive parents for each country. Agency fee: $6,800; Russia, $11,000; China, $3,200; Romania, $7,000; Mexico, $7,000; Costa Rica, $6,000; Honduras, $10,000.

My agency: Offers confidential adoptions.

Does your agency provide videotapes of children needing adoption? Yes in some countries.

Are you an adoptive parent, adopted person, or birthparent? Adoptive parent.

In how many cases with your agency has an adoptive parent been placed with a child but lost the child due to a birthparent challenge? 0

Has your agency lost any adoption litigation filed against you by an adoptive parent or birthparent? No.

MISSOURI

ADOPTION ADVOCATES

Respondent: Susan Sarachih, Adoption Specialist
In charge of social services: Susan Sarachih
3100 Broadway, Suite 218, Kansas City, MO 64111
(816) 753-1881 • Fax: (816) 753-5551
www.adoptionadvocates.com

Agency provides services for: International adoption; U.S. adoption; children with special needs; homestudy if parents working with another agency; postplacement services.

What states do your adoptive parent clients come from? Missouri, Kansas.

Services provided adopting parents: Required readings of books and/or articles on adoption.

States/countries your birthparents/adopted children come from: Missouri, Kansas.

What was the goal of your agency when first organized? What is the goal of your agency now? Counseling. Now: Adoption and counseling.

Nonrelative children placed in 1998: 10

Percent of adoptive placements under 6 mos.: 100%

Special expertise of staff: Licensed social workers; attorney.

In 1998, what was the average time from when a prospective adoptive parent applied to when he or she received a homestudy? 1 mo.

Average time from homestudy to placement of child: 18 mos.

What made you decide to work in the adoption field? New opportunity in social work.

Agency criteria for adoptive parents you work with: Married at least 2 years; at least 21 years of age. Number of children in home is looked at on individual basis. We have no age limits, but birthmothers do.

How do you screen adoptive parents? Consult interview; police and child abuse references; in-depth interviews.

How do you screen birthparents? Complete medical and social evaluation.

What percent of your U.S. adoptions are nonwhite children? 2%

Do you have a waiting list of prospective parents? Yes.

Is it all right if adopting parents you work with are on waiting lists of other agencies or attorneys? Yes.

Are your adoption fees based on a sliding scale? No.

Do you have an application fee? If yes, what is the amount of the application fee? Yes. $50

What is your homestudy fee (if a flat rate)? Domestic, $900; international, $1,200.

What is your placement fee? $1,000

Do adopting parents also pay fees for medical and hospital expenses for birthmother and baby when they have no insurance? If yes, what is the average fee paid? Yes. $2,400

My agency: Offers confidential adoptions; semi-open adoptions; meetings between birthparents and adoptive parents; birthparents pick adoptive parents from bios/resumes.

Does your agency provide videotapes of children needing adoption? Yes.

In how many cases with your agency has an adoptive parent been placed with a child but lost the child due to a birthparent challenge? 0

Has your agency lost any adoption litigation filed against you by an adoptive parent or birthparent? No.

CHILDREN'S HOPE INTL.

Respondent: Melody Zhang, Associate Director
In charge of social services: Kathy Smith, Director of Social Services
9229 Lackland Rd., St. Louis, MO 63114
(314) 890-0086 • Fax: (314) 427-4288
E-mail: melody@childrenshopeint.org • www.childrenshopeint.org
Year first licensed by state: 1993

Agency provides services for: International adoption; children with special needs; infants; homestudy if parents working with another agency; postplacement services.

What states do your adoptive parent clients come from? All states.

Services provided adopting parents: Classes with other prospective parents; required readings of books and/or articles on adoption; group discussions about adoption; parenting discussions; preadoption class to families free of charge if going through placement.

States/countries your birthparents/adopted children come from: China, Russia, Vietnam, Guatemala, India.

What was the goal of your agency when first organized? What is the goal of your agency now? To find homes for orphaned children in China. Now: Finding homes for orphans and providing humanitarian aid to children who remain in orphanages.

Nonrelative children placed in 1998: 200

Percent of adoptive placements under 6 mos.: 30%

Special expertise of staff: Adoptive parents on staff; licensed social workers; therapists.

In 1998, what was the average time from when a prospective adoptive parent applied to when he or she received a homestudy? 1–2 mos.

Average time from homestudy to placement of child: 8 mos.

What made you decide to work in the adoption field? I was led into the field by call (luck?) and I love it! Love to help children.

Agency criteria for adoptive parents you work with: 25–60 years of age (older parents for older children); 0–4 children [in the home already] or depends on country requirement. Stable safe home environment.

How do you screen adoptive parents? We rely on homestudy assessment to make sure the parents are stable, no abuse issues, meet all criteria of foreign country.

What kind of medical information do you seek on older children? Besides the medical form of information, we try to get as much detail about personality, schedule, medical history, etc.

What percent of your U.S. adoptions are nonwhite children? 80%

About what percent are children with medical problems? 5%

Do you have a waiting list of prospective parents? No.

Is it all right if adopting parents you work with are on waiting lists of other agencies or attorneys? No.

Are your adoption fees based on a sliding scale? No.

Do you have an application fee? If yes, what is the amount of the application fee? Yes. $100

What is your homestudy fee (if a flat rate)? $900 ($1,200 if not going through us for placement.)

Do adopting parents also pay fees for medical and hospital expenses for birthmother and baby when they have no insurance? No.

If applicable, what is the average document language translation fee? $400

If international adoption, what are average travel expenses? Varies from country to country; $3,000 average.

If you place children from other countries please list the estimated *entire* average cost to adoptive parents for each country. China, $15,000; Russia, $18,000; Vietnam, $15,000; Guatemala, $19,000; India, $16,000.

My agency: Offers confidential adoptions.

Does your agency provide videotapes of children needing adoption? Yes.

In how many cases with your agency has an adoptive parent been placed with a child but lost the child due to a birthparent challenge? 0

Has your agency lost any adoption litigation filed against you by an adoptive parent or birthparent? No.

THE CHILDREN'S HOME SOCIETY OF MISSOURI

Respondents: Robert Sheahan, President and Karen Nolte, Vice President
In charge of social services: Karen Nolte
9445 Litzsinger Rd., St. Louis, MO 63144
(314) 968-2350 • Fax: (314) 968-4239
Year first licensed by state: 1891

Agency provides services for: International adoption; U.S. adoption; children with special needs; infants; homestudy if parents working with another agency; postplacement services.

What states do your adoptive parent clients come from? Primarily Missouri. Out-of-state placements are primarily special needs.

Services provided adopting parents: Group discussions about adoption; parenting discussions.

States/countries your birthparents/adopted children come from: Missouri. International Partnership Program—13 countries including Asia, Eastern Europe, South America, India.

What was the goal of your agency when first organized? What is the goal of your agency now? Foster care and adoption. Now: Adoption and respite/residential services for children with developmental disabilities.

Nonrelative children placed in 1998: 20

Percent of adoptive placements under 6 mos.: 20%

Special expertise of staff: Licensed social workers; therapists; physician; attorney.

In 1998, what was the average time from when a prospective adoptive parent applied to when he or she received a homestudy? 1 mo. or less

Average time from homestudy to placement of child: 1–2 years

Agency criteria for adoptive parents you work with: For healthy Caucasian infant: Infertility; married 5 years; no other children. For minority, older, special needs child: These criteria don't apply.

How do you screen adoptive parents? Homestudy process.

What kind of medical information do you seek on older children? Same and current functioning and health history.

What percent of your U.S. adoptions are nonwhite children? 66%

About what percent are children with medical problems? 10%

Do you have a waiting list of prospective parents? Yes.

Is it all right if adopting parents you work with are on waiting lists of other agencies or attorneys? Yes.

Are your adoption fees based on a sliding scale? If yes, what are the sliding scale criteria? Yes. 12% annual income; 16% for special needs.

Do you have an application fee? No.

What is your homestudy fee (if a flat rate)? $1,000

What is your placement fee? Sliding scale criteria.

Do adopting parents also pay fees for medical and hospital expenses for birth-mother and baby when they have no insurance? No.

My agency: Offers confidential adoptions; semi-open adoptions; meetings between birthparents and adoptive parents; birthparents pick adoptive parents from bios/resumes.

Does your agency provide videotapes of children needing adoption? No.

In how many cases with your agency has an adoptive parent been placed with a child but lost the child due to a birthparent challenge? 0

Has your agency lost any adoption litigation filed against you by an adoptive parent or birthparent? No.

HIGHLANDS CHILD PLACEMENT SERVICES AND MATERNITY HOME

Respondent: Rev. Robert J. Michels, Administrator
In charge of social services: Julie Wilson
P.O. Box 300198, Kansas City, MO 64130-0198
(816) 924-6565 • Fax: (816) 924-3409
E-mail: revrhn@msn.com • www.highlandsmaternityhome.com
Year first licensed by state: 1966

Agency provides services for: U.S. adoption; infants.

What states do your adoptive parent clients come from? All states.

Services provided adopting parents: Classes with other prospective parents; required readings of books and/or articles on adoption; group discussions about adoption.

States/countries your birthparents/adopted children come from: All states.

What was the goal of your agency when first organized? What is the goal of your agency now? Adoption. Now: Same.

Nonrelative children placed in 1998: 7

Percent of adoptive placements under 6 mos.: 100%

Special expertise of staff: Licensed social workers; minister.

In 1998, what was the average time from when a prospective adoptive parent applied to when he or she received a homestudy? 3 years

Average time from homestudy to placement of child: 1 year

Agency criteria for adoptive parents you work with: Age 21–40; married 3 years; preference to couples with no children or no more than one child; preference to Assembly of God couples.

How do you screen adoptive parents? Applications, references, home visits.

How do you screen birthparents? Applications.

What percent of your U.S. adoptions are nonwhite children? 30%

About what percent are children with medical problems? 10%

Do you have a waiting list of prospective parents? Yes.

Is it all right if adopting parents you work with are on waiting lists of other agencies or attorneys? Yes.

Are your adoption fees based on a sliding scale? If yes, what are the sliding scale criteria? Yes. Based on combined income.

Do you have an application fee? If yes, what is the amount of the application fee? Yes. $25

What is your homestudy fee (if a flat rate)? $650

What is your placement fee? $4,000–12,000

Do adopting parents also pay fees for medical and hospital expenses for birthmother and baby when they have no insurance? No.

My agency: Offers confidential adoptions; semi-open adoptions; meetings between birthparents and adoptive parents; birthparents pick adoptive parents from bios/resumes.

Does your agency provide videotapes of children needing adoption? No.

In how many cases with your agency has an adoptive parent been placed with a child but lost the child due to a birthparent challenge? 0

Has your agency lost any adoption litigation filed against you by an adoptive parent or birthparent? No.

LIGHT HOUSE

Respondent: Shirley Gibson, LMSW, Director of Social Services
In charge of social services: Shirley Gibson
1409 East Meyer Blvd., Kansas City, MO 64131
(861) 361-2233 • Fax: (861) 361-8333
Year first licensed by state: 1985

Agency provides services for: U.S. adoption; postplacement services.

What states do your adoptive parent clients come from? All states.

Services provided adopting parents: Required readings of books and/or articles on adoption; initial adoption information meeting.

States/countries your birthparents/adopted children come from: Birthparents come from all over the United States.

What was the goal of your agency when first organized? What is the goal of your agency now? To offer an alternative to abortion to young women experiencing an unplanned pregnancy.

Nonrelative children placed in 1998: 7

Percent of adoptive placements under 6 mos.: 100%

Special expertise of staff: Licensed social workers.

In 1998, what was the average time from when a prospective adoptive parent applied to when he or she received a homestudy? Varies.

Average time from homestudy to placement of child: Varies. Birthmother chooses through nonidentifying profiles.

Agency criteria for adoptive parents you work with: 1. Husband and wife between ages of 25–40 at time of preapplication. 2. Husband and wife are Christians and active members of the same church. 3. Been married 3 years if first marriage and 5 years if either spouse has been divorced. 4. No more than one child in family, including children from previous marriages.

How do you screen adoptive parents? 1. Pre-application. 2. Formal application (references, child abuse check, police check, etc.). 3. Homestudy process.

How do you screen birthparents? Gather social and medical background on birthparents and their families.

What kind of medical information do you seek from birthparents? As much as possible.

Do you have a waiting list of prospective parents? Yes.

Is it all right if adopting parents you work with are on waiting lists of other agencies or attorneys? Yes.

Are your adoption fees based on a sliding scale? If yes, what are the sliding scale criteria? Yes. Based on adjusted gross income.

Do you have an application fee? If yes, what is the amount of the application fee? A preapplication fee and a formal application fee. Preapplication: $25; formal application: $500 when approved.

What is your placement fee? All adoption fees are included in our fee.

My agency: Offers confidential adoptions; semi-open adoptions; meetings between birthparents and adoptive parents; birthparents pick adoptive parents from bios/resumes.

Does your agency provide videotapes of children needing adoption? No.

In how many cases with your agency has an adoptive parent been placed with a child but lost the child due to a birthparent challenge? 0

Has your agency lost any adoption litigation filed against you by an adoptive parent or birthparent? No. Never had any litigation filed.

LOVE BASKET, INC.

Respondent: Frank R. Block, Executive Director
In charge of social services: Frank Block
10306 Hwy. 21, Hillsboro, MO 63050
(314) 797-4100 • Fax: (314) 789-4978
Year first licensed by state: 1982

Agency provides services for: International adoption; U.S. adoption; children with special needs; infants; homestudy if parents working with another agency; postplacement services.

What states do your adoptive parent clients come from? All states.

Services provided adopting parents: Required readings of books and/or articles on adoption; orientation meeting.

States/countries your birthparents/adopted children come from: Predominantly Missouri, Illinois, and Minnesota. Also India and Romania.

What was the goal of your agency when first organized? What is the goal of your agency now? Place baby girls from India with U.S. families. Now: Reach birthparents and destitute children with the ministry of adoption.

Nonrelative children placed in 1998: 51

Percent of adoptive placements under 6 mos.: 40%

Special expertise of staff: Adoptive parents on staff; licensed social workers; MSW; LCSW; ACSW.

In 1998, what was the average time from when a prospective adoptive parent applied to when he or she received a homestudy? 120 days

Average time from homestudy to placement of child: 18 mos.

What made you decide to work in the adoption field? Pro-life volunteer work lead to full-time "real job."

How do you screen adoptive parents? Application materials; child abuse/criminal screenings; orientation meetings; homestudy process.

How do you screen birthparents? Interviews; medical testing (social, HIV, etc.).

What kind of medical information do you seek from birthparents? Complete social and medical history.

What kind of medical information do you seek on older children? All hospital and pediatrician records plus complete social and medical history.

What percent of your U.S. adoptions are nonwhite children? 25%

Do you have a waiting list of prospective parents? Yes.

Is it all right if adopting parents you work with are on waiting lists of other agencies or attorneys? No.

Are your adoption fees based on a sliding scale? If yes, what are the sliding scale criteria? Yes. Adjusted gross income (1040s as evidence).

Do you have an application fee? If yes, what is the amount of the application fee?
Yes. $95

What is your homestudy fee (if a flat rate)? $1,000

What is your placement fee? Varies.

Do adopting parents also pay fees for medical and hospital expenses for birth-mother and baby when they have no insurance? If yes, what is the average fee paid? Yes. $1,500

If applicable, what is the average document language translation fee? $500

If international adoption, what are average travel expenses? $2,500

If you place children from other countries, please list the estimated *entire* average cost to adoptive parents for each country. India, $12,000; Romania, $11,000 plus travel for a total of $13,500.

My agency: Offers confidential adoptions; semi-open adoptions; meetings between birthparents and adoptive parents; birthparents pick adoptive parents from bios/resumes; full disclosure of names between birth and adoptive parents.

Does your agency provide videotapes of children needing adoption? No.

In how many cases with your agency has an adoptive parent been placed with a child but lost the child due to a birthparent challenge? 0

Has your agency lost any adoption litigation filed against you by an adoptive parent or birthparent? No.

SMALL WORLD ADOPTION FOUNDATION, INC.

Respondent: Brenda Henn, Director of Operations
In charge of social services: Brenda Henn
15480 Clayton Rd., Suite 101, Ballwin, MO 63011
(636) 207-9229 • Fax: (636) 207-9055
E-mail: staff@swaf.com • www.swaf.com
Year first licensed by state: 1994

Agency provides services for: International adoption; homestudy if parents working with another agency, postplacement services.

What states do your adoptive parent clients come from? We have placed children in 34 states, Puerto Rico, and Germany. We currently have clients in Guatemala and France waiting to finalize adoptions.

Services provided adopting parents: Classes with other prospective parents; required readings of books and/or articles on adoption; training seminars.

States/countries your birthparents/adopted children come from: Russia, Belarus, and Ukraine.

What was the goal of your agency when first organized? What is the goal of your agency now? In 1992, Small World was incorporated to provide relief to orphanages of St. Petersburg, Russia. I was working to adopt a child from Hungary. I was caught in a bad situation and forced to learn all about international adoption. I was asked to put together a program and did. For the first year, we worked under the umbrella of another agency. In 1994 we became fully licensed.

Nonrelative children placed in 1998: 120

Percent of adoptive placements under 6 mos.: 1% are younger than 6 mos. of age. 90% are between 6 mos. and 14 mos. of age.

Special expertise of staff: Adoptive parents on staff; licensed social workers; pediatricians who travel to Eastern Europe 3–4 times yearly to see the children and deliver relief items for the orphanage; Executive Director and Director of Foreign Children's Services speak fluent Russian and have the ability to oversee all aspects of the adoption process in the foreign country.

In 1998, what was the average time from when a prospective adoptive parent applied to when he or she received a homestudy? Small World families are encouraged to begin their homestudy process within a couple of weeks of acceptance into the adoption program.

Average time from homestudy to placement of child: Average time for clients to finalize their adoption in the foreign country was from 5–9 mos. from the point of application to the actual travel date.

What made you decide to work in the adoption field? My own terrible experience opened my eyes to the world of adoption. I believe adoption should be full of warm fuzzies and not a terrible experience one has to survive. I adore my child and want to help other people realize the joy of adoption and parenthood. I feel very blessed to be able to do this!

Agency criteria for adoptive parents you work with: Our primary prospective-parent criteria stem from the regulations of the foreign countries. For instance, in Belarus, all adopting parents must be 45 years old or younger. In the Ukraine, there are no age requirements. However, Small World does not place babies with adopting parents older than 50 years. Small World requires parents be married a minimum of 2 years, no more than two divorces. Single women may adopt. The foreign countries we work with do not allow single men to adopt.

How do you screen adoptive parents? Initially, when prospective adoptive families apply to Small World, they complete a comprehensive four-page application. Upon approval, parents receive contracts outlining the rights and responsibilities of both the agency and the prospective adoptive clients.

What kind of medical information do you seek on older children? For all Small World Adoption Foundation children, our pediatricians, who select the children, try to obtain as much information as possible about the child. They examine orphanage records for birthweights, Apgar scores, head circumferences, chest measurements, developmental milestones, etc. They look in the records for any information about birthparents plus ask the orphanage staff if they have any knowledge of the birthfamily.

What percent of your U.S. adoptions are nonwhite children? Less than 1%

About what percent are children with medical problems? Less than 10%

Do you have a waiting list of prospective parents? Yes.

Is it all right if adopting parents you work with are on waiting lists of other agencies or attorneys? Yes. Once a child is selected, they must agree to withdraw from all other agencies or programs.

Are your adoption fees based on a sliding scale? No.

Do you have an application fee? If yes, what is the amount of the application fee? Yes. $275

What is your homestudy fee (if a flat rate)? $1,150

What is your placement fee? The foreign country fee ranges from $8,500 to $15,000.

If you place children from other countries, please list the estimated *entire* average cost to adoptive parents for each country. For a non-special needs child under the age of 4, adoptive parents are told to expect to pay approximately $24,000 for everything.

My agency: Offers confidential adoptions.

Does your agency provide videotapes of children needing adoption? Yes

Are you an adoptive parent, adopted person, or birthparent? Adoptive parent.

In how many cases with your agency has an adoptive parent been placed with a child but lost the child due to a birthparent challenge? Approximately 25 times, clients have had to select another child because a birth relative came to the orphanage to get the child. If this happens, it usually happens early in the process. We have never had anyone travel to adopt their child be faced with a birthparent trying to take the child. In all cases, the client may immediately select another child. However, some clients may require some healing time before selecting another child. On rare occasions, prospective adoptive parents may be forced to select another child because our pediatricians discover the child may have developed an illness. They may choose to select another child, wait to see if the child improves, or adopt the child with the understanding that they may likely be parents of a special needs child.

Has your agency lost any adoption litigation filed against you by an adoptive parent or birthparent? No. Small World Adoption Foundation has never been sued.

UNIVERSAL ADOPTION SERVICES

Respondent: Pam Schantz Rich, Director
In charge of social services: Pam Schantz Rich
124 E. High St., Jefferson City, MO 65101
(573) 634-3733
E-mail: rich@socketis.net
Year first licensed by state: 1990

Agency provides services for: U.S. adoption; infants; homestudy if parents working with another agency; postplacement services; homestudies and consultation for international adoption.

What states do your adoptive parent clients come from? Missouri.

Services provided adopting parents: Required readings of books and/or articles on adoption; sometimes workshops on adoption.

States/countries your birthparents/adopted children come from: Missouri (unless ICPC).

What was the goal of your agency when first organized? What is the goal of your agency now? To place children who need permanent families with qualified families. Now: Same.

Nonrelative children placed in 1998: 4

Percent of adoptive placements under 6 mos.: 100%

Special expertise of staff: Adoptive parents on staff; licensed social workers; psychologists.

In 1998, what was the average time from when a prospective adoptive parent applied to when he or she received a homestudy? 8 weeks for international, 12 weeks for domestic.

Average time from homestudy to placement of child: 10 mos.

What made you decide to work in the adoption field? Saw need for birthparents to have a place to go besides the public sector ("welfare office").

Agency criteria for adoptive parents you work with: Domestic: aged between 25–40 (may be flexible) married 3 years.

How do you screen adoptive parents? Review application, discussion on phone or workshop.

What kind of medical information do you seek from birthparents? Birthparents complete a 13-page dossier, of which seven pages are biological history and medical.

About what percent are children with medical problems? 10%

Do you have a waiting list of prospective parents? Yes.

Is it all right if adopting parents you work with are on waiting lists of other agencies or attorneys? Yes.

Are your adoption fees based on a sliding scale? No.

Do you have an application fee? If yes, what is the amount of the application fee? Yes. $200

What is your homestudy fee (if a flat rate)? $1,000

What is your placement fee? $10,000, based on some direct costs.

My agency: Offers semi-open adoptions; meetings between birthparents and adoptive parents; birthparents pick adoptive parents from bios/resumes; offers full disclosure of names between birth and adoptive parents.

Does your agency provide videotapes of children needing adoption? No.

In how many cases with your agency has an adoptive parent been placed with a child but lost the child due to a birthparent challenge? 0

Has your agency lost any adoption litigation filed against you by an adoptive parent or birthparent? No.

MONTANA

CATHOLIC SOCIAL SERVICES FOR MONTANA

Respondent: Rosemary Miller, Director
In charge of social services: Rosemary Miller
P.O. Box 907, Helena, MT 59604
(406) 442-4130 • Fax: (406) 442-4192
E-mail: rmiller@mt.net
Year first licensed by state: 1970s

Agency provides services for: International adoption; U.S. adoption; children with special needs; infants; homestudy if parents working with another agency; postplacement services.

What states do your adoptive parent clients come from? Mostly Montana.

Services provided adopting parents: Classes with other prospective parents; required readings of books and/or articles on adoption; parenting discussions.

States/countries your birthparents/adopted children come from: Montana, China, Russia, Romania, India.

What was the goal of your agency when first organized? What is the goal of your agency now? Provide child residential care. Now: Adoption.

Nonrelative children placed in 1998: 65

Percent of adoptive placements under 6 mos.: Most.

Special expertise of staff: Licensed social workers; therapists.

In 1998, what was the average time from when a prospective adoptive parent applied to when he or she received a homestudy? 3–4 mos.

Average time from homestudy to placement of child: 12–18 mos.

What made you decide to work in the adoption field? Interest in children.

Agency criteria for adoptive parents you work with: Married and active in Christian Church.

How do you screen adoptive parents? Homestudy process and training.

How do you screen birthparents? We don't screen out birthparents.

What kind of medical information do you seek from birthparents? As much as we can obtain.

What kind of medical information do you seek on older children? As much as we can obtain.

What percent of your U.S. adoptions are nonwhite children? 2–3%

About what percent are children with medical problems? 5%

About what percent are children with emotional problems? 5% (risk of)

Do you have a waiting list of prospective parents? Yes.

Is it all right if adopting parents you work with are on waiting lists of other agencies or attorneys? Yes at inquiring stage, no if committed to our agency.

Are your adoption fees based on a sliding scale? If yes, what are the sliding scale criteria? Yes. Minimum of $4,000, maximum of $11,000.

Do you have an application fee? If yes, what is the amount of the application fee? Yes. $300

What is your homestudy fee (if a flat rate)? $1,000

What is your placement fee? 12% of gross income.

Do adopting parents also pay fees for medical and hospital expenses for birthmother and baby when they have no insurance? No.

My agency: Offers semi-open adoptions; meetings between birthparents and adoptive parents; birthparents pick adoptive parents from bios/resumes; full disclosure of names between birth and adoptive parents.

Does your agency provide videotapes of children needing adoption? No.

In how many cases with your agency has an adoptive parent been placed with a child but lost the child due to a birthparent challenge? 0

Has your agency lost any adoption litigation filed against you by an adoptive parent or birthparent? No.

NEBRASKA

NEBRASKA CHILDREN'S HOME SOCIETY

Respondent: Katherine G. Hoyt, Adoptive Parent Intake Coordinator
In charge of social services: Carol Krueger
3549 Fonetenelle Blvd., Omaha, NE 68104
(402) 451-0787 • Fax: (402) 451-0300
E-mail: nchomaha@radiks.net
Year first licensed by state: 1893

Agency provides services for: International adoption; children with special needs; infants; postplacement services; birthparent counseling.

What states do your adoptive parent clients come from? We are licensed to place with families in Nebraska only.

Services provided adopting parents: Classes with other prospective parents; group discussions about adoption; parenting discussions.

States/countries your birthparents/adopted children come from: Mostly Nebraska.

What was the goal of your agency when first organized? What is the goal of your agency now? "Caring for Nebraska's homeless, orphaned and dependent children." Now: "...committed to assisting children of all ages find permanent homes that provide safety and loving care. We are dedicated to providing counseling for birthparents, families and children entrusted to our care, as well as life-long support services we provide for all persons we care for through adoption, foster care and emergency shelter services."

Nonrelative children placed in 1998: Over 100

Percent of adoptive placements under 6 mos.: 84%

Special expertise of staff: Adoptive parents on staff; licensed social workers; therapists.

In 1998, what was the average time from when a prospective adoptive parent applied to when he or she received a homestudy? 1 year

What made you decide to work in the adoption field? Had been special needs teacher and high school counselor. Stayed home 20 years with four kids, wanted to return to work. Office not far from home (10 minutes by car).

Agency criteria for adoptive parents you work with: Resident of Nebraska; married at least 3 years.

How do you screen adoptive parents? Meetings; homework; interviews; references; police checks; cps [child protective services] checks; reading.

How do you screen birthparents? Meetings; homework; reading.

What kind of medical information do you seek from birthparents? As much as we can get from them and their extended families.

What kind of medical information do you seek on older children? Everything we can.

What percent of your U.S. adoptions are nonwhite children? 37%

About what percent are children with medical problems? 5%

About what percent are children with emotional problems? 5%

Is it all right if adopting parents you work with are on waiting lists of other agencies or attorneys? No.

Are your adoption fees based on a sliding scale? No. We have no fees.

Do you have an application fee? No.

What is your homestudy fee (if a flat rate)? 0

What is your placement fee? 0

My agency: Offers confidential adoptions; semi-open adoptions; meetings between birthparents and adoptive parents; birthparents pick adoptive parents from bios/resumes; full disclosure of names between birth and adoptive parents.

Does your agency provide videotapes of children needing adoption? No.

In how many cases with your agency has an adoptive parent been placed with a child but lost the child due to a birthparent challenge? 0

Has your agency lost any adoption litigation filed against you by an adoptive parent or birthparent? No.

Is there anything I have not asked you that is important? We have no fees but are supported by our adoptive families, not state or local monies, United Way, etc.

NEW HAMPSHIRE

NEW HOPE CHRISTIAN SERVICES

Respondent: Elizabeth Mexcur, Adoption Counselor
In charge of social services: Joyce Watts, MSW
210 Silk Form Rd., Concord, OH 03301
(603) 225-0992 • Fax: (603) 225-7400
Year first licensed by state: 1996

Agency provides services for: International adoption; children with special needs; infants.

What states do your adoptive parent clients come from? All states and Canada.

Services provided adopting parents: Required readings of books and/or articles on adoption; workshops; one-on-one counseling; recommend support groups.

States/countries your birthparents/adopted children come from: Russia, Romania, Ukraine.

What was the goal of your agency when first organized? What is the goal of your agency now? To place orphaned children into stable and loving homes. Now: Same, and relief programs.

Nonrelative children placed in 1998: 52

Special expertise of staff: Adoptive parents on staff; licensed social workers; adoption counselor.

In 1998, what was the average time from when a prospective adoptive parent applied to when he or she received a homestudy? 3–4 mos. for completion.

Average time from homestudy to placement of child: From the time we receive the application to the time they receive a child is 9–12 mos.

Agency criteria for adoptive parents you work with: It depends on the country they are interested in; the age of the parents is the biggest deal.

How do you screen adoptive parents? Through our application process.

What kind of medical information do you seek from birthparents? We use international clinics.

What kind of medical information do you seek on older children? International clinics.

Do you have a waiting list of prospective parents? No.

Is it all right if adopting parents you work with are on waiting lists of other agencies or attorneys? Yes.

Are your adoption fees based on a sliding scale? If yes, what are the sliding scale criteria? Yes. We give a discount for people adopting older children.

Do you have an application fee? If yes, what is the amount of the application fee? Yes. $150

What is your homestudy fee (if a flat rate)? $100 original homestudy.

What is your placement fee? Varies from country to country.

Do adopting parents also pay fees for medical and hospital expenses for birth-mother and baby when they have no insurance? No.

If international adoption, what are average travel expenses? $2,500–3,500

If you place children from other countries, please list the estimated *entire* average cost to adoptive parents for each country. Russia, $20,000; Romania, $17,000; Ukraine, $14,000; plus travel expenses estimated at $2,500–3,500.

My agency: Offers confidential adoptions.

Does your agency provide videotapes of children needing adoption? Yes.

Are you an adoptive parent, adopted person, or birthparent? Adopted person.

In how many cases with your agency has an adoptive parent been placed with a child but lost the child due to a birthparent challenge? 0

Has your agency lost any adoption litigation filed against you by an adoptive parent or birthparent? No.

NEW JERSEY

CHILDREN'S HOME SOCIETY

Respondent: Carolyn Bacher, Director of Operations
In charge of social services: Carolyn Bacher
929 Parkside Ave., Trenton, NJ 08618
(609) 695-6274 • Fax: (609) 394-5769
E-mail: cabacher@aol.com • www.princetonol.com/chsofnj
Year first licensed by state: 1984

Agency provides services for: International adoption; U.S. adoption; children with special needs; infants; homestudy if parents working with another agency; postplacement services.

What states do your adoptive parent clients come from? New Jersey, Pennsylvania.

Services provided adopting parents: Required readings of books and/or articles on adoption; group discussions about adoption; parenting discussions; support group for parents adopting from Bulgaria.

States/countries your birthparents/adopted children come from: New Jersey, Pennsylvania, Bulgaria, Russia, China.

What was the goal of your agency when first organized? What is the goal of your agency now? "Homes for the Homeless" orphanage care, foster care, adoption. Now: To provide at-risk children and their families with a range of services that empower them to achieve their potential.

Special expertise of staff: Adoptive parents on staff; licensed social workers; therapists; physician; attorney.

In 1998, what was the average time from when a prospective adoptive parent applied to when he or she received a homestudy? Complete homestudy 4 mos.

Average time from homestudy to placement of child: 6 mos.

What made you decide to work in the adoption field? We look for stable, loving, flexible families.

Agency criteria for adoptive parents you work with: No restrictions for hard-to-place children. Domestic, healthy Caucasian babies: no more than one child in home, finished with fertility work, under 40; international: rules of the country.

How do you screen birthparents? We accept all birthparents.

What kind of medical information do you seek from birthparents? New Jersey requires a 21-page family medical form.

What kind of medical information do you seek on older children? All medical and developmental information available.

What percent of your U.S. adoptions are nonwhite children? 59%

About what percent are children with medical problems? 29%

Do you have a waiting list of prospective parents? Yes.

Is it all right if adopting parents you work with are on waiting lists of other agencies or attorneys? No.

Are your adoption fees based on a sliding scale? If yes, what are the sliding scale criteria? Yes. Healthy domestic, 12% of annual income; hard-to-place, $350–4,000 based on income.

Do you have an application fee? If yes, what is the amount of the application fee? Yes. $800 (half refundable)

What is your homestudy fee (if a flat rate)? $800

What is your placement fee? None.

Do adopting parents also pay fees for medical and hospital expenses for birthmother and baby when they have no insurance? No.

If international adoption, what are average travel expenses? $2,000

If you place children from other countries, please list the estimated *entire* average cost to adoptive parents for each country. Bulgaria, $19,000; China, $21,000; Russia, $24,000.

My agency: Offers confidential adoptions; semi-open adoptions; meetings between birthparents and adoptive parents; birthparents pick adoptive parents from bios/resumes.

Does your agency provide videotapes of children needing adoption? Yes.

Are you an adoptive parent, adopted person, or birthparent? Adoptive parent.

In how many cases with your agency has an adoptive parent been placed with a child but lost the child due to a birthparent challenge? 0

Has your agency lost any adoption litigation filed against you by an adoptive parent or birthparent? No.

DOWNEY SIDE

Respondent: Carole Trewin, Area Director
In charge of social services: Carole Trewin
146 U.S. Route 130, Bordentown, NJ 08505
(609) 291-2784 • Fax: (609) 291-2787
Year first licensed by state: 1989

Agency provides services for: U.S. adoption; children with special needs; postplacement services.

What states do your adoptive parent clients come from? New Jersey.

Services provided adopting parents: Classes with other prospective parents; required readings of books and/or articles on adoption; group discussions about adoption; parenting discussions; eight-week parent preparation class called "Exploring Adoption;" support groups; newsletters.

States/countries your birthparents/adopted children come from: All states.

What was the goal of your agency when first organized? What is the goal of your agency now? Recruiting families for youth 7–17 years old who need permanent families. Essentially, to "prevent homelessness through relationship." Now: Same.

Nonrelative children placed in 1998: 60

Percent of adoptive placements under 6 mos.: 0%

Special expertise of staff: Adoptive parents on staff; licensed social workers.

In 1998, what was the average time from when a prospective adoptive parent applied to when he or she received a homestudy? 3 mos.

Average time from homestudy to placement of child: 6–9 mos.

What made you decide to work in the adoption field? Felt strongly that families should be committed to children and that families needed assistance to prevent adoption disruptions.

Agency criteria for adoptive parents you work with: We don't have any limits and we don't discriminate.

How do you screen adoptive parents? By CARI checks; federal and state fingerprint check; and our required eight-week parent preparation class, which allows parents an opportunity to explore their decision to adopt.

What kind of medical information do you seek on older children? All medical records that are available.

What percent of your U.S. adoptions are nonwhite children? 60%

About what percent are children with medical problems? 10%

About what percent are children with emotional problems? 90%

Do you have a waiting list of prospective parents? Yes.

Is it all right if adopting parents you work with are on waiting lists of other agencies or attorneys? No.

Are your adoption fees based on a sliding scale? No.

Do you have an application fee? If yes, what is the amount of the application fee? Yes. $75 per couple and $50 per individual.

What is your homestudy fee (if a flat rate)? 0

What is your placement fee? A negotiated contract with the child's placing agency.

Do adopting parents also pay fees for medical and hospital expenses for birthmother and baby when they have no insurance? No.

My agency: Offers confidential adoptions. Birthparents' rights are terminated legally before placement of a child.

Does your agency provide videotapes of children needing adoption? Yes.

Has your agency lost any adoption litigation filed against you by an adoptive parent or birthparent? No.

Is there anything I have not asked you that is important? Including our office in New Jersey, there are ten Downey Side agencies, in Missouri, Minnesota (2), Massachusetts, Connecticut, and New York (4).

GOLDEN CRADLE ADOPTION SERVICES

Respondent: Jared N. Rolshy, Executive Director
In charge of social services: Jared N. Rolshy
1050 Kings Highway N. #201, Cherry Hill, NJ 08034
(609) 667-2229 • Fax: (609) 667-5437
E-mail: gcadopt@erols.com • www.goldencradle.org
Year first licensed by state: 1980

Agency provides services for: International adoption; U.S. adoption; infants; homestudy if parents working with another agency; postplacement services.

What states do your adoptive parent clients come from? All states.

Services provided adopting parents: Classes with other prospective parents; group discussions about adoption; parenting discussions.

States/countries your birthparents/adopted children come from: All states, Albania, Ukraine, Russia, China.

What was the goal of your agency when first organized? What is the goal of your agency now? Provide birthmothers/fathers with a choice regarding unplanned pregnancy. Provide homes for children whose parents choose adoption. Provide children in need of permanent homes, adoptive families. Now: Same.

Nonrelative children placed in 1998: 35

Percent of adoptive placements under 6 mos.: 100%

Special expertise of staff: Adoptive parents on staff; licensed social workers; birthmothers.

In 1998, what was the average time from when a prospective adoptive parent applied to when he or she received a homestudy? 2 weeks–3 mos., depending on speed that client desires. Also depends on time it takes to get state and federal clearances.

Average time from homestudy to placement of child: 2 weeks–2 years; depends on program.

Agency criteria for adoptive parents you work with: No arbitrary eligibility standards.

How do you screen adoptive parents? Not screen, prepare. Homestudy, education sessions.

How do you screen birthparents? Not screen, prepare. Options counseling, medical information.

What kind of medical information do you seek from birthparents? Full record as available: mother's prenatal records, labor and delivery, state of New Jersey medical history form.

What kind of medical information do you seek on older children? Full record as available.

What percent of your U.S. adoptions are nonwhite children? 10–15%

Do you have a waiting list of prospective parents? No.

Is it all right if adopting parents you work with are on waiting lists of other agencies or attorneys? Yes.

Are your adoption fees based on a sliding scale? No.

Do you have an application fee? If yes, what is the amount of the application fee? Yes. $200

What is your homestudy fee (if a flat rate)? $800

What is your placement fee? Depends on program. $6,500–23,300

Do adopting parents also pay fees for medical and hospital expenses for birthmother and baby when they have no insurance? If yes, what is the average fee paid? Yes. $3,000–6,000

If international adoption, what are average travel expenses? Depends on country.

If you place children from other countries, please list the estimated *entire* average cost to adoptive parents for each country. International adoptions range from $22,000–30,000 including all costs, expenses, travel, etc.

My agency: Offers confidential adoptions; semi-open adoptions; meetings between birthparents and adoptive parents; birthparents pick adoptive parents from bios/resumes.

Does your agency provide videotapes of children needing adoption? Yes, international only.

In how many cases with your agency has an adoptive parent been placed with a child but lost the child due to a birthparent challenge? None in New Jersey since 1983.

Has your agency lost any adoption litigation filed against you by an adoptive parent or birthparent? No.

GROWING FAMILIES, INC. ADOPTION AGENCY

Respondent: Rose M. Santiago-Averbach, LCSW, Executive Director
In charge of social services: Rose M. Santiago-Averbach and Laura M. Krug, LCSW
178 South St., Freehold, NJ 07728
(732) 431-4330 • Fax: (732) 431-3884
E-mail: rosa53@aol.com
Year first licensed by state: 1989

Agency provides services for: International adoption; U.S. adoption; infants; homestudy if parents working with another agency; postplacement services; adoption complaint investigations; stepparent adoptions; counseling for adoptive families and children.

What states do your adoptive parent clients come from? New Jersey, Pennsylvania, New York.

Services provided adopting parents: Classes with other prospective parents; group discussions about adoption; parenting discussions.

States/countries your birthparents/adopted children come from: Guatemala, Russia, Mexico.

What was the goal of your agency when first organized? What is the goal of your agency now? Our primary goal was and is to match up available children with parents that truly want to adopt a child. Every child deserves a family. Now: Openness is very important. All documentation on the child has to be accurate, to ensure that the child gets the best parents available, that the child is loved, and that the adoptive family has received the best of their dreams. It's important that all members of the triad be happy.

Nonrelative children placed in 1998: 25

Percent of adoptive placements under 6 mos.: 100%

Special expertise of staff: Licensed social workers; therapists; attorney.

In 1998, what was the average time from when a prospective adoptive parent applied to when he or she received a homestudy? 1 week

Average time from homestudy to placement of child: 6 mos.

What made you decide to work in the adoption field? I originate from an adoptive family, my siblings are adopted, and my family is adopted.

Agency criteria for adoptive parents you work with: We are open. There are limited requirements. We must see a genuine want to parent a child. International children need homes and families that will love them forever.

How do you screen adoptive parents? They must qualify with state and federal fingerprints, their income, their desire to adopt. Their acceptance of a different culture and their openness regarding adoption.

How do you screen birthparents? We do not accept birthmothers abusing drugs or alcohol. We establish a relationship with the birthparents. We inform them of ways to keep their children before they are accepted as viable parents.

What kind of medical information do you seek from birthparents? DYFS-regulated information and additional information.

What kind of medical information do you seek on older children? We have to have neurological and psychological reports.

What percent of your U.S. adoptions are nonwhite children? Almost all are Hispanic-white.

Do you have a waiting list of prospective parents? No.

Is it all right if adopting parents you work with are on waiting lists of other agencies or attorneys? Yes, domestic. No, international.

Are your adoption fees based on a sliding scale? No.

Do you have an application fee? If yes, what is the amount of the application fee? Yes. $150

What is your homestudy fee (if a flat rate)? $600

What is your placement fee? Domestic, $7,000–10,000; identified adoption, $12,000; international, $3,000–4,000, with homestudy included.

Do adopting parents also pay fees for medical and hospital expenses for birthmother and baby when they have no insurance? If yes, what is the average fee paid? Yes. $5,000

If applicable, what is the average document language translation fee? $300 (Mexico). Guatemala, included in fees.

If international adoption, what are average travel expenses? Guatemala, approximately $800; Russia, approximately $2,800; Mexico, approximately $2,000.

If you place children from other countries, please list the estimated *entire* average cost to adoptive parents for each country. $10,000 (attorney fee); agency fee $3,500–4,000, including homestudy. Guatemala, $14,000 (attorney fee two attorneys); Mexico, $15,000 (birthmother and attorney fee) plus agency fee, $3,500; Russia, $9,000 (international fee), agency fee, $3,000.

My agency: Offers confidential adoptions; semi-open adoptions; meetings between birthparents and adoptive parents; birthparents pick adoptive parents from bios/resumes; full disclosure of names between birth and adoptive parents.

Does your agency provide videotapes of children needing adoption? Yes.

Are you an adoptive parent, adopted person, or birthparent? Adoptive parent.

In how many cases with your agency has an adoptive parent been placed with a child but lost the child due to a birthparent challenge? Never.

Has your agency lost any adoption litigation filed against you by an adoptive parent or birthparent? No.

REACHING OUT THRU INTERNATIONAL ADOPTION, INC.

Respondent: Jeannene Smith, Founder
In charge of social services: Leslie Breslau, Casework Supervisor
312 S. Lincoln Ave., Cherry Hill, NJ 08002
(609) 321-0777 • Fax: (609) 321-0809
E-mail: reachoutnj@aol.com
Year first licensed by state: 1998

Agency provides services for: International adoption; children with special needs; infants; homestudy if parents working with another agency; postplacement services.

What states do your adoptive parent clients come from? All states.

Services provided adopting parents: Classes with other prospective parents; group discussions about adoption; parenting discussions.

States/countries your birthparents/adopted children come from: China, Russia, Guatemala, Vietnam, Moldova, India.

What was the goal of your agency when first organized? What is the goal of your agency now? Child placement and humanitarian aid. Now: Same.

Nonrelative children placed in 1998: 92

Percent of adoptive placements under 6 mos.: 20%

Special expertise of staff: Adoptive parents on staff; licensed social workers; physician.

In 1998, what was the average time from when a prospective adoptive parent applied to when he or she received a homestudy? 10–12 weeks

Average time from homestudy to placement of child: 2–10 mos. depending on country.

What made you decide to work in the adoption field? Personal adoption experience.

Agency criteria for adoptive parents you work with: Flexible, depending on country requirements.

How do you screen adoptive parents? By state or country requirements and homestudy process.

What kind of medical information do you seek on older children? Varies by country.

About what percent are children with medical problems? 5%

Do you have a waiting list of prospective parents? No.

Is it all right if adopting parents you work with are on waiting lists of other agencies or attorneys? No.

Are your adoption fees based on a sliding scale? No.

Do you have an application fee? If yes, what is the amount of the application fee? Yes. $500

What is your homestudy fee (if a flat rate)? $800

What is your placement fee? $4,200–4,900 including application fee.

If applicable, what is the average document language translation fee? Varies by country.

If international adoption, what are average travel expenses? Varies by country.

If you place children from other countries, please list the estimated *entire* average cost to adoptive parents for each country. China, $14,810, including all travel costs; Russia, $16,200–17,605, including travel, meals, and lodging, depending on length of stay; Guatemala, $19,350, including travel, lodging, and meals; Vietnam, $20,175, including travel, lodging, and meals.

My agency: Offers confidential adoptions; meetings between birthparents and adoptive parents in Guatemala only.

Does your agency provide videotapes of children needing adoption? Yes, in some cases.

Are you an adoptive parent, adopted person, or birthparent? Adoptive parent.

In how many cases with your agency has an adoptive parent been placed with a child but lost the child due to a birthparent challenge? 0

Has your agency lost any adoption litigation filed against you by an adoptive parent or birthparent? No. Never any complaints or litigation filed.

NEW MEXICO

LA FAMILIA, INC.

Respondent: Megan Walsh, Adoption Coordinator
In charge of social services: Beverly Nomberg, Executive Director
707 Broadway SE #103, Albuquerque, NM 87102
(505) 766-9361 • Fax: (505) 766-9157
Year first licensed by state: 1989

Agency provides services for: International adoption; U.S. adoption; children with special needs; infants; homestudy if parents working with another agency; postplacement services.

What states do your adoptive parent clients come from? All states.

Services provided adopting parents: Classes with other prospective parents; required readings of books and/or articles on adoption; group discussions about adoption; parenting discussions; support group.

States/countries your birthparents/adopted children come from: All states, China, Russia, Thailand.

What was the goal of your agency when first organized? What is the goal of your agency now? Adoption. Now: Support services to all people: treatment foster care, adoption, senior services, outpatient counseling.

Nonrelative children placed in 1998: 22

Percent of adoptive placements under 6 mos.: 90%

Special expertise of staff: Adoptive parents on staff; licensed social workers; psychologists; therapists; attorney.

In 1998, what was the average time from when a prospective adoptive parent applied to when he or she received a homestudy? 2 mos.

Average time from homestudy to placement of child: 6 mos.–1 year

What made you decide to work in the adoption field? I enjoy helping people build families. I also enjoy working with birthfamilies and helping them preserve their self-esteem.

How do you screen adoptive parents? CYFD abuse and neglect checks; FBI; state and city fingerprint checks; medical screen.

What kind of medical information do you seek on older children? Developmental evaluations.

What percent of your U.S. adoptions are nonwhite children? 60%

About what percent are children with medical problems? 5%

About what percent are children with emotional problems? 10%

Do you have a waiting list of prospective parents? No.

Is it all right if adopting parents you work with are on waiting lists of other agencies or attorneys? Yes.

Are your adoption fees based on a sliding scale? No.

Do you have an application fee? If yes, what is the amount of the application fee? Yes. $100

What is your homestudy fee (if a flat rate)? $850

What is your placement fee? $3,500

Do adopting parents also pay fees for medical and hospital expenses for birthmother and baby when they have no insurance? If yes, what is the average fee paid? Yes. $4,000

My agency: Offers confidential adoptions; semi-open adoptions; meetings between birthparents and adoptive parents; birthparents pick adoptive parents from bios/resumes; full disclosure of names between birth and adoptive parents.

In how many cases with your agency has an adoptive parent been placed with a child but lost the child due to a birthparent challenge? 4

Has your agency lost any adoption litigation filed against you by an adoptive parent or birthparent? No.

RAINBOW HOUSE INTERNATIONAL

Respondent: Donna Clauss, Executive Director
In charge of social services: Rosalind Ogowa
19676 Hwy. 85, Belen, NM 87002
(505) 861-1234 • Fax: (505) 864-8420
E-mail: donna@rhi.org • www.rhi.org
Year first licensed by state: 1984

Agency provides services for: International adoption; U.S. adoption; children with special needs; infants; homestudy if parents working with another agency; postplacement services; postlegal counseling, preplacement education.

What states do your adoptive parent clients come from? All states.

Services provided adopting parents: Classes with other prospective parents; required readings of books and/or articles on adoption; group discussions about adoption; parenting discussions; postlegal counseling and education.

States/countries your birthparents/adopted children come from: All states, Korea, Vietnam, China, Thailand, India, Russia, Romania, Guatemala, Ecuador.

What was the goal of your agency when first organized? What is the goal of your agency now? To assist needy children throughout the world through aid, assistance, and adoption. Now: Same.

Nonrelative children placed in 1998: 100+

Special expertise of staff: Adoptive parents on staff; licensed social workers; psychologists; therapists.

In 1998, what was the average time from when a prospective adoptive parent applied to when he or she received a homestudy? Less than 6 mos.

Average time from homestudy to placement of child: Less than 4 mos.

What made you decide to work in the adoption field? I have done so all my life (since early childhood).

Agency criteria for adoptive parents you work with: Varies.

How do you screen adoptive parents? Through the use of good information that helps them to assess their candidacy. Educate them and provide relevant, up-to-date information.

What kind of medical information do you seek from birthparents? We have a comprehensive questionnaire.

What kind of medical information do you seek on older children? Complete.

What percent of your U.S. adoptions are nonwhite children? 99%

Do you have a waiting list of prospective parents? No.

Is it all right if adopting parents you work with are on waiting lists of other agencies or attorneys? No.

Are your adoption fees based on a sliding scale? No.

Do you have an application fee? If yes, what is the amount of the application fee? Yes. $150

What is your homestudy fee (if a flat rate)? $800

What is your placement fee? Varies by country.

Do adopting parents also pay fees for medical and hospital expenses for birth-mother and baby when they have no insurance? If yes, what is the average fee paid? Yes. Less than $7,000. We do very few domestic adoptions.

If international adoption, what are average travel expenses? Less than $7,000. Depends whether you are departing from East Coast or West Coast.

If you place children from other countries, please list the estimated *entire* average cost to adoptive parents for each country. Russia, $10,500; Korea, $12,500 (includes transportation); India, $13,500 (includes transportation); China, $9,500.

My agency: Offers confidential adoptions; semi-open adoptions; meetings between birthparents and adoptive parents; birthparents pick adoptive parents from bios/resumes.

Does your agency provide videotapes of children needing adoption? Yes.

Are you an adoptive parent, adopted person, or birthparent? Adoptive parent.

In how many cases with your agency has an adoptive parent been placed with a child but lost the child due to a birthparent challenge? 0

Has your agency lost any adoption litigation filed against you by an adoptive parent or birthparent? No.

TRIAD ADOPTION AND COUNSELING SERVICES, INC.

Respondent: Vonda C. Cheshire, Administrative Director
In charge of social services: Barbara Gatewood, MA, LPC
2811 Indian School Rd. NE, Albuquerque, NM 87106
(505) 266-0456 • Fax: (505) 255-6924
www.wrldcom.com/triad
Year first licensed by state: 1986

Agency provides services for: International adoption; U.S. adoption; children with special needs; infants; homestudy if parents working with another agency; postplacement services.

What states do your adoptive parent clients come from? All states except New York.

Services provided adopting parents: Classes with other prospective parents; required readings of books and/or articles on adoption; networking program with other adoptive parents.

States/countries your birthparents/adopted children come from: New Mexico.

What was the goal of your agency when first organized? What is the goal of your agency now? To facilitate open adoption in the state of New Mexico. Now: To continue to offer this service with supporting educational and community services.

Nonrelative children placed in 1998: 41

Percent of adoptive placements under 6 mos.: 90%

Special expertise of staff: Adoptive parents on staff; licensed counselors; adoptees.

In 1998, what was the average time from when a prospective adoptive parent applied to when he or she received a homestudy? 8–10 weeks

Average time from homestudy to placement of child: 1 week–18 mos.

What made you decide to work in the adoption field? Foster parenting.

Agency criteria for adoptive parents you work with: Must be of childbearing age; married at least 2 years; have a spiritual plan for the child; comfortable with and value open adoption; willing to travel to New Mexico.

How do you screen adoptive parents? Preplacement study; update/addendum of pre-placement study; attendance at one-day orientation; completion of required reading; completion of personal album for presentation to birthparents.

How do you screen birthparents? A desire to do what is in children's best interest and willingness to participate in placement plan with honesty and candor.

What kind of medical information do you seek from birthparents? Request their complete social medical form. Request medical records and photograph(s) of birthparents.

What percent of your U.S. adoptions are nonwhite children? Of 41 placements: 7 Anglo, 8 Hispanic, 3 biracial (African-American), 23 Anglo/Hispanic.

Do you have a waiting list of prospective parents? Yes.

Is it all right if adopting parents you work with are on waiting lists of other agencies or attorneys? Yes.

Are your adoption fees based on a sliding scale? No.

Do you have an application fee? If yes, what is the amount of the application fee? Yes. $65 fee to attend orientation class.

What is your homestudy fee (if a flat rate)? $950

What is your placement fee? $7,500

Do adopting parents also pay fees for medical and hospital expenses for birthmother and baby when they have no insurance? If yes, what is the average fee paid? Yes. $2,500 of $7,500 placement fee is applied to medical expenses; adoptive family is billed for the balance, $1,600–1,800.

My agency: Offers confidential adoptions; semi-open adoptions; meetings between birthparents and adoptive parents; birthparents pick adoptive parents from bios/resumes; full disclosure of names between birth and adoptive parents.

Does your agency provide videotapes of children needing adoption? No.

Are you an adoptive parent, adopted person, or birthparent? Adoptive parent.

In how many cases with your agency has an adoptive parent been placed with a child but lost the child due to a birthparent challenge? 0 as a result of legal challenge; approximately two times a year an infant will be placed immediately from hospital and birthmother will request child be returned within 48 hours.

Has your agency lost any adoption litigation filed against you by an adoptive parent or birthparent? No.

NEW YORK

COMMUNITY MATERNITY SERVICES

Respondent: Margaret Elliott, Associate Executive Director, Children's Services
27 N. Main Ave., Albany, NY 12203
(518) 482-8836 • Fax: (518) 482-5805
Year first licensed by state: 1929

Agency provides services for: International adoption; U.S. adoption; children with special needs; infants; postplacement services.

What states do your adoptive parent clients come from? New York.

Services provided adopting parents: Classes with other prospective parents; required readings of books and/or articles on adoption; group discussions about adoption; parenting discussions; presentation panels by birth, adoptive, and foster parents.

States/countries your birthparents/adopted children come from: New York.

What was the goal of your agency when first organized? What is the goal of your agency now? Multifaceted—to serve people in need. Now: Same.

Nonrelative children placed in 1998: 10

Percent of adoptive placements under 6 mos.: 75%

Special expertise of staff: Licensed social workers.

In 1998, what was the average time from when a prospective adoptive parent applied to when he or she received a homestudy? 18 mos.

Average time from homestudy to placement of child: 12 mos.

What made you decide to work in the adoption field? Interest in children; protecting and providing for their needs of safety and stability.

Agency criteria for adoptive parents you work with: CMS works with adoptive parents age 21and older of all backgrounds and family compositions.

How do you screen adoptive parents? Group process; individual family consultations; references; medical clearances; state central registry for child abuse clearance; fingerprinting.

How do you screen birthparents? Individual and family counseling.

What kind of medical information do you seek on older children? Any and all current medical information available, including well-child care, immunizations, and applicable special assessments.

What percent of your U.S. adoptions are nonwhite children? 30%

About what percent are children with medical problems? 20%

About what percent are children with emotional problems? 10%

Do you have a waiting list of prospective parents? Yes.

Is it all right if adopting parents you work with are on waiting lists of other agencies or attorneys? No.

Are your adoption fees based on a sliding scale? If yes, what are the sliding scale criteria? Yes. Domestic, 12% of income; foreign, 7% of income to a maximum of $3,000 (do not provide placement).

Do you have an application fee? If yes, what is the amount of the application fee? Yes. Preregistration fee, $75; domestic, $250 registration fee; foreign, $50 registration fee.

My agency: Offers semi-open adoptions; meetings between birthparents and adoptive parents; birthparents pick adoptive parents from bios/resumes; full disclosure of names between birth and adoptive parents.

Does your agency provide videotapes of children needing adoption? No.

In how many cases with your agency has an adoptive parent been placed with a child but lost the child due to a birthparent challenge? 0

Has your agency lost any adoption litigation filed against you by an adoptive parent or birthparent? No.

FAMILY CONNECTIONS, INC.

Respondent: Anita F. Stevens, Director
156 Port Watson St., P.O. Box 5555, Cortland, NY 13045
(607) 756-6574 • Fax: (607) 756-0373
E-mail: family@clarityconnect.com
Year first licensed by state: 1994

Agency provides services for: International adoption; U.S. adoption; children with special needs; infants; homestudy if parents working with another agency; postplacement services.

What states do your adoptive parent clients come from? New York, Pennsylvania (consultation), Texas, California. Mostly New York.

Services provided adopting parents: Classes with other prospective parents; parenting discussions.

States/countries your birthparents/adopted children come from: New York. Network with other agencies all over the United States.

What was the goal of your agency when first organized? What is the goal of your agency now? 1. To provide help and assistance to women experiencing an unplanned pregnancy. 2. To provide adoption services to children, birthparents, and adoptive parents. Now: Same except that we have grown to be able to maximize opportunities and allow adoptive parents to change their goals and still remain with the agency. For example, a family can switch from domestic to international adoption.

Nonrelative children placed in 1998: 19, not including international adoptions.

Percent of adoptive placements under 6 mos.: 90%

Special expertise of staff: Adoptive parents on staff; licensed social workers.

In 1998, what was the average time from when a prospective adoptive parent applied to when he or she received a homestudy? 2–3 mos., depending on turn-around of child abuse clearance.

Average time from homestudy to placement of child: I don't like averages. The longest a person currently has waited is 11–12 mos.

What made you decide to work in the adoption field? Pro-life political view led me to work with women dealing with unplanned pregnancy. When they decided to place infants, I acquired a wonderful passion to help birthmothers surrender with dignity and support. We assist birthparents to parent or choose adoption, creating an atmosphere that empowers them to choose what is best for them.

Agency criteria for adoptive parents you work with: New York state law does not allow agencies to discriminate. We have no criteria other than those imposed by the New York state law.

How do you screen adoptive parents? Through the homestudy process, using child abuse clearance, references, criminal clearance, education, verifying documents such as birth certificates, face-to-face meetings, and visits to home.

How do you screen birthparents? Face-to-face meeting; collect medical and social information; home visits.

What kind of medical information do you seek from birthparents? As much as they know or I can ask them. Medical form is about 10 pages long. Hospital medical records also required.

What kind of medical information do you seek on older children? Same as above plus medical records.

What percent of your U.S. adoptions are nonwhite children? 40–50%. 20–25% of adoptive parents are nonwhite.

About what percent are children with medical problems? About 10%

About what percent are children with emotional problems? About 10%

Do you have a waiting list of prospective parents? No.

Is it all right if adopting parents you work with are on waiting lists of other agencies or attorneys? Yes. The more opportunities they create for themselves, the better.

Are your adoption fees based on a sliding scale? No.

Do you have an application fee? If yes, what is the amount of the application fee? Yes. $500

What is your homestudy fee (if a flat rate)? $750 for domestic; $900 for foreign.

What is your placement fee? $6,500

Do adopting parents also pay fees for medical and hospital expenses for birthmother and baby when they have no insurance? Yes, but very rarely.

If international adoption, what are average travel expenses? Depends on country.

If you place children from other countries, please list the estimated *entire* average cost to adoptive parents for each country. Depends on age of children and country. Most expensive is $23,000, least expensive is $11,000–13,000.

My agency: Offers confidential adoptions; semi-open adoptions; meetings between birthparents and adoptive parents; birthparents pick adoptive parents from bios/resumes; full disclosure of names between birth and adoptive parents.

Does your agency provide videotapes of children needing adoption? No.

In how many cases with your agency has an adoptive parent been placed with a child but lost the child due to a birthparent challenge? 2 in 4 years. In New York state, there is usually a 30-day legal risk period. Usually birthparents sign a surrender within 30 days.

Has your agency lost any adoption litigation filed against you by an adoptive parent or birthparent? No.

HAPPY FAMILIES INFORMATION CENTER

Respondent: Judy Schwartz, Adoption Social Worker
In charge of social services: Judy Schwartz
3 Stone St., Coldspring, NY 10516
(914) 265-9272 • Fax: (914) 265-4731
E-mail: hfickids@aol.com • www.happyfamilies.org
Year first licensed by state: 1992

Agency provides services for: International adoption; children with special needs (international); infants; postplacement services.

What states do your adoptive parent clients come from? All states.

Services provided adopting parents: Classes with other prospective parents; required readings of books and/or articles on adoption; group discussions about adoption; parenting discussions; cultural seminar; older children adoption groups.

States/countries your birthparents/adopted children come from: Russia and Ukraine.

What was the goal of your agency when first organized? What is the goal of your agency now? To find loving homes for Russian orphans. At first this was only [children with] severe medical problems, special needs. Now healthy children are available. Now: To bring all available orphans to the United States to be placed with loving parents.

Nonrelative children placed in 1998: 70

Percent of adoptive placements under 6 mos.: 5%

Special expertise of staff: Adoptive parents on staff; licensed social workers. Our executive director is a licensed Russian psychiatrist.

In 1998, what was the average time from when a prospective adoptive parent applied to when he or she received a homestudy? 1 mo.

Average time from homestudy to placement of child: 6–9 mos.

What made you decide to work in the adoption field? I have always worked in child welfare as a social worker and my four children are adopted, one domestic, three Russian.

Agency criteria for adoptive parents you work with: Parents need to be over 18, no other limitations.

How do you screen adoptive parents? Interview, application, homestudy.

What kind of medical information do you seek from birthparents? We get whatever medical report is available.

What kind of medical information do you seek on older children? As much as is available.

Do you have a waiting list of prospective parents? No.

Is it all right if adopting parents you work with are on waiting lists of other agencies or attorneys? Yes.

Are your adoption fees based on a sliding scale? No.

Do you have an application fee? If yes, what is the amount of the application fee? Yes. $150

What is your homestudy fee (if a flat rate)? $1,000

What is your placement fee? $7,500

If applicable, what is the average document language translation fee? $300 per dossier.

If international adoption, what are average travel expenses? $1,000

If you place children from other countries, please list the estimated *entire* average cost to adoptive parents for each country. $15,000–19,000

My agency: Offers confidential adoptions.

Does your agency provide videotapes of children needing adoption? Yes.

Are you an adoptive parent, adopted person, or birthparent? Adoptive parent.

In how many cases with your agency has an adoptive parent been placed with a child but lost the child due to a birthparent challenge? 0

Has your agency lost any adoption litigation filed against you by an adoptive parent or birthparent? No.

NEW LIFE ADOPTION AGENCY, INC.

Respondent: Leah Murphy, Adoption Coordinator
In charge of social services: Cynthia Adamowsky, MSW, CSW, Executive Director
430 E. Genesee St., Suite 301, Syracuse, NY 13202
(315) 422-7300 • Fax: (315) 475-7727
E-mail: newlife@newlifeadoption.org • www.newlifeadoption.org
Year first licensed by state: 1986

Agency provides services for: International adoption; U.S. adoption; infants; homestudy if parents working with another agency; postplacement services.

What states do your adoptive parent clients come from? All states.

Services provided adopting parents: Classes with other prospective parents; group discussions about adoption; parenting discussions, if desired; orientation meetings; travel and country, culture classes; postplacement services.

States/countries your birthparents/adopted children come from: All states.

What is the goal of your agency now? The New Life philosophy is based on the premise that each child is entitled to a life in a nurturing family environment. New Life works with families sincerely committed to parenting in that kind of environment. Policies and screening practices are designed to include, rather than exclude, applicants from the adoption process. Each family is considered on an individual basis.

Nonrelative children placed in 1998: 100+

Special expertise of staff: Adoptive parents on staff; licensed social workers; attorney.

In 1998, what was the average time from when a prospective adoptive parent applied to when he or she received a homestudy? 2 mos.

Average time from homestudy to placement of child: Varies; international less than 18 mos.

Agency criteria for adoptive parents you work with: None; each case is considered on an individual basis.

How do you screen adoptive parents? Through application, homestudy process, fingerprinting, criminal and child abuse clearances.

How do you screen birthparents? Background information sheets, pregnancy verification, release for medical information.

What kind of medical information do you seek on older children? Case-by-case basis. All doctors' records.

Do you have a waiting list of prospective parents? No.

Is it all right if adopting parents you work with are on waiting lists of other agencies or attorneys? Yes.

Are your adoption fees based on a sliding scale? No.

Do you have an application fee? If yes, what is the amount of the application fee? Yes. $250

What is your homestudy fee (if a flat rate)? $1,000

What is your placement fee? $3,500

Do adopting parents also pay fees for medical and hospital expenses for birthmother and baby when they have no insurance? If yes, what is the average fee paid? Yes. $5,000–8,000

If applicable, what is the average document language translation fee? $300

If international adoption, what are average travel expenses? $1,500–3,500 depending on how many people travel.

If you place children from other countries, please list the estimated *entire* average cost to adoptive parents for each country. China, $17,000 for one person to travel.

My agency: Offers confidential adoptions; semi-open adoptions; meetings between birthparents and adoptive parents; birthparents pick adoptive parents from bios/resumes; full disclosure of names between birth and adoptive parents.

Does your agency provide videotapes of children needing adoption? No.

In how many cases with your agency has an adoptive parent been placed with a child but lost the child due to a birthparent challenge? 0

Has your agency lost any adoption litigation filed against you by an adoptive parent or birthparent? No.

SPENCE-CHAPIN SERVICES TO FAMILIES AND CHILDREN

Respondent: Sandra Ripberger, Communications Director
In charge of social services: Katharine S. Legg, Executive Director
6 E. 94th St., New York, NY 10128
(212) 369-0300
E-mail: info@spence-chapin.org • www.spence-chapin.org
Year first licensed by state: 1948

Agency provides services for: International adoption; U.S. adoption; children with special needs; infants; homestudy if parents working with another agency; postplacement services; adoption resource center; workshops and educational programs; "Adoption Awareness for Educators" workshops for teachers.

What states do your adoptive parent clients come from? Primarily New York, New Jersey, and Connecticut. For special needs placements, throughout the United States.

Services provided adopting parents: Classes with other prospective parents; required readings of books and/or articles on adoption; group discussions about adoption; parenting discussions.

States/countries your birthparents/adopted children come from: United States, Korea, China, Vietnam, Colombia, Ecuador, Guatemala, Russia, Moldova, Bulgaria.

What was the goal of your agency when first organized? What is the goal of your agency now? To find adoptive families for foundlings in New York. Now: To provide adoption and adoption-related services of the highest quality; to find adoptive homes for infants and children who need families.

Nonrelative children placed in 1998: 193

Percent of adoptive placements under 6 mos.: 50%

Special expertise of staff: Adoptive parents on staff; licensed social workers; therapists; physician; attorney.

In 1998, what was the average time from when a prospective adoptive parent applied to when he or she received a homestudy? 3–6 mos. completed.

Average time from homestudy to placement of child: 6–9 mos.

What made you decide to work in the adoption field? Several people here contributed to this information and agreed that helping families and children and birthparents as well, is important and satisfying work.

Agency criteria for adoptive parents you work with: The agency itself has no specific criteria besides the ability to parent a child; individual countries have particular requirements concerning age and the number of children in the home.

How do you screen adoptive parents? Personal interviews; personal and business references; health reports; fingerprints; state clearances.

How do you screen birthparents? Personal interviews and counseling; health forms. We do not screen any birthparents out; we find families prepared to accept particular medical needs.

What kind of medical information do you seek from birthparents? Full personal and family medical history.

What kind of medical information do you seek on older children? Most children placed who are over 1 year old are from abroad. We seek all information available so that families can evaluate it with the help of a pediatrician.

What percent of your U.S. adoptions are nonwhite children? 66%

About what percent are children with medical problems? 33%

Do you have a waiting list of prospective parents? No.

Is it all right if adopting parents you work with are on waiting lists of other agencies or attorneys? Yes.

Are your adoption fees based on a sliding scale? If yes, what are the sliding scale criteria? Yes. Income, other assets.

Do you have an application fee? If yes, what is the amount of the application fee? Yes. $100

What is your homestudy fee (if a flat rate)? These are included in the sliding scale fee.

What is your placement fee? These are included in the sliding scale fee.

Do adopting parents also pay fees for medical and hospital expenses for birthmother and baby when they have no insurance? No.

If applicable, what is the average document language translation fee? This too varies. In some programs it is included in the fee.

If international adoption, what are average travel expenses? We have no average and these vary very widely.

If you place children from other countries, please list the estimated *entire* average cost to adoptive parents for each country. Because each program varies with income and travel costs, it is more helpful to give a range. For single parents that is $15,000–17,000; for couples it is $17,000–20,000.

My agency: Offers confidential adoptions; semi-open adoptions; meetings between birthparents and adoptive parents; birthparents pick adoptive parents from bios/resumes; full disclosure of names between birth and adoptive parents.

Does your agency provide videotapes of children needing adoption? Yes for inter-country adoption.

In how many cases with your agency has an adoptive parent been placed with a child but lost the child due to a birthparent challenge? In 10 years, in 4 of 940 placements have children been returned to birthparents.

Has your agency lost any adoption litigation filed against you by an adoptive parent or birthparent? No.

NORTH CAROLINA

CHILDREN'S HOME SOCIETY OF NORTH CAROLINA

Respondent: Sandy M. Cook, Executive Director
In charge of social services: Sandy M. Cook
P.O. Box 14608, Greensboro, NC 27415-4608
(336) 274-1538 • Fax: (336) 274-0276
E-mail: chsnc@greensboro.com
Year first licensed by state: 1940

Agency provides services for: International adoption; U.S. adoption; children with special needs; infants; homestudy if parents working with another agency; postplacement services.

What states do your adoptive parent clients come from? North Carolina.

Services provided adopting parents: Classes with other prospective parents; required readings of books and/or articles on adoption; group discussions about adoption; parenting discussions.

States/countries your birthparents/adopted children come from: North Carolina.

What was the goal of your agency when first organized? What is the goal of your agency now? To find homes for children (1902). Now: To provide every child with a permanent, safe, and loving home.

Nonrelative children placed in 1998: 133

Percent of adoptive placements under 6 mos.: 40%

Special expertise of staff: Adoptive parents on staff; licensed social workers; attorney.

In 1998, what was the average time from when a prospective adoptive parent applied to when he or she received a homestudy? 3 mos.

Average time from homestudy to placement of child: 12 mos.

What made you decide to work in the adoption field? Interest in children's needs.

Agency criteria for adoptive parents you work with: Flexible. We are looking for safe, nurturing families. We look at the entire family circumstance.

How do you screen adoptive parents? MAPP-GS classes.

How do you screen birthparents? All clients are given an appointment.

What kind of medical information do you seek from birthparents? As much as possible.

What kind of medical information do you seek on older children? As much as possible.

What percent of your U.S. adoptions are nonwhite children? 59%

About what percent are children with medical problems? 30%

About what percent are children with emotional problems? 40%

Do you have a waiting list of prospective parents? Yes.

Is it all right if adopting parents you work with are on waiting lists of other agencies or attorneys? Yes. Some may; some programs limit to one agency.

Are your adoption fees based on a sliding scale? No.

Do you have an application fee? If yes, what is the amount of the application fee? Yes. $150; for special needs, no fees.

What is your homestudy fee (if a flat rate)? $1,400

What is your placement fee? $8,000

Do adopting parents also pay fees for medical and hospital expenses for birthmother and baby when they have no insurance? No.

My agency: Offers confidential adoptions; semi-open adoptions; meetings between birthparents and adoptive parents; birthparents pick adoptive parents from bios/resumes; full disclosure of names between birth and adoptive parents.

Does your agency provide videotapes of children needing adoption? Yes.

In how many cases with your agency has an adoptive parent been placed with a child but lost the child due to a birthparent challenge? 2

Has your agency lost any adoption litigation filed against you by an adoptive parent or birthparent? No.

FRANK ADOPTION CENTER

Respondent: Anne Liddicote, Executive Director
In charge of social services: Joan Harlow
2840 Plaza Pl., Suite 325, Raleigh, NC 27612
(800) 597-9135 • Fax: (919) 510-9137
E-mail: info@frankadopt.org • www.frankadopt.org
Year first licensed by state: 1994

Agency provides services for: International adoption; homestudy if parents working with another agency; postplacement services.

What states do your adoptive parent clients come from? All states.

Services provided adopting parents: Classes with other prospective parents; parenting discussions.

States/countries your birthparents/adopted children come from: Russia, Kazakhstan, Moldova.

What was the goal of your agency when first organized? What is the goal of your agency now? International adoption. Now: Same.

Nonrelative children placed in 1998: 257

Percent of adoptive placements under 6 mos.: 10%

Special expertise of staff: Adoptive parents on staff; licensed social workers; therapists; physician.

In 1998, what was the average time from when a prospective adoptive parent applied to when he or she received a homestudy? 2 mos.

Average time from homestudy to placement of child: 6–7 mos.

What made you decide to work in the adoption field? Being an adoptive parent, professional social worker.

Agency criteria for adoptive parents you work with: Very flexible; married 1 year or single woman; 45 years or younger for infant; open to children in home.

How do you screen adoptive parents? Home assessments, applications, telephone calls.

What kind of medical information do you seek from birthparents? As much as is allowed by the foreign court.

What kind of medical information do you seek on older children? As much as possible from hospital and orphanage records.

About what percent are children with medical problems? 15%

Do you have a waiting list of prospective parents? No.

Is it all right if adopting parents you work with are on waiting lists of other agencies or attorneys? No.

Are your adoption fees based on a sliding scale? No.

Do you have an application fee? If yes, what is the amount of the application fee? Yes. $300

What is your homestudy fee (if a flat rate)? $1,200

What is your placement fee? $3,300

If applicable, what is the average document language translation fee? $500

If international adoption, what are average travel expenses? $4,000

If you place children from other countries, please list the estimated *entire* average cost to adoptive parents for each country. Varies according to age of child. Highest is $23,000 for under 12 mos., then fee decreases.

My agency: Offers confidential adoptions.

Does your agency provide videotapes of children needing adoption? Yes.

Are you an adoptive parent, adopted person, or birthparent? Adoptive parent.

In how many cases with your agency has an adoptive parent been placed with a child but lost the child due to a birthparent challenge? 0

Has your agency lost any adoption litigation filed against you by an adoptive parent or birthparent? No.

LUTHERAN FAMILY SERVICES IN THE CAROLINAS

Respondent: Sandy Deutsch, Director of Adoptions
P.O. Box 12289, Raleigh, NC 27605
(919) 832-2620 • Fax: (919) 832-0591
E-mail: sandy-deutsch@usa.net
Year first licensed by state: 1986

Agency provides services for: Homestudy if parents working with another agency; post-placement services; assist with independent adoptions.

What states do your adoptive parent clients come from? North Carolina, South Carolina.

Services provided adopting parents: Classes with other prospective parents; required readings of books and/or articles on adoption; contact with other families who have already adopted and other resources as indicated.

States/countries your birthparents/adopted children come from: Networking with agencies placing from former Soviet Union, China, Korea, Thailand, India, Vietnam, Cambodia. All U.S. states for domestic placements.

What was the goal of your agency when first organized? What is the goal of your agency now? To help with international adoption for North Carolina families. Now: To find loving stable homes for children from all walks of life.

Nonrelative children placed in 1998: About 75

Percent of adoptive placements under 6 mos.: About 80%

Special expertise of staff: Adoptive parents on staff; licensed social workers.

In 1998, what was the average time from when a prospective adoptive parent applied to when he or she received a homestudy? 2 mos.

Average time from homestudy to placement of child: 1 year

What made you decide to work in the adoption field? Adoptive mother—wanted to "improve" my experience in the adoption arena.

Agency criteria for adoptive parents you work with: Stability of individual, marriage, and employment; commitment to parenthood (not pregnancy); flexibility; understanding or willingness to learn about adoption (trans-racial, etc.) issues.

How do you screen adoptive parents? Full homestudy based on several interviews, autobiographies, references. Participation in education workshop. Review application which asks for substantial information.

What percent of your U.S. adoptions are nonwhite children? About 15%

About what percent are children with medical problems? About 25%

About what percent are children with emotional problems? 25%

Do you have a waiting list of prospective parents? No.

Are your adoption fees based on a sliding scale? No.

Do you have an application fee? If yes, what is the amount of the application fee? Yes. $195

What is your homestudy fee (if a flat rate)? $1,350

Do adopting parents also pay fees for medical and hospital expenses for birth-mother and baby when they have no insurance? If yes, what is the average fee paid? Yes. Ceiling in North Carolina is $10,000.

If applicable, what is the average document language translation fee? Varies.

If international adoption, what are average travel expenses? Varies.

Are you an adoptive parent, adopted person, or birthparent? Adoptive parent.

In how many cases with your agency has an adoptive parent been placed with a child but lost the child due to a birthparent challenge? 10

Has your agency lost any adoption litigation filed against you by an adoptive parent or birthparent? No.

OHIO

ACTION ADOPTION SERVICES

Respondent: Patricia A. Hill, MSW, LSW, Executive Director
1927 N. Main St., Suite 2, Dayton, OH 45405
(937) 277-6101 • Fax: (937) 277-2962
E-mail: actionadopt@aol.com
Year first licensed by state: 1998

Agency provides services for: International adoption; U.S. adoption; children with special needs; infants; homestudy if parents working with another agency; postplacement services.

What states do your adoptive parent clients come from? All states, with a homestudy. Ohio families with or without homestudy.

Services provided adopting parents: Classes with other prospective parents; required readings of books and/or articles on adoption; group discussions about adoption; parenting discussions; post-adoption support groups; social events for adoptive families.

States/countries your birthparents/adopted children come from: Domestic, all states; international, China and Russia.

What was the goal of your agency when first organized? What is the goal of your agency now? Formed as adoption support group in 1993. Now: Primary goal is to place "waiting" children in the care of public child [services system—foster care].

Nonrelative children placed in 1998: 12

Special expertise of staff: Adoptive parents on staff; licensed social workers; therapists; physician; attorney.

In 1998, what was the average time from when a prospective adoptive parent applied to when he or she received a homestudy? 4 mos.

Average time from homestudy to placement of child: Less than 6 mos.

What made you decide to work in the adoption field? Adopted twenty special needs children and felt I could assist others.

Agency criteria for adoptive parents you work with: We are very flexible. There is a need for many different types of families to meet the needs of children.

How do you screen adoptive parents? Fingerprints (state and FBI per Ohio code); references; medical records; and 36 hours of pre-adoption training.

What kind of medical information do you seek on older children? As much as is available.

What percent of your U.S. adoptions are nonwhite children? 50%

About what percent are children with medical problems? 50%

About what percent are children with emotional problems? 50%

Do you have a waiting list of prospective parents? Yes, but short as we are quick to find children.

Is it all right if adopting parents you work with are on waiting lists of other agencies or attorneys? Yes. We often collaborate.

Are your adoption fees based on a sliding scale? No.

Do you have an application fee? No.

What is your homestudy fee (if a flat rate)? $1,100 for international or infant.

What is your placement fee? $2,000 for infant. No fees to families for children in the care of public agencies.

My agency: Offers confidential adoptions; semi-open adoptions; meetings between birthparents and adoptive parents; birthparents pick adoptive parents from bios/resumes.

Does your agency provide videotapes of children needing adoption? Yes.

Are you an adoptive parent, adopted person, or birthparent? Adoptive parent.

In how many cases with your agency has an adoptive parent been placed with a child but lost the child due to a birthparent challenge? 0

Has your agency lost any adoption litigation filed against you by an adoptive parent or birthparent? No.

ADOPT AMERICA NETWORK

Respondent: Beverly Moore, Adoptions Director
In charge of social services: Brit Eaton, Executive Director
1025 Reynolds Rd., Toledo, OH 43615
(419) 534-3350 • Fax: (419) 534-2995
E-mail: adoptamer@aol.com • www.adoptamerica.org

Agency provides services for: Children with special needs; postplacement services.

What states do your adoptive parent clients come from? All states.

Services provided adopting parents: Classes with other prospective parents; required readings of books and/or articles on adoption; group discussions about adoption; parenting discussions.

States/countries your birthparents/adopted children come from: All states.

What was the goal of your agency when first organized? What is the goal of your agency now? To find permanent, loving, adoptive homes for special needs children. Now: Same as above, but we are now an adoption agency that does homestudies, etc.

Nonrelative children placed in 1998: 125 (noncustodial, but matched 125 children that were placed).

Special expertise of staff: Adoptive parents on staff; licensed social workers.

In 1998, what was the average time from when a prospective adoptive parent applied to when he or she received a homestudy? About 6 mos.

Average time from homestudy to placement of child: Varies.

What made you decide to work in the adoption field? Have five adopted children and had biological special-needs daughter. Love the work!

Agency criteria for adoptive parents you work with: Must have homestudy. Very open.

How do you screen adoptive parents? Through training and homestudy process. They usually screen themselves.

What kind of medical information do you seek from birthparents? Regular medical from doctor.

What kind of medical information do you seek on older children? Regular medical.

What percent of your U.S. adoptions are nonwhite children? 65%

About what percent are children with medical problems? 40%

About what percent are children with emotional problems? Most have, just by being in the system.

Do you have a waiting list of prospective parents? Yes.

Is it all right if adopting parents you work with are on waiting lists of other agencies or attorneys? Yes.

Are your adoption fees based on a sliding scale? No fees.

Do you have an application fee? No.

Do adopting parents also pay fees for medical and hospital expenses for birth-mother and baby when they have no insurance? No.

Does your agency provide videotapes of children needing adoption? Yes, some.

Are you an adoptive parent, adopted person, or birthparent? Adoptive parent and adopted person.

ADOPTION BY GENTLE CARE

Respondent: Susan A. Zelasks, Executive Director
In charge of social services: Susan A. Zelasks
17 Brickel St., Columbus, OH 43215
(614) 469-0007 • Fax: (614) 621-2229
E-mail: gentle.care@worldnet.att.net • www.adoptgentlecare.com
Year first licensed by state: 1985

Agency provides services for: International adoption; U.S. adoption; infants; homestudy if parents working with another agency; postplacement services.

What states do your adoptive parent clients come from? All states.

Services provided adopting parents: Classes with other prospective parents; required readings of books and/or articles on adoption; group discussions about adoption; parenting discussions.

States/countries your birthparents/adopted children come from: Ohio, Russia.

What was the goal of your agency when first organized? What is the goal of your agency now? Our primary goal was to be a nondenominational, nonprofit, private child-placing agency licensed by the state of Ohio that provides adoption services throughout the state of Ohio as well as facilitates interstate and international placements. Now: Same.

Nonrelative children placed in 1998: 85

Percent of adoptive placements under 6 mos.: 100%

Special expertise of staff: Licensed social workers; attorney.

In 1998, what was the average time from when a prospective adoptive parent applied to when he or she received a homestudy? 6 weeks

Average time from homestudy to placement of child: 1 year

What made you decide to work in the adoption field? I felt it would be very worthwhile.

How do you screen adoptive parents? We review preapplications throughout the year and notify adopting parents of acceptance.

How do you screen birthparents? We meet with them.

What kind of medical information do you seek on older children? We do not facilitate placement of children over the age of 6 mos. except in an international program.

What percent of your U.S. adoptions are nonwhite children? 15%

Do you have a waiting list of prospective parents? Yes.

Is it all right if adopting parents you work with are on waiting lists of other agencies or attorneys? Yes.

Are your adoption fees based on a sliding scale? No.

Do you have an application fee? If yes, what is the amount of the application fee? Yes. $100

What is your homestudy fee (if a flat rate)? $1,200

What is your placement fee? Varies.

Do adopting parents also pay fees for medical and hospital expenses for birthmother and baby when they have no insurance? If yes, what is the average fee paid? Yes. $7,000

My agency: Offers confidential adoptions; semi-open adoptions; meetings between birthparents and adoptive parents; birthparents pick adoptive parents from bios/resumes; full disclosure of names between birth and adoptive parents.

Does your agency provide videotapes of children needing adoption? Yes.

In how many cases with your agency has an adoptive parent been placed with a child but lost the child due to a birthparent challenge? 0

Has your agency lost any adoption litigation filed against you by an adoptive parent or birthparent? No.

BUILDING BLOCKS ADOPTION SERVICE, INC.

Respondent: Denise Hubbard, President
In charge of social services: Carol Wilson
4387 Remsen Rd., Medina, OH 44256
(330) 725-5521 • Fax: (330) 725-7389
E-mail: dhubbard@pohio.net • www.buildingblocksadoption.com
Year first licensed by state: 1998

Agency provides services for: International adoption; children with special needs; infants; homestudy if parents working with another agency; postplacement services.

What states do your adoptive parent clients come from? All states.

Services provided adopting parents: Required readings of books and/or articles on adoption; parenting discussions.

States/countries your adopted children come from: Russia, Ukraine, Bulgaria, and Guatemala.

What is the goal of your agency now? Lower fees, all in one service, honesty, placing children in loving families.

Nonrelative children placed in 1998: 47

Percent of adoptive placements under 6 mos.: 80%

Special expertise of staff: Adoptive parents on staff; licensed social workers; physician; attorney.

In 1998, what was the average time from when a prospective adoptive parent applied to when he or she received a homestudy? 7 mos.

Average time from homestudy to placement of child: 4 mos.

What made you decide to work in the adoption field? Adopting our daughter.

Agency criteria for adoptive parents you work with: Over 25; current children doesn't matter; singles can adopt; no criminal record; financial stability.

How do you screen adoptive parents? Application process; criminal check; home-study assessment.

What kind of medical information do you seek on older children? Hepatitis A and C, TB, syphilis, HIV, standard physical.

About what percent are children with medical problems? 20%

About what percent are children with emotional problems? 20%

Do you have a waiting list of prospective parents? No.

Is it all right if adopting parents you work with are on waiting lists of other agencies or attorneys? Yes.

Are your adoption fees based on a sliding scale? No.

Do you have an application fee? If yes, what is the amount of the application fee? Yes. $200

What is your homestudy fee (if a flat rate)? $850

What is your placement fee? $100

Do adopting parents also pay fees for medical and hospital expenses for birth-mother and baby when they have no insurance? No.

If international adoption, what are average travel expenses? Under $5,000.

If you place children from other countries, please list the estimated *entire* average cost to adoptive parents for each country. Bulgaria, $14,000; Russia, $20,000; Ukraine, $20,000; Guatemala, $20,000. These include travel and all expenses.

My agency: Offers confidential adoptions.

Does your agency provide videotapes of children needing adoption? Yes.

Are you an adoptive parent, adopted person, or birthparent? Adoptive parent.

In how many cases with your agency has an adoptive parent been placed with a child but lost the child due to a birthparent challenge? 0

Has your agency lost any adoption litigation filed against you by an adoptive parent or birthparent? No.

THE CHILDREN'S HOME OF CINCINNATI

Respondent: Veronica A. Berry, Adoption Recruiter
In charge of social services: Jacqueline Thomas
5050 Madison Rd., Cincinnati, OH 45227
(513) 272-2800 • Fax: (513) 272-2807

Agency provides services for: International adoption; U.S. adoption; children with special needs; infants; homestudy if parents working with another agency; postplacement services; pregnancy counseling.

What states do your adoptive parent clients come from? All states, mainly Ohio.

Services provided adopting parents: Classes with other prospective parents; required readings of books and/or articles on adoption; group discussions about adoption; parenting discussions; post-adoption support group.

States/countries your birthparents/adopted children come from: All states. Will expand into international adoptions in June, 1999.

What was the goal of your agency when first organized? What is the goal of your agency now? To help find homes for children. Now: To facilitate the healthy development of children and their families by building on their individual strengths and reducing the risks of deterioration.

Nonrelative children placed in 1998: 6 infants

Percent of adoptive placements under 6 mos.: 100%

Special expertise of staff: Adoptive parents on staff; licensed social workers; therapists.

In 1998, what was the average time from when a prospective adoptive parent applied to when he or she received a homestudy? Started right away.

Average time from homestudy to placement of child: Less than 2 years

What made you decide to work in the adoption field? Because I am adoptive parent, I saw the need to help provide information to prospective adoptive parents.

Agency criteria for adoptive parents you work with: For healthy white infant adoptions can be no more than one nonspecial needs child under 18 already in the family. Applicants for special needs children are exempt.

How do you screen adoptive parents? Criminal record checks pursuant to Section 2151.86 of the Ohio Revised Code; references, interviews.

How do you screen birthparents? Serve all birthparents in the surrounding area.

What kind of medical information do you seek on older children? All information that is known.

What percent of your U.S. adoptions are nonwhite children? 80%

About what percent are children with medical problems? 10%

Do you have a waiting list of prospective parents? Yes.

Is it all right if adopting parents you work with are on waiting lists of other agencies or attorneys? No.

Are your adoption fees based on a sliding scale? If yes, what are the sliding scale criteria? Yes. 10% of gross income minus fees paid (maximum adoption fee will be $10,000).

Do you have an application fee? If yes, what is the amount of the application fee? Yes, for nonspecial needs only. $150

What is your homestudy fee (if a flat rate)? $1,500

What is your placement fee? 10% of gross income (maximum $10,000) minus fees already paid.

Do adopting parents also pay fees for medical and hospital expenses for birth-mother and baby when they have no insurance? No.

My agency: Offers confidential adoptions; semi-open adoptions; meetings between birthparents and adoptive parents; birthparents pick adoptive parents from bios/resumes; full disclosure of names between birth and adoptive parents.

Does your agency provide videotapes of children needing adoption? Yes.

Are you an adoptive parent, adopted person, or birthparent? Adoptive parent.

In how many cases with your agency has an adoptive parent been placed with a child but lost the child due to a birthparent challenge? 0

Has your agency lost any adoption litigation filed against you by an adoptive parent or birthparent? No.

FAMILY ADOPTION CONSULTANTS - OHIO OFFICE

Respondent: Karen Ristow, Assistant Ohio Administrator
In charge of social services: Barbara Irvin, Ohio Administrator
8536 Crow Dr., Suite 230, Macedonia, OH 44056
(330) 468-0673 • Fax: (330) 468-0678
E-mail: facohio@acclink.com • www.facadopt.org
Year first licensed by state: 1982

Agency provides services for: International adoption; children with special needs; infants; homestudy if parents working with another agency; postplacement services.

What states do your adoptive parent clients come from? Ohio families service by Ohio office; Michigan families by Michigan office. Can accept out-of-state families for some country programs, including China and Guatemala. Work with out-of-state families coordinated by the Michigan office.

Services provided adopting parents: Classes with other prospective parents; required readings of books and/or articles on adoption; group discussions about adoption; parenting discussions.

States/countries your birthparents/adopted children come from: Korea, Guatemala, China, Philippines. Network programs with other agencies for placement of children from other countries, including Russia.

What was the goal of your agency when first organized? What is the goal of your agency now? To find homes for waiting overseas children. Now: Same.

Percent of adoptive placements under 6 mos.: 15%

Special expertise of staff: Adoptive parents on staff; licensed social workers.

In 1998, what was the average time from when a prospective adoptive parent applied to when he or she received a homestudy? Application to completion of homestudy: 2–3 mos.

Average time from homestudy to placement of child: 6–8 mos.

What made you decide to work in the adoption field? Positive nature of work; meets the needs of families and children.

Agency criteria for adoptive parents you work with: No agency requirements; abide by requirements set by foreign country.

How do you screen adoptive parents? Follow state/INS requirements, including fingerprint clearance; child abuse clearance; must submit references; physical reports, etc.

What kind of medical information do you seek on older children? Varies depending on country program.

About what percent are children with medical problems? 5% require ongoing medical attention.

Do you have a waiting list of prospective parents? Yes, for some programs.

Is it all right if adopting parents you work with are on waiting lists of other agencies or attorneys? No.

Are your adoption fees based on a sliding scale? If yes, what are the sliding scale criteria? Yes, for homestudy only. [Based on] income of adoptive family.

Do you have an application fee? If yes, what is the amount of the application fee? Yes. $100

What is your homestudy fee (if a flat rate)? $900–1,500

What is your placement fee? Program fee depends on country program. Low of $7,000 to a high of $19,000.

If applicable, what is the average document language translation fee? $1,000

If you place children from other countries, please list the estimated *entire* average cost to adoptive parents for each country. Korea, $16,000 (including homestudy); Philippines, $13,000 (including homestudy); China, $20,000 (including homestudy); Guatemala, $25,000 (including homestudy).

Does your agency provide videotapes of children needing adoption? Yes.

In how many cases with your agency has an adoptive parent been placed with a child but lost the child due to a birthparent challenge? 0

Has your agency lost any adoption litigation filed against you by an adoptive parent or birthparent? No.

JEWISH FAMILY SERVICE

Respondent: Mimi Surloff, Adoption Coordinator
In charge of social services: Judith L. Rosenthal, PhD
83 N. Miller Rd. #202, Akron, OH 44333
(330) 867-3388 • Fax: (330) 867-3396
E-mail: mo1028@aol.com

Agency provides services for: International adoption; U.S. adoption; children with special needs; infants; homestudy if parents working with another agency; postplacement services; counseling for all members of an adoptive triad.

What states do your adoptive parent clients come from? Ohio only.

Services provided adopting parents: Classes with other prospective parents; required readings of books and/or articles on adoption; group discussions about adoption; parenting discussions.

States/countries your birthparents/adopted children come from: Ohio, China, Korea, Russia, Brazil.

What is the goal of your agency now? To enhance the mental, emotional, and social functioning of individuals, families, and groups. Counseling continues to be the core program of this agency.

Nonrelative children placed in 1998: 5

Percent of adoptive placements under 6 mos.: 0%

Special expertise of staff: Adoptive parents on staff; licensed social workers; psychologists; therapists.

In 1998, what was the average time from when a prospective adoptive parent applied to when he or she received a homestudy? 6 mos.

Average time from homestudy to placement of child: 3 mos.

What made you decide to work in the adoption field? My job placements led me to an adoption position initially.

Agency criteria for adoptive parents you work with: Ohio does not allow for any specific criteria that rules out adoptive parents [years married, age] other than marriage length of at least 1 year and age of at least 21. Our agency policy requires that for healthy Caucasian infant placements of children under our custody, the couple or individual must be Jewish.

How do you screen adoptive parents? Through the ODHS application information provided; through a police/criminal record check, and through an initial interview.

How do you screen birthparents? We see so few that we do not have a screening process. We assess individually if their needs fit the scope of our services.

What kind of medical information do you seek from birthparents? Ohio has a state-required form that is presented to birthparents for their provision of complete medical histories.

What kind of medical information do you seek on older children? There is also a state-required form to secure complete medical information for children.

What percent of your U.S. adoptions are nonwhite children? 0%

About what percent are children with medical problems? 40%

Do you have a waiting list of prospective parents? Yes.

Is it all right if adopting parents you work with are on waiting lists of other agencies or attorneys? Yes.

Are your adoption fees based on a sliding scale? If yes, what are the sliding scale criteria? Yes. For placement services only, income and number of people in family.

Do you have an application fee? If yes, what is the amount of the application fee? Yes. $200

What is your homestudy fee (if a flat rate)? $1,650

What is your placement fee? Sliding scale.

If international adoption, what are average travel expenses? $5,000

If you place children from other countries, please list the estimated *entire* average cost to adoptive parents for each country. We don't directly place these children, we facilitate the placements in cooperation with other programs. For those we've worked with, Russia averages $20,000, China, $15,000.

My agency: Offers confidential adoptions; semi-open adoptions; meetings between birthparents and adoptive parents; birthparents pick adoptive parents from bios/resumes.

Does your agency provide videotapes of children needing adoption? No.

Are you an adoptive parent, adopted person, or birthparent? Adoptive parent.

In how many cases with your agency has an adoptive parent been placed with a child but lost the child due to a birthparent challenge? 0

Has your agency lost any adoption litigation filed against you by an adoptive parent or birthparent? No.

MATHIS CARE, INC.

Respondent: Martin Mathis, Executive Director
In charge of social services: Mary Ann Jochim, LICSW
1191 W. Galbraith Rd., Cincinnati, OH 45231
(513) 522-7390 • Fax: (513) 522-9844
Year first licensed by state: 1997

Agency provides services for: U.S. adoption; children with special needs; homestudy if parents working with another agency; postplacement services.

What states do your adoptive parent clients come from? Ohio.

Services provided adopting parents: Classes with other prospective parents; required readings of books and/or articles on adoption; group discussions about adoption; parenting discussions.

States/countries your birthparents/adopted children come from: Ohio.

What was the goal of your agency when first organized? What is the goal of your agency now? To provide safe, loving, therapeutic environments for children in out-of-home placement. Now: Same.

Nonrelative children placed in 1998: 1

Special expertise of staff: Adoptive parents on staff; licensed social workers; therapists.

In 1998, what was the average time from when a prospective adoptive parent applied to when he or she received a homestudy? 6 mos.

Average time from homestudy to placement of child: 3 mos.

Agency criteria for adoptive parents you work with: Good health; adequate income; safe home; ability to advocate; willing to take children with special needs.

How do you screen adoptive parents? Individual and couple (family) interviews; home inspection; fire inspection; physical exams; fingerprint and background checks.

What kind of medical information do you seek on older children? Birth records if possible and all that may be available.

What percent of your U.S. adoptions are nonwhite children? 100%

About what percent are children with emotional problems? 100%

Do you have a waiting list of prospective parents? Yes.

Is it all right if adopting parents you work with are on waiting lists of other agencies or attorneys? Yes.

Are your adoption fees based on a sliding scale? No.

Do you have an application fee? No.

What is your homestudy fee (if a flat rate)? $1,000

My agency: Offers confidential adoptions.

Does your agency provide videotapes of children needing adoption? No.

Are you an adoptive parent, adopted person, or birthparent? Adoptive parent.

In how many cases with your agency has an adoptive parent been placed with a child but lost the child due to a birthparent challenge? 0

Has your agency lost any adoption litigation filed against you by an adoptive parent or birthparent? No.

PRIVATE ADOPTION SERVICES, INC.

Respondent: Carolyn Mussio Franke, Executive Director
In charge of social services: Carolyn M. Franke
3411 Michigan Ave., Cincinnati, OH 45208
(513) 871-5777 • Fax: (513) 871-8582
E-mail: adopt@fuse.net
Year first licensed by state: 1997

Agency provides services for: International adoption; U.S. adoption; children with special needs; infants; homestudy if parents working with another agency; postplacement services; counseling and training for adoptive couples.

What states do your adoptive parent clients come from? All states.

Services provided adopting parents: Classes with other prospective parents; required readings of books and/or articles on adoption; group discussions about adoption; parenting discussions; information about the adoption process; live speakers.

States/countries your birthparents/adopted children come from: Mostly Ohio, Kentucky, and Indiana.

What was the goal of your agency when first organized? What is the goal of your agency now? To find good homes for infants. Now: Same.

Nonrelative children placed in 1998: 50

Special expertise of staff: Adoptive parents on staff; licensed social workers; therapists; attorney; nurse.

In 1998, what was the average time from when a prospective adoptive parent applied to when he or she received a homestudy? 2 weeks

Average time from homestudy to placement of child: 1 year

What made you decide to work in the adoption field? My father was an obstetrician and sent me my first clients.

Agency criteria for adoptive parents you work with: No specific criteria.

How do you screen adoptive parents? They must pass the homestudy and follow through with 12 hours of training.

How do you screen birthparents? Through interviews and background checks.

What kind of medical information do you seek from birthparents? Twenty pages of questions.

What kind of medical information do you seek on older children? All doctors' records.

What percent of your U.S. adoptions are nonwhite children? 2%

Do you have a waiting list of prospective parents? Yes.

Is it all right if adopting parents you work with are on waiting lists of other agencies or attorneys? Yes.

Are your adoption fees based on a sliding scale? No.

Do you have an application fee? If yes, what is the amount of the application fee? Yes. $650

What is your homestudy fee (if a flat rate)? $1,200

What is your placement fee? $8,000

Do adopting parents also pay fees for medical and hospital expenses for birthmother and baby when they have no insurance? If yes, what is the average fee paid? Yes. $7,000

My agency: Offers confidential adoptions; semi-open adoptions; meetings between birthparents and adoptive parents; birthparents pick adoptive parents from bios/resumes; full disclosure of names between birth and adoptive parents.

Does your agency provide videotapes of children needing adoption? No.

In how many cases with your agency has an adoptive parent been placed with a child but lost the child due to a birthparent challenge? 0

Has your agency lost any adoption litigation filed against you by an adoptive parent or birthparent? No.

OKLAHOMA

ASSOCIATED CATHOLIC CHARITIES

Respondent: Julia Reed, LCSW, Director, Family Support Services
In charge of social services: Julia Reed
1501 N. Classen Blvd., Oklahoma City, OK 73106
(405) 523-3012 • Fax: (405) 523-3015
E-mail: jdreed.okc@worldnet.att.net • www.catholiccharitiesok.org
Year first licensed by state: 1912

Agency provides services for: U.S. adoption; infants; homestudy if parents working with another agency; postplacement services.

What states do your adoptive parent clients come from? Primarily Oklahoma.

Services provided adopting parents: Classes with other prospective parents; required readings of books and/or articles on adoption; parenting discussions.

States/countries your birthparents/adopted children come from: Primarily Oklahoma.

What was the goal of your agency when first organized? What is the goal of your agency now? To provide services to children, youth, and families. Now: Same. To put into practice gospel values of justice, love, compassion, and hope through service, empowerment, and advocacy.

Nonrelative children placed in 1998: 6

Percent of adoptive placements under 6 mos.: 100%

Special expertise of staff: Licensed social workers; therapists.

In 1998, what was the average time from when a prospective adoptive parent applied to when he or she received a homestudy? 1 year

Average time from homestudy to placement of child: 1 year

What made you decide to work in the adoption field? Children's issues.

Agency criteria for adoptive parents you work with: Must be 25–43 years old; married 3 years; attend a church (does not have to be Catholic).

How do you screen adoptive parents? Through homestudy process and criteria.

How do you screen birthparents? Counseling process.

What kind of medical information do you seek from birthparents? Required state medical and social history.

What kind of medical information do you seek on older children? Same.

Do you have a waiting list of prospective parents? Yes.

Is it all right if adopting parents you work with are on waiting lists of other agencies or attorneys? Yes (depends).

Are your adoption fees based on a sliding scale? If yes, what are the sliding scale criteria? Yes. Based on income (5%); does not exceed $11,000.

Do you have an application fee? No.

What is your homestudy fee (if a flat rate)? $800

What is your placement fee? $4,300 plus 5% of income, not to exceed $11,000.

My agency: Offers confidential adoptions; semi-open adoptions; meetings between birthparents and adoptive parents; birthparents pick adoptive parents from bios/resumes.

Does your agency provide videotapes of children needing adoption? No.

In how many cases with your agency has an adoptive parent been placed with a child but lost the child due to a birthparent challenge? 0

Has your agency lost any adoption litigation filed against you by an adoptive parent or birthparent? No.

ADOPTION CHOICES, INC.

Respondent: Virginia L. Frank, Executive Director
In charge of social services: Child Placement Supervisor
11212 N. May Ave., Suite 200, Oklahoma City, OK 73120
(405) 275-1388 • Fax: (405) 749-0412
E-mail: adoption@ionet.net • www.adoptionchoices.org
Year first licensed by state: 1998

Agency provides services for: U.S. adoption; international adoption; infants.

What states do your adoptive parent clients come from? Several from Georgia, Texas, and Pennsylvania, but other states as well.

Services provided adopting parents: Required readings of books and/or articles on adoption.

States/countries your birthparents/adopted children come from: Oklahoma, Kansas, California, Washington, Hawaii, Marshall Islands, Arkansas. A few other states as well.

Nonrelative children placed in 1998: 75

Percent of adoptive placements under 6 mos.: 95%

Special expertise of staff: Licensed social workers; nurse and employees with degrees in similar field; women who have placed a child for adoption.

Average time from homestudy to placement of child: 6–8 mos.

What made you decide to work in the adoption field? I was raised by a single mom and most of my friends were pregnant before high school graduation. I wanted to help women make good decisions for themselves and their children.

How do you screen birthparents? Initial phone interview, then a face-to-face interview.

What kind of medical information do you seek on older children? All available medical records from doctors and hospitals.

What percent of your U.S. adoptions are nonwhite children? 20%

Do you have a waiting list of prospective parents? Yes.

Is it all right if adopting parents you work with are on waiting lists of other agencies or attorneys? Yes.

Are your adoption fees based on a sliding scale? No.

Do you have an application fee? If yes, what is the amount of the application fee? Yes. $150

What is your homestudy fee (if a flat rate)? $600

What is your placement fee? $14,500

Do adopting parents also pay fees for medical and hospital expenses for birthmother and baby when they have no insurance? If yes, what is the average fee paid? Yes. $2,000–3,000

If applicable, what is the average document language translation fee? $500

If you place children from other countries, please list the estimated *entire* average cost to adoptive parents for each country. Republic of the Marshall Islands, $18,000 (includes medical).

My agency: Offers confidential adoptions; semi-open adoptions; meetings between birthparents and adoptive parents; birthparents pick adoptive parents from bios/resumes.

Does your agency provide videotapes of children needing adoption? No.

In how many cases with your agency has an adoptive parent been placed with a child but lost the child due to a birthparent challenge? 0

Has your agency lost any adoption litigation filed against you by an adoptive parent or birthparent? No.

DEACONESS HOME PREGNANCY AND ADOPTION SERVICES

Respondent: Dierdre L. McCool, Manager
In charge of social services: Debbie Espinosa
5300 N. Meridian, Suite 9, Oklahoma City, OK 73112
(405) 949-4200 • Fax: (405) 951-4081
Year first licensed by state: 1901

Agency provides services for: U.S. adoption; infants; homestudy if parents working with another agency; postplacement services.

What states do your adoptive parent clients come from? All states.

Services provided adopting parents: Group discussions about adoption.

States/countries your birthparents/adopted children come from: All states; mainly Oklahoma.

What was the goal of your agency when first organized? What is the goal of your agency now? To provide a refuge for women who became pregnant out of wedlock. Now: To help the woman in an unplanned pregnancy choose life for her child.

Nonrelative children placed in 1998: 13

Percent of adoptive placements under 6 mos.: 100%

Special expertise of staff: Psychologists; attorney; RN.

In 1998, what was the average time from when a prospective adoptive parent applied to when he or she received a homestudy? 4 mos.

Average time from homestudy to placement of child: 1 year

What made you decide to work in the adoption field? Felt like God called me here.

Agency criteria for adoptive parents you work with: Two-child limit unless accepting special needs; aged 21–45 (over 45 if accepting special needs); married at least 3 years; medically established that they cannot have biological children.

How do you screen adoptive parents? 1. Administer MMPI/Taylor Johnson. 2. Fingerprint checks, OSBI, FBI, sex offenders registry, Dept. of Public Safety, child abuse/neglect information check. 3. Ten reference letters and two interviews.

How do you screen birthparents? No screening except MMPI and STD/AIDS screening.

What kind of medical information do you seek from birthparents? As much as possible.

What percent of your U.S. adoptions are nonwhite children? 30–40%

About what percent are children with medical problems? Less than 10%

Do you have a waiting list of prospective parents? Yes.

Is it all right if adopting parents you work with are on waiting lists of other agencies or attorneys? Yes.

Are your adoption fees based on a sliding scale? No.

Do you have an application fee? If yes, what is the amount of the application fee? Yes. $600

What is your placement fee? $2,500

Do adopting parents also pay fees for medical and hospital expenses for birthmother and baby when they have no insurance? If yes, what is the average fee paid? Yes. $5,000–7,000

My agency: Offers confidential adoptions; semi-open adoptions; meetings between birthparents and adoptive parents; birthparents pick adoptive parents from bios/resumes; full disclosure of names between birth and adoptive parents.

Does your agency provide videotapes of children needing adoption? No.

In how many cases with your agency has an adoptive parent been placed with a child but lost the child due to a birthparent challenge? 0

Has your agency lost any adoption litigation filed against you by an adoptive parent or birthparent? No.

OREGON

ADVENTIST ADOPTION AND FAMILY SERVICES

Respondent: Julianne Bodnar, Assistant Director
In charge of social services: Julianne Bodnar
6040 SE Belmont St., Portland, OR 97215
(503) 232-1211 • Fax: (503) 232-4756
E-mail: adventistadoption@msn.com • www.tagnet.org/adventistadoption
Year first licensed by state: 1965 approx.

Agency provides services for: International adoption; children with special needs; infants; homestudy if parents working with another agency; postplacement services; birthparent counseling, mediation.

What states do your adoptive parent clients come from? All states for infant adoptions and birthparents. Oregon and Washington for special needs.

Services provided adopting parents: Classes with other prospective parents; required readings of books and/or articles on adoption; group discussions about adoption; parenting discussions.

States/countries your birthparents/adopted children come from: All states.

What was the goal of your agency when first organized? What is the goal of your agency now? To provide needed services for birthmothers and homes for unexpected babies. Now: To create successful families for all types of children needing homes.

Nonrelative children placed in 1998: 26

Percent of adoptive placements under 6 mos.: 7%

Special expertise of staff: Adoptive parents on staff; licensed social workers.

In 1998, what was the average time from when a prospective adoptive parent applied to when he or she received a homestudy? 3–4 weeks

Average time from homestudy to placement of child: 6–12 mos.

What made you decide to work in the adoption field? The joy of giving families children. I love working with children.

Agency criteria for adoptive parents you work with: Varies depending on type of adoption.

How do you screen adoptive parents? Preapplication reviewed by assistant director and case worker; references.

How do you screen birthparents? We counsel any birthparent, whether they place or not.

What kind of medical information do you seek on older children? State provides medical information on special needs children.

What percent of your U.S. adoptions are nonwhite children? 30%

About what percent are children with medical problems? 10%

About what percent are children with emotional problems? 30%

Do you have a waiting list of prospective parents? Yes.

Is it all right if adopting parents you work with are on waiting lists of other agencies or attorneys? Yes.

Are your adoption fees based on a sliding scale? No.

Do you have an application fee? If yes, what is the amount of the application fee? Yes. $125

What is your homestudy fee (if a flat rate)? Varies.

What is your placement fee? $12,000 for infant.

Do adopting parents also pay fees for medical and hospital expenses for birthmother and baby when they have no insurance? No, unless unusual expenses occur.

My agency: Offers confidential adoptions; semi-open adoptions; meetings between birthparents and adoptive parents; birthparents pick adoptive parents from bios/resumes; full disclosure of names between birth and adoptive parents.

Does your agency provide videotapes of children needing adoption? No.

In how many cases with your agency has an adoptive parent been placed with a child but lost the child due to a birthparent challenge? 0

Has your agency lost any adoption litigation filed against you by an adoptive parent or birthparent? No.

ASSOCIATED SERVICES FOR INTERNATIONAL ADOPTION (ASIA)

Respondent: Michael Z. Han, Director of International Adoptions
In charge of social services: Michael Z. Han
5935 Willow Ln., Lake Oswego, OR 97035-5344
(503) 697-6863 • Fax: (503) 697-6957
E-mail: info@asiadopt.org • www.asiadopt.org
Year first licensed by state: 1995

Agency provides services for: International adoption; children with special needs; infants; homestudy if parents working with another agency; postplacement services.

What states do your adoptive parent clients come from? All states.

Services provided adopting parents: Classes with other prospective parents; required readings of books and/or articles on adoption; group discussions about adoption; parenting discussions.

States/countries your birthparents/adopted children come from: China.

What was the goal of your agency when first organized? What is the goal of your agency now? To create a better future for children in orphanages and promote cultural awareness in intercountry adoption. Now: Same.

Nonrelative children placed in 1998: 50

Percent of adoptive placements under 6 mos.: 2%. All of the children we place are foreign orphans.

Special expertise of staff: Licensed social workers; adoptive parents on board; bilingual adoption workers.

In 1998, what was the average time from when a prospective adoptive parent applied to when he or she received a homestudy? 2 mos.

Average time from homestudy to placement of child: 8 mos.

What made you decide to work in the adoption field? Orphaned children and the desire to help them get into loving families.

Agency criteria for adoptive parents you work with: At least 30 years of age; married or single; with or without children; with reasonable income, health, and stability; without criminal and child abuse records.

How do you screen adoptive parents? Through adoptive homestudy investigation; background check; interviews; references, etc.

What kind of medical information do you seek on older children? Physical exam, some lab tests, information on child's development and social interaction.

About what percent are children with medical problems? 10%

Do you have a waiting list of prospective parents? No.

Is it all right if adopting parents you work with are on waiting lists of other agencies or attorneys? Yes.

Are your adoption fees based on a sliding scale? No.

Do you have an application fee? If yes, what is the amount of the application fee? Yes. $125

What is your homestudy fee (if a flat rate)? $950, including pre-adoption homestudy and postplacement study.

What is your placement fee? $3,500 (Not a placement fee; program coordination.)

Do adopting parents also pay fees for medical and hospital expenses for birthmother and baby when they have no insurance? No.

If international adoption, what are average travel expenses? $2,600

If you place children from other countries, please list the estimated *entire* average cost to adoptive parents for each country. China, $12,000–15,000 (including agency fee, overseas fee, travel expenses).

Does your agency provide videotapes of children needing adoption? Yes, only of certain "waiting children" who are older and have significant special needs.

Has your agency lost any adoption litigation filed against you by an adoptive parent or birthparent? No.

THE BOYS AND GIRLS AID SOCIETY OF OREGON

Respondent: Lauren Greenbaum, LCSW, Adoption Lead Clinician
018 SW Boundary Ct., Portland, OR 97201
(503) 222-9661 • Fax: (503) 224-5960
www.boysngirlsaid.citysearch.com

Agency provides services for: U.S. adoption; children with special needs; infants; homestudy if parents working with another agency; postplacement services.

What states do your adoptive parent clients come from? Oregon.

Services provided adopting parents: Classes with other prospective parents; required readings of books and/or articles on adoption; "buddy families."

States/countries your birthparents/adopted children come from: Oregon.

What was the goal of your agency when first organized? What is the goal of your agency now? We were a receiving home. The basic goal was to get orphans in off the streets. Now: "To help children grow by strengthening the capacity of the individual child and family and helping change the societal conditions of poverty, racism, and sexism which affect children's growth."

Nonrelative children placed in 1998: 30

Percent of adoptive placements under 6 mos.: 90%

Special expertise of staff: Adoptive parents on staff; licensed social workers; therapists; adoptees.

In 1998, what was the average time from when a prospective adoptive parent applied to when he or she received a homestudy? 2–3 mos.

Average time from homestudy to placement of child: 9–12 mos.

What made you decide to work in the adoption field? Just always had an interest. My best friend is adopted and I supported her through a search.

Agency criteria for adoptive parents you work with: Over 21; if a couple, cohabitating for at least 2 years; general health sufficient to care for child over time.

How do you screen adoptive parents? Application, interviews, criminal check, physical exam, financial statement, references.

How do you screen birthparents? Interviews, check in with obstetrician.

What percent of your U.S. adoptions are nonwhite children? 10–15%

About what percent are children with medical problems? Less than 5%

Do you have a waiting list of prospective parents? Yes.

Is it all right if adopting parents you work with are on waiting lists of other agencies or attorneys? No.

Are your adoption fees based on a sliding scale? If yes, what are the sliding scale criteria? Yes. 20% of gross combined income. Minimum is $9,000; maximum is $17,000. Includes all costs except attorney fees to file petition ($300–600). $1,750 due during study, balance at placement.

Do you have an application fee? If yes, what is the amount of the application fee? Yes. $75

What is your homestudy fee (if a flat rate)? $750 (deducted from sliding scale balance).

What is your placement fee? Sliding scale criteria.

Do adopting parents also pay fees for medical and hospital expenses for birthmother and baby when they have no insurance? No.

My agency: Offers semi-open adoptions; meetings between birthparents and adoptive parents; birthparents pick adoptive parents from bios/resumes; full disclosure of names between birth and adoptive parents.

Does your agency provide videotapes of children needing adoption? No.

In how many cases with your agency has an adoptive parent been placed with a child but lost the child due to a birthparent challenge? 0

Has your agency lost any adoption litigation filed against you by an adoptive parent or birthparent? No.

CASCADE INTERNATIONAL CHILDREN'S SERVICES

Respondent: Lisa Adams-Reese, Executive Director
In charge of social services: Julie Eagleson
153 E. Historical Columbia Run Hwy., Troutdale, OR 97060
(503) 665-1589 • Fax: (503) 665-7865
E-mail: CascadeICS@aol.com
Year first licensed by state: 1994

Agency provides services for: International adoption; children with special needs; infants, homestudy if parents working with another agency, postplacement services; education and support.

What states do your adoptive parent clients come from? All states.

Services provided adopting parents: Classes with other prospective parents; required readings of books and/or articles on adoption; group discussions about adoption; parenting discussions.

States/countries your birthparents/adopted children come from: India, Guatemala, China, Vietnam, Russia.

What was the goal of your agency when first organized? What is the goal of your agency now? To find homes for orphaned and abandoned children. Now: To create futures for orphans and abandoned children in developing countries through humanitarian aid and adoption.

Nonrelative children placed in 1998: 89

Percent of adoptive placements under 6 mos: 10%

Special expertise of staff: Adoptive parents on staff; licensed social workers.

In 1998, what was the average time from when a prospective adoptive parent applied to when he or she received a homestudy? 30 days

Average time from homestudy to placement of child: 10 mos.

What made you decide to work in the adoption field? Working with families and a personal interest in this field.

Agency criteria for adoptive parents you work with: Very flexible. Requirements vary by country.

How do you screen adoptive parents? Through interviews, police checks, and references.

How do you screen birthparents? We don't work directly with birthparents. The agency or attorney in country does this step.

What kind of medical information do you seek from birthparents? Most are cases of abandonment, so little information is available.

What kind of medical information do you seek on older children? We have a doctor screen the child for medical issues.

About what percent are children with medical problems? 5%

Do you have a waiting list of prospective parents? Yes.

Is it all right if adopting parents you work with are on waiting lists of other agencies or attorneys? Situational by individual case.

Are your adoption fees based on a sliding scale? No.

Do you have an application fee? If yes, what is the amount of the application fee? Yes. $100

What is your homestudy fee (if a flat rate)? $800 plus three postplacement reports, $400.

If applicable, what is the average document language translation fee? $300–500

If international adoption, what are average travel expenses? $3,000

If you place children from other countries, please list the estimated entire average cost to adoptive parents for each country. India, $15,000; China, $14,500; Guatemala $13,000–19,000; Vietnam, $17,000.

My agency: Offers confidential adoptions.

Does your agency provide videotapes of children needing adoption? Yes.

In how many cases with your agency has an adoptive parent been placed with a child but lost the child due to a birthparent challenge? 0

Has your agency lost any adoption litigation filed against you by an adoptive parent or birthparent? No.

HOLT INTERNATIONAL CHILDREN'S SERVICES

Respondent: John Aeby, Director of Communications
In charge of social services: Carole Stiles, Vice-President of Social Services
P.O. Box 2880, Eugene, OR 97402
(541) 687-2202 • Fax: (541) 683-6175
E-mail: info@holtintl.org • www.holtintl.org
Year first licensed by state: 1956

Agency provides services for: International adoption; U.S. adoption; children with special needs; infants; homestudy if parents working with another agency; postplacement services.

What states do your adoptive parent clients come from? All states.

Services provided adopting parents: Classes with other prospective parents; required readings of books and/or articles on adoption.

States/countries your birthparents/adopted children come from: China, Ecuador, Guatemala, Hong Kong, India, Korea, Philippines, Romania, Thailand, Vietnam.

What was the goal of your agency when first organized? What is the goal of your agency now? To help homeless children in Korea to be adopted by families in the United States. Now: Holt International Children's Services is dedicated to carrying out God's plan for every child to have a permanent, loving home through reuniting birth families, in-country adoption, and international adoption. "Every child deserves a home of his own." —Harry Holt, Founder, Holt International Children's Services.

Nonrelative children placed in 1998: 963

Percent of adoptive placements under 6 mos.: We do not track this figure. Under 2 years, it's 82.6%.

Special expertise of staff: Adoptive parents on staff; licensed social workers; attorney.

What kind of medical information do you seek on older children? As much as possible.

About what percent are children with medical problems? About 20%

Do you have a waiting list of prospective parents? Yes.

Are your adoption fees based on a sliding scale? If yes, what are the sliding scale criteria? Yes. For homestudy only, based on income.

Do you have an application fee? If yes, what is the amount of the application fee? Yes. $150

What is your homestudy fee (if a flat rate)? $1,200–2,200

What is your placement fee? The adoption fee is $2,890–9,660

If you place children from other countries, please list the estimated *entire* average cost to adoptive parents for each country. $1,525 and up to have the child escorted. Very complicated to estimate costs for parents who travel.

My agency: Offers confidential adoptions; semi-open adoptions; meetings between birthparents and adoptive parents; birthparents pick adoptive parents from bios/resumes; full disclosure of names between birth and adoptive parents.

Does your agency provide videotapes of children needing adoption? Yes.

Are you an adoptive parent, adopted person, or birthparent? Adoptive parent.

In how many cases with your agency has an adoptive parent been placed with a child but lost the child due to a birthparent challenge? 0

JOURNEYS OF THE HEART ADOPTION SERVICE

Respondent: Susan Tompkins, Executive Director
P.O. Box 482, Hillsboro, OR 97123
(503) 681-3075 • Fax: (503) 640-5834
E-mail: Journeys-heart@msn.com
Year first licensed by state: 1993 in Oregon, 1999 in Illinois.

Agency provides services for: International adoption; U.S. adoption; children with special needs; infants; postplacement services; education.

What states do your adoptive parent clients come from? All states.

Services provided adopting parents: Classes with other prospective parents.

States/countries your birthparents/adopted children come from: Oregon, China, Vietnam, Nepal, Pacific Islands, India, Guatemala.

What was the goal of your agency when first organized? What is the goal of your agency now? To place children in permanent, safe, and loving homes who may be in harm's way. Now: Same.

Nonrelative children placed in 1998: 109

Percent of adoptive placements under 6 mos.: 90%

Special expertise of staff: Adoptive parents on staff, attorney.

In 1998, what was the average time from when a prospective adoptive parent applied to when he or she received a homestudy? 1–2 mos.

Average time from homestudy to placement of child: 8–10 mos.

What made you decide to work in the adoption field? Adoption is my personal passion. Parent of three adopted children.

Agency criteria for adoptive parents you work with: Case-by-case basis.

How do you screen adoptive parents? Criminal and child abuse checks; medical; four references; social work assessment; check out all certificates.

How do you screen birthparents? We work with most birthparents. (Criminal, drug, mental illness, etc.)

What kind of medical information do you seek from birthparents? Lengthy state form, which is not always valid if birthparents are ill-informed or misinformed.

What kind of medical information do you seek on older children? Medical records if available. If none, medical assessment.

What percent of your U.S. adoptions are nonwhite children? 50%

What percent are children with medical problems? 5%

Do you have a waiting list of prospective parents? Yes.

Is it all right if adopting parents you work with are on waiting lists of other agencies or attorneys? Yes.

Are your adoption fees based on a sliding scale? No.

Do you have an application fee? If yes, what is the amount of the application fee? Yes. $250

What is your homestudy fee (if a flat rate)? $850

What is your placement fee? $14,000 for Oregon newborn; $18,000 for out-of-state newborn; $14,500 for Washington newborn.

Do adopting parents also pay fees for medical and hospital expenses for birth-mother and baby when they have no insurance? If yes, what is the average fee paid? Yes. First day of baby's hospital expense.

If international adoption, what are average travel expenses? $1,500–3,000

My agency: Offers confidential adoptions: semi-open adoptions; meetings between birthparents and adoptive parents; birthparents pick adoptive parents from bios/resumes; full disclosure of names between birth and adoptive parents.

Does your agency provide videotapes of children needing adoption? No.

Are you an adoptive parent, adopted person, or birthparent? Adoptive parent.

In how many cases with your agency has an adoptive parent been placed with a child but lost the child due to a birthparent challenge? 0

Has your agency lost any adoption litigation filed against you by an adoptive parent or birthparent? No.

ORPHANS OVERSEAS

Respondent: Jane Kincaid, Executive Director
In charge of social services: Lee Wise
14986 NW Cornell Rd., Portland, OR 97229
(503) 297-2006 • Fax: (503) 533-5836
Year first licensed by state: 1992

Agency provides services for: International adoption; U.S. adoption; infants; postplacement services; birthmother home/advocacy program.

What states do your adoptive parent clients come from? All states.

Services provided adopting parents: Classes with other prospective parents; required readings of books and/or articles on adoption; group discussions about adoption; parenting discussions.

States/countries your birthparents/adopted children come from: Vietnam, Russia, China, United States.

What was the goal of your agency when first organized? What is the goal of your agency now? To honor Christ by serving the needs of orphans worldwide. Now: Same.

Nonrelative children placed in 1998: 83

Percent of adoptive placements under 6 mos: 71%

Special expertise of staff: Adoptive parents on staff; licensed social workers; nurse.

In 1998, what was the average time from when a prospective adoptive parent applied to when he or she received a homestudy? 1 mo.

Average time from homestudy to placement of child: $4\frac{1}{2}$ mos.

What made you decide to work in the adoption field? I was adopted and have always had a passion to help others like me.

Agency criteria for adoptive parents you work with: None, other than foreign government regulations.

How do you screen adoptive parents? Application; interview; credit checks; MMPI-2 tests; reference letters; medical records; criminal checks.

How do you screen birthparents? Interview; application; medical report.

What kind of medical information do you seek from birthparents? Questionnaire.

What kind of medical information do you seek on older children? Medical report from locale where they live.

About what percent are children with medical problems? 6%

Do you have a waiting list of prospective parents? Yes.

Is it all right if adopting parents you work with are on waiting lists of other agencies or attorneys? Yes.

Are your adoption fees based on a sliding scale? No.

Do you have an application fee? If yes, what is the amount of the application fee? Yes. $250

What is your homestudy fee (if a flat rate)? $475

What is your placement fee? $425

Do adopting parents also pay fees for medical and hospital expenses for birthmother and baby when they have no insurance? If yes, what is the average fee paid? Yes. Under $5,000

If international adoption, what are average travel expenses? $4,000–5,000

If you place children from other countries, please list the estimated *entire* average cost to adoptive parents for each country. $10,000 plus travel.

My agency: Offers confidential adoptions; semi-open adoptions; meetings between birthparents and adoptive parents; birthparents pick adoptive parents from bios/resumes; full disclosure of names between birth and adoptive parents.

Does your agency provide videotapes of children needing adoption? No.

Are you an adoptive parent, adopted person, or birthparent? Adoptive parent, adopted person.

In how many cases with your agency has an adoptive parent been placed with a child but lost the child due to a birthparent challenge? 0

Has your agency lost any adoption litigation filed against you by an adoptive parent or birthparent? No.

PLAN LOVING ADOPTIONS NOW, INC.

Respondent: Katey McIntire, Public Relations
In charge of social services: Ann Scott, Executive Director
P.O. Box 667, McMinnville, OR 97128
(503) 472-8452 • Fax: (503) 472-0665
E-mail: info@planlovingadoptions.org • www.planlovingadoptions.org
Year first licensed by state: 1975

Agency provides services for: International adoption; U.S. adoption; children with special needs; infants; homestudy if parents working with another agency; postplacement services.

What states do your adoptive parent clients come from? All states. We also place children with U.S. citizens living abroad (military families).

Services provided adopting parents: Classes with other prospective parents; required readings of books and/or articles on adoption; group discussions about adoption; parenting discussions.

States/countries your birthparents/adopted children come from: Oregon, Georgia, Texas, Florida, Missouri, West Virginia, Washington, D.C., Indiana, Kentucky, Kansas, Illinois, Ohio, Bulgaria, China, Colombia, Costa Rica, Guatemala, India, Latvia, Liberia, Peru, Romania, Russia, Siberia, Sierra Leone, Ukraine, Vietnam.

What was the goal of your agency when first organized? What is the goal of your agency now? To place children and babies without homes in permanent families of their own. Now: Same: "Joining children and families through adoption" since 1975.

Nonrelative children placed in 1998: 215

Percent of adoptive placements under 6 mos.: 0%

Special expertise of staff: Adoptive parents on staff; licensed social workers; therapists; physician; attorney.

In 1998, what was the average time from when a prospective adoptive parent applied to when he or she received a homestudy? 9 mos.–1 year

Average time from homestudy to placement of child: 8–11 mos.

Agency criteria for adoptive parents you work with: Criteria based on country/program requirements; if married, must be for 1 year.

How do you screen adoptive parents? Application, criminal history check, homestudy, reference.

How do you screen birthparents? Professional counselors for domestic programs.

What kind of medical information do you seek from birthparents? We have them complete detailed medical history form.

What kind of medical information do you seek on older children? We seek as much information made available.

What percent of your U.S. adoptions are nonwhite children? 75%

Do you have a waiting list of prospective parents? Yes.

Is it all right if adopting parents you work with are on waiting lists of other agencies or attorneys? No.

Are your adoption fees based on a sliding scale? No.

Do you have an application fee? If yes, what is the amount of the application fee? Yes. $300

What is your homestudy fee (if a flat rate)? $650

What is your placement fee? Up to $25,000

Do adopting parents also pay fees for medical and hospital expenses for birth-mother and baby when they have no insurance? If yes, what is the average fee paid? Yes. $12,000–14,000

If applicable, what is the average document language translation fee? Depends on country.

If international adoption, what are average travel expenses? $2,000–4,000

My agency: Offers semi-open adoptions; meetings between birthparents and adoptive parents; birthparents pick adoptive parents from bios/resumes; full disclosure of names between birth and adoptive parents.

Does your agency provide videotapes of children needing adoption? No.

In how many cases with your agency has an adoptive parent been placed with a child but lost the child due to a birthparent challenge? 1

Has your agency lost any adoption litigation filed against you by an adoptive parent or birthparent? No.

Is there anything I have not asked you that is important? So many children—so few families

PENNSYLVANIA

ADOPTION HOMESTUDY ASSOCIATES

Respondent: Sherry Gold, President
1014 Centre School Way, West Chester, PA 19382
(610) 429-1001
Year first licensed by state: 1993

Agency provides services for: International adoption; U.S. adoption; homestudy if parents working with another agency, postplacement services. This agency does homestudies and postplacements only. Does not do child placing.

What states do your adoptive parent clients come from? Pennsylvania.

Services provided adopting parents: Counseling.

States/countries your birthparents/adopted children come from: Parents from Pennsylvania, children from anywhere in the United States or abroad. (We do not place children. We do only homestudies and postplacement reports.)

What was the goal of your agency when first organized? What is the goal of your agency now? To provide adoption homestudies and postplacement services. Now: Same, plus counseling is available.

Nonrelative children placed in 1998: 35

Percent of adoptive placements under 6 mos.: 95%

Special expertise by staff: Licensed social workers.

In 1998, what was the average time from when a prospective adoptive parent applied to when he or she received a homestudy? 2 mos.

What made you decide to work in the adoption field? It makes me happy to see couples fulfill a dream. (I had a stillborn daughter.)

Agency criteria for adoptive parents you work with: No age requirement or number of children. Couple must be healthy and have the finances necessary to raise a child, and a safe environment in which to raise the child.

How do you screen adoptive parents? 1. By telephone; 2. Office interview; 3. In-depth home visit.

Do you have a waiting list of prospective parents? No.

Is it all right if adopting parents you work with are on waiting lists of other agencies or attorneys? No.

Are your adoption fees based on a sliding scale? No.

Do you have an application fee? No.

What is your homestudy fee (if a flat rate)? $800 for domestic, $900 for international.

What is your placement fee? $175–200; $200 for first visit; $175 for subsequent visits.

Do adopting parents also pay fees for medical and hospital expenses for birthmother and baby when they have no insurance? No. Depends on state.

My agency: Encourages parents to consider all types of adoption. We hope their goals will be the same as the birthparents' goals regarding open adoption.

Does your agency provide videotapes of children needing adoption? No.

Has your agency lost any adoption litigation filed against you by an adoptive parent or birthparent? No.

ADOPTION SERVICES, INC.

Respondent: Vincent F. Berger, PhD, President
In charge of social services: Vincent F. Berger
28 Central Blvd., Camp Hill, PA 17011
(717) 737-3960, 800-943-0400 • Fax: (717) 731-0157
E-mail: mail@adoptionservices.org • www.adoptionservices.org
Year first licensed by state: 1985

Agency provides services for: International adoption; U.S. adoption; infants; homestudy if parents working with another agency; postplacement services.

What states do your adoptive parent clients come from? Worldwide (except New York as of this date).

Services provided adopting parents: Individual meetings/screenings (no groups).

States/countries your birthparents/adopted children come from: United States, China, Russia.

What was the goal of your agency when first organized? What is the goal of your agency now? To provide to pregnant women appropriate and comprehensive counseling as well as an accurate picture of adoption and how it can help them. Now: Same.

Nonrelative children placed in 1998: 61, not including foreign.

Percent of adoptive placements under 6 mos.: 95%

Special expertise of staff: Individually and extensively trained staff.

In 1998, what was the average time from when a prospective adoptive parent applied to when he or she received a homestudy? 6 mos.

Average time from homestudy to placement of child: 1 week–6 mos.

What made you decide to work in the adoption field? I have been a practicing psychologist for 30 years and saw the great need for an extensive presentation of the adoption alternative.

Agency criteria for adoptive parents you work with: Must maintain current child abuse, criminal record, and FBI clearances and pass our extensive screening process.

How do you screen adoptive parents? 1. Registration process (written); 2. Application (written); 3. In-office personal interviews (about 4 hours); 4. Home evaluation (about 1 hour).

How do you screen birthparents? Frequent phone conversations, detailed questionnaires including genetic health history, follow-up with hospital.

What kind of medical information do you seek on older children? Current physical exam report, including immunizations, detailed health history from birth.

What percent of your U.S. adoptions are nonwhite children? 10%

Do you have a waiting list of prospective parents? Yes.

Is it all right if adopting parents you work with are on waiting lists of other agencies or attorneys? Yes.

Are your adoption fees based on a sliding scale? No.

Do you have an application fee? If yes, what is the amount of the application fee? Yes. Registration, $575; application, $1,075.

What is your homestudy fee (if a flat rate)? $2,700

What is your placement fee? $12,900 plus travel (at $100 per hour).

Do adopting parents also pay fees for medical and hospital expenses for birthmother and baby when they have no insurance? If yes, what is the average fee paid? Yes. $6,000

If applicable, what is the average document language translation fee? Varies.

If international adoption, what are average travel expenses? $2,500 per person.

If you place children from other countries, please list the estimated *entire* average cost to adoptive parents for each country. China, $20,000 (including travel for two people); Russia, $24,000 (including travel for two people).

My agency: Offers confidential adoptions; semi-open adoptions; meetings between birthparents and adoptive parents; full disclosure of names between birth and adoptive parents.

Does your agency provide videotapes of children needing adoption? No.

In how many cases with your agency has an adoptive parent been placed with a child but lost the child due to a birthparent challenge? 0. (One parental rights have been terminated. Prior to parental right termination, 7–9%.)

Has your agency lost any adoption litigation filed against you by an adoptive parent or birthparent? No.

ADOPTIONS FROM THE HEART

Respondent: Maxine G. Chalker, Executive Director
In charge of social services: Maxine G. Chalker
30–31 Hampstead Circle, Wynnewood, PA 19096
(610) 642-7200 • Fax: (610) 642-7938
E-mail: infoafth@aol.com • www.adoptionsfromtheheart.org
Year first licensed by state: 1985

Agency provides services for: International adoption; U.S. adoption; infants; homestudy if parents working with another agency; postplacement services.

What states do your adoptive parent clients come from? All states for the international and minority programs; Pennsylvania, New Jersey, and Delaware for domestic Caucasian programs.

Services provided adopting parents: Classes with other prospective parents; required readings of books and/or articles on adoption; group discussions about adoption; parenting discussions.

States/countries your birthparents/adopted children come from: Pennsylvania, New Jersey, Delaware, New York, West Virginia, Virginia, China, Vietnam, Latvia, Moldova, Russia, Thailand.

What was the goal of your agency when first organized? What is the goal of your agency now? To provide quality, comprehensive, ongoing adoption services to all members of the adoption triangle in agency or private adoptions. Agency specializes in open adoption of U.S. infants. Now: Same except for last sentence.

Nonrelative children placed in 1998: 229

Percent of adoptive placements under 6 mos.: 24%

In 1998, what was the average time from when a prospective adoptive parent applied to when he or she received a homestudy? 1 year

Average time from homestudy to placement of child: No average with open adoption, but maybe 1–2 years.

What made you decide to work in the adoption field? I am an adoptee and have a BSW and MSW.

Agency criteria for adoptive parents you work with: Very flexible, but prefer 2 year relationships with married couples.

How do you screen adoptive parents? Individual interviews, group sessions, educational course, references, police and child abuse clearances.

How do you screen birthparents? Interviews, release of information to get medical and hospital records, lengthy questionnaire.

What kind of medical information do you seek on older children? No U.S. children over 1 year placed. International children come with medical information, depending on the country. Usually HIV and hepatitis B tests and immunizations.

What percent of your U.S. adoptions are nonwhite children? 78%

Do you have a waiting list of prospective parents? Yes.

Is it all right if adopting parents you work with are on waiting lists of other agencies or attorneys? Yes, as long as they keep us informed.

Are your adoption fees based on a sliding scale? No.

Do you have an application fee? If yes, what is the amount of the application fee? Yes. $400 for Caucasian; $150 for all other programs.

What is your homestudy fee (if a flat rate)? $800

What is your placement fee? $11,000 for Caucasian; $4,000 for minority; $7,000 for international.

Do adopting parents also pay fees for medical and hospital expenses for birthmother and baby when they have no insurance? If yes, what is the average fee paid? Yes. $200–8,000

If applicable, what is the average document language translation fee? $350

If international adoption, what are average travel expenses? $2,500

If you place children from other countries, please list the estimated *entire* average cost to adoptive parents for each country. Vietnam, $22,600; China, $17,235; Thailand, $14,446; Russia, $26,040; Latvia, $20,650; Moldova, $26,150; network programs in Guatemala, $24,250; Ukraine, $20,635.

My agency: Offers semi-open adoptions; meetings between birthparents and adoptive parents; birthparents pick adoptive parents from bios/resumes; full disclosure of names between birth and adoptive parents.

Does your agency provide videotapes of children needing adoption? Yes, for eastern European countries only.

Are you an adoptive parent, adopted person, or birthparent? Adopted person.

In how many cases with your agency has an adoptive parent been placed with a child but lost the child due to a birthparent challenge? 4 in 1999.

Has your agency lost any adoption litigation filed against you by an adoptive parent or birthparent? No.

ADOPTIONS INTERNATIONAL INC.

Respondent: H. Lipschutz, Administrator
In charge of social services: Hannah Wallace, Director
601 S. Tenth St., Philadelphia, PA 19147
(215) 238-9057 • Fax: (215) 592-0464
E-mail: hwall334@aol.com
Year first licensed by state: 1983

Agency provides services for: International adoption; homestudy if parents working with another agency; postplacement services. All our services are related to international adoption. We do not do U.S. adoptions.

What states do your adoptive parent clients come from? All states and abroad.

Services provided adopting parents: Group discussions about adoption; parenting discussions; adoption preparation; country counseling; homestudy; placement; and postplacement supervision.

States/countries your birthparents/adopted children come from: Guatemala, Romania, China, Honduras.

What was the goal of your agency when first organized? What is the goal of your agency now? To make possible new and permanent family bonds between homeless children from abroad with capable and caring U.S. families. Now: Same.

Nonrelative children placed in 1998: 48

Percent of adoptive placements under 6 mos.: 50%

Special expertise of staff: Adoptive parents on staff; licensed social workers; therapists; attorney.

In 1998, what was the average time from when a prospective adoptive parent applied to when he or she received a homestudy? 1 mo.–6 weeks

What made you decide to work in the adoption field? Director adopted a foreign child and saw the need for facilitation of services.

Agency criteria for adoptive parents you work with: That they meet all requirements of U.S. Immigration, their state, and the government of the country abroad. Minimum age, 25 years.

How do you screen adoptive parents? Through receiving, reviewing, and verifying documents; through the homestudy process; through counseling sessions.

How do you screen birthparents? References, police clearances, financial verification, counseling, homestudy.

What kind of medical information do you seek from birthparents? As much as possible.

What kind of medical information do you seek on older children? Medical evaluation, lab testing, psychological testing, as applicable.

Do you have a waiting list of prospective parents? Yes.

Are your adoption fees based on a sliding scale? If yes, what are the sliding scale criteria? Yes. For those with incomes under $45,000 a year.

Do you have an application fee? If yes, what is the amount of the application fee? Yes. $100 for full-service applicants, $250 for partial-service applicants.

What is your homestudy fee (if a flat rate)? Full-service fee is $4,500 plus application fee and includes homestudy and placement and postplacement supervision fees. Partial-service fee is $3,000 plus application fee and does not include homestudy or supervision.

Do adopting parents also pay fees for medical and hospital expenses for birthmother and baby when they have no insurance? No.

If international adoption, what are average travel expenses? Varies according to country.

Does your agency provide videotapes of children needing adoption? Yes.

In how many cases with your agency has an adoptive parent been placed with a child but lost the child due to a birthparent challenge? 0

Has your agency lost any adoption litigation filed against you by an adoptive parent or birthparent? No.

BEST NEST

Respondent: Chawn Frontera, Adoption Social Worker II
In charge of social services: Michelle Isgate, Site Administrator
325 Market St., Williamsport, PA 17701
(570) 321-9690 • Fax: (570) 321-1980
Year first licensed by state: 1988

Agency provides services for: Children with special needs.

What states do your adoptive parent clients come from? Pennsylvania.

Services provided adopting parents: Classes with other prospective parents; required readings of books and/or articles on adoption; group discussions about adoption; parenting discussions.

States/countries your birthparents/adopted children come from: Pennsylvania and occasionally out-of-state.

What was the goal of your agency when first organized? What is the goal of your agency now? Foster care for medically needy children. Now: Serving medically fragile children, permanency for children in care, same match services in adoptions.

Nonrelative children placed in 1998: 20

Special expertise of staff: Adoptive parents on staff; licensed social workers.

In 1998, what was the average time from when a prospective adoptive parent applied to when he or she received a homestudy? 1 year

Average time from homestudy to placement of child: 6 mos.–1 year

What made you decide to work in the adoption field? First job out of college. Now have a passion for kids and system improvement.

Agency criteria for adoptive parents you work with: Case-by-case determination.

How do you screen adoptive parents? Homestudy; references; clearances.

How do you screen birthparents? Most birthparents are so due to involuntary termination of rights.

What kind of medical information do you seek from birthparents? Pennsylvania medical history registry.

What kind of medical information do you seek on older children? All we can get.

What percent of your U.S. adoptions are nonwhite children? 95%

About what percent are children with medical problems? 60%

About what percent are children with emotional problems? 40%

Do you have a waiting list of prospective parents? Yes.

Is it all right if adopting parents you work with are on waiting lists of other agencies or attorneys? Yes.

Are your adoption fees based on a sliding scale? No.

Do you have an application fee? No.

What is your homestudy fee (if a flat rate)? 0

What is your placement fee? 0

Do adopting parents also pay fees for medical and hospital expenses for birthmother and baby when they have no insurance? No.

My agency: Offers confidential adoptions; semi-open adoptions; meetings between birthparents and adoptive parents; full disclosure of names between birth and adoptive parents.

Does your agency provide videotapes of children needing adoption? No.

In how many cases with your agency has an adoptive parent been placed with a child but lost the child due to a birthparent challenge? 0

Has your agency lost any adoption litigation filed against you by an adoptive parent or birthparent? No.

COMMON SENSE ADOPTION SERVICES

Respondent: Erin R. Jones, Associate Executive Director
In charge of social services: Lori J. Tecter, service information
5021 E. Trindle Rd., Mechanicsberg, PA 17055
(800) 445-2444 • Fax: (717) 766-8015
Year first licensed by state: 1992

Agency provides services for: International adoption; U.S. adoption; children with special needs; infants; homestudy if parents working with another agency; postplacement services; post-finalization and support services; prime contractor for statewide adoption network.

What states do your adoptive parent clients come from? Pennsylvania.

Services provided adopting parents: Classes with other prospective parents; required readings of books and/or articles on adoption; group discussions about adoption; parenting discussions; support groups; counseling.

States/countries your birthparents/adopted children come from: United States, Russia, China, Guatemala, Bulgaria.

What was the goal of your agency when first organized? What is the goal of your agency now? Serve children with special needs through adoption. Now: Same.

Nonrelative children placed in 1998: 25

Percent of adoptive placements under 6 mos.: Less than 5%

Special expertise of staff: Adoptive parents on staff; licensed social workers; therapists.

In 1998, what was the average time from when a prospective adoptive parent applied to when he or she received a homestudy? 2 mos. to completion.

Average time from homestudy to placement of child: 5 mos.

What made you decide to work in the adoption field? Desire to serve children waiting for permanency, especially those in the child welfare system.

Agency criteria for adoptive parents you work with: Applicants must be at least 21 years of age; couples must be married for 1 year; must be Pennsylvania residents.

How do you screen adoptive parents? According to regulatory and best-practice requirements.

How do you screen birthparents? Individual counseling and education.

What kind of medical information do you seek from birthparents? Full disclosure.

What kind of medical information do you seek on older children? Pennsylvania requires full disclosure of all available information on all children.

What percent of your U.S. adoptions are nonwhite children? 60–70%

About what percent are children with medical problems? 30–40%

About what percent are children with emotional problems? 90–100%

Do you have a waiting list of prospective parents? Yes.

Is it all right if adopting parents you work with are on waiting lists of other agencies or attorneys? No.

Are your adoption fees based on a sliding scale? No.

Do you have an application fee? No.

What is your homestudy fee (if a flat rate)? $1,200

What is your placement fee? We only charge for matching and supervision. When families request those services we charge $750 for networking, $1,800 for supervision.

Do adopting parents also pay fees for medical and hospital expenses for birthmother and baby when they have no insurance? No.

If applicable, what is the average document language translation fee? Depends on program. $500 average.

If you place children from other countries, please list the estimated _entire_ average cost to adoptive parents for each country. We work with several agents to place foreign children. The total cost of these average $20,000.

My agency: Offers confidential adoptions; semi-open adoptions; meetings between birthparents and adoptive parents; birthparents pick adoptive parents from bios/resumes; full disclosure of names between birth and adoptive parents.

Does your agency provide videotapes of children needing adoption? Yes.

In how many cases with your agency has an adoptive parent been placed with a child but lost the child due to a birthparent challenge? 0

Has your agency lost any adoption litigation filed against you by an adoptive parent or birthparent? No.

JEWISH FAMILY AND CHILDREN'S SERVICE

Respondent: Shelley Sanders, Manager of Adoption Services
10125 Verree Rd., Philadelphia, PA 19116
(215) 673-0100 ext. 139 • Fax: (215) 698-2148
E-mail: shelleys@jfcsphil.org
Year first licensed by state: 1855

Agency provides services for: International adoption; U.S. adoption; children with special needs; homestudy if parents working with another agency; postplacement services.

What states do your adoptive parent clients come from? International adoption, all states. Homestudies, Pennsylvania and New Jersey.

Services provided adopting parents: Group discussions about adoption.

States/countries your birthparents/adopted children come from: Russia, China, Romania, Estonia, Moldova.

What was the goal of your agency when first organized? What is the goal of your agency now? To care for indigent and destitute Jewish children. Now: Agency is a nonsectarian multiservice community agency.

Nonrelative children placed in 1998: Recently merged with agency that placed 100+

Special expertise of staff: Adoptive parents on staff; licensed social workers; psychologists; therapists.

In 1998, what was the average time from when a prospective adoptive parent applied to when he or she received a homestudy? 2 weeks

Agency criteria for adoptive parents you work with: Criteria are based on the needs of the child.

How do you screen adoptive parents? Interviews, medicals, criminal and child abuse clearances, home visit.

Do you have a waiting list of prospective parents? No.

Are your adoption fees based on a sliding scale? No.

Do you have an application fee? If yes, what is the amount of the application fee? Yes. $50 for homestudy; $500 for international program.

What is your homestudy fee? (if a flat rate)? $750

What is your placement fee? $4,000 agency fee for international adoption.

If applicable, what is the average document language translation fee? $350

My agency: Offers confidential adoptions; semi-open adoptions; meetings between birthparents and adoptive parents; birthparents pick adoptive parents from bios/resumes; full disclosure of names between birth and adoptive parents.

Does your agency provide videotapes of children needing adoption? Yes.

In how many cases with your agency has an adoptive parent been placed with a child but lost the child due to a birthparent challenge? 0

Has your agency lost any adoption litigation filed against you by an adoptive parent or birthparent? No.

KALEIDOSCOPE OF FAMILY SERVICES

Respondent: Debra Fox, Director
In charge of social services: Debra Fox, Carole Denenberg, and Martia Leventon
355 W. Lancaster Ave., Haverford, PA 19041
(610) 642-3322 • Fax: (610) 642-7731
Year first licensed by state: 1992

Agency provides services for: International adoption; children with special needs; infants; homestudy if parents working with another agency; postplacement services.

What states do your adoptive parent clients come from? All states.

Services provided adopting parents: Group discussions about adoption; parenting discussions; support groups.

States/countries your birthparents/adopted children come from: Primarily Pennsylvania.

What was the goal of your agency when first organized? What is the goal of your agency now? To find permanent loving homes for all babies, regardless of race, background, or circumstances. Now: Same.

Nonrelative children placed in 1998: Approximately 30

Percent of adoptive placements under 6 mos.: 100%

Special expertise of staff: Licensed social workers; therapists; attorney.

In 1998, what was the average time from when a prospective adoptive parent applied to when he or she received a homestudy? 6–8 weeks

Average time from homestudy to placement of child: 6 mos.

What made you decide to work in the adoption field? Interested in social service work. Wanted babies of all races to find good homes.

Agency criteria for adoptive parents you work with: Must be 21 or older; must have approved homestudy. Otherwise, analyze on a case-by-case basis.

How do you screen adoptive parents? Must have approved homestudy.

How do you screen birthparents? Telephone counseling; face-to-face counseling.

What kind of medical information do you seek from birthparents? Very detailed 20-page social and biological history.

What kind of medical information do you seek on older children? We do not place children over age 1.

What percent of your U.S. adoptions are nonwhite children? 98%

About what percent are children with medical problems? 50%

Do you have a waiting list of prospective parents? Yes.

Is it all right if adopting parents you work with are on waiting lists of other agencies or attorneys? Yes.

Are your adoption fees based on a sliding scale? No.

Do you have an application fee? If yes, what is the amount of the application fee? Yes. $25

What is your homestudy fee (if a flat rate)? $875

What is your placement fee? $8,150

Do adopting parents also pay fees for medical and hospital expenses for birthmother and baby when they have no insurance? Yes, varies widely.

My agency: Offers confidential adoptions; semi-open adoptions; meetings between birthparents and adoptive parents; birthparents pick adoptive parents from bios/resumes; full disclosure of names between birth and adoptive parents.

Does your agency provide videotapes of children needing adoption? No.

In how many cases with your agency has an adoptive parent been placed with a child but lost the child due to a birthparent challenge? 3

Has your agency lost any adoption litigation filed against you by an adoptive parent or birthparent? No.

MARIAN ADOPTION SERVICES

Respondent: Marlene Piasecki, Director
In charge of social services: Marlene Piasecki
600 N. Bethlehem Pike, Ambler, PA 19002
(215) 283-8522 • Fax: (215) 283-8955
E-mail: masadopt@aol.com
Year first licensed by state: 1993 in Pennsylvania; 1996 in New Jersey.

Agency provides services for: International adoption; U.S. adoption; children with special needs; infants; homestudy if parents working with another agency; postplacement services.

What states do your adoptive parent clients come from? Primarily Pennsylvania and New Jersey.

Services provided adopting parents: Parenting discussions.

States/countries your birthparents/adopted children come from: Primarily Pennsylvania and New Jersey, also Russia and China.

What is the goal of your agency now? To provide permanent homes for children.

Nonrelative children placed in 1998: 40

Special expertise of staff: Adoptive parents on staff; licensed social workers; psychologists; therapists; physician.

In 1998, what was the average time from when a prospective adoptive parent applied to when he or she received a homestudy? Less than 1 mo. to begin, 4 mos. to complete.

Average time from homestudy to placement of child: 3 mos. for African-American infants; 2 years for Caucasian infants; 1 year for international infants; 1 year for special needs adoption.

What made you decide to work in the adoption field? To provide placement homes for children.

Agency criteria for adoptive parents you work with: Aged 21 and over. If married, must be married 1 year. We accept singles.

How do you screen adoptive parents? Individual homestudy; child abuse and criminal clearance; references.

How do you screen birthparents? Individual interviews; medical history; birthfather and extended family whenever possible.

What kind of medical information do you seek on older children? All available medical records.

What percent of your U.S. adoptions are nonwhite children? 49%

About what percent are children with emotional problems? 8%

Do you have a waiting list of prospective parents? No.

Is it all right if adopting parents you work with are on waiting lists of other agencies or attorneys? Yes.

Are your adoption fees based on a sliding scale? No.

Do you have an application fee? If yes, what is the amount of the application fee? Yes. $175

What is your homestudy fee (if a flat rate)? $975

What is your placement fee? Depends on program.

Do adopting parents also pay fees for medical and hospital expenses for birthmother and baby when they have no insurance? If yes, what is the average fee paid? Yes, but this is very rare. $4,000

If international adoption, what are average travel expenses? We are a networking agency. We don't place directly from outside the United States.

If you place children from other countries, please list the estimated *entire* average cost to adoptive parents for each country. We tell families to assume about $25,000.

My agency: Offers confidential adoptions; semi-open adoptions; meetings between birthparents and adoptive parents; birthparents pick adoptive parents from bios/resumes; full disclosure of names between birth and adoptive parents.

Does your agency provide videotapes of children needing adoption? No.

Are you an adoptive parent, adopted person, or birthparent? Adoptive parent.

In how many cases with your agency has an adoptive parent been placed with a child but lost the child due to a birthparent challenge? In Pennsylvania it takes 3–4 mos. to complete a termination of parental rights. We had one birthparent who changed her mind before termination of parental rights. We have never had a completed termination of parental rights challenge.

Has your agency lost any adoption litigation filed against you by an adoptive parent or birthparent? No.

TRESSLER LUTHERAN SERVICES

Respondent: Barbara A. Holtan, MS, MSW, Director, Adoption Services
In charge of social services: Barbara A. Holtan
836 S. George St., York, PA 17403
(717) 845-9113 • Fax: (717) 852-8439
E-mail: barbholtan@bressler.org, TLS@bressler.org
Year first licensed by state: Special needs adoption program was formally implemented in 1972.

Agency provides services for: International adoption; U.S. adoption; children with special needs; infants (special needs); homestudy if parents working with another agency; postplacement services; foster care and adoption kinship.

What states do your adoptive parent clients come from? Pennsylvania, Maryland, Delaware.

Services provided adopting parents: Classes with other prospective parents; required readings of books and/or articles on adoption; group discussions about adoption; parenting discussions; support groups; newsletter; counseling.

States/countries your birthparents/adopted children come from: Anywhere.

What was the goal of your agency when first organized? What is the goal of your agency now? TLS has been around since 1868. I am answering questions in relation to adoption program.

Nonrelative children placed in 1998: 61

Special expertise of staff: Adoptive parents on staff; licensed social workers; therapists.

In 1998, what was the average time from when a prospective adoptive parent applied to when he or she received a homestudy? 3 mos., including required 20-hour family prep, once a week for 10 weeks.

Average time from homestudy to placement of child: 9 mos. is average; some are much faster, some take longer.

What made you decide to work in the adoption field? I became Tim's mom in April, 1975 (from Vietnam) and I was hooked!

How do you screen adoptive parents? We don't; we teach and expect self-assessment, and prospective parents screen themselves.

How do you screen birthparents? We serve and assist birthparents, we don't screen.

What kind of medical information do you seek from birthparents? Absolutely everything we can get.

What kind of medical information do you seek on older children? Same.

What percent of your U.S. adoptions are nonwhite children? 40%

About what percent are children with medical problems? 20%

About what percent are children with emotional problems? 85%

Do you have a waiting list of prospective parents? Yes.

Is it all right if adopting parents you work with are on waiting lists of other agencies or attorneys? Yes.

Are your adoption fees based on a sliding scale? No.

Do you have an application fee? No.

What is your homestudy fee (if a flat rate)? $425

What is your placement fee? No other fees are charged to parents.

My agency: Offers confidential adoptions; semi-open adoptions; meetings between birthparents and adoptive parents.

Does your agency provide videotapes of children needing adoption? Yes.

Are you an adoptive parent, adopted person, or birthparent? Adoptive parent.

In how many cases with your agency has an adoptive parent been placed with a child but lost the child due to a birthparent challenge? A tiny number. Six in 26 years.

Has your agency lost any adoption litigation filed against you by an adoptive parent or birthparent? No.

YOUR ADOPTION AGENCY, INC.

Respondent: Amy James, Director
In charge of social services: Amy James
RR2 Box 2638, Susquehanna, PA 18847
(570) 853-2022, (888) ADOPT-10 • Fax: (570) 853-4997
E-mail: adoption@epix.net • http://youradoption.com
Year first licensed by state: 1994

Agency provides services for: International adoption; U.S. adoption; children with special needs; infants; homestudy if parents working with another agency, postplacement services.

What states do your adoptive parent clients come from? Mostly Pennsylvania.

Services provided adopting parents: Classes with other prospective parents; required readings of books and/or articles on adoption; group discussions about adoption; parenting discussions; social events.

States/countries your birthparents/adopted children come from: Mostly Pennsylvania; developing a program in Guatemala.

What was the goal of your agency when first organized? What is the goal of your agency now? Infant adoption. Now: Infant and special needs adoption.

Nonrelative children placed in 1998: 8

Percent of adoptive placements under 6 mos.: 25%

Special expertise of staff: Adoptive parents on staff; licensed social workers.

In 1998, what was the average time from when a prospective adoptive parent applied to when he or she received a homestudy? Less than 1 mo.

Average time from homestudy to placement of child: About $1\frac{1}{2}$ years.

What made you decide to work in the adoption field? Adopting my daughter.

Agency criteria for adoptive parents you work with: We try to be as flexible as possible.

How do you screen adoptive parents? FBI check; state police and child abuse clearances; medical reports; references.

How do you screen birthparents? Interview; counseling; medical history.

What kind of medical information do you seek from birthparents? As complete as possible. Availability of birthfather's information varies.

What kind of medical information do you seek on older children? These children are typically in custody of county, which provides all available information.

What percent of your U.S. adoptions are nonwhite children? About 30%

About what percent are children with medical problems? About 10%

About what percent are children with emotional problems? About 20%

Do you have a waiting list of prospective parents? Yes.

Is it all right if adopting parents you work with are on waiting lists of other agencies or attorneys? Yes.

Are your adoption fees based on a sliding scale? No.

Do you have an application fee? If yes, what is the amount of the application fee? Yes. $100

What is your homestudy fee (if a flat rate)? $1,400

What is your placement fee? $6,000

If you place children from other countries, please list the estimated *entire* average cost to adoptive parents for each country. Program is being established, so don't know yet.

My agency: Offers confidential adoptions; semi-open adoptions; meetings between birthparents and adoptive parents; birthparents pick adoptive parents from bios/resumes; full disclosure of names between birth and adoptive parents.

Does your agency provide videotapes of children needing adoption? No.

Are you an adoptive parent, adopted person, or birthparent? Adoptive parent.

In how many cases with your agency has an adoptive parent been placed with a child but lost the child due to a birthparent challenge? 0

Has your agency lost any adoption litigation filed against you by an adoptive parent or birthparent? No.

RHODE ISLAND

ADOPTION OPTIONS

Respondent: Peg Boyle, LICSW, Adoption Social Worker
In charge of social services: Erin Minior, LICSW
229 Waterman St., Providence, RI 02906
(401) 331-5437 • Fax: (401) 331-5572
Year first licensed by state: 1938

Agency provides services for: U.S. adoption; infants; homestudy if parents working with another agency; postplacement services; finalization of adoptions; termination of parental rights.

What states do your adoptive parent clients come from? Rhode Island.

Services provided adopting parents: Classes with other prospective parents; group discussions about adoption;

States/countries your birthparents/adopted children come from: Rhode Island.

What was the goal of your agency when first organized? What is the goal of your agency now? To provide quality service to adoptive parents and birthparents. Now: Same.

Nonrelative children placed in 1998: 12

Percent of adoptive placements under 6 mos.: 100%

Special expertise of staff: Adoptive parents on staff; licensed social workers; therapists.

In 1998, what was the average time from when a prospective adoptive parent applied to when he or she received a homestudy? $2\frac{1}{2}$ mos.

Average time from homestudy to placement of child: 6 mos. (This was an unusual year!)

What made you decide to work in the adoption field? The opportunity to help people build families, as well as the complexity and challenge of the job.

Agency criteria for adoptive parents you work with: We do not have any criteria other than that the parents be able to provide a safe and loving home. Parents do need to provide evidence of financial security, physical health, etc.

How do you screen adoptive parents? We meet with parents approximately five or six times and request references. We ask questions relative to safety and security in the home. We also request clearances from the Department of Children, Youth, and Families, as well as the Attorney General's office.

How do you screen birthparents? We spend as much time as possible with birthparents and try to build a relationship. We assess for their needs and obtain as thorough a history as possible.

What percent of your U.S. adoptions are nonwhite children? 30%

About what percent are children with medical problems? 40%

Do you have a waiting list of prospective parents? Yes.

Is it all right if adopting parents you work with are on waiting lists of other agencies or attorneys? Yes.

Are your adoption fees based on a sliding scale? No.

Do you have an application fee? If yes, what is the amount of the application fee? Yes. $50

What is your homestudy fee (if a flat rate)? $1,500 for domestic homestudy; $1,700 for international homestudy.

What is your placement fee? $15,000

Do adopting parents also pay fees for medical and hospital expenses for birthmother and baby when they have no insurance? No.

My agency: Offers confidential adoptions; semi-open adoptions; meetings between birthparents and adoptive parents; birthparents pick adoptive parents from bios/resumes; full disclosure of names between birth and adoptive parents.

Does your agency provide videotapes of children needing adoption? No.

In how many cases with your agency has an adoptive parent been placed with a child but lost the child due to a birthparent challenge? 1. (Rights had not yet been terminated.)

Has your agency lost any adoption litigation filed against you by an adoptive parent or birthparent? No. (None filed.)

GIFT OF LIFE ADOPTION SERVICE, INC.

Respondent: Donna Ricci, President, Director
In charge of social services: Donna Ricci
1053 Park Ave., Cranston, RI 02910
(401) 943-6484 • Fax: (401) 943-6806
E-mail: 75317.1056@compuserve.com
Year first licensed by state: 1992

Agency provides services for: International adoption; U.S. adoption; children with special needs; infants; homestudy if parents working with another agency; postplacement services; adoption finalization services.

What states do your adoptive parent clients come from? All states.

Services provided adopting parents: Classes with other prospective parents; required readings of books and/or articles on adoption; group discussions about adoption; parenting discussions; private meeting with parents.

States/countries your birthparents/adopted children come from: United States, Russia, China, Guatemala.

What was the goal of your agency when first organized? What is the goal of your agency now? To find loving homes for children in need. Now: Same and also we are committed to providing humanitarian aid to orphanages overseas.

Nonrelative children placed in 1998: 100

Percent of adoptive placements under 6 mos.: 35%

Special expertise of staff: Adoptive parents on staff; licensed social workers; physician; attorney.

In 1998, what was the average time from when a prospective adoptive parent applied to when he or she received a homestudy? 1 mo.

Average time from homestudy to placement of child: 6 mos.

What made you decide to work in the adoption field? Personally I have adopted two children from Romania and I remain firmly committed to the cause.

Agency criteria for adoptive parents you work with: Our agency is very nonrestrictive. However, we must follow restrictions from foreign governments.

How do you screen adoptive parents? Personal meetings; references; police, child abuse, and FBI clearances; homestudy process, etc.

How do you screen birthparents? Social evaluation

What kind of medical information do you seek from birthparents? All information available.

What kind of medical information do you seek on older children? All information available.

What percent of your U.S. adoptions are nonwhite children? 0%

About what percent are children with medical problems? 5%

About what percent are children with emotional problems? 5%

Do you have a waiting list of prospective parents? Yes.

Is it all right if adopting parents you work with are on waiting lists of other agencies or attorneys? Yes.

Are your adoption fees based on a sliding scale? No.

Do you have an application fee? If yes, what is the amount of the application fee? Yes. $150

What is your homestudy fee (if a flat rate)? $2,250

What is your placement fee? Varies.

Do adopting parents also pay fees for medical and hospital expenses for birthmother and baby when they have no insurance? If yes, what is the average fee paid? Yes. Varies.

If international adoption, what are average travel expenses? $500–900 per person, round trip.

If applicable, what is the average document language translation fee? $300

If you place children from other countries, please list the estimated *entire* average cost to adoptive parents for each country. Russia, $20,000; China, $13,000; Guatemala, $22,000.

My agency: Offers confidential adoptions; semi-open adoptions; meetings between birthparents and adoptive parents; birthparents pick adoptive parents from bios/resumes; full disclosure of names between birth and adoptive parents.

Does your agency provide videotapes of children needing adoption? Yes.

Are you an adoptive parent, adopted person, or birthparent? Adoptive parent.

In how many cases with your agency has an adoptive parent been placed with a child but lost the child due to a birthparent challenge? 0

Has your agency lost any adoption litigation filed against you by an adoptive parent or birthparent? No.

LITTLE TREASURES ADOPTION SERVICES, INC.

Respondents: Eric H. and Maryanne Johnson, Directors
In charge of social services: Karen Cryan, LICW
P.O. Box 20555, Cranston, RI 02920
(401) 828-7747
E-mail: ltltreasur@aol.com
Year first licensed by state: 1996

Agency provides services for: International adoption; infants; homestudy if parents working with another agency; postplacement services.

What states do your adoptive parent clients come from? All states.

Services provided adopting parents: Parenting discussions. We give individual adoption preparation and education.

States/countries your birthparents/adopted children come from: We do not work directly with birthparents at this time. Children come from Guatemala, China, Cambodia, Romania, and Russia.

What was the goal of your agency when first organized? What is the goal of your agency now? Uniting children who need permanent, loving homes with families wanting to adopt children and to provide continued support throughout the process. Now: Same.

Nonrelative children placed in 1998: 5

Percent of adoptive placements under 6 mos.: Our children ranged from 0–3 years of age at the time of referral.

Special expertise of staff: Adoptive parents on staff; licensed social workers; attorney. Director has a background as a pediatric nurse.

In 1998, what was the average time from when a prospective adoptive parent applied to when he or she received a homestudy? 1 mo.

Average time from homestudy to placement of child: 6–7 mos.

What made you decide to work in the adoption field? We are the adoptive parents of two daughters born overseas and we have always been actively involved in the adoption world.

Agency criteria for adoptive parents you work with: We do not impose restrictions on adoptive parents or criteria other than the regulations set by INS or the country or state of the child's origin.

How do you screen adoptive parents? The homestudy process and the immigration process are our tools for screening parents.

What kind of medical information do you seek on older children? Full information or whatever is available.

Do you have a waiting list of prospective parents? Yes.

Is it all right if adopting parents you work with are on waiting lists of other agencies or attorneys? Yes.

Are your adoption fees based on a sliding scale? No.

Do you have an application fee? If yes, what is the amount of the application fee? Yes. $75

What is your homestudy fee (if a flat rate)? $1,200

What is your placement fee? It varies according to the country.

If international adoption, what are average travel expenses? Very variable; $500 per person to $3,000 per person, depending on country.

If you place children from other countries, please list the estimated *entire* average cost to adoptive parents for each country. Guatemala, $15,000; China, $11,000–13,000; Chile, $16,000; Romania, $13,000; Russia, $14,000.

Does your agency provide videotapes of children needing adoption? Yes, if available.

Are you an adoptive parent, adopted person, or birthparent? Adoptive parent.

In how many cases with your agency has an adoptive parent been placed with a child but lost the child due to a birthparent challenge? 0

Has your agency lost any adoption litigation filed against you by an adoptive parent or birthparent? No.

SOUTH CAROLINA

CHILDREN UNLIMITED, INC.

Respondent: Linda J. Eisele, Executive Director
In charge of social services: Linda J. Eisele
P.O. 11463, Columbia, SC 29211
(803) 799-8311 • Fax: (803) 765-0284
E-mail: cuadop@usit.net • http://children-unlimited.org
Year first licensed by state: 1977

Agency provides services for: U.S. adoption; children with special needs; postplacement services.

What states do your adoptive parent clients come from? South Carolina.

Services provided adopting parents: Classes with other prospective parents; required readings of books and/or articles on adoption; group discussions about adoption; parenting discussions; support group.

States/countries your birthparents/adopted children come from: Primarily South Carolina.

What was the goal of your agency when first organized? What is the goal of your agency now? Special needs adoption. Now: Permanency.

Nonrelative children placed in 1998: 29

Percent of adoptive placements under 6 mos.: 0%

Special expertise of staff: Adoptive parents on staff; licensed social workers; therapists; mediator.

In 1998, what was the average time from when a prospective adoptive parent applied to when he or she received a homestudy? 5 mos.

Average time from homestudy to placement of child: $5\frac{1}{2}$ mos.

What made you decide to work in the adoption field? I am an adoptive parent.

Agency criteria for adoptive parents you work with: Over 21, clear marital status (married or single).

How do you screen adoptive parents? Telephone intake and home visit.

What kind of medical information do you seek from birthparents? We cull everything we can from records available.

What kind of medical information do you seek on older children? Everything state will furnish and special information when indicated.

What percent of your U.S. adoptions are nonwhite children? 65%

About what percent are children with medical problems? 30%

About what percent are children with emotional problems? 100%

Do you have a waiting list of prospective parents? No.

Is it all right if adopting parents you work with are on waiting lists of other agencies or attorneys? No.

Are your adoption fees based on a sliding scale? No.

Do you have an application fee? No.

What is your homestudy fee (if a flat rate)? None.

What is your placement fee? None. No fees to parents.

My agency: Offers confidential adoptions; semi-open adoptions; meetings between birthparents and adoptive parents when state allows.

Does your agency provide videotapes of children needing adoption? Yes.

Are you an adoptive parent, adopted person, or birthparent? Adoptive parent.

In how many cases with your agency has an adoptive parent been placed with a child but lost the child due to a birthparent challenge? Never.

Has your agency lost any adoption litigation filed against you by an adoptive parent or birthparent? No.

TENNESSEE

ADOPTION COUNSELING SERVICES

Respondent: Ellen S. Rardin, Director
In charge of social services: Ellen S. Rardin
2185 Wickersham Ln., Germantown, TN 38139
(901) 753-9089 • Fax: (901) 753-9089
E-mail: ESRardin@aol.com
Year first licensed by state: 1992

Agency provides services for: International adoption; U.S. adoption; infants; homestudy if parents working with another agency; postplacement services; workshops; classes.

What states do your adoptive parent clients come from? Local, but occasionally other states.

Services provided adopting parents: Classes with other prospective parents; group discussions about adoption.

States/countries your birthparents/adopted children come from: Local.

What was the goal of your agency when first organized? What is the goal of your agency now? Provide consultation and education. Provide homestudies for international and domestic adoptions. Now: Same as above but facilitate adoptions as well.

Nonrelative children placed in 1998: 4

Percent of adoptive placements under 6 mos.: 100%

Special expertise of staff: Licensed social workers; therapists.

In 1998, what was the average time from when a prospective adoptive parent applied to when he or she received a homestudy? Upon appointment.

How do you screen adoptive parents? Readiness to adopt and willingness to learn.

How do you screen birthparents? Interview and 16 years of experience.

What kind of medical information do you seek from birthparents? Comprehensive testing for drugs, HIV.

What kind of medical information do you seek on older children? Comprehensive and pediatric exam.

What percent of your U.S. adoptions are nonwhite children? 15%

Do you have a waiting list of prospective parents? No.

Is it all right if adopting parents you work with are on waiting lists of other agencies or attorneys? Yes.

Are your adoption fees based on a sliding scale? No.

Do you have an application fee? No.

What is your homestudy fee (if a flat rate)? $500–1,400

What is your placement fee? $2,500

Do adopting parents also pay fees for medical and hospital expenses for birth-mother and baby when they have no insurance? If yes, what is the average fee paid? Yes. $10,000–16,000

My agency: Offers confidential adoptions; semi-open adoptions; meetings between birthparents and adoptive parents; birthparents pick adoptive parents from bios/resumes; full disclosure of names between birth and adoptive parents.

Does your agency provide videotapes of children needing adoption? No.

In how many cases with your agency has an adoptive parent been placed with a child but lost the child due to a birthparent challenge? 0

Has your agency lost any adoption litigation filed against you by an adoptive parent or birthparent? No.

CATHOLIC CHARITIES CARING CHOICES PROGRAM

Respondent: Donna T. Taylor, Department Director
30 White Bridge Rd., Nashville, TN 37205
(615) 352-3089 • Fax: (615) 352-8591
Year first licensed by state: 1970

Agency provides services for: International adoption; U.S. adoption; children with special needs; infants; homestudy if parents working with another agency; postplacement services.

What states do your adoptive parent clients come from? Tennessee.

Services provided adopting parents: Classes with other prospective parents; required readings of books and/or articles on adoption; group discussions about adoption; parenting discussions; seminars on international adoption issues. We provide homestudies for couples who have adopted from numerous countries: Russia, Guatemala, Vietnam, India, Latvia, etc.

States/countries your birthparents/adopted children come from: Tennessee, China.

What is the goal of your agency now? To provide professional homestudies to adoptive parents and supportive decision-making counseling for birthparents.

Nonrelative children placed in 1998: 12 domestic; assisted with 50 international adoptions.

Percent of adoptive placements under 6 mos.: Nearly all.

Special expertise of staff: Adoptive parents on staff; all staff have social work or psychology degree; two have masters in guidance/counseling; one has MSW.

In 1998, what was the average time from when a prospective adoptive parent applied to when he or she received a homestudy? For international and independent studies, there is no waiting time. Domestic adoptions are done in groups, generally, two to three times a year.

Average time from homestudy to placement of child: For first child, 18–24 mos.; for second child, 2–3 years.

Agency criteria for adoptive parents you work with: Will place up to two children in a home. Adoptive couples' median age is 45 years or less. Been married 3 years.

How do you screen adoptive parents? Information/intake sessions; individual sessions; fingerprint clearances; references; psychological testing and/or marriage counseling as indicated.

What kind of medical information do you seek from birthparents? Individual sessions; medical information from treating physician; other testing or counseling as needed.

What kind of medical information do you seek on older children? Hospital discharge and treating pediatrician's report.

What percent of your U.S. adoptions are nonwhite children? 25–30%

Do you have a waiting list of prospective parents? Yes.

Are your adoption fees based on a sliding scale? If yes, what are the sliding scale criteria? Yes. 15% for non-special needs (between $4,000–12,000); 8% for special needs (between $2,000–8,000).

Do you have an application fee? If yes, what is the amount of the application fee? Yes. $500

What is your homestudy fee (if a flat rate)? $1,400 for international; $800–1,000 for independent.

Do adopting parents also pay fees for medical and hospital expenses for birthmother and baby when they have no insurance? If yes, what is the average fee paid? Yes. $2,000

My agency: Offers semi-open adoptions; meetings between birthparents and adoptive parents; birthparents pick adoptive parents from bios/resumes; full disclosure of names between birth and adoptive parents.

Has your agency lost any adoption litigation filed against you by an adoptive parent or birthparent? No.

HEAVEN SENT CHILDREN

Respondent: Sandra DuCharme Russell
316 West Lytle St., Suite 110, Murfreesboro, TN 37310
(615) 898-0803 • Fax: (615) 898-1990
Year first licensed by state: 1991

Agency provides services for: International adoption; homestudy if parents working with another agency; postplacement services.

What states do your adoptive parent clients come from? Primarily Tennessee.

Services provided adopting parents: Workshops; homestudy; placement and postplacement supervision.

States/countries your birthparents/adopted children come from: Russia, Latvia, Korea, China, Guatemala, Vietnam.

What was the goal of your agency when first organized? What is the goal of your agency now? To find homes for children. Now: Same.

Nonrelative children placed in 1998: 66

Percent of adoptive placements under 6 mos.: 38%

Special expertise of staff: Adoptive parents on staff; licensed social workers; therapists.

In 1998, what was the average time from when a prospective adoptive parent applied to when he or she received a homestudy? 3 weeks to begin.

Average time from homestudy to placement of child: 9 mos.–1 year

What made you decide to work in the adoption field? I have always been surrounded by adoption and then became an adoptive parent and social worker.

Agency criteria for adoptive parents you work with: Must be 25–55 years old. No limit for children in home if capable of caring for them.

How do you screen adoptive parents? Application and interview.

How do you screen birthparents? Interview and application.

What kind of medical information do you seek from birthparents? Everything we can get legally.

What kind of medical information do you seek on older children? Everything we can get.

What percent of your U.S. adoptions are nonwhite children? 10%

About what percent are children with medical problems? 10%

About what percent are children with emotional problems? 5%

Do you have a waiting list of prospective parents? Yes.

Is it all right if adopting parents you work with are on waiting lists of other agencies or attorneys? Yes.

Are your adoption fees based on a sliding scale? If yes, what are the sliding scale criteria? Yes. Income-based: $6,000–12,000 for placement.

Do you have an application fee? If yes, what is the amount of the application fee? Yes. $100

What is your homestudy fee (if a flat rate)? $1,200 if domestic, $1,500 if international.

If international adoption, what are average travel expenses? Depends on country.

If applicable, what is the average document language translation fee? Depends on country.

If you place children from other countries, please list the estimated *entire* **average cost to adoptive parents for each country.** China, $14,500; Vietnam, $13,000.

My agency: Offers confidential adoptions; semi-open adoptions; meetings between birthparents and adoptive parents; birthparents pick adoptive parents from bios/resumes; full disclosure of names between birth and adoptive parents.

Does your agency provide videotapes of children needing adoption? Yes.

Are you an adoptive parent, adopted person, or birthparent? Adoptive parent.

In how many cases with your agency has an adoptive parent been placed with a child but lost the child due to a birthparent challenge? 0

Has your agency lost any adoption litigation filed against you by an adoptive parent or birthparent? No.

SMALL WORLD ADOPTION PROGRAMS

Respondent: Jim Savley, President
In charge of social services: Tom McDonald, Director of Adoptive Parent Services
401 Bonnaspring Dr., Hermitage, TN 37076
(615) 883-4372 • Fax: (615) 885-7582
E-mail: SWA@SWA.net • www.swa.net
Year first licensed by state: 1986

Agency provides services for: International adoption; U.S. adoption; children with special needs; infants; homestudy if parents working with another agency; postplacement services; birthparent services (counseling, etc.).

What states do your adoptive parent clients come from? All states and many foreign countries.

Services provided adopting parents: Classes with other prospective parents; required readings of books and articles on adoption; group discussions about adoption; parenting discussions; cultural training.

States/countries your birthparents/adopted children come from: China, Guatemala, Latvia, Romania, Quebec, Russia, Ukraine.

What was the goal of your agency when first organized? What is the goal of your agency now? To preserve and enhance the lives of children through adoption at home and around the world. Now: Same.

Nonrelative children placed in 1998: 104

Percent of adoptive placements under 6 mos.: 30%

Special expertise of staff: Adoptive parents on staff; licensed social workers; psychologists; therapists; attorney; labor and delivery nurse.

In 1998, what was the average time from when a prospective adoptive parent applied to when he or she received a homestudy? 4–6 weeks, dependent on fingerprint clearance time.

Average time from homestudy to placement of child: We measure profile to match; 6 mos.

What made you decide to work in the adoption field? A calling from God, which included the memory of my grandmother, who was an abandoned child and grew up without a permanent family.

Agency criteria for adoptive parents you work with: No age or number of children restrictions.

How do you screen adoptive parents? Questionnaire and personal interviews.

How do you screen birthparents? Personal interviews and psychological and medical testing.

What kind of medical information do you seek from birthparents? Use medical form.

What kind of medical information do you seek on older children? All available current information and significant history.

What percent of your U.S. adoptions are nonwhite children? 40%

Do you have a waiting list of prospective parents? No.

Is it all right if adopting parents you work with are on waiting lists of other agencies or attorneys? Yes.

Are your adoption fees based on a sliding scale? No.

Do you have an application fee? If yes, what is the amount of the application fee? Yes. $50

What is your homestudy fee (if a flat rate)? $500 for domestic; $800 for international.

What is your placement fee? $7,000 for white domestic; $5,900 for all international.

Do adopting parents also pay fees for medical and hospital expenses for birthmother and baby when they have no insurance? Rarely, but never without prior agreement.

If international adoption, what are average travel expenses? $2,000 for single adult; $3,000 per couple.

If applicable, what is the average document language translation fee? $1,000

If you place children from other countries, please list the estimated *entire* average cost to adoptive parents for each country. China, $12,000 plus $3,000 for travel ($15,000 total); Guatemala, $19,000 plus travel ($22,000 total); Latvia, Romania, Russia, Ukraine, $18,000 plus travel ($21,000 total).

Does your agency provide videotapes of children needing adoption? Yes.

In how many cases with your agency has an adoptive parent been placed with a child but lost the child due to a birthparent challenge? 0

Has your agency lost any adoption litigation filed against you by an adoptive parent or birthparent? No.

Is there anything else important about your agency? We are the holder of the registered trademark "Small World."

TEXAS

ABRAZO ADOPTION ASSOCIATES

Respondent: Elizabeth Vanderwerf, MS, MPC, LMFT, Executive Director
In charge of social services: Katherine Fromm, LMSW
10010 San Pedro, Suite 540, San Antonio, TX 78216
(210) 342-LOVE • Fax: (210) 342-6547
www.abrazo.org
Year first licensed by state: 1994

Agency provides services for: U.S. adoption; children with special needs; infants; home-study if parents working with another agency; postplacement services; birthparent counseling and support.

What states do your adoptive parent clients come from? All except New York and
   Connecticut.

Services provided adopting parents: Classes with other prospective parents; required
   readings of books and/or articles on adoption; group discussions about adoption;
   parenting discussions; Camp Abrazo, annual family reunion with parent workshops; national family network; Abrazo Adoption Institute; triannual newsletter;
   "Parents of Tomorrow" orientation weekends.

States/countries your birthparents/adopted children come from: Texas (and any
   other "state of need").

Nonrelative children placed in 1998: 60+

Percent of adoptive placements under 6 mos.: 95%

Special expertise of staff: Licensed social workers; therapists; birthparents on staff.

**In 1998, what was the average time from when a prospective adoptive parent
   applied to when he or she received a homestudy?** Families contract for homestudy in whatever time frame they choose.

Average time from homestudy to placement of child: 3–9 mos.

Agency criteria for adoptive parents you work with: Full-service program: Medically
   indicated infertility; minimum age of 25, married at least 1 year; financially sound;
   emotionally stable and comfortable with tenets of open adoption. Designated program: flexible.

How do you screen adoptive parents? Adoptive parents screens via inquiry, application, orientation participation, and/or homestudy content.

How do you screen birthparents? Birthparents are screened via intake counseling.

What kind of medical information do you seek from birthparents? Self-reported genetic history; prenatal records; HIV/RPR and/or all HOL/drug testing as indicated.

What kind of medical information do you seek on older children? Birth history;
   pediatric and immunization record; dental checks; developmental evaluation and
   psychological assessment.

What percent of your U.S. adoptions are nonwhite children? 15%

Do you have a waiting list of prospective parents? No.

Is it all right if adopting parents you work with are on waiting lists of other agencies or attorneys? Yes.

Are your adoption fees based on a sliding scale? No.

Do you have an application fee? If yes, what is the amount of the application fee? Yes. $125

What is your homestudy fee (if a flat rate)? $750 plus expenses.

What is your placement fee? $7,500 for full services; $5,500 for designated services; $3,500 for special needs.

Do adopting parents also pay fees for medical and hospital expenses for birthmother and baby when they have no insurance? If yes, what is the average fee paid? Yes. $8,500

My agency: Offers semi-open adoptions; meetings between birthparents and adoptive parents; birthparents pick adoptive parents from bios/resumes; full disclosure of names between birth and adoptive parents.

Does your agency provide videotapes of children needing adoption? No.

In how many cases with your agency has an adoptive parent been placed with a child but lost the child due to a birthparent challenge? 1

Has your agency lost any adoption litigation filed against you by an adoptive parent or birthparent? No.

ADOPTION SERVICES, INC.

Respondent: Eileen Anderson Stancukas, Director
In charge of social services: Eileen Anderson Stancukas
3500 Overton Park West, Fort Worth, TX 76109
(817) 921-0718 • Fax: (817) 924-4771
Year first licensed by state: 1987

Agency provides services for: International adoption; U.S. adoption; children with special needs; homestudy if parents working with another agency; postplacement services; counseling for all parties.

What states do your adoptive parent clients come from? Mainly Texas. Other states or foreign countries by special arrangement.

Services provided adopting parents: Classes with other prospective parents; required readings of books and/or articles on adoption; group discussions about adoption; parenting discussions; open adoption.

States/countries your birthparents/adopted children come from: All states.

What was the goal of your agency when first organized? What is the goal of your agency now? Homestudies for international adoption. Now: Help with all types of adoption other than actual placement.

Nonrelative children placed in 1998: 50+

Percent of adoptive placements under 6 mos.: 5%

Special expertise of staff: Adoptive parents on staff; licensed social workers.

In 1998, what was the average time from when a prospective adoptive parent applied to when he or she received a homestudy? 2–3 weeks to begin.

Average time from homestudy to placement of child: 9–12 mos.

What made you decide to work in the adoption field? Initially liked the people who hired me. Later, just enjoyed the field.

Agency criteria for adoptive parents you work with: Varies.

How do you screen adoptive parents? Personal discussion and information from other sources, if necessary.

How do you screen birthparents? Only accept those already matched with adoptive parents.

What kind of medical information do you seek from birthparents? As much as I can get; use State of Texas form.

What kind of medical information do you seek on older children? As much as possible; strongly suggest families consult with international adoption medical experts.

What percent of your U.S. adoptions are nonwhite children? 50%

About what percent are children with medical problems? 20%

Do you have a waiting list of prospective parents? No.

Are your adoption fees based on a sliding scale? No.

Do you have an application fee? No.

What is your homestudy fee (if a flat rate)? $950

Do adopting parents also pay fees for medical and hospital expenses for birthmother and baby when they have no insurance? No.

If international adoption, what are average travel expenses? Varies.

If applicable, what is the average document language translation fee? $250–500

Does your agency provide videotapes of children needing adoption? Yes.

Are you an adoptive parent, adopted person, or birthparent? Adoptive parent.

In how many cases with your agency has an adoptive parent been placed with a child but lost the child due to a birthparent challenge? 0

Has your agency lost any adoption litigation filed against you by an adoptive parent or birthparent? No.

ANDREL ADOPTIONS, INC.

Respondent: Vika Andrel, Executive Director
In charge of social services: Vika Andrel
3908 Manchaca Rd., Austin, TX 78704
(512) 448-4605
E-mail: vandrel@worldnet.att.net
Year first licensed by state: 1990

Agency provides services for: International adoption; U.S. adoption; infants; homestudy if parents working with another agency; postplacement services.

What states do your adoptive parent clients come from? All states and Canada.

Services provided adopting parents: Required readings of books and/or articles on adoption; group discussions about adoption; parenting discussions; advice on advertising.

States/countries your birthparents/adopted children come from: United States, Bulgaria, Mexico.

What was the goal of your agency when first organized? What is the goal of your agency now? To assist adoptive parents with legal process and provide good legal and therapeutic counseling to birth families. Now: Same, as well as finding safe and loving permanent homes for children in need.

Nonrelative children placed in 1998: 13

Percent of adoptive placements under 6 mos.: 100%

Special expertise of staff: Licensed social workers; attorney.

In 1998, what was the average time from when a prospective adoptive parent applied to when he or she received a homestudy? 2 mos., once required documents have been received.

Average time from homestudy to placement of child: 6 mos.

What made you decide to work in the adoption field? Gratification of witnessing a good placement.

Agency criteria for adoptive parents you work with: Varies by case.

How do you screen adoptive parents? Personal interview; criminal checks; assessment in their home.

How do you screen birthparents? Personal interview; collection of medical records.

What kind of medical information do you seek from birthparents? Complete medical history of family and all prenatal records.

What kind of medical information do you seek on older children? See above.

What percent of your U.S. adoptions are nonwhite children? 5%

Do you have a waiting list of prospective parents? Yes.

Is it all right if adopting parents you work with are on waiting lists of other agencies or attorneys? Yes.

Do you have an application fee? If yes, what is the amount of the application fee? Yes. $500

What is your homestudy fee (if a flat rate)? $1,200

What is your placement fee? $9,500

Do adopting parents also pay fees for medical and hospital expenses for birth-mother and baby when they have no insurance? If yes, what is the average fee paid? Yes. $5,000–8,000

If applicable, what is the average document language translation fee? $500–800

My agency: Offers confidential adoptions; semi-open adoptions; meetings between birthparents and adoptive parents; birthparents pick adoptive parents from bios/resumes; full disclosure of names between birth and adoptive parents.

Does your agency provide videotapes of children needing adoption? Yes.

In how many cases with your agency has an adoptive parent been placed with a child but lost the child due to a birthparent challenge? 0

Has your agency lost any adoption litigation filed against you by an adoptive parent or birthparent? No.

CRADLE OF LIFE ADOPTION AGENCY, INC.

Respondent: Mel W. Shelander, Director
In charge of social services: Gwyn Vail, Social Worker
245 North 14th St., Beaumont, TX 77701
(409) 832-3000 • Fax: (409) 833-3935
Year first licensed by state: 1989

Agency provides services for: International adoption; children with special needs; infants; homestudy if parents working with another agency; postplacement services.

What states do your adoptive parent clients come from? Mainly Texas.

Services provided adopting parents: Required readings of books and/or articles on adoption; parenting discussions.

States/countries your birthparents/adopted children come from: Texas.

What was the goal of your agency when first organized? What is the goal of your agency now? To provide adoption services. Now: Same.

Nonrelative children placed in 1998: 33

Percent of adoptive placements under 6 mos.: 90%

Special expertise of staff: Adoptive parents on staff; licensed social workers; attorney.

In 1998, what was the average time from when a prospective adoptive parent applied to when he or she received a homestudy? 4–5 mos.

Average time from homestudy to placement of child: 1 year if not less.

What made you decide to work in the adoption field? Adopting children.

Agency criteria for adoptive parents you work with: 24–45 years of age; preferably no more than three children already in the home.

How do you screen adoptive parents? Application and homestudy process.

How do you screen birthparents? Through counseling.

What percent of your U.S. adoptions are nonwhite children? 0%

Do you have a waiting list of prospective parents? Yes.

Is it all right if adopting parents you work with are on waiting lists of other agencies or attorneys? Yes.

Are your adoption fees based on a sliding scale? No.

Do you have an application fee? If yes, what is the amount of the application fee? Yes. $50

What is your homestudy fee (if a flat rate)? $1,500

What is your placement fee? $5,500–21,500

Do adopting parents also pay fees for medical and hospital expenses for birthmother and baby when they have no insurance? No.

My agency: Offers confidential adoptions; semi-open adoptions; meetings between birthparents and adoptive parents; birthparents pick adoptive parents from bios/resumes.

Does your agency provide videotapes of children needing adoption? No.

Are you an adoptive parent, adopted person, or birthparent? Adoptive parent.

In how many cases with your agency has an adoptive parent been placed with a child but lost the child due to a birthparent challenge? 1

Has your agency lost any adoption litigation filed against you by an adoptive parent or birthparent? No.

GLADNEY CENTER FOR ADOPTION

Respondent: Paige McCoy Smith, Marketing and Outreach Manager
In charge of social services: Martha Wynn, Vice President of Adoption Services
2300 Hemphill, Fort Worth, TX 76110
(800)-GLADNEY/ (817) 922-6000
www.gladney.org
Year first licensed by state: Agency started in 1887. Began placing children in 1994 in North Carolina; in 1988 New Jersey; in 1993 in Oklahoma; in 1989 in Louisiana; in 1983 in Connecticut; in 1984 in Arkansas; in 1978 in Kansas; in 1967 and 1989 in New York; in 1940 and 1977 in Texas.

Agency provides services for: International adoption; U.S. adoption; children with special needs; infants; postplacement services; maternity home for women planning adoption.

What states do your adoptive parent clients come from? All states.

Services provided adopting parents: Classes with other prospective parents; required readings of books and/or articles on adoption; group discussions about adoption; parenting discussions; auxiliary program.

States/countries your birthparents/adopted children come from: Birthparents: All states. Adopted children: United States, China, Russia, Guatemala, Romania, Mexico, Vietnam.

What was the goal of your agency when first organized? What is the goal of your agency now? To find homes for orphaned children. Now: Adoption agency and maternity home.

Nonrelative children placed in 1998: 354

Percent of adoptive placements under 6 mos.: 98% domestic; 0% international.

Special expertise of staff: Adoptive parents on staff; licensed social workers; psychologists; therapists; physician; attorney.

In 1998, what was the average time from when a prospective adoptive parent applied to when he or she received a homestudy? About a month.

Average time from homestudy to placement of child: 9 mos.

What made you decide to work in the adoption field? Committed to adoption mission.

Agency criteria for adoptive parents you work with: Domestic: Aged 24–45, married minimum 3 years; no more than three children currently in home; live in licensed state or auxiliary area. International: Varies depending on country.

How do you screen adoptive parents? Homestudy; medical reports; criminal checks; child abuse check; FBI fingerprint checks in New Jersey; INS approval for international.

How do you screen birthparents? Receive calls on 800 line and utilize counselors to provide assistance and gather information.

What kind of medical information do you seek from birthparents? In accordance with the laws and regulations of the states where we are licensed.

What percent of your U.S. adoptions are nonwhite children? 15% African-American and biracial.

Do you have a waiting list of prospective parents? Yes.

Is it all right if adopting parents you work with are on waiting lists of other agencies or attorneys? No.

Are your adoption fees based on a sliding scale? If yes, what are the sliding scale criteria? Yes, for domestic. [Based on] average of last 3 years' income tax returns.

Do you have an application fee? If yes, what is the amount of the application fee? Yes, for international. $300

What is your homestudy fee (if a flat rate)? $1,200–1,500

My agency: Offers confidential adoptions; semi-open adoptions with first names exchanged; meetings between birthparents and adoptive parents; birthparents pick adoptive parents from bios/resumes.

Does your agency provide videotapes of children needing adoption? Yes, international.

In how many cases with your agency has an adoptive parent been placed with a child but lost the child due to a birthparent challenge? 0

Has your agency lost any adoption litigation filed against you by an adoptive parent or birthparent? Yes.

HOPE COTTAGE PREGNANCY AND ADOPTION CENTER

Respondent: Doris Marshall, Director, International Adoption Services
In charge of social services: Doris Marshall
4209 McKinney Ave., Dallas, TX 75205
(214) 526-8721 • Fax: (214) 526-7168
www.hopecottage.org
Year first licensed by state: 1918

Agency provides services for: International adoption; U.S. adoption; infants; homestudy if parents working with another agency; postplacement services; free pregnancy counseling.

What states do your adoptive parent clients come from? Texas, 90%; other states, 10%.

Services provided adopting parents: Classes with other prospective parents; group discussions about adoption; parenting discussions.

States/countries your birthparents/adopted children come from: Adopted children from Texas, Romania, China, and India.

What was the goal of your agency when first organized? What is the goal of your agency now? To provide a home for the foundlings of Dallas County. Now: To provide services to pregnant women and assist families in adopting children.

Nonrelative children placed in 1998: 19

Percent of adoptive placements under 6 mos.: 80%

Special expertise of staff: Adoptive parents on staff; licensed social workers; attorney; licensed professional counselors.

In 1998, what was the average time from when a prospective adoptive parent applied to when he or she received a homestudy? 2 mos.

Average time from homestudy to placement of child: 14 mos.

Agency criteria for adoptive parents you work with: Couple must be legally married; financially able to parent child. We also work with single individuals.

How do you screen adoptive parents? Orientation; individual interview; adoption training; study.

How do you screen birthparents? If they need help we give it.

What kind of medical information do you seek on older children? Hospital birth records; medical records; HIV test results.

What percent of your U.S. adoptions are nonwhite children? 32%

About what percent are children with medical problems? 10%

Do you have a waiting list of prospective parents? Yes.

Is it all right if adopting parents you work with are on waiting lists of other agencies or attorneys? No.

Are your adoption fees based on a sliding scale? If yes, what are the sliding scale criteria? Yes. Percent of salary and graduated increases based on salary.

Do you have an application fee? No.

What is your homestudy fee (if a flat rate)? $1,400

What is your placement fee? $3,500–22,000

Do adopting parents also pay fees for medical and hospital expenses for birth-mother and baby when they have no insurance? If yes, what is the average fee paid? Yes. $4,000

If international adoption, what are average travel expenses? $5,000

If applicable, what is the average document language translation fee? $900

If you place children from other countries, please list the estimated _entire_ average cost to adoptive parents for each country. Romania, $23,700; India, $20,700; China, $15,800.

My agency: Offers confidential adoptions; semi-open adoptions; meetings between birthparents and adoptive parents; birthparents pick adoptive parents from bios/resumes; full disclosure of names between birth and adoptive parents.

Does your agency provide videotapes of children needing adoption? Yes, from Romania.

In how many cases with your agency has an adoptive parent been placed with a child but lost the child due to a birthparent challenge? 2

Has your agency lost any adoption litigation filed against you by an adoptive parent or birthparent? No.

GREAT WALL CHINA ADOPTION

Respondent: Leigh Anne Baseflug, Assistant Director
In charge of social services: Snow Wu, Executive Director
5555 N. Lamar #H-135, Austin, TX 78751
(512) 323-9595 • Fax: (512) 323-9599
E-mail: gwcadopt@eden.com • www.eden.com/~gwcadopt
Year first licensed by state: 1996

Agency provides services for: International adoption.

What states do your adoptive parent clients come from? All states plus any U.S. citizens who live abroad.

Services provided adopting parents: Classes with other prospective parents; group discussions about adoption; parenting discussions; Chinese culture training and travel preparation.

States/countries your birthparents/adopted children come from: China.

What was the goal of your agency when first organized? What is the goal of your agency now? To help orphaned children in China to find loving homes here in the United States. Now: Same.

Nonrelative children placed in 1998: Over 200

Percent of adoptive placements under 6 mos.: 29%

Special expertise of staff: Adoptive parents on staff; licensed social workers; psychologists; therapists.

In 1998, what was the average time from when a prospective adoptive parent applied to when he or she received a homestudy? 1–2 mos.

Average time from homestudy to placement of child: 1 mo.

Agency criteria for adoptive parents you work with: 30–60 years old, income average of $10,000 per person.

How do you screen adoptive parents? Prescreening via application; CANRIS; criminal background check; homestudy.

What kind of medical information do you seek on older children? We receive a standard medical check-up report from China.

What percent of your U.S. adoptions are nonwhite children? 100%

Do you have a waiting list of prospective parents? No.

Is it all right if adopting parents you work with are on waiting lists of other agencies or attorneys? Yes.

Are your adoption fees based on a sliding scale? No.

Do you have an application fee? If yes, what is the amount of the application fee? Yes. $200

What is your homestudy fee (if a flat rate)? $1,000

What is your placement fee? $4,000

Do adopting parents also pay fees for medical and hospital expenses for birthmother and baby when they have no insurance? No.

If international adoption, what are average travel expenses? $2,500 per adult.

If you place children from other countries, please list the estimated *entire* average cost to adoptive parents for each country. For married couple, about $15,000.

My agency: Offers confidential adoptions.

Does your agency provide videotapes of children needing adoption? No.

Has your agency lost any adoption litigation filed against you by an adoptive parent or birthparent? No.

INHERITANCE ADOPTIONS

Respondent: Vicky Payne, Director
P.O. Box 2563, Wichita Falls, TX 76307-2563
(940) 322-3678 • Fax: (940) 322-2386
E-mail: adopt@wf.net • www.inheritanceadoptions.org
Year first licensed by state: 1993

Agency provides services for: U.S. adoption; infants; homestudy if parents working with another agency; postplacement services; homestudy for international and private adoption.

What states do your adoptive parent clients come from? Texas and any state that the law allows.

Services provided adopting parents: Classes with other prospective parents; adoption support group.

States/countries your birthparents/adopted children come from: Texas and any state that the law allows.

What was the goal of your agency when first organized? What is the goal of your agency now? To offer alternatives to abortion and place (legally) adoptable children with Christian families. Now: Same.

Nonrelative children placed in 1998: 5

Percent of adoptive placements under 6 mos.: 98%

Special expertise of staff: Licensed social workers; director has business degree and legal background; certified open adoption practitioner.

In 1998, what was the average time from when a prospective adoptive parent applied to when he or she received a homestudy? 60–90 days

Average time from homestudy to placement of child: 60–90 days. 1999 has been longer.

What made you decide to work in the adoption field? Legalized abortion.

Agency criteria for adoptive parents you work with: Adoptive parents, aged 24–45.

How do you screen adoptive parents? They send $5 for information packet and first screen themselves. If they do not meet our requirements, they should not apply. Second screening is through application process, references, and homestudy, including letter from physicians. Prefer applicants to send $5 and request information packet rather than call. Licensed agencies in Texas must provide written information before applicant becomes a client.

How do you screen birthparents? Through contact and medical information.

What kind of medical information do you seek from birthparents? Family history of medical conditions; prenatal care and delivery medical records.

What kind of medical information do you seek on older children? For adoptive families: TB test for all ages and HIV test for children 16 or over. For placement: According to licensing requirements and doctor assessment.

What percent of your U.S. adoptions are nonwhite children? 25–35%

About what percent are children with medical problems? 20%

Do you have a waiting list of prospective parents? No.

Is it all right if adopting parents you work with are on waiting lists of other agencies or attorneys? Yes.

Are your adoption fees based on a sliding scale? No.

Do you have an application fee? If yes, what is the amount of the application fee? Yes. $50, nonrefundable.

What is your homestudy fee (if a flat rate)? $1,000

What is your placement fee? $6,500 ($3,000 can be used for medical expenses). Fees can change each year.

Do adopting parents also pay fees for medical and hospital expenses for birthmother and baby when they have no insurance? If yes, what is the average fee paid? Yes. $7,000–9,000

My agency: Offers confidential adoptions; semi-open adoptions; meetings between birthparents and adoptive parents; birthparents pick adoptive parents from bios/resumes; full disclosure of names between birth and adoptive parents.

Does your agency provide videotapes of children needing adoption? No.

In how many cases with your agency has an adoptive parent been placed with a child but lost the child due to a birthparent challenge? 1

Has your agency lost any adoption litigation filed against you by an adoptive parent or birthparent? No.

Is there anything I have not asked you that is important? Adoptive families should not feel guilty when they review the medical history of a child and decide to pass up the placement. But also, when that happens, they should not bad-mouth the agency to others because of their decision.

LOS NINOS INTERNATIONAL ADOPTION AGENCY

Respondent: Jean Nelson-Erichsen, LSW-MA-PA, Co-founder and Director
In charge of social services: Jean Nelson-Erichsen
1600 Lake Front Cir. #130, The Woodlands, TX 77380
(281) 363-2892 • Fax: (281) 297-4191
E-mail: jerichsen@losninos.org • www.losninos.org
Year first licensed by state: 1981

Agency provides services for: International adoption; postplacement services.

What states do your adoptive parent clients come from? All states.

Services provided adopting parents: Required readings of books and/or articles on adoption; eight-week correspondence course on international adoptive parenting.

States/countries your birthparents/adopted children come from: Bolivia, Bulgaria, China, Colombia, Ecuador, Guatemala, Honduras, Peru, Romania, Russia, Vietnam. Have plans for Kazakhstan.

What was the goal of your agency when first organized? What is the goal of your agency now? Aid and adoption. Now: Same.

Nonrelative children placed in 1998: 155

Percent of adoptive placements under 6 mos.: 25%

Special expertise of staff: Adoptive parents on staff; licensed social workers.

In 1998, what was the average time from when a prospective adoptive parent applied to when he or she received a homestudy? 3 mos.

Average time from homestudy to placement of child: 6–9 mos.

What made you decide to work in the adoption field? We adopted abroad and saw the needs of abandoned children first-hand.

Agency criteria for adoptive parents you work with: Must be 25–50 years old; childless or with children, all races and religions.

How do you screen adoptive parents? Interviews and certified social worker according to a guide, which meets state, foreign, INS, and COA standards.

What kind of medical information do you seek on older children? Everything the foreign country gives us.

Do you have a waiting list of prospective parents? Yes.

Is it all right if adopting parents you work with are on waiting lists of other agencies or attorneys? No.

Are your adoption fees based on a sliding scale? No.

Do you have an application fee? If yes, what is the amount of the application fee? Yes. $50 for preapproval, then $500 to process.

What is your homestudy fee (if a flat rate)? $1,000

What is your placement fee? Depends on country.

Do adopting parents also pay fees for medical and hospital expenses for birthmother and baby when they have no insurance? No.

If international adoption, what are average travel expenses? $3,000

If applicable, what is the average document language translation fee? $500

If you place children from other countries, please list the estimated *entire* average cost to adoptive parents for each country. China, $13,500; Eastern European countries, $18,000–20,000; Latin America except Guatemala, $16,000; Vietnam, $16,000; Guatemala, $22,000.

My agency: Offers confidential adoptions.

Does your agency provide videotapes of children needing adoption? Yes, from Europe.

In how many cases with your agency has an adoptive parent been placed with a child but lost the child due to a birthparent challenge? 0

Has your agency lost any adoption litigation filed against you by an adoptive parent or birthparent? No.

LUTHERAN SOCIAL SERVICES OF THE SOUTH, INC.

Respondent: Karalyn L. Heimlich, Director of Adoption and Related Activities
In charge of social services: Sam Sipes, COO
314 Highland Mall Blvd., Suite 200, Austin, TX 78752
(512) 454-4611 • Fax: (512) 454-9385
E-mail: karalynh@lsss.org • www.lsss.org
Year first licensed by state: 1940s.

Agency provides services for: International adoption; U.S. adoption; children with special needs; infants; homestudy if parents working with another agency; postplacement services.

What states do your adoptive parent clients come from? Texas and Louisiana.

Services provided adopting parents: Classes with other prospective parents; required readings of books and/or articles on adoption; parenting discussions.

States/countries your birthparents/adopted children come from: Texas, Eastern Europe; numerous other countries working cooperatively with other international agencies.

What was the goal of your agency when first organized? What is the goal of your agency now? To provide a home for orphans and old folks; to serve children, the elderly, and the poor. Now: Same.

Nonrelative children placed in 1998: 63

Special expertise of staff: Adoptive parents on staff; licensed social workers; LPCs.

In 1998, what was the average time from when a prospective adoptive parent applied to when he or she received a homestudy? Within 2 mos. of receipt of application.

Average time from homestudy to placement of child: 3 mos.–2 years, depending on type of child being adopted.

Agency criteria for adoptive parents you work with: Age 45 or under; no more than one child in the home; must be documented infertility or recommended not to get pregnant (for healthy infants from America). Criteria are waived for waiting children; international depends on country.

How do you screen adoptive parents? Screen by inquiry form.

What kind of medical information do you seek on older children? Everything that we can get.

What percent of your U.S. adoptions are nonwhite children? 40%

About what percent are children with medical problems? 5% (American)

Do you have a waiting list of prospective parents? Yes.

Is it all right if adopting parents you work with are on waiting lists of other agencies or attorneys? No.

Are your adoption fees based on a sliding scale? If yes, what are the sliding scale criteria? Yes. Based on program and income.

Do you have an application fee? If yes, what is the amount of the application fee? Yes. $200

What is your placement fee? Fee is based on program; nonsubsidized, $13,500–21,500; subsidized, $2,000–7,000; Eastern European, $14,800 plus travel.

Do adopting parents also pay fees for medical and hospital expenses for birth-mother and baby when they have no insurance? No.

If international adoption, what are average travel expenses? $7,000

If you place children from other countries, please list the estimated *entire* average cost to adoptive parents for each country. Russia and Moldova, $21,000–22,000.

My agency: Offers confidential adoptions; semi-open adoptions; meetings between birthparents and adoptive parents; birthparents pick adoptive parents from bios/resumes; full disclosure of names between birth and adoptive parents.

Does your agency provide videotapes of children needing adoption? Yes, international.

In how many cases with your agency has an adoptive parent been placed with a child but lost the child due to a birthparent challenge? 0

Has your agency lost any adoption litigation filed against you by an adoptive parent or birthparent? No.

NEW LIFE CHILDREN'S SERVICES

Respondent: Sara C. Black, Director
In charge of social services: Sara C. Black
19911 SH 249, Houston, TX 77070
(281) 955-1001 • Fax: (281) 955-0114
E-mail: nlcs@flash.net
Year first licensed by state: 1983

Agency provides services for: U.S. adoption; infants; homestudy if parents working with another agency; postplacement services.

What states do your adoptive parent clients come from? Primarily Texas (we only place special needs babies out of state).

Services provided adopting parents: Classes with other prospective parents; required readings of books and/or articles on adoption; group discussions about adoption; parenting discussions.

States/countries your birthparents/adopted children come from: Any state or country, but primarily Texas.

What was the goal of your agency when first organized? What is the goal of your agency now? To provide services to unwed mothers; to help them through a time of crisis, through the painful experience of giving up a child for adoption. Now: To provide counseling, emotional support, spiritual guidance, and practical assistance to women who find themselves in a crisis pregnancy. We believe every child is a miracle from God and deserves a chance to live. For those women wishing to explore adoption, we can provide the proper counseling and opportunities to select a family for her child.

Nonrelative children placed in 1998: 17

Percent of adoptive placements under 6 mos.: 99%

Special expertise of staff: Adoptive parents on staff; licensed social workers; RN.

In 1998, what was the average time from when a prospective adoptive parent applied to when he or she received a homestudy? 3–6 mos.

Average time from homestudy to placement of child: 4–6 mos.

Agency criteria for adoptive parents you work with: Christian two-parent families; active members in the same church; aged 21–39; married at least 3 years.

How do you screen adoptive parents? Pre-adoption conference; Christian questionnaire, references; CANRIS (child abuse) check; criminal history check through Texas Dept. of Protective and Regulatory Service; medical check-up and recommendation by physician.

How do you screen birthparents? Interview; intake information.

What kind of medical information do you seek on older children? As much as possible—all that is available.

What percent of your U.S. adoptions are nonwhite children? 25–30%

About what percent are children with medical problems? 10%

Do you have a waiting list of prospective parents? Yes.

Is it all right if adopting parents you work with are on waiting lists of other agencies or attorneys? No.

Are your adoption fees based on a sliding scale? No.

Do you have an application fee? No.

What is your homestudy fee (if a flat rate)? $1,500 for contract homestudy.

What is your placement fee? $5,000 for special needs; $14,000 for regular.

Do adopting parents also pay fees for medical and hospital expenses for birthmother and baby when they have no insurance? No.

My agency: Offers semi-open adoptions; meetings between birthparents and adoptive parents; birthparents pick adoptive parents from bios/resumes.

Does your agency provide videotapes of children needing adoption? No.

In how many cases with your agency has an adoptive parent been placed with a child but lost the child due to a birthparent challenge? 3

Has your agency lost any adoption litigation filed against you by an adoptive parent or birthparent? Yes.

PLACEMENT SERVICES AGENCY
Respondent: Barbara Silverman, LMSW-ACP
In charge of social services: Barbara Silverman
P.O. Box 799004, Dallas, TX 25379-9004
(972) 387-8312 • Fax: (972) 387-3312
Year first licensed by state: 1990

Agency provides services for: International adoption; U.S. adoption; homestudy if parents working with another agency; postplacement services; training and consultation; counseling services for all triad members.

What states do your adoptive parent clients come from? Texas usually.

Services provided adopting parents: Classes with other prospective parents; required readings of books and/or articles on adoption; group discussions about adoption; parenting discussions; infant care; counseling and consultation.

States/countries your birthparents/adopted children come from: I do not place directly, but most of my families adopt from Eastern Europe.

What was the goal of your agency when first organized? What is the goal of your agency now? Homestudies and postplacement. Now: Same and added stress on education and preparation of families.

Special expertise of staff: Licensed social workers; therapists.

In 1998, what was the average time from when a prospective adoptive parent applied to when he or she received a homestudy? 2 weeks

Average time from homestudy to placement of child: Varies (6–12 mos.).

What made you decide to work in the adoption field? Started in child placement with child welfare, did ICPC contract with state for 10 years, and evolved from there.

Agency criteria for adoptive parents you work with: None; depends on criteria of placing agency.

How do you screen adoptive parents? Interviews.

How do you screen birthparents? Interviews.

What kind of medical information do you seek on older children? Anything and everything.

Do you have a waiting list of prospective parents? No.

Is it all right if adopting parents you work with are on waiting lists of other agencies or attorneys? Yes.

Are your adoption fees based on a sliding scale? No.

Do you have an application fee? No.

What is your homestudy fee (if a flat rate)? $850 for domestic; $1,000 for international.

What is your placement fee? None.

Do adopting parents also pay fees for medical and hospital expenses for birthmother and baby when they have no insurance? No.

My agency: Offers meetings between birthparents and adoptive parents.

Does your agency provide videotapes of children needing adoption? No.

In how many cases with your agency has an adoptive parent been placed with a child but lost the child due to a birthparent challenge? 0

Has your agency lost any adoption litigation filed against you by an adoptive parent or birthparent? No.

SMITHLAWN MATERNITY HOME AND ADOPTION AGENCY

Respondent: Frances Phillips, Director of Maternity Services
In charge of social services: Tony Parnell, ACSW, LMSW-ACP
P.O. Box 6451, Lubbock, TX 79493-6451
(806) 745-2574 • Fax: (806) 748-1088
E-mail: smithlawn@door.net • www.door.net/smithlawn
Year first licensed by state: 1968

Agency provides services for: U.S. adoption; children with special needs; infants, post-placement services.

What states do your adoptive parent clients come from? Primarily Texas, but all states when able to work with the interstate compact.

Services provided adopting parents: Classes with other prospective parents; required readings of books and/or articles on adoption; group discussions about adoption; parenting discussions.

States/countries your birthparents/adopted children come from: Primarily United States; I have worked with virtually every state.

What was the goal of your agency when first organized? What is the goal of your agency now? To provide services to birthparents, children, and adoptive parents in a Christian setting. Now: Same.

Nonrelative children placed in 1998: 15

Percent of adoptive placements under 6 mos.: 100%

Special expertise of staff: Adoptive parents on staff; licensed social workers.

In 1998, what was the average time from when a prospective adoptive parent applied to when he or she received a homestudy? 4–5 mos.

Average time from homestudy to placement of child: 1–2 years.

What made you decide to work in the adoption field? Personal experience and to respond to a need.

Agency criteria for adoptive parents you work with: Normal child-rearing age; no limit to number of children; financial, marital, and emotional stability.

How do you screen adoptive parents? According to state minimum standards requirements.

How do you screen birthparents? Depending on their individual needs.

What kind of medical information do you seek from birthparents? All available family medical histories, hospital records, and birth histories.

What kind of medical information do you seek on older children? Same, plus medical record since birth.

What percent of your U.S. adoptions are nonwhite children? 25%

About what percent are children with medical problems? 3%

Do you have a waiting list of prospective parents? Yes.

Is it all right if adopting parents you work with are on waiting lists of other agencies or attorneys? Yes.

Are your adoption fees based on a sliding scale? If yes, what are the sliding scale criteria? Yes. Special needs of child and family income.

Do you have an application fee? No.

What is your homestudy fee (if a flat rate)? Not separate: It is part of the overall placement fee.

What is your placement fee? $4,000–15,000

My agency: Offers semi-open adoptions; meetings between birthparents and adoptive parents; birthparents pick adoptive parents from bios/resumes.

Does your agency provide videotapes of children needing adoption? No.

Are you an adoptive parent, adopted person, or birthparent? Adoptive parent.

In how many cases with your agency has an adoptive parent been placed with a child but lost the child due to a birthparent challenge? 1

Has your agency lost any adoption litigation filed against you by an adoptive parent or birthparent? No.

TEXAS CRADLE SOCIETY

Respondent: Carol Schmidt, MSW, LMSW, Executive Director
In charge of social services: Carol Schmidt
8600 Wurzbach, Suite 1110, San Antonio, TX 78240
(210) 614-0299 • Fax: (210) 614-0511
E-mail: txcradle@onr.com • www.onr.com/user/txcradle
Year first licensed by state: 1936

Agency provides services for: International adoption; U.S. adoption; children with special needs; infants; homestudy if parents working with another agency; postplacement services; search and reunion.

What states do your adoptive parent clients come from? For international, all states; for domestic, all states that do not require our agency to have a license from their state, such as New York.

Services provided adopting parents: Classes with other prospective parents; required readings of books and/or articles on adoption; group discussions about adoption; parenting discussions; support groups.

States/countries your birthparents/adopted children come from: Texas for birthparents; Romania and Russia for adopted children from orphanages.

What was the goal of your agency when first organized? What is the goal of your agency now? To provide housing for birthmothers in a dorm-type facility, to provide counseling to birthmothers and adoptive parents, and to place newborns and very young children for adoption. Now: To place newborns (domestic) after counseling with birthparents and adoptive parents, to place Romanian and Russian children, aged 6 mo.–16 years with U.S. citizens, and to support the triad during post-adoption.

Nonrelative children placed in 1998: 26

Percent of adoptive placements under 6 mos.: 99% of domestic under 6 mos.; none internationally under 6 mos.

Special expertise of staff: Licensed social workers; psychologists.

In 1998, what was the average time from when a prospective adoptive parent applied to when he or she received a homestudy? 3–6 weeks. Completion of homestudy process takes 2–3 mos.

Average time from homestudy to placement of child: 6–9 mos.

What made you decide to work in the adoption field? I believe that all relinquishments and placements are guided by the Lord, and that adoption is the work He has called me to do.

How do you screen adoptive parents? Must meet agency's criteria; must have favorable homestudy, including physicals, personal and employment references, and criminal and child abuse registry check.

How do you screen birthparents? Discuss with them their personal situation, including financial need, and their motivation for adoption. They must seem sincere in motivation, willing to give as much information as possible about birthfather, and have financial needs that do not exceed the agency's limits.

What kind of medical information do you seek on older children? Social and medical history of birthparents and their families; pediatric exam; dental exam; developmental assessment; immunizations.

What percent of your U.S. adoptions are nonwhite children? 10% with black in background; 50% with Hispanic in background.

About what percent are children with medical problems? 5% domestic newborns.

Do you have a waiting list of prospective parents? Yes.

Is it all right if adopting parents you work with are on waiting lists of other agencies or attorneys? No.

Are your adoption fees based on a sliding scale? No.

Do you have an application fee? If yes, what is the amount of the application fee? Yes. $125; also, $50 preapplication fee.

What is your homestudy fee (if a flat rate)? $750 for domestic; $850 for international.

What is your placement fee? $6,500 for domestic; $5,400 for international processing plus $4,500 for Romanian processing.

Do adopting parents also pay fees for medical and hospital expenses for birth-mother and baby when they have no insurance? If yes, what is the average fee paid? Yes. Most birthmothers qualify for Medicaid; about $4,500 for birthmother and $250 for baby.

If international adoption, what are average travel expenses? Romania, approximately $600 plus airfare (per couple); Russia, approximately $1,900–2,600, plus airfare (per couple).

If you place children from other countries, please list the estimated *entire* average cost to adoptive parents for each country. Romania, $10,500 (does not include airfare, homestudy, INS); Russia, $17,000–20,000 (does not include airfare, home-study, INS).

My agency: Offers confidential adoptions; semi-open adoptions; meetings between birthparents and adoptive parents; birthparents pick adoptive parents from bios/resumes; full disclosure of names between birth and adoptive parents.

Does your agency provide videotapes of children needing adoption? Yes, for international.

In how many cases with your agency has an adoptive parent been placed with a child but lost the child due to a birthparent challenge? 0

Has your agency lost any adoption litigation filed against you by an adoptive parent or birthparent? No.

UTAH

ADOPT AN ANGEL, INC.

Respondent: N. Ann Lamphere, Executive Director
In charge of social services: N. Ann Lamphere
254 West 400 South, Suite 320, Salt Lake City, UT 84101
(801) 537-1622 or (888) 423-6788 • Fax: (801) 359-6873
E-mail: annl@fia.net
Year first licensed by state: 1997

Agency provides services for: U.S. adoption; infants; homestudy if parents working with another agency; postplacement services.

What states do your adoptive parent clients come from? All states.

Services provided adopting parents: Classes with other prospective parents; required readings of books and/or articles on adoption; group discussions about adoption; parenting discussions; classes at community schools on how to adopt.

States/countries your birthparents/adopted children come from: All states.

What was the goal of your agency when first organized? What is the goal of your agency now? To place infants for adoption. Now: Same.

Nonrelative children placed in 1998: 8

Percent of adoptive placements under 6 mos.: 100%

Special expertise of staff: Adoptive parents on staff; licensed social workers; attorney.

In 1998, what was the average time from when a prospective adoptive parent applied to when he or she received a homestudy? 2–3 mos.

Average time from homestudy to placement of child: 2–3 mos.

What made you decide to work in the adoption field? Been in adoption field since 1976. Was adoptive parent, then adoption counselor.

Agency criteria for adoptive parents you work with: No age limit; no children limits; must be married for 1 year.

How do you screen adoptive parents? Meetings with them; homestudies; BCIs; reference letters; medical records.

How do you screen birthparents? Meetings, forms.

What kind of medical information do you seek from birthparents? We ask as much as possible.

What kind of medical information do you seek on older children? Do not do special needs, only infants.

What percent of your U.S. adoptions are nonwhite children? 10%

Do you have a waiting list of prospective parents? No.

Is it all right if adopting parents you work with are on waiting lists of other agencies or attorneys? Yes.

Are your adoption fees based on a sliding scale? If yes, what are the sliding scale criteria? Yes. $9,000 minimum; 15% over $60,000 to maximum of $18,000.

Do you have an application fee? If yes, what is the amount of the application fee? Yes. $250

What is your homestudy fee (if a flat rate)? $250

Do adopting parents also pay fees for medical and hospital expenses for birthmother and baby when they have no insurance? If yes, what is the average fee paid? Yes. $2,000–3,000

My agency: Offers confidential adoptions; semi-open adoptions; meetings between birthparents and adoptive parents; birthparents pick adoptive parents from bios/resumes; full disclosure of names between birth and adoptive parents.

Does your agency provide videotapes of children needing adoption? No.

Are you an adoptive parent, adopted person, or birthparent? Adoptive parent.

In how many cases with your agency has an adoptive parent been placed with a child but lost the child due to a birthparent challenge? 0. Utah's adoption laws are very strict.

Has your agency lost any adoption litigation filed against you by an adoptive parent or birthparent? No.

WASATCH INTERNATIONAL ADOPTIONS

Respondent: Kathy Kaiser, Executive Director
In charge of social services: Jeanne Hansel, MSW
2580 Jefferson Ave., Ogden, UT 84401
(801) 334-8683 • Fax: (801) 479-1301
E-mail: info@wiaa.org
Year first licensed by state: 1997

Agency provides services for: International adoption; homestudy if parents working with another agency; postplacement services; additional post-adoption services and classes.

What states do your adoptive parent clients come from? All states plus some overseas military families.

Services provided adopting parents: Classes with other prospective parents; required readings of books and/or articles on adoption; support groups for adoption parents; arranged get-togethers of children from some countries.

States/countries your birthparents/adopted children come from: Bulgaria, Moldova, Russia, Ukraine, Vietnam, China, Marshall Islands, Guatemala.

What was the goal of your agency when first organized? What is the goal of your agency now? To provide child assistance programs and homes for children, and adoption services at a reasonable cost to adoptive parents who desire to adopt needy children. Now: Same.

Nonrelative children placed in 1998: 50

Percent of adoptive placements under 6 mos.: 5%

Special expertise of staff: Adoptive parents on staff; licensed social workers; therapists.

In 1998, what was the average time from when a prospective adoptive parent applied to when he or she received a homestudy? 3 weeks

Average time from homestudy to placement of child: 3–12 mos., depending on country of placement.

What made you decide to work in the adoption field? My partner and I were overwhelmed at the need of children in other countries. I became actively involved in service projects that my grandson was adopted from. My partner began promoting international adoption in the country she adopted her child from in an effort to help the children she couldn't adopt herself. Eventually we worked with professionals who believed the same way we did to organize a board of directors and a new agency.

Agency criteria for adoptive parents you work with: Most of our guidelines for adoptive parents are set by the foreign country that the parents are adopting from. As a standard, we require that the child be not more than 45 years younger than the parents, that spouses have been married at least 2 years.

How do you screen adoptive parents? Review of initial application by a committee; state background criminal check and child abuse clearance; homestudy with evidence of supporting documents and psychological evaluation; review of homestudy by Director of Social Work and committee.

How do you screen birthparents? Presently not working in domestic adoption.

What kind of medical information do you seek on older children? Anything we can get! All available medical information is provided to parents as well as a personal assessment by foreign agents.

About what percent are children with medical problems? 30%

About what percent are children with emotional problems? Because most of the children come from an orphanage or extreme poverty, I would say that all of our children come with some type of emotional problem. It's the reality of international adoption.

Do you have a waiting list of prospective parents? Yes, for infants.

Is it all right if adopting parents you work with are on waiting lists of other agencies or attorneys? No.

Are your adoption fees based on a sliding scale? No.

Do you have an application fee? No.

What is your homestudy fee (if a flat rate)? $600

What is your placement fee? $1,800

If international adoption, what are average travel expenses? Varies by adoption because of individual expenses to fly to the particular country, the time of year, age of the child, etc.

If applicable, what is the average document language translation fee? $500–1,000

If you place children from other countries, please list the estimated *entire* average cost to adoptive parents for each country. The average cost for our adoptions, with travel, is about $17,000, with a low of $13,000 for Marshall Islands and a high of $23,000 for Guatemala.

My agency: Offers confidential adoptions; semi-open adoptions; meetings between birthparents and adoptive parents; full disclosure of names between birth and adoptive parents.

Does your agency provide videotapes of children needing adoption? Yes, from some countries.

Has your agency lost any adoption litigation filed against you by an adoptive parent or birthparent? No.

VERMONT

ADOPTION ADVOCATES, INC.

Respondent: Ann Clark, Director
In charge of social services: Ann Clark
P.O. Box 521, Shelburne, VT 05482-6531
(802) 985-8289
Year first licensed by state: 1996

Agency provides services for: International adoption; U.S. adoption; children with special needs; infants; homestudy if parents working with another agency; postplacement services; post-adoption services and support groups.

What states do your adoptive parent clients come from? Vermont.

Services provided adopting parents: Classes with other prospective parents; required readings of books and/or articles on adoption; group discussions about adoption; parenting discussions.

States/countries your birthparents/adopted children come from: Many.

What was the goal of your agency when first organized? What is the goal of your agency now? Comprehensive adoption agency. Now: Same.

Nonrelative children placed in 1998: 13

Percent of adoptive placements under 6 mos.: 50%

Special expertise of staff: Adoptive parents on staff; licensed social workers; therapists.

In 1998, what was the average time from when a prospective adoptive parent applied to when he or she received a homestudy? 2 mos.

Average time from homestudy to placement of child: 9 mos.

What made you decide to work in the adoption field? I am an adoptive parent and saw the need to better educate and support adoptive families.

Agency criteria for adoptive parents you work with: None.

How do you screen adoptive parents? Extensive social work interviews; child abuse and neglect and criminal records check; reference checks.

What kind of medical information do you seek on older children? Everything.

What percent of your U.S. adoptions are nonwhite children? 50%

About what percent are children with medical problems? 50%

About what percent are children with emotional problems? 30%

Do you have a waiting list of prospective parents? Yes.

Is it all right if adopting parents you work with are on waiting lists of other agencies or attorneys? Yes

Are your adoption fees based on a sliding scale? If yes, what are the sliding scale criteria? Yes. 5% of family's annual income; minimum fee for homestudy is $1,000, maximum fee is $1,800.

Do you have an application fee? No.

What is your homestudy fee (if a flat rate)? Please see sliding scale criteria question.

What is your placement fee? Don't do direct placements.

If international adoption, what are average travel expenses? $2,000

If applicable, what is the average document language translation fee? Varies.

If you place children from other countries, please list the estimated *entire* average cost to adoptive parents for each country. China, $14,500; Russia, $18,000; Cambodia, $13,000; Vietnam, $15,000; Ethiopia, $2,000.

Does your agency provide videotapes of children needing adoption? Yes.

Are you an adoptive parent, adopted person, or birthparent? Adoptive parent.

In how many cases with your agency has an adoptive parent been placed with a child but lost the child due to a birthparent challenge? 0

Has your agency lost any adoption litigation filed against you by an adoptive parent or birthparent? No.

VERMONT CHILDREN'S AID SOCIETY

Respondent: Dorsey Naylor, LICSW, Director of Adoption Services
In charge of social services: Dorsey Naylor
79 Weaver St., P.O. Box 127, Winooski, VT 05404
(802) 655-0006 • Fax: (802) 655-0073
E-mail: vtcas@aol.com • www.vermontchildrensaid.org
Year first licensed by state: 1918

Agency provides services for: International adoption; U.S. adoption; infants; homestudy if parents working with another agency; postplacement services; post-adoption services.

What states do your adoptive parent clients come from? Vermont; New Hampshire, Sullivan, Grafton, and Cheshire Counties; New York, areas bordering Vermont.

Services provided adopting parents: Classes with other prospective parents; required readings of books and/or articles on adoption; group discussions about adoption; parenting discussions.

States/countries your birthparents/adopted children come from: All states.

What was the goal of your agency when first organized? What is the goal of your agency now? To support and strengthen families and to provide permanent homes for children. Now: Same.

Nonrelative children placed in 1998: 44

Percent of adoptive placements under 6 mos.: Of the twenty-one domestic placements, 90%; of the 23 international placements, 40%.

Special expertise of staff: Licensed social workers; psychologists.

In 1998, what was the average time from when a prospective adoptive parent applied to when he or she received a homestudy? 2–3 mos. from start of homestudy to completion.

Average time from homestudy to placement of child: 1 year.

Agency criteria for adoptive parents you work with: No more than 45 years between the age of the parent and the age of the child; no more than six children in the home.

How do you screen adoptive parents? Fingerprint FBI clearance; child abuse and neglect clearance; domestic violence check in family court; child support verification; intensive and extensive interview process in the office and home by MSW social workers.

How do you screen birthparents? We have a pregnancy counseling program open to anyone through which we provide counseling.

What kind of medical information do you seek on older children? Complete medical records.

What percent of your U.S. adoptions are nonwhite children? 75%

About what percent are children with medical problems? 5%

About what percent are children with emotional problems? 10%

Do you have a waiting list of prospective parents? Yes.

Is it all right if adopting parents you work with are on waiting lists of other agencies or attorneys? Yes.

Are your adoption fees based on a sliding scale? If yes, what are the sliding scale criteria? Yes. 5% of income on scale of $1,250–$2,500 for comprehensive services.

Do you have an application fee? If yes, what is the amount of the application fee? Yes. $35

What is your homestudy fee (if a flat rate)? $800 flat fee for agency adoptions; $1,200–2,500 for comprehensive adoption services, including homestudy, postplacement, and finalizations for adoption through other agencies.

What is your placement fee? $8,000–14,000, based on 10% of total income.

Do adopting parents also pay fees for medical and hospital expenses for birthmother and baby when they have no insurance? If yes, what is the average fee paid? Yes. Rarely happens, but occasional payment up to $500.

If international adoption, what are average travel expenses? Depends on the country.

If you place children from other countries, please list the estimated *entire* average cost to adoptive parents for each country. We do not have our own international programs, but work through other well-established agencies such as Holt Children's International and Children's Home Society of Minnesota.

My agency: Offers confidential adoptions; semi-open adoptions; meetings between birthparents and adoptive parents; birthparents pick adoptive parents from bios/resumes.

Does your agency provide videotapes of children needing adoption? No.

In how many cases with your agency has an adoptive parent been placed with a child but lost the child due to a birthparent challenge? 0

Has your agency lost any adoption litigation filed against you by an adoptive parent or birthparent? No.

VIRGINIA

COMMONWEALTH CATHOLIC CHARITIES

Respondent: Barbara Smith, Adoption Coordinator
In charge of social services: Margarite B. Savage, MSW, Regional Program Coordinator, Southwest Virginia
P.O. Box 6565, Richmond, VA 23230-0565
(804) 285-5900 or (540) 344-5107 • Fax: (804) 285-9130 or (540) 344-2748
E-mail: comcathric@aol.com • members.aol.com/comcathric/index.html
Year first licensed by state: 1923

Agency provides services for: U.S. adoption; international adoption; children with special needs; infants; homestudy if parents working with another agency; postplacement services.

What states do your adoptive parent clients come from? Virginia for local adoptions, other states for Romanian adoptions.

Services provided adopting parents: Classes with other prospective parents; required readings of books and/or articles on adoption; group discussions about adoption; parenting discussions.

States/countries your birthparents/adopted children come from: Virginia, Romania. Network with other U.S.-based agencies for children from Bolivia, China, Korea, Philippines, Thailand, Russia, India, Chile, Colombia, El Salvador, and Guatemala, etc.

What was the goal of your agency when first organized? What is the goal of your agency now? To provide human care services within the community. Now: In response to the Catholic mission, to respect diversity, promote human dignity, and value families, Commonwealth Catholic Charities provides quality, compassionate human services to all people, especially the most vulnerable.

Nonrelative children placed in 1998: 84

Percent of adoptive placements under 6 mos.: 48%

Special expertise of staff: Adoptive parents on staff; licensed social workers; therapists.

In 1998, what was the average time from when a prospective adoptive parent applied to when he or she received a homestudy? 3–6 mos.

Average time from homestudy to placement of child: 18 mos.

What made you decide to work in the adoption field? I am an adoptive parent.

Agency criteria for adoptive parents you work with: Domestic adoption of a
Caucasian infant can be up to age 45; must have been married 3 years; must be
childless or have one adopted child. Our requirements are more flexible for special
needs and minority children. International programs have individual requirements
set by country. We have found Romania to be flexible with their requirements.

How do you screen adoptive parents? According to Virginia guidelines; individual
homestudy; group homestudy sessions; medical evaluation by physician; psychological evaluation; police clearance; CPS search; DMV report; personal references.

How do you screen birthparents? Individual counseling, following Virginia child-placing guidelines.

What percent of your U.S. adoptions are nonwhite children? 39%

About what percent are children with medical problems? 7%

Do you have a waiting list of prospective parents? Yes, for U.S. Caucasian infants.

**Is it all right if adopting parents you work with are on waiting lists of other agen-
cies or attorneys?** No.

**Are your adoption fees based on a sliding scale? If yes, what are the sliding scale
criteria?** Yes. Based on family's annual income.

Do you have an application fee? If yes, what is the amount of the application fee?
Yes. $175

What is your homestudy fee (if a flat rate)? $1,700, including homestudy and
postplacement.

What is your placement fee? Varies and may be subsidized, depending on the needs of
the child.

**Do adopting parents also pay fees for medical and hospital expenses for birth-
mother and baby when they have no insurance? If yes, what is the average fee
paid?** Yes. $5,000

If international adoption, what are average travel expenses? $3,000–4,000

**If you place children from other countries, please list the estimated *entire* average
cost to adoptive parents for each country.** Romania, $20,000 (includes U.S. and
Romanian fees plus travel costs).

My agency: Offers confidential adoptions; semi-open adoptions; meetings between
birthparents and adoptive parents; birthparents pick adoptive parents from
bios/resumes; full disclosure of names between birth and adoptive parents.

Does your agency provide videotapes of children needing adoption? Yes (Romania).

Are you an adoptive parent, adopted person, or birthparent? Adoptive parent.

**In how many cases with your agency has an adoptive parent been placed with a
child but lost the child due to a birthparent challenge?** 0

**Has your agency lost any adoption litigation filed against you by an adoptive parent
or birthparent?** No.

JEWISH FAMILY SERVICE OF TIDEWATER, INC.

Respondent: Debra Mayer, LCWS, Director of Adoption and Clinical Services
In charge of social services: Debra Mayer
5520 Greenwich Rd., Suite 202, Virginia Beach, VA 23462
(757) 473-2695 • Fax: (757) 473-2699
Year first licensed by state: 1969

Agency provides services for: International adoption; U.S. adoption; infants; homestudy if parents working with another agency; postplacement services.

What states do your adoptive parent clients come from? Virginia.

Services provided adopting parents: Required readings of books and/or articles on adoption; parenting discussions.

States/countries your birthparents/adopted children come from: Virginia.

What was the goal of your agency when first organized? What is the goal of your agency now? Nonprofit family service agency. Now: Same.

Nonrelative children placed in 1998: 11

Percent of adoptive placements under 6 mos.: 100%

Special expertise of staff: Licensed social workers; therapists.

In 1998, what was the average time from when a prospective adoptive parent applied to when he or she received a homestudy? 8 weeks to complete homestudy.

Average time from homestudy to placement of child: 6 mos.

What made you decide to work in the adoption field? Agency service, child advocate.

Agency criteria for adoptive parents you work with: For agency placements only, must be 40 years old or younger; up to three children in home; married 3 years.

How do you screen adoptive parents? Using state standards.

How do you screen birthparents? Using pregnancy counseling skills.

Do you have a waiting list of prospective parents? Yes.

Is it all right if adopting parents you work with are on waiting lists of other agencies or attorneys? Yes.

Are your adoption fees based on a sliding scale? If yes, what are the sliding scale criteria? Yes. 15% of annual gross income.

Do you have an application fee? No.

What is your homestudy fee (if a flat rate)? $1,200

What is your placement fee? Sliding scale up to $10,000

Do adopting parents also pay fees for medical and hospital expenses for birthmother and baby when they have no insurance? Yes. Varies.

If you place children from other countries, please list the estimated *entire* average cost to adoptive parents for each country. Agency provides homestudy and postplacement only; does not provide placements for international adoption.

My agency: Offers confidential adoptions; semi-open adoptions; meetings between birthparents and adoptive parents; birthparents pick adoptive parents from bios/resumes; full disclosure of names between birth and adoptive parents.

Does your agency provide videotapes of children needing adoption? No.

In how many cases with your agency has an adoptive parent been placed with a child but lost the child due to a birthparent challenge? 0

Has your agency lost any adoption litigation filed against you by an adoptive parent or birthparent? No.

WASHINGTON

ADOPTION ADVOCATES INTERNATIONAL

Respondent: Merrily Ripley, Executive Director
In charge of social services: Kathy Barner, Director of Social Services
401 E. Front St., Port Angeles, WA 98362
(360) 452-4777 • Fax: (360) 452-1107
Year first licensed by state: 1983

Agency provides services for: International adoption; U.S. adoption; children with special needs; infants; homestudy if parents working with another agency; postplacement services; adoption support paperwork for Washington families.

What states do your adoptive parent clients come from? All states as well as U.S. citizens living abroad.

Services provided adopting parents: Classes with other prospective parents; required readings of books and/or articles on adoption.

States/countries your birthparents/adopted children come from: All states, China, India, Vietnam, Romania, Ethiopia, Bulgaria, Thailand.

What was the goal of your agency when first organized? What is the goal of your agency now? To find families for special needs children, older, large sibling groups, and physically challenged children, and to provide them with the support, advice, and resources to make the adoptions successful. Now: Although we now place many infants and healthy children, we are still committed to building families for those who wait longer through no fault of their own.

Nonrelative children placed in 1998: 116

Percent of adoptive placements under 6 mos.: 7%

Special expertise of staff: Adoptive parents on staff; licensed social workers; many of our adoption counselors who work directly with families are psychologists.

In 1998, what was the average time from when a prospective adoptive parent applied to when he or she received a homestudy? Less than 1 mo. Counselor contracts requires completion, before 1 mo. barring problems.

Average time from homestudy to placement of child: There is no real "average" due to the big difference in programs. Most families have a child within a year.

What made you decide to work in the adoption field? We had adopted several children and others were asking us about the process. We thought long and hard before deciding to use the knowledge and skills we'd gained to create an agency more geared to the concerns of adoptive parents.

Agency criteria for adoptive parents you work with: It varies, depending on the rules of various foreign countries. The agency itself is flexible and looks only to the best interests of the children as a guideline.

How do you screen adoptive parents? All parents must complete our homestudy and in-home orientation process, meeting criteria established by the agency and states in which they live.

What kind of medical information do you seek from birthparents? We seek any and all that is available. It ranges from extensive to negligible.

What kind of medical information do you seek on older children? Same as above, although all infants and children in foreign and domestic care have health records from the time of their out-of-home placement. Children with special needs often have more comprehensive records, which we encourage prospective parents to take to their own physicians for consultation.

What percent of your U.S. adoptions are nonwhite children? 41%

About what percent are children with medical problems? 13%

Do you have a waiting list of prospective parents? Yes.

Is it all right if adopting parents you work with are on waiting lists of other agencies or attorneys? No.

Are your adoption fees based on a sliding scale? If yes, what are the sliding scale criteria? Yes. Gross income scale from under $24,999 to over $125,000.

Do you have an application fee? If yes, what is the amount of the application fee? Yes. $100

What is your homestudy fee (if a flat rate)? Homestudy and placement fees range from $900-1,600 for Washington and Alaska families. Out-of-state, $1,300–2,000 for adoption processing.

Do adopting parents also pay fees for medical and hospital expenses for birthmother and baby when they have no insurance? No.

If applicable, what is the average document language translation fee? Depends on country and what state families live in.

If you place children from other countries, please list the estimated *entire* average cost to adoptive parents for each country. China, $13,500; Thailand, $7,500–8,000; Romania, $12,000–16,000; Vietnam, $15,000; Ethiopia, $10,000; India, $12,400; Bulgaria, $13,700; East and West Coast, Europe and Asia, several hundred variations possible.

My agency: Offers confidential adoptions; semi-open adoptions.

Does your agency provide videotapes of children needing adoption? Yes.

Are you an adoptive parent, adopted person, or birthparent? Adoptive parent.

In how many cases with your agency has an adoptive parent been placed with a child but lost the child due to a birthparent challenge? 0

Has your agency lost any adoption litigation filed against you by an adoptive parent or birthparent? No.

Is there anything I have not asked you that is important? As the adoptive mother of 18 and an adoption professional for over 23 years, I have learned that adoption is a process that requires extraordinary amounts of commitment, energy, love, strength, and personal stability. Add "sense of humor" to these ingredients and one has a recipe for success.

AMERICANS ADOPTING ORPHANS

Respondents: David B. Ptasnik and Cynthia M. Ptasnik, Co-directors
In charge of social services: David B. Ptasnik
12345 Lake City Way NE, Suite 2001, Seattle, WA 98125
(206) 524-5437 • Fax: (206) 527-2001
E-mail: aao@orphans.com • www.orphans.com
Year first licensed by state: 1995

Agency provides services for: International adoption; children with special needs; infants; homestudy if parents working with another agency; postplacement services.

What states do your adoptive parent clients come from? All states including U.S. citizens living abroad.

Services provided adopting parents: Classes with other prospective parents; group discussions about adoption; parenting discussions; waiting family support meetings; bookstore with books and videos for purchase. Also each semester we offer a schedule of 12–20 classes for parents (culture, language, child care, adoption issues, parenting, etc.).

States/countries your birthparents/adopted children come from: China and Vietnam. Our agency has divided the adoption process into steps; at each step we offer multiple levels of service so that parents decide their level of participation and the fees they may pay.

What was the goal of your agency when first organized? What is the goal of your agency now? To provide a higher level of service and more options to parents to encourage more families to adopt. Now: Same.

Nonrelative children placed in 1998: 78

Percent of adoptive placements under 6 mos.: 25%

Special expertise of staff: Adoptive parents on staff; licensed social workers; psychologists; therapists; adoptee on staff; pediatrics nurse; Chinese-speaking staff.

In 1998, what was the average time from when a prospective adoptive parent applied to when he or she received a homestudy? 3–4 mos.

Average time from homestudy to placement of child: 7–8 mos.

What made you decide to work in the adoption field? Family connections to adoption. David Ptasnik, co-director, is an adoptee. David and his wife have adopted two kids themselves.

Agency criteria for adoptive parents you work with: We do not place restrictions on prospective adoptive parents other than those of the U.S. Immigration and Naturalization Service and the countries with which we work. Mainly families for China need to be 30 years of age or older and earn at least 125% of the national poverty guidelines. For Vietnam, parents can be 25 years old and up.

How do you screen adoptive parents? Our application form is our main tool. It's a basic reality check—what is the family's income (does it meet INS and China/Vietnam guidelines), stable relationship (married around a year), is there a history of substance abuse, child abuse, domestic violence, etc.? Basically, is it an okay time in the family's life to add a child to the fold?

What kind of medical information do you seek from birthparents? With China and Vietnam, the children are anonymously abandoned and no birthparent or prenatal information is available.

What kind of medical information do you seek on older children? All children assigned to families have had basic physical exams, including measurements (height, weight), review of body systems, lab tests for hepatitis B, and passport-sized photo. We offer the option of obtaining additional medical information for our China adoptions, including developmental assessment and social history with up-to-date photos (and videos if available).

Do you have a waiting list of prospective parents? No.

Is it all right if adopting parents you work with are on waiting lists of other agencies or attorneys? Yes.

Are your adoption fees based on a sliding scale? If yes, what are the sliding scale criteria? Yes. Multiple levels of service chosen by family.

Do you have an application fee? If yes, what is the amount of the application fee? Yes. $100

What is your homestudy fee (if a flat rate)? $500–700; local parents may select from among 6–8 homestudy providers with whom we've contracted or they may locate their own homestudy provider within guidelines.

What is your placement fee? Our fee breakdown does not include a placement fee per se; however, our total agency fees vary according to level of service chosen by parents (beginning at $1,500).

If international adoption, what are average travel expenses? $2,000 per traveling parent.

If applicable, what is the average document language translation fee? $200

If you place children from other countries, please list the estimated *entire* average cost to adoptive parents for each country. China, $9,000 (including adoption tax credit); Vietnam, $14,000 (including adoption tax credit).

Does your agency provide videotapes of children needing adoption? Yes.

Are you an adoptive parent, adopted person, or birthparent? Adoptive parent, adopted person.

In how many cases with your agency has an adoptive parent been placed with a child but lost the child due to a birthparent challenge? 0

BETHANY CHRISTIAN SERVICES
Respondent: Edna Kuipers, Executive Director
19936 Ballinger Way NE #D, Seattle, WA 98155
(206) 367-4604 • Fax: (206) 367-1860
E-mail: bcswashsea@aol.com • www.bethany.org
Year first licensed by state: 1984

Agency provides services for: International adoption; U.S. adoption; children with special needs; infants; homestudy if parents working with another agency; postplacement services; receiving care for King County.

What states do your adoptive parent clients come from? Washington, Oregon, Idaho, Alaska.

Services provided adopting parents: Classes with other prospective parents.

States/countries your birthparents/adopted children come from: Washington and Oregon for domestic; Asia, Eastern Europe, South America for international.

What was the goal of your agency when first organized? What is the goal of your agency now? To provide free pregnancy counseling for women with unplanned pregnancies and provide the option of adoption to them. Now: To provide services to women experiencing unplanned pregnancies and to find families for children who continue to wait in foster care and orphanages.

Nonrelative children placed in 1998: 58

Percent of adoptive placements under 6 mos.: 40%

Special expertise of staff: Adoptive parents on staff; licensed social workers.

In 1998, what was the average time from when a prospective adoptive parent applied to when he or she received a homestudy? 7 mos.

Average time from homestudy to placement of child: 12 mos.

What made you decide to work in the adoption field? Desire to have a positive influence on children and families.

Agency criteria for adoptive parents you work with: No age requirements unless specified by international countries. Families over 40 have a more difficult time in infant program. Christian families in infant program.

How do you screen adoptive parents? Initial telephone screening, preliminary application.

How do you screen birthparents? Do not screen them; will work with anyone requesting our services.

What kind of medical information do you seek from birthparents? Social and medical history.

What kind of medical information do you seek on older children? Child's medical and family background report.

What percent of your U.S. adoptions are nonwhite children? 40%

About what percent are children with medical problems? 10%

About what percent are children with emotional problems? 50%

Do you have a waiting list of prospective parents? Yes.

Is it all right if adopting parents you work with are on waiting lists of other agencies or attorneys? Private networking encouraged; other agencies not.

Are your adoption fees based on a sliding scale? If yes, what are the sliding scale criteria? Yes. [Based on] annual gross family income.

Do you have an application fee? If yes, what is the amount of the application fee? Yes. Preliminary, $50; formal, $500.

What is your homestudy fee (if a flat rate)? $800

What is your placement fee? Varies with program. Infant, $8,000–15,000; special needs, $1,000–4,000.

Do adopting parents also pay fees for medical and hospital expenses for birthmother and baby when they have no insurance? If yes, what is the average fee paid? Yes. $1,000

If international adoption, what are average travel expenses? $1,000–2,000

If applicable, what is the average document language translation fee? Varies. Sometimes included in fee or could be up to $1,000.

If you place children from other countries, please list the estimated *entire* average cost to adoptive parents for each country. (Does not include travel.) Korea, $13,400; China, $11,000; India, $8,700; Philippines, $8,700; Romania, $12,200; Albania, $12,200; Russia, $12,700–20,700; Bulgaria, $14,500; Columbia, $10,500; Guatemala, $19,200; Costa Rica, $8,000.

My agency: Offers confidential adoptions; semi-open adoptions; meetings between birthparents and adoptive parents; birthparents pick adoptive parents from bios/resumes.

Does your agency provide videotapes of children needing adoption? No.

In how many cases with your agency has an adoptive parent been placed with a child but lost the child due to a birthparent challenge? 0

Has your agency lost any adoption litigation filed against you by an adoptive parent or birthparent? Cases were settled.

MEDINA CHILDREN'S SERVICES

Respondent: Marylee Killinger, Director, Adoption Services (retired 9/1/99)
In charge of social services: Mary Ann Curran, MA
123 16th Ave., Seattle, WA 98122
(206) 461-4520 • Fax: (206) 461-8372
E-mail: medina@medinachild.org • www.medinachild.org
Year first licensed by state: 1922

Agency provides services for: U.S. adoption; children with special needs; infants; home-study if parents working with another agency; postplacement services; homestudies if adopting independently; support services for international adoption: homestudies and postplacements.

What states do your adoptive parent clients come from? Washington.

Services provided adopting parents: Classes with other prospective parents; required readings of books and/or articles on adoption; group discussions about adoption; specific classes for infant adoption; international; special needs; networking.

States/countries your birthparents/adopted children come from: Washington, Oregon.

What was the goal of your agency when first organized? What is the goal of your agency now? Maternity services for unwed mothers and adoption of babies and children in orphanages. Now: Placement of all kinds of children into loving, stable homes.

Nonrelative children placed in 1998: 40

Percent of adoptive placements under 6 mos.: 60%

Special expertise of staff: Adoptive parents on staff; licensed social workers.

In 1998, what was the average time from when a prospective adoptive parent applied to when he or she received a homestudy? Started within 3 weeks.

Average time from homestudy to placement of child: 7 mos. for infant.

What made you decide to work in the adoption field? As an adoptive parent, I saw the amazing benefits to children and families of adoption.

Agency criteria for adoptive parents you work with: None—anyone may apply.

How do you screen adoptive parents? Lengthy homestudy; educational process; references; lengthy writing assignments.

How do you screen birthparents? Develop relationships with them, as extensive a background, as is possible.

What kind of medical information do you seek from birthparents? All of the above, for birthparents plus all medical, psychological, and social history of child.

What percent of your U.S. adoptions are nonwhite children? 20%

About what percent are children with medical problems? 10%

About what percent are children with emotional problems? 70%

Do you have a waiting list of prospective parents? Yes, for infants; no for older or special needs.

Is it all right if adopting parents you work with are on waiting lists of other agencies or attorneys? No.

Are your adoption fees based on a sliding scale? If yes, what are the sliding scale criteria? Yes. Gross income of family.

Do you have an application fee? If yes, what is the amount of the application fee? Yes. $60

What is your homestudy fee (if a flat rate)? $750–1,000

What is your placement fee? For infant, $7,500–16,000; for older child, $1,350–3,200.

My agency: Offers semi-open adoptions; meetings between birthparents and adoptive parents; birthparents pick adoptive parents from bios/resumes.

Does your agency provide videotapes of children needing adoption? No.

Are you an adoptive parent, adopted person, or birthparent? Adoptive parent.

In how many cases with your agency has an adoptive parent been placed with a child but lost the child due to a birthparent challenge? 0

Has your agency lost any adoption litigation filed against you by an adoptive parent or birthparent? No.

NEW HOPE CHILD AND FAMILY AGENCY

Respondent: Agnes Havlis, Executive Director
In charge of social services: Agnes Havlis
2611 NE 125 St., Suite 146, Seattle, WA 98125
(206) 363-1800 • Fax: (206) 363-0318
E-mail: info@newhopekids.org • www.newhopekids.org
Year first licensed by state: 1974

Agency provides services for: International adoption; U.S. adoption; children with special needs (Washington State only); infants; homestudy if parents working with another agency; postplacement services; birthparent services.

What states do your adoptive parent clients come from? For domestic, Washington, Oregon, Idaho, and Nevada; for international, all states.

Services provided adopting parents: Classes with other prospective parents; required readings of books and/or articles on adoption; group discussions about adoption; parenting discussions.

States/countries your birthparents/adopted children come from: United States, China, Russia, and Romania.

What was the goal of your agency when first organized? What is the goal of your agency now? Children should have quality permanent homes when they cannot be raised by their birthparents. New Hope works actively and compassionately to provide children and their families with solutions that best meet the child's need for a safe, stable, and nurturing home. Now: Same.

Nonrelative children placed in 1998: 180

Percent of adoptive placements under 6 mos.: 90% for domestic.

Special expertise of staff: Adoptive parents on staff; licensed social workers.

In 1998, what was the average time from when a prospective adoptive parent applied to when he or she received a homestudy? 1–2 mos.

Average time from homestudy to placement of child: 6–12 mos.

Agency criteria for adoptive parents you work with: Depends on the program.

How do you screen adoptive parents? Application; homestudy; orientation (two-day training).

How do you screen birthparents? In-person counseling; prenatal records; background information sheets.

What kind of medical information do you seek from birthparents? Complete medical history; prenatal records; brief medical history on their parents and their siblings.

What kind of medical information do you seek on older children? Complete from prenatal to present.

What percent of your U.S. adoptions are nonwhite children? 10%

About what percent are children with medical problems? 10%

About what percent are children with emotional problems? 15%

Do you have a waiting list of prospective parents? Yes.

Is it all right if adopting parents you work with are on waiting lists of other agencies or attorneys? No.

Are your adoption fees based on a sliding scale? If yes, what are the sliding scale criteria? No for all programs but special needs. Special needs adoptions are based on income.

Do you have an application fee? If yes, what is the amount of the application fee? Yes. $50

What is your homestudy fee (if a flat rate)? $850 for domestic.

What is your placement fee? Varies by program.

Do adopting parents also pay fees for medical and hospital expenses for birthmother and baby when they have no insurance? If yes, what is the average fee paid? Yes. For baby only, not birthmother. $800

If international adoption, what are average travel expenses? $2,000–3,000

If applicable, what is the average document language translation fee? $450

If you place children from other countries, please list the estimated *entire* average cost to adoptive parents for each country. China, $12,000 plus travel expenses; Romania, $16,000, plus travel expenses; Russia, $16,000–18,000, depending on region, plus travel expenses.

My agency: Offers confidential adoptions; semi-open adoptions; meetings between birthparents and adoptive parents; birthparents pick adoptive parents from bios/resumes; full disclosure of names between birth and adoptive parents.

Does your agency provide videotapes of children needing adoption? Yes, for international.

In how many cases with your agency has an adoptive parent been placed with a child but lost the child due to a birthparent challenge? 0

Has your agency lost any adoption litigation filed against you by an adoptive parent or birthparent? No.

WEST VIRGINIA

BURLINGTON UNITED METHODIST FAMILY SERVICES

Respondent: Donna McCune, Area Supervisor
In charge of social services: Janice Cannon, Vice President/Community Based Services
P.O. Box 370, Scott Depot, WV 25560
(304) 757-9127 • Fax: (304) 757-9136
E-mail: adoption@zoomnet.net
Year first licensed by state: 1950s

Agency provides services for: International adoption; U.S. adoption; children with special needs; infants; homestudy if parents working with another agency; postplacement services; birthparent services.

What states do your adoptive parent clients come from? West Virginia and Maryland.

Services provided adopting parents: Classes with other prospective parents; required readings of books and/or articles on adoption; group discussions about adoption.

States/countries your birthparents/adopted children come from: West Virginia and Maryland.

What is the goal of your agency now? Burlington United Methodist Family Services, Inc. is a charitable human services organization whose mission is to bring growth and wholeness to family life. This is accomplished by providing a variety of caring and supportive residential and community based services to infants, children, youth, and families.

Nonrelative children placed in 1998: 84

Percent of adoptive placements under 6 mos.: 10%

Special expertise of staff: Adoptive parents on staff; licensed social workers.

In 1998, what was the average time from when a prospective adoptive parent applied to when he or she received a homestudy? 2 mos.

Average time from homestudy to placement of child: 1–2 years for newborn relinquished to agency; 1 year or less for international.

Agency criteria for adoptive parents you work with: Varies.

How do you screen adoptive parents? Telephone, mail, or personal interviews.

How do you screen birthparents? Personal interviews.

What kind of medical information do you seek from birthparents? All that is available on child and extended family members.

What percent of your U.S. adoptions are nonwhite children? 30–40%

About what percent are children with medical problems? 30–40%

Do you have a waiting list of prospective parents? Yes.

Is it all right if adopting parents you work with are on waiting lists of other agencies or attorneys? Yes.

Are your adoption fees based on a sliding scale? Yes, on domestic and special needs relinquished directly to agency; no on international.

Do you have an application fee? If yes, what is the amount of the application fee? Yes. $200

What is your homestudy fee (if a flat rate)? Varies.

Do adopting parents also pay fees for medical and hospital expenses for birthmother and baby when they have no insurance? If yes, what is the average fee paid? Yes. Varies.

If you place children from other countries, please list the estimated *entire* average cost to adoptive parents for each country. We work in cooperation with international placing agencies.

My agency: Offers confidential adoptions; semi-open adoptions; meetings between birthparents and adoptive parents; birthparents pick adoptive parents from bios/resumes; full disclosure of names between birth and adoptive parents.

Does your agency provide videotapes of children needing adoption? No.

In how many cases with your agency has an adoptive parent been placed with a child but lost the child due to a birthparent challenge? 0

Has your agency lost any adoption litigation filed against you by an adoptive parent or birthparent? No.

WISCONSIN

THE ADOPTION OPTION, INC.

Respondent: Roberta Fries, MSW, ACSW, Director
In charge of social services: Roberta Fries
1804 Chapman Dr., Waukesha, WI 53189
(414) 544-4278
Year first licensed by state: 1985

Agency provides services for: International adoption; U.S. adoption; children with special needs; infants; homestudy if parents working with another agency; postplacement services; birthparent counseling.

What states do your adoptive parent clients come from? Wisconsin.

Services provided adopting parents: Referral to adoptive parent support groups.

States/countries your birthparents/adopted children come from: Any state, Latin American countries, China and Asian countries, India, Russia, Ukraine, Romania.

What was the goal of your agency when first organized? What is the goal of your agency now? To provide children who need stable, permanent, loving, nurturing families and parents with them. Now: Same.

Nonrelative children placed in 1998: 20

Percent of adoptive placements under 6 mos.: 35% in 1998

Special expertise of staff: Adoptive parents on staff; licensed social workers.

In 1998, what was the average time from when a prospective adoptive parent applied to when he or she received a homestudy? 30 days

Average time from homestudy to placement of child: 6–12 mos.

What made you decide to work in the adoption field? I had experience doing stepparent and relative adoptions when I worked for the county in the 1970s and I enjoyed it.

Agency criteria for adoptive parents you work with: Very open and flexible; no age limit; no religious requirement; no minimum number of children in the home; each case decided on its own merits.

How do you screen adoptive parents? Interviews; home visit; medical reports; reference letters; criminal record checks; child abuse record checks.

How do you screen birthparents? Interviews.

What kind of medical information do you seek from birthparents? The Wisconsin Medical-Genetic history form; pregnancy and delivery information.

What kind of medical information do you seek on older children? I have a medical form for the doctor to fill out.

What percent of your U.S. adoptions are nonwhite children? 33%

About what percent are children with emotional problems? 15%, not usually severe.

Do you have a waiting list of prospective parents? No.

Is it all right if adopting parents you work with are on waiting lists of other agencies or attorneys? No.

Are your adoption fees based on a sliding scale? No.

Do you have an application fee? No.

What is your homestudy fee (if a flat rate)? $1,800

Do adopting parents also pay fees for medical and hospital expenses for birthmother and baby when they have no insurance? If yes, what is the average fee paid? Yes. Varies.

If you place children from other countries, please list the estimated *entire* average cost to adoptive parents for each country. I just do the homestudy and postplacement. The clients work with an international agency.

My agency: Offers confidential adoptions; semi-open adoptions; meetings between birthparents and adoptive parents; birthparents pick adoptive parents from bios/resumes; full disclosure of names between birth and adoptive parents.

Does your agency provide videotapes of children needing adoption? No.

In how many cases with your agency has an adoptive parent been placed with a child but lost the child due to a birthparent challenge? 0

Has your agency lost any adoption litigation filed against you by an adoptive parent or birthparent? No. Never had any.

CATHOLIC CHARITIES OF THE ARCHDIOCESE OF MILWAUKEE, INC.

Respondent: Marilyn Metz, Child Welfare Supervisor
In charge of social services: Diane Knight, Director of Program Services
2021 N. 60th St., Milwaukee, WI 53208
(414) 771-2881 • Fax: (414) 771-6095
E-mail: mmetz@ccmke.org • www.ccmke.org
Year first licensed by state: 1920

Agency provides services for: International adoption; U.S. adoption; children with special needs; infants.

What states do your adoptive parent clients come from? Primarily Wisconsin, as agency is licensed in Wisconsin. We also do interstate adoption.

Services provided adopting parents: Classes with other prospective parents; required readings of books and/or articles on adoption; group discussions about adoption; six-week educational classes.

States/countries your birthparents/adopted children come from: Primarily Wisconsin.

What was the goal of your agency when first organized? What is the goal of your agency now? Original goal centered around care for the unwed mother and child. Now: 1. To position Catholic Charities as the valued provider of individual and family services. 2. To provide quality services that strengthen and empower individuals and families with diverse communities.

Nonrelative children placed in 1998: 37

Percent of adoptive placements under 6 mos.: 100%

Special expertise of staff: Adoptive parents on staff; licensed social workers; therapists.

In 1998, what was the average time from when a prospective adoptive parent applied to when he or she received a homestudy? Most homestudies are completed within 8 weeks.

Average time from homestudy to placement of child: It varies; agency adoption may take 2–3 years.

What made you decide to work in the adoption field? I work primarily with children as a teacher and family therapist. My parent raised foster children.

Agency criteria for adoptive parents you work with: Follow Wisconsin state guidelines; will participate in open adoptions.

How do you screen adoptive parents? Through background checks; local police; local DSS; DMV; State of Wisconsin Department of Justice; three personal references.

How do you screen birthparents? We don't screen. Our intake process consists of a questionnaire that all pregnant women fill out which determines eligibility for our state Medicaid program. However, we take all birthparents.

What kind of medical information do you seek from birthparents? Medical/genetic state form on birthmother and alleged father. Also, labor, delivery, and birth records of infant.

What percent of your U.S. adoptions are nonwhite children? 28%

Do you have a waiting list of prospective parents? Yes.

Is it all right if adopting parents you work with are on waiting lists of other agencies or attorneys? No.

Are your adoption fees based on a sliding scale? Fees are a flat fee for traditional infant program. However, special needs children are sometimes placed on a reduced fee, according to income of adopting parents.

Do you have an application fee? No.

What is your homestudy fee (if a flat rate)? Depends on type of adoption.

What is your placement fee? Depends on type of adoption.

If you place children from other countries, please list the estimated *entire* average cost to adoptive parents for each country. We only do homestudy and postplacement services for international adoptions.

My agency: Offers confidential adoptions; semi-open adoptions; meetings between birthparents and adoptive parents; birthparents pick adoptive parents from bios/resumes; full disclosure of names between birth and adoptive parents.

Does your agency provide videotapes of children needing adoption? No.

In how many cases with your agency has an adoptive parent been placed with a child but lost the child due to a birthparent challenge? 0

Has your agency lost any adoption litigation filed against you by an adoptive parent or birthparent? No.

CATHOLIC CHARITIES

Respondent: Grace Mrozinski, Adoption Specialist
3311 Prairie Ave., Beloit, WI 53511
(608) 365-3665 or (608) 821-3100 • Fax: (608) 365-1279 or (608) 821-3125
Year first licensed by state: 1948

Agency provides services for: International adoption; U.S. adoption; infants; postplacement services.

What states do your adoptive parent clients come from? Wisconsin.

Services provided adopting parents: Required readings of books and/or articles on adoption; parenting discussions.

States/countries your birthparents/adopted children come from: Wisconsin, Russia.

What was the goal of your agency when first organized? What is the goal of your agency now? Child welfare agency—adoption, foster care for infants. Now: To provide permanency for children.

Nonrelative children placed in 1998: 14

Percent of adoptive placements under 6 mos.: 90%

Special expertise of staff: Licensed social workers; therapists; attorney.

In 1998, what was the average time from when a prospective adoptive parent applied to when he or she received a homestudy? 6 weeks–2 mos.

Average time from homestudy to placement of child: 2 years

What made you decide to work in the adoption field? The challenge and the need for all children legally free to be adopted and have a permanent family.

Agency criteria for adoptive parents you work with: Infertile; married 2 years; no children if desire to adopt infant; aged 45–50.

How do you screen adoptive parents? Individual informational interview with couple interested in adoption. Explain all types of adoption: infant, foreign, older children, special needs children, stepparent/relative.

What kind of medical information do you seek on older children? Request medical information from agency having custody of child.

What percent of your U.S. adoptions are nonwhite children? 5%

Do you have a waiting list of prospective parents? Yes.

Is it all right if adopting parents you work with are on waiting lists of other agencies or attorneys? No.

Are your adoption fees based on a sliding scale? No.

Do you have an application fee? If yes, what is the amount of the application fee? Yes. $100

What is your homestudy fee (if a flat rate)? $10,000

What is your placement fee? Included in above.

Do adopting parents also pay fees for medical and hospital expenses for birthmother and baby when they have no insurance? If yes, what is the average fee paid? Yes. $1,200–3,000; varies case-by-case.

If international adoption, what are average travel expenses? Depends on country.

If you place children from other countries, please list the estimated *entire* average cost to adoptive parents for each country. Russia, $20,000–25,000.

My agency: Offers confidential adoptions; semi-open adoptions; meetings between birthparents and adoptive parents; birthparents pick adoptive parents from bios/resumes.

Does your agency provide videotapes of children needing adoption? No.

Has your agency lost any adoption litigation filed against you by an adoptive parent or birthparent? No.

PAUQUETTE CHILDREN'S SERVICES

Respondent: Lynn C. Tool, Supervisor of Adoptions
In charge of social services: Lynn C. Tool
315 West Conant, Portage, WI 53901-7937
(608) 742-8004 • Fax: (608) 742-7937
E-mail: adopt@palacenet.net
Year first licensed by state: 1982

Agency provides services for: International adoption; U.S. adoption; infants; homestudy if parents working with another agency; postplacement services.

What states do your adoptive parent clients come from? Wisconsin for homestudy and postplacement services; all states for international programs and independent adoptions.

Services provided adopting parents: Classes with other prospective parents; required readings of books and/or articles on adoption; group discussions about adoption; parenting discussions; pre- and postplacement adoption counseling.

States/countries your birthparents/adopted children come from: Wisconsin and other states, India, Mexico, Russia, China, Guatemala, Bolivia, Vietnam, Korea, Haiti, Brazil, Colombia.

What was the goal of your agency when first organized? What is the goal of your agency now? International adoption. At the time our agency was started, international adoptions were very difficult or impossible in Wisconsin. Now: To provide a wide range of adoption services.

Nonrelative children placed in 1998: 100

Percent of adoptive placements under 6 mos.: 75%

Special expertise of staff: Adoptive parents on staff; licensed social workers; therapists.

In 1998, what was the average time from when a prospective adoptive parent applied to when he or she received a homestudy? 2 weeks

Average time from homestudy to placement of child: 12 mos.

What made you decide to work in the adoption field? I find the work rewarding and interesting. Since I began working in the field, my husband and I adopted four children so my work is also a personal interest.

Agency criteria for adoptive parents you work with: Must be 21–50 years old; married 1 year; singles accepted; infertility not required; no family size or religious requirements.

How do you screen adoptive parents? Homestudy and interviews; extensive background check including criminal history, child abuse, etc.; references/financial information; recent physical exam.

How do you screen birthparents? Birthparents provide medical, genetic, and social history; social worker. interviews.

What kind of medical information do you seek on older children? We don't place children over age 1.

What percent of your U.S. adoptions are nonwhite children? 40%

About what percent are children with medical problems? 0–5%

Do you have a waiting list of prospective parents? Yes.

Is it all right if adopting parents you work with are on waiting lists of other agencies or attorneys? Yes.

Are your adoption fees based on a sliding scale? No.

Do you have an application fee? No.

What is your homestudy fee (if a flat rate)? $3,000, including postplacement and all other agency services. We have a flat fee of $3,000 that includes homestudy, dossier preparation, yearly updates if necessary, postplacement, finalization, re-adoption assistance with obtaining citizenship.

What is your placement fee? $10,500. (If we place the child this includes medical, legal, foster care, and birthparent counseling costs.)

Do adopting parents also pay fees for medical and hospital expenses for birthmother and baby when they have no insurance? No.

If international adoption, what are average travel expenses? Varies; Mexico is a lot less expensive than India.

My agency: Offers confidential adoptions; semi-open adoptions; meetings between birthparents and adoptive parents; birthparents pick adoptive parents from bios/resumes; full disclosure of names between birth and adoptive parents.

Does your agency provide videotapes of children needing adoption? Yes, sometimes.

Are you an adoptive parent, adopted person, or birthparent? Adoptive parent.

In how many cases with your agency has an adoptive parent been placed with a child but lost the child due to a birthparent challenge? 0

Has your agency lost any adoption litigation filed against you by an adoptive parent or birthparent? No.

SPECIAL BEGINNINGS ADOPTION SERVICES

Respondent: Donna M. Strayer, Program Director
In charge of social services: Donna M. Strayer
237 South St., Waukesha, WI 53186
(414) 896-3600 • Fax: (414) 896-3601
Year first licensed by state: 1992

Agency provides services for: International adoption; U.S. adoption; infants; homestudy if parents working with another agency; postplacement services;

What states do your adoptive parent clients come from? Wisconsin.

Services provided adopting parents: Individual meetings.

States/countries your birthparents/adopted children come from: Wisconsin and Russia.

Nonrelative children placed in 1998: 27

Percent of adoptive placements under 6 mos.: 100%

Special expertise of staff: Licensed social workers; therapists.

In 1998, what was the average time from when a prospective adoptive parent applied to when he or she received a homestudy? 6–8 weeks.

What made you decide to work in the adoption field? I am a birthparent.

Agency criteria for adoptive parents you work with: Married 3 years; completed infertility treatment.

How do you screen adoptive parents? Individual meeting; clearance checks; letter of reference; medical clearance.

How do you screen birthparents? Personal interviews.

What kind of medical information do you seek from birthparents? Medical genetic form used by the State of Wisconsin.

What percent of your U.S. adoptions are nonwhite children? 25%

About what percent are children with medical problems? 5%

Do you have a waiting list of prospective parents? Yes.

Is it all right if adopting parents you work with are on waiting lists of other agencies or attorneys? No.

Are your adoption fees based on a sliding scale? If yes, what are the sliding scale criteria? Yes. 10% of taxable income, $7,000–10,500.

Do you have an application fee? If yes, what is the amount of the application fee? Yes, but only for Russia. Russia, $200; other, none.

What is your homestudy fee (if a flat rate)? $1,800

What is your placement fee? $7,000–10,500

Do adopting parents also pay fees for medical and hospital expenses for birthmother and baby when they have no insurance? If yes, what is the average fee paid? Yes. $1,500

If international adoption, what are average travel expenses? $6,000

If you place children from other countries, please list the estimated *entire* average cost to adoptive parents for each country. Russia, $20,000–23,000.

My agency: Offers semi-open adoptions; meetings between birthparents and adoptive parents; birthparents pick adoptive parents from bios/resumes; full disclosure of names between birth and adoptive parents.

Does your agency provide videotapes of children needing adoption? Yes, for Russia.

Are you an adoptive parent, adopted person, or birthparent? Birthparent.

In how many cases with your agency has an adoptive parent been placed with a child but lost the child due to a birthparent challenge? 0

Has your agency lost any adoption litigation filed against you by an adoptive parent or birthparent? No.

WYOMING

WYOMING CHILDREN'S SOCIETY

Respondent: Carol Lindly, Director
In charge of social services: Carol Lindly
P.O. Box 105, Cheyenne, WY 82003
(307) 632-7619 • Fax: (307) 632-3056
Year first licensed by state: 1911

Agency provides services for: International adoption; U.S. adoption; children with special needs; infants; homestudy if parents working with another agency; postplacement services.

What states do your adoptive parent clients come from? Primarily Wyoming.

Services provided adopting parents: Classes with other prospective parents; special needs adoption training.

States/countries your birthparents/adopted children come from: Birthparents from Wyoming; children from United States and international.

What was the goal of your agency when first organized? What is the goal of your agency now? Orphanage and home for unwed mothers. Now: Adoption, child-placing agency.

Nonrelative children placed in 1998: 35

Percent of adoptive placements under 6 mos.: 35%

Special expertise of staff: Adoptive parents on staff; licensed social workers.

In 1998, what was the average time from when a prospective adoptive parent applied to when he or she received a homestudy? 4–12 weeks

Average time from homestudy to placement of child: 1 year

What made you decide to work in the adoption field? I am an adoptive parent and have years of child welfare work.

Agency criteria for adoptive parents you work with: Must be over 21 years old; Wyoming residents.

How do you screen adoptive parents? Application process; homestudy interviews; and occasionally psychological testing.

How do you screen birthparents? Establish a relationship; gather information through numerous meetings.

What kind of medical information do you seek on older children? We request a current medical and social history, and school and psychological report if appropriate.

What percent of your U.S. adoptions are nonwhite children? Less than 10%

About what percent are children with medical problems? Less than 10%

About what percent are children with emotional problems? 30% special needs adoption.

Do you have a waiting list of prospective parents? Yes.

Is it all right if adopting parents you work with are on waiting lists of other agencies or attorneys? Yes.

Are your adoption fees based on a sliding scale? If yes, what are the sliding scale criteria? Yes. For infant adoption, 15% of gross annual income up to $10,000; for special needs adoption, no placement fee.

Do you have an application fee? If yes, what is the amount of the application fee? Yes. $100

What is your homestudy fee (if a flat rate)? $700

What is your placement fee? See sliding scale criteria question.

Do adopting parents also pay fees for medical and hospital expenses for birthmother and baby when they have no insurance? If yes, what is the average fee paid? Yes. $6,000

If you place children from other countries, please list the estimated *entire* average cost to adoptive parents for each country. We do homestudy, assist with INS and postplacement. The family selects an international agency as the placing agency.

My agency: Offers confidential adoptions; semi-open adoptions; meetings between birthparents and adoptive parents; birthparents pick adoptive parents from bios/resumes; full disclosure of names between birth and adoptive parents.

Does your agency provide videotapes of children needing adoption? No.

Are you an adoptive parent, adopted person, or birthparent? Adoptive parent.

In how many cases with your agency has an adoptive parent been placed with a child but lost the child due to a birthparent challenge? 0

Has your agency lost any adoption litigation filed against you by an adoptive parent or birthparent? No.

OUTSIDE THE UNITED STATES

I have information on one American social worker living in Germany who does home-studies for Americans who live in Europe. I've adapted his information to my agency questionnaire format. As with agencies and attorneys, I do not endorse this social worker or any other, and families should thoroughly investigate every adoption contact before making a commitment.

GERALD BOWMAN

Veldener Str. 52
80687 Munich Germany
Telephone from U.S.: 011-49-89-5601-7944
From elsewhere: 0049-89-5601-7944
E-mail: GeraldBowman@compuserve.com or 101546.03@compuserve.com

Agency provides services for: Homestudy; postplacement services; parental preparation; education for individuals or groups.

What states do your adoptive parent clients come from? They come from every state in the United States. I do both international and domestic homestudies.

Nonrelative children placed in 1998: I did 12 homestudies in 1998.

Special expertise of staff: I am a licensed social worker and a therapist.

In 1998, what was the average time from when a prospective adoptive parent applied to when he or she received a homestudy? This varies but generally within a month. I can also do them quicker if it is necessary.

What made you decide to work in the adoption field? I fell into it by accident. I was requested to do a homestudy by a couple wishing to adopt. Because I am a licensed clinical social worker, my services are requested often. Because of my expertise, I have gained more referrals. I have dome homestudies in the United States and postplacement visits in Europe.

Do you have a waiting list of prospective parents? Yes.

What is your homestudy fee (if a flat rate)? $750 plus travel overnight if outside Germany. $650 plus travel and overnight if inside Germany. I seek the most reasonable means of travel, such as staying over on a Saturday.

What is your placement fee? $200 plus travel. $100 for telephone follow-up.

What is the most common mistake you see adopting parents make? Being unrealistic, but this usually comes from lack of information, preparation, etc. I think that what I see with some agencies is that they do not respond or talk to couples enough that live broad.

In how many cases with your agency has an adoptive parent been placed with a child but lost the child due to a birthparent challenge? None that I have been involved with.

Have you lost any adoption litigation filed against you by an adoptive parent or birthparent? No.

CHAPTER THREE

ALL ABOUT
ADOPTION ATTORNEYS

Thousands of people successfully adopt their children—usually infants—using the assistance of an adoption attorney. As discussed earlier, the adoption attorney's role varies depending on state laws. In some states, attorneys can assist families to identify pregnant women who wish to place their babies for adoption, while in others, the family must find the birthmother themselves and then the lawyer can provide legal help.

The common denominator among the attorneys I listed here is that they urge prospective parents to find a good attorney early on, one who is experienced in the laws of their state. I have encapsulated some key advice of several adoption attorneys in the following table and in the top ten tips from the attorneys responding to my questionnaire.

Then I provide an excellent essay written by a highly experienced and talented attorney, Sam Totaro, Jr., who describes how you can find a good attorney and establish a positive working rapport while you work together toward your goal of adopting a baby. Following Mr. Totaro's essay is a list of attorneys who work with clients throughout the country, as well as in Canada and elsewhere.

An extensive section on the responses from the attorneys themselves to my questionnaire is the next and largest section of this chapter.

FROM ATTORNEYS: HOW WOULD YOU ADVISE PROSPECTIVE ADOPTERS JUST STARTING OUT?

- Be wise consumers of adoption services. Thoroughly check out the person/agency/attorney/facilitator *before* laying out funds.—Douglas Donnelly, Santa Barbara, CA
- Register with a reputable attorney or agency and believe it will happen!—Linda McIntyre, Delray Beach, FL
- Get a good agency, a good lawyer and good doctor who can answer medical questions. "Good" means they know what they are doing and can get along with the adopting parent.—Deborah Crouse Cobb, Edwardsville, IL
- Look into all of your available options, interview attorneys and agencies, and then settle upon an attorney or agency whom you trust, whom you believe is experienced

339

in the area of adoption law, and with whom you believe you have the greatest chance of success.—Steve Kirsh, Indianapolis, IN

- 1. Be comfortable to be an adoptive parent. 2. Put the past behind and look to the future. 3. Do not be desperate. 4. Do not cut corners. 5. Educate yourself as to the realities.—Aaron Britvan, Woodbury, NY

- Be cautious, never offer money to birthmothers and be aware that the process may take awhile.—Chana Mesberg, Waccubuc, NY

- Patience, patience, patience. Explore every opportunity you find.—Mary Smith, Toledo, OH

- Be aware that it is possible to adopt. Proper effort (spreading the word) will enhance chances of finding a child sooner.—Laurence H. Spiegel, Lake Oswego, OR

- Read everything you can find. Find a support group—talk to adoptees, adoptive families, and adoption professionals. Gather information to realistically understand the process.—Vika Andrel, Austin, TX

- Tell everyone they know or meet that they are interested in adopting. It is amazing how some of these contacts are made.—Melody B. Royall, Houston, TX

- Make sure you consult with a qualified adoption attorney. General practitioners should *not* try to do adoption work.—Kurt M. Hughes, Burlington, VT

TOP TEN TIPS FROM ADOPTION ATTORNEYS

1. Hire an experienced adoption attorney and don't wait too long to do so. Don't hire your uncle's tax attorney or your friend's lawyer who handles accidents.
2. Don't be in a such a big rush that you make mistakes and act rashly. Calm down.
3. Listen to your attorney and don't assume outsiders know more. You hired him or her for legal advice, so why not follow it?
4. Be proactive. Let people know you want to adopt rather than remaining passive and idle.
5. Don't complain about things the attorney can't help, such as court costs or events he or she has no control over.
6. Be understanding of birthparents and see them as real people—because they are real people.
7. Don't assume the attorney will promise you a perfect child. If he or she does, run the other way.
8. Ask a lot of questions. Attorneys say that too many people keep their questions to themselves. If a couple, tell each other what the attorney said. Husbands and wives should not ask the same questions.
9. Be careful. Avoid jumping into situations that may be risky. Don't agree to something and then expect your attorney to save you. Ask for help first.
10. Avoid desperation. Desperate people don't think straight and can commit to bad situations or make serious mistakes.

WHAT DO ATTORNEYS LIKE BEST ABOUT ADOPTIVE PARENTS?

The following are a sampling of responses.

- Seeing their eyes light up when they see the child for the first time and getting pictures from them letting us know everything is going well for them. Feedback is important.—Bryant Whitmire, AL
- Their intense love and commitment to the child they are adopting. Unconditional desire to be good parents. Their joy and appreciation for the wonderful gift they have received.—Mary Verdier, AZ
- Sharing their joy.—Jed Somit, CA
- Almost without exception, they are warm, generous, loving people who are understanding, giving, and caring parents.—Cynthia Stump Swanson, FL
- I like everything about the adoption field without exception and I wish it was all I did.—John Hirschfeld, IL
- Their gratitude. The Christmas cards with pictures of the children!—Colleen Marea Quinn, VA
- Most are caring, intelligent, wonderful people.—Margaret Cunniff Holm, WA

OPTIMIZING YOUR RELATIONSHIP WITH YOUR ADOPTION ATTORNEY

Sam Totaro, Jr.

Generally, when people think of the role of an attorney in an adoption, they imagine it to be primarily the preparation of legal documents, making court appearances at the time of termination of parental rights, and giving legal advice. Unfortunately, most judges think the same. However, an attorney who specializes in adoption offers the client special knowledge, skills and valuable resources in the adoption community that the general practitioner does not have. These special abilities can be the difference between an adoption placement that runs smoothly and one that falls apart at the last minute.

There are important advantages to using an experienced and capable adoption attorney, especially when you are planning an independent or "private" adoption. As a specialist, the adoption attorney will know the many special laws and legal procedures of adoption that exist in different states. Don't trust that a family law lawyer has that special skill. Most law schools do not teach even one course in adoption, but rather adoption attorneys obtain their skills and abilities over a long period of time during private practice.

An adoption attorney will have greater insight into whether or not there is a red flag in the adoption—whether there are any concerns that would cause you to decide to not proceed with this birthparent. This insight can only be gained through extensive experience working with birthparents and adoptive parents.

An adoption attorney will also have numerous contacts in the local adoption community to refer either you or your birthparent for additional counseling. This is especially important if you are contemplating an interstate adoption. An adoption attorney will also have contacts in other states to provide those services, which are so crucial in making certain that the adoption is completed successfully. The attorney will be able to ensure that the birthmother is referred to a physician who is pro-adoption, or to an appropriate counselor if an issue arises with the birthfather.

One of the most important reasons to retain an adoption attorney is that he or she may often have the ability to introduce you to a birthparent who is contemplating adoption. Most adoption attorneys have established relationships with others in the pregnancy-related fields and are often thought of first when referrals are made for placements. Some even have their own programs of networking for birthmothers, such as national advertising programs. However, be careful, because a few states do not allow anyone other than licensed agencies to locate and introduce birthparents to prospective adoptive parents.

In those states, adoption attorneys generally advise you on the methods of locating birthparents for yourself, then perform the necessary legal work thereafter, including coordinating everything during the birthmother's pregnancy, the birth of the baby, and the placement of the baby with the adoptive parents. It is always beneficial to consult with an adoption attorney in the beginning of your quest, even though you may contemplate doing the networking for a birthmother by yourself. The attorney will be invaluable in reviewing with you the laws of the states in which you contemplate networking, and make sure that what you plan on doing is allowed in that state.

Choosing an Adoption Attorney

For many people, the adoption of a child is the single most important thing they will ever do in their lives. Choosing the right attorney is critical to ensuring that the process works for both you and the birthparents. The quality of service, depth of knowledge, fairness of fees, and other important factors can and will vary greatly from attorney to attorney, even among those who are adoption attorneys.

In selecting an adoption attorney, do exactly what you would do if you were selecting a physician or surgeon. Your first stop would not be the yellow pages. Nor should your first stop be the local bar association, because they will only recommend a family law lawyer.

Instead, your first stop on your way to selecting an adoption attorney is to ask others who have adopted successfully whom they used. Most people are referred to their doctors or other specialists in the same way. If you ask three or four people in your area which attorney they used, often the same name will surface. Those who have had a good experience will gladly tell you who they have used, as will those who have had a bad experience.

Another method of selecting a qualified adoption attorney is to obtain a list of members of the American Academy of Adoption Attorneys, which is a national organization of attorneys, law professors, and judges whose practice has an emphasis in adoption. Its members need to have extensive experience in adoption, especially interstate adoptions, before they are admitted into membership. Additionally, they often have the extensive contacts in other states that are so critical in ensuring that an adoption runs smoothly. You can reach the American Academy of Adoption Attorneys at 202-832-2222, or P.O. Box 33053, Washington, DC 20033-0053.

Important Do's and Don'ts

In interviewing an attorney, or even after you have selected one, there are numerous things that you should know to ensure that your relationship with your adoption attorney runs as smoothly as you want your adoption to run. The following list of do's and don'ts is not exhaustive, but should help you in finding that right person to help you create your family:

- After you make your appointment with the attorney, make sure that you try to keep it. Attorneys have numerous clients and, just like doctors, can use the time allocated for your appointment if you don't show. If for some reason you can't keep your appointment, be courteous and cancel as early as possible. When coming to the appointment, plan to get there as early as possible. Expect traffic delays, or getting lost, since it is your first visit to the office, And, by all means, if you are running late, call the attorney's office so they can plan their time accordingly. This advice may sound so natural, but you would be surprised at how many times adoptive parents make appointments and then do not show or arrive late with no explanation whatsoever.
- Both husband and wife should always attend the first meeting with the attorney together. So many times, the appointment is made for both, but only one appears for the meeting. The excuse always is that the other spouse is very busy and couldn't make it. Is he or she going to be too busy to go to the hospital to pick up the baby? I always question the commitment of both spouses when only one attends the initial meeting.
- Before arriving at the initial consultation, do some homework. Read some books or articles on adoption. Become familiar with the terminology in adoption. Talk to your friends and relatives who have adopted and become familiar with open and closed adoptions. Talk to each other, and discuss what type of adoption you would be comfortable with. And always bring a list of questions or areas of concern that you wish to discuss with the attorney.

During Your First Consultation

At the initial consultation, discuss with the attorney the following questions regarding qualifications:

- How much of the attorney's practice is devoted to adoption?
- How many adoptions does the attorney do annually? Although this number varies from area to area, most adoption attorneys do at least 25 to 30 adoptions annually, with some doing in excess of 100.
- What is the average time before you can expect to be selected by a birthmother? Don't expect guarantees, but an attorney should be able to give you an estimate of what the average length of time before selection was last year and should know how many of his or her clients were not successful at all.
- Ask specifically whether the attorney has a networking program to find birthparents, or whether you will do the networking. It has been reported that most successful adoption attorneys locate the birthparents for their clients in at least one-half of the adoptions they handle on a yearly basis.
- Make sure the attorney completely outlines his or her fees, as well as what the anticipated expenses would be. Ask to see a copy of the attorney's fee agreement and take it home with you. As with most professionals, expect to pay more for the services of

an attorney with more experience than for one with less. Most attorneys charge by the amount of time for each individual case. Others charge a flat fee. Even if the charge is by the hour, ask what he or she would estimate the fee to be without any complications. A good attorney will be able to estimate within a few hundred dollars. It is important to remember that the only product an attorney has to sell is his or her time and advice. Therefore, be prepared to be charged for telephone calls. Decide in advance which one of you will make the phone call (or do a conference call). It is very irritating to an adoption attorney to get back-to-back telephone calls from the husband and then the wife asking the same questions. I always wonder whether spouses cease talking to each other after they contemplate adopting. If you want to use this practice, be ready to pay twice for the same information,

- In reviewing the fee agreement, determine what fees are required in advance and what amount is nonrefundable. Also, be prepared to pay for the initial consultation. When making the appointment, ask whether there is a charge for the initial consultation, which will generally last one to two hours.

- Does the attorney seem not only professional, but also reasonably emotionally sensitive? Do you think that he or she can relate well to a birthparent? What are the attorney's practices in having contact with you or the birthparents in the evenings or on weekends? The attorney should be accessible at all times, not only during normal business hours. However, don't take advantage of this accessibility. If a question or concern is not an emergency, then save it until the next day. Adoption attorneys have families and want to spend time with them, and it is also important that they spend their off hours on real emergencies.

- Never expect guarantees of any type. Any attorney who guarantees a result does not have the experience that is necessary in an adoption. If every birthparent came from a mold, any attorney could handle this case for you. However, birthparents are as varied as the general population. A good adoption attorney can only give you advice based upon his or her experience—nothing more!

- At times you may find it necessary to seek a second opinion. Your adoption attorney is giving you advice based upon years of experience. When seeking a second opinion, consult with another adoption attorney, not your best friend who adopted or your cousin who is a commercial real estate lawyer. Many times adoptive parents will confront their lawyer with the statement that it wasn't done that way when their cousin adopted. Each case is different, and you can never expect the same analysis in two different cases. Take your advice from a qualified adoption attorney.

- Expect your lawyer to take time and answer your questions. Expect to pay for his or her time in doing so. However, don't ask questions concerning situations that may never occur. We realize most adoptive parents need to know what may happen in every contingency, but trust your lawyer to tell you what you need to know when you need to know it.

- Be accessible yourself. If you are going away for an extended vacation (more than a few days) let your attorney know. There is nothing more frustrating than trying to track down adoptive parents in an emergency situation.

There are many risks that you may take in an adoption. One of them should not be the attorney that you are using.

Sam Totaro, Jr. is a partner in the Bensalem, Pennsylvania law firm of Kellis Totaro & Soffer. During his career, Mr. Totaro has been involved in over 3,000 adoptions, representing agencies, adoptive parents, and birthparents. He is a member of the American Bar Association and of the Executive Committee of the Adoption Committee of the Family Law Section. Mr. Totaro served on the Board of Directors of the National Council for Adoption in Washington, DC and is a past president of the American Academy of Adoption Attorneys as well as the current vice president of the Pennsylvania Academy of Adoption Attorneys. He is also a member of the Hague Alliance, a coalition of adoption agencies, organizations, and professionals convened to advise the U.S. State Department on the implementation of the Hague Convention on Intercountry Adoption.

ATTORNEYS WHO WORK WITH ADOPTIVE PARENTS IN ALL OR MOST STATES, IN CANADA, AND IN OTHER COUNTRIES

Name of Attorney	State	Adoptive Parents Come From
Philip J. McCarthy	AZ	United States
Kathryn A. Pidgeon	AZ	Many states and Canada
Daniel T. Ziskin	AZ	United States
Eugene T. Kelley	AR	United States, Canada, other countries
David Baum	CA	United States and Canada
Timothy J. Blied	CA	United States
D. Durand Cook	CA	United States and Canada
Douglas R. Donnelly	CA	United States and Europe
Diane Michelsen	CA	United States and other countries
David J. Radis	CA	United States
M.D. Widelock	CA	United States and Canada
Nanci R. Worcestser	CA	United States
W. Thomas Beltz	CO	United States
Linda W. McIntyre	FL	United States
Mary Ann Scherer	FL	United States
Michael A. Shorstein	FL	United States, Canada, and Europe
Jeanne T. Tate	FL	United States and other countries
Rhonda Fishbein	GA	United States
Linda E. F. Lach	HI	United States, Australia, England, and Germany
John T. Hawley	ID	United States, Canada, and other countries
Deborah Crouse Cobb	IL	United States, Canada, and England
H. Joseph Gitlin	IL	United States
Susan F. Grammer	IL	United States
John C. Hirschfeld	IL	United States and other countries
Steven M. Kirsh	IN	United States and Europe
Lori L. Klockau	IA	United States and Europe
Ross S. Randall	IA	United States, Israel, and Europe
Jill Bremyer-Archer	KS	United States

CONTINUES

ATTORNEYS WHO WORK WITH ADOPTIVE PARENTS IN ALL OR MOST STATES, IN CANADA, AND IN OTHER COUNTRIES, CONTINUED

Name of Attorney	State	Adoptive Parents Come From
Alan A. Hazlett	KS	United States and Europe
Elisabeth Goldman	KY	United States
Leslie Scherr	MD	United States and Europe
Carolyn H. Thaler	MD	United States and Europe
Gary A. Debele	MN	United States and other countries
Steven L. Gawron	MN	United States
Judith D. Vincent	MN	United States and Europe
James W. Miskowski	NJ	United States
Harold O. Atencio	NM	United States
Aaron Britvan	NY	United States
Michael S. Goldstein	NY	United States and other countries
Suzanne B. Nichols	NY	United States and other countries
Golda Zimmerman	NY	United States
Shelley Ballard	NC	United States
Jerry M. Johnson	OH	United States
W. R. Cubbage	OK	United States
Catherine M. Dexter	OR	United States and Europe
Susan C. Moffet	OR	United States and other countries
Laurence H. Spiegel	OR	United States and other countries
Debra Fox	PA	United States, Canada, and Europe
Tara Gutterman	PA	United States
Mary Ann Petrillo	PA	United States
Vika Andrel	TX	United States and Canada
David C. Cole	TX	United States
Irv W. Queal	TX	United States
Melody B. Royall	TX	United States
Kurt M. Hughes	VT	United States and Canada
David T. Daulton	WA	United States
Rita L. Bender	WA	United States and Europe
Mark M. Demaray	WA	United States, Canada, and Europe
Albert G. Lirhus	WA	United States, Canada, and Europe
Stephen W. Hayes	WI	United States and Europe

INDIVIDUAL LISTING OF ADOPTION ATTORNEYS

Cautionary Note: The information that follows was drawn from the responses of adoption attorneys in the United States to an adoption attorney questionnaire I submitted in the spring of 1999. In some cases, so much information was provided to me that I could not include it all.

Inclusion in this book is in no way a guarantee of the services of the attorney nor should it be considered an endorsement. Readers should thoroughly check out any attorney before applying. Do not retain an attorney until you have considered at least several attorneys, for comparison purposes.

The information provided here may have changed since April 1999; you should verify policies, fees, and other data. The purpose of providing this information is to give readers not only data on each attorney but also information that can be used for comparison purposes.

I have checked and double-checked the received questionnaires and my transcribed data, but errors of omission and commission may have crept in; if so, they were purely accidental and I apologize in advance for them.

ALABAMA

BRYANT A. WHITMIRE, JR.

215 North 21st St., Suite 501, Birmingham, AL 35203-3722
(205) 324-6631 • Fax: (205) 324-6632
E-mail: dwhitm8871@aol.com

What are your office hours when you accept calls from adoptive parents?
8 a.m.–5:30 p.m., CST

Education: BA in history, University of Richmond, 1979; JD, University of Alabama, 1972

What states or countries do your adoptive parents come from? Primarily from the state of Alabama, but I do a substantial amount of interstate compacts, so I have represented couples from all over the United States.

What states or countries do your birthparents/adopted children come from? Primarily from the state of Alabama, but I do a substantial amount of interstate compacts, so I have represented couples from all over the United States.

Are other attorneys in your law firm active in adoption? No.

In what year did you begin legal work in adoptions? 1979

How many nonrelative adoptions did you arrange in 1998? 70–80

About how many children have you placed since you started? Alabama law only allows two actual placements a year by an individual or attorney.

About what percent of your work is devoted to adoption? 80%

In 1998, what was the average time from when a prospective adoptive parent retained you to the placement of a child? Indefinite.

What made you decide to work in the adoption field? My wife was experiencing difficulty in becoming pregnant, and we were attempting to adopt when she became pregnant.

Do you have any criteria for adoptive parents, such as age, number of children in the home, etc., and if so, what are they? I have no set criteria other than that they are a couple I will be comfortable working with to accomplish the adoption, and that they would be good parents. Also that the couple's homestudy must be completed by a licensed agency or person who does homestudies.

What percent of your adoptions are infants under 6 mos.? 90%

Do you have a waiting list of prospective parents? Yes.

Is it all right if adopting parents are on waiting lists of other attorneys or agencies? Yes.

Do you charge adoptive parents for a first phone consultation? No.

Do you charge adoptive parents for a first office consultation, and if yes, what is the fee? Yes; $150.

Do you charge a retainer fee, and if yes, what is it and when is it payable? Yes. $1,500, payable when the couple has been selected by a birthmother and the adoption process begins.

What are your legal fees, not including retainer, and when are they payable? Hourly retainer is applied to total hours and balance is due on completion of adoption.

Will adoptive parents pay a separate attorney for the birthmother? Birthmother is not always represented by an attorney.

What are the approximate fees for medical and hospital expenses for the birthmother and baby, when they have no insurance? $6,000–10,000

What are the approximate homestudy fees in your state? $1,200

If living expenses for a birthmother are allowed, what is the average amount paid? $500

In how many of your cases has an adoptive parent lost a placed child due to a birthparent challenge? 0

Have you lost any adoption litigation filed against you by an adoptive parent or birthparent? No.

In about what percentage of your adoptions do adopting parents and birthparents know each other's first and last names? 50%

Are you a member of the American Academy of Adoption Attorneys and/or the National Council for Adoption? American Academy of Adoption Attorneys.

ARIZONA

PHILIP J. MCCARTHY, JR.

Hufford, Horstman, Mongini, Parnell, and McCarthy
323 N. Leroux St., Flagstaff, AZ 86001
(520) 774-1453 • Fax: (520) 779-3621
E-mail: pjm@hzmzlaw.com

What are your office hours when you accept calls from adoptive parents?
8 a.m.–5 p.m. Arizona time

Education: BS, Northern Arizona University, 1974; JD, Creighton University, 1980

What states or countries do your adoptive parents come from? All states.

What states or countries do your birthparents/adopted children come from? Primarily western United States.

Are other attorneys in your law firm active in adoption? Yes.

In what year did you begin legal work in adoptions? 1981

How many nonrelative adoptions did you arrange in 1998? 4

About how many children have you placed since you started? 22

About what percent of your work is devoted to adoption? 25%

In 1998, what was the average time from when a prospective adoptive parent retained you to the placement of a child? 1 year

What made you decide to work in the adoption field? Before law school, I worked in programs to assist children. I was also a Vista volunteer and worked in a program for victims of domestic violence.

Do you have any criteria for adoptive parents, such as age, number of children in the home, etc.? No.

What percent of your adoptions are infants under 6 mos.? 90%

Do you have a waiting list of prospective parents? No.

Is it all right if adopting parents are on waiting lists of other attorneys or agencies? Yes.

Do you charge adoptive parents for a first phone consultation, and if yes, what is the fee? Yes; $150 per hour.

Do you charge adoptive parents for a first office consultation, and if yes, what is the fee? Yes; $150 per hour.

Do you charge a retainer fee, and if yes, what is it and when is it payable? Yes. $2,000 for in-state adoption; $3,000 for interstate adoption; $3,500 for Indian Child Welfare Act adoption.

What are your legal fees, not including retainer, and when are they payable? $150 per hour, and $75 paralegal time plus costs.

Will adoptive parents pay a separate attorney for the birthmother? Yes.

What are the approximate fees for medical and hospital expenses for the birthmother and baby, when they have no insurance? Case-by-case, can't give answer.

What are the approximate homestudy fees in your state? $1,000

If living expenses for a birthmother are allowed, what is the average amount paid? $500–1,000. In Arizona, living expenses can only be paid if approved by the court.

In how many of your cases has an adoptive parent lost a placed child due to a birthparent challenge? None.

Have you lost any adoption litigation filed against you by an adoptive parent or birthparent? No.

In about what percentage of your adoptions do adopting parents and birthparents know each other's first and last names? 20%

Are you a member of the American Academy of Adoption Attorneys and/or the National Council for Adoption? American Academy of Adoption Attorneys.

Is there anything I have not asked you that is important? I handle a great many Indian Child Welfare Act adoptions. I am licensed to practice in Arizona, Alaska, Missouri, Nebraska. I am licensed to practice in Hopi, Navajo, and White Mountain Apache Tribal Courts. I am licensed to practice before the U.S. Supreme Court.

KATHRYN A. PIDGEON, PC

8433 N. Black Canyon Hwy., Suite 100, Phoenix, AZ 85021
(602) 371-1317 • Fax: (602) 371-1506
E-mail: skp3@aol.com

What are your office hours when you accept calls from adoptive parents? 8:30 a.m.–5 p.m., MST

Education: BA in English, SUNY Plattsburgh, 1977; JD, University of Miami, 1981

What states or countries do your adoptive parents come from? Arizona, various states across country, and Canada.

What states or countries do your birthparents/adopted children come from? Arizona.

Are other attorneys in your law firm active in adoption? No. Sole practitioner.

In what year did you begin legal work in adoptions? 1989

How many nonrelative adoptions did you arrange in 1998? 40+

About how many children have you placed since you started? 250

About what percent of your work is devoted to adoption? 75%

In 1998, what was the average time from when a prospective adoptive parent retained you to the placement of a child? 1 year

What made you decide to work in the adoption field? My practice is exclusively devoted to children. Love adoption work, love making families!

Do you have any criteria for adoptive parents, such as age, number of children in the home, etc., and if so, what are they? No, only that they have a homestudy.

What percent of your adoptions are infants under 6 mos.? 90%

Do you have a waiting list of prospective parents? Yes.

Is it all right if adopting parents are on waiting lists of other attorneys or agencies? Yes.

Do you charge adoptive parents for a first phone consultation? No.

Do you charge adoptive parents for a first office consultation, and if yes, what is the fee? Yes; $150 for consultation.

Do you charge a retainer fee, and if yes, what is it and when is it payable? Yes. $2,000 for in-state. $3,000 for interstate; when we have a match.

What are your legal fees, not including retainer, and when are they payable? $175 per hour.

Will adoptive parents pay a separate attorney for the birthmother, and if yes, what are approximate legal fees? Yes; $2,000.

What are the approximate fees for medical and hospital expenses for the birthmother and baby, when they have no insurance? $5,000

What are the approximate homestudy fees in your state? $800

If living expenses for a birthmother are allowed, what is the average amount paid? $2,000; need court approval.

In how many of your cases has an adoptive parent lost a placed child due to a birthparent challenge? None.

Have you lost any adoption litigation filed against you by an adoptive parent or birthparent? No.

In about what percentage of your adoptions do adopting parents and birthparents know each other's first and last names? 50%

Are you a member of the American Academy of Adoption Attorneys and/or the National Council for Adoption? American Academy of Adoption Attorneys.

MARY L. VERDIER

Law Offices of Mary L. Verdier
2800 N. Central Ave., Suite 1400, Phoenix, AZ 85004
(602) 997-4367 • Fax: (602) 279-4129
E-mail: mverdier@extremezone.com

What are your office hours when you accept calls from adoptive parents? 9 a.m.–4 p.m., MST

Education: BS in political science, Arizona State University, 1976; JD, Arizona State University College of Law, 1979

What states or countries do your adoptive parents come from? United States, mostly Arizona, also Minnesota, New York, Illinois, Florida, Texas, Colorado, others.

What states or countries do your birthparents/adopted children come from? Arizona, many states, Mexico, Canada, Russia, Korea, Pakistan, Scotland.

Are other attorneys in your law firm active in adoption? No.

In what year did you begin legal work in adoptions? 1986

How many nonrelative adoptions did you arrange in 1998? Approxmately 15

About how many children have you placed since you started? Approximately 200

About what percent of your work is devoted to adoption? 70%

In 1998, what was the average time from when a prospective adoptive parent retained you to the placement of a child? This is difficult to estimate because many of my clients have already been placed when they retain my firm.

What made you decide to work in the adoption field? I have been a child welfare attorney since I became a lawyer. I love helping children find permanent families. I have represented hundreds of children in dependencies and represent foster parents, grandparents, and prospective adoptive parents who want to provide permanent homes for kids. I was a juvenile court commissioner from 1986 to 1990 and handled all the adoption hearings in Phoenix.

Do you have any criteria for adoptive parents, such as age, number of children in the home, etc., and if so, what are they? No. In Arizona, adoptive parents must be certified by our court to adopt. My criteria for Arizona families is that they be certified. I do not have requirements for out-of-state families as long as they have a current homestudy.

What percent of your adoptions are infants under 6 mos.? 70%

Do you have a waiting list of prospective parents? Yes.

Is it all right if adopting parents are on waiting lists of other attorneys or agencies? Yes. In fact, I encourage it.

Do you charge adoptive parents for a first phone consultation? No.

Do you charge adoptive parents for a first office consultation, and if yes, what is the fee? Yes; $185/hour.

Do you charge a retainer fee, and if yes, what is it and when is it payable? Yes. $1,200–1,500 for in-state; $2,500 for out-of-state (payable in advance).

What are your legal fees, not including retainer, and when are they payable? $185/hour. Total depends on the complications of the case, such as ICPC [interstate] issues, ICWA [Indian Child Welfare], necessity of termination, whether birthmother has own attorney, etc.

Will adoptive parents pay a separate attorney for the birthmother, and if yes, what are approximate legal fees? Yes; $1,500–2,000.

What are the approximate fees for medical and hospital expenses for the birthmother and baby, when they have no insurance? $2,000–4,000. The Arizona indigent health care program requires out-of-state adoptive parents to reimburse the birthmother's medical costs.

What are the approximate homestudy fees in your state? $1,000

If living expenses for a birthmother are allowed, what is the average amount paid? $500–1,000

If you manage international adoptions, what is the average fee for translating documents? Varies according to translator, language, and number of documents; approximately $200–300.

In how many of your cases has an adoptive parent lost a placed child due to a birthparent challenge? 2

Have you lost any adoption litigation filed against you by an adoptive parent or birthparent? No.

In about what percentage of your adoptions do adopting parents and birthparents know each other's first and last names? 80%

Are you a member of the American Academy of Adoption Attorneys and/or the National Council for Adoption? American Academy of Adoption Attorneys.

DANIEL I. ZISKIN, PC

3309 North Second St., Phoenix, AZ 85012
(602) 234-2280 • Fax: (602) 234-0013
E-mail: dan@adopt.com

What are your office hours when you accept calls from adoptive parents?
8:30 a.m.–5:30 p.m., MST

Education: BA, Arizona State University, 1971; JD, Arizona State University, 1975

What states or countries do your adoptive parents come from? Arizona and all other states.

What states or countries do your birthparents/adopted children come from? All states.

Are other attorneys in your law firm active in adoption? No.

In what year did you begin legal work in adoptions? 1982

How many nonrelative adoptions did you arrange in 1998? 30

About how many children have you placed since you started? 500

About what percent of your work is devoted to adoption? 60%

In 1998, what was the average time from when a prospective adoptive parent retained you to the placement of a child? Unable to compute.

What made you decide to work in the adoption field? My wife and I decided to adopt and then did so.

Do you have any criteria for adoptive parents, such as age, number of children in the home, etc., and if so, what are they? They must be good people.

What percent of your adoptions are infants under 6 mos.? 95%

Do you have a waiting list of prospective parents? Yes.

Is it all right if adopting parents are on waiting lists of other attorneys or agencies? Yes.

Do you charge adoptive parents for a first phone consultation? No.

Do you charge adoptive parents for a first office consultation, and if yes, what is the fee? Yes; $175/hour.

Do you charge a retainer fee, and if yes, what is it and when is it payable? Yes. $1,500–2,500, payable after initial consultation.

What are your legal fees, not including retainer, and when are they payable? $175/hour plus costs, payable monthly as accumulated.

Will adoptive parents pay a separate attorney for the birthmother, and if yes, what are approximate legal fees? If she retains one. Unknown, depends on attorney.

What are the approximate fees for medical and hospital expenses for the birthmother and baby, when they have no insurance? $5,500–12,000 depending on complications.

What are the approximate homestudy fees in your state? $750–1,000

If living expenses for a birthmother are allowed, what is the average amount paid? $500–1,200 monthly.

Are you an adoptive parent, adopted person, or birthparent? Adoptive parent.

In how many of your cases has an adoptive parent lost a placed child due to a birthparent challenge? None.

Have you lost any adoption litigation filed against you by an adoptive parent or birthparent? No. None filed against me personally. However, some have been contested.

In about what percentage of your adoptions do adopting parents and birthparents know each other's first and last names? 50%

Are you a member of the American Academy of Adoption Attorneys and/or the National Council for Adoption? American Academy of Adoption Attorneys.

ARKANSAS

EUGENE T. KELLEY

Kelley Law Firm
222 W. Walnut, Rogers, AR 72756
(501) 636-1051 • Fax: (501) 636-1663
E-mail: kelley@arkansasusa.com

What are your office hours when you accept calls from adoptive parents? 8 a.m.–5 p.m., CT

Education: Villanova, 1958; Seton Hall, 1959–1960; BSBA, University of Arkansas, 1961; JD, Law School 1968

What states or countries do your adoptive parents come from? All states, Canada, Mexico, England, Germany, Australia.

What states or countries do your birthparents/adopted children come from? Arkansas and adjoining states.

Are other attorneys in your law firm active in adoption? Yes.

In what year did you begin legal work in adoptions? 1980

How many nonrelative adoptions did you arrange in 1998? 47

About how many children have you placed since you started? 450

About what percent of your work is devoted to adoption? 75%

In 1998, what was the average time from when a prospective adoptive parent retained you to the placement of a child? 11 mos.

What made you decide to work in the adoption field? I thought that I could make a difference.

Do you have any criteria for adoptive parents, such as age, number of children in the home, etc., and if so, what are they? Stable marriage; flexible, easy-going; financially secure; willing to work as a team; prefer childless, one child in home at most; combined ages of adopting parents not to exceed 81.

What percent of your adoptions are infants under 6 mos.? 95%

Do you have a waiting list of prospective parents? Yes.

Is it all right if adopting parents are on waiting lists of other attorneys or agencies? Yes.

Do you charge adoptive parents for a first phone consultation? No.

Do you charge adoptive parents for a first office consultation, and if yes, what is the fee? Yes; $375 (three hours).

Do you charge a retainer fee, and if yes, what is it and when is it payable? Yes; $3,000 on engagement.

What are your legal fees, not including retainer, and when are they payable? Varies.

Will adoptive parents pay a separate attorney for the birthmother? No.

What are the approximate fees for medical and hospital expenses for the birthmother and baby, when they have no insurance? $4,500

What are the approximate homestudy fees in your state? $500

If living expenses for a birthmother are allowed, what is the average amount paid? Court approved living expenses based on need.

In how many of your cases has an adoptive parent lost a placed child due to a birthparent challenge? One, and that case is still pending and expecting a positive outcome.

Have you lost any adoption litigation filed against you by an adoptive parent or birthparent? See answer to previous question.

In about what percentage of your adoptions do adopting parents and birthparents know each other's first and last names? Given names in no cases.

Are you a member of the American Academy of Adoption Attorneys and/or the National Council for Adoption? American Academy of Adoption Attorneys.

CALIFORNIA

G. DARLENE ANDERSON

Law Offices of G. Darlene Anderson
127 E. Third Ave., Suite 202, Escondido, CA 92025-4201
(760) 743-4700 • Fax: (760) 743-6218
E-mail: gdaadopt@home.com

What are your office hours when you accept calls from adoptive parents?
9 a.m.–5 p.m., PT

Education: JD, University of San Diego, 1981

What states or countries do your adoptive parents come from? California, primarily.

What states or countries do your birthparents/adopted children come from?
California, primarily.

Are other attorneys in your law firm active in adoption? No. Sole practitioner.

In what year did you begin legal work in adoptions? 1982

How many nonrelative adoptions did you arrange in 1998? 20

About how many children have you placed since you started? 350

About what percent of your work is devoted to adoption? 90%

In 1998, what was the average time from when a prospective adoptive parent retained you to the placement of a child? 1–2 years.

What percent of your adoptions are infants under 6 mos.? 99%

Do you have a waiting list of prospective parents? Yes.

Is it all right if adopting parents are on waiting lists of other attorneys or agencies?
Yes.

Do you charge adoptive parents for a first phone consultation? No.

Do you charge adoptive parents for a first office consultation, and if yes, what is the fee? Yes; $350.

Do you charge a retainer fee, and if yes, what is it and when is it payable? Yes. One-third of total cost of adoption, due upon commitment to a specific adoption match.

What are your legal fees, not including retainer, and when are they payable? Fees vary according to circumstances; payment is due when commitment to specific adoption match occurs.

Will adoptive parents pay a separate attorney for the birthmother, and if yes, what are approximate legal fees? Yes. Depends on circumstances.

What are the approximate fees for medical and hospital expenses for the birthmother and baby, when they have no insurance? $5,000–6,000

What are the approximate homestudy fees in your state? $1,250

If living expenses for a birthmother are allowed, what is the average amount paid?
Depends on circumstances.

Have you lost any adoption litigation filed against you by an adoptive parent or birthparent? No.

In about what percentage of your adoptions do adopting parents and birthparents know each other's first and last names? 100%

Are you a member of the American Academy of Adoption Attorneys and/or the National Council for Adoption? American Academy of Adoption Attorneys. Also a member of Academy of California Adoption Lawyers.

DAVID H. BAUM

The Law Offices of David H. Baum
16255 Ventura Blvd., Suite 704, Encino, CA 91436
(818) 501-8355
E-mail: adoptlaw@ix.netcom.com • www.adoptlaw.com

What are your office hours when you accept calls from adoptive parents?
9 a.m.–5 p.m. PT, but also available by pager 24 hours a day.

Education: BA with high honors in English and American literature, Brandeis University 1975; JD, Loyola School of Law, 1978

What states or countries do your adoptive parents come from? Throughout the United States and Canada.

What states or countries do your birthparents/adopted children come from?
Throughout the United States, Canada, and Europe.

Are other attorneys in your law firm active in adoption? No.

In what year did you begin legal work in adoptions? 1978

How many nonrelative adoptions did you arrange in 1998? 50+

About how many children have you placed since you started? Hundreds.

About what percent of your work is devoted to adoption? 80%

In 1998, what was the average time from when a prospective adoptive parent retained you to the placement of a child? Under one year.

What made you decide to work in the adoption field? My decision to emphasize adoption law in my practice was an outgrowth of my own adoption experience as an adopting parent and my commitment to the goals of improving the quality of life for children.

Do you have any criteria for adoptive parents, such as age, number of children in the home, etc.? None other than required by the State of California.

What percent of your adoptions are infants under 6 mos.? 99%

Do you have a waiting list of prospective parents? No.

Is it all right if adopting parents are on waiting lists of other attorneys or agencies? Yes.

Do you charge adoptive parents for a first phone consultation? No.

Do you charge for a first-time office visit from an adoptive parent client? Yes; $225 per hour for consultation time, charged in increments of tenths of an hour.

Do you charge a retainer fee, and if yes, what is it and when is it payable? Yes. Retainer is quoted at time of retention and may vary, depending on work to be performed and scope of that retention. Terms of payment are tailored to meet client finances whenever possible.

What are your legal fees, not including retainer, and when are they payable? My fees depend on the tasks performed and are billed as performed.

Will adoptive parents pay a separate attorney for the birthmother, and if yes, what are approximate legal fees? If appropriate or required on a case-by-case basis. Yes as required under California law. $500 or such other sum as may be agreed on per the California statutes.

What are the approximate fees for medical and hospital expenses for the birthmother and baby, when they have no insurance? $3,500

What are the approximate homestudy fees in your state? $1,250

If living expenses for a birthmother are allowed, what is the average amount paid? Varies.

Are you an adoptive parent, adopted person, or birthparent? Adoptive parent.

In how many of your cases has an adoptive parent lost a placed child due to a birthparent challenge? None.

Have you lost any adoption litigation filed against you by an adoptive parent or birthparent? I've never been sued by an adoptive or birthparent.

In about what percentage of your adoptions do adopting parents and birthparents know each other's first and last names? 95%

Are you a member of the American Academy of Adoption Attorneys and/or the National Council for Adoption? American Academy of Adoption Attorneys and National Council for Adoption. Also president of the Academy of California Adoption Lawyers.

TIMOTHY J. BLIED

Schmiesing Blied and Mackey
2260 N. State College Blvd., Fullerton, CA 92830-1361
(714) 257-3388 • Fax: (714) 990-3826
E-mail: sbm@aol.com

What are your office hours when you accept calls from adoptive parents?
8:30 a.m.–5 p.m., PT

Education: JD, Pepperdine University, 1978

What states or countries do your adoptive parents come from? United States.

What states or countries do your birthparents/adopted children come from? United States.

Are other attorneys in your law firm active in adoption? No.

In what year did you begin legal work in adoptions? 1979

How many nonrelative adoptions did you arrange in 1998? 60

About how many children have you placed since you started? 1,100

About what percent of your work is devoted to adoption? 50%

In 1998, what was the average time from when a prospective adoptive parent retained you to the placement of a child? 6–18 mos.

What made you decide to work in the adoption field? Have two adopted children.

Do you have any criteria for adoptive parents, such as age, number of children in the home, etc.? No.

What percent of your adoptions are infants under 6 mos.? 95%

Do you have a waiting list of prospective parents? Yes.

Is it all right if adopting parents are on waiting lists of other attorneys or agencies? Yes.

Do you charge adoptive parents for a first phone consultation? No.

Do you charge adoptive parents for a first office consultation, and if yes, what is the fee? Yes; $500.

What are your legal fees, not including retainer, and when are they payable? Fixed fee between $2,500–4,500, based on parts of adoption.

Will adoptive parents pay a separate attorney for the birthmother, and if yes, what are approximate legal fees? Maybe, but only if birthmother wants a separate attorney. Minimum of $500.

What are the approximate fees for medical and hospital expenses for the birthmother and baby, when they have no insurance? $3,000 minimum, no maximum.

What are the approximate homestudy fees in your state? $1,250

If living expenses for a birthmother are allowed, what is the average amount paid? Varies greatly.

Are you an adoptive parent, adopted person, or birthparent? Adoptive parent.

In how many of your cases has an adoptive parent lost a placed child due to a birthparent challenge? 1%

Have you lost any adoption litigation filed against you by an adoptive parent or birthparent? No.

In about what percentage of your adoptions do adopting parents and birthparents know each other's first and last names? 100%

Are you a member of the American Academy of Adoption Attorneys and/or the National Council for Adoption? American Academy of Adoption Attorneys.

D. DURAND COOK, ESQ.

8383 Wilshire Blvd. #1030, Beverly Hills, CA 90211
(323) 655-2601 • Fax: (323) 852-0871
E-mail: openadopt@aol.com • www.adoption-option.com

What are your office hours when you accept calls from adoptive parents?
9 a.m.–5:30 p.m., PT

Education: BS, Loma Linda University, 1962; JD, California Western School of Law, 1965

What states or countries do your adoptive parents come from? United States, Mexico, Canada, Cayman Islands.

What states or countries do your birthparents/adopted children come from? United States, Mexico.

Are other attorneys in your law firm active in adoption? No.

In what year did you begin legal work in adoptions? 1974

How many nonrelative adoptions did you arrange in 1998? Approximately 85

About how many children have you placed since you started? Approximately 3,000

About what percent of your work is devoted to adoption? 100%

In 1998, what was the average time from when a prospective adoptive parent retained you to the placement of a child? 9 mos.

What made you decide to work in the adoption field? To make a difference in people's lives.

Do you have any criteria for adoptive parents, such as age, number of children in the home, etc., and if so, what are they? They have or will have a qualified homestudy.

What percent of your adoptions are infants under 6 mos.? 98%

Do you have a waiting list of prospective parents? Yes.

Is it all right if adopting parents are on waiting lists of other attorneys or agencies? Yes.

Do you charge adoptive parents for a first phone consultation? No.

Do you charge adoptive parents for a first office consultation? No.

Do you charge a retainer fee, and if yes, what is it and when is it payable? Yes. $850 the day we meet at a six-hour adoption conference.

What are your legal fees, not including retainer, and when are they payable? Varies.

Will adoptive parents pay a separate attorney for the birthmother, and if yes, what are approximate legal fees? Sometimes; $500.

What are the approximate fees for medical and hospital expenses for the birthmother and baby, when they have no insurance? Approximately $6,000.

What are the approximate homestudy fees in your state? Varies.

If living expenses for a birthmother are allowed, what is the average amount paid? $4,000

If you manage international adoptions, what is the average fee for translating documents? $350

In how many of your cases has an adoptive parent lost a placed child due to a birthparent challenge? 5–10%

Have you lost any adoption litigation filed against you by an adoptive parent or birthparent? No.

In about what percentage of your adoptions do adopting parents and birthparents know each other's first and last names? 95%

Are you a member of the American Academy of Adoption Attorneys and/or the National Council for Adoption? American Academy of Adoption Attorneys

---

DOUGLAS R. DONNELLY

976 Garden St., Santa Barbara, CA 93101
(805) 962-0988 • Fax: (805) 966-2993
E-mail: adoption@ix.netcom.com

What are your office hours when you accept calls from adoptive parents?
9 a.m.–5 p.m., PT

Education: BA, political science, Westmont College (cum laude), 1974; JD, Loyola University Law School, 1977

What states or countries do your adoptive parents come from? Nearly all states and some European countries.

What states or countries do your birthparents/adopted children come from? Same.

Are other attorneys in your law firm active in adoption? No.

In what year did you begin legal work in adoptions? 1979

How many nonrelative adoptions did you arrange in 1998? 90

About how many children have you placed since you started? 1,200–1,500 (assisted in placement). Under California law, it is a misdemeanor for anyone other than a birthparent or a licensed agency to place a child.

About what percent of your work is devoted to adoption? 98%

In 1998, what was the average time from when a prospective adoptive parent retained you to the placement of a child? Impossible to say; ranges from 3 hours to never.

What made you decide to work in the adoption field? Adoptive father of two.

Do you have any criteria for adoptive parents, such as age, number of children in the home, etc., and if so, what are they? Flexible criteria.

What percent of your adoptions are infants under 6 mos.? 99%

Do you have a waiting list of prospective parents? Yes.

Is it all right if adopting parents are on waiting lists of other attorneys or agencies? Yes.

Do you charge adoptive parents for a first phone consultation? No. Office consultation is required.

Do you charge adoptive parents for a first office consultation, and if yes, what is the fee? Yes; $240 per hour, up to maximum of two hours.

Do you charge a retainer fee? No.

What are your legal fees, not including retainer, and when are they payable? Billed monthly, "pay as you go," calculated at $240 an hour.

Will adoptive parents pay a separate attorney for the birthmother, and if yes, what are approximate legal fees? Possibly. California law requires that separate legal counsel be offered at expense of adopting parent. Most birthmothers will decline this offer. $500–1,500.

What are the approximate fees for medical and hospital expenses for the birthmother and baby, when they have no insurance? $7,000

What are the approximate homestudy fees in your state? $1,250

If living expenses for a birthmother are allowed, what is the average amount paid? Varies widely.

Are you an adoptive parent, adopted person, or birthparent? Adoptive parent.

In how many of your cases has an adoptive parent lost a placed child due to a birthparent challenge? 8

Have you lost any adoption litigation filed against you by an adoptive parent or birthparent? No.

In about what percentage of your adoptions do adopting parents and birthparents know each other's first and last names? 100%

Are you a member of the American Academy of Adoption Attorneys and/or the National Council for Adoption? American Academy of Adoption Attorneys and National Council for Adoption.

Is there anything I have not asked you that is important? Also a member of Academy of California Adoption Lawyers.

RANDALL B. HICKS

Law Offices of Randall B. Hicks
6690 Alessandro Blvd., Suite D, Riverside, CA 92506
(909) 789-6800
E-mail: ranhicks@aol.com

What are your office hours when you accept calls from adoptive parents?
9 a.m.–12 p.m., 1 p.m.–5 p.m., PT

Education: BA, California State University, Fullerton, 1976; MS California State University Long Beach, 1980; JD, Pepperdine University School of Law, 1986

What states or countries do your adoptive parents come from? California.

What states or countries do your birthparents/adopted children come from? California for domestic; Ukraine for international.

Are other attorneys in your law firm active in adoption? No.

In what year did you begin legal work in adoptions? 1986

How many nonrelative adoptions did you arrange in 1998? About 60

About how many children have you placed since you started? 700+

About what percent of your work is devoted to adoption? 100%

In 1998, what was the average time from when a prospective adoptive parent retained you to the placement of a child? 8 mos. for domestic; 6 mos. for international.

What made you decide to work in the adoption field? Desire to work with and help people. Four years a volunteer social worker, prelaw practice.

Do you have any criteria for adoptive parents, such as age, number of children in the home, etc.? No, just confirm readiness and appropriateness to adopt.

What percent of your adoptions are infants under 6 mos.? Domestic are 98% newborn; international 1–5 years old.

Do you have a waiting list of prospective parents? Yes.

Is it all right if adopting parents are on waiting lists of other attorneys or agencies? Yes.

Do you charge adoptive parents for a first phone consultation? No.

Do you charge adoptive parents for a first office consultation, and if yes, what is the fee? Yes; $475 for 2–3 hours.

Do you charge a retainer fee? No.

What are your legal fees, not including retainer, and when are they payable? For domestic, three payments of $1,650 as they progress through adoption. Only stage one is due to start process. For international full program fee is $8,850.

Will adoptive parents pay a separate attorney for the birthmother? Usually no.

What are the approximate fees for medical and hospital expenses for the birthmother and baby, when they have no insurance? 70% have Medi-Cal (California Medicaid) or insurance. If not, average fee is $4,100.

What are the approximate homestudy fees in your state? For independent, $1,250; for agency (private), $3,200, pre- and postplacement.

If living expenses for a birthmother are allowed, what is the average amount paid? 30% need help. Of these, average is $600 monthly for 3 months.

If you manage international adoptions, what is the average fee for translating documents? My program fee ($8,850) covers all legal work, dossier preparation, translation, orphanage donation, all services of translators, drivers in Ukraine, re-adoption. Only homestudy and travel not included.

In how many of your cases has an adoptive parent lost a placed child due to a birthparent challenge? About 4% of adoptions fail.

Have you lost any adoption litigation filed against you by an adoptive parent or birthparent? No.

In about what percentage of your adoptions do adopting parents and birthparents know each other's first and last names? For domestic, 100%; for international, 0%.

Are you a member of the American Academy of Adoption Attorneys and/or the National Council for Adoption? American Academy of Adoption Attorneys.

Is there anything I have not asked you that is important? Also a member of the Academy of California Adoption Lawyers (ACAC).

DIANE MICHELSEN

Law Offices of Diane Michelsen
3190 Old Tunnel Rd., Lafayette, CA 94549-4133
(925) 945-1880 • Fax: (925) 933-6807
E-mail: diane@lodm.com • www.lodm.com

What are your office hours when you accept calls from adoptive parents?
9 a.m.–5 p.m., PT

Education: BA in social science, University of California, Berkeley, 1968; MSW, San Francisco State University, 1974; JD, Golden Gate University School of Law, 1979

What states or countries do your adoptive parents come from? 50% from California, 50% from outside of California (including outside of the United States).

What states or countries do your birthparents/adopted children come from? 50% from California, 50% from outside of California.

Are other attorneys in your law firm active in adoption? Yes.

In what year did you begin legal work in adoptions? 1982

How many nonrelative adoptions did you arrange in 1998? 85+

About how many children have you placed since you started? 2,000

About what percent of your work is devoted to adoption? 85%

In 1998, what was the average time from when a prospective adoptive parent retained you to the placement of a child? Ranges from 2 days to 2 years (heavy grouping 8–11 mos.).

What made you decide to work in the adoption field? It was a calling.

Do you have any criteria for adoptive parents, such as age, number of children in the home, etc., and if so, what are they? If adoptive parents live in California, I must meet with them. If I feel it would be okay if one of my children was placed in their home, I will work with them. If not, I will not represent them. I do not discriminate based on gender, religion, sexual orientation, age, or marital status.

What percent of your adoptions are infants under 6 mos.? 99.8%

Do you have a waiting list of prospective parents? No.

Is it all right if adopting parents are on waiting lists of other attorneys or agencies? Yes.

Do you charge adoptive parents for a first phone consultation, and if yes, what is the fee? Yes; the first 15 minutes are free. Usually the first genuine consult lasts approximately 2 hours and the maximum charge is usually $500.

Do you charge adoptive parents for a first office consultation, and if yes, what is the fee? Yes; see above.

Do you charge a retainer fee, and if yes, what is it and when is it payable? Yes; $4,000. This fee encompasses services for 12 mos. or through the birthparents' signing of the relinquishment/adoption placement agreement, whichever occurs first. The fee covers ongoing consultations, screening of prospective adoptive situations, efforts to gather social and medical information about the birthparents, verification of pregnancy, birthmother trust administration, referrals to counselors and agencies as needed, preparation of the adopting family for the baby's arrival, and preplacement legal work involved in an uncontested adoption.

What are your legal fees, not including retainer, and when are they payable? Interstate compact on placement of children, $1,000; proceedings to determine father/child relationship, $1,000–1,500; proceedings to obtain permission to remove child from county, $300; court appearance as necessary, $300–1,200; order for issuance of passport, $300; postplacement services/finalization, $1,000, for independent, $500 for agency.

Will adoptive parents pay a separate attorney for the birthmother, and if yes, what are approximate legal fees? Sometimes. Up to $5,700, average $500.

What are the approximate fees for medical and hospital expenses for the birthmother and baby, when they have no insurance? Range $3,000–11,000, average $8,000.

What are the approximate homestudy fees in your state? $1,000–2,000

If living expenses for a birthmother are allowed, what is the average amount paid? $4,500

Are you an adoptive parent, adopted person, or birthparent? Adoptive parent.

In how many of your cases has an adoptive parent lost a placed child due to a birthparent challenge? 0

Have you lost any adoption litigation filed against you by an adoptive parent or birthparent? No.

In about what percentage of your adoptions do adopting parents and birthparents know each other's first and last names? 93%

Are you a member of the American Academy of Adoption Attorneys and/or the National Council for Adoption? American Academy of Adoption Attorneys.

DAVID J. RADIS

Law Offices of David J. Radis
1901 Avenue of the Stars, 20th Floor, Los Angeles, CA 90067
(310) 552-0536 • Fax: (310) 552-0713
E-mail: radis@radis-adopt.com • www.radis-adopt.com

What are your office hours when you accept calls from adoptive parents?
8:30 a.m.–6 p.m., PT

Education: BA in comparative government, California State University, Northridge, 1971; JD, Southwestern University Law School, 1974

What states or countries do your adoptive parents come from? United States.

What states or countries do your birthparents/adopted children come from? United States.

Are other attorneys in your law firm active in adoption? No.

In what year did you begin legal work in adoptions? 1976

How many nonrelative adoptions did you arrange in 1998? 101

About how many children have you placed since you started? 2,600

About what percent of your work is devoted to adoption? 98%

In 1998, what was the average time from when a prospective adoptive parent retained you to the placement of a child? 9 mos. to $1\frac{1}{2}$ years

What made you decide to work in the adoption field? Win-win attitude.

Do you have any criteria for adoptive parents, such as age, number of children in the home, etc.? None.

What percent of your adoptions are infants under 6 mos.? 99%

Do you have a waiting list of prospective parents? Yes.

Is it all right if adopting parents are on waiting lists of other attorneys or agencies? Yes.

Do you charge adoptive parents for a first phone consultation? No.

Do you charge adoptive parents for a first office consultation, and if yes, what is the fee? Yes; $500–700, depending on time involved in meeting.

Do you charge a retainer fee, and if yes, what is it and when is it payable? Yes; $4,500.

What are your legal fees, not including retainer, and when are they payable? $4,500 flat rate, payable in advance; $500 nonrefundable; $4,000 refundable.

Will adoptive parents pay a separate attorney for the birthmother, and if yes, what are approximate legal fees? Yes; $500 minimum.

What are the approximate fees for medical and hospital expenses for the birthmother and baby, when they have no insurance? $5,000–7,500

What are the approximate homestudy fees in your state? $1,250

If living expenses for a birthmother are allowed, what is the average amount paid? $1,200–1,500 per month.

In how many of your cases has an adoptive parent been placed with a child but lost the child due to a birthparent challenge? 14

Have you lost any adoption litigation filed against you by an adoptive parent or birthparent? No.

In about what percentage of your adoptions do adopting parents and birthparents know each other's first and last names? 96%

Are you a member of the American Academy of Adoption Attorneys and/or the National Council for Adoption? American Academy of Adoption Attorneys.

Is there anything I have not asked you that is important? I am a founding fellow of the Academy of California Adoption Lawyers.

JED SOMIT

1440 Broadway #910, Oakland, CA 94612
(510) 839-3215 • Fax: (510) 839-7041
E-mail: jedsomit@pacbell.net

What are your office hours when you accept calls from adoptive parents? 9 a.m.–5 p.m., PT

Education: BA in general studies, Harvard College, 1973; JD, Baltimore School of Law (University of California at Berkeley), 1976

What states or countries do your adoptive parents come from? California.

What states or countries do your birthparents/adopted children come from? California.

Are other attorneys in your law firm active in adoption? No.

In what year did you begin legal work in adoptions? 1982

How many nonrelative adoptions did you arrange in 1998? 3

About how many children have you placed since you started? 200

About what percent of your work is devoted to adoption? 30%

What made you decide to work in the adoption field? Interest in adoption; have three adopted children.

Do you have any criteria for adoptive parents, such as age, number of children in the home, etc.? No.

What percent of your adoptions are infants under 6 mos.? 90%

Do you have a waiting list of prospective parents? No.

Is it all right if adopting parents are on waiting lists of other attorneys or agencies? Yes.

Do you charge adoptive parents for a first phone consultation? No.

Do you charge adoptive parents for a first office consultation, and if yes, what is the fee? Yes; $250/hour.

Do you charge a retainer fee, and if yes, what is it and when is it payable? Yes. Deposit (not retainer) due on major litigation, deciding to go forward on adoption. Varies by case and client's resources.

What are your legal fees, not including retainer, and when are they payable? $250/hour, billed monthly.

Will adoptive parents pay a separate attorney for the birthmother? Yes.

What are the approximate fees for medical and hospital expenses for the birthmother and baby, when they have no insurance? $2,000

What are the approximate homestudy fees in your state? $1,500

If living expenses for a birthmother are allowed, what is the average amount paid? $3,500

Are you an adoptive parent, adopted person, or birthparent? Adoptive parent.

Have you lost any adoption litigation filed against you by an adoptive parent or birthparent? Yes.

In about what percentage of your adoptions do adopting parents and birthparents know each other's first and last names? 100%

Are you a member of the American Academy of Adoption Attorneys and/or the National Council for Adoption? American Academy of Adoption Attorneys.

Is there anything I have not asked you that is important? My practice is adoption law. I do not generally find children. I represent parties in adoption proceedings, including contested adoptions, and in general litigation related to adoption. I handle many different, unusual and contested adoption matters.

M. D. WIDELOCK

O'Neil and Widelock
5401 California Ave., #300, Bakersfield, CA 93309
(661) 325-6950 • Fax: (661) 325-7882
E-mail: OandW@thestork.com • www.thestork.com

What are your office hours when you accept calls from adoptive parents?
8 a.m.–5 p.m., PT. However, attorney or paralegal is available 24 hours a day, 7 days a week, 365 days a year.

Education: JD, Western State University, 1985

What states or countries do your adoptive parents come from? Every state from Maine to Alaska, and Canada.

What states or countries do your birthparents/adopted children come from? Nearly every state from Alaska to Maine, Canada, Mexico, Central and South America, and Ireland.

Are other attorneys in your law firm active in adoption? No.

In what year did you begin legal work in adoptions? 1988

How many nonrelative adoptions did you arrange in 1998? 75+

About how many children have you placed since you started? 1,000+

About what percent of your work is devoted to adoption? 100%, although my practice does include surrogacy, which I view as a preplanned adoption.

In 1998, what was the average time from when a prospective adoptive parent retained you to the placement of a child? About 6 mos.

What made you decide to work in the adoption field? I made a special appearance at a final adoption hearing for an out-of-town adoption attorney. The experience enlightened me. It was the first time I was in court when everyone was smiling. My clients, whom I had just met, kissed me, the judge thanked me, and I felt a strong sense of accomplishment. I was no longer dividing families (divorce law). I was helping to create them.

Do you have any criteria for adoptive parents, such as age, number of children in the home, etc., and if so, what are they? No. My only criteria is that the prospective adoptive parents maintain a strong desire to provide a loving, emotionally and financially stable home for the child they seek to adopt.

What percent of your adoptions are infants under 6 mos.? 99%. They are almost always newborns.

Do you have a waiting list of prospective parents? Yes. But no one waits very long. Approximately 2–3 weeks.

Is it all right if adopting parents are on waiting lists of other attorneys or agencies? Yes.

Do you charge adoptive parents for a first phone consultation? No. Our adoption survival kit is available at no cost to prospective adoptive parents as well.

Do you charge adoptive parents for a first office consultation, and if yes, what is the fee? Yes. This is usually our consultation, which lasts approximately 90 minutes and can be conducted in person, by telephone, or by video conference. Fee is $350.

Do you charge a retainer fee, and if yes, what is it and when is it payable? Yes; $4,000, which is a flat fee for a routine adoption, payable when services commence.

What are your legal fees, not including retainer, and when are they payable? My legal fee and retainer are one and the same. (See remarks for previous question.) $4,000 is a flat fee for a routine adoption. There are no hourly billings. My clients can contact me whenever they desire.

Will adoptive parents pay a separate attorney for the birthmother, and if yes, what are approximate legal fees? Varies. If birthmother desires separate representation, Yes. If the state in which she resides requires separate representation, yes. Otherwise, additional counsel may not be necessary. Approximate legal fees vary; $500 minimum.

What are the approximate fees for medical and hospital expenses for the birthmother and baby, when they have no insurance? Routine delivery, $3,500–5,000 obstetrical and hospital costs, although most birthmothers qualify for Medi-Cal or Medicaid.

What are the approximate homestudy fees in your state? $1,250 if performed by California Dept. of Social Services. Higher fees if performed by private agency.

If living expenses for a birthmother are allowed, what is the average amount paid? Varies, depending on birthmother's circumstances (e.g., is she two months along or is she in her ninth month? Is she living with family? Is she employed?). Each case is different.

In how many of your cases has an adoptive parent lost a placed child due to a birthparent challenge? Legal challenge (3).

Have you lost any adoption litigation filed against you by an adoptive parent or birthparent? No. No litigation ever filed.

In about what percentage of your adoptions do adopting parents and birthparents know each other's first and last names? 99%

Are you a member of the American Academy of Adoption Attorneys and/or the National Council for Adoption? American Academy of Adoption Attorneys.

Is there anything I have not asked you that is important? Total cost of adoption? Average total cost of adoption, including birthmother expenses, is $10,000 to $15,000.

NANCI R. WORCESTER

Adoption Center of Northern California
210 Magnolia Ave., Auburn, CA 95603
(530) 888-1311 • Fax: (530) 888-7529
E-mail: nrwadopt@quik.com • www.adopting.org/nrw.html

What are your office hours when you accept calls from adoptive parents? 9 a.m.–5 p.m., PT; accept calls 24 hours, answering service forwards.

Education: BA, in Psychology, University of California, Los Angeles, 1974; JD, Southwestern University School of Law, 1981

What states or countries do your adoptive parents come from? Any state.

What states or countries do your birthparents/adopted children come from? Any state.

Are other attorneys in your law firm active in adoption? No.

In what year did you begin legal work in adoptions? 1985

How many nonrelative adoptions did you arrange in 1998? 30

About what percent of your work is devoted to adoption? 100%

In 1998, what was the average time from when a prospective adoptive parent retained you to the placement of a child? 9 mos.

What made you decide to work in the adoption field? My personal experience with infertility and adoption of my children.

Do you have any criteria for adoptive parents, such as age, number of children in the home, etc.? No.

What percent of your adoptions are infants under 6 mos.? 98%

Do you have a waiting list of prospective parents? Yes.

Is it all right if adopting parents are on waiting lists of other attorneys or agencies? Yes.

Do you charge for a first phone consultation from adoptive parents? No.

Do you charge adoptive parents for a first office consultation, and if yes, what is the fee? No, if it is a brief half-hour "getting to know you" meeting. Yes, if it is a $2\frac{1}{2}$ to 3 hour counseling session: $500 for counseling session.

Do you charge a retainer fee, and if yes, what is it and when is it payable? Yes; $1,500, on representation.

What are your legal fees, not including retainer, and when are they payable? $2,500

Will adoptive parents pay a separate attorney for the birthmother, and if yes, what are approximate legal fees? Yes; $500–1,500.

What are the approximate fees for medical and hospital expenses for the birthmother and baby, when they have no insurance? $6,500 for normal vaginal birth and 24-hour stay.

What are the approximate homestudy fees in your state? $1,500 for agency $1,200 for state independent.

If living expenses for a birthmother are allowed, what is the average amount paid? $2,000

Are you an adoptive parent, adopted person, or birthparent? Adoptive parent.

In how many of your cases has an adoptive parent lost a placed child due to a birthparent challenge? Never.

Have you lost any adoption litigation filed against you by an adoptive parent or birthparent? No.

In about what percentage of your adoptions do adopting parents and birthparents know each other's first and last names? 100%

Are you a member of the American Academy of Adoption Attorneys and/or the National Council for Adoption? American Academy of Adoption Attorneys.

Is there anything I have not asked you that is important? I am a strong advocate for open adoption. I feel adoption should be looked on like a marriage. A child joins a new family, but is not related to them. However, he or she does not lose contact with their own relatives by virtue of the "marriage."

COLORADO

W. THOMAS BELTZ

Beltz Law Firm
729 S. Cascade, Colorado Springs, CO 80903
(719) 473-4444 • Fax: (719) 444-0186

What are your office hours when you accept calls from adoptive parents?
8 a.m.–6 p.m., MST

Education: BS in multidisciplinary social science, Michigan State University, 1970; JD, Washington University (St. Louis) Law School, 1973

What states or countries do your adoptive parents come from? All states.

What states or countries do your birthparents/adopted children come from? All states.

Are other attorneys in your law firm active in adoption? Yes. Daniel A. West.

In what year did you begin legal work in adoptions? 1974

How many nonrelative adoptions did you arrange in 1998? 75, not arranged, but performed legal work for.

About how many children have you placed since you started? I have handled more than 1,000 adoptions, but I do not do the placements.

About what percent of your work is devoted to adoption? 75%

In 1998, what was the average time from when a prospective adoptive parent retained you to the placement of a child? I have designated adoptions. I don't make placements.

What made you decide to work in the adoption field? To do something meaningful.

Do you have any criteria for adoptive parents, such as age, number of children in the home, etc.? No.

What percent of your adoptions are infants under 6 mos.? 85%

Do you have a waiting list of prospective parents? No.

Is it all right if adopting parents are on waiting lists of other attorneys or agencies? Yes.

Do you charge adoptive parents for a first phone consultation? No, unless retained thereafter.

Do you charge adoptive parents for a first office consultation? No, unless retained thereafter.

Do you charge a retainer fee, and if yes, what is it and when is it payable? Yes. At time fee agreement is signed; depends on the facts as to amount.

What are your legal fees, not including retainer, and when are they payable? $175/hour payable within 30 days of billing.

Will adoptive parents pay a separate attorney for the birthmother? No, not typically.

What are the approximate fees for medical and hospital expenses for the birthmother and baby, when they have no insurance? Typically covered by Medicaid or health insurance.

What are the approximate homestudy fees in your state? $2,000

If living expenses for a birthmother are allowed, what is the average amount paid? Less than $1,000.

In how many of your cases has an adoptive parent lost a placed child due to a birthparent challenge? None after a court hearing, about 50 who changed mind before court.

Have you lost any adoption litigation filed against you by an adoptive parent or birthparent? No.

In about what percentage of your adoptions do adopting parents and birthparents know each other's first and last names? 80%

Are you a member of the American Academy of Adoption Attorneys and/or the National Council for Adoption? American Academy of Adoption Attorneys.

CONNECTICUT

JANET S. STULTING

Shipman and Goodwin, LLP
One American Row, Hartford, CT 06103-2819
(860) 251-5000 • Fax: (860) 251-5199
E-mail: jstulting@goodwin.com

What are your office hours when you accept calls from adoptive parents? 9 a.m.–5 p.m., ET

Education: BA in French and art history, University of Connecticut, 1991; JD, University of Connecticut Law School, 1980

What states or countries do your adoptive parents come from? Various.

What states or countries do your birthparents/adopted children come from? Various.

Are other attorneys in your law firm active in adoption? No.

In what year did you begin legal work in adoptions? 1986

How many nonrelative adoptions did you arrange in 1998? Connecticut permits agency and identified adoptions. Attorneys do not arrange or place children with adoptive parents.

About what percent of your work is devoted to adoption? 50%

What made you decide to work in the adoption field? The opportunity presented itself and I found the work to be extremely rewarding.

Do you have any criteria for adoptive parents, such as age, number of children in the home, etc.? No.

Do you charge adoptive parents for a first phone consultation? No.

Do you charge adoptive parents for a first office consultation, and if yes, what is the fee? Yes. My hourly rate in 1999 is $245.

Do you charge a retainer fee, and if yes, what is it and when is it payable? Yes. Varies.

What are your legal fees, not including retainer, and when are they payable? Varies.

Will adoptive parents pay a separate attorney for the birthmother? No.

What are the approximate fees for medical and hospital expenses for the birthmother and baby, when they have no insurance? $3,000

What are the approximate homestudy fees in your state? $1,200–1,500

If living expenses for a birthmother are allowed, what is the average amount paid? $1,500 is maximum permitted.

In how many of your cases has an adoptive parent lost a placed child due to a birthparent challenge? None.

Have you lost any adoption litigation filed against you by an adoptive parent or birthparent? No.

In about what percentage of your adoptions do adopting parents and birthparents know each other's first and last names? Very few.

Are you a member of the American Academy of Adoption Attorneys and/or the National Council for Adoption? American Academy of Adoption Attorneys.

DISTRICT OF COLUMBIA

MICHAEL P. BENTZEN

Davis and Bentzen
888 17th St. NW, #1075, Washington, DC 20006
(202) 452-8553 • Fax: (202) 293-8973
E-mail: mbentzen@aol.com

What are your office hours when you accept calls from adoptive parents?
9 a.m.–6 p.m., ES/OST

Education: BA in economics, DePaul University, 1960; JD, (with honors) George Washington University Law School, 1964

What states or countries do your adoptive parents come from? I have represented adoptive parents from Maryland, Virginia, District of Columbia, Tennessee, and New York.

What states or countries do your birthparents/adopted children come from? The adoptive couples I represent have adopted children from Maryland, Virginia, Kentucky, North Carolina, Russia, Korea, Colombia, Vietnam, and China.

Are other attorneys in your law firm active in adoption? No.

In what year did you begin legal work in adoptions? 1968

How many nonrelative adoptions did you arrange in 1998? I do not arrange adoptions.

About how many children have you placed since you started? I do not place children in adoption.

About what percent of your work is devoted to adoption? 5–10%

In 1998, what was the average time from when a prospective adoptive parent retained you to the placement of a child? The parents (adoptive) usually have identified the child when I am retained.

What made you decide to work in the adoption field? I adopted my son through Barker in 1968 and became professionally involved from that time.

Do you have any criteria for adoptive parents, such as age, number of children in the home, etc.? I do not place children. If a couple does not appear to meet agency eligibility requirements, I try to assist in finding a source which will accept them.

Do you charge adoptive parents for a first phone consultation? No.

Do you charge adoptive parents for a first office consultation? Usually not.

Do you charge a retainer fee, and if yes, what is it and when is it payable? Yes; $500 on agreement that I will represent the client.

What are your legal fees, not including retainer, and when are they payable? $250 per hour, billed monthly.

Will adoptive parents pay a separate attorney for the birthmother? Depends on jurisdiction(s) involved.

What are the approximate fees for medical and hospital expenses for the birthmother and baby, when they have no insurance? $8,000–10,000. Would be more with complications.

What are the approximate homestudy fees in your state? $1,600. Can be less.

If living expenses for a birthmother are allowed, what is the average amount paid? Not allowed in Maryland.

Are you an adoptive parent, adopted person, or birthparent? Adoptive parent.

In how many of your cases has an adoptive parent lost a placed child due to a birthparent challenge? 0

Have you lost any adoption litigation filed against you by an adoptive parent or birthparent? No.

In about what percentage of your adoptions do adopting parents and birthparents know each other's first and last names? 20–40%

Are you a member of the American Academy of Adoption Attorneys and/or the National Council for Adoption? National Council For Adoption.

MARK T. MCDERMOTT

Joseph, McDermott and Reiner
1050 17th St. NW, #700, Washington, DC 20036
(202) 331-1955 • Fax: (202) 293-2309
E-mail: mcdermtm@aol.com

What are your office hours when you accept calls from adoptive parents?
9:30 a.m.–5:30 p.m., EST

Education: BS, Indiana University 1970; JD, Indiana University Law School, 1974

What states or countries do your adoptive parents come from? District of Columbia, Maryland, Virginia, and elsewhere.

What states or countries do your birthparents/adopted children come from? All states.

Are other attorneys in your law firm active in adoption? Yes.

In what year did you begin legal work in adoptions? 1985

How many nonrelative adoptions did you arrange in 1998? 80

About how many children have you placed since you started? 900

About what percent of your work is devoted to adoption? 70%

In 1998, what was the average time from when a prospective adoptive parent retained you to the placement of a child? 6 mos.–1 year

What made you decide to work in the adoption field? I am an adoptive parent.

What percent of your adoptions are infants under 6 mos.? 95%

Do you have a waiting list of prospective parents? No.

Is it all right if adopting parents are on waiting lists of other attorneys or agencies? Yes.

Do you charge adoptive parents for a first phone consultation? No.

Do you charge adoptive parents for a first office consultation? No.

Do you charge a retainer fee? No.

What are your legal fees, not including retainer, and when are they payable? Hourly fees payable monthly as services are rendered.

Will adoptive parents pay a separate attorney for the birthmother, and if yes, what are approximate legal fees? Yes; $1,500.

What are the approximate fees for medical and hospital expenses for the birthmother and baby, when they have no insurance? $5,000

What are the approximate homestudy fees in your state? $1,200

Are you an adoptive parent, adopted person, or birthparent? Adoptive parent.

In how many of your cases has an adoptive parent lost a placed child due to a birth-parent challenge? 15–20, if "challenge" includes change of mind during the revocation period allowed by law.

Have you lost any adoption litigation filed against you by an adoptive parent or birthparent? No.

In about what percentage of your adoptions do adopting parents and birthparents know each other's first and last names? 30%

Are you a member of the American Academy of Adoption Attorneys and/or the National Council for Adoption? American Academy of Adoption Attorneys and National Council for Adoption.

Is there anything I have not asked you that is important? I am a past president of the American Academy of Adoption Attorneys.

FLORIDA

LINDA W. MCINTYRE

98 SE 6th Ave., Suite 1, Delray Beach, FL 33483
(561) 279-2297

What are your office hours when you accept calls from adoptive parents?
9 a.m.–5 p.m., ET

Education: BS, University of Minnesota, 1966; JD, Nova Southeastern University, 1984

What states or countries do your adoptive parents come from? All states.

What states or countries do your birthparents/adopted children come from? All states.

Are other attorneys in your law firm active in adoption? No.

In what year did you begin legal work in adoptions? 1984

How many nonrelative adoptions did you arrange in 1998? 50+

About how many children have you placed since you started? 800+

About what percent of your work is devoted to adoption? 85%

In 1998, what was the average time from when a prospective adoptive parent retained you to the placement of a child? 6 mos.

What percent of your adoptions are infants under 6 mos.? 98%

Do you have a waiting list of prospective parents? Yes.

Is it all right if adopting parents are on waiting lists of other attorneys or agencies? Yes.

Do you charge adoptive parents for a first phone consultation, and if yes, what is the fee? No phone consultation. I must meet all applicants in person. There is an application fee for this consultation. It varies, depending on circumstances; there is no fee for applications wanting biracial placements.

Do you charge adoptive parents for a first office consultation, and if yes, what is the fee? Yes; it varies.

Do you charge a retainer fee, and if yes, what is it and when is it payable? Yes. It varies depending on the nature of the work.

What are your legal fees, not including retainer, and when are they payable? Based on time and hourly rate or flat rate.

Will adoptive parents pay a separate attorney for the birthmother, and if yes, what are approximate legal fees? Yes; $500–750 (at this time) plus expenses.

What are the approximate fees for medical and hospital expenses for the birthmother and baby, when they have no insurance? $3,000–6,000

What are the approximate homestudy fees in your state? $850–1,500

If living expenses for a birthmother are allowed, what is the average amount paid? It varies.

In how many of your cases has an adoptive parent lost a placed child due to a birthparent challenge? None.

Have you lost any adoption litigation filed against you by an adoptive parent or birthparent? No.

In about what percentage of your adoptions do adopting parents and birthparents know each other's first and last names? 25% or less.

Are you a member of the American Academy of Adoption Attorneys and/or the National Council for Adoption? American Academy of Adoption Attorneys and National Council for Adoption.

MARY ANN SCHERER

2734 East Oakland Park Blvd., Ft. Lauderdale, FL 33306
(954) 564-6900 • Fax: (954) 564-0187

What are your office hours when you accept calls from adoptive parents? 9 a.m.–5 p.m., ET

Education: BS in nursing University of Miami, 1974; JD, Nova University, 1977

What states or countries do your adoptive parents come from? All states.

What states or countries do your birthparents/adopted children come from? All states, India, Russia, China, Poland, Guatemala.

Are other attorneys in your law firm active in adoption? Yes.

In what year did you begin legal work in adoptions? 1979

How many nonrelative adoptions did you arrange in 1998? 60

About how many children have you placed since you started? 4,000

About what percent of your work is devoted to adoption? 80%

In 1998, what was the average time from when a prospective adoptive parent retained you to the placement of a child? 3 mos.–1 year

What made you decide to work in the adoption field? Love for children, empathy for childless couples, empathy for unwed mothers and other mothers whose circumstances require them to make an adoption plan.

What percent of your adoptions are infants under 6 mos.? 80%

Do you have a waiting list of prospective parents? Yes.

Is it all right if adopting parents are on waiting lists of other attorneys or agencies? Yes.

Do you charge adoptive parents for a first phone consultation? No.

Do you charge adoptive parents for a first office consultation, and if yes, what is the fee? Yes; $200.

Do you charge a retainer fee? No.

What are your legal fees, not including retainer, and when are they payable? Depending on work to be done, $1,500–5,000; one-third down, balance on completion of adoption.

Will adoptive parents pay a separate attorney for the birthmother, and if yes, what are approximate legal fees? Yes; $500–1,000.

What are the approximate fees for medical and hospital expenses for the birthmother and baby, when they have no insurance? $2,000 for hospital; $2,000–3,000 for gynecologist; $500 for tests (medical/sonogram); $200 for pediatrician.

What are the approximate homestudy fees in your state? $850–1,500

If living expenses for a birthmother are allowed, what is the average amount paid? Varies, based on needs of mother.

In how many of your cases has an adoptive parent lost a placed child due to a birthparent challenge? 0

Have you lost any adoption litigation filed against you by an adoptive parent or birthparent? No.

In about what percentage of your adoptions do adopting parents and birthparents know each other's first and last names? 2%

Are you a member of the American Academy of Adoption Attorneys and/or the National Council for Adoption? American Academy of Adoption Attorneys.

MICHAEL A. SHORSTEIN

Shorstein and Kelly, Attorneys at Law, PA
1660 Prudential Dr. #402, Jacksonville, FL 32207
(904) 348-6400
E-mail: adoption@ibm.net • www.adoptionattorneyfla.com

What are your office hours when you accept calls from adoptive parents?
8:30 a.m.–5:30 p.m., ET

Education: BS in accounting, University of Florida School of Accounting, 1980; CPA, Florida, 1983; JD, Florida State University College of Law, 1985

What states or countries do your adoptive parents come from? United States, Canada, Europe.

What states or countries do your birthparents/adopted children come from?
Florida.

Are other attorneys in your law firm active in adoption? Yes.

In what year did you begin legal work in adoptions? 1990

How many nonrelative adoptions did you arrange in 1998? Approximately 100.

About how many children have you placed since you started? Over 700

About what percent of your work is devoted to adoption? 100%

What percent of your adoptions are infants under 6 mos.? 100%

Do you have a waiting list of prospective parents? Yes.

Is it all right if adopting parents are on waiting lists of other attorneys or agencies?
Yes.

Do you charge adoptive parents for a first phone consultation? No.

Do you charge adoptive parents for a first office consultation, and if yes, what is the fee? Yes; $200.

Do you charge a retainer fee, and if yes, what is it and when is it payable? Yes. Variable.

What are your legal fees, not including retainer, and when are they payable?
Variable.

Will adoptive parents pay a separate attorney for the birthmother? No.

What are the approximate fees for medical and hospital expenses for the birthmother and baby, when they have no insurance? $10,000

What are the approximate homestudy fees in your state? $1,000–1,500

If living expenses for a birthmother are allowed, what is the average amount paid?
Variable.

In how many of your cases has an adoptive parent lost a placed child due to a birthparent challenge? 0

Have you lost any adoption litigation filed against you by an adoptive parent or birthparent? No.

In about what percentage of your adoptions do adopting parents and birthparents know each other's first and last names? 10%

Are you a member of the American Academy of Adoption Attorneys and/or the National Council for Adoption? American Academy of Adoption Attorneys.

CYNTHIA STUMP SWANSON

Swanson and Sperling, PA
500 E. University Ave., Suite C, Gainesville, FL 32601
(352) 375-5602 • Fax: (352) 373-7292
E-mail: swansonc@earthlink.net

What are your office hours when you accept calls from adoptive parents?
8:30 a.m.–5:30 p.m., ET

Education: BS in political science, Florida State University, 1975; JD, University of Florida, 1981

What states or countries do your adoptive parents come from? Florida.

What states or countries do your birthparents/adopted children come from? Any state is a possibility; mostly from Florida and Arizona.

Are other attorneys in your law firm active in adoption? No.

In what year did you begin legal work in adoptions? 1985

How many nonrelative adoptions did you arrange in 1998? 20

About how many children have you placed since you started? About 250.

About what percent of your work is devoted to adoption? 15%

In 1998, what was the average time from when a prospective adoptive parent retained you to the placement of a child? 10 mos.

Do you have any criteria for adoptive parents, such as age, number of children in the home, etc.? No.

What percent of your adoptions are infants under 6 mos.? 100%, except for international adoptions, which are finalized here and all of which are older than 6 mos.

Do you have a waiting list of prospective parents? Yes.

Is it all right if adopting parents are on waiting lists of other attorneys or agencies? Yes.

Do you charge adoptive parents for a first phone consultation? No, I don't do phone consultations.

Do you charge adoptive parents for a first office consultation, and if yes, what is the fee? Yes; $250/hour.

Do you charge a retainer fee, and if yes, what is it and when is it payable? Yes. $1,000 minimum, nonrefundable retainer paid when a match is made. In addition, at that time, adoptive parents have to pay entire amount we have estimated the adoption will cost.

What are your legal fees, not including retainer, and when are they payable?
$250/hour for me; $50/hour for adoption assistant. At the time a match is made, we estimate all fees and costs, all of which have to be paid at that time.

Will adoptive parents pay a separate attorney for the birthmother, and if yes, what are approximate legal fees? Sometimes. $150/hour to $200/hour, depending on that attorney's rate.

What are the approximate fees for medical and hospital expenses for the birthmother and baby, when they have no insurance? $7,000 if birthmother is in the Gainesville area.

What are the approximate homestudy fees in your state? $750–1,500

If living expenses for a birthmother are allowed, what is the average amount paid? Varies with each situation.

Are you an adoptive parent, adopted person, or birthparent? Adoptive parent.

In how many of your cases has an adoptive parent lost a placed child due to a birthparent challenge? 0

Have you lost any adoption litigation filed against you by an adoptive parent or birthparent? No.

In about what percentage of your adoptions do adopting parents and birthparents know each other's first and last names? 2% or less; just first names, about 95%.

Are you a member of the American Academy of Adoption Attorneys and/or the National Council for Adoption? American Academy of Adoption Attorneys.

Is there anything I have not asked you that is important? Under present Florida law, attorneys cannot place children with parents who don't live in Florida (except special needs children). There is no point in out-of-Florida parents contacting Florida attorneys unless they are interested in special needs kids.

JEANNE T. TATE

418 W. Platt St., Suite B, Tampa, FL 33606-2244
(813) 258-3355 • Fax: (813) 258-3373
E-mail: jeanne@jtatelaw.com

What are your office hours when you accept calls from adoptive parents?
8 a.m.–5:30 p.m., ET

Education: BS in journalism, University of Florida, 1978; JD, University of Florida, 1981

What states or countries do your adoptive parents come from? All states and foreign countries.

What states or countries do your birthparents/adopted children come from? All states.

Are other attorneys in your law firm active in adoption? No, solo practice.

In what year did you begin legal work in adoptions? 1982

How many nonrelative adoptions did you arrange in 1998? 50+

About how many children have you placed since you started? 500+

About what percent of your work is devoted to adoption? 100%

In 1998, what was the average time from when a prospective adoptive parent retained you to the placement of a child? 12–20 mos.

What made you decide to work in the adoption field? I greatly enjoy assisting birthparents in their search for a dream family to adopt their child as well as assisting adoptive parents fulfill their dream of becoming a family. I cannot think of a greater calling—I often say and feel like I am doing God's work.

Do you have any criteria for adoptive parents, such as age, number of children in the home, etc.? No.

What percent of your adoptions are infants under 6 mos.? 95%

Do you have a waiting list of prospective parents? Yes.

Is it all right if adopting parents are on waiting lists of other attorneys or agencies? Yes.

Do you charge adoptive parents for a first phone consultation? No.

Do you charge adoptive parents for a first office consultation? No.

Do you charge a retainer fee? No. All fees are due at the time of placement. No fees due for disrupted placements.

What are your legal fees, not including retainer, and when are they payable? Varies dependent on the circumstances. Generally no more than $6,000.

Will adoptive parents pay a separate attorney for the birthmother? No.

What are the approximate fees for medical and hospital expenses for the birthmother and baby, when they have no insurance? $7,000

What are the approximate homestudy fees in your state? $900–1,200

If living expenses for a birthmother are allowed, what is the average amount paid? $4,000–6,000

In how many of your cases has an adoptive parent lost a placed child due to a birthparent challenge? 0

Have you lost any adoption litigation filed against you by an adoptive parent or birthparent? No.

In about what percentage of your adoptions do adopting parents and birthparents know each other's first and last names? 1%

Are you a member of the American Academy of Adoption Attorneys and/or the National Council for Adoption? American Academy of Adoption Attorneys.

GEORGIA

RHONDA FISHBEIN

17 Executive Park Dr., Suite 480, Atlanta, GA 30329
(404) 248-9205 • Fax: (404) 248-0419
E-mail: rlfishbein@aol.com

What are your office hours when you accept calls from adoptive parents?
9 a.m.–5 p.m., ET

Education: BA in psychology, New York University, 1971; MA in counseling, New York University, 1975; JD, Benjamin N. Cardozo School of Law, 1982

What states or countries do your adoptive parents come from? All states.

What states or countries do your birthparents/adopted children come from?
Georgia (50%) and rest of the United States.

Are other attorneys in your law firm active in adoption? No.

In what year did you begin legal work in adoptions? 1987

How many nonrelative adoptions did you arrange in 1998? 20–30 through my work as director of licensed agency; 25 independent adoptions through law practice where clients were active in the process of identifying birthparents.

About how many children have you placed since you started? 200

About what percent of your work is devoted to adoption? 100%

In 1998, what was the average time from when a prospective adoptive parent retained you to the placement of a child? 1 year

What made you decide to work in the adoption field? I went to law school to work in the family law area. I knew that I wanted to combine my law degree and my counseling degree. In 1987, my husband and I adopted our first child and I decided to focus on adoption law.

Do you have any criteria for adoptive parents, such as age, number of children in the home, etc., and if so, what are they? Flexible, case-by-case.

What percent of your adoptions are infants under 6 mos.? 95%

Do you have a waiting list of prospective parents? No.

Is it all right if adopting parents are on waiting lists of other attorneys or agencies? Yes.

Do you charge adoptive parents for a first phone consultation? No.

Do you charge adoptive parents for a first office consultation, and if yes, what is the fee? Yes. $225 for $1\frac{1}{2}$- to 2-hour meeting.

Do you charge a retainer fee, and if yes, what is it and when is it payable? Yes; $850 on retaining me (this is an advance payment fee). If birthmother is already identified when I am contacted by prospective clients, retainer is $2,500 (this is an advance payment fee).

What are your legal fees, not including retainer, and when are they payable? $175 per hour. Billing is done monthly.

Will adoptive parents pay a separate attorney for the birthmother? Depends on law in state in which birthmother resides. Georgia law does not require independent representation.

What are the approximate fees for medical and hospital expenses for the birthmother and baby, when they have no insurance? $8,000–9,000 for normal delivery.

What are the approximate homestudy fees in your state? $900–1,000 (domestic)

If living expenses for a birthmother are allowed, what is the average amount paid? Only agency can help with living expenses. Average amount paid by agencies is $400/month.

Are you an adoptive parent, adopted person, or birthparent? Adoptive parent.

In how many of your cases has an adoptive parent lost a placed child due to a birthparent challenge? 1

Have you lost any adoption litigation filed against you by an adoptive parent or birthparent? No.

In about what percentage of your adoptions do adopting parents and birthparents know each other's first and last names? 10%

Are you a member of the American Academy of Adoption Attorneys and/or the National Council for Adoption? American Academy of Adoption Attorneys.

HAWAII

LINDA E. F. LACH

Adoption Law Office of Linda E. F. Lach, A Law Corporation
4473 Pahe'e St., Suite R, Lihue, HI 96766
(808) 245-8000 • Fax: (808) 246-2605
www.youcanadopt.com

What are your office hours when you accept calls from adoptive parents? 8 a.m.–5 p.m., Hawaiian, M–F or by arrangement.

Education: BS in business, Babson College, 1973; MBA in business, Babson College, 1974; JD, Georgetown University, 1977

What states or countries do your adoptive parents come from? United States, Australia, England, Germany, etc.

What states or countries do your birthparents/adopted children come from? United States, Marshall Islands, Mexico, others on occasion.

Are other attorneys in your law firm active in adoption? N/A

In what year did you begin legal work in adoptions? 1984

How many nonrelative adoptions did you arrange in 1998? 25

About how many children have you placed since you started? 500

About what percent of your work is devoted to adoption? 100%

In 1998, what was the average time from when a prospective adoptive parent retained you to the placement of a child? 3–4 mos.

What made you decide to work in the adoption field? The suggestion of my law partner (an adoptive parent).

Do you have any criteria for adoptive parents, such as age, number of children in the home, etc., and if so, what are they? No.

What percent of your adoptions are infants under 6 mos.? 95%

Do you have a waiting list of prospective parents? Yes.

Is it all right if adopting parents are on waiting lists of other attorneys or agencies? Yes.

Do you charge adoptive parents for a first phone consultation? No.

Do you charge adoptive parents for a first office consultation? No.

Do you charge a retainer fee, and if yes, what is it and when is it payable? Yes. $2,000, payable when I begin to search for a child for a client.

What are your legal fees, not including retainer, and when are they payable? If adoption takes place in Hawaii, $7,500 at placement. If only birth takes place in Hawaii, $5,000 at placement. If birth and adoption are elsewhere, $3,000 at placement.

Will adoptive parents pay a separate attorney for the birthmother, and if yes, what are approximate legal fees? If birthparent wants one. Always offered. Varies.

What are the approximate fees for medical and hospital expenses for the birthmother and baby, when they have no insurance? $5,000 here.

What are the approximate homestudy fees in your state? $1,200–1,500

If living expenses for a birthmother are allowed, what is the average amount paid? Never calculated the average; it varies enormously.

In how many of your cases has an adoptive parent lost a placed child due to a birthparent challenge? 2

Have you lost any adoption litigation filed against you by an adoptive parent or birthparent? No.

In about what percentage of your adoptions do adopting parents and birthparents know each other's first and last names? Maybe 80%, by choice.

IDAHO

ALFRED E. BARRUS

Barrus Law Office
Box 487, Burly, ID 83318
(280) 678-1155 • Fax: (280) 678-1166

What are your office hours when you accept calls from adoptive parents?
9 a.m.–5 p.m., MT

Education: BA, Bryce, 1971; JD, University of Idaho Law School, 1974

What states or countries do your adoptive parents come from? Idaho and Western United States.

What states or countries do your birthparents/adopted children come from? Idaho and Western United States.

Are other attorneys in your law firm active in adoption? No.

In what year did you begin legal work in adoptions? 1975

How many nonrelative adoptions did you arrange in 1998? 14

About how many children have you placed since you started? 300+

About what percent of your work is devoted to adoption? 20%

What made you decide to work in the adoption field? I have five adopted children of my own and enjoy helping others become parents.

Do you have any criteria for adoptive parents, such as age, number of children in the home, etc.? No.

What percent of your adoptions are infants under 6 mos.? 95%

Do you have a waiting list of prospective parents? Yes.

Is it all right if adopting parents are on waiting lists of other attorneys or agencies? Yes.

Do you charge adoptive parents for a first phone consultation? No.

Do you charge adoptive parents for a first office consultation? No.

Do you charge a retainer fee, and if yes, what is it and when is it payable? Yes. $1,500 at time of agreement.

What are your legal fees, not including retainer, and when are they payable? $125 per hour for time involved.

Will adoptive parents pay a separate attorney for the birthmother, and if yes, what are approximate legal fees? Yes; $500–1,000.

What are the approximate fees for medical and hospital expenses for the birthmother and baby, when they have no insurance? $3,000

What are the approximate homestudy fees in your state? $500

If living expenses for a birthmother are allowed, what is the average amount paid? Not allowed.

Are you an adoptive parent, adopted person, or birthparent? Adoptive parent.

In how many of your cases has an adoptive parent lost a placed child due to a birthparent challenge? 0

Have you lost any adoption litigation filed against you by an adoptive parent or birthparent? No.

In about what percentage of your adoptions do adopting parents and birthparents know each other's first and last names? 50%

Are you a member of the American Academy of Adoption Attorneys and/or the National Council for Adoption? American Academy of Adoption Attorneys.

JOHN T. HAWLEY, JR.

202 N. 9th St., Suite 205, Boise, ID 83702
(208) 336-6686 • Fax: (208) 336-2088
E-mail: jthidaho@aol.com

What are your office hours when you accept calls from adoptive parents?
9 a.m.–5:30 p.m., MT

Education: BS in journalism (with honors), University of Idaho, 1976; JD, Gonzaga University, 1980

What states or countries do your adoptive parents come from? I have worked with adoptive parents from Germany, Italy, Switzerland, Canada, Mexico, Philippines, Japan; have also worked with couples from 40 states, Idaho, California, Washington, Oregon, Nevada, Arizona, Utah, Texas, Wisconsin, New York, New Jersey, Florida, etc.

What states or countries do your birthparents/adopted children come from? Children/birthparents from Idaho, Washington, Oregon, California, New Hampshire, Texas, Arizona, Missouri. Foreign children from China, Romania, Philippines.

Are other attorneys in your law firm active in adoption? No.

In what year did you begin legal work in adoptions? 1984

How many nonrelative adoptions did you arrange in 1998? 10

About how many children have you placed since you started? 75–80

About what percent of your work is devoted to adoption? 75%

In 1998, what was the average time from when a prospective adoptive parent retained you to the placement of a child? Not sure—varies.

What made you decide to work in the adoption field? I assisted two couples to adopt children in the early 1980s and decided that this was an area of law where I could obtain positive results and really help people begin families. Every year my involvement in adoption work has increased.

Do you have any criteria for adoptive parents, such as age, number of children in the home, etc.? No restrictions, although I have not had much success with adoptive couples who have three or more children in the home.

What percent of your adoptions are infants under 6 mos.? 80–85%

Do you have a waiting list of prospective parents? No. I will accept profiles from any/all prospective adoptive parents and keep them on file without charge.

Is it all right if adopting parents are on waiting lists of other attorneys or agencies? Yes.

Do you charge adoptive parents for a first phone consultation? No.

Do you charge adoptive parents for a first office consultation, and if yes, what is the fee? No, if brief. If lengthy, $125 per hour.

Do you charge a retainer fee, and if yes, what is it and when is it payable? Yes. $1,500–5,000 when couple is matched with birthmother. If I located the birthmother, the fee is generally $5,000.

What are your legal fees, not including retainer, and when are they payable? $125 per hour. Interstate adoptions usually run in the $1,200–1,800 range. If I locate and counsel birthmom, $5,000.

Will adoptive parents pay a separate attorney for the birthmother, and if yes, what are approximate legal fees? Yes. Varies greatly; depends on extent of legal work.

What are the approximate fees for medical and hospital expenses for the birthmother and baby, when they have no insurance? $6,000

What are the approximate homestudy fees in your state? $850–1,200

If living expenses for a birthmother are allowed, what is the average amount paid? Not permitted in Idaho.

If you manage international adoptions, what is the average fee for translating documents? Varies greatly.

In how many of your cases has an adoptive parent lost a placed child due to a birthparent challenge? 0. I have had a few cases where the birthmother could not go through with placement, usually before she consented to terminate parental rights.

Have you lost any adoption litigation filed against you by an adoptive parent or birthparent? No.

In about what percentage of your adoptions do adopting parents and birthparents know each other's first and last names? 50%

Are you a member of the American Academy of Adoption Attorneys and/or the National Council for Adoption? American Academy of Adoption Attorneys.

Is there anything I have not asked you that is important? Idaho law requires birthmother (and birthfather if available) to execute consents to terminate parental rights in court after child is born. Once this occurs, it becomes a final and irrevocable decision.

ILLINOIS

DEBORAH CROUSE COBB

Crouse Cobb and Bays
#2 Sunset Hills Executive Park, Suite 4C, Edwardsville, IL 62025-3712
(618) 692-6300 • Fax: (618) 692-9831
E-mail: complaw@mvp.net

What are your office hours when you accept calls from adoptive parents?
9 a.m.–2:30 p.m., ET

Education: BA in English and home economics education, Eastern Illinois University, 1976; JD, Washington University School of Law, St. Louis, 1983

What states or countries do your adoptive parents come from? Throughout the United States, Canada, and England.

What states or countries do your birthparents/adopted children come from? Illinois, Missouri, and throughout the United States. We also handle international adoptions.

Are other attorneys in your law firm active in adoption? Yes.

In what year did you begin legal work in adoptions? 1985

How many nonrelative adoptions did you arrange in 1998? Uncertain. The office finalized more than 150 unrelated adoptions, but we didn't keep track of how placement occurred.

About how many children have you placed since you started? In Illinois I facilitate, I cannot place.

About what percent of your work is devoted to adoption? 90%

In 1998, what was the average time from when a prospective adoptive parent retained you to the placement of a child? 1 year

Do you have any criteria for adoptive parents, such as age, number of children in the home, etc., and if so, what are they? Yes; they must have homestudy and foster care licenses if required by their state.

What percent of your adoptions are infants under 6 mos.? 70%

Do you have a waiting list of prospective parents? Yes.

Is it all right if adopting parents are on waiting lists of other attorneys or agencies? Yes.

Do you charge adoptive parents for a first phone consultation? No.

Do you charge adoptive parents for a first office consultation, and if yes, what is the fee? Depends—we offer a free first consultation if they come to a monthly group meeting. If they want a private session we charge $200.

Do you charge a retainer fee, and if yes, what is it and when is it payable? Yes; $300.

What are your legal fees, not including retainer, and when are they payable? Depends on type of case; payable as billed.

Will adoptive parents pay a separate attorney for the birthmother, and if yes, what are approximate legal fees? Depends on situation. $500 average.

What are the approximate fees for medical and hospital expenses for the birthmother and baby, when they have no insurance? $6,000 for vaginal; $10,000 for caesarean.

What are the approximate homestudy fees in your state? $1,500

If living expenses for a birthmother are allowed, what is the average amount paid? $2,000

In how many of your cases has an adoptive parent lost a placed child due to a birthparent challenge? 2

Have you lost any adoption litigation filed against you by an adoptive parent or birthparent? No.

In about what percentage of your adoptions do adopting parents and birthparents know each other's first and last names? 20–25%

Are you a member of the American Academy of Adoption Attorneys and/or the National Council For Adoption? American Academy of Adoption Attorneys.

TERRI FINESMITH HORWICH

Bush-Joseph and Horwich
20 N. Wacker Dr. #3710, Chicago, IL 60606
(312) 541-1149 • Fax: (312) 629-5499
E-mail: tfhorwich@infertility-law.com

What are your office hours when you accept calls from adoptive parents? 9 a.m.–5 p.m., CT

Education: BA in psychology, University of Wisconsin, Madison, 1981; JD, Northwestern University, 1984

What states or countries do your adoptive parents come from? Primarily Illinois, but other states as well where birthparent resides in Illinois.

What states or countries do your birthparents/adopted children come from? Primarily Illinois, but other states and countries as well.

Are other attorneys in your law firm active in adoption? Yes. (Firm practices only adoption and infertility law.)

In what year did you begin legal work in adoptions? 1993

About how many children have you placed since you started? Provided legal services for 150.

About what percent of your work is devoted to adoption? 60%

In 1998, what was the average time from when a prospective adoptive parent retained you to the placement of a child? 9 mos.

What made you decide to work in the adoption field? The hope that I could help others experience the joy I found when I adopted my son, but with less uncertainty and more support in the process.

Do you have any criteria for adoptive parents, such as age, number of children in the home, etc., and if so, what are they? Willingness to comply with applicable laws and procedures.

What percent of your adoptions are infants under 6 mos.? 80%

Do you have a waiting list of prospective parents? No.

Is it all right if adopting parents are on waiting lists of other attorneys or agencies? Yes.

Do you charge adoptive parents for a first phone consultation? No.

Do you charge adoptive parents for a first office consultation, and if yes, what is the fee? Yes. Fee charged if client seeking specific legal advice rather than overview or interviewing firm. Up to $175.

Do you charge a retainer fee, and if yes, what is it and when is it payable? Yes. $1,000 when firm retained to handle adoption. This is a deposit toward fees, not separate fee.

What are your legal fees, not including retainer, and when are they payable? $140–175/hour, payable monthly after retainer applied.

Will adoptive parents pay a separate attorney for the birthmother? Not usually.

What are the approximate fees for medical and hospital expenses for the birthmother and baby, when they have no insurance? $3,000–7,000.

What are the approximate homestudy fees in your state? $1,200–2,500

If living expenses for a birthmother are allowed, what is the average amount paid? $0–5,000

Are you an adoptive parent, adopted person, or birthparent? Adoptive parent.

In how many of your cases has an adoptive parent lost a placed child due to a birthparent challenge? 2

Have you lost any adoption litigation filed against you by an adoptive parent or birthparent? No.

In about what percentage of your adoptions do adopting parents and birthparents know each other's first and last names? 10%

Are you a member of the American Academy of Adoption Attorneys and/or the National Council for Adoption? American Academy of Adoption Attorneys.

H. JOSEPH GITLIN

Gitlin & Gitlin
111 Dean St., Woodstock, IL 60098
(815) 338-0021 • Fax: (815) 338-0544
www.Gitlin.com

What are your office hours when you accept calls from adoptive parents? 8:15 a.m.–4:15 p.m., CT

Education: Undergrad, Depaul University, Chicago; Depaul University Law School, 1959

What states or countries do your adoptive parents come from? United States.

Are other attorneys in your law firm active in adoption? Yes.

In what year did you begin legal work in adoptions? 1960

How many nonrelative adoptions did you arrange in 1998? I do not arrange adoptions. I represent petitioners in adoption proceedings.

About how many children have you placed since you started? I do not place children.

About what percent of your work is devoted to adoption? 10%

What made you decide to work in the adoption field? It is part of family law practice.

Do you have any criteria for adoptive parents, such as age, number of children in the home, etc., and if so, what are they? No.

What percent of your adoptions are infants under 6 mos.? Most.

Do you have a waiting list of prospective parents? Yes.

Is it all right if adopting parents are on waiting lists of other attorneys or agencies? Yes.

Do you charge adoptive parents for a first phone consultation? No.

Do you charge adoptive parents for a first office consultation, and if yes, what is the fee? Yes. Minimum consult fee is $150.

Do you charge a retainer fee, and if yes, what is it and when is it payable? Yes. Varies from case to case, depending on complexity. It is payable before any work is done on the case.

What are your legal fees, not including retainer, and when are they payable? Hourly basis. Depends on lawyer in firm doing the work. Retainer is credit against services.

Will adoptive parents pay a separate attorney for the birthmother? No.

What are the approximate fees for medical and hospital expenses for the birthmother and baby, when they have no insurance? Variable, depending on hospital, physician, etc.

What are the approximate homestudy fees in your state? Varies from county to county.

If living expenses for a birthmother are allowed, what is the average amount paid? Too variable to state average.

In how many of your cases has an adoptive parent lost a placed child due to a birthparent challenge? None except in those cases where I represented the birthparent who was challenging the adoption.

Have you lost any adoption litigation filed against you by an adoptive parent or birthparent? No.

In about what percentage of your adoptions do adopting parents and birthparents know each other's first and last names? Some but rarely.

Are you a member of the American Academy of Adoption Attorneys and/or the National Council for Adoption? American Academy of Adoption Attorneys.

SUSAN F. GRAMMER

P.O. Box 111, Bethalto, IL 62010
(618) 259-2113 • Fax: (618) 259-2111
E-mail: gfglaw1@aol.com

What are your office hours when you accept calls from adoptive parents?
9 a.m.–6 p.m., CT

Education: BS, University of Illinois, 1972; MS in communicative disorders, Northwestern University, 1973; JD, Washington University School of Law, 1982

What states or countries do your adoptive parents come from? United States.

What states or countries do your birthparents/adopted children come from? United States.

Are other attorneys in your law firm active in adoption? N/A

In what year did you begin legal work in adoptions? 1983

How many nonrelative adoptions did you arrange in 1998? Several.

About how many children have you placed since you started? Many.

In 1998, what was the average time from when a prospective adoptive parent retained you to the placement of a child? 1 year

What made you decide to work in the adoption field? My brother adopted two children; many of my friends wanted to adopt.

Do you have any criteria for adoptive parents, such as age, number of children in the home, etc., and if so, what are they? No.

What percent of your adoptions are infants under 6 mos.? 100%

Do you have a waiting list of prospective parents? Yes.

Is it all right if adopting parents are on waiting lists of other attorneys or agencies? Yes.

Do you charge adoptive parents for a first phone consultation? No.

Do you charge adoptive parents for a first office consultation, and if yes, what is the fee? Yes. For a three-hour adoption counseling session, $400.

Do you charge a retainer fee, and if yes, what is it and when is it payable? Yes. $3,500 when birthmother is identified (then billed out at $125/hour plus costs).

What are your legal fees, not including retainer, and when are they payable? $125/hour plus costs.

Will adoptive parents pay a separate attorney for the birthmother, and if yes, what are approximate legal fees? Yes; $400.

What are the approximate fees for medical and hospital expenses for the birthmother and baby, when they have no insurance? $8,500 more or less.

What are the approximate homestudy fees in your state? $850, preplacement; $850, postplacement.

If living expenses for a birthmother are allowed, what is the average amount paid? Whatever court allows.

In how many of your cases has an adoptive parent lost a placed child due to a birth-parent challenge? 0

Have you lost any adoption litigation filed against you by an adoptive parent or birthparent? No.

In about what percentage of your adoptions do adopting parents and birthparents know each other's first and last names? 5%

Are you a member of the American Academy of Adoption Attorneys and/or the National Council for Adoption? American Academy of Adoption Attorneys.

JOHN C. HIRSCHFELD

Meyer, Capel, Hirschfeld, Muncy, Jahn and Aldeen, PC
P.O. Box 6750, Champaign, IL 61826-6750
(217) 352-1800 • Fax: (217) 352-1083

What are your office hours when you accept calls from adoptive parents? 24 hours per day at our 800 number, which is 1-800-265-4848.

Education: BA in history, University of Notre Dame, 1958; JD, University of Notre Dame Law School, 1961

What states or countries do your adoptive parents come from? All states and numerous countries.

What states or countries do your birthparents/adopted children come from? All states and numerous countries.

Are other attorneys in your law firm active in adoption? Yes.

In what year did you begin legal work in adoptions? 1961

How many nonrelative adoptions did you arrange in 1998? 100

About how many children have you placed since you started? Several thousand.

About what percent of your work is devoted to adoption? 40%

In 1998, what was the average time from when a prospective adoptive parent retained you to the placement of a child? Less than 2 years.

What made you decide to work in the adoption field? I had started my own law practice in 1961 and an agency asked me if I would represent them in an adoption matter. I have gone on from there.

What percent of your adoptions are infants under 6 mos.? 80%

Do you have a waiting list of prospective parents? Yes.

Is it all right if adopting parents are on waiting lists of other attorneys or agencies? Yes.

Do you charge adoptive parents for a first phone consultation? No.

Do you charge adoptive parents for a first office consultation? No.

Do you charge a retainer fee? No.

What are your legal fees, not including retainer, and when are they payable? These vary by the difficulty of the case.

Will adoptive parents pay a separate attorney for the birthmother, and if yes, what are approximate legal fees? Sometimes; $500.

What are the approximate fees for medical and hospital expenses for the birthmother and baby, when they have no insurance? $3,000

What are the approximate homestudy fees in your state? $1,500

If living expenses for a birthmother are allowed, what is the average amount paid? These vary from case to case.

If you manage international adoptions, what is the average fee for translating documents? Very low since I live in Champaign, Illinois and have translation facilities available at the University of Illinois.

In how many of your cases has an adoptive parent lost a placed child due to a birthparent challenge? 0

Have you lost any adoption litigation filed against you by an adoptive parent or birthparent? No.

In about what percentage of your adoptions do adopting parents and birthparents know each other's first and last names? 25%

Are you a member of the American Academy of Adoption Attorneys and/or the National Council for Adoption? American Academy of Adoption Attorneys (a founding member).

INDIANA

STEVEN M. KIRSH

Kirsh & Kirsh, PC
401 Pennsylvania Pkwy., Suite 370, Indianapolis, IN 46280
(317) 575-5555 • Fax: (317) 575-5631
E-mail: kirsh.adoption@worldnet.att.net • www.indianaadoption.com

What are your office hours when you accept calls from adoptive parents? 24 hours a day, 7 days a week.

Education: BA in history, Dartmouth College, 1976; JD, Indiana University of Law, 1979

What states or countries do your adoptive parents come from? Primarily the United States, but we also have a number of clients from Holland and Switzerland.

What states or countries do your birthparents/adopted children come from? United States.

Are other attorneys in your law firm active in adoption? Yes.

In what year did you begin legal work in adoptions? 1982

How many nonrelative adoptions did you arrange in 1998? 152

About how many children have you placed since you started? 2000+

About what percent of your work is devoted to adoption? 100%

In 1998, what was the average time from when a prospective adoptive parent retained you to the placement of a child? 1 year

What made you decide to work in the adoption field? The personal satisfaction that I receive from this work in knowing that everyone benefits from the process. The adoptive parents have a child that they could not otherwise have, the birthmother has a good solution to a difficult problem, and the baby receives a wonderful home and the opportunity for a bright future.

Do you have any criteria for adoptive parents, such as age, number of children in the home, etc., and if so, what are they? All adoptive parents with whom we work must have a homestudy prepared by a licensed, child-placing agency. The specifics, such as their age, number of children, etc., is determined more by the requests of the birthparents than by any artificial requirements of our firm.

What percent of your adoptions are infants under 6 mos.? 100%

Do you have a waiting list of prospective parents? Yes.

Is it all right if adopting parents are on waiting lists of other attorneys or agencies? Yes.

Do you charge adoptive parents for a first phone consultation? No.

Do you charge adoptive parents for a first office consultation? No.

Do you charge a retainer fee, and if yes, what is it and when is it payable? Yes. $750 payable whenever the prospective adoptive parents decide to retain our services.

What are your legal fees, not including retainer, and when are they payable? Our fees range from $2,750 to $7,250, depending on the case. In general, our fees are not payable until the time of placement.

Will adoptive parents pay a separate attorney for the birthmother, and if yes, what are approximate legal fees? Not generally. When a fee is charged, it is usually between $500 and $1,500.

What are the approximate fees for medical and hospital expenses for the birthmother and baby, when they have no insurance? $7,000

What are the approximate homestudy fees in your state? $1,500

If living expenses for a birthmother are allowed, what is the average amount paid? It is very hard to estimate. Each case is different.

In how many of your cases has an adoptive parent lost a placed child due to a birthparent challenge? None.

Have you lost any adoption litigation filed against you by an adoptive parent or birthparent? No.

In about what percentage of your adoptions do adopting parents and birthparents know each other's first and last names? Less than 5%.

Are you a member of the American Academy of Adoption Attorneys and/or the National Council for Adoption? American Academy of Adoption Attorneys and National Council for Adoption.

IOWA

LORI L. KLOCKAU

Bray and Klockau
402 S. Linn, Iowa City, IA 52240
(319) 338-7968 • Fax: (319) 354-4871

What are your office hours when you accept calls from adoptive parents?
8 a.m.–5 p.m., CT

Education: BS, University of Iowa, 1980; MA, University of Iowa, 1982; JD, University of Iowa, 1991

What states or countries do your adoptive parents come from? All over the United States, Norway, Sweden, England.

What states or countries do your birthparents/adopted children come from? Iowa.

Are other attorneys in your law firm active in adoption? No.

In what year did you begin legal work in adoptions? 1991

How many nonrelative adoptions did you arrange in 1998? 21

About how many children have you placed since you started? 150+

About what percent of your work is devoted to adoption? 50%

In 1998, what was the average time from when a prospective adoptive parent retained you to the placement of a child? Variable. Some years the waiting time is short, sometimes it is longer.

What made you decide to work in the adoption field? I believe it is the most important thing that I can do with a law degree.

Do you have any criteria for adoptive parents, such as age, number of children in the home, etc., and if so, what are they? They must have a current homestudy, but I have no constraints because of age, number of children in the home, etc.

What percent of your adoptions are infants under 6 mos.? 98%

Do you have a waiting list of prospective parents? Yes.

Is it all right if adopting parents are on waiting lists of other attorneys or agencies? Yes.

Do you charge adoptive parents for a first phone consultation, and if yes, what is the fee? Yes; $100.

Do you charge adoptive parents for a first office consultation, and if yes, what is the fee? Yes; $100.

Do you charge a retainer fee, and if yes, what is it and when is it payable? Yes. The retainer varies due to case circumstances, whether the case involves an interstate placement or whether the case may be contested. Retainers are usually $4,000–5,000. I ask for a retainer when the placement is imminent and likely to occur.

What are your legal fees, not including retainer, and when are they payable? Legal fees are paid from the retainer.

Will adoptive parents pay a separate attorney for the birthmother, and if yes, what are approximate legal fees? In some cases, but not usually. Total legal fees including court costs, other costs are usually $5,000–7,500.

What are the approximate fees for medical and hospital expenses for the birthmother and baby, when they have no insurance? $4,000–10,000

What are the approximate homestudy fees in your state? $500–1,200

If living expenses for a birthmother are allowed, what is the average amount paid? This also varies from a few hundred dollars to several thousand. Often no expenses are paid at all.

If you manage international adoptions, what is the average fee for translating documents? $300–1,000

In how many of your cases has an adoptive parent lost a placed child due to a birthparent challenge? 1

Have you lost any adoption litigation filed against you by an adoptive parent or birthparent? No.

In about what percentage of your adoptions do adopting parents and birthparents know each other's first and last names? 25%

Are you a member of the American Academy of Adoption Attorneys and/or the National Council for Adoption? American Academy of Adoption Attorneys and National Council for Adoption.

Is there anything I have not asked you that is important? In my state (and most others) adoptive parents find out medical and social background of birthparents. They need to be aware that independent placement is not legal in all states, so they need to find out before working with some placements if it is legal. Most importantly, there are only certain things which can be paid for on behalf of a birthmother in this state.

ROSS S. RANDALL

Randall, Griffin, Nelson and Hawbaker, PLC
P.O. Box 120, Waterloo, IA 50704-1020
(319) 291-6161 • Fax: (319) 291-6193
E-mail: randall@rgnh.com

What are your office hours when you accept calls from adoptive parents?
8 a.m.–5 p.m., CT

Education: BA in political science, 1965; JD, Drake University Law School, 1968

What states or countries do your adoptive parents come from? Continental United States, Europe, and Israel.

What states or countries do your birthparents/adopted children come from? Primarily the continental United States.

Are other attorneys in your law firm active in adoption? Yes.

In what year did you begin legal work in adoptions? 1968

How many nonrelative adoptions did you arrange in 1998? 12

About how many children have you placed since you started? Over 200

About what percent of your work is devoted to adoption? 20%

In 1998, what was the average time from when a prospective adoptive parent retained you to the placement of a child? Variable.

What made you decide to work in the adoption field? My wife and I always planned to adopt one or two children in addition to having our own family. After we married we found we were unable to conceive a child and proceeded to adopt. Our children consist of two children born in the United States, two born in Vietnam and one born in Peru.

Do you have any criteria for adoptive parents, such as age, number of children in the home, etc., and if so, what are they? My criteria are that the prospective adoptive parents have a stable marriage and relationship and will be loving, patient, and caring parents of any child they are fortunate enough to adopt.

What percent of your adoptions are infants under 6 mos.? 95%

Do you have a waiting list of prospective parents? Yes.

Is it all right if adopting parents are on waiting lists of other attorneys or agencies? Yes.

Do you charge adoptive parents for a first phone consultation? No.

Do you charge adoptive parents for a first office consultation? No.

Do you charge a retainer fee, and if yes, what is it and when is it payable? Yes. $3,000 is deposited in my firm's trust account prior to the initiation of a petition for termination of parental rights or the birth of the child.

What are your legal fees, not including retainer, and when are they payable? $150/hour deducted from trust account based on hours devoted to case.

Will adoptive parents pay a separate attorney for the birthmother, and if yes, what are approximate legal fees? Yes. Birthparents are advised that I represent the adoptive couple and they should seek their own legal representation. This is rare, but when it occurs, it is approximately $250 for the attorney to represent each birthparent.

What are the approximate fees for medical and hospital expenses for the birthmother and baby, when they have no insurance? $5,000–12,000

What are the approximate homestudy fees in your state? $350

If living expenses for a birthmother are allowed, what is the average amount paid?
$500

Are you an adoptive parent, adopted person, or birthparent? Adoptive parent.

In how many of your cases has an adoptive parent lost a placed child due to a birthparent challenge? 2

Have you lost any adoption litigation filed against you by an adoptive parent or birthparent? No.

In about what percentage of your adoptions do adopting parents and birthparents know each other's first and last names? 50%

Are you a member of the American Academy of Adoption Attorneys and/or the National Council for Adoption? American Academy of Adoption Attorneys.

KANSAS

JILL BREMYER-ARCHER

Bremyer & Wise, PA
P.O. Box 1146, McPherson, KS 67460
(316) 241-0554 • Fax: (316) 241-7692
E-mail: jbarcher@bwisecounsel.com

What are your office hours when you accept calls from adoptive parents?
8 a.m.–5:30 p.m., CT

Education: BS in family and child development, Kansas State, 1973; MS in family and child development, Kansas State, 1974; JD, Washburn University Law School, 1979

What states or countries do your adoptive parents come from? United States.

What states or countries do your birthparents/adopted children come from? United States.

Are other attorneys in your law firm active in adoption? No.

In what year did you begin legal work in adoptions? 1984

How many nonrelative adoptions did you arrange in 1998? 6

About how many children have you placed since you started? 110

About what percent of your work is devoted to adoption? 10%

What made you decide to work in the adoption field? I have a background in family and child development and our law firm has a long history of handling adoptions.

Do you have any criteria for adoptive parents, such as age, number of children in the home, etc., and if so, what are they? The only criteria for adoptive parents is that a clinically licensed social worker has approved them for adoption through a home assessment.

What percent of your adoptions are infants under 6 mos.? 80%

Do you have a waiting list of prospective parents? Yes.

Is it all right if adopting parents are on waiting lists of other attorneys or agencies? Yes.

Do you charge adoptive parents for a first phone consultation? No.

Do you charge adoptive parents for a first office consultation? No.

Do you charge a retainer fee, and if yes, what is it and when is it payable? Yes. Fee varies. Payable at the time a birthmother makes a commitment to adoptive couple.

What are your legal fees, not including retainer, and when are they payable? On a case-by-case basis.

Will adoptive parents pay a separate attorney for the birthmother? No, unless the birthmother is a minor or unless the birthmother has requested to have her own attorney.

What are the approximate fees for medical and hospital expenses for the birthmother and baby, when they have no insurance? Varies.

What are the approximate homestudy fees in your state? Varies.

If living expenses for a birthmother are allowed, what is the average amount paid? Varies.

In how many of your cases has an adoptive parent lost a placed child due to a birthparent challenge? 0

Have you lost any adoption litigation filed against you by an adoptive parent or birthparent? No.

In about what percentage of your adoptions do adopting parents and birthparents know each other's first and last names? 30%

Are you a member of the American Academy of Adoption Attorneys and/or the National Council for Adoption? American Academy of Adoption Attorneys.

ALLAN A. HAZLETT

Hazlett Law Offices
1608 SW Mulvane St., Topeka, KS 66604-2746
(785) 232-2011 • Fax: (785) 232-5214
E-mail: ksadoptlaw@aol.com • www.lawyers.com/adoptionlaw

What are your office hours when you accept calls from adoptive parents? 8 a.m.–5 p.m., CT

Education: Undergraduate degree in accounting, University of Kansas, 1965; JD, University of Kansas School of Law, 1967

What states or countries do your adoptive parents come from? I have clients all over the United States. Additionally, I have clients in the United Kingdom, Poland and Germany.

What states or countries do your birthparents/adopted children come from? I work with domestic adoptions at this time. I work with birthparents from all states.

Are other attorneys in your law firm active in adoption? No. I am a solo practitioner.

In what year did you begin legal work in adoptions? 1987

How many nonrelative adoptions did you arrange in 1998? 38

About how many children have you placed since you started? 300+

About what percent of your work is devoted to adoption? 100%

In 1998, what was the average time from when a prospective adoptive parent retained you to the placement of a child? Less than one year, usually around 4–6 mos.

What made you decide to work in the adoption field? I started doing adoptions when a birthmother walked in my door and wanted to place her child for adoption. That led to doing several more, and I enjoyed working with birthparents and adoptive couples. After several years of doing adoptions, I decided to accept only adoption cases.

Do you have any criteria for adoptive parents, such as age, number of children in the home, etc.? We have no specific restrictions, other than they must have an approved homestudy.

What percent of your adoptions are infants under 6 mos.? 98%

Do you have a waiting list of prospective parents? No.

Is it all right if adopting parents are on waiting lists of other attorneys or agencies? Yes. I encourage all my clients to diligently search all options to find birthparents.

Do you charge adoptive parents for a first phone consultation? No.

Do you charge adoptive parents for a first office consultation? No.

Do you charge a retainer fee, and if yes, what is it and when is it payable? Yes. I charge a $500 retainer only when the couple actively starts to use my services to search for a birthmother and I participate in that search.

What are your legal fees, not including retainer, and when are they payable? My legal fees vary depending on the work involved. Each case is different.

Will adoptive parents pay a separate attorney for the birthmother? No. If the adoption is done in Kansas, only a minor birthmother must have separate counsel.

What are the approximate fees for medical and hospital expenses for the birthmother and baby, when they have no insurance? $7,000–8,000.

What are the approximate homestudy fees in your state? Generally $250–1,200.

If living expenses for a birthmother are allowed, what is the average amount paid? $500–1,000 a month.

Are you an adoptive parent, adopted person, or birthparent? Adopted person.

In how many of your cases has an adoptive parent lost a placed child due to a birthparent challenge? None.

Have you lost any adoption litigation filed against you by an adoptive parent or birthparent? No.

In about what percentage of your adoptions do adopting parents and birthparents know each other's first and last names? They all know at least first names. We leave it up to them how much further the relationship will go.

Are you a member of the American Academy of Adoption Attorneys and/or the National Council for Adoption? American Academy of Adoption Attorneys.

KENTUCKY

ELISABETH GOLDMAN

118 Old Lafayette Ave., Lexington, KY 40502
(606) 252-2325 • Fax: (606) 252-2325
E-mail: elliegold@aol.com

What are your office hours when you accept calls from adoptive parents?
9 a.m.–5 p.m., ET

Education: BA in economics, Queens College, 1964; JD, University of Kentucky College of Law, 1975

What states or countries do your adoptive parents come from? United States.

What states or countries do your birthparents/adopted children come from? United States.

Are other attorneys in your law firm active in adoption? No.

In what year did you begin legal work in adoptions? 1978

How many nonrelative adoptions did you arrange in 1998? 10+

About how many children have you placed since you started? 200+

About what percent of your work is devoted to adoption? 100%

Do you have any criteria for adoptive parents, such as age, number of children in the home, etc.? No.

What percent of your adoptions are infants under 6 mos.? All.

Is it all right if adopting parents are on waiting lists of other attorneys or agencies? Yes.

Do you charge adoptive parents for a first phone consultation? No.

Do you charge adoptive parents for a first office consultation, and if yes, what is the fee? Yes; minimum $150.

Do you charge a retainer fee? No further fees until after birthmother makes a selection.

What are your legal fees, not including retainer, and when are they payable?
$150/hour, payable when estimate is presented.

Will adoptive parents pay a separate attorney for the birthmother, and if yes, what are approximate legal fees? Yes; $3,000–4,000.

What are the approximate fees for medical and hospital expenses for the birth-mother and baby, when they have no insurance? $7,500

What are the approximate homestudy fees in your state? Free by state agency.

If living expenses for a birthmother are allowed, what is the average amount paid? $1,000/month

In how many of your cases has an adoptive parent lost a placed child due to a birth-parent challenge? 0

Have you lost any adoption litigation filed against you by an adoptive parent or birthparent? No.

In about what percentage of your adoptions do adopting parents and birthparents know each other's first and last names? 50%

Are you a member of the American Academy of Adoption Attorneys and/or the National Council for Adoption? American Academy of Adoption Attorneys.

MASSACHUSETTS

KAREN K. GREENBERG

Konowitz and Greenberg
110 Cedar St., Suite 250, Wellesley Hills, MA 02481
(781) 237-0033 • Fax: (781) 235-2755

What are your office hours when you accept calls from adoptive parents? 9 a.m.–5:30 p.m., ET

Education: BS in education (Dean's and President's List), Boston University, 1972; MS in education, Wheelock College, 1979; JD, Suffolk Law School, 1983

What states or countries do your adoptive parents come from? Mostly Massachusetts, occasionally out of state.

What states or countries do your birthparents/adopted children come from? All states, Russia, China, Vietnam, South America, Columbia.

Are other attorneys in your law firm active in adoption? No.

In what year did you begin legal work in adoptions? 1983

How many nonrelative adoptions did you arrange in 1998? Massachusetts is an agency state, and attorneys may not arrange adoptions. I represent many birthparents, adoptive families, single adoptive parents, and two agencies.

About how many children have you placed since you started? See previous response.

About what percent of your work is devoted to adoption? 65%

In 1998, what was the average time from when a prospective adoptive parent retained you to the placement of a child? 9 mos. or less

What made you decide to work in the adoption field? I have two children I adopted myself.

Do you have any criteria for adoptive parents, such as age, number of children in the home, etc.? No.

What percent of your adoptions are infants under 6 mos.? 99%

Is it all right if adopting parents are on waiting lists of other attorneys or agencies?
Yes.

Do you charge adoptive parents for a first phone consultation, and if yes, what is the fee? It will depend on the length of the call and depth of information. $175 an hour; 10-minute minimum.

Do you charge adoptive parents for a first office consultation, and if yes, what is the fee? Yes; $175 per hour.

Do you charge a retainer fee, and if yes, what is it and when is it payable? It depends on the situation. $750 and up—varies.

What are your legal fees, not including retainer, and when are they payable? Finalization, $850; termination of birthparent rights, $600; all other services are at my hourly rate. Payment varies.

Will adoptive parents pay a separate attorney for the birthmother, and if yes, what are approximate legal fees? Yes. Varies.

What are the approximate fees for medical and hospital expenses for the birthmother and baby, when they have no insurance? $3,600

What are the approximate homestudy fees in your state? $2,500

If living expenses for a birthmother are allowed, what is the average amount paid?
Massachusetts allows living expenses for lodging, food, clothing, and utilities, not to exceed $980 a month, not for more than six months during pregnancy, and six weeks after the child is born.

If you manage international adoptions, what is the average fee for translating documents? Varies.

Are you an adoptive parent, adopted person, or birthparent? Adoptive parent.

In how many of your cases has an adoptive parent lost a placed child due to a birthparent challenge? 1%

Have you lost any adoption litigation filed against you by an adoptive parent or birthparent? No.

In about what percentage of your adoptions do adopting parents and birthparents know each other's first and last names? 40%

Are you a member of the American Academy of Adoption Attorneys and/or the National Council for Adoption? American Academy of Adoption Attorneys.

PAULA MACKIN, ESQ.

Law Offices of Paula Mackin
233 Needham St., 5th Fl., Newton, MA 02464
(617) 332-0781 • Fax: (617) 244-6511
E-mail: mackinb@aol.com

What are your office hours when you accept calls from adoptive parents?
9 a.m.–5 p.m., ET; voicemail 24 hours a day.

Education: BS in languages (Spanish, French, and Portuguese), Georgetown University, 1971; JD, George Washington University, 1974

What states or countries do your adoptive parents come from? Primarily Massachusetts.

What states or countries do your birthparents/adopted children come from? All states, many foreign countries.

Are other attorneys in your law firm active in adoption? Yes.

In what year did you begin legal work in adoptions? 1975. (1991, became exclusively adoptions.)

How many nonrelative adoptions did you arrange in 1998? Approximately 100 in Massachusetts, only agencies may facilitate adoptions. I represent adopters and pre-adoptive parents with issues with agencies, birthparents, etc.

About what percent of your work is devoted to adoption? 95%

In 1998, what was the average time from when a prospective adoptive parent retained you to the placement of a child? Varied.

What made you decide to work in the adoption field? I have devoted my practice to children's issues since 1975 and am an adoptive parent of two.

Do you have any criteria for adoptive parents, such as age, number of children in the home, etc.? No.

What percent of your adoptions are infants under 6 mos.? 85%+

Do you have a waiting list of prospective parents? No.

Is it all right if adopting parents are on waiting lists of other attorneys or agencies? Yes.

Do you charge adoptive parents for a first phone consultation? No.

Do you charge adoptive parents for a first office consultation, and if yes, what is the fee? Yes. $175 per hour but reduced rate for the first-time adoptions and public-sector adoptions.

Do you charge a retainer fee? Depends/varies.

What are your legal fees, not including retainer, and when are they payable? Within 30 days of invoice.

Will adoptive parents pay a separate attorney for the birthmother, and if yes, what are approximate legal fees? Yes. Varies.

What are the approximate fees for medical and hospital expenses for the birthmother and baby, when they have no insurance? Varies.

What are the approximate homestudy fees in your state? $875–3,000

If living expenses for a birthmother are allowed, what is the average amount paid? Varies. Payments to Massachusetts birthmothers are controlled by regulations.

If you manage international adoptions, what is the average fee for translating documents? Varies.

Are you an adoptive parent, adopted person, or birthparent? Adoptive parent.

In how many of your cases has an adoptive parent lost a placed child due to a birthparent challenge? 1; Several dozen threatened, however.

Have you lost any adoption litigation filed against you by an adoptive parent or birthparent? No.

In about what percentage of your adoptions do adopting parents and birthparents know each other's first and last names? Approximately 30%

Are you a member of the American Academy of Adoption Attorneys and/or the National Council for Adoption? American Academy of Adoption Attorneys.

MARYLAND

NATALIE H. REES

The Law Offices of Natalie H. Rees, PA
The Mercantile Towson Bldg., 409 Washington Ave., Suite 920
Baltimore, MD 21204-4905
(410) 494-8080 • Fax: (410) 494-8082

What are your office hours when you accept calls from adoptive parents?
8:30 a.m.–5:30 p.m., weekdays, ET

Education: BA, University of Maryland, 1972; MA, Johns Hopkins University, 1974; JD, University of Baltimore School of Law, 1977

What states or countries do your adoptive parents come from? Only Maryland.

What states or countries do your birthparents/adopted children come from? All states.

Are other attorneys in your law firm active in adoption? No. I am a solo practitioner.

In what year did you begin legal work in adoptions? 1978

How many nonrelative adoptions did you arrange in 1998? Attorneys in Maryland are not permitted to arrange adoptions. I handle approximately 25 independent adoptions per year, including stepmother adoptions arising out of surrogacy by artificial insemination arrangements.

About how many children have you placed since you started? Attorneys in Maryland are not permitted to place adoptions. In the past 21 years, I have handled over 1,000 adoptions (including surrogacy and donor egg procedures).

About what percent of your work is devoted to adoption? 60% (including surrogacy and donor egg procedures).

In 1998, what was the average time from when a prospective adoptive parent retained you to the placement of a child? 3–5 mos. to find a pregnant birthmother interested in placing for adoption, followed by the time left in the pregnancy.

What made you decide to work in the adoption field? Since I began practicing law in 1979, my entire practice has focused on children—custody, paternity, abuse and neglect, adoption, surrogacy, donor egg, etc.

Do you have any criteria for adoptive parents, such as age, number of children in the home, etc.? None. I work with singles or couples of any age, race, gender, sexual orientation, nationality, etc.

What percent of your adoptions are infants under 6 mos.? 100%

Do you have a waiting list of prospective parents? No.

Is it all right if adopting parents are on waiting lists of other attorneys or agencies? Yes.

Do you charge adoptive parents for a first phone consultation? I do not do phone consultation. Prospective adoptive parents must come to my office for a three-hour consultation.

Do you charge adoptive parents for a first office consultation, and if yes, what is the fee? Yes. A fee of $425 is charged for a three-hour consultation, a letter summarizing the initial consultation, and unlimited assistance during the search period.

Do you charge a retainer fee, and if yes, what is it and when is it payable? Yes. I bill out my time at $200/hour. The initial retainer fee of $4,000 for twenty hours of work is payable in advance. Most adoptions do not exceed the $4,000 retainer.

What are your legal fees, not including retainer, and when are they payable? See previous answer.

Will adoptive parents pay a separate attorney for the birthmother, and if yes, what are approximate legal fees? Yes. It depends on the jurisdiction where the birthmother is located.

What are the approximate fees for medical and hospital expenses for the birthmother and baby, when they have no insurance? $4,000–5,000

What are the approximate homestudy fees in your state? $1,000–1,500, but a homestudy is not required for in-state placements.

If living expenses for a birthmother are allowed, what is the average amount paid? Not allowed in Maryland.

In how many of your cases has an adoptive parent lost a placed child due to a birthparent challenge? In over 1,000 adoptions, only five fall-throughs have occurred after the placement was made.

Have you lost any adoption litigation filed against you by an adoptive parent or birthparent? No.

In about what percentage of your adoptions do adopting parents and birthparents know each other's first and last names? Almost all.

Are you a member of the American Academy of Adoption Attorneys and/or the National Council for Adoption? American Academy of Adoption Attorneys.

LESLIE SCHERR

Pasternak and Fidis, PC
7735 Old Georgetown Rd., #1100, Bethesda, MD 20814-6130
(301) 656-8850 • Fax: (301) 656-3053
E-mail: ls@pasternakfidis.com

What are your office hours when you accept calls from adoptive parents?
9 a.m.–5 p.m., ET

Education: BA, Queens College, NW; LLB, Columbia University, School of Law

What states or countries do your adoptive parents come from? All over the United States, Italy, France.

What states or countries do your birthparents/adopted children come from? All over the United States, China, Russia, Romania, Vietnam, Nepal.

Are other attorneys in your law firm active in adoption? Yes.

In what year did you begin legal work in adoptions? 1968

How many nonrelative adoptions did you arrange in 1998? Arranged none.

About how many children have you placed since you started? Placed none.

About what percent of your work is devoted to adoption? 60%

In 1998, what was the average time from when a prospective adoptive parent retained you to the placement of a child? 8 mos.

What made you decide to work in the adoption field? We have adopted two children (now no longer children).

Do you have any criteria for adoptive parents, such as age, number of children in the home, etc., and if so, what are they? No.

What percent of your adoptions are infants under 6 mos.? 98% of domestic; some foreign.

Do you have a waiting list of prospective parents? Yes.

Is it all right if adopting parents are on waiting lists of other attorneys or agencies? Yes.

Do you charge adoptive parents for a first phone consultation? No.

Do you charge adoptive parents for a first office consultation, and if yes, what is the fee? Yes; $300 per hour.

Do you charge a retainer fee, and if yes, what is it and when is it payable? Yes. Depends on whether it is a routine adoption case ($1,000) or a contested case ($5,000+).

What are your legal fees, not including retainer, and when are they payable? $300/hour, [billed] monthly.

Will adoptive parents pay a separate attorney for the birthmother, and if yes, what are approximate legal fees? Yes; $300–500.

What are the approximate fees for medical and hospital expenses for the birth-mother and baby, when they have no insurance? $7,000–15,000

What are the approximate homestudy fees in your state? $1,350

If living expenses for a birthmother are allowed, what is the average amount paid? Not allowed in Maryland.

Are you an adoptive parent, adopted person, or birthparent? Adoptive parent.

In how many of your cases has an adoptive parent lost a placed child due to a birth-parent challenge? One out of approximately 45 cases.

Have you lost any adoption litigation filed against you by an adoptive parent or birthparent? No.

In about what percentage of your adoptions do adopting parents and birthparents know each other's first and last names? 90%

Are you a member of the American Academy of Adoption Attorneys and/or the National Council for Adoption? American Academy of Adoption Attorneys.

CAROLYN H. THALER

29 W. Susquehanna Ave., Suite 205, Towson, MD 21204
(410) 828-6627 • Fax: (410) 296-3719

What are your office hours when you accept calls from adoptive parents?
9 a.m.–5 p.m., ET, Monday–Friday.

Education: BA, University of Maryland; JD, University of Baltimore, 1974

What states or countries do your adoptive parents come from? All over the United States and Europe.

What states or countries do your birthparents/adopted children come from? Throughout the United States.

Are other attorneys in your law firm active in adoption? Yes.

In what year did you begin legal work in adoptions? 1983

How many nonrelative adoptions did you arrange in 1998? Maryland statute prohibits attorneys arranging adoptions.

About how many children have you placed since you started? I have been involved with hundreds of adoption cases.

About what percent of your work is devoted to adoption? 80%

In 1998, what was the average time from when a prospective adoptive parent retained you to the placement of a child? 6 mos.–1 year

What made you decide to work in the adoption field? I adopted two children through the independent adoption method. They are now aged 14 and 15 and we have had a wonderful adoption experience.

Do you have any criteria for adoptive parents, such as age, number of children in the home, etc.? No.

What percent of your adoptions are infants under 6 mos.? 99%

Do you have a waiting list of prospective parents? No.

Is it all right if adopting parents are on waiting lists of other attorneys or agencies? Yes.

Do you charge adoptive parents for a first phone consultation? No.

Do you charge adoptive parents for a first office consultation, and if yes, what is the fee? Yes. It depends on the situation and the individual's ability to pay.

Do you charge a retainer fee, and if yes, what is it and when is it payable? Yes; $3,500.

What are your legal fees, not including retainer, and when are they payable? $180 per hour. Look at each situation on a case-by-case basis.

Will adoptive parents pay a separate attorney for the birthmother, and if yes, what are approximate legal fees? Yes; $2,500–3,000. In Maryland separate legal counsel.

What are the approximate fees for medical and hospital expenses for the birthmother and baby, when they have no insurance? $3,000–5,000

What are the approximate homestudy fees in your state? $1,200–1,800

If living expenses for a birthmother are allowed, what is the average amount paid? Not allowed.

Are you an adoptive parent, adopted person, or birthparent? Adoptive parent.

Have you lost any adoption litigation filed against you by an adoptive parent or birthparent? No.

In about what percentage of your adoptions do adopting parents and birthparents know each other's first and last names? 95%

Are you a member of the American Academy of Adoption Attorneys and/or the National Council for Adoption? American Academy of Adoption Attorneys.

Is there anything I have not asked you that is important? I would suggest that the adoptive parents take every opportunity to get to know the birthparents of the child. It is extremely helpful to the adoptive parents but mostly to the child.

MICHIGAN

HERBERT A. BRAIL

Keane and Keane
930 Mason, Dearborn, MI 48124
(313) 278-8775 • Fax: (313) 278-1767
E-mail: brail@provide.net

What are your office hours when you accept calls from adoptive parents?
9 a.m.–5 p.m., ET

Education: BA, Albino College, 1977; JD, Wayne State University Law School, 1981

What states or countries do your adoptive parents come from? I handle cases in Michigan and interstate.

What states or countries do your birthparents/adopted children come from? Primarily Michigan, also interstate as indicated above.

Are other attorneys in your law firm active in adoption? No.

In what year did you begin legal work in adoptions? 1989

How many nonrelative adoptions did you arrange in 1998? 15

About how many children have you placed since you started? Approximately 200 cases. I do not place. The birthparent places the child.

About what percent of your work is devoted to adoption? 50%

In 1998, what was the average time from when a prospective adoptive parent retained you to the placement of a child? 4–5 mos.

What made you decide to work in the adoption field? Personal and professional motivation.

Do you have any criteria for adoptive parents, such as age, number of children in the home, etc., and if so, what are they? Must have approved homestudy.

What percent of your adoptions are infants under 6 mos.? 80%

Do you have a waiting list of prospective parents? No.

Is it all right if adopting parents are on waiting lists of other attorneys or agencies? Yes.

Do you charge adoptive parents for a first phone consultation? No.

Do you charge adoptive parents for a first office consultation, and if yes, what is the fee? Yes; $125 per hour.

Do you charge a retainer fee, and if yes, what is it and when is it payable? Yes. $2,500 if unrelated, $1,500 if relative of a birthparent, payable at first meeting.

What are your legal fees, not including retainer, and when are they payable? Above.

Will adoptive parents pay a separate attorney for the birthmother, and if yes, what are approximate legal fees? Yes; $1,500–2,500.

What are the approximate fees for medical and hospital expenses for the birthmother and baby, when they have no insurance? Adoptive parents pay the actual costs, $8,000–10,000.

What are the approximate homestudy fees in your state? $950

If living expenses for a birthmother are allowed, what is the average amount paid? $2,000–3,000

Are you an adoptive parent, adopted person, or birthparent? Adoptive parent.

In how many of your cases has an adoptive parent lost a placed child due to a birthparent challenge? 10%

Have you lost any adoption litigation filed against you by an adoptive parent or birthparent? No. Adoption litigation never has happened.

In about what percentage of your adoptions do adopting parents and birthparents know each other's first and last names? 90%

Are you a member of the American Academy of Adoption Attorneys and/or the National Council for Adoption? American Academy of Adoption Attorneys.

Is there anything I have not asked you that is important? I am affiliated with an adoption agency, the Keane Center for Adoption.

MONICA FARRIS LINKNER

Adoption Law Center, PC
3250 Coolidge Hwy., Berkley, MI 48072
(248) 548-1588 • Fax: (248) 546-8858
E-mail: monica@adoptionlawcenterpc.com • www.adoptionlawcenterpc.com

What are your office hours when you accept calls from adoptive parents?
9 a.m.–5 p.m., ET

Education: BA in anthropology (Magna cum Laude, Phi Beta Kappa), Wayne State University, 1972; JD, Wayne State University, 1977; graduate credits in adoption studies, Southern Connecticut State University, 1992

What states or countries do your adoptive parents come from? Anywhere in the United States, but primarily from Michigan.

What states or countries do your birthparents/adopted children come from? Anywhere in the United States, but primarily from Michigan.

Are other attorneys in your law firm active in adoption? No.

In what year did you begin legal work in adoptions? 1993

How many nonrelative adoptions did you arrange in 1998? 42

About how many children have you placed since you started? 150

About what percent of your work is devoted to adoption? 95%

In 1998, what was the average time from when a prospective adoptive parent retained you to the placement of a child? 6–18 mos.

What made you decide to work in the adoption field? Personal experience as an adoptive parent and as an advocate for adoption law reform in Michigan.

Do you have any criteria for adoptive parents, such as age, number of children in the home, etc.? No, only that they be found suitable on homestudy.

What percent of your adoptions are infants under 6 mos.? 85%

Do you have a waiting list of prospective parents? It's not really a list, but a pool, from which a birthmother can select families she wants to consider as adoptive families for her child.

Is it all right if adopting parents are on waiting lists of other attorneys or agencies? Yes.

Do you charge adoptive parents for a first phone consultation, and if yes, what is the fee? No, if it's an inquiry call. If it's a full consult appointment, we charge $175 (standard hourly rate).

Do you charge adoptive parents for a first office consultation, and if yes, what is the fee? Yes; $175 (standard hourly rate).

Do you charge a retainer fee, and if yes, what is it and when is it payable? Yes. $1,000 if client not yet connected with birthmother; $2,500 if connected; payable when client retains us.

What are your legal fees, not including retainer, and when are they payable? $175 per hour, which we bill against retainer as work is performed; client is billed directly when retainer is used up and is expected to pay monthly bills; account must be current by time of finalization.

Will adoptive parents pay a separate attorney for the birthmother, and if yes, what are approximate legal fees? Yes. I do not represent birthparent(s) in same adoption in which I represent adoptive parents, so it would depend on what birthmother's attorney charges.

What are the approximate fees for medical and hospital expenses for the birthmother and baby, when they have no insurance? Variable. (Note: The vast majority of birthmothers we work with have either Medicaid or private insurance.)

What are the approximate homestudy fees in your state? $850–1,100 in southern half of state; higher in northern half.

If living expenses for a birthmother are allowed, what is the average amount paid? $3,000–5,000

Are you an adoptive parent, adopted person, or birthparent? Adoptive parent.

In how many of your cases has an adoptive parent lost a placed child due to a birthparent challenge? 6 (due to change of mind).

Have you lost any adoption litigation filed against you by an adoptive parent or birthparent? No. None has been filed.

In about what percentage of your adoptions do adopting parents and birthparents know each other's first and last names? 50%

Are you a member of the American Academy of Adoption Attorneys and/or the National Council for Adoption? American Academy of Adoption Attorneys.

MINNESOTA

GARY A. DEBELE

Walling and Berg, PA
Suite 1550, 121 South Eighth St., Minneapolis, MN 55402
(612) 340-1150 • Fax: (612) 340-1154
E-mail: gad@walling-berg.com

What are your office hours when you accept calls from adoptive parents?
8 a.m.–5 p.m., CT

Education: JD, University of Minnesota Law School, 1987

What states or countries do your adoptive parents come from? Any state and any country.

What states or countries do your birthparents/adopted children come from? Any state and any country.

Are other attorneys in your law firm active in adoption? Yes.

In what year did you begin legal work in adoptions? 1991

How many nonrelative adoptions did you arrange in 1998? In Minnesota, lawyers are prohibited from arranging adoptions or matching birthparents to adoptive parents. We are only allowed to do the legal work once the match has occurred.

About how many children have you placed since you started? See response to previous question.

About what percent of your work is devoted to adoption? 30–40%

In 1998, what was the average time from when a prospective adoptive parent retained you to the placement of a child? Varies significantly from case to case.

What made you decide to work in the adoption field? A desire to help people from all walks of life build loving and nurturing families for children, as well as interest in the legal issues involved in adoption.

Do you have any criteria for adoptive parents, such as age, number of children in the home, etc.? I have no restrictive criteria and am willing to consider legal representation in any adoption.

Do you charge adoptive parents for a first phone consultation, and if yes, what is the fee? Depends on the extent of the phone conversation; standard hourly rate of $165.

Do you charge adoptive parents for a first office consultation, and if yes, what is the fee? Standard hourly rate of $165.

Do you charge a retainer fee, and if yes, what is it and when is it payable? Yes. Depends on nature and complexity of the case.

What are your legal fees, not including retainer, and when are they payable? My hourly rate is $165 and we generally ask for a retainer ranging from $750 to $2,500 or more depending on the complexity of the case.

Will adoptive parents pay a separate attorney for the birthmother? Depends on the circumstances of the case.

What are the approximate fees for medical and hospital expenses for the birthmother and baby, when they have no insurance? This varies so significantly from case to case, I am unable to provide an approximate amount.

What are the approximate homestudy fees in your state? Ranges from $2,000 to more than $5,000.

If living expenses for a birthmother are allowed, what is the average amount paid?
This varies so significantly from case to case, I am unable to provide an approximate amount.

In how many of your cases has an adoptive parent lost a placed child due to a birthparent challenge? Do not have statistics.

Have you lost any adoption litigation filed against you by an adoptive parent or birthparent? Not relevant.

Are you a member of the American Academy of Adoption Attorneys and/or the National Council for Adoption? American Academy of Adoption Attorneys.

STEVEN L. GAWRON

Gawron and Associates, PA
2850 Metro Dr., Suite 429, Bloomington, MN 55425
(612) 854-4483 • Fax: (612) 854-2103
E-mail: sgawron@minnesotalawyer.com • www.minnesotalawyer.com

What are your office hours when you accept calls from adoptive parents?
8 a.m.–5 p.m., CT

Education: AA and AS, North Hennepin Community College, 1972; BS, University of Minnesota, 1974; JD, William Mitchell College of Law, 1980

What states or countries do your adoptive parents come from? All states.

What states or countries do your birthparents/adopted children come from?
Minnesota.

Are other attorneys in your law firm active in adoption? No.

In what year did you begin legal work in adoptions? 1984

How many nonrelative adoptions did you arrange in 1998? 30+

About how many children have you placed since you started? 300+

About what percent of your work is devoted to adoption? 20%

In 1998, what was the average time from when a prospective adoptive parent retained you to the placement of a child? 90 days

What made you decide to work in the adoption field? I have three adopted children.

Do you have any criteria for adoptive parents, such as age, number of children in the home, etc.? None.

What percent of your adoptions are infants under 6 mos.? 40%

Do you have a waiting list of prospective parents? No.

Is it all right if adopting parents are on waiting lists of other attorneys or agencies?
Yes.

Do you charge adoptive parents for a first phone consultation? No.

Do you charge adoptive parents for a first office consultation, and if yes, what is the fee? No, generally; if yes, varies.

Do you charge a retainer fee, and if yes, what is it and when is it payable? Yes. Varies based on complexity of issues. Payable at initiation of attorney-client relationship.

What are your legal fees, not including retainer, and when are they payable? Varies.

Will adoptive parents pay a separate attorney for the birthmother, and if yes, what are approximate legal fees? Yes; $500–1,000.

What are the approximate fees for medical and hospital expenses for the birthmother and baby, when they have no insurance? Varies.

What are the approximate homestudy fees in your state? $2,500–5,000

If living expenses for a birthmother are allowed, what is the average amount paid? Minimal.

If you manage international adoptions, what is the average fee for translating documents? Client generally retains translation services.

Are you an adoptive parent, adopted person, or birthparent? Adoptive parent.

In how many of your cases has an adoptive parent lost a placed child due to a birthparent challenge? 0

Have you lost any adoption litigation filed against you by an adoptive parent or birthparent? No.

In about what percentage of your adoptions do adopting parents and birthparents know each other's first and last names? 80%

Are you a member of the American Academy of Adoption Attorneys and/or the National Council for Adoption? American Academy of Adoption Attorneys.

Is there anything I have not asked you that is important? I am a founding member of the Minnesota Academy of Adoption Attorneys.

JODY OLLYVER DeSMIDT

Walling and Berg, PA
121 South 8th St. #1550, Minneapolis, MN 55042
(612) 335-4284 • Fax: (612) 340-1154
E-mail: jod@walling-berg.com

What are your office hours when you accept calls from adoptive parents?
9 a.m.–5:30 p.m., CT

Education: BA in political science, University of Minnesota, 1979; JD, William Mitchell College of Law, 1982

Are other attorneys in your law firm active in adoption? Yes.

In what year did you begin legal work in adoptions? 1986

How many nonrelative adoptions did you arrange in 1998? None. Minnesota law prohibits attorneys from arranging or placing children for adoption.

About how many children have you placed since you started? None. Minnesota law prohibits attorneys from arranging or placing children for adoption.

About what percent of your work is devoted to adoption? 75%

What made you decide to work in the adoption field? I find the work enjoyable and feel it to be very helpful to others.

Do you have any criteria for adoptive parents, such as age, number of children in the home, etc.? No.

Do you have a waiting list of prospective parents? No.

Is it all right if adopting parents are on waiting lists of other attorneys or agencies? Yes.

Do you charge adoptive parents for a first phone consultation? No.

Do you charge adoptive parents for a first office consultation, and if yes, what is the fee? Yes; $95 for an initial consultation.

Do you charge a retainer fee, and if yes, what is it and when is it payable? Yes. The retainer depends on the type of adoption but varies from $750 to $3,500, payable when work begins.

What are your legal fees, not including retainer, and when are they payable? The retainer is an estimate of the legal fees. However, fees are billed on an hourly basis.

Will adoptive parents pay a separate attorney for the birthmother, and if yes, what are approximate legal fees? Yes; $1,500–2,000.

What are the approximate fees for medical and hospital expenses for the birthmother and baby, when they have no insurance? $4,000–6,000 for uncomplicated delivery.

What are the approximate homestudy fees in your state? $2,200–5,500

If living expenses for a birthmother are allowed, what is the average amount paid? $1,500

Have you lost any adoption litigation filed against you by an adoptive parent or birthparent? No.

In about what percentage of your adoptions do adopting parents and birthparents know each other's first and last names? 80%

Are you a member of the American Academy of Adoption Attorneys and/or the National Council for Adoption? American Academy of Adoption Attorneys.

JUDITH D. VINCENT

Vincent Law Office
111 Third Ave. South, Suite 240, Minneapolis, MN 55401
(612) 332-7772 • Fax: (612) 332-1839
E-mail: vinc009@tc.umn.edu

What are your office hours when you accept calls from adoptive parents?
8 a.m.–5 p.m., CT

Education: BA, State University of New York at Buffalo, 1965; JD, University of Minnesota, 1978

What states or countries do your adoptive parents come from? All states and European countries.

What states or countries do your birthparents/adopted children come from? All states.

In what year did you begin legal work in adoptions? 1978

How many nonrelative adoptions did you arrange in 1998? Minnesota law does not allow attorneys to arrange adoptions.

About how many children have you placed since you started? Minnesota law does not allow attorneys to place children for adoption.

About what percent of your work is devoted to adoption? 99%

What made you decide to work in the adoption field? I am an adoptive mother and grandmother. I absolutely love the work involved in creating new families.

Do you have any criteria for adoptive parents, such as age, number of children in the home, etc.? None.

What percent of your adoptions are infants under 6 mos.? 90%

Do you have a waiting list of prospective parents? No.

Is it all right if adopting parents are on waiting lists of other attorneys or agencies? Yes.

Do you charge adoptive parents for a first phone consultation? No.

Do you charge adoptive parents for a first office consultation, and if yes, what is the fee? Yes; $125.

Do you charge a retainer fee, and if yes, what is it and when is it payable? Yes. Varies depending on type of case, anywhere from $300 to $2,000.

What are your legal fees, not including retainer, and when are they payable? Varies. $195 per hour if hourly; flat fees for certain cases. Generally retainer in amount of estimated cost due when work begins.

Will adoptive parents pay a separate attorney for the birthmother, and if yes, what are approximate legal fees? Yes; $1,200.

What are the approximate fees for medical and hospital expenses for the birthmother and baby, when they have no insurance? $4,000–6,000

What are the approximate homestudy fees in your state? $2,000–4,000

If living expenses for a birthmother are allowed, what is the average amount paid? $1,000

Are you an adoptive parent, adopted person, or birthparent? Adoptive parent.

In how many of your cases has an adoptive parent lost a placed child due to a birthparent challenge? About 8%

Have you lost any adoption litigation filed against you by an adoptive parent or birthparent? No.

In about what percentage of your adoptions do adopting parents and birthparents know each other's first and last names? 50%

Are you a member of the American Academy of Adoption Attorneys and/or the National Council for Adoption? American Academy of Adoption Attorneys.

MISSOURI

SANFORD KRIGEL

Krigel & Krigel, PC
4550 Belleview, Kansas City, MO 64111
(816) 756-5800 • Fax: (816) 756-1999
E-mail: skrigel95@aol.com

What are your office hours when you accept calls from adoptive parents?
8 a.m.–5:30 p.m., CT

Education: BA, Urban Studies University of Pennsylvania, 1973; JD, St. Louis University School of Law, 1976

What states or countries do your adoptive parents come from? Mostly Missouri and Kansas.

What states or countries do your birthparents/adopted children come from? Mostly Missouri and Kansas.

Are other attorneys in your law firm active in adoption? Yes.

In what year did you begin legal work in adoptions? 1976

About what percent of your work is devoted to adoption? 25%

Do you have any criteria for adoptive parents, such as age, number of children in the home, etc., and if so, what are they? Must have a homestudy from a qualified social worker recommending client for adoption.

What percent of your adoptions are infants under 6 mos.? 75%

Do you have a waiting list of prospective parents? Yes.

Is it all right if adopting parents are on waiting lists of other attorneys or agencies? Yes.

Do you charge adoptive parents for a first phone consultation? No.

Do you charge adoptive parents for a first office consultation, and if yes, what is the fee? Yes. Based on hourly rate.

Do you charge a retainer fee, and if yes, what is it and when is it payable? Yes. Varies.

What are your legal fees, not including retainer, and when are they payable? Varies; on hourly basis.

Will adoptive parents pay a separate attorney for the birthmother, and if yes, what are approximate legal fees? Yes. Varies.

What are the approximate fees for medical and hospital expenses for the birthmother and baby, when they have no insurance? $3,000 and up.

What are the approximate homestudy fees in your state? $750–1,200

If living expenses for a birthmother are allowed, what is the average amount paid? Varies.

In how many of your cases has an adoptive parent lost a placed child due to a birthparent challenge? 0

Have you lost any adoption litigation filed against you by an adoptive parent or birthparent? No.

In about what percentage of your adoptions do adopting parents and birthparents know each other's first and last names? 75%

Are you a member of the American Academy of Adoption Attorneys and/or the National Council for Adoption? American Academy of Adoption Attorneys.

NEW HAMPSHIRE

MARGARET CUNNANE HALL
37 High St., Milford, NH 03055
(603) 673-8323 • Fax: (603) 672-2348

What are your office hours when you accept calls from adoptive parents? 8:30 a.m.–5 p.m., ET

Education: BA in psychology and anthropology, University of Massachusetts, Boston, 1974; JD, New England School of Law, 1978

What states or countries do your adoptive parents come from? New Hampshire.

What states or countries do your birthparents/adopted children come from? California, Arizona, Massachusetts, New Hampshire, New York.

Are other attorneys in your law firm active in adoption? N/A

In what year did you begin legal work in adoptions? 1984

How many nonrelative adoptions did you arrange in 1998? 20

About how many children have you placed since you started? 250–300

About what percent of your work is devoted to adoption? 40%

In 1998, what was the average time from when a prospective adoptive parent retained you to the placement of a child? 9 mos.–1 year

What made you decide to work in the adoption field? My children are adopted.

Do you have any criteria for adoptive parents, such as age, number of children in the home, etc.? None, except they need to complete a homestudy.

What percent of your adoptions are infants under 6 mos.? 100%

Do you have a waiting list of prospective parents? Yes.

Is it all right if adopting parents are on waiting lists of other attorneys or agencies? Yes.

Do you charge adoptive parents for a first phone consultation? No.

Do you charge for a first-time office visit from an adoptive parent client? Yes; $160.

Do you charge a retainer fee, and if yes, what is it and when is it payable? Yes. $1,500–2,500 when birthfamily and adoptive family are matched.

What are your legal fees, not including retainer, and when are they payable? $160/hour as earned.

Will adoptive parents pay a separate attorney for the birthmother, and if yes, what are approximate legal fees? Yes; $3,000–5,000.

What are the approximate fees for medical and hospital expenses for the birthmother and baby, when they have no insurance? $5,000–7,000

What are the approximate homestudy fees in your state? $1,500

If living expenses for a birthmother are allowed, what is the average amount paid? $500–1,500

Are you an adoptive parent, adopted person, or birthparent? Adoptive parent.

In how many of your cases has an adoptive parent lost a placed child due to a birthparent challenge? Twice.

Have you lost any adoption litigation filed against you by an adoptive parent or birthparent? No.

In about what percentage of your adoptions do adopting parents and birthparents know each other's first and last names? Less than 5%

Are you a member of the American Academy of Adoption Attorneys and/or the National Council for Adoption? American Academy of Adoption Attorneys.

NEW JERSEY

JAMES W. MISKOWSKI

MacFall, Riedl and Miskowski
45 N. Brood St., Ridgewood, NJ 07451
(201) 445-4600 • Fax: (201) 617-0715

What are your office hours when you accept calls from adoptive parents? 7 a.m.–6 p.m., ET

Education: JD, St. John's University School of Law, 1974

What states or countries do your adoptive parents come from? Nationally.

What states or countries do your birthparents/adopted children come from? Nationally.

Are other attorneys in your law firm active in adoption? Yes.

In what year did you begin legal work in adoptions? 1986

How many nonrelative adoptions did you arrange in 1998? 90+

About how many children have you placed since you started? 1,000

About what percent of your work is devoted to adoption? 90%

In 1998, what was the average time from when a prospective adoptive parent retained you to the placement of a child? 6–8 mos.

What made you decide to work in the adoption field? Adopted parent and drafted legislation that changed the adoption laws in New Jersey.

Do you have any criteria for adoptive parents, such as age, number of children in the home, etc.? No.

What percent of your adoptions are infants under 6 mos.? 98%

Do you have a waiting list of prospective parents? Yes.

Is it all right if adopting parents are on waiting lists of other attorneys or agencies? Yes.

Do you charge adoptive parents for a first phone consultation? No.

Do you charge adoptive parents for a first office consultation, and if yes, what is the fee? Yes; $350.

Do you charge a retainer fee, and if yes, what is it and when is it payable? Yes; $2,500.

What are your legal fees, not including retainer, and when are they payable? Average $4,000; varies depending on complexity of legal work.

Will adoptive parents pay a separate attorney for the birthmother, and if yes, what are approximate legal fees? Yes; $1,500.

What are the approximate fees for medical and hospital expenses for the birthmother and baby, when they have no insurance? $4,000

What are the approximate homestudy fees in your state? $750

If living expenses for a birthmother are allowed, what is the average amount paid? Varies; $0–5,000.

Are you an adoptive parent, adopted person, or birthparent? Adoptive parent.

In how many of your cases has an adoptive parent lost a placed child due to a birthparent challenge? 3%

Have you lost any adoption litigation filed against you by an adoptive parent or birthparent? No.

In about what percentage of your adoptions do adopting parents and birthparents know each other's first and last names? First names only.

Are you a member of the American Academy of Adoption Attorneys and/or the National Council for Adoption? American Academy of Adoption Attorneys.

DEBORAH STEINCOLOR, ESQ.
329 Bellevelle Ave., Bloomfield, NJ 10022
(973) 743-7500 or (212) 421-7807

What are your office hours when you accept calls from adoptive parents?
9:30 a.m.–4 p.m., ET

Education: BA in English, New York University, 1979; JD, Delaware Law School, 1981

What states or countries do your adoptive parents come from? New Jersey, New York, Connecticut primarily.

What states or countries do your birthparents/adopted children come from? Most states.

Are other attorneys in your law firm active in adoption? No.

In what year did you begin legal work in adoptions? 1987

How many nonrelative adoptions did you arrange in 1998? 41

About how many children have you placed since you started? Not children, but adoptions. Not placed, but participated in approximately 1,600. For seven years I was employed in a high-volume adoption practice.

About what percent of your work is devoted to adoption? 100%

In 1998, what was the average time from when a prospective adoptive parent retained you to the placement of a child? 6 mos.–1 year

What made you decide to work in the adoption field? I was frustrated providing legal services in other areas of the law. I interviewed with a major adoption practitioner. It is the only area of law in which I experience a great deal of satisfaction in providing compassionate services to my clients.

Do you have any criteria for adoptive parents, such as age, number of children in the home, etc., and if so, what are they? They are required to meet legal qualifications in accordance with their state's laws.

What percent of your adoptions are infants under 6 mos.? 99.9%

Is it all right if adopting parents are on waiting lists of other attorneys or agencies? Yes.

Do you charge adoptive parents for a first phone consultation? No.

Do you charge adoptive parents for a first office consultation, and if yes, what is the fee? Yes; $200–400.

Do you charge a retainer fee, and if yes, what is it and when is it payable? Yes. $1,000–2,000 due when my clients sign an agreement discussing the services I will render and fees.

What are your legal fees, not including retainer, and when are they payable? Average fees are $2,500–5,000, depending on what type of services I am providing.

Will adoptive parents pay a separate attorney for the birthmother, and if yes, what are approximate legal fees? Yes. Average $1,500–2,500.

What are the approximate fees for medical and hospital expenses for the birthmother and baby, when they have no insurance? $7,000 for vaginal delivery.

What are the approximate homestudy fees in your state? New York, $500 private social worker; $800 for agency; New Jersey, $700–900.

If living expenses for a birthmother are allowed, what is the average amount paid? Utilities, rent made directly to utility companies, landlords.

In how many of your cases has an adoptive parent lost a placed child due to a birthparent challenge? 0

Have you lost any adoption litigation filed against you by an adoptive parent or birthparent? N/A

In about what percentage of your adoptions do adopting parents and birthparents know each other's first and last names? Approximately 5%. This issue is not legally regulated. Every family has their own privacy/disclosure opinion that should be respected.

Are you a member of the American Academy of Adoption Attorneys and/or the National Council for Adoption? American Academy of Adoption Attorneys.

TOBY SOLOMON

354 Eisenhower Pkwy., Livingston, NJ 07039
(973) 533-0078 • Fax: (973) 533-0466
E-mail: tsolo@mindspring.com • www.tobysolomon.com

What are your office hours when you accept calls from adoptive parents? 9 a.m.–5 p.m., ET, or any time I am available in the office.

Education: BS, Ohio State University; MA, Columbia University; JD, Seton Hall Law School, cum laude, 1983

What states or countries do your adoptive parents come from? New Jersey.

What states or countries do your birthparents/adopted children come from? All states.

Are other attorneys in your law firm active in adoption? Yes.

In what year did you begin legal work in adoptions? 1986

How many nonrelative adoptions did you arrange in 1998? Do not keep count.

About how many children have you placed since you started? Do not keep count.

About what percent of your work is devoted to adoption? 25%

In 1998, what was the average time from when a prospective adoptive parent retained you to the placement of a child? 6 mos.

What made you decide to work in the adoption field? Special interest in children and children's rights.

What percent of your adoptions are infants under 6 mos.? Majority.

Do you have a waiting list of prospective parents? Yes, a small number.

Is it all right if adopting parents are on waiting lists of other attorneys or agencies? Yes.

Do you charge adoptive parents for a first phone consultation? No.

Do you charge adoptive parents for a first office consultation, and if yes, what is the fee? Yes; $250.

Do you charge a retainer fee, and if yes, what is it and when is it payable? Yes. Approximate retainer fee is $3,000 and is due upon being retained.

What are your legal fees, not including retainer, and when are they payable? $250 per hour, payable when billed if retainer amount has been used.

Will adoptive parents pay a separate attorney for the birthmother, and if yes, what are approximate legal fees? Yes; $2,500–4,000.

What are the approximate fees for medical and hospital expenses for the birthmother and baby, when they have no insurance? This expense varies from state to state.

What are the approximate homestudy fees in your state? $750

If living expenses for a birthmother are allowed, what is the average amount paid? Reasonable living expenses; Varies.

In how many of your cases has an adoptive parent lost a placed child due to a birthparent challenge? N/A

Have you lost any adoption litigation filed against you by an adoptive parent or birthparent? No.

In about what percentage of your adoptions do adopting parents and birthparents know each other's first and last names? Approximately 80%

Are you a member of the American Academy of Adoption Attorneys and/or the National Council for Adoption? American Academy of Adoption Attorneys.

NEW MEXICO

HAROLD O. ATENCIO

Atencio and Associates
P.O. Box 66468, Albuquerque, NM 87193-6468
(505) 839-9111 • Fax: (505) 839-0888
E-mail: hatencio@aol.com

What are your office hours when you accept calls from adoptive parents?
8:30 a.m.–5 p.m., MT

Education: Bachelor of University Studies (cum laude), University of New Mexico, 1985; JD, University of New Mexico, 1988

What states or countries do your adoptive parents come from? United States, China.

What states or countries do your birthparents/adopted children come from? United States, China.

Are other attorneys in your law firm active in adoption? No.

In what year did you begin legal work in adoptions? 1995

How many nonrelative adoptions did you arrange in 1998? I participated in approximately 30 to 40.

About how many children have you placed since you started? None. It's illegal for an attorney to place children in New Mexico.

About what percent of your work is devoted to adoption? 35%

What made you decide to work in the adoption field? Watching my sister-in-law adopt three children. (I was retained to perform the legal work in her next two).

Do you have any criteria for adoptive parents, such as age, number of children in the home, etc.? No.

What percent of your adoptions are infants under 6 mos.? 95%

Do you have a waiting list of prospective parents? No.

Is it all right if adopting parents are on waiting lists of other attorneys or agencies? Yes.

Do you charge adoptive parents for a first phone consultation? No.

Do you charge adoptive parents for a first office consultation, and if yes, what is the fee? Yes; $125/hour (usually one hour).

Do you charge a retainer fee, and if yes, what is it and when is it payable? Yes. It depends on the type of adoption.

What are your legal fees, not including retainer, and when are they payable? $125/hour unless a flat fee is negotiated.

Will adoptive parents pay a separate attorney for the birthmother, and if yes, what are approximate legal fees? Yes. Depends on state where birthmother is located.

What are the approximate fees for medical and hospital expenses for the birthmother and baby, when they have no insurance? Varies too widely to give meaningful information.

What are the approximate homestudy fees in your state? $1,000

If living expenses for a birthmother are allowed, what is the average amount paid? Agencies will make these payments.

In how many of your cases has an adoptive parent lost a placed child due to a birthparent challenge? 0. But some adoptions have not gone through because a birthparent exercised their right to change their mind before the applicable law made a relinquishment final and binding.

Have you lost any adoption litigation filed against you by an adoptive parent or birthparent? No.

In about what percentage of your adoptions do adopting parents and birthparents know each other's first and last names? 50%

Are you a member of the American Academy of Adoption Attorneys and/or the National Council for Adoption? American Academy of Adoption Attorneys.

NEW YORK

AARON BRITVAN, COUNSELLOR-AT-LAW

7600 Jericho Turnpike, Woodbury, NY 11797
(516) 496-2222 • Fax: (516) 496-3450
E-mail: adoptbrit@aol.com • www.usaprofit.com/britvan

What are your office hours when you accept calls from adoptive parents?
9 a.m.–5 p.m., ET. Anytime by answering machine.

Education: BS, New York University, 1958; Bachelor of Law, Brooklyn Law School, 1961

What states or countries do your adoptive parents come from? All states.

What states or countries do your birthparents/adopted children come from? All states.

Are other attorneys in your law firm active in adoption? Yes.

In what year did you begin legal work in adoptions? 1975

How many nonrelative adoptions did you arrange in 1998? Do not arrange, but assist; 125.

About how many children have you placed since you started? 3,500

About what percent of your work is devoted to adoption? 100%

In 1998, what was the average time from when a prospective adoptive parent retained you to the placement of a child? 10 mos.

What made you decide to counsel in the adoption field? I am an adoptive parent.

Do you have any criteria for adoptive parents, such as age, number of children in the home, etc., and if so, what are they? Subject to being certified by local court.

What percent of your adoptions are infants under 6 mos.? 99%

Do you have a waiting list of prospective parents? Yes.

Is it all right if adopting parents are on waiting lists of other attorneys or agencies? Yes.

Do you charge adoptive parents for a first phone consultation? No.

Do you charge adoptive parents for a first office consultation, and if yes, what is the fee? Yes; if for formal consultation, which runs $2\frac{1}{2}$ hours, $350.

Do you charge a retainer fee? No.

What are your legal fees, not including retainer, and when are they payable? $250 per hour, maximum of $3,750, payable at end.

Will adoptive parents pay a separate attorney for the birthmother, and if yes, what are approximate legal fees? Yes; $1,500.

What are the approximate fees for medical and hospital expenses for the birthmother and baby, when they have no insurance? $6,000

What are the approximate homestudy fees in your state? $400

If living expenses for a birthmother are allowed, what is the average amount paid? Reasonable living expenses related to pregnancy for 3–4 mos.

Are you an adoptive parent, adopted person, or birthparent? Adoptive parent.

In how many of your cases has an adoptive parent lost a placed child due to a birthparent challenge? 0

Have you lost any adoption litigation filed against you by an adoptive parent or birthparent? No.

In about what percentage of your adoptions do adopting parents and birthparents know each other's first and last names? 2%

Are you a member of the American Academy of Adoption Attorneys and/or the National Council for Adoption? National Council for Adoption.

Is there anything I have not asked you that is important? I am Chair of the Adoption Committee, New York State Bar Association.

ROBIN A. FLEISCHNER, ATTORNEY AT LAW

NY office: 11 Riverside Dr., Suite 14MW, New York, NY 10023
NJ Office: 374 Millburn Ave., Millburn, NJ 07041
New York: (212) 362-6945; New Jersey: (973) 376-6623 • Fax: (212) 875-1431
E-mail: raflaw@aol.com

What are your office hours when you accept calls from adoptive parents? 9 a.m.–5 p.m., Monday–Friday, ET

Education: JD, Benjamin N. Cardozo School of Law, 1980

What states or countries do your adoptive parents come from? New York and New Jersey.

What states or countries do your birthparents/adopted children come from? All states.

Are other attorneys in your law firm active in adoption? No.

In what year did you begin legal work in adoptions? 1986

How many nonrelative adoptions did you arrange in 1998? 50

About how many children have you placed since you started? 500

About what percent of your work is devoted to adoption? 100%

In 1998, what was the average time from when a prospective adoptive parent retained you to the placement of a child? 1 year

What made you decide to work in the adoption field? I am an adoptive parent.

Do you have any criteria for adoptive parents, such as age, number of children in the home, etc., and if so, what are they? They must qualify in a homestudy.

What percent of your adoptions are infants under 6 mos.? All.

Do you have a waiting list of prospective parents? Yes.

Is it all right if adopting parents are on waiting lists of other attorneys or agencies? Yes.

Do you charge adoptive parents for a first phone consultation, and if yes, what is the fee? Yes; $400.

Do you charge adoptive parents for a first office consultation, and if yes, what is the fee? Yes; $400.

Do you charge a retainer fee, and if yes, what is it and when is it payable? Yes; $1,000.

What are your legal fees, not including retainer, and when are they payable? $3,000, payable 30 days prior to birth of adoptive child.

Will adoptive parents pay a separate attorney for the birthmother, and if yes, what are approximate legal fees? Yes. Varies.

What are the approximate fees for medical and hospital expenses for the birthmother and baby, when they have no insurance? Varies.

What are the approximate homestudy fees in your state? $500–750

If living expenses for a birthmother are allowed, what is the average amount paid? $3,000

Are you an adoptive parent, adopted person, or birthparent? Adoptive parent.

In how many of your cases has an adoptive parent lost a placed child due to a birthparent challenge? None.

Have you lost any adoption litigation filed against you by an adoptive parent or birthparent? No.

In about what percentage of your adoptions do adopting parents and birthparents know each other's first and last names? 10% of adoptive parents are willing to disclose their identity, but most birthparents are willing to disclose theirs.

Are you a member of the American Academy of Adoption Attorneys and/or the National Council for Adoption? American Academy of Adoption Attorneys.

GREGORY A. FRANKLIN, ESQ.

Goldman, Newman, Shiner and Franklin, LLP
95 Allens Creek Rd., Bldg. 1, Suite. 104, Rochester, NY 14618-3227
(716) 442-0540 • Fax: (716) 442-6889
E-mail: gafadopt@eznet.net • www.Adoption.com/Franklin/

What are your office hours when you accept calls from adoptive parents? 9 a.m.–5 p.m., ET

Education: BA, Grinnell College, 1978; JD, Fordham University School of Law, 1984

What states or countries do your adoptive parents come from? Domestic, New York State; international, United States, Western Europe, and Canada.

What states or countries do your birthparents/adopted children come from? United States and worldwide.

Are other attorneys in your law firm active in adoption? Yes.

In what year did you begin legal work in adoptions? 1990

How many nonrelative adoptions did you arrange in 1998? New York State attorneys may not arrange adoptions. I represented clients in 75 completed adoptions in 1998.

About how many children have you placed since you started? 500

About what percent of your work is devoted to adoption? 90%

In 1998, what was the average time from when a prospective adoptive parent retained you to the placement of a child? Varies.

What made you decide to work in the adoption field? My wife and I adopted our son in 1990, from Chile. I felt that I would bring my personal experience to this practice of law.

Do you have any criteria for adoptive parents, such as age, number of children in the home, etc.? None, other than general ethical and moral criteria.

What percent of your adoptions are infants under 6 mos.? 75%

Do you have a waiting list of prospective parents? No.

Is it all right if adopting parents are on waiting lists of other attorneys or agencies? Yes.

Do you charge adoptive parents for a first phone consultation? No.

Do you charge adoptive parents for a first office consultation? No.

Do you charge a retainer fee, and if yes, what is it and when is it payable? Yes; $500, when retained.

What are your legal fees, not including retainer, and when are they payable? $150/hour, payable when billed.

Will adoptive parents pay a separate attorney for the birthmother, and if yes, what are approximate legal fees? Yes. Varies.

What are the approximate fees for medical and hospital expenses for the birthmother and baby, when they have no insurance? $2,500

What are the approximate homestudy fees in your state? $400–1,500

If living expenses for a birthmother are allowed, what is the average amount paid? $2,000

If you manage international adoptions, what is the average fee for translating documents? $350

Are you an adoptive parent, adopted person, or birthparent? Adoptive parent.

In how many of your cases has an adoptive parent lost a placed child due to a birthparent challenge? 5

Have you lost any adoption litigation filed against you by an adoptive parent or birthparent? No.

In about what percentage of your adoptions do adopting parents and birthparents know each other's first and last names? 70%

Are you a member of the American Academy of Adoption Attorneys and/or the National Council for Adoption? American Academy of Adoption Attorneys and National Council for Adoption.

MICHAEL S. GOLDSTEIN

62 Bowman Ave., Rye Brook, NY 10573
(914) 939-1111 • Fax: (914) 939-2369
E-mail: adoptgold@aol.com

What are your office hours when you accept calls from adoptive parents?
9 a.m.–5 p.m., ET

Education: BS, SUNY Stony Brook; JD, Fordham Law School; MSW, Syracuse University

What states or countries do your adoptive parents come from? Worldwide.

What states or countries do your birthparents/adopted children come from? Worldwide.

Are other attorneys in your law firm active in adoption? Yes.

In what year did you begin legal work in adoptions? 1982

How many nonrelative adoptions did you arrange in 1998? 100+

About how many children have you placed since you started? 1,500+

About what percent of your work is devoted to adoption? 98%

In 1998, what was the average time from when a prospective adoptive parent retained you to the placement of a child? 1 year

What made you decide to work in the adoption field? Emotionally rewarding field and I am an adoptive parent myself and in the social work counseling field.

Do you have any criteria for adoptive parents, such as age, number of children in the home, etc.? No; must be approved by homestudy.

What percent of your adoptions are infants under 6 mos.? 95%

Do you have a waiting list of prospective parents? No.

Is it all right if adopting parents are on waiting lists of other attorneys or agencies? Yes.

Do you charge adoptive parents for a first phone consultation? No.

Do you charge adoptive parents for a first office consultation, and if yes, what is the fee? Yes; fees vary for $1\frac{1}{2}$ to 2 hours private consultation.

Do you charge a retainer fee, and if yes, what is it and when is it payable? Yes. Varies; payable before services.

What are your legal fees, not including retainer, and when are they payable? Varies.

Will adoptive parents pay a separate attorney for the birthmother, and if yes, what are approximate legal fees? Yes. Varies.

What are the approximate fees for medical and hospital expenses for the birthmother and baby, when they have no insurance? Varies.

What are the approximate homestudy fees in your state? $500

If living expenses for a birthmother are allowed, what is the average amount paid? Varies.

If you manage international adoptions, what is the average fee for translating documents? Varies.

Are you an adoptive parent, adopted person, or birthparent? Adoptive parent.

In how many of your cases has an adoptive parent lost a placed child due to a birthparent challenge? None.

Have you lost any adoption litigation filed against you by an adoptive parent or birthparent? No.

In about what percentage of your adoptions do adopting parents and birthparents know each other's first and last names? 5%

Are you a member of the American Academy of Adoption Attorneys and/or the National Council for Adoption? American Academy of Adoption Attorneys.

STEPHEN LEWIN, ESQ.

Irwin, Lewin, Cohen and Lewin, PC
845 Third Ave., Suite 1400, New York, NY 10022
(212) 759-2600 • Fax: (212) 593-1318
E-mail: s.lewin@ilel-law.com

What are your office hours when you accept calls from adoptive parents? 9 a.m.–6:30 p.m., ET

Education: BA, Franklin and Marshall College, 1971; JD, Brooklyn Law School, 1977

What states or countries do your adoptive parents come from? New York.

What states or countries do your birthparents/adopted children come from? Throughout the United States and the rest of the world.

Are other attorneys in your law firm active in adoption? No.

In what year did you begin legal work in adoptions? 1984

How many nonrelative adoptions did you arrange in 1998? It is illegal for an attorney to arrange adoptions under New York law.

About how many children have you placed since you started? It is illegal for an attorney to arrange adoptions under New York law.

About what percent of your work is devoted to adoption? 33%

In 1998, what was the average time from when a prospective adoptive parent retained you to the placement of a child? 6 mos.–1 year, depending on whether it is an international or domestic adoption.

What made you decide to work in the adoption field? My brother's adoption on his own 15 years ago and my relationship with a social worker whose expertise was infertility counseling.

Do you have any criteria for adoptive parents, such as age, number of children in the home, etc.? None.

What percent of your adoptions are infants under 6 mos.? Most, except for step- or second-parent adoption.

Do you have a waiting list of prospective parents? Yes.

Is it all right if adopting parents are on waiting lists of other attorneys or agencies? Yes.

Do you charge adoptive parents for a first phone consultation? No.

Do you charge adoptive parents for a first office consultation, and if yes, what is the fee? Yes; varies, but only if longer than $\frac{1}{2}$ hour.

Do you charge a retainer fee, and if yes, what is it and when is it payable? Yes. Varies, but initially $2,500.

What are your legal fees, not including retainer, and when are they payable? Varies and subject to court approval. Approximately $4,000–5,000.

Will adoptive parents pay a separate attorney for the birthmother, and if yes, what are approximate legal fees? Yes. Varies, depending on geography and amount of work performed.

What are the approximate fees for medical and hospital expenses for the birthmother and baby, when they have no insurance? Varies, depending on geography and amount of medical and hospital work incurred.

What are the approximate homestudy fees in your state? $500–1,000

If living expenses for a birthmother are allowed, what is the average amount paid? Between 0 and $5,000, subject to court approval.

If you manage international adoptions, what is the average fee for translating documents? Most agencies perform this as part of agency costs.

In how many of your cases has an adoptive parent lost a placed child due to a birthparent challenge? 2

Have you lost any adoption litigation filed against you by an adoptive parent or birthparent? No.

In about what percentage of your adoptions do adopting parents and birthparents know each other's first and last names? First names for all, last names for very few.

Are you a member of the American Academy of Adoption Attorneys and/or the National Council for Adoption? American Academy of Adoption Attorneys.

CHANA (FORMERLY CHRISTINE) MESBERG

28 Hilltop Rd., Waccabuc, NY 10597
(914) 669-5401 • Fax: (914) 669-8105
E-mail: cmesberg@aol.com

What are your office hours when you accept calls from adoptive parents?
9 a.m.–5 p.m., ET

Education: BA, Brandeis University, 1975; JD, Pace University, 1986

What states or countries do your adoptive parents come from? Many in the United States; some international (readoptions) Russia, China, India.

Are other attorneys in your law firm active in adoption? No.

In what year did you begin legal work in adoptions? 1986

How many nonrelative adoptions did you arrange in 1998? 30–40, estimated.

About how many children have you placed since you started? Several hundred.

About what percent of your work is devoted to adoption? 100%

In 1998, what was the average time from when a prospective adoptive parent retained you to the placement of a child? 1 year

What made you decide to work in the adoption field? We adopted our younger daughter.

Do you have any criteria for adoptive parents, such as age, number of children in the home, etc.? No.

What percent of your adoptions are infants under 6 mos.? 95%

Do you have a waiting list of prospective parents? Yes.

Is it all right if adopting parents are on waiting lists of other attorneys or agencies? Yes.

Do you charge adoptive parents for a first phone consultation? No.

Do you charge adoptive parents for a first office consultation, and if yes, what is the fee? Yes; $200.

Do you charge a retainer fee, and if yes, what is it and when is it payable? Yes; $1,500, payable on being retained.

What are your legal fees, not including retainer, and when are they payable? $2,250 at time of placement.

Will adoptive parents pay a separate attorney for the birthmother, and if yes, what are approximate legal fees? Yes; $750–3,500.

What are the approximate fees for medical and hospital expenses for the birthmother and baby, when they have no insurance? $5,000–6,000

What are the approximate homestudy fees in your state? $450–550

If living expenses for a birthmother are allowed, what is the average amount paid? $2,000

Are you an adoptive parent, adopted person, or birthparent? Adoptive parent.

In how many of your cases has an adoptive parent lost a placed child due to a birthparent challenge? None.

Have you lost any adoption litigation filed against you by an adoptive parent or birthparent? No.

In about what percentage of your adoptions do adopting parents and birthparents know each other's first and last names? 10%

Are you a member of the American Academy of Adoption Attorneys and/or the National Council for Adoption? American Academy of Adoption Attorneys.

SUZANNE B. NICHOLS

Rosenstock Lowe and Nichols
70 West Red Oak Ln., White Plains, NY 10604
(914) 697-4870 • Fax: (914) 697-4888

What are your office hours when you accept calls from adoptive parents?
9 a.m.–5 p.m., ET

Education: BS, Boston University, 1971; MA in counseling, George Washington University, 1974; JD, New York Law School, 1984

What states or countries do your adoptive parents come from? New York, New Jersey, Pennsylvania, Missouri, Illinois, Connecticut, Florida, Maryland, Virginia, Italy, Spain, Ecuador, France, England, Australia.

What states or countries do your birthparents/adopted children come from? Throughout the United States, Hungary, Ukraine.

Are other attorneys in your law firm active in adoption? Yes, part-time.

In what year did you begin legal work in adoptions? 1989

How many nonrelative adoptions did you arrange in 1998? 60

About how many children have you placed since you started? Approximately 600

About what percent of your work is devoted to adoption? 100%

In 1998, what was the average time from when a prospective adoptive parent retained you to the placement of a child? 5–8 mos.

What made you decide to work in the adoption field? I am able to combine my education and work experience in the field of counseling with my legal background.

Do you have any criteria for adoptive parents, such as age, number of children in the home, etc.? None.

What percent of your adoptions are infants under 6 mos.? Approximately 70%

Is it all right if adopting parents are on waiting lists of other attorneys or agencies? Yes.

Do you charge adoptive parents for a first phone consultation? No.

Do you charge adoptive parents for a first office consultation, and if yes, what is the fee? Yes; $500 for a $1\frac{1}{2}$- to $2\frac{1}{2}$-hour consultation.

Do you charge a retainer fee, and if yes, what is it and when is it payable? Yes. $1,000 is required when clients sign a retainer letter.

What are your legal fees, not including retainer, and when are they payable? $4,000; $1,500 is due at the commencement of the case and $2,500 is due when the baby is ready for placement.

Will adoptive parents pay a separate attorney for the birthmother, and if yes, what are approximate legal fees? Yes; $1,500–3,000.

What are the approximate fees for medical and hospital expenses for the birthmother and baby, when they have no insurance? $6,000–8,000

What are the approximate homestudy fees in your state? $500–800

If living expenses for a birthmother are allowed, what is the average amount paid? $2,000–3,000

If you manage international adoptions, what is the average fee for translating documents? I find this depends on the country. Hungary, $1,200–1,600; Ukraine, much higher.

In how many of your cases has an adoptive parent lost a placed child due to a birthparent challenge? I have never even been part of a challenged adoption. Birthparents have changed their minds prior to and immediately after birth, as well as a day or two after placement, but never after signing.

Have you lost any adoption litigation filed against you by an adoptive parent or birthparent? No.

In about what percentage of your adoptions do adopting parents and birthparents know each other's first and last names? Always first names are known. Very rarely do they exchange last names.

Are you a member of the American Academy of Adoption Attorneys and/or the National Council for Adoption? American Academy of Adoption Attorneys and National Council for Adoption.

ANNE REYNOLDS COPPS

126 State St., Albany, NY 12207
(518) 436-4170 • Fax: (518) 436-1456

What are your office hours when you accept calls from adoptive parents? 8:30 a.m.–5:30 p.m., ET

Education: BA in political science, State University of New York, Albany, 1978; JD, Union University, Albany Law School, 1981

What states or countries do your adoptive parents come from? New York.

What states or countries do your birthparents/adopted children come from? All states, Russia, China, Lithuania, Romania, Guatemala, Vietnam.

Are other attorneys in your law firm active in adoption? No.

In what year did you begin legal work in adoptions? 1981

How many nonrelative adoptions did you arrange in 1998? In New York, attorneys cannot make the match as counsel to adoptive parents or birthparents. We represented approximately 50 families.

About how many children have you placed since you started? In New York attorneys cannot place children.

About what percent of your work is devoted to adoption? 50%

In 1998, what was the average time from when a prospective adoptive parent retained you to the placement of a child? 1–2 years

What made you decide to work in the adoption field? It is very pleasant to help create families rather than go work in other fields of law such as matrimonial or banking law.

Do you have any criteria for adoptive parents, such as age, number of children in the home, etc.? No.

What percent of your adoptions are infants under 6 mos.? Approximately 75%

Do you have a waiting list of prospective parents? No.

Do you charge adoptive parents for a first phone consultation, and if yes, what is the fee? Yes; $140 per hour.

Do you charge adoptive parents for a first office consultation, and if yes, what is the fee? Yes; $140 per hour.

Do you charge a retainer fee, and if yes, what is it and when is it payable? Yes; $750, when retained.

What are your legal fees, not including retainer, and when are they payable? Hourly, as billed monthly.

Will adoptive parents pay a separate attorney for the birthmother, and if yes, what are approximate legal fees? Yes. Depends on the situation and the attorney she selects.

What are the approximate fees for medical and hospital expenses for the birthmother and baby, when they have no insurance? $5,000

What are the approximate homestudy fees in your state? $750–1,000

If living expenses for a birthmother are allowed, what is the average amount paid? It varies widely.

In how many of your cases has an adoptive parent lost a placed child due to a birthparent challenge? 0

Have you lost any adoption litigation filed against you by an adoptive parent or birthparent? No.

In about what percentage of your adoptions do adopting parents and birthparents know each other's first and last names? 90%

Are you a member of the American Academy of Adoption Attorneys and/or the National Council for Adoption? American Academy of Adoption Attorneys.

Is there anything I have not asked you that is important? Yes. I strongly encourage my families to offer to pay for counseling for the birthmother. I strongly urge them to accept counseling to help her make her decision and to help her live with her decision.

BEN ROSIN

Rosin and Reiniger
630 Third Ave., New York, NY 10017
(212) 972-5430 • Fax: (212) 972-5835
E-mail: benrosin@aol.com

What are your office hours when you accept calls from adoptive parents?
9 a.m.–5 p.m., ET

Education: BA, Middlebury College, 1962; LLB, Columbia University School of Law, 1965

What states or countries do your adoptive parents come from? New York.

What states or countries do your birthparents/adopted children come from? All states.

Are other attorneys in your law firm active in adoption? Yes.

In what year did you begin legal work in adoptions? 1969

How many nonrelative adoptions did you arrange in 1998? New York lawyers represent adoptive couples or birthparents, or act as law guardian; we do not arrange (or put together or facilitate) adoptions. I was the attorney in approximately 60 adoptions in 1998.

About how many children have you placed since you started? See response above. I've been involved as lawyer in over 400 adoptions.

About what percent of your work is devoted to adoption? 50%

In 1998, what was the average time from when a prospective adoptive parent retained you to the placement of a child? 6–18 mos.

What made you decide to work in the adoption field? I am an adoptive parent; I have been a foster parent to 14 children; and I have been involved in child welfare (foster care) since 1969.

Do you have any criteria for adoptive parents, such as age, number of children in the home, etc.? No, only that they are fit to parent and that is determined by the homestudy.

What percent of your adoptions are infants under 6 mos.? None. Under New York law it takes about 6 to 9 months.

Do you have a waiting list of prospective parents? Yes.

Is it all right if adopting parents are on waiting lists of other attorneys or agencies? Yes.

Do you charge adoptive parents for a first phone consultation? No.

Do you charge adoptive parents for a first office consultation, and if yes, what is the fee? Yes; $200 for a consultation of about one hour.

Do you charge a retainer fee, and if yes, what is it and when is it payable? Yes. For an independent adoption, $4,000, payable as follows: $1,000; then $1,500 when a child is placed, and $1,500 on completion of the adoption (fully refundable to extent not earned if adoption is not completed by us).

Will adoptive parents pay a separate attorney for the birthmother, and if yes, what are approximate legal fees? Yes; $1,500–2,500.

What are the approximate fees for medical and hospital expenses for the birthmother and baby, when they have no insurance? $8,000–10,000

What are the approximate homestudy fees in your state? $500

If living expenses for a birthmother are allowed, what is the average amount paid? $1,500 a month, usually allowed 2 mos. before birth and one after, unless caesarean section, then 6–8 weeks.

Are you an adoptive parent, adopted person, or birthparent? Adoptive parent.

In how many of your cases has an adoptive parent lost a placed child due to a birthparent challenge? One that I can recall.

Have you lost any adoption litigation filed against you by an adoptive parent or birthparent? No.

In about what percentage of your adoptions do adopting parents and birthparents know each other's first and last names? 15 to 20%

Are you a member of the American Academy of Adoption Attorneys and/or the National Council for Adoption? American Academy of Adoption Attorneys.

GOLDA ZIMMERMAN, ESQ.

430 E. Genesee St., Suite 203, Syracuse, NY 13202
(315) 475-3322

What are your office hours when you accept calls from adoptive parents? 9 a.m.–5 p.m., ET

Education: BS, Boston University, 1971; MS, University of Kansas, 1974; JD, Syracuse University College of Law, 1980; Adjunct Professor of Law, Syracuse University College of Law since 1990; editor and author, Adoption Law in New York, published by the Bar Association in 1997.

What states or countries do your adoptive parents come from? All states.

What states or countries do your birthparents/adopted children come from? All states.

Are other attorneys in your law firm active in adoption? No.

In what year did you begin legal work in adoptions? 1984

How many nonrelative adoptions did you arrange in 1998? New York does not allow attorneys to participate in placement activity.

About what percent of your work is devoted to adoption? 50%

In 1998, what was the average time from when a prospective adoptive parent retained you to the placement of a child? Varies, birthparent chooses family.

What made you decide to work in the adoption field? I am an adoptive parent.

Do you have any criteria for adoptive parents, such as age, number of children in the home, etc.? None.

What percent of your adoptions are infants under 6 mos.? Domestic adoptions are newborns, international adoptions vary.

Do you have a waiting list of prospective parents? No.

Is it all right if adopting parents are on waiting lists of other attorneys or agencies? Yes.

Do you charge for a first phone consultation? No. I do not do telephone consultations; I find them to be a disservice to prospective adoptive parents.

Do you charge adoptive parents for a first office consultation, and if yes, what is the fee? Yes; $250 for a two- to three-hour consultation.

Do you charge a retainer fee, and if yes, what is it and when is it payable? Yes. The fee depends on the legal work required and is payable on signing of the written retainer agreement.

What are your legal fees, not including retainer, and when are they payable? I escrow the estimated budget for the case after the adoptive parent(s) identify a prospective case.

Will adoptive parents pay a separate attorney for the birthmother? Yes. This is required under New York law. I cannot represent both parties.

What are the approximate fees for medical and hospital expenses for the birthmother and baby, when they have no insurance? $5,000–9,000

What are the approximate homestudy fees in your state? $1,000–2,500 paid directly to provider (not paid to attorney).

If living expenses for a birthmother are allowed, what is the average amount paid? Varies. I use a three-pronged test approved by courts in New York: 1. Is the expense pregnancy-related; 2. Is it medically necessary; 3. Is it reasonable?

If you manage international adoptions, what is the average fee for translating documents? This fee, $300, is paid directly to the provider.

Are you an adoptive parent, adopted person, or birthparent? Adoptive parent.

In how many of your cases has an adoptive parent lost a placed child due to a birthparent challenge? One agency placement where I represented the adoptive parents and another attorney represented the agency. One private placement where I represented the birthparent who was successful in obtaining return of her child.

Have you lost any adoption litigation filed against you by an adoptive parent or birthparent? No. I never had any adoption litigation filed against me.

In about what percentage of your adoptions do adopting parents and birthparents know each other's first and last names? Varies; case-by-case basis.

Are you a member of the American Academy of Adoption Attorneys and/or the National Council For Adoption? American Academy of Adoption Attorneys.

NORTH CAROLINA

SHELLEY B. BALLARD (FORMERLY SHELLEY BALLARD BOSTICK)

Gorman and Associates
7422 Carmel Executive Park, Suite 200, Charlotte, NC 28226
(704) 544-2500 • Fax: (704) 544-2596
E-mail: sbballard1@aol.com

What are your office hours when you accept calls from adoptive parents?
8:30 a.m.–5 p.m., ET

Education: BS in engineering science, Vanderbilt University, 1979; JD, Northwestern University, 1987

What states or countries do your adoptive parents come from? North Carolina, primarily.

What states or countries do your birthparents/adopted children come from? All states.

Are other attorneys in your law firm active in adoption? No.

In what year did you begin legal work in adoptions? 1988

How many nonrelative adoptions did you arrange in 1998? I rarely arrange adoptions; the parties locate each other.

About how many children have you placed since you started? 12 (where I brought the parties together).

About what percent of your work is devoted to adoption? 20%

In 1998, what was the average time from when a prospective adoptive parent retained you to the placement of a child? 6–9 mos.

What made you decide to work in the adoption field? Adoptive parent of two.

Do you have any criteria for adoptive parents, such as age, number of children in the home, etc.? No.

What percent of your adoptions are infants under 6 mos.? Private adoptions: 99%

Do you have a waiting list of prospective parents? No.

Is it all right if adopting parents are on waiting lists of other attorneys or agencies? Yes.

Do you charge adoptive parents for a first phone consultation? No.

Do you charge adoptive parents for a first office consultation? No.

Do you charge a retainer fee, and if yes, what is it and when is it payable? Yes. Depends on the case, range is 0 to $3,000, payable when retained.

What are your legal fees, not including retainer, and when are they payable? $150/hour; some flat fees (depends on case); billed monthly.

Will adoptive parents pay a separate attorney for the birthmother, and if yes, what are approximate legal fees? Sometimes, if birthmother requests. Wide variation.

What are the approximate fees for medical and hospital expenses for the birthmother and baby, when they have no insurance? Wide variation.

What are the approximate homestudy fees in your state? $1,150–2,000 in private agencies.

If living expenses for a birthmother are allowed, what is the average amount paid? Varies; ordinary and reasonable.

Are you an adoptive parent, adopted person, or birthparent? Adoptive parent.

In how many of your cases has an adoptive parent lost a placed child due to a birthparent challenge? 0

Have you lost any adoption litigation filed against you by an adoptive parent or birthparent? No.

In about what percentage of your adoptions do adopting parents and birthparents know each other's first and last names? In North Carolina, 100% of private agencies are full disclosure.

Are you a member of the American Academy of Adoption Attorneys and/or the National Council for Adoption? American Academy of Adoption Attorneys.

W. DAVID THURMAN

Bush, Thurman and Wilson, PA
803 E. Trade St., Charlotte, NC 28202
(704) 377-4164 • Fax: (704) 377-5503
E-mail: wdtatbtw@aol.com

What are your office hours when you accept calls from adoptive parents? 9 a.m.–4 p.m., ET

Education: BA, University of North Carolina, 1980; JD, University of North Carolina, 1983

What states or countries do your adoptive parents come from? Multiple.

What states or countries do your birthparents/adopted children come from? North Carolina.

Are other attorneys in your law firm active in adoption? No.

In what year did you begin legal work in adoptions? 1985

How many nonrelative adoptions did you arrange in 1998? N/A. Note: Attorneys in North Carolina do not perform placements.

About how many children have you placed since you started? N/A

About what percent of your work is devoted to adoption? 40%

What made you decide to work in the adoption field? The work is personal, important, and fulfilling.

Do you have any criteria for adoptive parents, such as age, number of children in the home, etc.? No.

What percent of your adoptions are infants under 6 mos.? 95%

Do you have a waiting list of prospective parents? No.

Is it all right if adopting parents are on waiting lists of other attorneys or agencies? Yes.

Do you charge adoptive parents for a first phone consultation? No.

Do you charge adoptive parents for a first office consultation, and if yes, what is the fee? Yes; $75.

Do you charge a retainer fee, and if yes, what is it and when is it payable? Yes; $2,000, payable initially.

What are your legal fees, not including retainer, and when are they payable? $150–200 per hour.

Will adoptive parents pay a separate attorney for the birthmother? No.

What are the approximate fees for medical and hospital expenses for the birthmother and baby, when they have no insurance? $4,500

What are the approximate homestudy fees in your state? $1,500

If living expenses for a birthmother are allowed, what is the average amount paid? $500/month

In how many of your cases has an adoptive parent lost a placed child due to a birthparent challenge? 0. A few placements failed due to birthparent consent revocation.

Have you lost any adoption litigation filed against you by an adoptive parent or birthparent? No.

In about what percentage of your adoptions do adopting parents and birthparents know each other's first and last names? 75%

Are you a member of the American Academy of Adoption Attorneys and/or the National Council for Adoption? American Academy of Adoption Attorneys.

Is there anything that I have not asked you that is important? Information not for use in specific adoption situations.

OHIO

SUSAN GARNER EISENMAN

338 South High St., Columbus, OH 43215
(614) 222-0540 • Fax: (614) 222-0543
E-mail: adoptohio@aol.com

What are your office hours when you accept calls from adoptive parents?
8:30 a.m.–5 p.m., EST

What states or countries do your adoptive parents come from? Mostly Ohio and surrounding states.

What states or countries do your birthparents/adopted children come from? Mostly Ohio and surrounding states.

Are other attorneys in your law firm active in adoption? No.

In what year did you begin legal work in adoptions? 1983

How many nonrelative adoptions did you arrange in 1998? 50+

About how many children have you placed since you started? 800–1,000

About what percent of your work is devoted to adoption? 97%

In 1998, what was the average time from when a prospective adoptive parent retained you to the placement of a child? 18 mos.

What made you decide to work in the adoption field? I am an adoptive parent. I helped to form Resolve of Ohio and New Roots Adoption Families.

Do you have any criteria for adoptive parents, such as age, number of children in the home, etc.? We don't have office criteria; however, we will advise clients that birthparents often prefer younger parents without children.

What percent of your adoptions are infants under 6 mos.? Approximately 99% of unrelated adoptions.

Do you have a waiting list of prospective parents? Yes.

Is it all right if adopting parents are on waiting lists of other attorneys or agencies? Yes.

Do you charge adoptive parents for a first phone consultation, and if yes, what is the fee? Not typically, unless call becomes very lengthy (half hour to hour).

Do you charge adoptive parents for a first office consultation, and if yes, what is the fee? Yes; $125 for an options appointment.

Do you charge a retainer fee, and if yes, what is it and when is it payable? Yes. Varies depending on the type of adoption.

What are your legal fees, not including retainer, and when are they payable? $180/hr, payable on receipt of statement. $65/hour for paralegal.

Will adoptive parents pay a separate attorney for the birthmother, and if yes, what are approximate legal fees? Yes, if she has one. Varies.

What are the approximate fees for medical and hospital expenses for the birth-mother and baby, when they have no insurance? Varies.

What are the approximate homestudy fees in your state? Varies depending on agency or court.

Are you an adoptive parent, adopted person, or birthparent? Adoptive parent.

In how many of your cases has an adoptive parent lost a placed child due to a birth-parent challenge? 1 case.

Have you lost any adoption litigation filed against you by an adoptive parent or birthparent? No.

In about what percentage of your adoptions do adopting parents and birthparents know each other's first and last names? 60%

Are you a member of the American Academy of Adoption Attorneys and/or the National Council for Adoption? American Academy of Adoption Attorneys.

JERRY M. JOHNSON

Hunt, Moritz, Johnson and Ebbeskotte
400 West North St., Lima, OH 45801
(419) 222-1040 • Fax: (419) 227-1826

What are your office hours when you accept calls from adoptive parents?
8 a.m.–5 p.m., EST

Education: BS, Ohio Northern University, 1971; JD, Ohio Northern University, 1975

What states or countries do your adoptive parents come from? Throughout the continental United States.

What states or countries do your birthparents/adopted children come from? Throughout the continental United States.

Are other attorneys in your law firm active in adoption? No.

In what year did you begin legal work in adoptions? 1979

How many nonrelative adoptions did you arrange in 1998? 20

About how many children have you placed since you started? 350

About what percent of your work is devoted to adoption? 25%

In 1998, what was the average time from when a prospective adoptive parent re-tained you to the placement of a child? Unable to determine.

What made you decide to work in the adoption field? After the first successful adop-tion, was able to see the positive influence upon the adoptive couple. Further saw the need for time and compassion for the birthmother.

Do you have any criteria for adoptive parents, such as age, number of children in the home, etc., and if so, what are they? Willing to work with any suitable family.

What percent of your adoptions are infants under 6 mos.? 100%

Do you have a waiting list of prospective parents? Yes.

Is it all right if adopting parents are on waiting lists of other attorneys or agencies? Yes.

Do you charge adoptive parents for a first phone consultation? No.

Do you charge adoptive parents for a first office consultation, and if yes, what is the fee? Yes; $60.

Do you charge a retainer fee? No.

What are your legal fees, not including retainer, and when are they payable? Hourly rate of $150 based on time spent; payable prior to placement.

Will adoptive parents pay a separate attorney for the birthmother, and if yes, what are approximate legal fees? Yes; $3,500.

What are the approximate fees for medical and hospital expenses for the birthmother and baby, when they have no insurance? $6,000–7,000

What are the approximate homestudy fees in your state? $750–800

In how many of your cases has an adoptive parent lost a placed child due to a birthparent challenge? 0

Have you lost any adoption litigation filed against you by an adoptive parent or birthparent? No.

In about what percentage of your adoptions do adopting parents and birthparents know each other's first and last names? 90–95% last names, 100% first names.

Are you a member of the American Academy of Adoption Attorneys and/or the National Council for Adoption? American Academy of Adoption Attorneys and National Council for Adoption.

MARY E. SMITH

Shindler, Neff, Holmes and Schlageter, LLP
1200 Edison Plaza; 300 Madison Ave., Toledo, OH 43604
(419) 243-6281 • Fax: (419) 243-0129

What are your office hours when you accept calls from adoptive parents? 9 a.m.–5 p.m., ET

Education: BA in English, Mary Manse College, 1965; JD, University of Toledo, 1984

What states or countries do your adoptive parents come from? Primarily Ohio.

What states or countries do your birthparents/adopted children come from? Primarily Ohio.

Are other attorneys in your law firm active in adoption? No.

In what year did you begin legal work in adoptions? 1985

How many nonrelative adoptions did you arrange in 1998? 15

About how many children have you placed since you started? 400, estimated

About what percent of your work is devoted to adoption? 20%

In 1998, what was the average time from when a prospective adoptive parent retained you to the placement of a child? Unknown.

Do you have any criteria for adoptive parents, such as age, number of children in the home, etc.? No.

What percent of your adoptions are infants under 6 mos.? 100%

Do you have a waiting list of prospective parents? Yes.

Is it all right if adopting parents are on waiting lists of other attorneys or agencies? Yes.

Do you charge adoptive parents for a first phone consultation? No.

Do you charge adoptive parents for a first office consultation, and if yes, what is the fee? Yes; $100.

Do you charge a retainer fee, and if yes, what is it and when is it payable? Yes. Only when matched.

What are your legal fees, not including retainer, and when are they payable? $175 per hour.

Will adoptive parents pay a separate attorney for the birthmother, and if yes, what are approximate legal fees? Yes. Depends on that attorney's rates.

What are the approximate fees for medical and hospital expenses for the birthmother and baby, when they have no insurance? $3,500

What are the approximate homestudy fees in your state? $1,500, estimated.

If living expenses for a birthmother are allowed, what is the average amount paid? Not allowed.

Are you an adoptive parent, adopted person, or birthparent? Adoptive parent.

In how many of your cases has an adoptive parent lost a placed child due to a birthparent challenge? 0

Have you lost any adoption litigation filed against you by an adoptive parent or birthparent? No.

In about what percentage of your adoptions do adopting parents and birthparents know each other's first and last names? 40%

Are you a member of the American Academy of Adoption Attorneys and/or the National Council for Adoption? American Academy of Adoption Attorneys.

OKLAHOMA

CYNTHIA CALIBANI, ATTORNEY AT LAW

207 SW 3rd St., Lawton, OK 73501
(580) 248-1199 • Fax: (580) 248-1806

What are your office hours when you accept calls from adoptive parents?
10 a.m.–5 p.m., CT

Education: BA in communications, Oklahoma State University, 1981; JD, Oklahoma City University, 1986

What states or countries do your adoptive parents come from? Mainly Oklahoma, have done many interstate adoptions.

What states or countries do your birthparents/adopted children come from? United States.

Are other attorneys in your law firm active in adoption? No.

In what year did you begin legal work in adoptions? 1987

How many nonrelative adoptions did you arrange in 1998? 15

About how many children have you placed since you started? 200

About what percent of your work is devoted to adoption? 50%

In 1998, what was the average time from when a prospective adoptive parent retained you to the placement of a child? 18 mos.

What made you decide to work in the adoption field? Love of children.

Do you have any criteria for adoptive parents, such as age, number of children in the home, etc.? No.

What percent of your adoptions are infants under 6 mos.? 90%

Do you have a waiting list of prospective parents? Yes.

Is it all right if adopting parents are on waiting lists of other attorneys or agencies? Yes.

Do you charge adoptive parents for a first phone consultation? No.

Do you charge adoptive parents for a first office consultation? No.

Do you charge a retainer fee, and if yes, what is it and when is it payable? Yes; $1,500, payable on receipt of a reliable lead with a birthmother.

What are your legal fees, not including retainer, and when are they payable? $1,000 in addition to retainer and costs.

Will adoptive parents pay a separate attorney for the birthmother, and if yes, what are approximate legal fees? Yes; $750–1,500.

What are the approximate fees for medical and hospital expenses for the birthmother and baby, when they have no insurance? $8,000

What are the approximate homestudy fees in your state? $450–700

If living expenses for a birthmother are allowed, what is the average amount paid? $1,000

In how many of your cases has an adoptive parent lost a placed child due to a birthparent challenge? 1

Have you lost any adoption litigation filed against you by an adoptive parent or birthparent? No.

In about what percentage of your adoptions do adopting parents and birthparents know each other's first and last names? 15%

Are you a member of the American Academy of Adoption Attorneys and/or the National Council for Adoption? American Academy of Adoption Attorneys.

W. R. CUBBAGE
P.O. Box 550, Cushing, OK 74023
(918) 225-2464 • Fax: (918) 225-9292

What are your office hours when you accept calls from adoptive parents?
8 a.m.–5 p.m., CT

Education: BA in journalism, University of Oklahoma; 1966, JD, University of Tulsa, 1969

What states or countries do your adoptive parents come from? Throughout the lower 48 states.

What states or countries do your birthparents/adopted children come from? Same as above.

Are other attorneys in your law firm active in adoption? No.

In what year did you begin legal work in adoptions? 1969

About what percent of your work is devoted to adoption? 20%

What made you decide to work in the adoption field? The results.

Do you have a waiting list of prospective parents? Yes.

Is it all right if adopting parents are on waiting lists of other attorneys or agencies? Yes.

Do you charge adoptive parents for a first phone consultation? No.

Do you charge adoptive parents for a first office consultation? No.

Do you charge a retainer fee, and if yes, what is it and when is it payable? Yes; $1,500, payable on receipt of agreement letter.

What are your legal fees, not including retainer, and when are they payable? Varies. Hourly rate of $125, payable on monthly billing.

Will adoptive parents pay a separate attorney for the birthmother, and if yes, what are approximate legal fees? Yes. Varies.

What are the approximate fees for medical and hospital expenses for the birthmother and baby, when they have no insurance? $5,000 and up.

What are the approximate homestudy fees in your state? $500 and up.

If living expenses for a birthmother are allowed, what is the average amount paid? Varies.

In how many of your cases has an adoptive parent lost a placed child due to a birthparent challenge? One.

Have you lost any adoption litigation filed against you by an adoptive parent or birthparent? No.

In about what percentage of your adoptions do adopting parents and birthparents know each other's first and last names? 50%

Are you a member of the American Academy of Adoption Attorneys and/or the National Council for Adoption? American Academy of Adoption Attorneys.

Phyllis L. Zimmerman, Attorney at Law

15 W. 6th St., Suite 1220, Tulsa, OK 74119-5444
(918) 582-6151 • Fax: (918) 582-6153

What are your office hours when you accept calls from adoptive parents?
9 a.m.–4 p.m., CT

Education: BS in business administration, Tulsa University, 1952; JD, Washington College of Law, American University, 1963

What states or countries do your adoptive parents come from? Oklahoma, Texas, Kansas, Missouri, California, Virginia, New Mexico.

What states or countries do your birthparents/adopted children come from? Same as above, only with children from Romania, China, Russia, Guatemala, Peru, India, and Korea.

Are other attorneys in your law firm active in adoption? No.

In what year did you begin legal work in adoptions? 1964

How many nonrelative adoptions did you arrange in 1998? 30

About how many children have you placed since you started? Close to 1,000.

About what percent of your work is devoted to adoption? 90%

In 1998, what was the average time from when a prospective adoptive parent retained you to the placement of a child? About a year.

What made you decide to work in the adoption field? I love children and felt this was a way for me to feel I made a difference in some lives. Also, my first adoption was for my sister and her husband, who asked me to help them find a child. It was so satisfying that I decided to continue. (This child is now a 32-year-old man with a wife and children of his own.)

Do you have any criteria for adoptive parents, such as age, number of children in the home, etc., and if so, what are they? Only that they have a Christian home. I don't care what denomination, only that the child gets some values from being in a Christian home. I have no criteria as to age or number of children in the home, but birthmothers seem to choose people with no children in their home.

What percent of your adoptions are infants under 6 mos.? 80%

Do you have a waiting list of prospective parents? Yes.

Is it all right if adopting parents are on waiting lists of other attorneys or agencies? Yes, I encourage it.

Do you charge adoptive parents for a first phone consultation? No.

Do you charge adoptive parents for a first office consultation, and if yes, what is the fee? Yes; depends on length of visit, $50–150.

Do you charge a retainer fee? No.

What are your legal fees, not including retainer, and when are they payable? Anywhere from $1,000 to $5,000, half payable when they get the child, the other half when the adoption is completed.

Will adoptive parents pay a separate attorney for the birthmother, and if yes, what are approximate legal fees? Yes; $500.

What are the approximate fees for medical and hospital expenses for the birthmother and baby, when they have no insurance? $5,000–8,000

What are the approximate homestudy fees in your state? $500

If living expenses for a birthmother are allowed, what is the average amount paid? About $2,000.

In how many of your cases has an adoptive parent lost a placed child due to a birthparent challenge? 3 or 4

Have you lost any adoption litigation filed against you by an adoptive parent or birthparent? No.

In about what percentage of your adoptions do adopting parents and birthparents know each other's first and last names? 0%

Are you a member of the American Academy of Adoption Attorneys and/or the National Council for Adoption? American Academy of Adoption Attorneys.

OREGON

JOHN CHALLY

Bouneff and Chally
825 NE Multnomah, Suite 1125, Portland, OR 97232
(503) 238-9720
E-mail: bounchal@worldstar.com • www.worldstar.com/~bounchal

What are your office hours when you accept calls from adoptive parents?
8 a.m.–5 p.m., PT

Education: University of the Pacific, 1972; University of the Pacific McGeorge School of Law, 1976

What states or countries do your adoptive parents come from? The majority of our clients are from Oregon. We work with adoptive families from all states and countries.

What states or countries do your birthparents/adopted children come from? Mostly Oregon and Washington.

Are other attorneys in your law firm active in adoption? Yes.

In what year did you begin legal work in adoptions? 1975

How many nonrelative adoptions did you arrange in 1998? 40

About how many children have you placed since you started? Thousands.

About what percent of your work is devoted to adoption? 70%

In 1998, what was the average time from when a prospective adoptive parent retained you to the placement of a child? 6 mos.

What made you decide to work in the adoption field? It was a much needed alternative to a busy litigation practice. It is more creative and fulfilling than most legal work.

Do you have any criteria for adoptive parents, such as age, number of children in the home, etc., and if so, what are they? Adoptive parents will be more successful if they are interested in some openness with the birthparents. Most birthparents want some postplacement contact or visitation.

What percent of your adoptions are infants under 6 mos.? 99%

Do you have a waiting list of prospective parents? No.

Is it all right if adopting parents are on waiting lists of other attorneys or agencies? Yes.

Do you charge adoptive parents for a first phone consultation? No.

Do you charge adoptive parents for a first office consultation, and if yes, what is the fee? Yes; $195.

Do you charge a retainer fee, and if yes, what is it and when is it payable? Yes. It depends on the estimated cost of a specific adoption. It is usually half of the estimated legal fee/cost.

What are your legal fees, not including retainer, and when are they payable? Agency adoption finalizations, $500 plus costs; independent adoptions, $1,500–4,000 plus costs.

Will adoptive parents pay a separate attorney for the birthmother, and if yes, what are approximate legal fees? Yes; $1,000–2,500.

What are the approximate fees for medical and hospital expenses for the birthmother and baby, when they have no insurance? $5,000–20,000 (caesarean section).

What are the approximate homestudy fees in your state? $794 for homestudy, $675 for postplacement report/visits.

If living expenses for a birthmother are allowed, what is the average amount paid? Reasonable fees of $1,000 to $1,750 per month for several months.

In how many of your cases has an adoptive parent lost a placed child due to a birthparent challenge? I am an adoption litigation attorney and take cases from attorneys and agencies when an adoption becomes contested.

Have you lost any adoption litigation filed against you by an adoptive parent or birthparent? No.

In about what percentage of your adoptions do adopting parents and birthparents know each other's first and last names? 99%

Are you a member of the American Academy of Adoption Attorneys and/or the National Council for Adoption? American Academy of Adoption Attorneys.

CATHERINE M. DEXTER

Dexter and Moffet
921 SW Washington #865, Portland, OR 97205
(503) 222-2474 • Fax: (503) 274-7888
E-mail: dexter.moffet@hevanet.com

What are your office hours when you accept calls from adoptive parents?
8:30 a.m.–5 p.m., Monday–Friday, PT

Education: BA in history, Michigan State University, 1977; JD, Northwestern School of Law at Lewis and Clark College, 1982

What states or countries do your adoptive parents come from? All states in the United States, Canada, England, Sweden, Italy.

What states or countries do your birthparents/adopted children come from? United States.

Are other attorneys in your law firm active in adoption? Yes.

In what year did you begin legal work in adoptions? 1983

How many nonrelative adoptions did you arrange in 1998? About 60

About how many children have you placed since you started? 500+

About what percent of your work is devoted to adoption? 98%

In 1998, what was the average time from when a prospective adoptive parent retained you to the placement of a child? 1 year

What made you decide to work in the adoption field? It is a positive area of the law; I like helping to create families.

Do you have any criteria for adoptive parents, such as age, number of children in the home, etc.? No; they need to pass a homestudy.

What percent of your adoptions are infants under 6 mos.? 90%

Do you have a waiting list of prospective parents? Yes.

Is it all right if adopting parents are on waiting lists of other attorneys or agencies? Yes.

Do you charge adoptive parents for a first phone consultation? No. We will answer some questions on the phone. A $300 office or phone consultation is required before we open a file.

Do you charge adoptive parents for a first office consultation, and if yes, what is the fee? Yes; $300.

Do you charge a retainer fee? No.

What are your legal fees, not including retainer, and when are they payable? We charge at an hourly rate for time spent.

Will adoptive parents pay a separate attorney for the birthmother, and if yes, what are approximate legal fees? Yes; $1,000.

What are the approximate fees for medical and hospital expenses for the birthmother and baby, when they have no insurance? $8,500

What are the approximate homestudy fees in your state? $1,100

If living expenses for a birthmother are allowed, what is the average amount paid? $2,500

In how many of your cases has an adoptive parent lost a placed child due to a birthparent challenge? Less than 1%.

Have you lost any adoption litigation filed against you by an adoptive parent or birthparent? No.

In about what percentage of your adoptions do adopting parents and birthparents know each other's first and last names? 40%

Are you a member of the American Academy of Adoption Attorneys and/or the National Council for Adoption? American Academy of Adoption Attorneys.

SUSAN C. MOFFET

Dexter and Moffet
921 SW Washington, Suite 865, Portland, OR 97205
(503) 222-2474 • Fax: (503) 274-7888
E-mail: dexter.moffet@hevanet.com

What are your office hours when you accept calls from adoptive parents?
8:30 a.m.–5 p.m. Monday–Friday, PT

Education: BS in business administration/finance law and BS in psychology, Portland State University, 1983; JD, Northwestern School of Law at Lewis and Clark College, 1986

What states or countries do your adoptive parents come from? All states in the United States; Canada, England, France, Italy, Saudi Arabia, etc.

What states or countries do your birthparents/adopted children come from? United States.

Are other attorneys in your law firm active in adoption? Yes.

In what year did you begin legal work in adoptions? 1984 (as legal assistance)

How many nonrelative adoptions did you arrange in 1998? 60

About how many children have you placed since you started? 500+

About what percent of your work is devoted to adoption? 100%

In 1998, what was the average time from when a prospective adoptive parent retained you to the placement of a child? 1 year

What made you decide to work in the adoption field? I enjoy the work; I enjoy helping families come together.

Do you have any criteria for adoptive parents, such as age, number of children in the home, etc.? No; they need to pass a homestudy.

What percent of your adoptions are infants under 6 mos.? 90%

Do you have a waiting list of prospective parents? Yes.

Is it all right if adopting parents are on waiting lists of other attorneys or agencies? Yes.

Do you charge adoptive parents for a first phone consultation, and if yes, what is the fee? No; we will charge a $300 consultation fee before opening a file, but answer general inquiring questions without charge.

Do you charge adoptive parents for a first office consultation, and if yes, what is the fee? Yes; $300 for a two-hour conference.

Do you charge a retainer fee? No. Unless the adopting parent comes to us with a birthmother lead; then we charge $1,000 retainer to begin work.

What are your legal fees, not including retainer, and when are they payable? At an hourly rate, based on actual time spent; payable within 30 days of billing.

Will adoptive parents pay a separate attorney for the birthmother, and if yes, what are approximate legal fees? Yes; $1,000.

What are the approximate fees for medical and hospital expenses for the birthmother and baby, when they have no insurance? $8,000–9,000

What are the approximate homestudy fees in your state? $1,100

If living expenses for a birthmother are allowed, what is the average amount paid? $2,500

In how many of your cases has an adoptive parent lost a placed child due to a birthparent challenge? Less than 1%

Have you lost any adoption litigation filed against you by an adoptive parent or birthparent? No.

In about what percentage of your adoptions do adopting parents and birthparents know each other's first and last names? 30%

Are you a member of the American Academy of Adoption Attorneys and/or the National Council for Adoption? American Academy of Adoption Attorneys.

LAURENCE H. SPIEGEL

P.O. Box 1708, Lake Oswego, OR 97035
(503) 635-7773 • Fax: (503) 635-1526
E-mail: cbspiegel@juno.com

What are your office hours when you accept calls from adoptive parents?
8:30 a.m.–5 p.m. Monday–Friday, PT

Education: BA, United States International University, 1969; MLS, Syracuse University, 1973; JD, Lewis and Clark Law School, 1981

What states or countries do your adoptive parents come from? Can be any state or country.

What states or countries do your birthparents/adopted children come from? Can be any state or country.

Are other attorneys in your law firm active in adoption? No.

In what year did you begin legal work in adoptions? 1981

How many nonrelative adoptions did you arrange in 1998? 20

About how many children have you placed since you started? 300

About what percent of your work is devoted to adoption? 99%

In 1998, what was the average time from when a prospective adoptive parent retained you to the placement of a child? Less than one year, depending on circumstances.

What made you decide to work in the adoption field? Personal infertility and ultimate adoptions.

Do you have any criteria for adoptive parents, such as age, number of children in the home, etc., and if so, what are they? Must be approved in homestudy by licensed adoption agency. This can be before or after initial meeting.

What percent of your adoptions are infants under 6 mos.? 95%

Do you have a waiting list of prospective parents? No.

Is it all right if adopting parents are on waiting lists of other attorneys or agencies? Yes.

Do you charge adoptive parents for a first phone consultation, and if yes, what is the fee? Yes; $120 per hour, $200 maximum.

Do you charge adoptive parents for a first office consultation, and if yes, what is the fee? Yes; $120 per hour, $200 maximum.

Do you charge a retainer fee, and if yes, what is it and when is it payable? Yes; $600, payable after initial conference.

What are your legal fees, not including retainer, and when are they payable? $120 per hour.

Will adoptive parents pay a separate attorney for the birthmother, and if yes, what are approximate legal fees? Yes. Depends on what that attorney charges.

What are the approximate fees for medical and hospital expenses for the birthmother and baby, when they have no insurance? $6,000

What are the approximate homestudy fees in your state? $495 preplacement, $545 postplacement.

If living expenses for a birthmother are allowed, what is the average amount paid? $3,000

If you manage international adoptions, what is the average fee for translating documents? Depends on how much needs to be translated.

Are you an adoptive parent, adopted person, or birthparent? Adoptive parent.

In how many of your cases has an adoptive parent lost a placed child due to a birthparent challenge? One under current Oregon law.

Have you lost any adoption litigation filed against you by an adoptive parent or birthparent? No.

In about what percentage of your adoptions do adopting parents and birthparents know each other's first and last names? 80%

Are you a member of the American Academy of Adoption Attorneys and/or the National Council for Adoption? American Academy of Adoption Attorneys.

PENNSYLVANIA

DENISE M. BIERLY, ESQUIRE

Delafield, McGee, Jones and Kauffman
300 South Allen St., Suite 300, State College, PA 16801-4841
(814) 237-6278 • Fax: (814) 237-3660

What are your office hours when you accept calls from adoptive parents?
8:30 a.m.–5 p.m., Tuesday and Thursdays; 8:30 a.m.–11:30 a.m., Fridays, ET

Education: BA, in speech communications, Pennsylvania State University, 1987; JD, Dickinson School of Law, 1990

What states or countries do your adoptive parents come from? Pennsylvania, Virginia, Texas.

What states or countries do your birthparents/adopted children come from?
Pennsylvania, New Jersey, New York, Virginia, Tennessee, Ohio, Russia, Bolivia, Vietnam.

Are other attorneys in your law firm active in adoption? No.

In what year did you begin legal work in adoptions? 1990

How many nonrelative adoptions did you arrange in 1998? 12

About how many children have you placed since you started? 50

About what percent of your work is devoted to adoption? 60%

In 1998, what was the average time from when a prospective adoptive parent retained you to the placement of a child? 2 years

What made you decide to work in the adoption field? I am an adoptive parent. I enjoy the practice of adoption.

Do you have any criteria for adoptive parents, such as age, number of children in the home, etc.? No written criteria.

What percent of your adoptions are infants under 6 mos.? 99%

Do you have a waiting list of prospective parents? Yes.

Is it all right if adopting parents are on waiting lists of other attorneys or agencies? Yes.

Do you charge adoptive parents for a first phone consultation, and if yes, what is the fee? Yes; I request that they come to an office conference; $60.

Do you charge adoptive parents for a first office consultation, and if yes, what is the fee? Yes; $60.

Do you charge a retainer fee, and if yes, what is it and when is it payable? Yes; $2,000 at the time of placement.

What are your legal fees, not including retainer, and when are they payable? $110–125 per hour, payable monthly.

Will adoptive parents pay a separate attorney for the birthmother, and if yes, what are approximate legal fees? Yes; $1,000.

What are the approximate fees for medical and hospital expenses for the birthmother and baby, when they have no insurance? $5,000

What are the approximate homestudy fees in your state? $1,000

If living expenses for a birthmother are allowed, what is the average amount paid? $300

Are you an adoptive parent, adopted person, or birthparent? Adoptive parent.

In how many of your cases has an adoptive parent lost a placed child due to a birthparent challenge? 3

Have you lost any adoption litigation filed against you by an adoptive parent or birthparent? Yes.

In about what percentage of your adoptions do adopting parents and birthparents know each other's first and last names? 50%

Are you a member of the American Academy of Adoption Attorneys and/or the National Council for Adoption? American Academy of Adoption Attorneys.

DEBRA FOX

Fox and Leventon
355 W. Lancaster Ave., Haverford, PA 19041
(610) 896-4832 • Fax: (610) 642-7731

What are your office hours when you accept calls from adoptive parents?
9 a.m.–5 p.m., ET

Education: BA in liberal arts, George Washington University, 1982; JD, Temple University School of Law, 1985

What states or countries do your adoptive parents come from? Many states in United States, Canada, and Europe.

What states or countries do your birthparents/adopted children come from? Primarily Pennsylvania, but many other states as well.

Are other attorneys in your law firm active in adoption? Yes.

In what year did you begin legal work in adoptions? 1985

How many nonrelative adoptions did you arrange in 1998? Approximately 35

About how many children have you placed since you started? 500

About what percent of your work is devoted to adoption? 100%

In 1998, what was the average time from when a prospective adoptive parent retained you to the placement of a child? I do not help families identify children in my law practice. However, in the agency which I direct, the wait is approximately 6 mos. for special needs and African-American infants.

What made you decide to work in the adoption field? I wanted to work in a nonadversarial area of the law, helping people in a very direct way.

Do you have any criteria for adoptive parents, such as age, number of children in the home, etc., and if so, what are they? Must have an approved homestudy. Otherwise there are no preset criteria. Each family is evaluated on a case-by-case basis.

What percent of your adoptions are infants under 6 mos.? 100%

Do you have a waiting list of prospective parents? Yes for the agency, not for the law practice.

Is it all right if adopting parents are on waiting lists of other attorneys or agencies? Yes.

Do you charge adoptive parents for a first phone consultation? No.

Do you charge adoptive parents for a first office consultation, and if yes, what is the fee? Yes; approximately $100.

Do you charge a retainer fee, and if yes, what is it and when is it payable? Yes. It depends on complexity of case. Clients are charged on an hourly basis. Fee is payable on return of retainer letter to office at outset of case.

What are your legal fees, not including retainer, and when are they payable? It depends on complexity of case. Clients are charged on an hourly basis. Fee is payable on return of retainer letter to office at outset of case.

Will adoptive parents pay a separate attorney for the birthmother, and if yes, what are approximate legal fees? Depends on what state birthmother is from and whether such payments are legal in that state. Depends on complexity of case.

What are the approximate fees for medical and hospital expenses for the birthmother and baby, when they have no insurance? Varies too much to state amount.

What are the approximate homestudy fees in your state? $800–1,200

If living expenses for a birthmother are allowed, what is the average amount paid? Not allowed.

In how many of your cases has an adoptive parent lost a placed child due to a birthparent challenge? Less than 1%

Have you lost any adoption litigation filed against you by an adoptive parent or birthparent? Yes.

In about what percentage of your adoptions do adopting parents and birthparents know each other's first and last names? 20%

Are you a member of the American Academy of Adoption Attorneys and/or the National Council for Adoption? American Academy of Adoption Attorneys.

TARA GUTTERMAN

4701 Pine St., J-7, Philadelphia, PA 19143
(215) 748-1441
E-mail: taralaw@aol.com

What are your office hours when you accept calls from adoptive parents?
10 a.m.–5 p.m., ET

What states or countries do your adoptive parents come from? All states.

What states or countries do your birthparents/adopted children come from? Pennsylvania and New Jersey.

Are other attorneys in your law firm active in adoption? Yes.

In what year did you begin legal work in adoptions? 1991

How many nonrelative adoptions did you arrange in 1998? 55

About how many children have you placed since you started? 300

About what percent of your work is devoted to adoption? 100%

In 1998, what was the average time from when a prospective adoptive parent retained you to the placement of a child? 3 mos.

What made you decide to work in the adoption field? Finding stability for children early in life.

Do you have any criteria for adoptive parents, such as age, number of children in the home, etc., and if so, what are they? 21 years of age. No other limits.

What percent of your adoptions are infants under 6 mos.? 100%

Do you have a waiting list of prospective parents? Yes.

Is it all right if adopting parents are on waiting lists of other attorneys or agencies? Yes.

Do you charge adoptive parents for a first phone consultation? No.

Do you charge adoptive parents for a first office consultation? No.

Do you charge a retainer fee? No.

What are your legal fees, not including retainer, and when are they payable? $2,200 at time of placement.

Will adoptive parents pay a separate attorney for the birthmother? No.

What are the approximate homestudy fees in your state? $800–1,000

If living expenses for a birthmother are allowed, what is the average amount paid? $500

In how many of your cases has an adoptive parent lost a placed child due to a birth-parent challenge? 2

Have you lost any adoption litigation filed against you by an adoptive parent or birthparent? No.

In about what percentage of your adoptions do adopting parents and birthparents know each other's first and last names? 0%

Are you a member of the American Academy of Adoption Attorneys and/or the National Council for Adoption? American Academy of Adoption Attorneys.

MARY ANN PETRILLO, ATTORNEY AT LAW

156 Clay Pike, North Huntingdon, PA 15642
(724) 861-8333 • Fax: (724) 861-9594
E-mail: Mapster1@aol.com

What are your office hours when you accept calls from adoptive parents? All hours. I give my home and cell phone number to them for evening and weekend emergencies. Babies wait until I'm on vacation or during the weekend to be born! They especially love the holidays.

Education: BA in sociology, BA in law enforcement, Mercyhurst College, 1980; JD, University of Pittsburgh School of Law, 1983

What states or countries do your adoptive parents come from? All.

What states or countries do your birthparents/adopted children come from? All.

Are other attorneys in your law firm active in adoption? No, I am a sole practitioner.

In what year did you begin legal work in adoptions? 1983

How many nonrelative adoptions did you arrange in 1998? I do not necessarily arrange adoptions, but I have been an intermediary on occasion. I normally initiate and complete the legal process for 60+ adoptions per year.

About how many children have you placed since you started? Private attorneys in Pennsylvania do not place children. Throughout my career, I have initiated or overseen hundreds of adoptions.

About what percent of your work is devoted to adoption? 60–70%

In 1998, what was the average time from when a prospective adoptive parent retained you to the placement of a child? It depends—anywhere from instantaneously (phone calls from a hospital, parent or other professional that a child has been born) to a few years.

What made you decide to work in the adoption field? Adoption is an integral part of my life. I am an adoptive parent and an adoption advocate who has testified before the Pennsylvania Senate for needed adoption reforms. Being both an adoptive mom and an adoption attorney allows me to understand the requisite sensitivity which is needed for all members of the adoption triad while proceeding legally with the case. I truly feel that it's my life's calling.

Do you have any criteria for adoptive parents, such as age, number of children in the home, etc.? No. Each situation should be viewed individually.

What percent of your adoptions are infants under 6 mos.? 50% or more.

Do you have a waiting list of prospective parents? Yes.

Is it all right if adopting parents are on waiting lists of other attorneys or agencies? Yes.

Do you charge adoptive parents for a first phone consultation? No, but a thorough office consultation is highly recommended.

Do you charge adoptive parents for a first office consultation, and if yes, what is the fee? Yes; $150.

Do you charge a retainer fee, and if yes, what is it and when is it payable? Yes. Between $1,500 and $2,000, payable when there has been an adoption plan made between the birthparents and the adoptive family.

What are your legal fees, not including retainer, and when are they payable? I charge against the retainer at the rate of $150 per hour.

Will adoptive parents pay a separate attorney for the birthmother? Sometimes. It depends on the situation.

What are the approximate fees for medical and hospital expenses for the birthmother and baby, when they have no insurance? Rarely an issue; medical care can usually be arranged.

What are the approximate homestudy fees in your state? $1,000–1,500

If living expenses for a birthmother are allowed, what is the average amount paid? Not allowed.

If you manage international adoptions, what is the average fee for translating documents? I normally assist clients in post-adoption registration of decrees, name changes, obtaining new birth certificates, etc. The documents are usually already translated from the county of origin.

Are you an adoptive parent, adopted person, or birthparent? Adoptive parent.

In how many of your cases has an adoptive parent lost a placed child due to a birthparent challenge? In a few cases birthparents have changed their minds during the normal revocation or consent period, but I have never been involved with the loss of a child after the court hearing or termination of parental rights.

Have you lost any adoption litigation filed against you by an adoptive parent or birthparent? No.

In about what percentage of your adoptions do adopting parents and birthparents know each other's first and last names? 50%

Are you a member of the American Academy of Adoption Attorneys and/or the National Council for Adoption? American Academy of Adoption Attorneys.

SAMUEL C. TOTARO, JR.

Kellis Totaro and Soffer
Four Greenwood Square, Suite 100, Bensalem, PA 19020
(215) 244-1045 • Fax: (215) 244-0641
E-mail: totaro@bellatlantic.net

What are your office hours when you accept calls from adoptive parents?
9 a.m.–5 p.m., ET

Education: BS, Ursinus College, 1969; JD, University of Memphis, 1974

What states or countries do your adoptive parents come from? Pennsylvania.

What states or countries do your birthparents/adopted children come from? All
states; some from foreign countries.

Are other attorneys in your law firm active in adoption? No.

In what year did you begin legal work in adoptions? 1980

How many nonrelative adoptions did you arrange in 1998? 75

About how many children have you placed since you started? Over 3,000

About what percent of your work is devoted to adoption? 40%

In 1998, what was the average time from when a prospective adoptive parent retained you to the placement of a child? 1 year

What made you decide to work in the adoption field? I enjoy working with families
who are eager to create a family, rather than other family law work where they use
a child to drive a wedge between families.

**Do you have any criteria for adoptive parents, such as age, number of children in
the home, etc., and if so, what are they?** No more than two children.

What percent of your adoptions are infants under 6 mos.? 100%

Do you have a waiting list of prospective parents? No.

Is it all right if adopting parents are on waiting lists of other attorneys or agencies?
Yes.

Do you charge adoptive parents for a first phone consultation? No.

**Do you charge adoptive parents for a first office consultation, and if yes, what is the
fee?** Yes; $195.

Do you charge a retainer fee, and if yes, what is it and when is it payable? Yes; $750,
payable when retained.

What are your legal fees, not including retainer, and when are they payable? Varies;
interstate placement is flat fee of $2,500–3,000; intrastate is on time basis (approximately $3,500).

**Will adoptive parents pay a separate attorney for the birthmother, and if yes, what
are approximate legal fees?** Yes. Depends on attorney (approximately $2,500).

What are the approximate fees for medical and hospital expenses for the birthmother and baby, when they have no insurance? $8,500 and up.

What are the approximate homestudy fees in your state? $800

If living expenses for a birthmother are allowed, what is the average amount paid? Not allowed.

Are you an adoptive parent, adopted person, or birthparent? Adoptive parent.

In how many of your cases has an adoptive parent lost a placed child due to a birthparent challenge? Maybe one or two cases a year.

Have you lost any adoption litigation filed against you by an adoptive parent or birthparent? No.

In about what percentage of your adoptions do adopting parents and birthparents know each other's first and last names? Vast majority.

Are you a member of the American Academy of Adoption Attorneys and/or the National Council for Adoption? American Academy of Adoption Attorneys and past president (1996–1997) of the American Academy of Adoption Attorneys.

SOUTH CAROLINA

RICHARD C. BELL

1535 Sam Rittenberg Blvd. NE, Suite E, Charleston, SC 29407
(843) 556-3391 • Fax: (843) 556-3496
E-mail: rcbadopts@aol.com • www.alovingchoice.com

What are your office hours when you accept calls from adoptive parents? 9 a.m.–5 p.m., ET

Education: BS in premed, Clemson University, 1967; JD, University of South Carolina, 1973; MA in history, College of Charleston, 1996; EID, United States Sports Academy, 1999

What states or countries do your adoptive parents come from? Domestic, South Carolina; international, all over.

What states or countries do your birthparents/adopted children come from? All over.

Are other attorneys in your law firm active in adoption? No.

In what year did you begin legal work in adoptions? 1982

How many nonrelative adoptions did you arrange in 1998? 60

About how many children have you placed since you started? 375

About what percent of your work is devoted to adoption? 100%

In 1998, what was the average time from when a prospective adoptive parent retained you to the placement of a child? 10 mos.

What made you decide to work in the adoption field? Adopted two girls, in 1982 and 1984.

Do you have any criteria for adoptive parents, such as age, number of children in the home, etc., and if so, what are they? No criteria but if seeking a white child must be South Carolina residents, but from anywhere for mixed racial (this is because South Carolina restricts placements).

What percent of your adoptions are infants under 6 mos.? 99%

Do you have a waiting list of prospective parents? Yes.

Is it all right if adopting parents are on waiting lists of other attorneys or agencies? Yes.

Do you charge adoptive parents for a first phone consultation? No.

Do you charge adoptive parents for a first office consultation? No.

Do you charge a retainer fee, and if yes, what is it and when is it payable? Yes. $750, payable to A Loving Choice Adoption Agency.

What are your legal fees, not including retainer, and when are they payable? Agency fees, $5,750, payable in two parts, beginning after a month; legal fees, approximately $2,000.

Will adoptive parents pay a separate attorney for the birthmother? No.

What are the approximate fees for medical and hospital expenses for the birthmother and baby, when they have no insurance? $4,000–6,000

What are the approximate homestudy fees in your state? $500–1,000

If living expenses for a birthmother are allowed, what is the average amount paid? $750–1,250

If you manage international adoptions, what is the average fee for translating documents? $500–700

Are you an adoptive parent, adopted person, or birthparent? Adoptive parent.

In how many of your cases has an adoptive parent lost a placed child due to a birthparent challenge? One

Have you lost any adoption litigation filed against you by an adoptive parent or birthparent? No.

In about what percentage of your adoptions do adopting parents and birthparents know each other's first and last names? 1%

FREDERICK M. CORLEY, ATTORNEY AT LAW

704 Prince St.
P.O. Box 2265, Beaufort, SC 29901-2265
(843) 524-3200 • Fax: (843) 522-3221
E-mail: rcorley@islc.net

What are your office hours when you accept calls from adoptive parents?
9 a.m.–4 p.m., ET

Education: BA in government, Wofford College, 1973; JD, University of South Carolina, 1976

What states or countries do your adoptive parents come from? Mostly South Carolina, but I have dealt with adoptive parents from California, Colorado, North Carolina, and Georgia.

What states or countries do your birthparents/adopted children come from? Mostly South Carolina, but I have dealt with birthparents from Tennessee.

Are other attorneys in your law firm active in adoption? No.

In what year did you begin legal work in adoptions? 1979

How many nonrelative adoptions did you arrange in 1998? Approximately 20.

About how many children have you placed since you started? Approximately 200.

About what percent of your work is devoted to adoption? 25%

In 1998, what was the average time from when a prospective adoptive parent retained you to the placement of a child? Approximately 3 mos. (Please keep in mind that I only accept a retainer after a match is agreed on by the birthparents.)

What made you decide to work in the adoption field? There is no other field that can provide the kinds of satisfaction that placing a child in the arms of new parents brings.

Do you have any criteria for adoptive parents, such as age, number of children in the home, etc.? No. Such criteria are determined by individual birthparents and the law.

What percent of your adoptions are infants under 6 mos.? 75%

Do you have a waiting list of prospective parents? Yes.

Is it all right if adopting parents are on waiting lists of other attorneys or agencies? Yes.

Do you charge adoptive parents for a first phone consultation? No.

Do you charge adoptive parents for a first office consultation? No.

Do you charge a retainer fee, and if yes, what is it and when is it payable? Yes. A retainer of 50% of the estimated total fee is payable on matching adoptive parents with birthparents.

What are your legal fees, not including retainer, and when are they payable? The balance of legal fees are payable by the date of the final adoption hearing.

Will adoptive parents pay a separate attorney for the birthmother, and if yes, what are approximate legal fees? Yes. Varies greatly depending on the time necessarily expended by birthmother's attorney.

What are the approximate fees for medical and hospital expenses for the birthmother and baby, when they have no insurance? $3,000

What are the approximate homestudy fees in your state? $850

If living expenses for a birthmother are allowed, what is the average amount paid? Varies widely.

In how many of your cases has an adoptive parent lost a placed child due to a birth-parent challenge? None.

Have you lost any adoption litigation filed against you by an adoptive parent or birthparent? No.

In about what percentage of your adoptions do adopting parents and birthparents know each other's first and last names? 25%

Are you a member of the American Academy of Adoption Attorneys and/or the National Council for Adoption? American Academy of Adoption Attorneys.

THOMAS P. LOWNDES, JR.

P.O. Box 214, 128 Meeting St., Charleston, SC 29402
(843) 723-1688 • Fax: (843) 722-7439

What are your office hours when you accept calls from adoptive parents? 9 a.m.–5 p.m., ET

Education: BA, The Citadel, 1960; JD, University of South Carolina, 1966

What states or countries do your adoptive parents come from? Mostly Eastern and Southern United States.

What states or countries do your birthparents/adopted children come from? South Carolina predominantly.

Are other attorneys in your law firm active in adoption? No. No other lawyers in my practice.

In what year did you begin legal work in adoptions? 1966

How many nonrelative adoptions did you arrange in 1998? Do not monitor.

About how many children have you placed since you started? In over 30 years the office has handled over 1,300 files.

About what percent of your work is devoted to adoption? 60%

In 1998, what was the average time from when a prospective adoptive parent retained you to the placement of a child? Controlled by profile requirements.

Do you have any criteria for adoptive parents, such as age, number of children in the home, etc.? No, birthmothers request family profiles.

What percent of your adoptions are infants under 6 mos.? 95%

Do you have a waiting list of prospective parents? No. We place according to profiles requested by birthmothers, not according to calendar receipt of portfolios.

Is it all right if adopting parents are on waiting lists of other attorneys or agencies? Yes, absolutely.

Do you charge adoptive parents for a first phone consultation? No, if limited.

Do you charge adoptive parents for a first office consultation, and if yes, what is the fee? Yes; $100 for initial consultation outside of possible placement.

Do you charge a retainer fee, and if yes, what is it and when is it payable? Yes. Payable once a placement has been made, active working with birthmother: $1,500.

What are your legal fees, not including retainer, and when are they payable? $4,000 (+)

Will adoptive parents pay a separate attorney for the birthmother, and if yes, what are approximate legal fees? Yes; $1,500.

What are the approximate fees for medical and hospital expenses for the birth-mother and baby, when they have no insurance? $2,200 for obstetrics, $4,500 for hospital if no prepayment deposit plan available or exercised.

What are the approximate homestudy fees in your state? $500–1,200

If living expenses for a birthmother are allowed, what is the average amount paid? Law states it must be reasonable and necessary (based on circumstance).

In how many of your cases has an adoptive parent lost a placed child due to a birth-parent challenge? Career: fewer than 5.

Have you lost any adoption litigation filed against you by an adoptive parent or birthparent? No. Had voluntary relinquishment prior to filing of petition.

In about what percentage of your adoptions do adopting parents and birthparents know each other's first and last names? 1/3

Are you a member of the American Academy of Adoption Attorneys and/or the National Council for Adoption? American Academy of Adoption Attorneys.

Is there anything I have not asked you that is important? Number of placement is not as important as quality of the adoption. There are always larger agencies/private attorneys that produce volume and not quality adoption.

TENNESSEE

LISA L. COLLINS

Tuke Yopp and Sweeney, PLC
Nations Bank Plaza, Suite 1100, 414 Union St., Nashville, TN 37219
(615) 313-3335 • Fax: (615) 313-3310
E-mail: lcollins@tys.com

What are your office hours when you accept calls from adoptive parents? Anytime. Direct-dial number goes directly to my office/voicemail.

Education: BA, University of Tennessee, 1990; JD, Vanderbilt University, 1993

What states or countries do your adoptive parents come from? Mainly Tennessee, but accepting from all states.

What states or countries do your birthparents/adopted children come from? Mainly Tennessee, but also from all over the country.

Are other attorneys in your law firm active in adoption? Yes. Robert D. Tuke.

In what year did you begin legal work in adoptions? 1993

How many nonrelative adoptions did you arrange in 1998? I provided legal services in approximately 200 adoption-related cases. Attorneys in Tennessee are only allowed to provide legal services in adoptions. "Arrange" is difficult to define under Tennessee law.

About how many children have you placed since you started? Attorneys in Tennessee are not allowed by law to place children.

About what percent of your work is devoted to adoption? 100%

What made you decide to work in the adoption field? My interests in helping children and families.

Do you have any criteria for adoptive parents, such as age, number of children in the home, etc.? No. All adoptive parents must go through a homestudy process with a licensed child placing agency or LCSW.

What percent of your adoptions are infants under 6 mos.? 70%

Do you have a waiting list of prospective parents? Yes.

Is it all right if adopting parents are on waiting lists of other attorneys or agencies? Yes.

Do you charge adoptive parents for a first phone consultation? No.

Do you charge adoptive parents for a first office consultation, and if yes, what is the fee? Yes. Varies.

Do you charge a retainer fee, and if yes, what is it and when is it payable? Yes. Varies.

What are your legal fees, not including retainer, and when are they payable? Varies.

Will adoptive parents pay a separate attorney for the birthmother, and if yes, what are approximate legal fees? Yes. Varies.

What are the approximate fees for medical and hospital expenses for the birthmother and baby, when they have no insurance? Varies.

What are the approximate homestudy fees in your state? Varies.

If living expenses for a birthmother are allowed, what is the average amount paid? Varies.

In how many of your cases has an adoptive parent lost a placed child due to a birthparent challenge? Very few times have I had a contested litigation, but birthparents have changed their minds.

Have you lost any adoption litigation filed against you by an adoptive parent or birthparent? Don't understand question.

In about what percentage of your adoptions do adopting parents and birthparents know each other's first and last names? 90%

Are you a member of the American Academy of Adoption Attorneys and/or the National Council for Adoption? American Academy of Adoption Attorneys.

DAWN COPPOCK

2101 Doane Lane, Strawberry Plains, TN 37871
(423) 933-8173 • Fax: (423) 933-3272

What are your office hours when you accept calls from adoptive parents?
9 a.m.–5 p.m., Monday–Thursday, ET

Education: BS in management and business data processing, Carson-Newman College, 1983; JD, Marshall-Wythe School of Law, College of William and Mary, 1987

What states or countries do your adoptive parents come from? Almost all are from Tennessee.

What states or countries do your birthparents/adopted children come from? Most states and the usual countries active in international adoption.

Are other attorneys in your law firm active in adoption? No.

In what year did you begin legal work in adoptions? 1989

How many nonrelative adoptions did you arrange in 1998? Not arrange, but handled about 66.

About how many children have you placed since you started? In Tennessee, attorneys are not allowed to place children.

About what percent of your work is devoted to adoption? 100%

In 1998, what was the average time from when a prospective adoptive parent retained you to the placement of a child? 1 year

What made you decide to work in the adoption field? I love families and children. The legal issues are interesting and I enjoy the emotional/psychological issues as well.

Do you have any criteria for adoptive parents, such as age, number of children in the home, etc., and if so, what are they? Approved homestudy.

What percent of your adoptions are infants under 6 mos.? 90%

Do you have a waiting list of prospective parents? No.

Is it all right if adopting parents are on waiting lists of other attorneys or agencies? Yes.

Do you charge adoptive parents for a first phone consultation, and if yes, what is the fee? Not if under 10 minutes; $150 per hour if billed.

Do you charge adoptive parents for a first office consultation, and if yes, what is the fee? Yes; $150 per hour.

Do you charge a retainer fee, and if yes, what is it and when is it payable? Yes; $1,500–3,000, depending on situation. Due after initial meeting with birthmother.

What are your legal fees, not including retainer, and when are they payable? $150 per hour, payable within 30 days of billing.

Will adoptive parents pay a separate attorney for the birthmother, and if yes, what are approximate legal fees? Yes, if she requests one. $800–1,500

What are the approximate fees for medical and hospital expenses for the birth-mother and baby, when they have no insurance? $6,000–12,000

What are the approximate homestudy fees in your state? Homestudy, $1,000; supervision; $500–700.

If living expenses for a birthmother are allowed, what is the average amount paid? $1,000

In how many of your cases has an adoptive parent lost a placed child due to a birth-parent challenge? 2

Have you lost any adoption litigation filed against you by an adoptive parent or birthparent? No. There has been no litigation.

In about what percentage of your adoptions do adopting parents and birthparents know each other's first and last names? 90%

Are you a member of the American Academy of Adoption Attorneys and/or the National Council for Adoption? American Academy of Adoption Attorneys.

MICHAEL S. JENNINGS

Samples, Jennings and Pineda, PLLC
130 Jordan Dr., Chattanooga, TN 37421
(423) 892-2006 • Fax: (423) 892-1919
E-mail: sjplaw@mindspring.com

What are your office hours when you accept calls from adoptive parents? 8 a.m.–5:30 p.m., ET

Education: BA in political science, University of Georgia, 1981; JD, University of Georgia, 1984

What states or countries do your adoptive parents come from? Primarily in Tennessee and Georgia.

What states or countries do your birthparents/adopted children come from? Domestic adoptions, primarily in Tennessee and Georgia; international re-adoptions, primarily children from China, Vietnam, and Russia.

Are other attorneys in your law firm active in adoption? Yes.

In what year did you begin legal work in adoptions? 1987

How many nonrelative adoptions did you arrange in 1998? 15–20

About how many children have you placed since you started? Tennessee attorneys are not permitted to place children for adoption. We have helped approximately 50 birthmothers identify adoptive parents with whom they have placed their children.

About what percent of your work is devoted to adoption? 65%

In 1998, what was the average time from when a prospective adoptive parent retained you to the placement of a child? 1 year

What made you decide to work in the adoption field? I love children and am active in pro-life issues, so adoption is a natural career choice.

Do you have any criteria for adoptive parents, such as age, number of children in the home, etc.? No limiting criteria.

What percent of your adoptions are infants under 6 mos.? 95%

Do you have a waiting list of prospective parents? Yes.

Is it all right if adopting parents are on waiting lists of other attorneys or agencies? Yes.

Do you charge adoptive parents for a first phone consultation, and if yes, what is the fee? Yes; $135/hour.

Do you charge adoptive parents for a first office consultation, and if yes, what is the fee? Yes; $135/hour.

Do you charge a retainer fee, and if yes, what is it and when is it payable? Yes. Depends on circumstances. Retainer ranges from $1,000 to $2,500.

What are your legal fees, not including retainer, and when are they payable? For independent placements we bill all time at an hourly rate. Total fees generally range from $2,000 to $7,000.

Will adoptive parents pay a separate attorney for the birthmother, and if yes, what are approximate legal fees? Depends on circumstances; $1,500.

What are the approximate fees for medical and hospital expenses for the birthmother and baby, when they have no insurance? $3,500

What are the approximate homestudy fees in your state? $1,000

If living expenses for a birthmother are allowed, what is the average amount paid? $1,000

If you manage international adoptions, what is the average fee for translating documents? Depends on language.

In how many of your cases has an adoptive parent lost a placed child due to a birthparent challenge? 1

Have you lost any adoption litigation filed against you by an adoptive parent or birthparent? Yes.

In about what percentage of your adoptions do adopting parents and birthparents know each other's first and last names? 85%

Are you a member of the American Academy of Adoption Attorneys and/or the National Council for Adoption? American Academy of Adoption Attorneys.

TEXAS

VIKA ANDREL

3908 Manchara Rd., Austin, TX 78704
(512) 448-4605 • Fax: (512) 448-1905
E-mail: vandrel@worldnet.att.net

What are your office hours when you accept calls from adoptive parents?
9 a.m.–2 p.m., CT

Education: BA in modern languages, University of Denver, 1971; MLS, University of Texas-Austin, 1973; JD, University of Texas-Austin, 1984

What states or countries do your adoptive parents come from? All over the United States and Canada.

What states or countries do your birthparents/adopted children come from? All over the United States, Mexico, Bulgaria, and Sri Lanka.

Are other attorneys in your law firm active in adoption? No.

In what year did you begin legal work in adoptions? 1989

How many nonrelative adoptions did you arrange in 1998? 9

About how many children have you placed since you started? It is illegal for non-agency to place in Texas. I have facilitated about 700 adoptions.

About what percent of your work is devoted to adoption? 99%

In 1998, what was the average time from when a prospective adoptive parent retained you to the placement of a child? 5 mos.

What made you decide to work in the adoption field? After my first experience in adoption and the joy it brought (and relief) to the parties involved, it was an easy choice.

Do you have any criteria for adoptive parents, such as age, number of children in the home, etc., and if so, what are they? Case-by-case.

What percent of your adoptions are infants under 6 mos.? 99.9%

Do you have a waiting list of prospective parents? Yes.

Is it all right if adopting parents are on waiting lists of other attorneys or agencies? Yes.

Do you charge adoptive parents for a first phone consultation? No.

Do you charge adoptive parents for a first office consultation, and if yes, what is the fee? Yes; $165/hour, usually one-hour consultation.

Do you charge a retainer fee, and if yes, what is it and when is it payable? Yes; $6,000 due prior to services rendered.

Will adoptive parents pay a separate attorney for the birthmother? I represent the birthmother. If they [adoptive parents] desire, they can get another attorney to represent them.

What are approximate additional legal fees? $2,500–5,000

What are the approximate fees for medical and hospital expenses for the birthmother and baby, when they have no insurance? $5,000–8,000

What are the approximate homestudy fees in your state? Varies very widely.

If living expenses for a birthmother are allowed, what is the average amount paid? $4,000

If you manage international adoptions, what is the average fee for translating documents? $650

In how many of your cases has an adoptive parent lost a placed child due to a birthparent challenge? 0

Have you lost any adoption litigation filed against you by an adoptive parent or birthparent? No.

In about what percentage of your adoptions do adopting parents and birthparents know each other's first and last names? 50%, by their choosing.

Are you a member of the American Academy of Adoption Attorneys and/or the National Council for Adoption? American Academy of Adoption Attorneys.

DAVID C. COLE

8340 Meadow Rd., Suite 231, Dallas, TX 75231
(214) 363-5117 • Fax: (214) 750-1970
E-mail: kari@adoptionaccess.com

What are your office hours when you accept calls from adoptive parents?
8 a.m.–6 p.m., CT

Education: BA in history, University of Texas at Austin, 1980; JD, Pepperdine University School of Law, 1987

What states or countries do your adoptive parents come from? Every state.

What states or countries do your birthparents/adopted children come from? Texas.

Are other attorneys in your law firm active in adoption? No, solo practitioner.

In what year did you begin legal work in adoptions? 1994

How many nonrelative adoptions did you arrange in 1998? 15. Texas does not allow an attorney to arrange a placement unless your office is a licensed child-placing agency, which requires a masters' level social worker or counselor. I do quite a few child protective services adoptions, (100+).

About how many children have you placed since you started? 60. Texas does not allow an attorney to arrange a placement unless your office is a licensed child-placing agency, which requires a masters' level social worker or counselor.

About what percent of your work is devoted to adoption? 90%

What made you decide to work in the adoption field? I worked as an assistant district attorney for seven years doing child abuse [cases]; many of these children were placed in adoption.

Do you have any criteria for adoptive parents, such as age, number of children in the home, etc.? No.

What percent of your adoptions are infants under 6 mos.? 50%. I represent several agencies where all of their placements are infants. The child protective services placements are typically not infants.

Do you have a waiting list of prospective parents? No.

Is it all right if adopting parents are on waiting lists of other attorneys or agencies? Yes.

Do you charge adoptive parents for a first phone consultation? No.

Do you charge adoptive parents for a first office consultation? No.

Do you charge a retainer fee, and if yes, what is it and when is it payable? Yes. Hard costs of the adoption—filing fees, guardian fees, etc.—approximately $500, due at inception of case.

What are your legal fees, not including retainer, and when are they payable? Payable in full at adoption hearing. Fees vary, typically between $2,500 and $5,000 for private placement. CPS and agency adoption fees are much less.

Will adoptive parents pay a separate attorney for the birthmother? No.

What are the approximate fees for medical and hospital expenses for the birthmother and baby, when they have no insurance? $3,000 for vaginal delivery; $4,500 for caesarean section.

What are the approximate homestudy fees in your state? $250–600

If living expenses for a birthmother are allowed, what is the average amount paid? Not allowed [in Texas] except by licensed child placing agencies. $500–750/mo.

If you manage international adoptions, what is the average fee for translating documents? Varies greatly.

In how many of your cases has an adoptive parent lost a placed child due to a birthparent challenge? One, an adoption agency case.

Have you lost any adoption litigation filed against you by an adoptive parent or birthparent? No. Nothing has ever been filed.

In about what percentage of your adoptions do adopting parents and birthparents know each other's first and last names? 60%+

Are you a member of the American Academy of Adoption Attorneys and/or the National Council for Adoption? American Academy of Adoption Attorneys.

HEIDI BRUEGEL COX

The Gladney Center
2300 Hemphill, Fort Worth, TX 76110
(817) 922-6043 • Fax: (817) 926-8505
E-mail: Heidi@Gladney.org

What are your office hours when you accept calls from adoptive parents? 8:30 a.m.–5:00 p.m., CST

Education: BA in history, Trinity University, 1983; JD, Texas Tech School of Law, 1986

What states or countries do your adoptive parents come from? All states, United Kingdom, Germany, and France.

What states or countries do your birthparents/adopted children come from? All states.

Are other attorneys in your law firm active in adoption? Yes.

In what year did you begin legal work in adoptions? 1990

How many nonrelative adoptions did you arrange in 1998? 200 domestic; through agency, 150 international.

About how many children have you placed since you started? 1,500+

About what percent of your work is devoted to adoption? 100%

In 1998, what was the average time from when a prospective adoptive parent retained you to the placement of a child? 9–12 mos.

What made you decide to work in the adoption field? Interest in child advocacy.

Do you have any criteria for adoptive parents, such as age, number of children in the home, etc., and if so, what are they? Criteria vary depending on whether it's a domestic placement or international source and what requirements each country places on the adopting parents.

What percent of your adoptions are infants under 6 mos.? 99% domestic, 1% international.

Do you have a waiting list of prospective parents? Yes.

Is it all right if adopting parents are on waiting lists of other attorneys or agencies? No.

Do you charge adoptive parents for a first phone consultation? No.

Do you charge adoptive parents for a first office consultation? No.

Do you charge a retainer fee? No.

What are your legal fees, not including retainer, and when are they payable? Fee is part of the entire adoption fee.

Will adoptive parents pay a separate attorney for the birthmother? No.

What are the approximate homestudy fees in your state? $700–1,500. It's included in agency fee.

If living expenses for a birthmother are allowed, what is the average amount paid? Varies.

In how many of your cases has an adoptive parent lost a placed child due to a birthparent challenge? 0 after relinquishment.

Have you lost any adoption litigation filed against you by an adoptive parent or birthparent? No.

Are you a member of the American Academy of Adoption Attorneys and/or the National Council for Adoption? American Academy of Adoption Attorneys and National Council For Adoption.

IRV W. QUEAL

8117 Preston, #800, Dallas, TX 75225
(214) 696-3200 • Fax: (214) 696-5971

What are your office hours when you accept calls from adoptive parents?
8 a.m.–5:30 p.m., CT

Education: BBA, University of North Texas, 1967; JD, Southern Methodist University Law School, 1971

What states or countries do your adoptive parents come from? Everywhere in United States.

What states or countries do your birthparents/adopted children come from? United States.

Are other attorneys in your law firm active in adoption? No.

In what year did you begin legal work in adoptions? 1981

How many nonrelative adoptions did you arrange in 1998? Can't arrange for adoptions in Texas unless licensed by Texas agency.

About how many children have you placed since you started? Do not place children. Have averaged at least 15 adoption cases a year since 1984.

About what percent of your work is devoted to adoption? 20%

What made you decide to work in the adoption field? Opportunity.

What percent of your adoptions are infants under 6 mos.? 95%

Do you charge adoptive parents for a first phone consultation? No.

Do you charge adoptive parents for a first office consultation? No.

Do you charge a retainer fee, and if yes, what is it and when is it payable? Yes; $2,000 at $200/hour, payable with engagement letter execution.

What are your legal fees, not including retainer, and when are they payable? Only legal fees charged.

Will adoptive parents pay a separate attorney for the birthmother? No, unless necessary.

What are the approximate fees for medical and hospital expenses for the birthmother and baby, when they have no insurance? $5,000–7,500

What are the approximate homestudy fees in your state? $750–1,500

In how many of your cases has an adoptive parent lost a placed child due to a birthparent challenge? 3

Have you lost any adoption litigation filed against you by an adoptive parent or birthparent? N/A

In about what percentage of your adoptions do adopting parents and birthparents know each other's first and last names? 90%

Are you a member of the American Academy of Adoption Attorneys and/or the National Council for Adoption? American Academy of Adoption Attorneys.

MELODY B. ROYALL

The Royalls
13430 Northwest Freeway, Suite 150, Houston, TX 77040
(713) 462-6500 • Fax: (713) 462-6570

What are your office hours when you accept calls from adoptive parents?
  8:30 a.m.–5:30 p.m., CST

Education: BA in psychology, University of Texas, 1980; JD, University of Houston Law School, 1984

What states or countries do your adoptive parents come from? My clients are from all over the United States.

What states or countries do your birthparents/adopted children come from? The children come from all over the United States. Most of my international adoptions come from Russia, Korea, and China.

Are other attorneys in your law firm active in adoption? Yes.

In what year did you begin legal work in adoptions? 1984

How many nonrelative adoptions did you arrange in 1998? Attorneys in Texas are not permitted to arrange adoptions. We can only prepare the paperwork and handle the legal proceedings.

About what percent of your work is devoted to adoption? 40%

What made you decide to work in the adoption field? I joined my father's law firm when I graduated from law school and he had an active adoption practice. It is the pleasant side to a family law practice.

What percent of your adoptions are infants under 6 mos.? 99%

Do you charge adoptive parents for a first phone consultation, and if yes, what is the fee? Yes; $250 per hour.

Do you charge adoptive parents for a first office consultation, and if yes, what is the fee? Yes; $250 per hour.

Do you charge a retainer fee, and if yes, what is it and when is it payable? Yes. The amount varies depending on what will be involved in the case. In a consensual adoption it is $1,500 for an interstate case and $1,000 for an intrastate case. The retainer is payable prior to the rendering of services.

What are your legal fees, not including retainer, and when are they payable? All legal fees and expenses are charged against the retainer and the parents are billed monthly thereafter.

Will adoptive parents pay a separate attorney for the birthmother, and if yes, what are approximate legal fees? Yes. It is not required but it is encouraged; $200–400.

What are the approximate fees for medical and hospital expenses for the birthmother and baby, when they have no insurance? $5,000–10,000

What are the approximate homestudy fees in your state? $750–1,500

If living expenses for a birthmother are allowed, what is the average amount paid? These are not permitted in private adoptions [in Texas].

In how many of your cases has an adoptive parent lost a placed child due to a birth-parent challenge? 2 agency cases.

Have you lost any adoption litigation filed against you by an adoptive parent or birthparent? No. No suits filed.

In about what percentage of your adoptions do adopting parents and birthparents know each other's first and last names? 100% of private adoptions, 40% of agency adoptions.

Are you a member of the American Academy of Adoption Attorneys and/or the National Council for Adoption? American Academy of Adoption Attorneys.

ELLEN A. YARRELL, PC

1980 Post Oak Blvd., Suite 1720, Houston, TX 77056
(713) 621-3332 • Fax: (713) 621-3669

What are your office hours when you accept calls from adoptive parents? 8 a.m.–5 p.m., CT

Education: BFA, summa cum laude, University of Texas, 1971; JD, University of Texas School of Law, 1978; Attorneys Mediators Institute, 1994

What states or countries do your adoptive parents come from? Varies widely.

What states or countries do your birthparents/adopted children come from? Generally Texas.

Are other attorneys in your law firm active in adoption? No.

In what year did you begin legal work in adoptions? 1989

How many nonrelative adoptions did you arrange in 1998? 15+ independent, 50+ agency. Texas lawyers do not arrange adoptions; can only handle legal work.

About what percent of your work is devoted to adoption? 25%

What made you decide to work in the adoption field? I have an adopted son and a biological daughter. I think I understand the feelings and needs of both sides.

Do you charge adoptive parents for a first phone consultation? No.

Do you charge adoptive parents for a first office consultation, and if yes, what is the fee? Yes; $200 for initial consultation.

Do you charge a retainer fee, and if yes, what is it and when is it payable? Yes; $3,500 for independent placement; $1,000 for agency adoption, post-termination.

What are your legal fees, not including retainer, and when are they payable? As incurred.

Will adoptive parents pay a separate attorney for the birthmother, and if yes, what are approximate legal fees? Yes, if birthmother requests; $200–300.

What are the approximate fees for medical and hospital expenses for the birth-mother and baby, when they have no insurance? $5,000–10,000

What are the approximate homestudy fees in your state? $350–750

If living expenses for a birthmother are allowed, what is the average amount paid? Not allowed in independent adoption [in Texas].

Are you an adoptive parent, adopted person, or birthparent? Adoptive parent.

In how many of your cases has an adoptive parent lost a placed child due to a birth-parent challenge? None.

Have you lost any adoption litigation filed against you by an adoptive parent or birthparent? No.

In about what percentage of your adoptions do adopting parents and birthparents know each other's first and last names? Always in independent adoption.

Are you a member of the American Academy of Adoption Attorneys and/or the National Council for Adoption? American Academy of Adoption Attorneys.

VERMONT

KURT M. HUGHES

Murdoch and Hughes
P.O. Box 363, Burlington, VT 05402
(802) 864-9811 • Fax: (802) 864-4136
E-mail: mhlaw@adoptvt.com • www.adoptvt.com

What are your office hours when you accept calls from adoptive parents? 9 a.m.–5 p.m., ET

Education: BA, Colgate University, 1981; JD, Vermont Law School, 1984

What states or countries do your adoptive parents come from? United States and Canada.

What states or countries do your birthparents/adopted children come from? United States.

Are other attorneys in your law firm active in adoption? Yes.

In what year did you begin legal work in adoptions? 1995

How many nonrelative adoptions did you arrange in 1998? We do not "arrange" adoptions, we have completed 15–20.

About how many children have you placed since you started? Have completed more than 70 adoptions.

About what percent of your work is devoted to adoption? 30%

What made you decide to work in the adoption field? I was burned out on divorce work. I wanted to do something that made people happy. Our probate judge turned her adoption practice over to me.

Do you have any criteria for adoptive parents, such as age, number of children in the home, etc.? None.

What percent of your adoptions are infants under 6 mos.? 99%

Do you have a waiting list of prospective parents? Yes.

Is it all right if adopting parents are on waiting lists of other attorneys or agencies? Yes.

Do you charge adoptive parents for a first phone consultation? No.

Do you charge adoptive parents for a first office consultation? No.

Do you charge a retainer fee, and if yes, what is it and when is it payable? Yes; $1,500 payable when there is a viable match.

What are your legal fees, not including retainer, and when are they payable? Total [legal] fees, including retainer generally run $2,000–3,000.

Will adoptive parents pay a separate attorney for the birthmother, and if yes, what are approximate legal fees? Yes. It depends.

What are the approximate fees for medical and hospital expenses for the birthmother and baby, when they have no insurance? $2,500–5,000

What are the approximate homestudy fees in your state? $800–1,000

If living expenses for a birthmother are allowed, what is the average amount paid? It depends.

In how many of your cases has an adoptive parent lost a placed child due to a birthparent challenge? In one case, the birthmother revoked her consent within revocation period.

Have you lost any adoption litigation filed against you by an adoptive parent or birthparent? No.

In about what percentage of your adoptions do adopting parents and birthparents know each other's first and last names? Almost 100%.

Are you a member of the American Academy of Adoption Attorneys and/or the National Council for Adoption? American Academy of Adoption Attorneys.

VIRGINIA

DAVID T. DAULTON

The Berean Law Group, PC
125 St. Paul's Blvd., Suite 302, Norfolk, VA 23510
(757) 622-0225 • Fax: (757) 622-0791

What are your office hours when you accept calls from adoptive parents? 9 a.m.–5 p.m., ET

Education: BS in business administration, Arizona State, 1987; JD, CBN University School of Law (now Regent University), 1990

What states or countries do your adoptive parents come from? All states.

What states or countries do your birthparents/adopted children come from? All states, many foreign countries.

Are other attorneys in your law firm active in adoption? No.

In what year did you begin legal work in adoptions? 1991

How many nonrelative adoptions did you arrange in 1998? 70

About how many children have you placed since you started? In Virginia, attorneys are not child-placing agencies. However, on a purely gratis basis, I have helped place about eight children.

About what percent of your work is devoted to adoption? 40%

In 1998, what was the average time from when a prospective adoptive parent retained you to the placement of a child? Not really applicable. Under Virginia law, attorneys do not place children.

What made you decide to work in the adoption field? I am an adoptive parent three times over, so far. There are a lot of children who need parents, and it is emotionally and spiritually very rewarding.

Do you have any criteria for adoptive parents, such as age, number of children in the home, etc., and if so, what are they? They must have, in most adoptions, an approved homestudy.

What percent of your adoptions are infants under 6 mos.? 85%

Do you have a waiting list of prospective parents? Yes.

Is it all right if adopting parents are on waiting lists of other attorneys or agencies? Yes.

Do you charge adoptive parents for a first phone consultation? No.

Do you charge adoptive parents for a first office consultation, and if yes, what is the fee? Yes; $75.

Do you charge a retainer fee, and if yes, what is it and when is it payable? Yes. I work on payment plans. Agency is flat fee of $350. Domestic and foreign adoption is flat fee of $400. Stepparent and parental placement are based on hourly rate of $180/hour; average stepparent adoption is about $650; average parental placement is about $1,800; average ICPC (Interstate Compact on the Placement of Children) is about $2,500. All of my hourly retainer clients receive an itemized bill of my time each month.

What are your legal fees, not including retainer, and when are they payable? Initial retainer is an estimate of entire fees. If more time is needed, I bill additional fees. If less time or work is needed, I refund the balance.

Will adoptive parents pay a separate attorney for the birthmother, and if yes, what are approximate legal fees? Yes, I always recommend it. It is permitted but optional under Virginia laws; $500.

What are the approximate fees for medical and hospital expenses for the birthmother and baby, when they have no insurance? $1,800–2,400, but it is rare that we cannot get coverage somehow.

What are the approximate homestudy fees in your state? $1,200–2,400

If living expenses for a birthmother are allowed, what is the average amount paid? $800

If you manage international adoptions, what is the average fee for translating documents? $30/hour

Are you an adoptive parent, adopted person, or birthparent? Adoptive parent.

In how many of your cases has an adoptive parent lost a placed child due to a birthparent challenge? 3

Have you lost any adoption litigation filed against you by an adoptive parent or birthparent? No.

In about what percentage of your adoptions do adopting parents and birthparents know each other's first and last names? 50%

Are you a member of the American Academy of Adoption Attorneys and/or the National Council for Adoption? American Academy of Adoption Attorneys and National Council for Adoption.

Is there anything I have not asked you that is important? I specialize in helping to place handicapped, African-American, special needs, and other different adoptions.

BETSY H. PHILLIPS

Phillips and Morrison
Irongate at Spring Hill, Rt. 4 Box 179-P, Rustburg, VA 24588
(804) 821-5022 • Fax: (804) 821-6092

What are your office hours when you accept calls from adoptive parents? 8:30 a.m.–4 p.m., ET

Education: BA in English, University of LaVerne, 1973; JD, University of Richmond, 1983

What states or countries do your adoptive parents come from? All over eastern seaboard. Have had a few in California and Midwest.

What states or countries do your birthparents/adopted children come from? Several from Philippines, one from Romania, two from Texas, several from North Carolina.

Are other attorneys in your law firm active in adoption? No.

In what year did you begin legal work in adoptions? 1984

How many nonrelative adoptions did you arrange in 1998? 5+

About how many children have you placed since you started? None. I do not place. I handle parental placements, agency placements, and contested adoptions.

About what percent of your work is devoted to adoption? 20%

In 1998, what was the average time from when a prospective adoptive parent retained you to the placement of a child? 150 days agency placement; 6 mos. on contested parental placement.

What made you decide to work in the adoption field? Private agency opened in Lynchburg my first year of practice.

Do you have any criteria for adoptive parents, such as age, number of children in the home, etc.? I do not place.

What percent of your adoptions are infants under 6 mos.? 90%

Do you have a waiting list of prospective parents? Yes.

Is it all right if adopting parents are on waiting lists of other attorneys or agencies? Yes.

Do you charge adoptive parents for a first office consultation, and if yes, what is the fee? Yes; $150/hour.

Do you charge a retainer fee, and if yes, what is it and when is it payable? Yes. $500 (agency) plus costs, $500 before filing, costs at conclusion. Contested, $2,000 up front and balance plus costs at conclusion.

What are your legal fees, not including retainer, and when are they payable? See previous answer.

Will adoptive parents pay a separate attorney for the birthmother, and if yes, what are approximate legal fees? Yes; $200–300.

What are the approximate fees for medical and hospital expenses for the birthmother and baby, when they have no insurance? Unknown to me.

What are the approximate homestudy fees in your state? $350 (DSS) to $2,000 (agency).

If living expenses for a birthmother are allowed, what is the average amount paid? Unknown.

In how many of your cases has an adoptive parent lost a placed child due to a birthparent challenge? 0

Have you lost any adoption litigation filed against you by an adoptive parent or birthparent? No.

In about what percentage of your adoptions do adopting parents and birthparents know each other's first and last names? 50%

Are you a member of the American Academy of Adoption Attorneys and/or the National Council for Adoption? American Academy of Adoption Attorneys.

COLLEEN MAREA QUINN

Cantor, Arkema, and Edmonds, PC
P.O. Box 561, 823 E. Main St., 15th Floor, Richmond, VA 23218-0561
(804) 644-1400 or (804) 343-4375 • Fax: (804) 644-9205
E-mail: colleenq@caevalaw.com • www.adoptionattorneys.org

What are your office hours when you accept calls from adoptive parents?
8:30 a.m.–5 p.m., ET

Education: BA in English and philosophy, College of William and Mary, 1985; JD, University of Virginia School of Law, 1988

What states or countries do your adoptive parents come from? All, but most frequently from Virginia.

What states or countries do your birthparents/adopted children come from? All, but most frequently from Virginia.

Are other attorneys in your law firm active in adoption? Yes.

In what year did you begin legal work in adoptions? 1989

How many nonrelative adoptions did you arrange in 1998? Approximately 25–30

About how many children have you placed since you started? 200+

About what percent of your work is devoted to adoption? 20%

In 1998, what was the average time from when a prospective adoptive parent retained you to the placement of a child? 4 mos.

What made you decide to work in the adoption field? The "win-win" and heartwarming feeling of a successful placement.

Do you have any criteria for adoptive parents, such as age, number of children in the home, etc.? I have no restrictions.

What percent of your adoptions are infants under 6 mos.? 90%

Do you have a waiting list of prospective parents? Yes.

Is it all right if adopting parents are on waiting lists of other attorneys or agencies? Yes.

Do you charge adoptive parents for a first phone consultation? No.

Do you charge adoptive parents for a first office consultation, and if yes, what is the fee? Yes; $175/hour.

Do you charge a retainer fee? No.

What are your legal fees, not including retainer, and when are they payable? $175/hour, monthly bills provided to clients.

Will adoptive parents pay a separate attorney for the birthmother, and if yes, what are approximate legal fees? Yes; $500–1,500.

What are the approximate fees for medical and hospital expenses for the birthmother and baby, when they have no insurance? $5,000–6,000

What are the approximate homestudy fees in your state? $800–2,000 (done on sliding scale).

If living expenses are allowed, what is the average amount paid? $300 a month.

In how many of your cases has an adoptive parent lost a placed child due to a birth-parent challenge? None, but in Virginia a birthparent has fifteen days to revoke consent. Only five birthmothers have exercised their right to revoke consent or have changed their minds after placement.

Have you lost any adoption litigation filed against you by an adoptive parent or birthparent? No.

In about what percentage of your adoptions do adopting parents and birthparents know each other's first and last names? 100%

Are you a member of the American Academy of Adoption Attorneys and/or the National Council for Adoption? American Academy of Adoption Attorneys.

STANTON PHILLIPS

Adoption Legal Services
2009 N. 14th St., Suite 510, Arlington, VA 22201
(703) 522-8800 • Fax: (703) 841-0845
E-mail: adoptlawr@aol.com • www.adoptionlawyer.net

What are your office hours when you accept calls from adoptive parents?
9 a.m.–5 p.m., ET

Education: BA, American University, 1976; JD, George Mason University School of Law, 1980

What states or countries do your adoptive parents come from? Primarily Virginia and District of Columbia.

What states or countries do your birthparents/adopted children come from? Virginia, District of Columbia, United States, and world.

Are other attorneys in your law firm active in adoption? No.

In what year did you begin legal work in adoptions? 1982

How many nonrelative adoptions did you arrange in 1998? 100+

About how many children have you placed since you started? 1,500

About what percent of your work is devoted to adoption? 100%

In 1998, what was the average time from when a prospective adoptive parent retained you to the placement of a child? 3 mos.

What made you decide to work in the adoption field? After being trained by area's retiring guru on adoption law, enjoyed intellectual stimulation of providing quality representation and protecting clients' interests when no other attorney was actively involved in adoptions in northern Virginia.

Do you have any criteria for adoptive parents, such as age, number of children in the home, etc.? No.

What percent of your adoptions are infants under 6 mos.? 90%

Do you have a waiting list of prospective parents? Yes.

Is it all right if adopting parents are on waiting lists of other attorneys or agencies? Yes.

Do you charge adoptive parents for a first phone consultation? No.

Do you charge adoptive parents for a first office consultation, and if yes, what is the fee? Yes. $100 for general consultation; $200 for private adoption consultation/training session.

Do you charge a retainer fee, and if yes, what is it and when is it payable? Yes. In private adoptions, $2,000; $1,000 when birthmother located; $1,000 in 30 days.

What are your legal fees, not including retainer, and when are they payable? $200/hour as needed.

Will adoptive parents pay a separate attorney for the birthmother, and if yes, what are approximate legal fees? Yes; $1,500.

What are the approximate fees for medical and hospital expenses for the birth-mother and baby, when they have no insurance? $8,000

What are the approximate homestudy fees in your state? $1,200

If living expenses for a birthmother are allowed, what is the average amount paid? $800

In how many of your cases has an adoptive parent lost a placed child due to a birth-parent challenge? 3: 2 cases prior to giving consent; 1 case during revocation period.

Have you lost any adoption litigation filed against you by an adoptive parent or birthparent? No.

In about what percentage of your adoptions do adopting parents and birthparents know each other's first and last names? 98%

Are you a member of the American Academy of Adoption Attorneys and/or the National Council for Adoption? American Academy of Adoption Attorneys.

RODNEY M. POOLE

Poole and Poole Attorneys
2800 Patterson Ave., Richmond, VA 23221
(804) 358-6669 • Fax: (804) 358-5290
E-mail: Rpooleadop@aol.com

What are your office hours when you accept calls from adoptive parents? 8 a.m.–5 p.m., ET

Education: BSBA, University of Richmond, 1969; JD, University of Virginia, 1973

What states or countries do your adoptive parents come from? Virginia.

What states or countries do your birthparents/adopted children come from? United States and all foreign countries.

Are other attorneys in your law firm active in adoption? No.

In what year did you begin legal work in adoptions? 1973

How many nonrelative adoptions did you arrange in 1998? None. Virginia does not permit attorneys to arrange an adoption. I participated in 45 nonrelative adoptions in 1998.

About how many children have you placed since you started? None. Virginia does not allow attorneys to place. I have been involved in over 1,000 adoptions in my career.

About what percent of your work is devoted to adoption? 60%

What made you decide to work in the adoption field? My father practiced in adoption after having been a foster care child in his youth.

Do you have any criteria for adoptive parents, such as age, number of children in the home, etc.? No.

What percent of your adoptions are infants under 6 mos.? 80%

Do you have a waiting list of prospective parents? Yes.

Is it all right if adopting parents are on waiting lists of other attorneys or agencies? Yes.

Do you charge adoptive parents for a first phone consultation? No.

Do you charge adoptive parents for a first office consultation, and if yes, what is the fee? Yes; about $275.

Do you charge a retainer fee, and if yes, what is it and when is it payable? Yes; $3,000, three weeks prior to birth.

What are your legal fees, not including retainer, and when are they payable? $200 per hour/hourly rate.

Will adoptive parents pay a separate attorney for the birthmother, and if yes, what are approximate legal fees? Yes; $500–800.

What are the approximate fees for medical and hospital expenses for the birthmother and baby, when they have no insurance? $6,000–12,000

What are the approximate homestudy fees in your state? $1,200–2,000

If living expenses for a birthmother are allowed, what is the average amount paid? $1,000/month

Are you an adoptive parent, adopted person, or birthparent? Adoptive parent.

In how many of your cases has an adoptive parent lost a placed child due to a birthparent challenge? 0

Have you lost any adoption litigation filed against you by an adoptive parent or birthparent? No.

In about what percentage of your adoptions do adopting parents and birthparents know each other's first and last names? 95%

Are you a member of the American Academy of Adoption Attorneys and/or the National Council for Adoption? American Academy of Adoption Attorneys.

NANCY D. POSTER

P.O. Box 197, Great Falls, VA 22066
(703) 759-1560 • Fax: (703) 759-6512
E-mail: ndposter@erols.com

What are your office hours when you accept calls from adoptive parents?
9 a.m.–5 p.m., ET

Education: BA in English, Wayne State University, 1971; JD, Detroit College of Law, 1980

What states or countries do your adoptive parents come from? Virginia, Maryland, District of Columbia.

What states or countries do your birthparents/adopted children come from? Mostly Virginia, Maryland, District of Columbia; some from Eastern Europe, China, Latin America.

Are other attorneys in your law firm active in adoption? N/A

In what year did you begin legal work in adoptions? 1984

How many nonrelative adoptions did you arrange in 1998? Did not arrange, but acted as counsel in about 50.

About how many children have you placed since you started? Cannot place children in my jurisdiction.

About what percent of your work is devoted to adoption? 90%

What made you decide to work in the adoption field? Liked the positive nature of the field—very different than other areas of the law.

What percent of your adoptions are infants under 6 mos.? 98%

Do you have a waiting list of prospective parents? No.

Is it all right if adopting parents are on waiting lists of other attorneys or agencies? N/A

Do you charge adoptive parents for a first phone consultation? No.

Do you charge adoptive parents for a first office consultation, and if yes, what is the fee? Yes; hourly rate of $225.

Do you charge a retainer fee, and if yes, what is it and when is it payable? Yes; $2,500 on identification of birthparents.

What are your legal fees, not including retainer, and when are they payable? Hourly rate of $225, no flat fee.

Will adoptive parents pay a separate attorney for the birthmother, and if yes, what are approximate legal fees? Yes; $1,500.

What are the approximate fees for medical and hospital expenses for the birthmother and baby, when they have no insurance? $6,000

What are the approximate homestudy fees in your state? $1,500

If living expenses for a birthmother are allowed, what is the average amount paid? $1,000

In how many of your cases has an adoptive parent lost a placed child due to a birth-parent challenge? 4

Have you lost any adoption litigation filed against you by an adoptive parent or birthparent? Yes.

In about what percentage of your adoptions do adopting parents and birthparents know each other's first and last names? 98%

Are you a member of the American Academy of Adoption Attorneys and/or the National Council for Adoption? American Academy of Adoption Attorneys.

WASHINGTON

RITA L. BENDER

Skellenger Bender
1301 Fifth Ave., Suite 3401, Seattle, WA 98101
(206) 623-6501 • Fax: (206) 447-1973
E-mail: rbender@skellengerbender.com

What are your office hours when you accept calls from adoptive parents? 8:30 a.m.–5:30 p.m., PT; also evenings and weekends if necessary.

Education: BA, University of the City of New York, 1964; JD, Rutgers School of Law, 1968

What states or countries do your adoptive parents come from? All over the United States and numerous European countries.

What states or countries do your birthparents/adopted children come from? All over the United States. Some children from South America, Central America, Asia.

Are other attorneys in your law firm active in adoption? Yes.

In what year did you begin legal work in adoptions? 1982

How many nonrelative adoptions did you arrange in 1998? 55

About how many children have you placed since you started? 600+

About what percent of your work is devoted to adoption? 50%

In 1998, what was the average time from when a prospective adoptive parent retained you to the placement of a child? Tremendous variability. 10–12 mos.

What made you decide to work in the adoption field? I believe in adoption. I am a parent of adoption. It is important that adoptive parents and birthparents have competent and caring legal representation.

Do you have any criteria for adoptive parents, such as age, number of children in the home, etc.? No, except that family must have a favorable homestudy.

What percent of your adoptions are infants under 6 mos.? 98%

Do you have a waiting list of prospective parents? Yes.

Is it all right if adopting parents are on waiting lists of other attorneys or agencies? Yes. It is more accurate to say there are families seeking to adopt than that there is a waiting list, which implies passivity on the part of the families.

Do you charge adoptive parents for a first phone consultation, and if yes, what is the fee? Yes; $175 per hour if we do an extensive consultation. A brief telephone call is not charged.

Do you charge adoptive parents for a first office consultation, and if yes, what is the fee? Yes; $175 per hour.

Do you charge a retainer fee, and if yes, what is it and when is it payable? Yes. Usually $1,000 when birthmother and adoptive parents decide to work together. Sometimes varies with the projected work on a particular case.

What are your legal fees, not including retainer, and when are they payable? $175 per hour, billed and due in month when work is done for client.

Will adoptive parents pay a separate attorney for the birthmother, and if yes, what are approximate legal fees? Yes. Sometimes birthmother waives counsel. If local, under $1,000.

What are the approximate fees for medical and hospital expenses for the birthmother and baby, when they have no insurance? $5,500+. Depends on whether birthmother needs caesarean-section, extra days in hospital, etc.

What are the approximate homestudy fees in your state? $500 if done by private social worker.

If living expenses for a birthmother are allowed, what is the average amount paid? Varies with circumstances. Must be approved by court; $2,000–4,000.

If you manage international adoptions, what is the average fee for translating documents? $300–400

Are you an adoptive parent, adopted person, or birthparent? Adoptive parent.

In how many of your cases has an adoptive parent lost a placed child due to a birthparent challenge? If you mean after the child has gone home with the adoptive parent, never.

Have you lost any adoption litigation filed against you by an adoptive parent or birthparent? No.

In about what percentage of your adoptions do adopting parents and birthparents know each other's first and last names? 65%

Are you a member of the American Academy of Adoption Attorneys and/or the National Council for Adoption? American Academy of Adoption Attorneys.

MARK M. DEMARAY

Beresford, Booth and Demaray
1420 5th Ave., #3650, Seattle, WA 98101
(206) 682-4000 • Fax: (206) 682-4004
E-mail: markdemaray@msn.com

What are your office hours when you accept calls from adoptive parents?
8:30 a.m.–5 p.m., PT

Education: BA, University of Washington, 1976; JD, Lewis and Clark Law School, 1981

What states or countries do your adoptive parents come from? All states, United Kingdom, France, Germany, Canada.

What states or countries do your birthparents/adopted children come from? Often Washington, many other states, occasionally other countries.

Are other attorneys in your law firm active in adoption? Yes.

In what year did you begin legal work in adoptions? 1982

How many nonrelative adoptions did you arrange in 1998? Approximately 75

About how many children have you placed since you started? Estimated 700–800

About what percent of your work is devoted to adoption? 90%

In 1998, what was the average time from when a prospective adoptive parent retained you to the placement of a child? 1 year

What made you decide to work in the adoption field? I am an adoptive parent of two children and I feel it is a positive area of law practice.

Do you have any criteria for adoptive parents, such as age, number of children in the home, etc.? I set no criteria.

What percent of your adoptions are infants under 6 mos.? 95%

Do you have a waiting list of prospective parents? Yes.

Is it all right if adopting parents are on waiting lists of other attorneys or agencies? Yes.

Do you charge adoptive parents for a first phone consultation? No.

Do you charge adoptive parents for a first office consultation, and if yes, what is the fee? Yes; $75.

Do you charge a retainer fee, and if yes, what is it and when is it payable? Yes. Depends on case and anticipated costs and fees.

What are your legal fees, not including retainer, and when are they payable? Hourly fees for time spent working with clients; often request advance retainer based on anticipated costs.

Will adoptive parents pay a separate attorney for the birthmother, and if yes, what are approximate legal fees? Yes, sometimes. Depends on case and birthparent needs.

What are the approximate fees for medical and hospital expenses for the birthmother and baby, when they have no insurance? $7,000–8,000

What are the approximate homestudy fees in your state? $500–1,000

If living expenses for a birthmother are allowed, what is the average amount paid? Depends on circumstances and court approval.

If you manage international adoptions, what is the average fee for translating documents? Usually $500 to $1,000 to do a complete finalization or re-adoption.

Are you an adoptive parent, adopted person, or birthparent? Adoptive parent.

In how many of your cases has an adoptive parent lost a placed child due to a birthparent challenge? 0

Have you lost any adoption litigation filed against you by an adoptive parent or birthparent? No.

In about what percentage of your adoptions do adopting parents and birthparents know each other's first and last names? 25–50%

Are you a member of the American Academy of Adoption Attorneys and/or the National Council for Adoption? American Academy of Adoption Attorneys.

MARGARET CUNNIFF HOLM

Connolly, Holm, Tacon, and Meserve
201 W. 5th, #301, Olympia, WA 98501
(360) 943-6747 • Fax: (360) 943-9651
E-mail: chtm@aol.com

What are your office hours when you accept calls from adoptive parents? 9a.m.–2 p.m., PT

Education: AA in nursing, Chicago City College, 1975; BA in psychology, California State University, 1977; JD, Seattle University, 1982

What states or countries do your adoptive parents come from? Washington, California.

What states or countries do your birthparents/adopted children come from? Washington, Oregon, California, Idaho.

Are other attorneys in your law firm active in adoption? No.

In what year did you begin legal work in adoptions? 1985

How many nonrelative adoptions did you arrange in 1998? 20

About how many children have you placed since you started? 200+

About what percent of your work is devoted to adoption? 30%

In 1998, what was the average time from when a prospective adoptive parent retained you to the placement of a child? 1 year

What made you decide to work in the adoption field? Knowledge of resources, interest in children welfare, infertility issues. Health care background.

Do you have any criteria for adoptive parents, such as age, number of children in the home, etc.? No. Must have court approved homestudy.

What percent of your adoptions are infants under 6 mos.? 80%

Do you have a waiting list of prospective parents? No.

Is it all right if adopting parents are on waiting lists of other attorneys or agencies? Yes.

Do you charge adoptive parents for a first phone consultation, and if yes, what is the fee? Yes; $160 per hour.

Do you charge adoptive parents for a first office consultation, and if yes, what is the fee? Yes; $160 per hour.

Do you charge a retainer fee, and if yes, what is it and when is it payable? Yes; $1,200 when clients are matched.

What are your legal fees, not including retainer, and when are they payable? $160 per hour; average cost of adoption $4,000.

Will adoptive parents pay a separate attorney for the birthmother? If necessary.

What are the approximate fees for medical and hospital expenses for the birthmother and baby, when they have no insurance? Unknown.

What are the approximate homestudy fees in your state? $650

If living expenses for a birthmother are allowed, what is the average amount paid? $800–1,000

In how many of your cases has an adoptive parent lost a placed child due to a birthparent challenge? 0

Have you lost any adoption litigation filed against you by an adoptive parent or birthparent? No.

In about what percentage of your adoptions do adopting parents and birthparents know each other's first and last names? 40%

Are you a member of the American Academy of Adoption Attorneys and/or the National Council for Adoption? American Academy of Adoption Attorneys.

ALBERT G. LIRHUS

Dubuar, Lirhus, and Engel, LLP
2200 6th Ave., Suite 1122, Seattle, WA 98121
(206) 728-5858 • Fax: (206) 728-5863
E-mail: lirhus@dle-law.com • www.dle-law.com

What are your office hours when you accept calls from adoptive parents? 8:30 a.m.–5 p.m., PT

Education: BA in business administration, University of Washington, 1968; JD, University of Washington School of Law, 1973

What states or countries do your adoptive parents come from? United States, France, England, Germany, Canada.

What states or countries do your birthparents/adopted children come from? Primarily Washington but also from almost all other states in the country.

Are other attorneys in your law firm active in adoption? Yes. Other attorneys in the law firm provide backup for me.

In what year did you begin legal work in adoptions? 1987 is when major emphasis in the field began.

How many nonrelative adoptions did you arrange in 1998? 85

About how many children have you placed since you started? Several hundred. (Actually, in Washington, the birthmothers generally make the "placement".)

About what percent of your work is devoted to adoption? 90–95%

What made you decide to work in the adoption field? In about 1987, I had the opportunity to assist in a number of adoption cases and I simply fell in love with this field of practice.

Do you have any criteria for adoptive parents, such as age, number of children in the home, etc.? No. However, most adoptive parents with whom I am working either have or are in the process of obtaining a homestudy.

What percent of your adoptions are infants under 6 mos.? 95% or more of the independent adoptions involve infants under the age of six months.

Is it all right if adopting parents are on waiting lists of other attorneys or agencies? Yes.

Do you charge adoptive parents for a first phone consultation? No.

Do you charge adoptive parents for a first office consultation? No.

Do you charge a retainer fee, and if yes, what is it and when is it payable? Yes. My retainer fee is generally $1,000, payable when the adoptive parents have been selected by the birthmother and/or birthfather.

What are your legal fees, not including retainer, and when are they payable? My legal fees depend on the amount of work and type of work that is done on behalf of my clients. Clients are billed generally on a monthly basis and payment is due on receipt.

Will adoptive parents pay a separate attorney for the birthmother? Yes, if the birthmother desires to be represented by her own counsel. Birthmothers are advised of this right and some will obtain separate counsel and some won't.

What are the approximate fees for medical and hospital expenses for the birthmother and baby, when they have no insurance? $3,500 to $6,000 for prenatal care and hospital expenses. However, this fee may vary with the amount of services required, depending on the medical circumstances of the birthmother and the child.

If living expenses for a birthmother are allowed, what is the average amount paid? $300–1,000 a month. (This figure varies widely because these expenses are to be approved by the court in advance and depend completely on the circumstances of the birthmother.)

If you manage international adoptions, what is the average fee for translating documents? Translations are done by translators from the court-approved list. Their charges vary.

In how many of your cases has an adoptive parent lost a placed child due to a birth-parent challenge? 0

Have you lost any adoption litigation filed against you by an adoptive parent or birthparent? No.

In about what percentage of your adoptions do adopting parents and birthparents know each other's first and last names? Approximately 35%

Are you a member of the American Academy of Adoption Attorneys and/or the National Council for Adoption? American Academy of Adoption Attorneys.

WISCONSIN

STEPHEN W. HAYES

von Briesen, Purtell and Roper, SC
735 Water St., Suite 1000, Milwaukee, WI 53202
(414) 287-1220 • Fax: (414) 273-7897
E-mail: shayes@vonbriesen.com or swhayes@execpc.com • www.vonbriesen.com or www.adoption.com

What are your office hours when you accept calls from adoptive parents?
8 a.m.–6 p.m., CT

Education: BA in history/romance languages, DePauw University, 1966; JD, University of Illinois College of Law, 1969

What states or countries do your adoptive parents come from? Throughout the United States and parts of Europe.

What states or countries do your birthparents/adopted children come from? Throughout the United States, Latin America, Southeast Asia, and Eastern Europe.

Are other attorneys in your law firm active in adoption? Yes.

In what year did you begin legal work in adoptions? 1969

How many nonrelative adoptions did you arrange in 1998? I participated in 110 non-relative adoptions.

About how many children have you placed since you started? I have been involved in the "placement of" over 2,000 children since I began work in the adoption field. In Wisconsin, lawyers do not place children. The above number reflects the cases in which I have done the legal work involving termination of parental rights and adoption.

About what percent of your work is devoted to adoption? 60–70%

What made you decide to work in the adoption field? First major case I handled was an adoption case which went to the U.S. Supreme Court. I began to represent an increasing number of agencies and private clients in the field and truly love it. Nothing is more satisfying than making a child part of a wonderful family.

Do you have any criteria for adoptive parents, such as age, number of children in the home, etc.? No such criteria.

What percent of your adoptions are infants under 6 mos.? 90%

Do you have a waiting list of prospective parents? No.

Do you charge adoptive parents for a first phone consultation? No.

Do you charge adoptive parents for a first office consultation, and if yes, what is the fee? Yes; $125.

Do you charge a retainer fee, and if yes, what is it and when is it payable? Yes. If client is out-of-state, full expected fee and costs. If client is in-state, $1,300. Payable before we begin work.

What are your legal fees, not including retainer, and when are they payable? Legal fees depend upon the nature and extent of the work performed. Fee estimates given in advance.

Will adoptive parents pay a separate attorney for the birthmother, and if yes, what are approximate legal fees? No, not required, but often birthmothers do have an attorney. Depends on circumstances of representation.

What are the approximate fees for medical and hospital expenses for the birthmother and baby, when they have no insurance? $4,000–6,000

What are the approximate homestudy fees in your state? $1,500

If living expenses for a birthmother are allowed, what is the average amount paid? $1,000 ceiling; average is below that.

If you manage international adoptions, what is the average fee for translating documents? $25 per page

In how many of your cases has an adoptive parent lost a placed child due to a birthparent challenge? None. I did litigate one case to the Wisconsin Supreme Court on behalf of an adoptive couple who did lose a child. It was not my case originally.

Have you lost any adoption litigation filed against you by an adoptive parent or birthparent? No.

In about what percentage of your adoptions do adopting parents and birthparents know each other's first and last names? 75%

Are you a member of the American Academy of Adoption Attorneys and/or the National Council for Adoption? American Academy of Adoption Attorneys.

CHAPTER FOUR

ADOPTING IN CANADA

"**A**re you going to say *anything* at all about Canadians adopting children?" asked one adoptive parent, who added, "Most books just ignore us." My heart sank when I heard that statement, because I too have been guilty of ignoring people from Canada who wish to adopt children.

So, here's a chapter dedicated to Canadians adopting children, including an essay written by a Canadian mother, followed by lists of Canadian adoption agencies and adoptive parent groups. Jennifer Smart is extremely knowledgeable about the ins and outs of adopting in Canada, and I think you'll be impressed.

THE FACE OF ADOPTION IN CANADA

Jennifer Smart

I'm a very modern adoptive mother, with two children, one adopted internationally and one domestically. Adopting them has been a great education, both in how to adopt in Canada and in how to raise sometimes-challenging kids.

I admit that I have an advantage over most mothers: I'm an occupational therapist with experience working with children, and I enjoy sharing the knowledge I've gleaned in the magazine that I edit, *Post-adoption Helper.*

Had I not adopted in the 1990s, the result might have been much different, because the face of adoption in Canada has changed greatly over recent decades.

We no longer live in the 1950s and 1960s when adoptions were controlled by public (government) agencies, which placed the children relinquished by birthmothers. Couples received the children according to their place on the waiting list, with minimal matching.

Today most single mothers parent their babies rather than choosing adoption, due in part to the financial support available. As a result, the number of newborn adoptions in Ontario, for example, has declined from over 400 a year in the mid-1980s to between 210 and 230 in the late 1990s. In the 1993 National Adoption Study, Dr. Michael Sobol found that of single pregnant women under 25, only two percent chose to place their child for adoption.

If they do choose adoption, today's birthparents take an active role in deciding how their adoption plan will proceed. They often choose private adoption, through an agency or licensee. In most cases, birthmothers don't see a public agency as offering as much choice to them, and they are also averse to using a public agency overly focussed on child protection versus adoption. As a result, many more children are adopted privately than publicly.

But in the last decade, international adoption has eclipsed both public and private adoptions of Canadian-born children. In 1998, there were 2,222 children adopted from abroad but only about 1,400 children were adopted domestically.

If you've decided to adopt, one major choice to make is, which will it be: Domestic public adoption, domestic private adoption, or international adoption? The age, health, and race of children available, the total cost of doing the adoption, and the time it takes from start to finish will likely be your main criteria.

Public Adoptions

One big advantage of domestic public adoption is there are no fees. But the big disadvantage is that the wait is interminable for a healthy infant (seven-year waiting lists!) although the wait is much shorter if you choose a child with special needs. The wait for a child with special needs could be as brief as about a year.

The children will likely require an adjustment period and be at risk for behavioral or learning problems due to high-risk backgrounds (genetic, prenatal, and postnatal). You will be working with a public agency whose role it will be to find the best family for that child, not a specific child for your family. It is true, however, that you will be able to access post-adoption support from the public agency.

Private Adoptions

Domestic private adoption fees range from about $2,500 to $10,000. That covers the initial consultation, homestudy, foster care, postplacement reports, documents, court costs, and birthmother costs (counseling, preparing a social history, travel expenses). The children are usually newborns and may or may not have a prenatal history indicating alcohol or drug use, poor nutrition, and a genetic disposition to learning or behavioral disabilities. Keep in mind that adopting privately, or adopting a newborn, does not guarantee that your child will not have some special need.

There is no chronological waiting list with private adoptions—you have to be chosen by the birthmother when your profile is presented, along with several others. You can expect to wait anywhere from three to five years and may well experience emotional disappointments along the way because the birthparents may change their minds about the adoption. (I'll explain this further later on in this essay.)

You might be able to shorten the wait by:

- Registering with several agencies
- Getting the word out that you are pursuing adoption
- Having a family whose profile happens to appeal to a particular birthmother.

Consents are signed after birth and can be revoked within a certain time period, requiring you to give the baby back. You will be responsible for all costs, including birthmother counseling, even if the birthmother changes her mind and keeps her baby.

International Adoptions

International adoption fees range from $12,000 to $25,000, with the average currently about $19,000. That includes facilitator or agency fees, out-of-country fees, and travel to the country. An international adoption can happen quickly and some babies arrive home as soon as six months after referral. Children come from a variety of backgrounds—orphanages, foster care, and birth families—and can have significant risk factors that you need to consider. Depending on the country, the agency can often fulfill your desire for a certain age, sex, and race of child.

International adoption also includes adopting from the United States, but few Canadians make this choice, due to much higher costs for adopting a Caucasian newborn (especially medical care). However, there are some affordable programs for adopting mixed-race and African-American babies from the United States which a number of Canadians have used. Some have chosen to adopt special needs children from the United States because they can receive subsidies to help cover the extra costs of raising them. Subsidies are now becoming more common in Canada.

To help you make your choice, here are more details on public, private and international adoption.

1. The Canadian Public Adoption System

Few reliable numbers on adoption, foster children, or children in care (living in group homes, treatment facilities, or independently in apartments in the community) are kept by provincial or federal governments. In April 1999, when I talked with Judy Grove, Executive Director of the Adoption Council of Canada, she estimated there were over 50,000 children in Canada currently in foster care, with about 14,500 being permanent Crown wards of the government. A "Crown ward" is a child who is legally under the care of the public agency (a ward of the state) and for whom the parents are no longer responsible. They are a subset of the children in care.

One-third of those in foster care, about 16,000, will never return permanently to their parents, but only a tiny fraction, about 1,700 a year, will be adopted out of the system. The rest are stuck in foster care. As Judy commented, "We keep better track of used cars than we do of our children, and that's a disgrace."

How do children become available for domestic public adoption in Canada? Children come into care in the public system because of neglect or abuse. Only a small number of infants are placed, with the birthmother's assistance. When a judge decides the parents are not able to care for the child, the child becomes a Crown ward and the public agency, for example, the Children's Aid Society in Ontario, becomes completely responsible for their care. However, if the judge issues an access order allowing the biological parent to visit the child, then in most provinces, this action makes the child ineligible to be adopted.

In Ontario, of 4,400 Crown wards, about three-quarters have such access orders. That leaves 1,232 children free for public adoption but, as Judy Grove noted, they are not being moved through the system. Take Toronto Metro Children's Aid Society, the largest public agency in Ontario: It had 1,831 children in care at the end of 1997. During that year, it placed 79 children.

Native children account for a high percentage of all children in foster care. In Canada it's very difficult, and in some places illegal, for nonnatives to adopt native children. Native families do not adopt all the native waiting children. As a result, many native children live with white foster families and the children have no hope of gaining a permanent family. If you have documented native ancestry you will be able to adopt native children quite quickly.

Who are the children placed by public agencies? Most public adoptions are of children with special needs. The typical child at placement is about two years old and comes from a poor background with an unstable family life, which resulted in the child coming into care. Substance abuse plays a large role: About one half of children placed are prenatally exposed to crack/cocaine, alcohol, or heroin. Birthparents often have mental health disorders or developmental handicaps, and there is a history of abuse or neglect. Limited social or medical histories of the birthparents are available.

Who may adopt from public agencies? In most provinces, married couples, single people, and common-law couples may apply to adopt. Québec and British Columbia allow same-sex couples to adopt. Most public agencies seem to prefer that parents finalize their first adoption before starting a second one. Both parents may have full-time jobs, but it is expected that one parent will take an initial parental leave to care for the child.

How long will a public adoption take? The waiting time before matching a child with a family varies considerably, depending on the parents' flexibility around specific attributes of the child, such as age, ethnic background, race, and health status. The process of training, homestudy, and approval is usually under twelve months. If you want a healthy infant, you will join a waiting list, which is typically seven years long. If you will consider a child with special needs who is available now, you might be able to adopt within a year or sooner.

How do I complete the public adoption process? Call the agency in your area. You will be asked to attend an intake group to learn how the system works. If you are still interested, there is a police check, and an adoption worker will be assigned to you. You may have to take preparatory educational classes. You make a formal application, complete with family background, social history, and at least three personal references. At this point the homestudy will be done by a public agency social worker. In most provinces, homestudies completed by private practitioners are not accepted by public agencies and have to be redone. During this time you need to have a medical exam. Once you have been approved, a meeting is held to match you with a child.

How does the public agency match a child to your family? The public agency will determine the child's history and the risks, and then draw up a list of the qualities needed in an adoptive parent. At an adoption planning conference, the child's service worker, their supervisor, the adoption worker, the foster parents who care for the child, and the supervisor of adoption might all be present. They will review the information on the approved families. A racial match for the child is also a consideration. If there is a match, the child is placed with you. There is a probation period, which varies in different provinces, to monitor how the child is doing in your home. The adoption is finalized in court.

Other options where approved adoptive parents can locate waiting children. Some provincial government agencies host regular presentations to profile waiting children for social workers and approved adoptive parents, such as Ontario's Adoption Resource Exchange in Toronto. Call your provincial coordinator for more information.

Canada's Waiting Children. The Adoption Council of Canada's Waiting Children Project was set up to find families for the thousands of Canadian children waiting for permanent homes. It is funded by the Dave Thomas Foundation for Adoption and Wendy's Restaurants. In the first three months of the Project over 1,100 information packages, including profiles and photos of waiting children, were mailed out by ACC Executive Director Judy Grove in Ottawa. The first placement resulting from the program happened just in time for Valentine's Day, 1999; two Manitoba children joined their new family in Newfoundland. For more information, call 1-888-54-ADOPT.

2. Private Adoption in Canada

All provinces except Québec allow private adoption. In Québec, you must apply to the director of youth protection in your area in order to adopt a Québec child.

What is the role of the provincial ministries? All private adoption is regulated by the provincial government ministries through their adoption units. They license individuals and agencies to place children for adoption, approve the social workers to conduct homestudies, and monitor the performance of licensees and social workers. When a private adoption is proposed, the ministry reviews and approves the private placement.

What does a licensee do? To adopt privately you must contact a licensee (an individual or a nonprofit agency licensed by your provincial ministry) because only licensees may place children privately. The licensee must obtain the ministry's approval to the adoption before the child may be legally placed with you.

The licensee must ensure that the birthparent has counseling available throughout the process and has an opportunity for independent legal advice before signing consents to the adoption. The counselor helps the birthparents sort through adoption issues, options, family selection, social history production, and pre- and postplacement counseling. After the consents have been signed and the revocation period has expired, the licensee assumes care of the child until legal completion.

What is a homestudy? After meeting a licensee, your next step is to start the homestudy. You will work with a social worker approved by your provincial ministry. The homestudy is a process to gather information about you, which can be shared with the birthparents in a nonidentifying way. It's a chance for you to learn more about parenting adopted children, open and closed adoptions, and disclosure registries. The homestudy gathers medical, police, financial, marital, and reference data together in one report.

How do you find birthmothers seeking to place their baby?   After your homestudy is done, it is time to let family, friends, work colleagues, church members, adoption agencies, and other licensees know of your interest to adopt. Ask your doctor to remember you if he or she has a patient considering placing a child for adoption. Some hopeful adopting parents send profiles to doctors across their province, place ads in community newspapers, rent an 800 phone number, and buy a cellular phone to be always available to answer calls.

What do birthmothers want in an adoptive family?   Birthmothers want adoptive families with or without other children but who have lots of extended family, who generally are two-parent families, who are rural or urban dwellers, who are financially secure, who have a solid marriage, who are of a similar ethnic background, and who are energetic with healthy lifestyles. Certain religious, educational, and employment criteria are also important.

Many birthmothers want adoptive mothers to take the ten-week adoption leave after the placement. Increasingly, birthmothers want some degree of openness in the adoption. This can range from just a regular exchange of (nonidentifying) pictures and letters, to frequent visits between birthparents and the adoptive family.

What happens after a birthmother is found?   Although you might have found a birthmother, the licensee must provide her with at least three family profiles. Your profile will include your letter of introduction as well as photographs, such as marriage pictures, family photos, pictures of other children in the family, and so forth.

If you find you are not chosen by a birthmother, you are still responsible for the cost up to this point.

Why weren't you chosen?   When you are not chosen by birthmothers, it's a good idea to ask why not. Most often, the birthparents find that profiled families have much to offer but select families based on similarity of family interests, experiences, values, and religion. You need to continually reassess your adoption plans. If you find you are not chosen because, for example, you are over 40, you may wish to change your plan of adopting a newborn and either consider adopting an older child or turn to international adoption.

What is in birthparent's social history?   If you are chosen by a birthparent, you will be presented with her social and medical histories. You need to assess the child's history of health issues and special needs. If you have medical concerns, consult your doctor. Information about prenatal exposure to alcohol or drugs is available from specialized clinics such as the MotheRisk Program in Toronto (Dr. Gideon Koren, (416) 813-6780).

You may be asked to meet the birthparents in a nonidentifying meeting, introduced by first name only. It seems both birthparents and adoptive parents are quite interested to meet each other, to say thank-you to each other, and to talk of the future. Most adoptions are not fully open, with exchanges of identities between the adoptive parents and the birthparents.

What does the ministry do?   The ministry reviews all the documents to ensure that the match is suitable, that the birthparents have had adequate opportunity to select a family, and that you are a suitable candidate. The ministry strongly encourages birthfather involvement and also seeks to obtain the best medical history possible. Satisfied the match is suitable, the ministry approves the placement.

What happens when the baby is born?   Once the baby is born, it is usual for birthparents to care for the child before they leave the hospital. With the help of the counselor, the birthparents again review their plan. If they wish to proceed with the adoption, they then release their child to the licensee. Often birthmothers leave the hospital 24 hours after birth. The child is frequently released from the hospital 24 to 48 hours after birth to the adoptive parents, with the understanding that the birthparents have not yet signed the consent forms.

What is involved in giving consent?   There are varying time restrictions in each province for both the signing of consent and the time during which consent can be revoked. Ask your ministry for the criteria for your province.

What is the revocation period?   During the revocation period, the birthparents have the right to terminate their adoption plan and the child must be returned to them. If this period expires without a revocation, the consent becomes irrevocable and the adoption continues.

What are the postplacement requirements?   Generally, you must arrange for your child to visit a doctor within a few days of release from the hospital. The social worker who did the homestudy must start several home visits, the last occurring six months after placement. The home visits ensure that both you and the child are adjusting appropriately. Then the social worker sends a report on the child's adjustment to the licensee, who forwards it to the ministry. If all is in order, the ministry authorizes the licensee to obtain an Adoption Order. The Adoption Order is granted in court, most often before the child reaches his or her first birthday. At this time your status changes to that of legal parent and your child joins your kinship lines.

Can you adopt from another province?   To adopt from another province you must use a licensee with an additional term in their license, which covers that province.

3. International Adoption for Canadians

If you've chosen international adoption, welcome to the majority! When you take the figure of only about 1,400 babies a year adopted domestically and compare it to an estimated 16,000 couples seeking to adopt, you can see why more and more look beyond the borders, to countries like China, Russia, Haiti, Romania, and Vietnam.

Follow the steps. Yes, I know—adopting *ought* to be as easy as giving birth to your own, but it isn't. And international adoption is another level more complicated than domestic. Still, the steps are clear, and I'll discuss them roughly in the order that you would follow. It may seem quite daunting, but it works, as thousands of Canadian families can attest.

One complication is that international adoption rules vary (although not greatly) in the thirteen jurisdictions of Canada (the ten provinces and three territories). Happily, each jurisdiction has a central authority you can consult; the adoption coordinator will send you free information on special requirements.

Choose a country. For many, the first decision is which country. I'm going to suggest a quick answer: Go where the successful people go. The following chart tells it all.

ADOPTIONS TO CANADA, 1998

Leading 20 countries, by province

	NS	NB	QC	ON	MN	SK	AB	BC	Total
China	12	10	494	293	1	16	22	50	901
India	0	0	5	94	6	1	16	56	178
Russia	7	0	50	82	0	4	0	16	160
Haiti	0	2	112	12	0	0	9	20	156
Romania	0	1	41	23	1	4	19	2	91
Jamaica	0	0	0	80	1	0	1	3	85
Philippines	1	3	8	31	8	4	8	16	79
Vietnam	0	0	62	12	0	0	2	3	79
U.S.A.	0	1	2	35	3	1	3	33	78
Guatemala	0	1	13	39	2	0	2	13	70
Thailand	0	0	38	5	1	0	0	3	47
Cambodia	0	0	19	0	0	3	0	1	23
Taiwan	0	0	17	1	1	1	0	3	23
Colombia	0	0	21	1	0	0	0	0	22
Guyana	0	0	0	15	1	0	0	1	17
Ukraine	0	0	0	10	3	0	0	2	15
Ghana	0	0	2	8	0	0	0	3	13
Ethiopia	0	0	0	10	0	0	1	1	12
Hong Kong	0	0	2	9	0	0	0	1	12
Mexico	0	0	4	3	0	1	0	2	10
Total (*all countries*)	22	18	915	828	29	40	91	274	2,222

Notes

- Figures include both relative and nonrelative adoptions. For some countries (e.g., India, Jamaica, Philippines) adoptions of relatives predominate.
- The table shows the top twenty sending countries and the top eight receiving provinces. (Remainder: Newfoundland 4; Yukon, 1; others, 0.)
- Totals are for all countries and all provinces.
- Data from Claire Lord, Program Specialist, Citizenship and Immigration Canada, (613) 941-9024, http://cicnet.ci.gc.ca/

Time and money. Adoption fees may influence your choice. Here are total costs (approximately) of an adoption from some top countries (excluding those with many relative adoptions).

U.S.A.	$25,000+
Guatemala	$24,000
Russia	$20,000
Romania	$19,000
Vietnam	$19,000
China	$17,000
Haiti	$12,000

The time it takes to adopt may also concern you. Typically, an international adoption will take twelve to eighteen months, from start to child in your home. With some countries you often find times under a year and even under nine months (China, Vietnam).

Details of the costs and time in the top twenty countries, plus the process in each, can be found in *Canadian Guide to Intercountry Adoption.* Published by Adoption Helper in 1999. See the end of this essay for more information.

Hague Convention: To protect the children. In May 1993, sixty-six countries, including Canada and the United States, agreed on the Hague Convention on Intercountry Adoption. The Hague Convention sets standards and procedures for international adoptions. For adoptions between countries that have ratified it, the Convention promises greater protection from exploitation for children, birthparents, and adoptive parents. An increasing number of countries and provinces continue to ratify the Convention. To learn whether Hague rules apply in your province and in the country you have chosen, contact your provincial adoption coordinator.

Choose an agency. Having chosen the country to adopt your child from, you then select an agency that is expert in the process for that country. The agency will help you with paperwork, travel and escort arrangements, and pre- and post-adoption support.

I recommend short-listing two or three agencies, then interviewing them and checking references. Before you sign a contract with an adoption agency or facilitator, be clear on the fee structure and the services provided. When must fees be paid? What is refundable if the process stops at a given stage?

You can find Canadian adoption agencies on-line at Family Helper (www.family helper.net/ad/adagyc.html) and in *Canadian Guide to Intercountry Adoption* (which also has a questionnaire for agencies). [Editor's note: Be sure to check the Canadian agency responses to our questionnaire in this chapter.]

Hire a social worker. You will need to hire an approved social worker to conduct a homestudy for international adoption. It's like a homestudy for domestic adoption—assessing your abilities as a parent—plus you name the country from where you want to adopt. The homestudy is one of the documents required by the authorities abroad. The social worker will meet you to discuss issues—racial, ethnic, bonding, and special needs—surrounding intercountry adoption.

Files on the move. You will also need to provide medical, financial, and police reports, and letters of reference, all appended to the homestudy and submitted to your provincial ministry of social services. The ministry grants you a letter of recommendation, generally good for eighteen months, assuring the foreign authority that you are a suitable adoptive parent. Your whole file goes abroad, reaching the adoption authority there, which approves your application. You may spend some months on a waiting list before matching starts.

National Adoption Desk. The National Adoption Desk (NAD) in Ottawa was set up in 1975 and serves all provinces and territories except Québec. NAD sets up adoption programs, or informal arrangements, under which we agree with another country on procedures for placing children in Canadian homes.

Countries with such arrangements are China, Colombia, Haiti, Hong Kong, Jamaica, Peru, Philippines, Romania, St. Vincent, and Thailand. When you deal with those countries, files and proposals flow between your provincial ministry and the foreign adoption authority via NAD.

For more information, write to: NAD, 5th Floor, Phase IV, Place du Portage, 140 Promenade du Portage, Hull, Québec K1A 0J9, or call (819) 953-8000, or fax (819) 953-1115. In Québec, contact the Secrétariat à l'adoption internationale, 201 boul. Crémazie est-RC, Montreal, Québec H2M 1L2, (514) 873-5226, fax (514) 873-1709.

Matching. How you will be matched with your child varies by country.

- Some countries match a child with you and send a photo and description; you decide whether to adopt the child (China, Haiti, Vietnam).
- Some countries maintain a central registry of available children, from which you (or your agent) choose (Romania, Russia).
- Your agency may have a selection of children available for adoption—photo, description, medical record—from which you choose (Guatemala).

Flying abroad.

1. Usually one or both parents must go to the country to pick up the child; rarely, escorts are allowed (Haiti).
2. You receive your child and stay (with your child) the required time, which varies from two days (Guatemala) to two weeks (China) to many weeks. A social worker may visit to see how your child is doing.
3. You appear in court and the judge issues the adoption decree. Your child is legally yours! (With some countries the adoption is finalized in court after you return home.)

Flying home with your new child   Under the new (and most welcome) Federal Citizenship Act, introduced in Parliament in December 1998 and probably in force when you read this, children adopted overseas (that is, whose adoption is finalized in a court abroad) will be granted automatic Canadian citizenship—no visa is needed to enter the country.

However, if the adoption is finalized in Canada (i.e., when adopting from Hong Kong, India, Jamaica, Philippines, or Thailand), then you must first apply for your child's landed immigrant visa before he or she enters Canada. For that, you file an "Undertaking of Assistance (sponsorship)" with Immigration Canada's Case Processing Centre, Box 895, Postal Stn. U, Toronto, Ont. M8Z 5P9, fax (905) 507-2486. Once back in Canada you apply for your child's citizenship.

Follow-up.   Countries often request progress reports for a year or more after you return home. These post-adoption reports may be letters and photos from you, or reports prepared by your social worker (at your expense).

Still have questions?   A great starting point, when filling in the information gaps, is the Adoption Council of Canada (180 Argyle Ave., Suite 329, Ottawa, Ont. K2P 1B7, (613) 235-1566, 1-888-542-3678, fax (613) 235-1728, e-mail acc@adoption.ca, Web site www.adoption.ca) or one of the provincial adoption associations or support groups. You can also find a list of support groups on-line at Family Helper (www.helping.com/family/ad/adsup.html).

Adoption Helper is a useful Canadian publication that focuses on international adoption. It's $32 a year, from Robin Hilborn, 185 Panoramic Dr., Sault Ste. Marie, Ont. P6B 6E3. He is also the source for the *Canadian Guide to Intercountry Adoption* (2nd ed., 1999, $12).

Don't forget that post-adoption phase, namely the rest of your life with your adopted child. Support groups can help here, too, as can magazines such as my own Post-adoption Helper, available from Robin Hilborn, 185 Panoramic Dr., Sault Ste. Marie, Ont. P6B 6E3

Jennifer Smart lives in Sault Ste. Marie, Ontario. She trained in college as a fish and wildlife technician *and worked in the wilds of northern Ontario, netting fish and counting moose. Later she attended university and became* an occupational therapist. *Her interest in adoption began as she struggled with unsuccessful infertility treatment. She has two children, a son who arrived from Korea as an infant, and a daughter who arrived as a newborn from Ontario. She has been active in the adoption field and in 1997 received an Ontario Adoption Award for her work on behalf of adoption in Ontario.*

Ms. Smart has presented workshops for adoptive parents at major adoption conferences. Currently she is editor of Post-adoption Helper, *a magazine devoted to supporting adoptive parents with raising their children, and she still makes time for her OT practice.*

Inclusion in the following list of adoption organizations in Canada does not in any way constitute endorsement or approval. Anyone wishing to consider using the services of any of these organizations should be sure to check them out thoroughly. (There are also many more organizations in Canada involved in placing children; this is only a partial listing.)

CANADIAN CHILD-PLACING ORGANIZATIONS

ALBERTA

ADOPTION OPTIONS

Respondent: Marilyn Shinyei, Director (Edmonton)
In charge of social services: Marilyn Shinyei, Linda Edney (Calgary)
#320, 9707 110 St., Edmonton, Alberta T5K 2L9
(780) 433-5656 • FAX: (780) 447-4763
E-mail: aoedm@adoptonoptions.com
Year first licensed: 1989

My agency provides services in: International adoption; postplacement services; search services.

What areas do your adoptive parent clients come from? Alberta.

Services provided to adopting parents: Classes with other prospective parents; required readings of books and/or article son adoption; group discussions about adoption; parenting discussions; bookstore; newsletter.

What was the goal of your organization when first organized? What is the goal of your organization now? Agency organized in 1985 to provide comprehensive adoption service to people seeking alternatives to the ward (government) adoption program and independent and international adoptions on a not-for-profit basis. Now: This has changed little except that we are doing the above as a licensed agency and the alternatives have become mainstream: licensed agency placements, international programs, and some independent adoptions which we process for the families. Also we have expanded to be a licensed search agency.

How many nonrelative children did your organization place in 1998? 57

What percent of your adoptive placements are infants under 6 mos.? 95%+

Do staff members have special expertise? Licensed social workers, all BSW or MSW and registered. Several are also adoptive parents and one is a reunited birthmother.

In 1998, what was the average time from when a prospective adoptive parent applied to when he or she received a homestudy? This is dependent on the speed with which they complete their paperwork. Homestudy is done within 90 days of their paperwork being received.

In 1998, what was the average time from the homestudy to the placement of a child? 12 mos.

What made you decide to work in the adoption field? Being an adoptive parent, I became involved in leadership training and adoption discussion groups, then founded the Adoptive Parents Association of Alberta. Eventually requests from birthparents pushed us to offer an alternative to government adoption. Also, I believed in open adoption and open records from the start!

What are your criteria for adoptive parents? Must be over 18 and residents of Alberta.

How do you screen adoptive parents? Medical records; three references; criminal record checks; child abuse information system check; parent preparation seminar; full home assessment by qualified social worker.

How do you screen birthparents? By having them complete medical/social forms.

What percent of your Canadian-born children are nonwhite? 33%

Do you have a waiting list of prospective parents? Yes.

Is it all right if adopting parents are on the waiting lists of other agencies or attorneys? Yes for other agencies. No for attorneys—this is illegal in Alberta.

Do you have an application fee? If yes, what is the amount of the application fee? Yes; $600.

What is your homestudy fee? $1,100

What is your placement fee? $2,300. Our total fees are $6,400 Canadian.

Do adopting parents also pay fees for medical and hospital expenses for the birthmother and baby? No—this is Canada—all expenses are covered. They might pay $40/day for a private room and there is a third-party medical required on the baby, which is paid for.

If you place children from other countries, please list the estimated entire average cost to adoptive parents for each country. We don't place children from other countries, but families must use our services to do an international adoption in terms of preparation seminars, home assessment, etc. The cost is $1,900. Postplacement reports are extra.

My agency: Offers meetings between birthparents and adoptive parents; lets birthparents pick adoptive parents from biographies/resumes; offers full disclosure of names between birth and adoptive parents.

How would you advise prospective adopters just starting out? To do their homework, find out what their options are, talk to other adopters, and be open about open adoption.

What is the most annoying thing adopting parents do to adoption organizations? They call too frequently to see what's happening. We suggest every 3 mos. would be okay.

Are you an adoptive parent, adopted person, or birthparent? Adoptive parent.

Has your agency lost any adoption litigation filed against you by an adoptive parent or birthparent? No.

CHRISTIAN ADOPTION SERVICES

Respondent: Wendy Robinson, BSW, Program Director
In charge of social services: Wendy Robinson
204-11625 Elbor Dr. SW, Calgary, Alberta T2W 1G8
(403) 256-3224 • FAX: (403) 256-8367
E-mail: w-robinson@home.com
Year first licensed: 1989. We are licensed to operate only in Alberta.

My agency provides services in: International adoption; infants; homestudy if parents working with another agency; postplacement services; training.

What areas do your adoptive parent clients come from? Alberta.

Services provided to adopting parents: Classes with other prospective parents; required readings of books or articles on adoption; group discussions about adoption.

What countries do your birthparents/adopted children come from? United States, Haiti, China, Romania, Jamaica.

What was the goal of your organization when first organized? To support birthparents in unplanned pregnancies and encourage them to carry the child to term. If adoption was their choice, to provide an evangelical Christian family.

How many nonrelative children did your organization place in 1998? Domestic, 20; international, 40.

What percent of your adoptive placements are infants under 6 mos.? 99%

Do staff members have special expertise? Adoptive parents on staff; licensed social workers; pastor.

In 1998, what was the average time from when a prospective adoptive parent applied to when he or she received a homestudy? 6 weeks

In 1998, what was the average time from the homestudy to the placement of a child? 16 mos. for domestic; 9 mos. for international.

What made you decide to work in the adoption field? I was a foster parent when I returned to university. After working in Jamaican orphanages, I wanted to find out about adoption—to make a difference.

What are your criteria for adoptive parents? For domestic, must be unable to conceive, active Christians, able to sign a statement of faith. For international, must meet government standards and the criteria of the country sending the child.

How do you screen adoptive parents? Training, interview, homestudy.

How do you screen birthparents? Government social and family history forms.

What kind of medical information do you seek on children over 1 year old? Adoptions are open, so the adopting couple can ask what they want.

What percent of your Canadian-born children are nonwhite? 5%

Do you have a waiting list of prospective parents? Yes.

Is it all right if adopting parents are on the waiting lists of other agencies or attorneys? Yes.

Do you have an application fee? If yes, what is the amount of the application fee? Yes. $250 for domestic; $50 for international.

What is your homestudy fee? $1,000

What is your placement fee? $3,500. Adopting parents also pay expenses for counselling for birthmother and travel to see birthmother. About $800.

If you place children from other countries, please list the estimated entire average cost to adoptive parents for each country. Haiti, $12,000; Romania, $16,000; China, $16,000.

My agency: Offers meetings between birthparents and adoptive parents; lets birthparents pick adoptive parents from biographies/resumes; full disclosure of names between birth and adoptive parents; birthmother can have confidentiality, but adoptive parents are not likely to get a child if they want this.

How would you advise prospective adopters just starting out? To take the courses and then decide how to proceed.

What is the most annoying thing adopting parents do to adoption organizations? Looking at the colour over the health of a child.

What statement do you wish you could make adoptive parents memorize? "There can never be too many people to love a child." "Nobody 'owns' a child. We all share them for a while."

Are you an adoptive parent, adopted person, or birthparent? Adoptive parent. Also, foster parent for 25 years.

In how many cases with your agency has an adoptive parent lost a child due to birthparent challenge? Once, in 1990, a child returned to a birthfather.

Has your agency lost any adoption litigation filed against you by an adoptive parent or birthparent? No.

ADOPTION SERVICES, CROSSROADS COUNSELLING CENTRE

Respondent: Lisa Parkin, Adoption Services Program Director
In charge of social services: Lisa Parkin
202 542 7 St. South, Lethbridge, Alberta T1J 2H1
(403) 327-7080 • Fax: (403) 327-7282
E-mail: croads@telusplanet.net • www.crossroadscounselling.com
Year first licensed: 1992

My agency provides services in: International adoption; children with special needs; infants; homestudy if parents working with another agency; postplacement services; search and reunion; finalization of private direct placements; counselling.

What areas do your adoptive parent clients come from? Alberta.

Services provided to adopting parents: Group discussions about adoption; parenting discussions; adoptive parenting workshops; able to provide support groups/workshops according to interest and need; workshop/training component through viewing videos.

What countries do your birthparents/adopted children come from? Romania, China, Haiti, Philippines, Russia, United States; others are possibilities.

What was the goal of your organization when first organized? What is the goal of your organization now? To provide high-quality, professional adoption services for birthparents and adoptive parents in our area (southern Alberta) and throughout the province of Alberta. Now: Same.

How many nonrelative children did your organization place in 1998? 10

What percent of your adoptive placements are infants under 6 mos.? 80%

Do staff members have special expertise? Adoptive parents on staff; licensed social workers; psychologists; therapists.

In 1998, what was the average time from when a prospective adoptive parent applied to when he or she received a homestudy? 3 mos.

In 1998, what was the average time from the homestudy to the placement of a child? 18 mos.

What made you decide to work in the adoption field? I began working in social work as a child/family therapist. I saw many attachment issues in families; this eventually drew me into the field of adoption.

What are your criteria for adoptive parents? They must be legally married and meet the other requirements of Alberta Family and Social Services (AFSS).

How do you screen adoptive parents? We follow the guidelines and regulations set out for us by Alberta Family and Social Services, by whom we are licensed. We initially meet with prospective adoptive parents to answer their questions and educate them. They then view a training video. If they choose to proceed, they must be approved through the guidelines of home assessments set out by AFSS.

How do you screen birthparents? There are no formal screening procedures. We begin counselling to determine their situation. If the matched adoptive parents request it, we can have a criminal record check and medical screening done.

What kind of medical information do you seek on children over 1 year old? We would have a doctor do a physical exam and write a report.

What percent of your Canadian-born children are nonwhite? 20–30%

About what percent are children with medical problems? 10–15%

Do you have a waiting list of prospective parents? Yes.

Is it all right if adopting parents are on the waiting lists of other agencies or attorneys? Yes for agencies, no for attorneys.

Do you have an application fee? If yes, what is the amount of the application fee? Yes. As of April 1999, $425.

What is your homestudy fee? $1,100

What is your placement fee? $2,565 (including all fees, $5,910).

My agency: Offers meetings between birthparents and adoptive parents; lets birthparents pick adoptive parents from biographies/resumes; offers full disclosure of names between birth and adoptive parents.

How would you advise prospective adopters just starting out? Gather as much information as possible on adoption and on various agencies. Make choices based on as much information as possible.

What is the most annoying thing adopting parents do to adoption organizations? Expect an immediate placement. Do not take into consideration that they are not the only couple we are working with.

What is the most common mistake you see adopting parents make? Rushing into situations; not heeding our warnings about the risks involved.

In how many cases with your agency has an adoptive parent lost a child due to birthparent challenge? None. Twice a birthmother has changed her mind within the ten-day period after consent in which she may do so. In one of those two cases, the birthmother returned the child to the adoptive parents.

BRITISH COLUMBIA

CHOICES ADOPTION & COUNSELLING SERVICES

Respondent: Joyce H. Masselink, Executive Director
In charge of social services: Joyce H. Masselink
#309-1095 McKenzie Ave., Victoria, British Columbia V8P 2L5
(250) 479-9811 • Fax: (250) 479-9850
E-mail: choices@pacificcoast.net
Year first licensed: 1996

My agency provides services in: International adoption; children with special needs; infants; homestudy if parents working with another agency; postplacement service; birthparent and post-adoption counselling.

What areas do your adoptive parent clients come from? British Columbia.

Services provided to adopting parents: Classes with other prospective parents; required reading books and articles on adoption; group discussions about adoption; parenting discussions; counselling and support.

What countries do your birthparents/adopted children come from? United States, Ukraine, Russia, Romania, China, Haiti, Guatemala, India, Pakistan, Vietnam, South Africa, and any other country that applicants have identified and wish to work with to obtain a child by adoption.

What was the goal of your organization when first organized? What is the goal of your organization now? To provide a continuum of services to individuals, couples, families, and groups. These services are to include counselling, education, and information regarding adoption issues and making decisions regarding adoption planning as well as becoming a family by adoption. Now: Same.

How many nonrelative children did your organization place in 1998? 29

What percent of your adoptive placements are infants under 6 mos.? 43%.

Do staff members have special expertise? Licensed social workers; attorney.

In 1998, what was the average time from when a prospective adoptive parent applied to when he or she received a homestudy? 3–6 mos.

In 1998, what was the average time from the homestudy to the placement of a child? 1–2 years

What made you decide to work in the adoption field? I have worked with various members of the adoption circle since 1962 and have found this a most interesting and rewarding field to work in.

What are your criteria for adoptive parents? For domestic (local) adoptions, applicant should not be able to have biological children. Intercountry criteria varies according to the country's requirements.

How do you screen adoptive parents? By education and a thorough interview process.

How do you screen birthparents? We interview them, obtain social and medical histories, and assist them to explore a range of options in planning for their expected child. We wish them to make a decision from a position of strength.

What kind of medical information do you seek from birthparents? Medical information on all members of their family of origin and everything that is known about the medical issues of the birthparents.

What kind of medical information do you seek on children over 1 year old? Everything that we can on their birthfamily and their own medical history from birth as well as prenatal history.

What percent of your Canadian-born children are nonwhite? Less than 1%

Do you have a waiting list of prospective parents? Yes.

Is it all right if adopting parents are on the waiting lists of other agencies or attorneys? Yes.

Do you have an application fee? If yes, what is the amount of the application fee? Yes; $250.

What is your homestudy fee? $2,250

What is your placement fee? $3,000–5,000, plus postplacement supervision costs (approximately $800) and completion costs $1,000 plus legal fees.

Do adopting parents also pay fees for medical and hospital expenses for the birthmother and baby? If yes, what is the average fee paid? Sometimes. Very little.

If you place children from other countries, please list the estimated entire average cost to adoptive parents for each country. $15,000–25,000 Canadian

My agency: Offers confidential adoptions; semi-open adoptions with first names exchanged; meetings between birthparents and adoptive parents; lets birthparents pick adoptive parents from biographies/resumes; full disclosure of names between birth and adoptive parents.

Does your agency provide videotapes of children needing adoption? Sometimes.

How would you advise prospective adopters just starting out? To read as much as they can about adoption, meet with other adopting parents, and attend courses and seminars on adoption.

What is the most annoying thing adopting parents do to adoption organizations? Challenging the costs, the wait, and the process.

What is the most common mistake you see adopting parents make? Taking on more than they are ready for.

What statement do you wish you could make adoptive parents memorize? "Adoption is a new journey. I will learn much about myself, my relationships, my capacity to parent, and about people, process, and cultures. I will grow in this process."

In how many cases with your agency has an adoptive parent lost a child due to birthparent challenge? None.

Has your agency lost any adoption litigation filed against you by an adoptive parent or birthparent? No.

SUNRISE ADOPTION CENTRE

Respondent: Douglas Chalke, Executive Director
In charge of social services: Rea Flamer
IBM Tower at Pacific Centre, #1500-701 West Georgia St., Vancouver, British Columbia V7Y 1E9
(604) 984-2488 • Fax: (604) 980-6469
Year first licensed: 1997

My agency provides services in: International adoption; infants; homestudy if parents working with another agency; postplacement services.

What areas do your adoptive parent clients come from? British Columbia.

Services provided to adopting parents: Classes with other prospective parents; required readings of books and/or articles on adoption; group discussions about adoption; parenting discussions; government-required adoption education course.

What countries do your birthparents/adopted children come from? United States, China, Russia, Ukraine, Canada, Guatemala, El Salvador, Georgia, Kazakhstan.

What percent of your adoptive placements are infants under 6 mos.? 100% for local, 20% for intercountry.

Do staff members have special expertise? Licensed social workers; attorney.

In 1998, what was the average time from when a prospective adoptive parent applied to when he or she received a homestudy? 3 mos.

In 1998, what was the average time from the homestudy to the placement of a child? 1 year

What made you decide to work in the adoption field? To provide options to infertile couples.

What are your criteria for adoptive parents? They must be approved by a social worker and provide numerous medical and record checks.

How do you screen adoptive parents? Through social worker interviews, etc.

How do you screen birthparents? Interviews with experienced social workers.

What kind of medical information do you seek from birthparents? Medical and hospital records, drug and alcohol checks.

What kind of medical information do you seek on children over 1 year old? Past medical records, current blood work.

What percent of your Canadian-born children are nonwhite? 10%

About what percent are children with medical problems? 15%

About what percent are children with emotional problems? 15%

Do you have a waiting list of prospective parents? Yes.

Is it all right if adopting parents are on the waiting lists of other agencies or attorneys? Yes.

Do you have an application fee? If yes, what is the amount of the application fee? Yes; $350.

What is your homestudy fee? $1,800

What is your placement fee? $4,250

Do adopting parents also pay fees for medical and hospital expenses for the birthmother and baby? In Canada, it's covered by public health insurance.

If applicable, what is the average document translation fee? $100

If you assist international adoptions, what are the average travel expenses? $5,000

If you place children from other countries, please list the estimated entire average cost to adoptive parents for each country. Fees are all in Canadian dollars. China, $19,500; Russia, $24,000; United States, $15,000–30,000; Guatemala, $25,000.

My agency: Offers confidential adoptions; "semi-open" adoptions; meetings between birthparents and adoptive parents; lets birthparents pick adoptive parents from biographies/resumes; full disclosure of names between birth and adoptive parents.

How would you advise prospective adopters just starting out? Keep an open mind and learn as much as possible about your options before making a decision.

What is the most annoying thing adopting parents do to adoption organizations? Treat us with a lack of respect.

What is the most common mistake you see adopting parents make? Become emotionally involved and unable to step back and rationally assess a situation.

What statement do you wish you could make adoptive parents memorize? "Be careful what you wish for; do not take on more than you can handle."

In how many cases with your agency has an adoptive parent lost a child due to birthparent challenge? None.

Has your agency lost any adoption litigation filed against you by an adoptive parent or birthparent? No.

NOVA SCOTIA

CHILDREN FROM CHINA

Respondent: Linda Kirby
In charge of social services: Susan Drysdale
6528 London St., Halifax, Nova Scotia B3L 1X6
(902) 454-5559
E-mail: Kirbquig@istar.ca

My agency provides services in: International adoption.

What areas do your adoptive parent clients come from? Nova Scotia.

Services provided to adopting parents: Classes with other prospective parents; required readings of books and/or articles on adoption; group discussions about adoption; parenting discussions; assistance with paperwork, translations, and escort.

What countries do your birthparents/adopted children come from? China.

What is the goal of your organization now? To continue to assist in the formation of families.

How many nonrelative children did your organization place in 1998? 7

Do staff members have special expertise? Adoptive parents on staff; attorney.

In 1998, what was the average time from when a prospective adoptive parent applied to when he or she received a homestudy? 4 mos.

In 1998, what was the average time from the homestudy to the placement of a child? 10 mos.

What made you decide to work in the adoption field? Adoptive parent of three myself.

What are your criteria for adoptive parents? Approved homestudy required.

Do you have a waiting list of prospective parents? No.

Is it all right if adopting parents are on the waiting lists of other agencies or attorneys? Yes.

Do you have an application fee? No.

What is your placement fee? $1,500

If you place children from other countries, please list the estimated entire average cost to adoptive parents for each country. $18,000

Are you an adoptive parent, adopted person, or birthparent? Adoptive parent and adopted person.

Has your agency lost any adoption litigation filed against you by an adoptive parent or birthparent? No.

ONTARIO

ADOPTION DIRECTIONS

Respondent: Alison Pentland-Folk
5 L'Estrange Place, Toronto, ON M6S 4S6
(416) 767-8154 • Fax: (416) 767-8154
E-mail address: apf@goodmedia.com

My agency provides services in: Domestic adoption; postplacement services; preplacement education; resource referral; advocacy; crisis intervention for process problems; one-on-one services.

What areas do your adoptive parent clients come from? Across Canada by e-mail or phone. Personal appointments for residents of southwestern Ontario.

What countries do your birthparents/adopted children come from? All countries.

What was the goal of your organization when first organized? Pre- and postplacement support and resource for prospective adoptive parents in intercountry adoption in manner that serves the needs of the prospective adoptive parent while maintaining the rights of the child and birthfamily.

How many nonrelative children did your organization place in 1998? I have worked with over 800 families since 1991. Almost all these families are parenting now, adopting, on average, toddler-aged children within 15 mos. of contacting me.

What made you decide to work in the adoption field? Uncertainty during my own adoptions led me to mentor families.

Is it all right if adopting parents are on the waiting lists of other agencies or attorneys? Yes.

Do you have an application fee? If yes, what is the amount of the application fee? My consultation fee is $90 per hour. Most appointments are two hours for $180, which includes my resource guide.

How would you advise prospective adopters just starting out? Gather as much information as you can in as broad a context as possible. Short-list at least three different countries (can include domestic) and become an expert in each. Join a support group and meet others. Take time for yourself. Have patience and humour.

What is the most annoying thing adopting parents do to adoption organizations? Their expectations are usually too high. They give away their power.

What statement do you wish you could make adoptive parents memorize? Be open. Trust your instincts. Be curious. No question is too stupid. Be concise with your agency and have your family and support group hold your hand.

Are you an adoptive parent, adopted person, or birthparent? Adoptive parent.

BEGINNINGS COUNSELLING, ADOPTION SERVICES OF ONTARIO, INC.

Respondent: Susan Chapman, Executive Director
In charge of social services: Susan Chapman
1 Young St., Suite 308, Hamilton, Ontario L8N 1T8
(905) 528-6665 • Fax: (905) 528-6589
Year first licensed: 1994

My agency provides services in: Infants with special needs; infants; postplacement services.

What areas do your adoptive parent clients come from? Ontario only.

Services provided to adopting parents: Readings of books and/or articles on adoption; group discussions about adoption.

What countries do your birthparents/adopted children come from? Ontario.

How many nonrelative children did your organization place in 1998? 10

What percent of your adoptive placements are infants under 6 mos.? 100%

Do staff members have special expertise? Adoptive parents on staff, licensed social workers.

In 1998, what was the average time from when a prospective adoptive parent applied to when he or she received a homestudy? 3 years. Could be less or more, depending on number of birthparents and range of acceptance of adoptive applicants.

In 1998, what was the average time from the homestudy to the placement of a child? 2 years

What made you decide to work in the adoption field? Used to work for provincial child welfare agency in adoption.

How do you screen adoptive parents? Homestudies, training.

How do you screen birthparents? Counselling, offer support groups.

What kind of medical information do you seek from birthparents? As complete as possible, including extended family (parents, grandparents).

What percent of your Canadian-born children are nonwhite? Less than 1%

About what percent are children with medical problems? 30%

Do you have a waiting list of prospective parents? Yes.

Is it all right if adopting parents are on the waiting lists of other agencies or attorneys? Yes.

Do you have an application fee? If yes, what is the amount of the application fee? Yes. $150

What is your homestudy fee? $850

What is your placement fee? $1,425, plus other costs, such as pregnancy counselling, supervision of placement, etc. Fees are reviewed annually.

My agency: Offers confidential adoptions; semi-open adoptions with first names exchanged; meetings between birthparents and adoptive parents; lets birthparents pick adoptive parents from biographies/resumes; full disclosure of names between birth and adoptive parents (if all parties request this, not the norm.)

How would you advise prospective adopters just starting out? Advocate for themselves—as broad a base as they are comfortable, locally, internationally.

What is the most common mistake you see adopting parents make? Not exploring all their options.

In how many cases with your agency has an adoptive parent lost a child due to birthparent challenge? None.

Has your agency lost any adoption litigation filed against you by an adoptive parent or birthparent? No.

CANADIAN HOMES FOR RUSSIAN CHILDREN (CHRC)

Respondent: Arnie Gotfryd, Executive Director
In charge of social services: Lidia Vidmonte
3727 Chesswood Dr., Toronto, Ontario M3Y 2P6
(416) 630-2472 • Fax: 416-630-3712
www.helping.com/family/ad/chrc.html
Year first licensed: Registered in 1994.

My agency provides services in: International adoption.

What areas do your adoptive parent clients come from? Ontario, Québec, British Columbia, Manitoba, Alberta, Saskatchewan, Nova Scotia.

Services provided to adopting parents: Group discussions about adoption; parenting discussions; seminars; family reunions; consultations.

What countries do your birthparents/adopted children come from? Russia, Ukraine, Canada, United States.

What was the goal of your organization when first organized? The goal of our organization is to unite homeless children with caring, adoptive parents in a healthy family.

How many nonrelative children did your organization place in 1998? 23

What percent of your adoptive placements are infants under 6 mos.? 9%

Do staff members have special expertise? Licensed social workers; physician; attorney; rabbi.

In 1998, what was the average time from when a prospective adoptive parent applied to when he or she received a homestudy? 3 mos.

In 1998, what was the average time from the homestudy to the placement of a child? 6 mos.

What made you decide to work in the adoption field? Executive director's previous experience was at a Toronto community centre providing educational and recreational programs for immigrant children of Russian-speaking families.

What are your criteria for adoptive parents? Single and older applicants may apply. May have children at home.

How do you screen adoptive parents? Application form, interview, favourable recommendation from licensed social worker, government approvals during process.

What kind of medical information do you seek on children over 1 year old? Detailed history and independent professional examination by a Canadian government–approved, designated medical practitioner.

Do you have a waiting list of prospective parents? No.

Is it all right if adopting parents are on the waiting lists of other agencies or attorneys? Yes.

Are your adoption fees based on a sliding scale? If yes, what are the sliding scale criteria? Yes. Adoption subsidies are available from time to time, based on the board of directors' review of demonstrated financial need and availability of funds.

Do you have an application fee? If yes, what is the amount of the application fee? Yes; $360 Canadian.

If you place children from other countries, please list the estimated entire average cost to adoptive parents for each country. Russia, $30,000 Canadian.

Does your agency provide videotapes of children needing adoption? Yes.

What is the most common mistake you see adopting parents make? Having rigid expectations of timing within the process.

What statement do you wish you could make adoptive parents memorize? We do the work, but God makes it happen.

THE CHILDREN'S BRIDGE

Respondent: Jennifer Dawson, Chief Administrative Officer
In charge of social services: Martha Maslen, MSW, Executive Director
1400 Clyde Ave., Suite 221, Nepean, Ontario K2G 2J2
(613) 226-2112 • Fax: (613) 226-8843
E-mail: cbridge@direct-internet.net • www.childrensbridge.com

My agency provides services in: International adoption; children from China with special needs; postplacement services; preadoption services via "Families-In-Waiting" groups and workshops, "Well Baby Clinics," to provide tips on caring for a baby.

What areas do your adoptive parent clients come from? Primarily from Canada; however, we have assisted families in the United States, France, Japan, Sweden, Hong Kong, and living within China.

Services provided to adopting parents: Classes with prospective group discussions about adoption; readings of book and adoption articles; parenting discussions and classes; pretravel meeting; monthly update bulletins to inform families of file progression; quarterly newsletter written by adoptive parents for adoptive parents; post-adoption support groups; "Families-In-Waiting" events; annual conference; annual national picnic held on August Civic Holiday.

What countries do your birthparents/adopted children come from? China and Vietnam.

What was the goal of your organization when first organized? What is the goal of your organization now? To build families through adoption. Now: Our goal has never changed, although we are now also interested in building the family as a whole. We work toward enabling families to make good adoption choices through education.

How many nonrelative children did your organization place in 1998? Over 130

What percent of your adoptive placements are infants under 6 mos.? Less than 1%

Do staff members have special expertise? Both our key office staff are adopted. Our executive director has a masters in social work and has worked in adoption for over 13 years. Our administrator is an adoptive mother of two children from China.

In 1998, what was the average time from when a prospective adoptive parent applied to when he or she received a homestudy? An average homestudy in the Province of Ontario takes 2–3 mos. to complete. The Ontario Provincial government then requires several months to review and approve the families for international adoption. These timelines change depending on which province in Canada the family resides, or the state process in the United States.

In 1998, what was the average time from the homestudy to the placement of a child? From the submission of a file in China to placement of a child is approximately 9 mos. In Vietnam, the average timeframe is 4 mos.

What made you decide to work in the adoption field? Our agency was founded on one person's journey overseas in 1991 and the word of mouth growth that ensued. We have now processed over 500 adoptions, primarily from China.

What are your criteria for adoptive parents? The Children's Bridge criteria for adoptive parents follow the guidelines of the sending countries we work with: China: Prospective parents must be over 30 years of age, married or single, with no criminal record. They may not be a common-law or same-sex couple. Vietnam: Younger prospective parents are welcome, married or single, with no criminal record.

How do you screen adoptive parents? Adoptive parents must have an approved homestudy and meet the criteria of the sending country.

What kind of medical information do you seek on children over 1 year old? We do follow-up with all our children's social welfare institutes to get updated information regarding the child's growth and development.

Do you have a waiting list of prospective parents? No. The sending countries do have waiting lists. This is the cause of the 9 mos. to placement in China.

Do you have an application fee? If yes, what is the amount of the application fee? Yes; $25.

What is your homestudy fee? Homestudies in Canada are primarily completed by private, approved social workers within their own provincial boundaries. The fees they charge range from $500–1,500.

What is your placement fee? $1,500 Canadian

If you place children from other countries, please list the estimated entire average cost to adoptive parents for each country. China, $17,000–18,000 Canadian; Vietnam, $20,000 Canadian.

Does your agency provide videotapes of children needing adoption? No.

How would you advise prospective adopters just starting out? We would advise anyone starting to look at international adoption to RESEARCH: Research the country. Research the agency: how many adoptions? How long has the agency been in business? Can you contact other adoptive parents? Is it for profit or nonprofit? What pre- and post-adoption services does the agency provide? Research how a multicultural adoption may affect your family. Research the rules and regulations of your own country, province, or state around the homestudy and immigration process.

What is the most annoying thing adopting parents do to adoption organizations? The most annoying thing that families do to adoption organizations is fail to read carefully all of the information that their agency sends to them. Many agencies provide their clients with an abundance of information relating to the processing of the adoption. Families often do not read this very crucial information.

What is the most common mistake you see adopting parents make? The most common mistake we see adopting parents make is not being realistic about the age and circumstances of the children they are adopting. They sometimes ask the agency to make guarantees around the health of children and the age of the child they are looking to adopt. Everyone wants the youngest child possible, but the reality is that someone will be offered a child a little older than they had dreamed of.

What statement do you wish you could make adoptive parents memorize? Be flexible.

In how many cases with your agency has an adoptive parent lost a child due to birthparent challenge? None.

Has your agency lost any adoption litigation filed against you by an adoptive parent or birthparent? No.

Is there anything that I have not asked you that is important? Children's Bridge strongly recommends its families participate in as many pre- and post-adoption services as possible. The wait for families and the adjustment once the child is home are all eased when done with others in the same position.

OPEN ARMS TO INTERNATIONAL ADOPTION

Respondent: Deborah Maw, Executive Director
In charge of social services: Deborah Maw
14 Roxborough St. W., Toronto, Ontario M5R 1T8
(416) 966-0294 • Fax: (416) 966-0187
E-mail: openarms@pathcom.com

My agency provides services in: International adoption.

Services provided to adopting parents: Classes with other prospective parents; readings of books and/or articles on adoption; group discussions about adoption.

What areas do your adoptive parent clients come from? China.

What was the goal of your organization when first organized? What is the goal of your organization now? To assist Ontario residents in adopting children from China. Now: To help Canadian families complete international adoptions.

How many nonrelative children did your organization place in 1998? 90 (approximate)

Do staff members have special expertise? Adoptive parents on staff.

In 1998, what was the average time from when a prospective adoptive parent applied to when he or she received a homestudy? 3 mos.

In 1998, what was the average time from the homestudy to the placement of a child? 11 mos.

What made you decide to work in the adoption field? I am an adoptive parent and wanted to help others experience my joy.

What are your criteria for adoptive parents? Aged 30–60. Number of children depends on each individual family and provincial guidelines. Our agency does not conduct homestudies—these are done by a government-approved group of social workers. Must be in good health, no criminal record, and have sufficient financial means to care for a child.

How do you screen adoptive parents? Homestudy: If approved by the provincial government, we accept the adoptive parents without further screening measures. However, if the agency found itself in a situation where the well-being of a child was questionable, measures would be taken with the appropriate authorities to protect the child's well-being.

What kind of medical information do you seek on children over 1 year old? Subject to information provided by Chinese authorities. These children tend to be very healthy.

About what percent are children with medical problems? Minor medical problems: 5%

Is it all right if adopting parents are on the waiting lists of other agencies or attorneys? No.

Do you have an application fee? No.

What is your placement fee? $950 plus tax

If you place children from other countries, please list the estimated entire average cost to adoptive parents for each country. China, including airfare and donation to orphanage; $16,000–17,000 Canadian.

How would you advise prospective adopters just starting out? Research: Speak to other adoptive families; talk to social workers; read; question motives honestly.

What is the most annoying thing adopting parents do to adoption organizations? Fail to inform the agency of changes in their circumstances until a proposal is made.

Are you an adoptive parent, adopted person, or birthparent? Adoptive parent.

Has your agency lost any adoption litigation filed against you by an adoptive parent or birthparent? No.

SASKATCHEWAN

CHRISTIAN COUNSELLING SERVICES—PREGNANCY COUNSELLING AND ADOPTIONS

Respondent: Glennis Wallace, Agency Program Supervisor
1125 Louise Ave., Saskatoon, SK S7H 2P8
(306) 244-9836 • Fax: (306) 244-9987
Year first licensed: 1997 and renewed every three years.

My agency provides services in: Children with special needs; infants; postplacement services; homestudy for parents with our agency; counselling to birthparents.

What areas do your adoptive parent clients come from? Saskatchewan.

Services provided to adopting parents: Classes with other prospective parents; required reading of books or articles on adoption; group discussions about adoption; homestudy; postplacement follow-up and support.

What countries do your birthparents/adopted children come from? Canada.

What was the goal of your organization when first organized? What is the goal of your organization now? To pioneer open adoption in Saskatchewan. Now: To provide services to birthparents facing an unplanned pregnancy. To provide services to couples dealing with infertility. To facilitate adoption placements.

How many nonrelative children did your organization place in 1998? 18

What percent of your adoptive placements are infants under 6 mos.? 95%

Do staff members have special expertise? Licensed social workers; therapists.

In 1998, what was the average time from when a prospective adoptive parent applied to when he or she received a homestudy? In the past 5 years, the average time from a couple applying to our waiting list to having a child in their home was 2 years.

What made you decide to work in the adoption field? Requests from the community.

How do you screen adoptive parents? We do an intake with each couple giving them information about adoption in general and our agency specifically. After obtaining this information, they make the decision with respect to applying to our waiting list or not.

What kind of medical information do you seek from birthparents? They complete lengthy forms asking for health and history information.

What kind of medical information do you seek on children over 1 year old? Obtain physician/medical reports. Have psychological assessments done if appropriate.

What percent of your Canadian-born children are nonwhite? 20%

About what percent are children with medical problems? 5%

Do you have a waiting list of prospective parents? Yes.

Is it all right if adopting parents are on the waiting lists of other agencies or attorneys? Yes, if agencies.

Do you have an application fee? If yes, what is the amount of the application fee? Yes; $250.

What is your homestudy fee? $1,200

What is your placement fee? $3,400. This fee covers many aspects and is payable over a period of time.

My agency: Offers confidential adoptions; semi-open adoptions, with first names exchanged; meetings between birthparents and adoptive parents; lets birthparents pick adoptive parents from biographies/resumes; full disclosure of names between birth and adoptive parents.

How would you advise prospective adopters just starting out? Apply to waiting list right away; be honest about the type of child you feel you could parent; meet other adoptive parents; join a support group.

What is the most annoying thing adopting parents do to adoption organizations? Say anything to get a child.

What is the most common mistake you see adopting parents make? Agreeing to things they are not ready for.

What statement do you wish you could make adoptive parents memorize? If you are desperate to have a child you are not ready to adopt.

Has your agency lost any adoption litigation filed against you by an adoptive parent or birthparent? No.

ADOPTIVE PARENT GROUPS IN CANADA

This is only a partial listing of the many adoptive parent support groups in Canada.

BRITISH COLUMBIA

Adoptive Parents Association of British Columbia
#205, 15463-104th Ave., Surrey, BC V3R 1N9
(604) 588-7300 • Fax: (604) 588-1388
E-mail: info@baadoption.com • www.bcadoption.com

Society of Special Needs Adoptive Parents
Suite 1150, 409 Granville St., United Kingdom Building, Vancouver, BC V6C 1T2
(604) 687-3144 or (800) 663-7627 • Fax: (604) 687-3364
E-mail: snap@snap.bc.ca

NEWFOUNDLAND

Nick and Doreen Westera
35 Creston Pl., St. John's, Newfoundland A1E 5W2
(709) 745-1201

ONTARIO

Adoption Council of Ontario
Adoption Resource Centre
3216 Yonge St., 2nd Floor, Toronto, ON M4N 2L2
(416) 482-0021 • Fax: (416) 482-1586
E-mail: aco@adoption.ca • www.interlog.com/~hwhs/aco/

OTTAWA

Open Door Society of Ottawa
Box 9141, Stn. T, Ottawa K1G 3T8
(613) 236-0432

QUÉBEC

La Federation des Parents Adoptants du Québec
42 Seminaire boul. South, St.-Jean-sur-Richelieu, Québec J3B 7M6
(514) 990-5307 • Fax: (450) 358-2000 (attn. F. Auger)
E-mail: fauger@oerlikon.ca • http://pages.infinit.net/bregi/adoption/index.html

SASKATCHEWAN

Saskatchewan Adoptive Parents Association, Inc.
Diana Dereski, Executive Director
203–510 Cynthia Street, Saskatoon, Saskatchewan S7L 7K7
(306) 665-7272 • Fax: (306) 665-7274
E-mail: adoptive.parents@sk.sympatico.ca • www3.sk.sympatico.ca/adoption

For more adoptive parent support groups, try the Family Helper at
www.helping.com/family/ad/adsup.html.

CHAPTER FIVE

ADOPTIVE PARENT SUPPORT GROUPS

When I was first interested in adopting a baby, rather a long time ago (my son is now 14) I hoped to talk to other people who had adopted or wanted to adopt. But there was no one to talk to in my area. So I found and joined the nearest group, over a hundred miles away, and they generously answered my many questions on their "Adoption Warmline" telephone. I also attended a few meetings and found this group to be comprised of wonderful and helpful people.

After my husband and I adopted our son, I decided that the area that I lived in still needed a support group. So I started one, in spite of not ever having done such a thing in my life. It just seemed like the right thing to do. Others have taken over the reins since the late 1980s.

I am telling you this because if you are interested in adopting a child, I urge you to find an adoptive parent support group so you can "network" with others who seek to adopt or with others who have already adopted. You may find many advantages from this contact, and by far the biggest one is that it may lead you to your child.

In the following essay, Alan Wasserman, the president of an excellent adoptive parent group in New York, captures the key points that you need to know about adoptive parent groups.

THE VALUE OF ADOPTIVE PARENT SUPPORT GROUPS: GUIDING YOU ON THE ADOPTION ROAD

Alan Wasserman

The Adoption Road offers many possible paths to those who make their first tentative steps upon it. And as you move along, each path that you encounter means yet another choice you must make. In fact, the very first decision is *if* you should adopt. Can you really love and parent a child who is not yours biologically? An adoptive parent group can help you with this decision—by listening to members, sharing your concerns and even by observing adoptive parents interact with their children.

If you decide to adopt a child—or at least, to explore adoption as an option—and you're thinking about the many choices to consider, ask yourself this question: Why go it alone? An adoptive parent support group can serve as your tour guide on the sometimes complicated Adoption Road. And they are not just bored young adults telling you about the nice painting here or the lovely view over there. Instead, they are actively involved people who have been-there, done-that, and they really want to share what they know.

Once you decide to take the adoption path—or you're pretty sure that you will, and you're gathering more information—there are many questions to consider, questions such as the age of the child you wish to adopt, the gender, the race, the nationality. There are also issues to consider, such as the time involved to adopt, the expenses, and the type of adoption you wish to pursue.

An adoptive parent support group can help you find the answers as you traverse the rough patches on your adoption path. Members can also help you figure out what questions you should be asking your attorney or social worker.

Adoptive Parent Support Groups and the Decision to Adopt

When you attend an adoptive parent support group meeting, you gain an opportunity to speak to other people who have already been down the path you are now traveling. For example, if your decision to adopt was made as a result of infertility, you'll find many people in the group who have been through the same infertility treatments, operations, and counseling that you have undergone.

In most adoptive parent support groups, some members have experienced the trials of infertility, and therefore, will be empathetic to your circumstances. In adoptions that stem from infertility, part of the decision to adopt involves putting aside the emotional baggage that has resulted from your experiences going through infertility.

Adoptive parent support groups can help you by debunking adoption myths and addressing your fears. By far the most valuable part of being a member of a parent support group is the networking that occurs. Many people in the group have had the same kind of doubts that new people entering the group are experiencing. Group members realize the importance of talking about those doubts and discussing how they put them aside and moved forward. Learning that your concerns are normal can help you to focus on the true issue of deciding whether you wish to become a parent.

Many adoptive parent support groups permit or encourage their children to attend meetings and social functions. Seeing the children of adoptive parents is often the most positive and direct form of feedback. They succeeded! You can succeed too. You can begin to imagine yourself feeding a baby or taking an older child to the carnival. The interaction between parents and their adopted children can be most comforting to those thinking of adopting. All of this factual and emotional information can then be used to help you determine if you wish to adopt.

What Adoptive Parent Support Groups Are Not. Adoption support groups are not adoption agencies. They don't locate or place children. In fact, in some states, such third-party intervention is illegal. Adoptive parent support groups are not providers of legal services. They don't provide homestudies or legal representation during the course of an adoption.

If a group claims to be a support organization and provides such services, it's probably an adoption agency that provides some adoption support as part of their services.

Most adoptive parent support groups are made up of volunteers. Those groups with a salaried staff usually pay for professionals to provide particular services such as advocacy, and grant writing. If a group is comprised of only paid staff and charges for a menu of services, then generally it isn't a parent support group, although it may provide support. Some adoptive parent support groups, however, provide services for which they charge, such as childcare workshops, CPR courses, or arranging for guest speakers on adoption-related topics. But such services are usually ancillary to the primary purpose of the organization.

Adoptive Parent Support Groups and the Adoption Process. Once you decide to adopt, the questions you had before can greatly multiply! An adoptive parent support group can provide an enormous amount of help in determining which method of adoption best suits your needs. In fact, you may find that you are your own worst enemy while making these decisions. Your fears and fantasies surrounding adoption and the adoption process and even parenting itself can spiral out of control at a time when you'd like to be at your most rational. Support group members can empathize and also set you straight on the realities of adopting.

Sometimes it's the little things that really help when you're trying to adopt a child. For example, here's one of my favorite pieces of advice, and it came from my adoptive parent group: If you're trying to adopt independently (an adoption where you seek out birthparents who wish to place their child with you) then place a picture of a smiling face near the telephone. It could be a yellow smiley face or a drawing or a photograph, but it should convey *big smile*. This depiction, placed where you can't *not* see it when you talk on the phone, will help remind you to smile when you answer the phone. Why? Because when there is a smile on your face, there is a smile in your voice.

Helping You Individualize the Adoption Decision

Another path on the Adoption Road to your child starts with a filtering process. You must decide which method of adoption suits your lifestyle, your visions of family, and your economic realities. At adoptive parent support group meetings, you'll meet people traveling the road to adoption alongside you. You might think they would be competitive, but instead most support group members are co-travelers who share information, support, and helpful hints they've picked up.

It's also likely that many people in the group have successfully adopted using the same method you are pursuing. You'll usually find people just ahead of you in the process and just behind you. You'll also meet people who have completed the adoption process and are willing to share their current experiences. You can directly address your concerns to them. If you have a problem, you can count on the fact that someone there has already encountered it and addressed it. You not only learn from other members' successes but also are able to avoid their mistakes.

Sometimes you'll find that *you* will be a provider of information, if you choose to be. At a time when you are feeling extremely dependent, an adoptive parent support group allows you to take on the role of a helper even when you feel the most helpless. This kind of ego support is very important during this period of time.

While agencies and adoption professionals may be very helpful in explaining the adoption process, they cannot provide you with the emotional support you need to help you survive the roller coaster ride of the adoption process. A good parent support group provides this level of emotional support.

Many groups offer access to adoption resources, which can aid in your filtering process. For example, a panel of adoption attorneys may be guest speakers at one meeting; a group of adoption agencies may offer adoption information about foster care; international placement or private placement adoptions may be available at another one. Social workers may explain what a homestudy is all about, or a group of birthparents or adult adoptees may discuss their experiences. All these presentations can aid in your decision-making process. Some groups offer preadoption workshops with a wide range of information on adoption options in one comprehensive format.

The Importance of Networking

After you select your primary adoption path, an adoptive parent support group can provide a wide range of experiences to help you choose which agency, attorney, social worker, facilitator, and so forth, will best fulfill your adoption plan. Again, networking is the key. Let's say you decide to pursue an independent adoption. It is usually wise to use an adoption attorney to aid in this process. But which attorney?

You can narrow the field down by reading books and you can check references. You can go to authorities such as the attorney general's office to see if there have been any complaints against a particular attorney. But how do you make that final decision? Asking a friend or neighbor who has adopted using that attorney is a start, but that is only one opinion. You really need more information. Why? Let's say you are considering using Mr. Smith, Esq. as your adoption attorney. You ask your friend who used Mr. Smith for her opinion.

Your friend was told the expenses associated with the adoption would be about $25,000 and she would adopt within one year. But your friend connected with the birthparents of her child very quickly. The birthmother was eight months pregnant and had medical insurance. The time that elapsed from the beginning of the process until placement of the child in your friend's home took five months and the expenses were $8,000, much lower that she anticipated. That lawyer was a saint!

Let's change the scenario. Your friend used the same reputable lawyer, Mr. Smith, but the circumstances were very different. Your friend did not make contact with the birthparents quickly, which resulted in more advertising expenses than she had anticipated. When a connection with the birthparents were made, the birthmother was six months pregnant and needed financial support (within the legal guidelines); the birthparents had no medical insurance and the birthmother needed a caesarean section during the birth. The adoptive parents were expected to pay the entire medical bill. The process leading up to the placement of the child into your friend's home took twenty months and expenses soared above expectations. That lawyer was the devil incarnate! But he was the same honorable man—it was the circumstances that were different.

For you to determine if Mr. Smith is the right choice, you really need a larger group of opinions. That is where networking can prove invaluable. In an adoptive parent support group you may find twenty people who used Mr. Smith as an attorney. You might also learn about Ms. Jones, Esq., another attorney, whom you had never heard of before. You now have additional options because you networked before you made your decision.

The interaction with other members of the adoptive parent support group will enable you to get much greater detail on the attorney you are thinking of using. You can find out how attentive each attorney is to clients; how effective and efficient his or her office staff is; how sensitive he or she is to the birth parents needs; and so forth. You can only get this level of detail by interviewing an attorney's clients. An adoptive parent support group meeting is a place where you can find many of an attorney's clients in one location, which enables you to interview them.

Meeting so many people from the adoption community in one place can help you choose adoption professionals with more confidence. The same scenario holds true for the selection of an agency, a social worker, a facilitator, and even a country of origin in an international adoption.

Because of the emotional imperative to move forward in building a family, people sometimes forget that they have rights in the adoption process. A support group helps to re-empower its members by reminding them that they are paying for a service from adoption professionals rather than for the privilege of being a parent.

Members are advised to use the same level of consumer consciousness they would use in procuring any other service. Prospective adoptive parents can be armed with a list of detailed questions that enable them to make decisions about which adoption professionals to hire and how to choose the method of adoption that best meets their needs.

Adoptive Parent Support Groups Role During the Adoption Process. Once your choice of adoption options is made and your path selected, an adoptive support group is still valuable. Nearly all groups recognize the need for emotional support during the adoption process. Up to now, the adoption process has been proactive. You made the decision to adopt, you selected the method of adoption that best suits you, you selected the agency, facilitator, or attorney that you needed for the process to go forward, and so on.

Now you wait. You must wait for a birthparent, agency, or facilitator to call you. You must wait for your paperwork to be processed. Maybe you're waiting for a videotape of a child you might wish to adopt from another country. Time slows way down during this period, and doubts and anxiety can replace the exhilaration you may have experienced moving through the process.

Many support groups have mechanisms to address these anxieties. Some assign you a "buddy" you can call to get situational questions answered. The buddy is also there for emotional support. Other groups offer a "warm line," which is basically telephone access to caring individuals who are there when a member needs them. Other groups offer "waiting workshops," where you meet periodically to exchange information with other members who are also waiting. It is here that you get the needed reinforcement that adoptions are in fact happening. Many groups will offer social activities where members can go to get their minds off of their individual situations. They can choose to network with other adoptive parents at these functions as well.

Another valuable aspect of being part of an adoptive parent support group during your adoption process is that many of the adoption resources available are aware of the networking powers of adoptive parent groups. With numbers comes power. Most support groups have a very strong feedback system so that if a member is treated unfairly, the group becomes aware of it. As adoptive parent support groups are usually one of the first places people go when entering the adoption process, your membership in an organization may help resolve minor misunderstandings, because the adoption resource does not want to get a bad reputation with the group.

Parenthood and Beyond: Adoptive Parent Support Groups Still Have a Role

Adoption doesn't end with the placement of a child in your home. Issues may arise through the years, and many groups provide post-adoption support. What kind of issues? Issues such as when and how to tell a child that he or she was adopted and how to cope with family, friends, and neighbors on adoption topics. They can often provide practical advice and suggestions.

Parenting topics in general are also discussed. Adoptive parent support groups also provide a positive reinforcement system for children who were adopted. Many groups provide social functions aimed at children so they can meet each other and realize that adoption is not an unusual event. Many children form bonds by meeting at these events, and this helps them forge a more positive image of themselves.

Types of Adoptive Parent Support Groups.   There are a variety of adoptive parent support groups. Some groups help members who want to adopt both babies, older children, children from other countries, and children from the United States. Other groups concentrate on specific niches, such as children adopted from China or Russia or children who were in foster care.

The very first adoptive parent support group formed in North America was the Adoptive Parents Committee, Inc. (APC) in New York. Thirteen people formed APC in 1955. They decided that the best way to get the support they needed was to rely on each other. APC is still flourishing today. I know—this is the group that has helped me for fifteen years, from my decision to adopt through the issues my now-teenaged son is raising.

Adoptive Parent Support Groups and Support for Children.   Many adoptive parent support groups have some form of a children's relief committee. These committees provide a wide range of support for children both locally and around the world. People may be asked to bring items to a meeting (such as toothbrushes) so that they can be sent to children who need them. Holiday presents are often collected and distributed to groups where children would otherwise get nothing for the holidays. Many groups pay a fee to larger groups, such as Save the Children, so that the needs of a child can be met.

While support for underprivileged children is not the primary function of most adoptive groups, many take some action along these lines as a statement of their commitment to improving the lives of children. For people waiting to bring a child into their home, these little efforts reinforce the precious nature of children and provide an outlet for people to feel they can help children in general while waiting for a specific child(ren) to become part of their family.

Support on the decision to adopt, support during the process of selecting a method of adoption, support during the adoption process, support with parenting issues, support on adoption advocacy and support for underprivileged children are just some of the benefits of adoptive parent support groups.

You may find that your adoptive parent group helps set you on the Adoption Road and guides you through the sometimes-circuitous course that eventually leads you to your child! When you think about it, with everything they have to offer, why wouldn't someone considering adoption want to become involved with these very worthy organizations?

Alan Wasserman is the vice president of the Adoptive Parents Committee Board of Governors and president of the New York City Chapter of the Adoptive Parents Committee. The Adoptive Parents Committee is a popular and effective adoptive parents group, with chapters in New York and New Jersey. (See the list of parent groups.) Alan has also co-authored an article on adoption in both the 1998 and the 1999 editions of Microsoft Encarta Encyclopedia. He and his wife are the parents of a son.

Editor's Note: To find a support group, check the list that follows. Contact several groups and attend at least one meeting, preferably two. If there's no group near you, call the closest group—even if it's in another state. Often groups know about other groups and can tell you about a new group that's just forming in your area. You may also find that a support group member in another area can become your telephone or e-mail friend, providing you with practical advice and emotional hand-holding as you move closer to your child.

ADOPTIVE PARENT SUPPORT GROUPS IN THE UNITED STATES*

Support groups are primarily run by volunteers who have full-time jobs doing something else. These people take time from their busy lives to network and assist others.

Some support groups list their phone numbers, while others prefer not to. The same is true of e-mail addresses. However you contact them, expect a caring and enthusiastic person to respond but remember that they also have lives, so try to keep your questions reasonably brief.

The following is a listing of adoptive parent groups nationwide. Other groups have formed and are forming all the time; it is impossible to list them all. Please also keep in mind that adoptive parent support group leaders change periodically. It is possible that errors of omission or commission may have occurred, although I tried to be as careful as possible.

---

* Canadian adoptive parent support groups are listed in Chapter 4.

ALABAMA

Alabama Friends of Adoption
P.O. Box 1453, Huntsville, AL 35807

Families with Children from China
25 Welton Dr., Madison, AL 35757
Parents of International Children
9710 Dortmond Dr., Huntsville, AL 35803

ALASKA

Anchorage Adoptive Parents Association
550 W. Seventh Ave., Suite 1320, Anchorage, AK 99501

Valley Adoptive Parents Association
P.O. Box 931, Palmer, AK 99645

CALIFORNIA

Families with Children from China
Wendy Williams
2529 K St., Eureka, CA 95501
wjwsimon@aol.com

Families with Children from China
P.O. Box 251785, Los Angeles, CA 90025
(310) 4789-1608

San Francisco Bay Area Families with Children from China
1036 Tennessee St., San Francisco, CA 94107-3016
www.fwcc.org

CONNECTICUT

Connecticut Friends of Adopted Children
P.O. Box 3246, Waterbury, CT 06705

Families with Children from China
P.O. Box 101, Thompson, CT 06277

FLORIDA

Families with Children from China
13611 SW 110 Terr., Miami, FL 33186
DeeJ5656@aol.com

Parents Adoption Lifeline, Inc.
11228 Monet Ridge Rd., Palm Beach Gardens, FL 33410
(561) 844-8282

People Adopting Children Everywhere (PACE)
318 W. Osceola Ln., Cocoa Beach, FL 32931
(407) 799-1928

Tallahassee Families with Asian Children
3940 Leane Dr., Tallahassee, FL 32308
foleyvideo@aol.com

GEORGIA

Reaching Out Step by Step (ROSS)
P.O. Box 278, Pavo, GA 31778

ILLINOIS

Adoptive Families Today
P.O. Box 1726, Barrington, IL 60011-1726
(847) 382-0859
www.adoptivefamiliestoday.org

Stars of David International, Inc.
3175 Commercial Ave., Suite 100, Northbrook, IL 60062-1915
(800) STAR-349 or (847) 509-9929 • Fax: (847) 509-9545
StarsDavid@aol.com • www.starsofdavid.org

INDIANA

FRUA
10236 Bent Tree Ln., Fishers, IN 46038
(317) 598-9566
rick@nerdsoncall.com

OURS Through Adoption
RR 3, 104 Water St., Monroeville, IN 46773-9301

IOWA

Families with Children from China
656 W. 5th St., Dubuque, IA 52001-6613
(319) 556-1085
Csmart@univ.dbq.edu

KANSAS

Families with Children from China
Kim Burghart
(785) 862-KIDS
sburghart@cjnetworks.com • www.cjnetworks.com/~sburghart/

KENTUCKY

Families with Children from China
3533 Colneck Ln., Lexington, KY 40502
KFrederich@aol.com

PACK, Inc.
139 Highland Dr., Madisonville, KY 42431-9154

LOUISIANA

Louisiana Eastern European Adoptive Families
1420 Rue Bayonne, Mandeville, LA 70471
(504) 727-1074

MAINE

Adoptive Families of Maine
129 Sunderland Dr., Auburn, ME 04210

Central Maine Area Adoption Group
7 Noyer St., Waterville, ME 04901

Maine Families with Children from Asia
280 Blanchard Rd., Cumberland, ME 04021

MASSACHUSETTS

Families with Children from China
31 Central St., Acton, MA 01720

Open Door Society of Mass., Inc.
1750 Washington St., Holliston, MA 01746-2234

MICHIGAN

All Doing Our Part Together (ADOPT)
6939 Shields Ct., Saginaw, MI 48609
(517) 781-2089

Families with Children from China
3790 Pioneer Rd., Osseo, MI 49266

Michigan Association of Single Adoptive Parents (MASAP)
946 Forest, Westland, MI 48186
(734) 729-6989

MINNESOTA

Families with Children from China
P.O. Box 11867, St. Paul, MN 55111

FRUA-Minnesota
c/o Nina Wallestad
2475 Bridle Creek Trail, Chanhassen, MN 55317

MONTANA

Families with Children from China
3753 Gymnast Way, Billings, MT 59102

Gathering International Families Together (GIFT)
1001 Harrison Ave., Helena, MT 59601
jefferson21@juno.com

NEW HAMPSHIRE

Families with Children from China
5 Burnett St., Nashua, NH 03060-4931

Manchester Concern for Adoption
11 Davis Rd., Merrimack, NH 03054

Open Door Society of New Hampshire
P.O. Box 792, Derry, NH 03038
(603) 679-1099
odsnh@aol.com • http://members.aol.com/odsnh

New Jersey

Adoptive Parents Committee, New Jersey Chapter
P.O. Box 725, Ridgewood, NJ 07451
(210) 689-0995

Concerned Persons for Adoption
P.O. Box 179, Whippany, NJ 07981

New Jersey Chapter, Families for Russian and Ukrainian Adoption (NJFRUA)
904 Cain St., Belle Meade, NJ 08502
(908) 431-0318

New Jersey Friends Through Adoption
30 Endicott Dr., Great Meadows, NJ 07838

Rainbow Families
670 Oakley Pl., Oradell, NJ 07649
(201) 261-1148
PaulBek670@aol.com

New York

Adoptive Families Coalition
P.O. Box 603, Glenmont, NY 12077
(518) 448-5295
www.timesunion.com/communities/afc.htm

Adoptive Parents Committee
P.O. Box 3525, Church St. Station, New York, NY 10008-3525
(212) 304-8749
www.adoptiveparents.org

Adoptive Parents Committee, Hudson Region Chapter
P.O. Box 625, Hartsdale, NY 10530
(914) 997-7859

Adoptive Parents Committee, Long Island Chapter
P.O. Box 71, Bellmore, NY 11710
(516) 432-5753

Adoptive Families of Older children
149-32A Union Turnpike, Flushing, NY 11367

Families with Children from China—Rochester
P.O. Box 125, Fairport, NY 14450
makmd@Rochester.rr.com

Families with Children from China of Central New York
P.O. Box 5558, Syracuse, NY 13220
(315) 472-2111, ext. 3006

Friends of Children Everywhere
23 Snowbird Ln., Levittown, NY 11756
(516) 796-5927

New York Singles Adopting Children (NYSAC)
P.O. Box 472, Glen Oaks, NY 11004
(212) 259-9402
nysac@aol.com

Single Mothers by Choice
P.O. Box 1642, Grace Square Station, New York, NY 10028
(212) 988-0993

NORTH CAROLINA

Families with Children from China
6728 Tara Dr., Charlotte, NC 28211

OHIO

Greater Cleveland Families with Children from China
Edd Schultz
5900 SOM Center Rd., #104, Willoughby, OH 44094
(440) 942-9048
rthreadmag@aol.com

OREGON

Adoptive Families Unlimited
P.O. Box 40752, Eugene, OR 97404
(541) 688-1654

PENNSYLVANIA

Families with Children from China
2310 Spring Ln., Allentown, PA 18103-7721
(610) 791-2559
bobs@enter.net

Families with Children from China
515 Keystone Ave., Peckville, PA 18452

Families with Children from Asia
311 North Second St., Harrisburg, PA 17110

SOUTH CAROLINA
Families with Children from China
P.O. Box 801, North, SC 29112
chinamom@usit.net

TENNESSEE
Mid-South Families with Children from China
440 Burley Rd., Colliersville, TN 38017
(901) 853-7223
darrobertson@juno.com

Mountain Region Adoption Support Group
305 Ferndale Ln., Kingsport, TN 37660

VERMONT
The Chosen Children from Romania
P.O. Box 401, Barre, VT 05641-0401

Vermont Families Through Adoption
16 Aspen Dr., Essex Junction, VT 05452

VIRGINIA
Families with Children from China, Capital Area
9407 Fairpine Ln., Great Falls, VA 22066
klmpa@aol.com

Families Through Adoption
935 South George Washington Hwy., Chesapeake, VA 23323

Families for Russian and Ukrainian Adoption (FRUA)
P.O. Box 2944, Merrifield, VA 22116
(703) 560-6184
www.frua.org

Korean Focus for Adoptive Families
1906 Sword Ln., Alexandria, VA 22308
(703) 799-0591
www.helping.com/family/pa/kfaf.htm

WEST VIRGINIA

From China with Love
455 Vine St., St. Albans, WV 25177-3289
tjspencer@worldnet.att.net

WISCONSIN

Adoptive Families of Greater Milwaukee
15385 Glenora Ct., New Berlin, WI 53151

Families with Children from China
850 N. 119th St., Wauwatosa, WI 53226
414-453-4480
downing@csd.uwm.edu

Special Needs Adoption Support Group (SNAP)
5209 Aiport Rd., Stevens Point, WI 54481
nhavl991@uwsp.edu

CHAPTER SIX

ADOPTING A BABY IN THE UNITED STATES

Your yearning for a baby can be so intense that it's like an obsession. Many women who are caught up in the throes of baby longing say that everywhere they go, they see women who are pregnant or pushing baby strollers. Once you decide to adopt, however, you can transform and channel that obsession into the actions needed to succeed at adopting your baby. And after you adopt your infant, you'll join the ranks of women (at least 25,000 per year) who no longer see those expectant or new moms everywhere they turn—unless it's to share a happy smile or a helpful hint.

Of course, men want to adopt babies too, and I don't want to be sexist here. It's just that men don't seem to have the punched-in-the-stomach kind of distressed feeling that women who want a baby can sometimes feel when they are caught up in baby longing. Or, if men have it, they don't talk about it!

In this chapter, I'll offer helpful hints to lead you to adopt your domestic baby, including some basic and time-tested tactics. Following my advice is an excellent essay on open adoption by Maxine Chalker, executive director of Adoptions From the Heart.

After you read this chapter, if you haven't read Chapter 1 carefully, I urge you to go back and read it again. It offers important advice and information on birthmothers changing or not changing their minds about adoption, adoption fees, and other issues you need to understand to maximize your adoption effort. If you're from Canada, be sure to read Chapter 4, which offers important and comprehensive advice from author Jennifer Smart.

THE ADOPTION OPTION TEN-POINT PLAN TO ADOPT YOUR BABY IN THE UNITED STATES

Different people have different strategies to adopt (or, horrors, no strategy at all), and in this essay, I'll give you mine. First, I'll list my ten major points and then I'll explain each one to you.

1. Tell everyone you know that you want to adopt a baby.
2. Learn about and contact adoption agencies in and outside your area.

549

3. Learn about and contact adoption attorneys in and outside your area.
4. Join an adoptive parent group.
5. Figure out adoption costs and how to pay them.
6. Talk to people who have adopted.
7. Research adoption.
8. Maintain a positive mental attitude.
9. Discuss adoption with your spouse or significant other.
10. Choose an agency or attorney.

1. Tell Everyone You Know that You Want to Adopt A Baby

If you want to keep your desire to adopt a baby a deep dark secret, are you sure that you really want to adopt? It's the people who really get the word out to the world at large who are the most successful. Sure, there's a down side to doing this. Some people will tell you it's a dumb idea to adopt or that you can never succeed or other negative things. So what? There are nay-sayers to just about any positive act you can think of. I see adoption as a very positive act indeed. You should too.

So go ahead, tell your family, your friends, your coworkers, your minister or rabbi, your doctor, and the supermarket cashier (I am not kidding) that you want to adopt a baby. The more people who know that someone really nice (you!) is avidly interested in adopting, the higher the probability that someone you know will know someone else who may lead you to a birthmother and to your child.

Of course, while you are telling everyone that you want to adopt, you should also work on finding an adoption agency or attorney—a pivotal step. If you link to a pregnant woman through your networking contacts, you'll need professional help in a hurry. Which leads me to my second major point.

2. Learn About and Contact Adoption Agencies In and Outside Your Area

One way to learn about adoption agencies is to read this book. Find the agencies (Chapter 2) in your state and neighboring states. Read about agencies that place children nation-wide—there are many. Do they sound appealing? Ask for information. If they have a Web site, go there. Call and ask for brochures.

Ask for the names of others who have adopted through their agency. Contact the Better Business Bureau in your area to make sure no one has filed a complaint against the agency. Verify that the agency is licensed through the state. (See phone numbers for state licensing organizations in the Appendix.)

3. Learn About and Contact Adoption Attorneys In and Outside Your Area

Even if you're sure you don't want to adopt independently, investigate nonagency adoption anyway. Read Attorney Sam Totaro's essay on attorneys in Chapter 3. Then read the entries for attorneys in your state and neighboring states.

Despite what you may have heard, independent adoption is not "black market" or even "gray market." An adoption is either legal or not legal. Baby buying is illegal. Consulting an honorable attorney is one good way to adopt your baby. Maybe it will work for you. Or maybe an adoption agency would be better. You won't know unless you compare and contrast the available options.

4. Join an Adoptive Parent Group

In his essay on the value of adoptive parent groups in Chapter 5, Alan Wasserman explains how and why an adoptive parent group can help a prospective adopter. I agree with everything he says and, in fact, I think that an adoptive parent group is very often an integral part of success. You could succeed without joining one. But why would you want to make it hard on yourself and perhaps extend the time you wait?

5. Figure Out Adoption Costs and How to Pay Them

When most people want to make a major life change, they figure out how much it will cost and how to pay for it. Adoption is no different. Sure, it would be great if adoption were free, but in most cases, it costs money. Whether an adoption agency helps you or you adopt privately, there are almost always fees to be paid: the homestudy, application fees, placement fees, and so forth. The various fees (and averages) are covered in Chapter 1.

Once you know approximately how much the adoption will cost, you can decide whether you should finance the adoption with savings, assistance from your extended family, a loan from your credit union, a grant from your company, or other means. Some people set aside money every week.

6. Talk to People Who Have Adopted

In addition to the people in your adoptive parent group, talk to others who have adopted. Don't worry, you can find them. If you've followed my first step by telling everyone you know that you want to adopt, then some of those people will tell you that they've adopted a child or lead you to other contacts.

Some of them may tell you that what you really need to do is adopt a baby from China or the foster care system and maybe that isn't what you want to do. It's still good to talk to adoptive parents no matter how they adopted. Why? Because their success can reinforce the idea that you can and will succeed. You may also learn something valuable from these contacts—a fact that later becomes useful.

7. Research Adoption

Read about adoption. There are books that help as well as a plethora of information from adoption agencies and organizations. I have written several books myself, such as *The Complete Idiot's Guide to Adoption* (Macmillan, 1998) and *Is Adoption For You?* (John Wiley & Sons, 1998). Agencies and attorneys can often recommend other information sources.

Check out information on the Internet. There are far too many Web sites on adoption topics to list them all here. Many agencies and attorneys have Web sites. Check individual listings.

I have two major warnings about on-line services, although I think you can gain an enormous amount of information from the 'Net. First, don't believe something just because you saw it on the Internet. It may be inaccurate. Also, who said it and why is not always easy to figure out, so take it with that proverbial grain of salt.

The other warning is that people have a tendency on-line to accentuate the negative. Sure, there are problems and adoption is no perfect solution to child welfare problems. But for the most part, adoption is a very positive way to form families. Don't try to convince disgruntled adult adoptees or birthparents about this point because you never will. And sometimes these are the people who proliferate on Web sites or chat rooms. Don't get caught up in their issues. Which leads me to the next major point.

8. Maintain a Positive Mental Attitude

Everyone gets discouraged sometimes. If you feel a little down during your quest to reach your child, don't worry, it's normal. But don't let the black cloud hang over your head too long because it could impair your efforts toward success.

Do something fun. Go to the movies, read a hilarious book, go to the beach—do whatever makes you really happy. And tell yourself, "I will adopt my baby." Look at yourself in the mirror and say hello to the soon-to-be adoptive parent. Sound silly? Do it anyway! When you create and maintain a positive attitude, your brain helps you work on the actions that will help you adopt.

I also think it's a good idea to try to do something toward adopting every day or at least every other day. It doesn't have to be something hard. Read a flyer that someone sent you. Make a phone call. Tell someone you want to adopt a baby. Write an entry in your diary about how you feel. Or take another action that is somehow, even if only remotely, associated with adopting.

9. Discuss Adoption with Your Spouse or Significant Other

If you're married or in a long-term relationship, talk to that person about the kind of child you hope to adopt. Maybe your spouse has an idea different from yours; for example, you might be interested in adopting a biracial baby but figure, he or she would never go for that idea. Yet your spouse could be thinking the same thing! So talk about it. Verbalizing your plans can help you sort out your ideas.

10. Choose an Agency or Attorney

After careful research and discussion, make your choice. If you decide to work with a particular agency, in some cases, that agency will expect you to make a commitment to them and not be on anyone else's waiting list. (Check the agency listings in Chapters 2 and 4—this is one question I asked.) If you decide to work with an attorney, you may wish to contact other attorneys as well; often they don't mind if you are on the list of more than one attorney.

Conclusion

Is my Adoption Option ten-point plan foolproof? Why don't you tell me? I think it will work for most people and hope it will work for you. Tell me if I missed something or if you think one of the steps should be modified or replaced. I'd like to hear from you. My e-mail address is Adamec@aol.com.

Next, read Maxine Chalker's essay on open adoption. Many agencies in the United States strongly advocate open adoption and Ms. Chalker is an ardent supporter, too. After reading her essay, you may be too! Keep in mind that if you want to maintain some element of confidentiality—for example, you want to meet the birthmother but on a first-name basis only—many adoption agencies support this idea. There are also agencies that support complete confidentiality, particularly if favored by the birthmother. You may also find that a completely open adoption is a wonderful way to adopt your baby.

OPEN ADOPTION

Maxine G. Chalker, MSW/LSW, Founder and Executive Director of Adoptions From The Heart

Open adoption equals open communication between birthparents and adoptive parents. This communication can come in many forms in a semi-open adoption. Semi-open adoption usually involves personal meetings and the exchange of first names only, with the option of keeping in touch through an agency or attorney as the child grows up. With a truly open adoption, the two sets of parents have face-to-face meetings and exchange all identifying information, such as full names, phone numbers, and addresses.

Contrary to the popular fear, open adoption is *not* co-parenting. The adoptive parents have all legal rights and parental responsibilities, and they make all the parenting decisions. They don't need permission or agreement from the birthparents.

Adoption-placing organizations began practicing open adoption in the late 1970s and early 1980s, and open adoption gained increasing acceptance in the 1990s. Several reasons contributed to this increased positive feeling toward open adoption. One key reason was that pregnant women found that they were now in a position to choose the type of parents they wanted for their children. They also learned that there were many families eager to adopt and thus many families to choose from. On the adoptive parent side, with fewer infants available, families seeking to adopt found it necessary to consider open adoption and to learn more about it.

In addition, the adoptee and birthparent search movement brought their feelings and demands to the forefront of the media and the public. It became known that many adoptees and birthparents sought more information about each other. At the same time, the social work community began to feel that the traditional closed system was not benefiting the adoptive parents, birthparents, and, especially, the children who grew up with so many unanswered questions.

How Does Open Adoption Work with an Adoption Agency?

Adoptions facilitated by an adoption agency have many advantages. The social workers are specifically trained in the field of adoption and act as facilitators between the adoptive parents and birthparents to help them arrange a mutually agreeable relationship. Adoptive parents are able to meet one or more birthparents during their educational course and see for themselves that birthparents are just normal people they might meet in the grocery or drugstore. They are almost never drug addicts or prostitutes.

In an open adoption, birthparents pick the family that they want to raise their baby or child, based on written information on the adoptive parents, adoption resumes, videos, and personal meetings. A social worker usually prepares the birthparents for the personal meeting and sits in on the meeting, facilitating the conversation, which can be awkward at first.

Adoptive families are often encouraged to bring in pictures of their families so that they can be used as an icebreaker. After that first meeting, the birthparents and adopting parents may want future meetings before the birth. They may either have a social worker attend these meetings or they may decide to go it alone.

Open Adoption Can Be Very Emotional

Although I strongly favor open adoption, I also know that it isn't always easy. Emotions often run very high because unplanned parenthood and transferring the responsibility of a child to another family is a very wrenching decision. It's hard for the adoptive parents too, because they are scared and many of their uninformed friends are telling them they're crazy to do this. As a result, there are many tears shed by birthparents and adopting parents. But what the adults involved have to remember is that adoption is for the child. Sometimes they have to overcome their personal feelings and consider the "best interest of the child."

Birthparents Are Less Likely to Change Their Minds

Because open adoption gives birthparents the ability to design their own adoption plan, I have found that it gives them more power and control and they are, therefore, less likely to change their mind after the adoption placement. For them to do so would be admitting that they made an error and went against what *they* decided, rather than what was imposed on them.

Other Benefits of Open Adoption

Traditional closed adoption did not allow birthparents to know who the adoptive parents were and vice versa. This implied that these two sets of parents could not have a cooperative relationship and were even enemies, both seeking the love of the child. Traditional adoptions also instilled fear of the birthparents in the adoptive parents. The birthparents were never given the names, addresses, or phone numbers of the adoptive parents for fear that the birthparents would interfere in the child's life.

In every other field of social work, families are encouraged to take control of their lives, but it has not been so with families involved with adoption. The agency and its social workers or the attorneys doing private adoption made sure that the "right" decision was made and that the "right" home was found. They did not credit the parties involved with being able to make the best decision for themselves and their child.

Being There When Your Baby Is Born

Most birthparents will now allow, and even encourage, the adoptive parents to be in the delivery room, or at least in the hospital, for the birth of the baby. The adoptive family is usually chosen before the baby is born. This allows them time to shop and to buy baby supplies and become extremely excited about the anticipated birth. They also get to feel the emotional highs and lows of the childbirth experience.

Another issue is that birthparents are as fearful of rejection as adoptive parents are—and this never ceases to amaze me. Birthparents always ask "What if they don't like me?" They are in a very vulnerable position and need to be given the opportunity to be an important part of the process.

Open Adoption of Older Chilren

With older child adoptions, open adoption is often even more essential. Older children have had previous relationships and memories with birthparents, extended family members, foster parents, and others. It's important for adoptive parents to acknowledge that an older adopted child had a life before he or she entered the family. If they do not, this attitude invalidates the child's past experience, almost as if the adoptive parents expect the child to have a pre-adoption amnesia. If they try to ignore the child or change the subject when he or she talks about the past, it can be very distressing for the child.

When this happens, the child gets the message that part of his or her life was not important and not worth remembering, and that he or she may not have been any good before adoption. Even though the child's past life may have been troubled by abuse and neglect, it still happened and there were usually some positive experiences in the past as well.

Changing a child's first name, we now know, gives the same message. When possible, allowing some old relationships to continue enables children to feel whole and worthwhile.

My Experience with Adoption

As an adoptee myself and an adoption professional, I have experience with both traditional adoption at a public child welfare agency and with totally open and semi-open adoption at the agency that I founded in 1985. In the old system, I enjoyed the power and control of creating families and deciding which family received which child. The birth and foster parents were seen as being unimportant, even though the children were not newborn babies. However, after seeing many returning birthparents and adult adoptees, and after attending search group meetings of frustrated and anxious participants, I believed that adoption practice needed to change.

When beginning the practice of open adoption, I found that birthparents were able to do an excellent job of selecting parents, and better still, both birthparents and adoptive parents were more satisfied with the process. Adoptive parents did not have to wonder who their child's birthparents were—they already knew. They did not have to worry about conveying correct information about the birthparents to their child, because of information passed on by a third party that might be inaccurate or incomplete. They could have pictures, stay in touch with, and even see the birthparents and allow their children to know the truth about their roots and adoption story.

As for the birthparents, they no longer worried about the well-being of their child—they knew. Adopted children no longer wondered about their birthparents and the circumstances surrounding their adoption—they knew. What better way could there be than that?

What If There Are Misunderstandings?

If there is a misunderstanding between the birthparents and adoptive parents about the terms of their agreement in a semi-open adoption, a social worker can step in and facilitate a compromise. If the misunderstanding occurs after placement, the parties can still choose to come back to the agency for help, but one of the parties might refuse to cooperate at that point.

Interestingly enough, there seem to be more and more cases where adoptive parents contact the agency to open up their adoption rather then the reverse. They see others having a relationship with birthparents, and they see the value and want the agency to try to assist them in this effort.

An infrequent problem occurs when birthparents or adoptive parents want more or less contact after finalization. There is a different reaction between the two parties. For example, adoptive parents often do not get updates from birthparents and they are disappointed, but not devastated.

When adoptive parents neglect to send a yearly update or say that they will no longer do this, the birthparents become very angry and upset, and justifiably so. They were promised a certain amount and type of communication by the adoptive parents, and they feel that they were lied to and that the adoptive parents misrepresented their commitment to open adoption. They are usually right.

Adoptive parents should be careful what they agree to. At Adoptions From the Heart, we attempt to screen out prospective parents who say they are open to contact when they, in fact, just want a baby and would say yes to anything, not really planning to honor their agreement. That is also why we give them an educational course about open adoption and the value of it.

If an adoption is semi-open, we have both parties sign a written contract of how much and what type of contact there will be. However, the contract is not enforceable in Pennsylvania, New Jersey, and many other states. Delaware does allow for an open adoption agreement to be attached to the final adoption decree and thereby it becomes enforceable. It is possible to get the parties to agree that if there is a breach in the contract that their identifying information will be released to the other party—usually the names of the adoptive parents to the birthparents.

If the adoption is totally open, the parties can usually come to an agreement about any misunderstandings that may crop up. Very occasionally, they may wish to ask the agency social worker to advise them.

Conclusion

Open adoption successes have proven that adoptive parents and birthparents can most certainly work together to make the best plan for their child. The adoptive parents are gratified to know they are the "chosen ones." They feel satisfaction that the birthparents chose *them* and that they were given permission to be the parents of this child. They can also enjoy the shared expectation of childbirth. The birthparents feel their child will be safe and loved. And the child will be able to communicate with his or her birthparents, often as he or she grows up and becomes an adult. I see open adoption as a win-win-win form of adoption.

Maxine Chalker, MSW/LSW, is an adult adoptee who founded Adoptions From the Heart in 1985. (Maxine herself has done an adoption search and found her birthfamily living in a nearby area in Pennsylvania.)

The agency was originally started to promote open adoptions in the Delaware Valley. It was the first agency in the area to have birthparents select and meet adoptive parents before they gave birth, so they could have options and control of the adoption process.

Adoptions From the Heart has prospered because of the open adoption concept and is now located in five states. This private nonprofit agency has offices in Wynnewood, Lancaster, Allentown, and Pittsburgh, Pennsylvania, and in Wilmington, Delaware, Cherry Hill, New Jersey, and Morgantown, West Virginia. They are licensed in New York and have contract social workers there. Their services also include international adoption from a variety of countries. In 1998, Adoptions From the Heart placed 229 infants.

CHAPTER SEVEN

ADOPTING CHILDREN FROM OTHER COUNTRIES

If you are thinking about adopting a baby, toddler, or older child from outside the United States (or Canada, if you are Canadian), that sounds like a very exciting idea! I recommend you follow the following game plan and read Jean Erichsen's excellent advice on what to do just before and just after adopting a child from another country.

Explore Your Motives

Ask yourself why you wish to adopt a child from another country. Is it that you are drawn to children from a particular country? Or do you feel repelled by the idea of adopting a child from the United States because you fear a birthparent challenge? If so, please read about mothers changing their minds in Chapter 1. Then, if you still wish to adopt internationally, proceed!

Also keep in mind that some international adoptions have the potential of becoming open eventually because often identifying information is provided, such as in countries that formerly comprised the Soviet Union.

Are you thinking about adopting from another country primarily from a humanitarian or saviour-type motive? Or guilt over past U.S. actions, such as the Vietnam War? Children take an enormous amount of time and care, and if you want to save the world and that is your primary or sole motive for adopting, often it would be far better to donate money to a charitable cause. Adopt because you want to become a parent.

Do you want to adopt a child from another country because you've already adopted one child from that country and you want to give your child a sibling? I have talked to people whose sole motive was to give their current child a sister or brother. (By the way, this is a bad motive even if your child was adopted from your own country.) Children don't make good gifts and the child you already have will often be ungrateful, as will the child you adopt. Adopt because *you* want another child. It's okay if providing a sibling is a secondary reason, but it should not be your main reason. I know of an adoption that failed because the "old" sibling told Mommy to send the new kid away—and she did. This is truly heartbreaking.

Are you adopting an older child from another country because you don't want to adopt a foster child from the United States who was abused or neglected and might have emotional or medical problems? Please think again. Many people think that children who are four or five years old or older, and who grew up in an orphanage abroad, are inevitably in much better emotional and medical health than foster children in the United States. The fact is that most orphanages are bad places for children; children can be abused and neglected in orphanages. They often receive poor medical care while there. In addition, many children who live in orphanages first lived in a family where they received abusive and neglectful treatment similar to or worse than what is suffered by foster children in the United States.

I strongly support intercountry adoption, but I also know prepared parents are the best parents. Some ingenuous families think two children, aged five and seven, that they adopt from a foreign orphanage will be just like their neighbor's children, also aged five and seven but who have known only one family in one country. This is a dangerous and wrong assumption. The adopted children need time to adjust to a new country, new language, and new culture. They may be very fearful of leaving the only home they've ever known, even though it was an orphanage.

Is race an issue? Are you adopting a child from a particular Eastern European country because you want a Caucasian child? Many children, even from Russia, have dark skin and may be of mixed race. If skin color is important to you, you might wish to adopt a domestic-born child through an agency or an attorney.

Unprepared parents with mixed-up motives for adopting don't inevitably fail with their adoptions. But why risk it? Explore your motives and make sure that you want to adopt a child. If you're ambivalent and confused, read my book, *Is Adoption For You? The Information You Need to Make the Right Choice* (John Wiley & Sons, 1998).

Be sure to read Jean Erichsen's important essay on life after adopting. (It follows this essay.) Also read Dr. Jenista's helpful essay on the initial medical evaluation of an adopted child, in Chapter 9.

Contact the Nearest Adoptive Parent Group

Adoptive parents in parent groups love to talk about their children. They think adoption is a wonderful option. It can be exhilarating to talk with them! They are also a wealth of information, and can help explode any mistaken ideas you may have. They'll tell you about the pros and cons of adopting a child from another country and this information can really help you. You'll also gain the opportunity to see children from other countries, because adoptive parents often bring their children to all or some meetings.

Also, adoptive parents will be more honest about agencies, costs, consultants, and so forth because they usually have no vested interest. Many national and some local adoptive parent groups have Web sites. Be sure to read Alan Wasserman's valuable essay on adoptive parent groups in Chapter 5.

Find a Reputable Agency

There are many adoption agencies that handle intercountry adoptions and new ones seem to spring up constantly. Deal with an agency that has a track record and can point you to happy adoptive parents they have placed with children. Such agencies are more likely to be around later in case you have questions or problems. Check with the state licensing bureau to make sure the agency is still licensed and in good standing. (Phone numbers for the state licensing bureaus are available in the Appendix.)

If you have family members or trusted friends in another country, you may have contacts within that country that can help you adopt. If not, deal with agencies, attorneys, or facilitators in your own country whom you have checked out thoroughly. If a foreign lawyer charges you thousands of dollars and you find you have been cheated, what can you do? Usually nothing. But if you have a problem in the United States, there are many actions you can take and many organizations you can complain to.

Most adoption agencies are staffed by wonderful and caring people, but it's best to be vigilant. When you were single (or maybe you still are), would you marry a stranger who walked up to you and proposed? Hopefully not. What if a stranger offered you a fabulous investment if you'd only give him $25,000? You'd probably decline that offer, too. You aren't marrying the adoption agency director or buying stock in the agency, but if you engage their services, they are doing something very important for you and you want the best. (The best, by the way, isn't always the priciest agency.)

Learn About the Country Your Child Comes From

Most people planning a vacation abroad will try to learn a few words and phrases, like "yes," "no," and "where is the bathroom?" But I am constantly amazed by parents who travel to another country to adopt a child and have learned no words in that country's language. Even if the child you adopt is six or seven months old, words that are alien to you are not foreign to them.

You can ease the way considerably, particularly on the long plane ride home, if you know some basics. You don't have to become fluent in Russian, Chinese, Spanish, or any other language. In fact, you probably should not make that effort because often children rapidly pick up their new language. But learn some basics. Knowing some foreign words and phrases will also help you communicate with citizens of the other country during your stay there.

It's also a good idea to read current books and articles about the country to gain a feel for what it's like. Other adoptive parents probably have photos of their trips they will be thrilled to show you.

Remember, you may never have another chance to visit this country again, so make the most of it. Plan ahead and your stay there will be far more enjoyable.

Be Prepared Before You Travel

Of course you should also plan ahead before you depart. Are your shots up to date? Maybe you haven't had a tetanus shot since you were 18 and you're now 40. Get one! Find out what immunizations you and anyone who comes with you should receive. This information is available through adoptive parent groups and also should be available from your adoption agency.

Find out what items your child will need. Some adopting parents travel all the way to Russia and don't bring disposable diapers or any supplies whatsoever. Don't depend on the kindness of strangers when in a foreign country. Bring what you need. Don't forget prescribed medications you take and bring an extra week's worth, just in case. Keep medicines in their original bottles, to prove they are prescribed to you.

Get your passport in order and don't wait until the last week. Ask your agency to help you make a list of everything you need to do beforehand and check off items as you do them. Adopting a child from another country is a wonderful and exciting adventure! Thousands of parents each year can attest to this fact and maybe soon you will be one of them. If you are well-prepared and have a fairly good idea of what to expect, (you can never know everything), the experience will be far more positive.

What if you've adopted a child from another country used to another language and other customs? How can you help your baby, toddler or older child adapt? Jean Nelson-Erichsen, co-director of Los Ninos International Adoption Center, provides practical advice on not only helping your child cope but making sure you take care of a variety of important tasks.

YOUR NEW CHILD FROM ANOTHER COUNTRY: WHAT YOU SHOULD DO AND WHAT TO EXPECT

Jean Nelson-Erichsen, LSW, MA, APA,
Co-director of Los Ninos International Adoption Center

Want to try a new game called "The International Parenting Challenge?" Travel abroad and become the "instant parent" of a child over six months old. Guess when and what the child was fed and put to bed.

Meet your new child's needs for the next week or two in a developing country, where most people speak a different language and you are the foreigner. Take custody of your new son or daughter in a series of crowded apartments and hotel rooms.

Move through the international bureaucracy, focused on the goal ahead. Hold the child in your arms and at the same time always be prepared with the proper documents and on time for adoption and visa-related appointments.

A Game Many Have Played and Won—and You Can Too!

Sounds daunting? It is. Yet over 15,000 Americans began their first weeks as mothers and fathers this way in 1998 alone. They advanced through all the challenges while caring for their dear child and reached the finish line in time to fly home with their precious one.

You guessed it. The game doesn't exist—but there's no question that adopting abroad can be a lot like a marathon. And, as with a marathon, it's a very good idea to learn ahead of time what to expect. Some of the aforementioned tasks are much easier when you have an experienced bilingual representative who knows the drill. Nevertheless, adopting parents need to keep their minds on the process to make certain that they obtain what they need.

For example, once the final adoption decree is issued in the country, make sure you get the information you need before leaving the orphanage or the court where records are stored. The agency representative should obtain the social and medical history for the medical file that will be opened in the United States. (A list of the kind of information needed is available in the "Initial Medical Evaluation of the Adopted Child" by Dr. Jenista in Chapter 9.)

New parents must also learn to tune in quickly to signs or symptoms of physical or emotional distress in their child. Such problems are usually mild and you can keep to your itinerary. (If the child seems seriously ill, usually the adoption agency representative or the U.S. Embassy can help you find appropriate medical care.) You or your representative will make appointments for your child's photo, embassy-required medical examination, and visa appointment while you get packed for your journey home.

Getting Ready to Come Home

Many airlines require you to confirm your reservations 72 hours before flight time. Children under two are free if you hold them on your lap, but although it sounds very nice, it could be difficult to hold a child for so long and on such a long trip. A seat for a child usually costs about half the adult fare. You can also ask for the roomier bulkhead seats that have bassinets for infants. Better yet, if you can, fly business or first class.

Airlines insist that you show up at the airport two to four hours in advance. An early arrival may make it possible to change the location of your seats.

Call home before you leave so that your loved ones will be there to greet you. But do let them know about your "bonding in progress" and why you can't allow your child to be passed among well-wishers at the airport. They'll be disappointed, but they'll understand.

Sometimes Your Child May Need Medical Treatment in the Other Country

New parents may find that they need their representative to locate a doctor in the country where the child is from to treat a cold, flu, parasites, and/or skin ailments typical of institutionalized children. Or you may be able to wait until you get home to get treatment.

Sylvia and Jack were handed their baby girl, Jade, in China. They called our agency that night to say that after all the wonderful things they had heard about Chinese adoptions, they felt sad, worried, and disappointed. Sylvia said, "All of the babies looked listless. Ours was the worst of the bunch, really burning up with fever and sick." Jade was dazed, refused her bottle, thrashed around, and couldn't sleep.

Sylvia was crying when she told me over the phone that Jade looked like a bald, spindly, little old man. "We need a doctor," Jack said. "I want to get her checked out as soon as possible. This is our baby and I'll move heaven and earth to get her well." Our representative brought a doctor to the hotel, and he diagnosed the baby with malnutrition, rickets, and an ear infection. Jade's problems are common to institutionalized infants in developing countries.

Sylvia and Jack pulled themselves together and asked the doctor what they could do. They took turns feeding and medicating Jade around the clock. Within a week, the baby's condition had improved considerably. She was still emaciated, but she was alert and cooing. Since the new parents needed to be sure they were doing everything right, they made an appointment with their pediatrician for the day they got back.

Jade is doing well now and Sylvia and Jack are very glad that she is theirs!

Back Home with Your Child, Hooray!

Once you land, your greatest desire will be to be back in your own home again. You bring your child through the doorway of your home like the proverbial groom carrying his bride over the threshold. New life begins—love is everywhere! You're the center of attention as friends, neighbors, and relatives shower you with joy, good wishes, and presents.

"I never expected such an outpouring of affection," said Susan. She and her husband, Joel, had come home the night before with Tatiana, a Russian one-year-old they adopted. Nearly everyone they knew showed up at the airport to welcome them home. Tatiana was crying and exhausted by then, and Susan knew it would be a bad idea to linger and let everyone hold her.

"Tatiana was just getting used to me. I thought it would be a bad idea to hand her over to my sister just then. Initially, Tatiana tried to avoid me. She turned away when I held her. Now she won't let go of me, and I love it." Susan showers Tatiana with her sunny ways and the little one responds by looking pleased, at least momentarily. Tatiana seems overwhelmed by all the newness. She appears to be a bit small for her age but otherwise healthy.

Susan adjusted to motherhood easily. Childhood songs and games, long forgotten, sprung to her mind, and childhood terms of endearment appeared, "Out of nowhere," she said, even under stress in Russia. Susan shopped before she left for home. Her best buys were cassettes and CDs of children's music. Tatiana's eyes lit up whenever she heard it. She had heard the same tapes in the orphanage.

Kids Can Act Out Sometimes—It's Part of Parenting

Carol and George adopted two-year-old Katy in Romania. She had never shown any frustration at the orphanage, but it was a different story when Carol and George took her to Bucharest for her physical, photo, and visa appointment. Katy threw tantrums and screamed with fright and anger.

"My one wish is to help Katy feel secure with us. Sometimes when I put her down to play, she sits and rocks herself or stands and sways on her feet. If she hurts herself, she doesn't come to me for help. That worries me. I saw some children in the orphanage doing that. I know it means she was neglected," said Carol.

Katy's parents were comforted to know that there is free professional help available from their local Early Childhood Intervention program. Katy had calmed down by the time the child development specialist paid her first visit. Katy stopped rocking and swaying in less than two months. Even sooner than that, Carol, George, and Katy formed a strong attachment.

Making Home More Homey

Comfort is as important as medical issues. Sleeping is a basic need and deprivation can cause a lot of stress. One soothing balm is to keep a piece of the child's old clothing, no matter how ugly or worn, for a "lovey" from the first day the child is placed with you.

Sylvia made a "lovey" for Jade by wadding up her ragged infant undershirt and tucking it in with the baby's blankets. Infants and children instinctively seek familiar smells. The old undershirt carried the familiar scent of the orphanage. It may look dreary to you, but it signifies security to your child. Jack went shopping for wind-up things that ticked like a heart. Warmly and securely bundled, the baby relaxed with chimes of music boxes and musical toys.

Take Some Time Off: You're Entitled

By federal law, new parents are entitled to twelve weeks of unpaid leave from their jobs, if their employers have 50 or more workers. Medical insurance and other benefits are maintained during the leave. And the parents get the same or a similar job when they go back to work. With the luxury of being able to "nest" for twelve weeks, you can ease gently into your old time zone, introduce your child to all the new sensations, and bond tightly. You're on a parental honeymoon, just like a bride and groom. Responsibilities will come crowding in all too soon.

Home: The Early Days

Get back on your bearings. You're finally home with the child you longed for. The darling room you decorated is finally occupied. But not for long. Jade or Alex may not be able to sleep in the cute little bed. And you may want to keep your boy or girl as close to you as possible anyway. You want them to see what you see, hear what you hear, touch what you touch, and feel what you feel. You want to share the core of your being with them.

Social workers call the early days of placement "the honeymoon phase." Like a honeymoon, the adoptive adjustment begins with a lot of love, a feeling of fulfillment, and a desire for the best and brightest of futures. The honeymoon lasts as long as the personalities of the adoptive parents and the child perpetuate it.

The honeymoon is not a good time to let social pressures loom large in your life. Resist social pressure to entertain out-of-town friends and relatives for days at a time or to take a trip with your new child. Some people have taken their newly immigrated children straight to Disneyland and gotten them over-excited, and over-stimulated, and unraveled the bonding process. This is a bad idea! "Nesting" and "quiet" are key aspirations here.

Take charge of visits from friends and relatives and keep them short. Tell them your new hours. The main thing to remind them of is that you want the child to bond to you and you don't want him or her to be passed around to each person. You can also say you are worried about new bacteria and viruses that might be introduced.

There is something wonderful and exhilarating about this new communal bond and the rituals associated with a new life in your social group. If this is your first child, you will feel a change in status. You're really a family now and will gladly take on the responsibilities. You're going to give this child everything you've got in terms of energy, time, and financial resources.

During nap times, begin the child's "life story book" with the items you've collected. Every child needs an account of their beginnings, adoption, and journey home conveyed by words, pictures, photographs, and documents.

If you have a baby, you'll need to work on time management. Decide how much you can really do in one day and don't let yourself get too tired. If your child is older than an infant, make a schedule and set some household rules for meals, naps, and playtime so that the child has a schedule—she or he is used to a very rigid one and feels more secure this way.

Learning to Set Boundaries

For children over age two, you may need to set limits and boundaries of acceptable behavior. As one wise social worker said, "If you wouldn't put up with rowdy behavior or temper tantrums from a child born to you, don't put up with it just because the child had a sad life up until now. All children need rules in order to feel secure." If you already have children in the family, get them involved. Ask them to help write the new household rules. They'll love it!

Education Is Important

One of the first concerns expressed by many parents of newly adopted children over two is language and education. Most newly arrived children get so excited over their abrupt change to a new environment that they may appear to have attention deficit disorder (ADD) or attention deficit hyperactivity disorder (ADHD). Therapist and adoption expert Claudia Jewett calls it "newness panic" and indeed it is. But do not rush your child off to the nearest psychiatrist or psychologist because you're convinced your child needs Ritalin. Instead, give your child a chance to adapt to such radical changes in his or her life.

Just where to place a child in school, especially a child who does not speak English, can be a baffling decision. Ask local school authorities for assistance. You also may need to check out all the public and private schools in your area. You may need to decide whether English as a second language (ESL) classes will help or hinder your child. After several months, you will be able to tell if your child might need appropriate ESL classes or a basic educational plan adapted to his or her needs.

Parents who want to help a child under age five learn the language quickly find that it can get tricky when they try to get outside help. And if passing a child around among strangers frightens the little one, imagine what strangers speaking the child's own native language does. "Another move coming up," he or she probably thinks. Children six and up will probably be able to sort this out and will benefit from being with people who speak their native language, with this caveat: Before you let them talk to your child, be sure to discuss adoption with them. If they have a lot of backward notions, they might do your child more harm than good.

You might decide to enlist an English tutor for an elementary school child instead. The child can always take classes in his or her native language later. You may wish to focus on just English for now.

Health Issues

When babies are adopted, most parents focus on health issues. One of your first responsibilities is to consult a pediatrician who has hopefully been lined up beforehand. Adjustments in formulas, solid foods, and schedules are made at this time.

A complete health screening should be arranged in the near future as well. A record for the schedule of innoculations is created for children who may or may not have had those that are required. Screening tests will be spread out over weeks or even months. During testing, your pediatrician may find questionable items in lab results that can scare you. You may need to visit several specialists to rule out health problems indicated by lab tests or to begin treatment on those that exist.

A dental examination should be scheduled for a child over 18 months. Teeth are routinely neglected among the poor and institutionalized. Your child may require substantial dentistry to ensure the health of permanent teeth.

Let your health insurance provider know that you have an addition to your family; they must be notified within thirty days of your child's placement or adoption.

Do know that Public Law 104-191, the Kennedy Kassenbaum bill, bans group insurance carriers from excluding pre-existing or undiagnosed conditions. If you have health insurance that covers your family, your new child will be covered too, despite any medical problems he may have.

Extra Help Is Available

Many previously institutionalized infants and toddlers benefit from Early Childhood Intervention (ECI) Programs available for children between one and three through county and the public school systems.

ECI programs are state and federal programs that provide services free of charge. ECI addresses cognitive, gross and fine motor skills, language, speech, social, emotional, and self-help skills. Children with a medical diagnosis with a high probability of delays are also eligible. ECI services are provided in home or community settings. Nurses, teachers, and social workers show families how to help their children reach their potential through education and therapy services. You can find the program nearest you by calling your county health and social services or find them on the Internet at www.nectas.unc.edu/PartC/ptccoord.html.

Your Child Has Been Home Nearly Six Weeks! What to Do

Relax and enjoy your child! Visit daycare facilities and nurseries. You may have done this before, but now your eye is more discerning. You, above all people, know exactly what your child needs.

If your social worker has not visited you already, call and arrange for a visit. The social worker who helped you prepare for this child will be delighted to see you together. He or she can give you helpful advice, make observations you may have missed, and recommend community resources. The report that social workers write on your family's adjustment is sent to the child-placing entity abroad according to that country's requirements.

Contact Government Agencies

Many adopters believe that adopting in their county of residence is all they need to make their child an American citizen. Not so. American citizenship is not bestowed automatically. You owe it to your child to obtain citizenship as soon as possible. Do it now because you might forget later. After your child is 18, it will be harder for him or her to obtain citizenship, even though he or she may have lived here nearly all his or her life.

The phone number for requesting Immigration and Naturalization Service forms is (800) 870-3676. Call INS and request Form N-634, Application for Citizenship in Behalf of an Adopted Child, to apply for your child's U.S. citizenship. If only one spouse is a U.S. citizen, order Form N-600. Send in photocopies of the documents listed on the form.

Be sure to include the following statement, "Copies of the documents being submitted are exact photocopies of original documents. I understand that I may be required to submit original documents to an immigration official at a later date." Then sign and date it.

If you didn't receive a second set of original documents while you were abroad or you lost them, request Form G-884, "Request for Return of Original Documents."

After you file the N-634 or N-600, INS will notify you of the citizenship hearing. If your child's name must be changed by a re-affirmation or re-adoption, you might decide to wait for the new decree before you file. Otherwise you will have to get the child's name changed on the U.S. citizenship certificate with a Form N-565. If you lose the citizenship certificate, the same form is used for a replacement.

Another government agency that you will need forms from is the Social Security Administration. Call (800) 722-1213 and ask for Form SS-5. Social Security Administration employees will need photocopies of the adoption or guardianship decree and a birth certificate, preferably in English; the child's passport, including the page showing the A-number on the INS stamp; and your identification, such as a passport, driver's license, or military I.D. (but not a birth certificate).

If officials tell you that they want to see originals, take them in person and retain them. Do not mail originals. It's too easy for things to get lost in the mail, even if you send them by certified mail. Also, you'll need the originals again later. Supposedly, the Social Security Administration will accept documents in other languages, but it is preferable to get these documents translated beforehand. Later on, if you decide to change the child's name, you will need to notify the Social Security Administration. Your child will retain the same number.

Don't forget the Internal Revenue Service, another federal agency that needs to be contacted about your new child. Order IRS Form W-7, Individual Taxpayer Identification number. With this form you can complete your tax return and get your adoption tax credit. Also obtain INS Form 8839, Qualified Adoption Expenses, which can be used in conjunction with your adoption agency's receipt for the legal expenses you paid. You may be able to locate these forms on the IRS Web site, www.irs.ustreas.gov, or call (800) 829-1040.

The Social Security number as well as the INS and IRS forms allow you to start new money-saving ventures. You can open savings accounts for your child, as described below. And you can apply for a tax credit for yourself of up to $5,000. Congress may raise this to $10,000 in the future.

Planning Ahead for Your Child's Future

If you've received gifts of money for your child, you may wish to plan ahead and open an educational individual retirement account. You can set aside up to $500 a year after federal income taxes. Your child will not have to pay taxes on the money or its future earnings if it is used for college expenses. Or you can open a custodial account with your child's name and Social Security number.

Make a will or revise your current will. Choose a guardian for your child who will be the executor of your estate. Read your life insurance policy. Take a look at the beneficiaries of your life insurance and 401 (k) retirement funds. This is the time to make changes.

Three Months After Your Child Is Home

Your family leave is over. You head back to work and go through separation anxiety, just as much as your child does. Conversely, the emotional and financial toll of separation might make you decide that one of you should stay home with your little honey.

Three or six months after you immigrate your child, depending on the laws in your state, your agency will complete the social work supervision and prepare documents for an adoption, in the case of a guardianship, or a re-affirmation or re-adoption in the case of a foreign final adoption decree. This is the time to make a name change official. Many legal experts believe that an adoption in the United States protects the child's right to inherit.

During that same time, you will receive an alien registration card in the mail. You triggered the issuance of the card when you turned in the envelope with your original adoption documents from the American consulate to an INS official at the airport. The card is mailed to the address you stated on the I-600. If you moved, the card will not be forwarded. If you didn't receive the form, get INS Form G-731, Inquiry about Status of I-551 Alien Registration Card. If you lost the card, order INS Form I-90, Application to Replace Alien Registration Card.

When you are called in for the citizenship hearing, take the originals requested on the N-634 or N-600 to present to the official. At that time, you will surrender your child's alien registration card and receive the certificate of citizenship.

Now get a passport for your child. This will be his or her identification from now on. Protect the certificate in a bank vault after you copy down the number. Citizenship bestows all the rights and privileges of an American. Your child will qualify for federal programs, college loans, and be able to travel abroad and re-enter the United States without a problem.

Enjoy Parenthood!

If you've followed my instructions, then you've accomplished everything required of you and more. As you nested, fed, snuggled, rested, and took care of the "things to do," you created a family that is emotionally secure, legally protected, and financially stable.

And if there were such a game as "The International Parenting Challenge," you would be the winner!

Jean Nelson-Erichsen, LSW, MA, APA is co-director of Los Ninos (Children's) International Adoption Center (The Woodlands, Texas), which she helped found in 1981. (Web site: www.losninos.org.) She has been interviewed on CNN Insight. Ms. Nelson-Erichsen is an expert on intercountry adoption. She is also an adoptive parent and co-author of How to Adopt Internationally *(Fort Worth, Texas: Mesa House Publishing, 2000).*

CHAPTER EIGHT

ADOPTING OLDER CHILDREN AND CHILDREN WITH SPECIAL NEEDS

It's important to understand that "special needs" are really in the eyes of the beholder. Families, public (government) and private agencies, the laws, and the courts may all have very different definitions of "special needs." Thus, a family needs to understand its own limits and find out how its agency or social worker defines special needs. Some physicians and some social workers consider all children in foster care to have special needs. Keep in mind that medical special needs are very different from social, emotional, and behavioral special needs. Many families find medical problems far less daunting than emotional problems.

An experienced adoptive mother and advocate for children with special needs, Peggy Soule provides a realistic view of adopting children with special needs from her thirty-three years of experience.

MYTHS AND REALITIES OF CHILDREN WITH SPECIAL NEEDS

Peggy Soule

This article was written with the help of Michele, Marge, Jim, Jackie, Judie, Carl, Judith, Dave, Josie, Linda, Paul, Lynda, John, Carolyn, and all the other adoptive parents who hung in there with us, laughed with us, and supported us as we raised our children. Together as adoptive parents we learned from one another, leaned on one another, and cared for each other. We grew together, became close friends, and forever have a bond that connects us. We still need each other and will always be there for one another.

There are many myths about adopting children with special needs and there are also important realities to be aware of. In this essay, I discuss the primary myths and realities that you need to know about, if you are considering adopting any child.

The Biggest Myth: "Love Is Enough"

The greatest myth in adoption is that "love is enough!" I used to believe that if only I loved the child deeply enough, then all would be well. But nothing could be further from the truth. Unfortunately, parental love and total commitment cannot solve all problems. This is true whether the child was born to you or adopted by you.

There are many reasons why love is not enough. The child you've adopted may have loved and lost before on his or her journey through the child welfare system and learned to erect barriers. Some of the child's problems may be rooted in his or her genetic make-up and no more easily changed than the color of his or her eyes. The child may equate intimacy with the sexual abuse he or she has experienced. Some troubled children believe their adoptive parents to be just plain "nuts" for having taken them in, and they behave accordingly.

Reality: No Child Is Perfect

At some point, all children present some sort of parenting challenge and all children have some sort of special need in their lives. Yet some children appear to move easily through life, successfully meeting their own special needs. They make a parent feel good. You begin to believe that they are succeeding thanks to your parenting skills. Others are difficult to parent from the beginning and do not respond to those techniques that you know are right. You think you are a terrible parent and begin to question yourself.

Whether your children come to you as infants, toddlers, or teenagers, there is never enough information. An infant labeled healthy can become a child with attention deficit disorder (ADD), alcohol-related problems, or severe mental health problems. Caring parents start to wonder what they did wrong and shoulder the blame themselves, certain that if they had done it right they would have had the perfect child. One parent said to me, "If we only had Tim and John I would think we were great parents. If we only had Mary and Sam I would believe we were terrible parents. I now know we have very little to do with their behaviors, and we must not judge ourselves. We are not responsible for their successes or their failures."

What is really important is how you deal with the child over the years and how you accept and respond to their needs and problems. You begin to understand that the genes children are born with have an incredible effect on them; you understand that any child separated from his or her birthfamily suffers loss; you learn that you have no idea whether the birthmother ever used drugs or alcohol during pregnancy and whether there was any effect on the fetus.

You realize how good it is that a child has a parent or two who cares and is there to help. You learn to reach out to others and not blame yourself. You get all sorts of advice and support from other parents; the ones with similar problems are the most comforting to you, and you and your family do go on.

Remember that many families parenting birthchildren also experience pain. They, too, are raising children with disabilities, children who will die, children who are unable to learn from experience. They are struggling to make it work just as adoptive families are.

Myth: Bonding Is Always Automatic

Children don't automatically bond to you when you adopt them and parents cannot automatically plug into a loving relationship either. This can lead to confusion, fear, and self-doubt. Babies are usually easy to love because they smile in response to your caring and are so dependent on you. It is fortunate that this happens because when they grow to become terrible twos, driving you crazy, you know you still love them.

Love may not come easily when the two-year-old who is placed in your home is feeling both sad and angry. I remember how easy it was to connect when we adopted infants two weeks and younger, but I have worked with people adopting an eight-month-old who could not bond.

Children may reject a new family because they were already attached to the previous family or may have trouble attaching to anyone. I adopted a two-year-old and did not feel that instant love I had experienced with infants. I thought something was wrong with me until I shared with my neighbor, who had also adopted a two-year-old at about the same time, that I didn't love my child. She confessed to me that she didn't love her son either. We both knew then that it wasn't us. These two-year-olds both traveled rough roads en route to becoming responsible thirty-year-olds, but there is now no question of our mutual love.

Adopting a child is comparable to involvement in an arranged marriage: You want to love this new person you never knew before. But it is not easy to love a stranger, especially a belligerent teenager who comes to live with you. The warm loving feeling you seek comes slowly when there is no reciprocity. Some children never attach. Your love may never get beyond the basic love of commitment, but that is okay. While not warm and fuzzy, it is still a powerful force.

When my husband and I adopted an eleven-year-old child and then a nine-year-old child, I no longer expected instant bonding, and wasn't upset when it did not happen. In fact, the nine-year-old was so difficult that, as much as we were committed to him, no one in our family really liked him for the first two years. However, once his ADD was diagnosed and he was treated with Ritalin, it was possible for him to change from the kid in school who was always in trouble, and who hung out with other low-achievers, to the kid who took pride in making the honor roll. Six years after he was adopted he died in an accident while he was an exchange student in Spain. I will never forget the reaction of our entire family. None of us realized how much we had bonded to him until he died.

Myth: You Can Mold Your Child

Too many parents believe in the myth that if they have great expectations and high standards, then the kids will live up to them. Instead, you need to be ready to tailor expectations, changing goals as special needs develop or become apparent. You need to be open and flexible. This does not mean you let the child run wild, doing whatever he or she wants, because he or she was abused before. You use love and limits to help the child achieve his or her own best potential.

Reality: Sometimes the Special Need Isn't What You Expected

Some adoptive parents seek children with clearly identified special needs such as ADD, cerebral palsy, a speech defect, or Down syndrome. In this situation, there is an opportunity to learn about the condition and meet others who have similar children. If you decide you can parent such a child, your expectations for your child are likely to be realistic. You learn that a child with mental retardation may never be totally self-sufficient; you learn that a child with fetal alcohol syndrome will have trouble learning cause and effect and may end up in the juvenile justice system.

But beware of the misleading sense of security such information can foster. The problems you encounter may include some that are totally different from your expectations. I always remember one father saying to me, "I thought we were getting a 'healthy' dying child with AIDS. I never expected the worst case of ADD, which is what is challenging our family to the limit and driving me crazy." The family expected that the child would die; they didn't expect the extreme attention deficit behavior he exhibited. This comment was said "tongue-in-cheek" to another adoptive parent, whom he knew would understand the humor that he used to cover his pain.

Special needs are varied, unpredictable, and often change with time. The visible ones are perhaps easier to identify and prepare for. You learn what to expect. It is the behavioral issues, the defiance, and the lack of caring that get to you. A child who has been sexually abused and who then becomes a perpetrator within your home can undo the whole family.

Educate yourself on the significance of what has happened to the child so you can understand what might happen. Never believe that all the important information is available or has been revealed. Many of the older children being placed today have been sexually abused. That does not mean they all will become perpetrators, but the social worker needs to discuss this possibility, recommending appropriate precautions. Knowledge, preparation, and education are vital in the placement of waiting children. Keep the healthy people healthy within your home. Protect and help your children cope with the disabilities of others.

Myth: Racism Doesn't Exist Anymore

Love alone cannot prepare you to parent a child of a different race. If you are white and adopting a child of another race you soon learn race matters in America. As a white mother who adopted an African-American infant I was sure I would not be aware of his color. How wrong I was. His beautiful skin is part of who he is, and I see it clearly every time I hug him—even today at thirty years of age. It is also what the police see when he is driving a car.

Unfortunately, racism is alive and well. It was the African-American adoptive parents in our parent group who embraced the white parents adopting children of other races and said, "We will be the bridge for you. You will need our help as you parent your children to cope with racism in America." If you are white and adopting a child of another race, it is wise to connect with that child's community before the child comes to your home. We chose to live in the city, making sure our children attended schools with a diverse population.

Reality: Adoption (and Life) Are Risks

The reality is that adoption is a risk, as is life. You can make an incredible difference in the life of a son or daughter through their adult lives. The difference you make may not be what you planned. Possibly you may never know the difference you make. One family recalled, "We had to continually rethink our expectations and let the children be part of setting them. I always remember those holiday letters where people bragged about how well their kids were doing in college or in their careers. I celebrated when my kid who struggled all through high school got into the local community college."

One mother said: "When my eighteen-year-old was pregnant and unmarried I was very upset. It was the doctor who looked at me and said, 'She is a success, not a failure.'" The girl was the first of her birthfamily to graduate from high school; she had waited until eighteen to have a child; the father was someone she had dated for four years; she was not using drugs. The mother began to look at her daughter in a different way, realizing that the adoptive family had made a difference. Today this woman has two children, lives with the father of the children, and is an excellent parent. She has health care for the children, although not for herself. She needs help from public assistance at times when the father is out of work, but she is making it. Today the adoptive mom knows that this is how success is measured.

Maybe you had hoped to get a child with developmental delays through high school, and were initially disappointed when his achievement stopped at the fifth grade level, but he can live independently. Perhaps a teenager gets pregnant and has a child, but you realize that without the support of your family she might have had three children. A boy gets into trouble with the law and spends time in prison. With a family for support he has someone to advocate for him in the justice system, someone to come home to, and someone to help him find an apartment and a job so he can make it on his own.

Myth: Adopted Children Are Always Grateful

Some people have the image of "saving" a child. They assume that the child will come to realize how fortunate he or she was to have been adopted. Experienced adoptive parents, however, don't expect this. They realize that before adoption comes the loss of the birthfamily.

Rewards come at odd times, and they may not be what you expected. Sometimes the small victories in life are what sustain us. Redefining success becomes an ongoing process. A child in special education makes an apron for you and hands it to you when you are in the bathroom, her first gift after a year in your home. A twenty-year-old who had sent you a Mother's Day card when growing up with "my" crossed out (Happy Mother's Day to ~~My~~ Mother) doesn't send cards any more but is always there for you when the family is in crisis.

One mom told me that even her children who had been most damaged and had had a hard time connecting to the family came through when their dad fell off a ladder. They were all at the hospital within four hours.

Don't expect instant gratification. Rewards may be delayed for years. For a while, your reward may be simply knowing that you tried to make a difference. It is amazing to hear the couples who have parented very difficult children talk about the kids when they are in their thirties. Some families have waited that long to form a close relationship; others have accepted that whatever relationship they have as okay.

My husband and I have found that the greatest rewards in our lives stemmed from our willingness to take risks and to open our lives and our family to others. Even heartbreak has taught us about love. We have never found a door closing without another one opening, and if we walked through it, family, friends, and strangers comforted us, and we learned more about life and love.

Reality: Sometimes You Need Outside Help

An absolute truth is that you will need support. Don't even start to think that you can do this alone. As one friend said, "Don't make the mistake of thinking you are not like those other adoptive families. This is who you are. This is who you need."

Other families who understand will sustain you and care for you. Some professionals understand the issues, but many do not. Those who have adopted themselves and may have experienced what you are going through are such a comfort to work with. Others may try to blame you for your children's problems. The bias of some professionals is to blame the family, especially the mother. One mom kept this magnet on her refrigerator, "If it's not bacterial or viral, it must be maternal."

I am always amazed when I talk with families who are at their wits' end with their children's behavior. So often they are afraid to tell that their daughter has flunked out of school or that their son is into drugs. When I share with a family what our children have done or what other families have experienced, they seem surprised that they are not alone. Often I will mail them a copy of the tape, *To Hell and Back,* a recording of a workshop done at a North American Council on Adoptable Children (NACAC) conference by a panel of experienced adoptive parents. The stories these families relate make listeners laugh and cry. Other parents in pain immediately connect to these families and realize they are not alone.

Adoption support should begin with the adoption homestudy. Adoption advocates across the country are pushing for services for families and children. It is so sad to see families trying to cope alone, receiving no support and blaming themselves or the child welfare system. Remember that there is no quick fix.

As Dee Paddock, adoptive parent and family psychotherapist says, "We need families who can manage, not fix." Many of us have parented children with very special needs, and what we needed was help in getting through it. You need someone you can tell anything to, even "I hate her today, I've had it! I'm not sure if I can survive. My marriage is in trouble."

Have someone to go to lunch or a movie with, someone to share a joke or a good laugh. We used to have a contest in our parent group to decide who would get the reward of the week for having the kid who did the worst thing. I won the week that four of my kids slipped out at night, with both parents home and in bed, to steal a car. As my husband said, "The family that steals together stays together." Another friend, after having been called back from a trip to Russia because one of her children had been arrested for attempted murder, said to me, "Do I win this week?" Adoptive parent humor is unique.

One friend's advice to adoptive parents is, "Be real, be humble." You are always learning. Someone always has a better story. Share with others. It is amazing how many of us have healed as we have helped others in pain. Often a situation is put in perspective by sharing.

Many families rely on their faith and belief in a higher being throughout this adoption journey. They find strength and comfort from their place of worship or their own spiritual beliefs. They choose to take on troubled children because they want to give something back to others. It is their faith that helps them go forward in times of stress and trouble.

Don't shoulder all the trouble. Let it go. I remember when my fifteen-year-old son had died, one son was in treatment for alcoholism, another one was being evaluated for alcoholism, and one daughter was on the street. I went to a meeting of parents whose children were being evaluated for drug abuse and we were all expressing how we were doing. I remember saying, "I can't cope with all of this. I have to let it fall off my shoulders and take care of myself." So often the families who had children in drug treatment began to heal because the parents went to Alanon, where they learned how to take care of themselves. Many of us began to live by the serenity prayer so well known to the Alcoholics Anonymous (AA) community: "God, grant me the serenity to accept the things I cannot change, the courage to change the things I can, and the wisdom to know the difference."

The love your child truly needs is the commitment and the willingness to stick with him or her, through thick and thin. Sometimes this means getting outside help, sending them to residential treatment centers, putting them out of the home temporarily. Rather than rejecting them, it means you are trying to get them the help they need. Some of the most committed families I have ever known had to put their children in other places to keep them from hurting themselves and others in the home. The pain was incredible; the commitment was always there.

You will not survive if you do not take good care of yourself. Family after family has told me this. Get yourself lots of love; know what you can do and what you cannot do. Know when you need a break, and figure out how to make it happen. Take time to be with your spouse, significant other, or good friend. Nurture your adult relationships. "Have good sex," emphasizes one adoptive parent.

One of the families I knew scheduled a date once a week without the kids. If they couldn't go out they fed the kids early and shared a special meal in the dining room with no kids allowed. They had two rules: No talk about the kids and no talk about money. It was hard at first, but soon they discovered they could discuss books, movies, ideas, and even dreams. It can be so hard to give ourselves permission to be good to ourselves, but it is so important. Families adopting children with special needs must take care of themselves or they will have nothing left to give to others.

A sense of humor helps immeasurably. The ability to laugh, to see things in perspective, and not take yourself too seriously has brought many a family through a crisis.

Reality: Sometimes Adoption "Grows" on You!

Many families who adopt children with special needs go back for more. There must be something to this stuff if families who take on these challenges go back again and again for other children. Somehow the parenting of children with special needs brings out the best and sometimes the worst in us. We are forever learning, forever changing, and forever hoping.

It's been said that adoption may be the only cure known to modern medicine for some of the children and their needs. I believe this is true. To be cared for, nurtured, listened to, cuddled—all are necessary for healing to take place. I believe families are the best therapists if they can be supported and helped as they take on the task of parenting the abused, the neglected, and the disabled in body and soul. Adoption is the only cure for thousands of children who wait.

Family is what our country is built on—family not just for children but for adults, too. It always haunts me to think about what will happen to the children who never find families. Where will they spend holidays as adults, whose weddings will they attend, whose funerals? Who will be the grandparents to their children? Where will they turn as adults when they need help and support?

Children with special needs are a joy, a pain, a heartache, a challenge, and a trip into the unknown. Adoption is not for the faint-hearted or for careful, cautious people afraid to take a risk to make a difference. For lots of families adoption was the way they were made, the way they changed, and the way they grew. Try it, but connect with those who have gone before you. They will help you, guide you, laugh with you, and welcome you into the wonderful world of adoption.

Peggy Soule and her husband Dave adopted six children, four of whom were considered children with special needs. All of them have presented challenges, including the healthy white infants. Together, as parents, Peggy and Dave have dealt with the death of a child, drugs in the home, unplanned pregnancies, sexual abuse, and jail. Today the five living children are responsible adults who bring joy, happiness, and love into the lives of their children, significant others, and their parents.

Peggy is the executive director of Children Awaiting Parents, the national organization that publishes The CAP Book, *and with the National Adoption Center co-sponsors* Faces of Adoption: America's Waiting Children *(www.adopt.org). Both are directories with pictures and descriptions of children with special needs awaiting adoption. Dave is a pediatrician and cares for many adopted children with special needs.*

CHAPTER NINE

WHAT YOU NEED TO KNOW AFTER YOU ADOPT

This chapter offers suggestions about things to do after you adopt. For example, what kind of medical examination and tests will your child need? Whether you adopt a baby or an older child from the United States, or a child from another country, it's important that your child receive a thorough medical examination soon after she or he arrives home. Jerri Ann Jenista, a pediatrician and adoptive mother of five, provides practical advice in her essay, "Initial Medical Evaluation of the Adopted Child."

R. Dubucs's essay, "Food and the Adopted Child," is important information for adoptive parents. Why food? Because food is not only what we all need to survive but it's also a nurturing, cultural, and emotional issue. Sometimes children overeat, horde food, or have a variety of other food-related quirks.

Lastly, how do you explain adoption to your child, as well as to others with nice (and pesky) questions? Read my essay for some basics on dealing with that toughie.

INITIAL MEDICAL EVALUATION OF THE ADOPTED CHILD

Jerri Ann Jenista, M.D.

The process leading to adoption is always fraught with anxiety. Parental concerns may vary with the type of adoption, but all parents have worries: an ill child's health; legal challenges to the adoption; or concerns about their ability to parent a child. The first medical evaluation after a child's placement is often viewed as an extension of the adoption process.

Parental Perception of the Pediatrician or Family Doctor

Some families see the first doctor's visit as an obstacle before "living happily ever after." Eager to begin parenting, they may minimize a physician's concerns about risk factors in a child's past or the current developmental or medical status. Such concerns may be dismissed by parents as "inexperience with this kind of child." But sometimes a parent also

579

dismisses an opportunity to recognize serious issues early and begin education and intervention when a problem may be far easier to resolve.

Other parents perceive the first check-up as a "stamp of approval" that they have adopted the right child. Any concerns raised by a physician may exacerbate fears that they have missed something very wrong. If no issues are raised, parents may feel the doctor is dismissing their worries too easily.

A few parents regard the first visit as a problem-solving session; a time to lay out all concerns and develop a plan to address them. If a physician sets priorities and delays evaluation of some issues until later, a parent may feel that the doctor is not "experienced enough in adoption."

Finally, some parents view the first check-up as an interim step to referrals to "real experts:" Medical or surgical consultants, psychologists, or others who assess and treat potential or existing problems.

Advantages of the Pediatric Specialist

If your birthchild was born with spina bifida or hypothyroidism, he or she would see specialists for that birth defect but would still get immunizations and well child check-ups at the doctor's office. If your older child developed chronic renal failure or leukemia, his or her regular doctor would still treat colds and sprained ankles, and acne. Your child's primary care doctor, usually a pediatrician, family practitioner, or general family doctor, is skilled in the care of children and an expert on the two main tasks of childhood: normal growth and development. These specialists in pediatrics recognize acceptable patterns of growth and development as well as deviations from those patterns. They provide the following:

- *Continuity of care over the first twenty years of a child's life.* A primary care doctor is often the only professional who knows a child through all stages of growth and development. Consultant specialists for heart disease, an orthopedic problem, or cerebral palsy may have long-term relationships but only on one aspect. Numerous studies show that children who receive medical care only in specialty clinics have much higher rates of incomplete immunizations, missed routine screening tests, such as vision and hearing, and unaddressed developmental issues, especially puberty and sexuality.
- *A "medical home."* When a child has complex or multiple medical or developmental issues, he or she is likely to be cared for by many consultants. Sometimes this care is provided in a multidisciplinary clinic, such as a spina bifida or cleft palate clinic. Often the child sees specialists in medical, surgical, counseling, and educational fields, but none have direct contact with each other. The pediatric specialist is often the only professional who "sees the whole picture" and can help the family deal with conflicting advice, set priorities for different procedures and therapies, and put into perspective the child's chronic condition as only a part of his or her whole life.
- *Comprehensive care.* Every child, no matter the special issues, needs well-child care: the array of preventive services essential to optimal growth and development. We often think of well-child care as immunizations, hearing and vision tests, and a "school physical." Today's pediatric specialist has a broader agenda: safety issues,

proper nutrition, choice of child care, "normal" behavioral problems, discipline at different ages, the effects of divorce, puberty, and sexuality, violence prevention, and early brain development.

Pediatric Specialists' Experience with Adoption

In the past, physicians' education about adoption and foster care was sketchy at best. In a popular pediatric textbook of twenty years ago, adoption was covered in a half a page out of 1,876 pages, that focused almost exclusively on infant adoption. Foster care received one sentence in a section on parental separation and death. In contrast, in Dershewitz's text with 1,106 pages, *Ambulatory Pediatric Care,* published by Lippincott-Raven, in 1999, foster children earned $4\frac{1}{2}$ pages and adoption 11 pages.

Following a recent article in the *American Academy of Pediatrics News,* almost 300 pediatricians requested additional information about adoption resources for their patients. There are no data, but I wonder if pediatric professionals adopt children at a higher rate than the general population. In the children's emergency room where I work, we have six physicians who are adoptive parents (and another waiting to adopt) and sixteen nurses who are adoptive parents (with two families waiting to adopt).

Adoption is common in pediatric practice. About 50,000 of the 3.5 million U.S. newborns, over one percent of infants born annually, were adopted. Add 36,000 children adopted from foster care and 16,000 adopted internationally and it's likely any pediatrician gains one or two adopted children per year. This is far higher than rates of children with juvenile arthritis, diabetes, cleft palate, or cystic fibrosis, all of whom are cared for in a typical pediatric practice.

Although, in some regions, children adopted from foster care or internationally attend a specialty clinic for the initial medical evaluation, most are examined by the physician who will be the long-term health care provider. Even children evaluated in specialty clinics eventually return to a primary care physician.

Solutions to Parental Concerns

Many concerns expressed by parents about a physician's "lack of experience with adoption" are valid. But remember, the doctor has many other skills that will be more important over the life of a child. I believe the solution is to better educate the primary care doctor. This education is already happening, as mentioned, in books, articles, and personal experience with adoption. Professional organizations such as the American Academy of Pediatrics and the Child Welfare League of America have or are developing standards of care for children in foster care or who will be adopted.

Patients are a very powerful motivating force in the doctor's education. For example, I know about ornithine transcarbamylase deficiency because I had an affected family in my practice. A "Dear Doctor" letter from an agency or the court, or a review article from a professional publication, can go far in improving the physician's knowledge and performance.

The medical evaluation needed at or before adoption is not complicated, and most pediatric experts already have the necessary skills. They may need a little prompting to make sure all important issues are addressed in a timely and efficient manner. There are many ways to achieve this goal. Some social service agencies have a checklist to be completed by the attending physician for a child in foster care at the point of referral for adoption. Sometimes, the local juvenile judge requires certain standards to be met before accepting a petition to adopt. Agencies may require a family to get a minimum set of tests and examinations before recommending they proceed with finalization.

A Suggested Set of Standards

Advances in "adoption medicine" are proceeding rapidly and gaining recognition in general pediatric practice. But until principles of adoption practice become mainstream, pediatric practitioners need reminders of what to do. The checklists at the end of this article are suggestions similar to standards being developed by pediatric and child welfare experts.

Domestic Newborn Adoption

The medical evaluation at adoption varies with the age and circumstances of the child. There is no one medical form for every adopted child. For example, the medical evaluation of a newborn consists mostly of reviewing a child's past history: genetic, ethnic, and perinatal risks to which the child has been exposed. The physical examination is not as important in a very young infant, since most medical care is dictated by a child's risk factors rather than physical condition.

For example, if the birthmother is a known IV drug user, the baby is screened for effects of drugs and/or alcohol and for infectious diseases such as syphilis, hepatitis B and C, HIV, and tuberculosis, regardless of whether the baby has signs or symptoms of disease. Similarly, the risks of being born at twenty-eight weeks gestation, weighing 750 grams are well known; a particular protocol of studies will be followed, regardless of the child's apparent condition.

The medically informed reader may comment that the above evaluation of the newborn is not specific to adoption. That is true, but, without an adequate history, it's much harder to practice good medicine. Adoption medicine for a very young baby is really collecting the history.

Adoption from Foster Care

Over half the children adopted from foster care have already lived with their adoptive families. Theoretically, the child should have had a complete medical evaluation at entrance into foster care and the foster or adoptive parent should have monitored medical progress. Some children have received medical care in a multidisciplinary foster care clinic. However, foster parents often have no access to a child's records in previous homes. Medical care is often fragmented and haphazard. A few jurisdictions have instituted a "medical passport" plan, in which an abbreviated medical history booklet follows a child no matter who cares for him or her. But this is not the norm for most children.

The medical evaluation of a child adopted from foster care places equal emphasis on history and current examination. Because the information needed is complex and often scattered, this first evaluation may be spread over several visits. Not all evaluations will be performed by the primary physician, but he or she should act as case manager in helping parents schedule and complete visits and assess the final picture obtained. Whenever possible, this comprehensive evaluation should be done before filing a petition to adopt, as the findings may alter the amount of adoption subsidy the child may require.

The Internationally Adopted Child

In a way, the medical evaluation of the immigrant adopted child may be the simplest. Prior medical records are often nonexistent, incomplete, inaccurate, or even falsified—thus the initial evaluation is protocol-driven. There is little room for individual decision-making on which tests to order and which examinations to perform on a child from overseas. This is one situation where "one size fits all" does apply.

One exception may be a young infant from Korean foster care. For those children, medical records tend to be complete and accurate. The medical evaluation is much more like the domestic newborn, with the additional needs only for infectious disease screening and updating immunizations to U.S. standards.

For all other children, accompanying medical documents should be reviewed carefully, but all tests, diagnoses, immunizations, and evaluations should be reconfirmed. Many children will have accurate medical records but there is no way to know in advance which records are trustworthy.

Because the history is so often unavailable or incomplete, the medical evaluation of the internationally adopted child is almost all test- and examination-oriented. No part of the evaluation should be eliminated without a very good reason. "He looks too healthy," "we'll wait and see if she develops any symptoms," "all tests were negative over there," or "she's too sick/malnourished/tired/upset" are not good reasons to skip the recommended evaluation.

In studies of children attending international adoption clinics who had been seen previously by their own physicians, most missed diagnoses were due to errors of omission. The doctor could have found the disease or condition if he or she had done a standard evaluation. Parent's fears of a doctor missing an "exotic" condition are usually unfounded. Diseases such as malaria are highly unusual.

Because of the numbers of tests needed, the need to complete immunization series, the parent's unfamiliarity with the child, and, sometimes, a child's lack of language proficiency, the comprehensive evaluation will be spread out over several weeks. Children with multiple medical issues may face an overwhelming number of interventions. The physician should help the family set priorities about which problems should be addressed first. But care should be taken that no part of the recommended evaluation is forgotten.

Take-home Message

As the practice of adoption medicine becomes more widespread and sophisticated, we are beginning to get a much better idea of the medical risks and outcomes for this special group of children. In particular, it is becoming increasingly clear that lessons learned from one kind of adoption also apply to other kinds of adoption. For example, we have a fairly clear understanding of the extensive mental health needs of children adopted from U.S. foster care.

We are becoming more aware that those same needs are found in children who have lived in orphanages overseas following an involuntary termination of parental rights because of abuse or neglect. Similarly, infectious diseases found in children overseas are found in increasing numbers in U.S. adopted children who lived in homeless shelters or other adverse environments. There may soon be only one kind of adoption evaluation applying to all children of adverse social backgrounds.

Even so, it is important to remember that, despite their special needs, all adopted children need basic pediatric care to achieve optimal growth and development. A primary care physician should be involved with the initial evaluation and management of every adopted child. Every child was a child, before he or she was an adopted child.

Information to Be Collected or Reviewed at the Initial Medical Evaluation of an Adopted Newborn

- Past and current health conditions of each birthparent, including any ongoing treatments
- History of any mental health diagnosis or treatment in either birthparent
- Ethnic origins of the birthparents
- Family history of medical conditions, including the birthparents' siblings and parents
- Any known genetic disorders in the extended families
- Lifestyle of the birthparents
- Description of any substance use during pregnancy, including over-the-counter medications, prescription drugs, tobacco, alcohol, and illegal drugs
- Description of the pregnancy, labor, and delivery
- Any screening tests of the mother or child for infectious diseases, toxins, or drugs
- Newborn discharge physical examination with a description of any unusual aspects of the nursery course
- Results of the newborn metabolic screen
- Preadoption testing under special circumstances

Information to Be Collected or Reviewed at the Initial Medical Evaluation of an Older Adopted Child

History

- As complete a birthfamily history as possible, including that of siblings. Preferably, all the information collected for a newborn should be included.
- Chronology of the child's care in custody, with birthparents, relatives, and foster families and reasons for each change in placement
- Record of immunizations
- List of all past major medical diagnoses, allergies, medications, and injuries
- Discharge summary for any hospitalizations
- Copy of any specialist consultations
- Summary of any psychiatric hospitalization or treatment
- Copy of special education evaluations, school records, and individual education plan
- Records of dental care or procedures
- Assessment of risk for prenatal drug or alcohol exposure
- Evidence for any past physical, emotional, or sexual abuse
- Assessment of risk for HIV, hepatitis B and C, and sexually transmitted diseases

Examination

- Complete physical examination, focusing on acute and chronic medical conditions
- Growth and nutritional status
- Examination for scars, bruises, deformities, or other evidence of past abuse
- Genital or gynecologic examination or testing of any child with symptoms or suspected to have been sexually abused
- Examination for features of fetal alcohol syndrome (FAS) or other alcohol-related disorders in the child with suspected prenatal alcohol exposure
- Dental evaluation
- Immunization update
- Age-appropriate screening tests (such as vision or blood pressure); repetition of screening tests of younger ages if there are no records that they were performed
- Screening tests for infectious diseases as indicated by the child's history
- Complete developmental/educational evaluation (may be deferred to second visit)
- Mental health assessment (to be reviewed at every visit)
- Plan referrals for any specialist consultations

Initial Evaluation for a Child Adopted Internationally

- Complete physical examination
- Assessment of growth
- Evaluation for nutritional disorders, especially iron deficiency, lead poisoning, rickets, and iodine deficient hypothyroidism
- Documentation of bruises, scars, or deformities from past medical procedures or abuse
- Preliminary assessment of age (final determination may be deferred as long as a year)
- Begin/repeat immunizations or check antibody titers
- Screening tests for all children: VDRL or other syphilis screening test; Mantoux or PPD skin test, regardless of past history of BCG vaccine; Hepatitis B serology (surface antigen, core and surface antibody); HIV 112 screening, PCR or viral culture in the child under 2 years; stool specimens for intestinal parasites; complete blood count/urinalysis; Hepatitis C serology for children from Eastern Europe, former Soviet Union, and China.
- Assessment of vision, hearing and dental health
- Age-appropriate screening tests and any tests for younger ages that may have been missed
- Genital/gynecologic examination/testing of any child with symptoms or suspected to have been sexually abused
- Examination for features of fetal alcohol syndrome (FAS) or other alcohol-related disorders in the child with suspected prenatal alcohol exposure
- Developmental/educational assessment (may be deferred to later visit)
- Speech/language assessment (may be deferred to the second visit)
- Mental health assessment for older children or those with known past problems (to be assessed at every visit as child gains language competence)

- Plan for referrals for testing or specialist evaluations for any previously diagnosed condition or new diagnosis suspected at initial evaluation
- Review risks for ethnically related conditions, such as thalassemia syndromes in Asian children

Jerri Ann Jenista, MD, is a pediatrician specializing in infectious diseases and the medical issues of adopted children. She is a single adoptive mother of five children. Dr. Jenista is the editor of Adoption/Medical News, *a publication that covers medical issues affecting children in the United States and other countries. Dr. Jenista has traveled abroad to visit orphanages and hospitals in Russia, India, and other countries. She has also reviewed over 5,000 videotapes and medical records of children waiting to be adopted, providing her medical opinion to prospective parents. Dr. Jenista is a member of the American Academy of Pediatrics National Committee on Early Childhood, Adoption and Dependent Care. She is a frequent speaker nationwide on medical issues affecting adopted children.*

Sometimes food can be an issue when children are adopted, whether it is because they eat too much or too little, or are used to different foods. R. Dubucs offers interesting and helpful advice for new parents.

FOOD AND THE ADOPTED CHILD

R. Dubucs

When Jeremy was adopted at age one from Central America, his brunette hair had a reddish tint, his skin had an unhealthy pallor, and his body was very thin except for a distended belly. Jeremy was diagnosed with malnutrition and the pediatrician prescribed unlimited food for Jeremy for one year.

During that year, Jeremy ate large quantities of food. He often drank five bottles of baby formula a night and ate three large meals and multiple snacks a day. In fact, he ate so much that his parents worried that he would make himself sick.

When introduced to new food, Jeremy always made a face, as if to say, "I'll eat it, but I won't like it." Then, if he really did not like the food, he ate only two servings. Otherwise he had three or more servings. The only new food Jeremy rejected during the entire year was a dill pickle.

Catch-Up Growth, the Paramount Importance of Food, and Control

The result was a big increase in height and weight. When Jeremy arrived in the United States, he ranked only in the twenty-fifth percentile in height for his age. (In other words, of one hundred American boys his age, seventy-five were taller than him.) But by the time of the check-up for his second birthday, Jeremy's weight and height had increased, and he was at the fiftieth percentile. His hearty food consumption had resulted in catch-ups in weight and height.

Jeremy's growth that year was not gradual. Rather, it resembled an accordion's movement. He would get plumper and plumper, until well-meaning friends of the family would suggest a diet. Within a week of the advice, Jeremy would shoot up in height and become almost slender. Then he would repeat the accordion process.

Some pediatricians prescribe unlimited food for an adopted child for a full year after his arrival, regardless of the child's native country, age, and weight during that year. Such pediatricians understand the concept of catch-up growth, as illustrated by the story of Jeremy.

For Jeremy, as for other deprived children, food for a time assumed an overriding importance. This paramount importance was expressed in contradictory ways. For example, sometimes Jeremy became hysterical if his food was a few minutes slow in arriving. However, he also threw away food and, like other toddlers, used food as a means of exerting control in his life.

To signal that he had temporarily finished drinking or eating, Jeremy would throw the bottle or the remaining food. On stroller rides, he repeatedly tossed his bottle into the dirt. Jeremy's family solved the beverage-throwing problem by purchasing a bottle strap that attaches to strollers. Jeremy still threw the bottle, but it could not hit the ground, because of the short strap. However, the food-throwing problem was more complicated.

While most toddlers throw food, few throw it like Jeremy. A splat mat or two are sufficient to contain the mess of most toddlers. In contrast, Jeremy, who had a great throwing arm even as a one-year-old, sometimes threw food all over the kitchen and into the two adjoining rooms.

The adoption agency advised Jeremy's family not to stop Jeremy from throwing food until he turned three. According to the agency staff, the food throwing was an effort by a child to whom food is desperately important to exert some control over his environment. Of course, in some cases, food throwing may mean that the child isn't hungry any more and is bored—but that was not true for Jeremy.

Jeremy is now four. Happily, he no longer throws food, but, with all that practice, his throwing arm is sensational! He still has a hearty appetite and a willingness to try almost any new food. He is sturdy but not overweight. In fact, he eats less as a four-year-old than he did as a one-year-old. Jeremy's parents are glad they ignored their friends' advice and followed the pediatrician's unlimited-food advice.

Hoarding and Hiding Food

Some adoptive parents of children with a history of food deprivation find that their child hoards and hides food. This phenomenon is illustrated by the story of Lucy, aged five.

Lucy arrived in the United States after years of insufficient nourishment. Having known days without food, she had learned to plan ahead for those times. Soon after her parents noticed an infestation of ants in her bedroom, they discovered the cause. Lucy had been pocketing extra food from the table to hide under her bed, for the expected future times of want.

Assurances that Lucy would always have ample food in her home clearly left the child unconvinced. Lucy's parents came up with a plan that proved to be a success. They assigned Lucy a kitchen closet shelf that was hers alone, and they kept it stocked with food such as cereal. At first, Lucy would check frequently to make sure that her shelf was well stocked. After awhile, she did not need to check so often. Eventually, she became satisfied that she would not go hungry.

Food Stealing and Food Punishment

One toddler emerged malnourished from a foreign orphanage where big children stole from little children. The following year, he got into trouble at play school for snatching food from other children's plates during lunch. The teacher was angry because the "greedy" child was "stealing food." A quiet talk between the child's mother and the teacher resulted in greater understanding on the part of the teacher and extra servings for the child, which soon eliminated the problem.

This boy's parents never deprive him of dinner or a dessert for misbehavior. A child with a history of hunger needs to be convinced that he will not go hungry in his home.

Lactose Intolerance, Bottle Propping, and Delayed Self-Feeding

Not all feeding issues involving adopted children stem from a history of malnutrition or a post-infancy adoption. Three such feeding issues are illustrated by the story of Randy.

When Randy's adoptive parents first met him in Latin America, Randy was a healthy and sturdy three-month-old baby. By asking questions about his baby formula, Randy's new parents discovered that Randy, like a high percentage of Hispanic, Asian, and African children, was lactose-intolerant. Randy's parents were able to solve his problem of intolerance to milk simply by substituting soy formula for a milk-based formula. When Randy is older, he, like many other children, may outgrow this problem and drink milk without adverse effects.

Randy's family also discovered that Randy was accustomed to eating lying down. Although he loved to be held, he clearly did not know how to eat in an upright position, even in his new mother's arms. While being fed, he kept trying to assume a horizontal position. It appears that Randy, like many other babies from orphanages, had been fed lying down, with no one around and the bottle propped in position. This feeding position is potentially dangerous, because it increases the danger of choking and of ear infections. With patience, Randy became accustomed to eating in an upright position.

Randy's parents, who were prevented from adopting Randy until he was eight months old, discovered the third feeding issue at the time of the adoption. Some older infants and toddlers, including Randy, arrive from foreign countries with no idea how to feed themselves.

The usual explanation is that in cultures in which becoming independent at an early age is disfavored, children are inhibited from feeding themselves until they are older. However, in other orphanages, such as in Russia or China, children are expected to be completely independent at feeding by the age of twelve months.

The first time eight-month-old Randy was handed a cracker, he seemed surprised at the thought of feeding himself. While he could hold the cracker, he had no idea how to convey it to his mouth. He waited, perplexed, for it to be fed to him. Similarly, when he was bottle-fed in his new mother's arms, he made no effort to hold the bottle and looked surprised when she handed it to him.

After Randy's mother began teaching him to feed himself, things moved quickly. Probably because of being older than many American babies at the start of self-feeding, he learned fast. Once the boy could feed himself, he refused to be fed by anyone else. Always a picky eater, he became even more so after he could control what entered his mouth. At age two Randy, when offered food he did not like, would turn his head away and say, "No way!"

Adopted children, like birthchildren, can be hearty eaters or finicky eaters who drive their mothers crazy. Randy is now four. His personal food taboos still include meat, poultry, fish, and vegetables, and he eats primarily bread, cereal, and fruit. Nonetheless, according to his pediatrician, Randy is doing very well and is healthy, despite his bizarre diet. Following the pediatrician's advice, Randy's family does not force-feed him foods he dislikes but does give him a vitamin daily.

How parents themselves perceive food preferences can be important. For example, researchers studied twins, adopted separately at birth. One family told researchers that the child was fine except she was terribly finicky about eating. No matter how hard they tried or what they did, she would only eat foods with cinnamon on them. They said it was really making them crazy. Then the researchers interviewed the other family. They didn't mention any food problems so the curious researchers asked if there were any. "Oh no!" said the parents. "As long as we put cinnamon on her food, she'll eat anything."

Mixed Reactions to Native Food

Initially, older children adopted internationally may be homesick for their native land and crave their native food. Sympathetic adoptive parents have tried to include this food in some meals. In addition, some parents have treated their child to a meal in a restaurant of his or her native culture. In some cases the child was delighted. In other cases, including Tommy's, the child reacted negatively, to his parents' surprise.

Tommy, born in Korea, became agitated when his adoptive parents took him to a Korean restaurant in the United States. In the parents' opinion, Tommy had started identifying with American culture and disengaging from Korean culture. The boy misinterpreted the trip to a restaurant run by Koreans as an effort by his parents to send him back to his old life. He was upset at the prospect of losing his new family and new life. Someday, after Tommy has become convinced of the permanency of his family, he should enjoy eating Korean food and meeting Koreans.

Appetite Increase Following Deprivation, Food Gorging, and the Link Between Nonfood Deprivation and Food Problems

Not all speedy weight gains following an adoption placement signal deprivation of food. Many adoptive parents (including Randy's) have found that their new child, though well-nourished, wants to eat much more and more frequently than expected. Somehow, being the center of a parent's love and attention quickly results in big appetite increases and weight and height gains for many adopted children.

Some adopted children, including children without a known history of malnutrition, have such huge appetites that they gorge themselves with food to the point of having stomachaches or vomiting. Courtney is an example.

Courtney was adopted from a Russian orphanage when she was about five years old. To her adoptive parents' surprise, she did not know when she was full. This is not an unusual scenario because in some orphanages, the children are expected to eat what is on the plate in front of them and there are no preferences or seconds. Thus, many children do not know when they are hungry or full.

Courtney occasionally ate so much that she vomited. A child who did not get enough to eat before the adoption (which is true for many children from orphanages) may not know his food limits or believe that food will always be available. Thus, Courtney's food gorging may stem from food deprivation. However, some children overeat even though they are not *physically* hungry.

There is a link in some cases between nonfood deprivation before the adoption and food gorging or other food problems after the adoption. Food gorging, food hoarding, and food stealing have all been equated with an attempt to fill up the emptiness the child feels inside. In other words, a child starved for affection or with other unmet needs, like some obese adults with unmet needs, may look to food for comfort.

According to some sources, gorging, hoarding, and stealing can be linked to maternal deprivation, inadequate early parenting, or attachment disorders. Maternal deprivation has even been said to be a contributing cause of malnutrition, as well as failure to thrive.

Breast-Feeding

Yet another food issue concerns breast-feeding. Many adoptive mothers are saddened at the thought of their child having missed the breast-feeding experience. It is technically possible for a mother who has not given birth to breast-feed her adopted child, but complete successes in this area are rare. For women considering pursuing this option, the La Leche League is a source for information about breast-feeding an adopted child. (The league, which is listed in most telephone books, can provide, among other things, a booklet on nursing an adopted baby.)

In any event, two things should be kept in mind about breast-feeding. First, some adoptive parents have discovered that their child did experience breast-feeding before the adoption. Second, not only can food be love, but bottle-feeding a preschooler in the new parent's arms is both food and love. In other words, a child does not need to suck at his or her mother's breast to feel safe and loved in her arms.

Conclusion

Sometimes food-related issues may arise with an adopted child. Most of the issues discussed here are linked to a child's past physical or emotional malnutrition or a hungering for both food and love. Of course, there are also medical issues that may be associated with feeding disorders as well—such as malabsorption, micronutrient deficiencies, parasites, and infections—so parents should rule out these problems with a thorough examination by a pediatrician before assuming that food issues are primarily behavioral issues.

For new parents of children with food problems, I have a message: Time, love, plenty of good food, and a sense of humor can help you and your child through. For our adopted children, I also have a message: Eat, drink (milk or a soy substitute), and be merry!

R. Dubucs is an adoptive mother and freelance writer.

EXPLAINING ADOPTION TO YOUR CHILD AND TO OTHERS

Christine Adamec

Explaining adoption to your child and to others is certainly doable, although when it comes to your child, it is not (or should not be) a one-time experience followed by "Whew! I'm glad *that* is over!" This essay offers some basic tips on what to do and what not to do when explaining adoption to your child and others.

Common Extremes

Adoptive parents seem to err at two ends of the spectrum when they make mistakes about explaining adoption to their children or to other people. At one end, they don't talk about adoption at all, try to hide the fact that their child was adopted, and hope that if they are very very good parents, the child will never know or think about being adopted or ask any questions. If anyone in or outside the family alludes to the adoption, the adoptive parents become defensive or upset. Let's call these scared parents the Inwardly Obsessed Parents

Inwardly Obsessed Parents (Inwards, for short) warn everyone in the family not to tell the child that he or she was adopted or even to talk about adoption at all. They change the channel if the subject comes up on television. The Inwards also decide they won't tell the child he or she was adopted because it might be upsetting. Or they convince themselves they will tell the child when the time is "right"—which it never is. Unfortunately, at some point most adopted people do find out they were adopted and this information can be devastating. They may wonder, what else did you lie to me about?

At the other end of the extreme, and far more prominent, are the adoptive parents who blurt everything out and talk incessantly about adoption. Let's call this person who is obsessed with adoption, the Outwardly Obsessed Parent, or an Outward. "Outwards" are defensive or even offensive, when it comes to adoption. Everything somehow links back to the adoption, good or bad.

In their zeal to do things "right," they buy their child ten or more children's books on adoption. They also worry about adoption constantly. One adoptive mother was very upset that the teacher at the Jewish preschool that her daughter attended was planning lessons to teach the children about Hanukkah and the teacher had turned down the mother's offer to provide the children with several days' instruction on adoption. The mother was convinced the preschool teacher was "anti-adoption."

When the child has any problems (and all children have some problem at some point), the Outward parent loudly attributes it to bad genes or the pain of being adopted. It can't be just within-the-normal-range annoying behavior. Oh no! It must be adoption! (Sometimes Inwards fear this as well.)

Of course, it is true that children are sometimes sad about not being born to the family that's raising them and that is a natural feeling. But when her child says, "I wish I grew in your tummy, Mommy," the Outward Mom panics. What should she do now? Take the child to a psychologist? Redouble her efforts at being a perfect parent? Buy some more children's books about adoption? In most cases, none of the above!

Instead, she should realize that the child loves her so much he or she wishes they shared a biological closeness. The mother probably wishes it too, and should say so.

Outward Mom (and sometimes Outward Dad, although I have seen this more commonly in mothers) also takes pains to tell the whole world about her adopted child. If a stranger tells her that her child looks "just like you," Outward Mom immediately states, or at least feels pressured to say, that the child is not hers by birth but was adopted. What should she say instead? How about "thank you."

The Outward Mom also always clutches up when strangers say, "Where did she get those gorgeous eyes?" (This is also a common reaction among new adoptive parents, but usually wears off in a month or so.) Outward Mom doesn't realize that this is usually a rhetorical question, meant as a compliment, to which one says, simply (again), "thank you."

Sometimes adopted children look very different from their parents, in skin color or other features. Rude people may say, "Is she really your child?" The answer "yes" is not a lie. Adoption is the legal transfer of all parental rights and obligations. This means that the child is "really yours."

Outwards, both moms and dads, are also known to vent their frustrations through Internet newsgroups and chat rooms and their posts are read globally. Negative members can argue for days over various issues, when their time would be far better spent bonding with their child and building on the child's belief that he or she is in a "forever family."

So how do you do it "right"? How do you explain adoption perfectly, to your child and to your family and friends? There is no one perfect way. But here are some suggestions.

Explaining Adoption to Your Child

The key factor to keep in mind about explaining adoption is your child's age. You can explain adoption a hundred times to a two-year-old and very little will sink in. Some parents think that they can somehow impress their positive thoughts about adoption on a child's brain engrams, through sheer repetition. But it doesn't work that way. However, the child *can* tell by your tone how you feel about adoption. Think about the child's feelings when you talk about this to adults in his or her presence.

Children grow and develop in fairly predictable stages. The preschool child, aged four or five, generally will believe anything you say about adoption. If you are happy about it, then the child is happy about it. He or she may have some sad moments about the idea of not coming from Mommy's "tummy," but these are transient. As a result of the relative ease of explaining adoption to young children, many parents tell themselves, hey, this isn't so bad, and they may think that the explaining part is over forever.

But the fact is that the issue of adoption should be revisited. Not weekly or monthly and maybe not even yearly. But at some point, the school-aged child will need to learn more about what adoption is. The older child's intellectual capacity and thinking skills are greater than they were when he or she was four. However, the ten-year-old child still is very different from an adult, and most preadolescents think in very black-and-white terms. Any subtleties elude them. For this reason, it's best to avoid explanations such as "Your birthmother chose adoption because she loved you." To a ten-year-old, the obvious next thought is, "Well, you love me too, don't you? Does that mean that you might have me adopted?"

The fact is that the birthparents may have chosen adoption for many different reasons, including love, but it was not love alone that lead them to choose adoption. It may have been a desire for the child to have a better life or to have two parents or to live in a safer environment—or any number of reasons, but it was not love alone. Thus, it's best to avoid relying on the "she loved you" explanation, which doesn't work for most children anyway. Instead, tell them the reason the adoption occurred, if you know, and in simple terms. If you don't know the reason, one explanation that covers a lot of ground is "she was not ready to be a parent and wanted you to be raised by someone who was ready." (I am using "she" because most children's questions center around birthmothers rather than birthfathers. However, this explanation also works for birthfathers; just change the pronouns.)

It's also important to make it clear that the adoption was not the child's "fault." Many children think that they must have been adopted because they were unattractive or stupid or just plain bad, and of course this is not true. Even if a child is born disabled, and is placed for adoption because of the disability, the fact is that it was the birthparents who were unready to be parents and who wanted someone who was ready.

Avoid blaming the birthparents. Don't depict them as stupid or bad people because if you do so, you run the risk of the child eventually wondering whether he or she is inherently stupid or bad. Even if the birthparents were child abusers, the fact is that they were unready to be parents. Conversely, don't depict birthparents as saintly either. The best course is a moderate one: The birthparents were "regular" people who made a difficult decision.

When your child becomes an adolescent, the issue of adoption should be revisited yet again. Your teenager may know other adolescents who have babies and decided to parent them or certainly he or she knows that this happens often. Because of his or her developing sexuality, as well as an increased reasoning capacity, many more questions can arise about adoption, and sometimes teens won't like the answers. They may even disbelieve you: Many adolescents fantasize that their biological mother was a beautiful and/or rich rock star or television personality. Or they may imagine that she was a prostitute who died of AIDS.

The reality for most adopted children is that their biological parents were average people, whether they were average people in the United States or average people in their country of origin. They may have been poor people by U.S. or Canadian standards, if the child was born in another country. But they were probably average for the area. They didn't have the resources to be parents, whether for personal or societal issues.

Here are a few helpful hints to keep in mind, and I recommend you also review the table that follows of common explanations for adoption, why they are problematic, and explanations that may work better.

1. If you make a mistake explaining adoption, you'll have other chances. Don't panic if you think you have botched the job.
2. Don't try to explain adoption when you or your child are upset. Keep explanations to a minimum at such a time and tell the child you'll talk about it later. And do talk about it later.
3. Realize that practically every adopted child has said his "real parents" would not: send him to his room; refuse to buy him a video game; tell him he must go to bed

by a certain time on school nights and so forth. Calmly tell the child that you feel certain that his birthparents would set the same or similar limits. The reality is that you are the parents and it's up to you to make the rules.

4. Use occasional opportunities that come up to mention adoption to your school-aged child or teenager. For example, if you happen to watch a TV show about a teenaged girl with an unexpected pregnancy, you could mention adoption as a solution. Or if someone talks about adopting a child from Russia, you could mention that it seems that many people are adopting Russian children. Even seeing a sign for "adopting" a highway could provide an opportunity for saying how silly it is for people to equate adoption with cleaning up roads.

You can also use special and obvious occasions to bring up adoption, such as Mother's Day or the child's birthday. You could say, "I am so happy to be your Mom (or Dad) and so glad that your birthmother had you. I think about her on this special day."

Use this open-the-door strategy and then see what your child says. If she wants to talk about it, she will. If she's not interested, she won't. Don't force a conversation.

5. Consider your own feelings about adoption and about birthparents. Do you feel guilty about "taking away" another woman's child? If so, you may have a problem with feelings of entitlement and need to realize that when you adopt a child, the child is yours. You could talk about this with other adoptive parents. If the problem begins to loom huge in your life, you may wish to discuss it with a social worker or a therapist.

Avoid being an Inwardly Obsessed Parent or an Outwardly Obsessed Parent. Instead, love and enjoy your child throughout the ups and downs of parenting. Adoption truly is a loving option.

COMMON PROBLEM AND BETTER EXPLANATIONS FOR ADOPTION

Explanation	*Problem*	*Better Explanation*
Your birthmother placed you for adoption because she loved you.	Don't you love the child too? Does that mean you might have her or him adopted? Especially important with children under age 11 because of lack of abstract thinking.	She wasn't able to be a parent. She wanted you to have someone who was ready and able to be a parent.
It was because she was so poor.	Many poor women rear children, even in other countries.	She wanted you to have a better life than she could provide (if this is likely). If in another country, her culture may have had a very negative attitude about single women rearing children alone.
It was because she had other children.	Many people have more than one child.	She felt she could not parent more children. It was not your fault.

COMMON PROBLEM AND BETTER EXPLANATIONS FOR ADOPTION, CONTINUED

Explanation	*Problem*	*Better Explanation*
She was only a teenager.	Many teenagers parent children.	She felt she was too young to be a good mother.
She wasn't married.	Many unmarried women parent children.	She wanted you to have a parent who was ready to take care of you.
God wanted you to be adopted.	Why didn't God help the birthparents?	Some children come by birth and some by adoption—as Moses did. We feel it's part of God's unknowable plan.
She was abusive/alcoholic/drug addict and the state took you away from her.	Why didn't someone else in the family step in and help?	Her behavior showed she was unable to be a good parent. Family members were unable to help.

Talking To Others About Adoption

Another difficult aspect for many people is what and how much to tell others about their child's adoption. Should you tell them everything or nothing? The answer is that you should gauge the situation. And, in most cases, you take a middle road. It is rarely necessary to tell your sister-in-law that you were worried about your child even before you adopted her because the birthmother had been known to drink once in awhile. In fact, if you do tell her, you can nearly count on her expecting your child to show signs of fetal alcohol syndrome as a child, and, when grown, to become an alcoholic. The sad truth is that people tend to remember (and exaggerate) negative information much longer than positive facts you may share about your child.

In the first flush of adopting, however, it's hard to not tell everyone, including the bank teller at the drive through window, everything there is to know about your child's background. But it's best to think of your child first and whether or not it will benefit the child for others to know personal details about his or her genetic background and adoption.

In the fairly rare cases when people badger you for information that you don't wish to divulge—and when saying something like "I don't wish to discuss that," or "that is private" isn't working—my advice is either to say nothing or to ask, "Why are you asking?" You may have to do this more than once, but usually the message gets across.

Another tactic is to change the subject. "Oh my goodness, look at the time! I have to run!"

In this essay, I'm including a table of frequently heard statements that really aggravate many adoptive parents, along with some possible responses that might work for you. Do keep in mind, however, that often when people ask questions about adoption it's because they are interested in adopting a child themselves. Or maybe they think a relative might adopt. So don't be too quick to attribute negative motives to the person curious about adoption.

Also remember that your child will be watching you and listening to what you say to others about adoption in general and his or her adoption in particular. If you present a positive view while at the same time refusing to divulge personal information, your child will notice and may model his or her behavior on yours.

You Have to Tell Somebody!

What if you're bursting at the seams and you just have to discuss something personal about your child with others? Rather than talking to a family member, it might help to talk to someone in an adoptive parent support group. Or if you adopted through an adoption agency, call them and ask if they have any information. They may have gathered new data on whatever the problem is since the time when you were placed with your child.

If it's a medical issue, don't ask your Aunt Mary about it, even if she's a physician. Better to ask your own pediatrician. Do keep in mind that doctors are humans and have their own biases (mostly positive!) about adoption. But they may not know the latest information about some medical problems, particularly those faced by children adopted from an orphanage. If you are really worried about a specific medical issue and don't think your doctor can help, contact an international adoption medical specialist. Remember, all doctors are very busy and these doctors are even busier than most, so keep your question brief and listen when they talk to you.

Here are a few physicians you might call:

Dr. Jerri Ann Jenista: (734) 668-0419

Dr. Jane Ellen Aronson: (516) 663-4417 (voice mail)

Dr. Sarah Springer: (412) 575-5805

Keep The Child's Best Interests In Mind

If the premise that underlies your explanations about adoption is that the child's needs—which are not, by the way, always the same as the child's wants—are paramount in explaining adoption, and if you are being realistic, then you should do fine.

When people ask you probing questions and it seems to you that you might actually have to be rude to stop the interrogation (after you have tried simple explanations, politeness, ignoring them, distractions, and other tactics that usually work for you), here's what I'd recommend. Default to rude, if the other choice is not in your child's best interests. Put your child first. The stranger or pushy relative will forget about it, but your child may not. Put your child first.

EXPLAINING ADOPTION TO OTHER PEOPLE: COMMON QUESTIONS AND SOME SERIOUS AND SILLY ANSWERS

Question	Serious Answer	Using Humor
How much did she cost?	Do you mean what were the fees? I'd have to look that up. But why don't you call the (name of) agency? I'm sure they can help you!	Oh, about a million dollars. But she's worth it!
Is there something wrong with him?	There might be something wrong with that question.	Yes! He hates carrots.

EXPLAINING ADOPTION TO OTHER PEOPLE:
COMMON QUESTIONS AND SOME SERIOUS AND SILLY ANSWERS , CONTINUED

Question	*Serious Answer*	*Using Humor*
You are such saints! I could never take on somebody else's problems.	We're not saints and we're lucky to have our child.	Hold on. I need to adjust my halo here.
How do you know he won't grow up to become a criminal/ insane/a drug addict/alcoholic/ other bad thing?	No child comes with guarantees. We'll try to be good parents, but if any problems happen, as they can with any family, we'll deal with them.	Actually, I was counting on him becoming an Olympic athlete, like Scott Hamilton. Or maybe president, like Gerald Ford. Both of them were adopted.
I guess she'll be bilingual.	Of course, she won't! Unless she takes lessons.	She was eight months old when we adopted her, so it's pretty doubtful. But hey! You never know!
It's good that you adopted an Asian child! They are neat, clean, and obedient. Also, smart!	Children are affected a lot by parents who raise them, too.	Let's hope! The stereotype might actually hold true.
It's so good that you adopted a Russian child who looks like you. No one will ever know.	We want her to know that she was adopted and to be proud of her heritage and interested in her homeland.	The Cold War is over! It's just fine to be Russian now.
Are they real brother/sister?	They sure are! Adoption confers full familyhood.	They certainly argue like siblings! Yes, I guess they must be.
Do you know who the real father is?	Adoptive fathers are real.	Let me introduce you to my husband... (If married. This works best with close family members.)

APPENDIX

NATIONAL ADOPTION ORGANIZATIONS

American Academy of Adoption Attorneys
P.O. Box 33053
Washington, DC 20033-0053
(202) 832-2222
www.adoptionattorneys.org

Children Awaiting Parents (CAP)
700 Exchange St.
Rochester, NY 14608
(716) 232-5110

The Dave Thomas Foundation for Adoption
4288 West Dublin Granville Rd.
Dublin, OH 43017
(614) 764-8454

The Evan B. Donaldson Adoption Institute
120 Wall St., 20th Floor
New York, NY 10005
(212) 269-5080

Families with Children from China
255 W. 90th St., #11C
New York, NY 10024
http://fwcc.org/fccinfo.htm

Families for Russian and Ukrainian Adoption (FRUA)
P.O. Box 2944
Merrifield, VA 22116
(703) 560-6184
www.frua.org

Joint Council on International Children's Services
7 Cheverly Circle
Cheverly, MD 20785
(301) 322-1906

National Adoption Center
1500 Walnut St., Suite 701
Philadelphia, PA 19102
(800) 862-36778

National Adoption Information Clearinghouse
330 C St. SW
Washington, DC 20447
(888) 251-0075
www.calib.com.naic/index.htm

National Council for Adoption
1930 Seventeenth St. NW
Washington, DC 20009-6207
(202) 328-1200
www.ncfa-us.org

National Council for Single Adoptive Parents
P.O. Box 15084
Chevy Chase, MD 20825

North American Council on Adoptable Children (NACAC)
970 Raymond Ave.
St. Paul, MN 55114-1149
(612) 644-3036

RESOLVE
1310 Broadway
Somerville, MA 02144-1731
(617) 623-0744
www.resolve.org

Stars of David International, Inc.
3175 Commercial Ave.
Northbrook, IL 60062-1915
(708) 509-9929

STATE SOCIAL SERVICES OFFICES

Alabama Office of Adoption
Alabama Department of Human Resources
50 N. Ripley St.
Montgomery AL 36130
(334) 242-9500

Alaska Division of Family and Youth Services
Box 110630
Juneau, AK 99811-0630
(907) 265-5080

Arizona Department of Economic Security
P.O Box 6123
Phoenix, AZ 85005
(602) 542-2359

Arkansas Department of Human Services
Division of Children and Family Services
P.O. Box 1437
Little Rock, AR 72203-1437

California Department of Social Services
744 P St., M/S 19-69
Sacramento, CA 95814
(916) 445-3146

Colorado Department of Children and Families
1575 Sherman St.
Denver, CO 80203
(303) 866-3209

Department of Children and Families
505 Hudson St.
Hartford, CT
(203) 238-6640

Delaware Division of Child Protective Services
1825 Faulkland Rd.
Wilmington, DE 19805
(302) 633-2655

Adoption and Placement Resources
609 H St. NE, 3rd Floor
Washington, DC 20002
(202) 724-8602

Florida Department of Human Services
1317 Winewood Blvd.
Tallahassee, FL 32399
(850) 488-2383

Georgia Department of Human Resources
Division of Family and Child Services
2 Peachtree St. NW, Suite 414
Atlanta, GA 30303
(404) 657-3560

Hawaii Department of Human Services
810 Richards St., 4th Floor
Honolulu, HI 96813
(808) 548-5698

Department of Health and Welfare
Division of Family and Community Services
P.O. Box 83720
Boise, ID 83720
(208) 334-5700

Illinois Department of Children and Family Services
406 East Monroe St.
Springfield, IL 62701-1498
(217) 524-2411

Division of Family and Children
Bureau of Family Protection
402 W. Washington St., Rm. W364
Indianapolis, IN 46204-2739
(888) 204-7466

Iowa Department of Human Services
Hoover State Office Building, 5th Floor
Des Moines, IA 50319
(515) 281-5358

Kansas Department of Social and Rehabilitative Services
300 SW Oakley, West Hall
Topeka, KS 66606
(913) 296-8138

Kentucky Cabinet for Human Resources
275 E. Main St., 6th Floor
Frankfort, KY 40621
(502) 564-2147

Louisiana Department of Social Services
Office of Community Services
P.O. Box 3318
Baton Rouge, LA 70821
(504) 342-2297

Maine Department of Human Services
11 State House Station
August, ME 04333-0011
(207) 287-5060

Massachusetts Department of Social Services
24 Farnsworth St.
Boston, MA 02210
(617) 727-0900

Michigan Department of Social Services
P.O. Box 30037
Lansing MI 48909
(517) 373-4021

Minnesota Department of Human Services
444 Lafayette Rd., 2nd Floor
St. Paul, MN 55155-3831
(612) 296-3740

Mississippi Department of Social Services
750 North State St.
Jackson, MS 39202
(601) 359-4500

Missouri Division of Family Services
P.O. Box 88
Jefferson City, MO 65101
(573) 751-2502

Department of Public Health and Human Services
P.O. Box 8005
Helena, MT 59620
(406) 444-5919

Nebraska Department of Social Services
P.O. Box 95026
Lincoln, NE 68509
(402) 471-9331

Nevada Children and Family Services
6171 W. Charleston Blvd., Bldg. 15
Las Vegas, NV 89158

New Hampshire Department of Health and Human Services
Children, Youth, and Families
6 Hazen Dr.
Concord, NH 03301
(603) 486-7650

New Jersey Division of Youth and Family Service
50 East State St., CN 717
Trenton, NJ 08625
(609) 292-9139

Children's Bureau
Placement Services Section
P.O. Drawer 5160
PERA Building, Rm. 252
Santa Fe, NM 87502
(505) 827-8456

New York State Department of Social Services
40 N. Pearl St.
Albany, NY 12243
(518) 473-2868

North Carolina Department of Human Resources
325 N. Salisbury St.
Raleigh, NC 27603
(919) 733-3801

North Dakota Department of Human Services
State Capitol Building
600 East Blvd.
Bismarck, ND 58505
(701) 328-4805

Ohio Department of Human Services
65 East State St., 5th Floor
Columbus, OH 43266-0423
(614) 466-9274

Oklahoma Department of Human Services
P.O. Box 25352
Oklahoma City, OK 73125
(405) 521-2475

Oregon Department of Human Services
Children's Services Division
500 Summer St. NE
Salem, OR 97310
(503) 945-5689

Pennsylvania Department of Public Welfare
Office of Children, Youth, and Families
Health and Welfare Bldg. Annex
P.O Box 2675
Harrisburg, PA 17105
(717) 787-7756

Rhode Island Department of Children and Their Families
610 Mt. Pleasant Ave., Bldg. 5
Providence, RI 02908
(401) 457-4548

South Carolina Department of Social Service
P.O. Box 1520
Columbia, SC 29202
(803) 734-6095

South Dakota Department of Social Services
Richard F. Kneip Building
700 Governors Dr.
Pierre, SD 57501
(605) 773-3227

Tennessee Department of Human Services
400 Deaderick St.
Nashville, TN 37248
(615) 741-5935

Texas Department of Human Services
Agency Mail Code E-55
701 W. 51st
Austin, TX 78714
(512) 438-3412

Utah Department of Social Services
Division of Family Services
120 N. 200 West, Suite 225
Salt Lake City, UT 84103
(801) 538-4080

Vermont Division of Social Services
103 S. Main St.
Waterbury, VT 05671
(802) 241-2131

Virginia Department of Social Services
Theater Row Bldg.
730 East Broad St.
Richmond, VA 23219
(804) 692-1273

Washington Department of Social and Health Services
Children's Administration
14th and Jefferson
P.O. Box 45713
Olympia, WA 98504
(360) 902-7968

Department of Human Services
Capitol Complex
Bldg. 6, Rm. B850
Charleston, WV 25305
(304) 558-7980

Wisconsin Department of Health and Social Services
1 West Wilson St.
P.O. Box 8916
Madison, WI 53708
(608) 266-3595

Wyoming Department of Family Services
Hathaway Building, Rm. 319
Cheyenne, WY 82002
(307) 777-3570

TELEPHONE NUMBERS OF STATE LICENSING DEPARTMENTS

Alabama	(334) 242-9500
Alaska	(907) 465-2817
Arkansas	(501) 682-8590
Arizona	(602) 542-2289
California	(916) 657-2346
Colorado	(800) 799-5876
Connecticut	(860) 550-6390
Delaware	(302) 739-6596
District of Columbia	(202) 727-7226
Florida	(850) 487-2383
Georgia	(404) 657-5562
Hawaii	(808) 586-5698
Idaho	(208) 334-5700
Illinois	(217) 785-2513
Indiana	(317) 232-3476

Iowa	(515) 281-3186
Kansas	913) 296-1270
Kentucky	(502) 564-2800
Louisiana	(504) 922-0015
Maine	(207) 287-5060
Maryland	(410) 767-7903
Minnesota	(612) 297-7014
Massachusetts	(617) 727-0900
Michigan	(517) 373-8183
Mississippi	(601) 359-4994
Missouri	(573) 751-4920
Montana	(405) 444-5919
Nebraska	(402) 471-9138
Nevada	(702) 486-7650
New Hampshire	(603) 271-4711
New Jersey	(609) 292-8255
New Mexico	(505) 827-8478
New York	(518) 474-9447
North Carolina	(919) 733-9464
North Dakota	(701) 328-4805
Ohio	(614) 466-3822
Oklahoma	(405) 521-3561
Oregon	(503) 945-5728
Pennsylvania	(717) 787-7759
Rhode Island	(401) 457-4763
South Carolina	(803) 734-5670
South Dakota	(605) 773-3227
Tennessee	(615) 313-4744
Texas	(512) 438-3242
Utah	(801) 538-4235
Vermont	(802) 241-2159
Virginia	(804) 692-1787
Washington	(360) 902-7992
West Virginia	(304) 232-4411
Wisconsin	(608) 266-0415
Wyoming	(307) 777-6479

RECOMMENDED READING

Books

How to Adopt Internationally: A Guide for Agency-Directed and Independent Adoptions, Jean Nelson-Erichsen and Heino R. Erichsen (Fort Worth, TX: Mesa House Publishing, 2000).

Is Adoption For You? The Information You Need to Make the Right Choice, Christine Adamec (New York: John Wiley and Sons, 1998).

Report on Intercountry Adoption, International Concerns for Children. (Send $25 to: 911 Cypress Dr., Boulder, CO 80303.)

Periodicals/Newsletters

Adoptive Families (published six times a year)
Adoptive Families of America
2309 Como Ave.
St. Paul, MN 55108
(612) 645-9955

Adoption/Medical News (published ten times a year)
Adoption Advocates Press
1921 Ohio St. NE, Suite P
Palm Bay, FL 32907
(407) 724-0815

Roots & Wings Adoption Magazine (published four times a year)
P.O. Box 577
Hackettstown, NJ 07840
(908) 813-8252

QUICK REFERENCE ADOPTION GLOSSARY

Adoptee An adopted child or adult.

Adoption Transfer of parental rights to adopting family. After finalization of adoption, adoptive parents have full parental rights and obligations.

Adoption agency Organization that is licensed by the state to place children with families. Some agencies are restricted to performing homestudies only.

Adoptive parent Person who has adopted a child in accordance with applicable state and federal laws. All parental rights and responsibilities are conveyed after finalization.

Adoptive parent support group Group designed to provide information and assistance to current and prospective adoptive parents. Usually run by volunteers.

Application fee Fee paid to adoption agency at beginning of process.

Attorney Person with law degree who is licensed to practice law. Attorneys' involvement varies according to state laws. In some states attorneys may handle legal paperwork only, while in other states attorneys assist adoptive parents with all or most of the adoption process.

Birthfather Biological father of adopted child.

Birthmother Woman who placed her biological child for adoption.

Designated adoption Term used by some agencies to describe cases in which birthparents and adoptive parents locate each other before coming to the agency for assistance.

Domestic adoption The adoption of a child from one's own country; for example, the adoption of a child from the United States by an American or the adoption of a Canadian child by a Canadian.

Finalization Court decree of legal adoption. It is extremely difficult to overturn a finalized adoption.

Foster/adopt Refers to a program in which a foster child is placed with a family in the belief that the child may become eligible to be adopted.

Foster parent Person who cares for a child legally in the custody of the state or county. Does not have all the rights and obligations of a parent.

Homestudy Assessment and evaluation of adoptive parent applicants.

Independent adoption or private adoption Refers to adoptions that are not arranged by agencies, although an agency may do the homestudy.

International or intercountry adoption The adoption of a child from another country; for example, the adoption of a child not born in the United States by an American or a child not born in Canada by a Canadian.

Interstate Compact (ICPC) Agreement between U.S. states as to how an interstate adoption is handled.

Placement fee A fee paid to adoption agency on placement of the child.

Postplacement services Home visits, advice, and other services offered to adoptive parents after a child is placed but before the adoption is finalized.

Sliding scale One fee method some adoption agencies use to charge adoptive applicants, based on a formula such as 15 percent of gross income. There is usually a minimum and maximum fee.

Social worker Person trained in social work field (with MSW or similar degree) or in social sciences. The social worker usually conducts the homestudy.

Special needs child A child with medical, emotional, or developmental problems. Also often used to refer to a healthy child who is non-Caucasian or a member of sibling group or to school aged children available for adoption.

Transracial adoption Adoption of a child by a person of another race or ethnic group. Generally is used to refer to white parents adopting black or biracial children.

Index